D0757903

PHILOSOPHY IN PROCESS

SUNY Series in Philosophy
Robert C. Neville, Editor

Philosophy
in process

VOLUME EIGHT
April 28, 1978 – July 28, 1980

Paul Weiss

State University of New York
ALBANY

Published by
State University of New York Press, Albany

© 1983 State University of New York

For information, address State University of New York
Press, State University Plaza, Albany, N.Y., 12246

Library of Congress Cataloging in Publication Data
(Revised for volume 8)

Weiss, Paul, 1901–
    Philosophy in Process.

    Vol. 8 issued in SUNY series in philosophy and published by the State University of New York Press.
    Includes index.
    CONTENTS: v. 1. 1955–1960.—v. 2. 1960–1964.—[etc.]
—v. 8. April 28, 1978–July 28, 1980.
    1. Philosophy—Collected works I. Title.
II. Series: SUNY series in philosophy.
B945.W396P5   191   63–14293
ISBN 0–8093–0401–5 (v. 1)

10   9   8   7   6   5   4   3   2   1

For *Hans Lenk*

Books by Paul Weiss

Beyond All Appearances (1974)
Cinematics (1975)
The Commonhealth (forthcoming)
First Considerations (1977)
The God We Seek (1964)
History: Written and Lived (1962)
The Making of Men (1967)
Man's Freedom (1950)
Modes of Being (1958)
Nature and Man (1947)
Nine Basic Arts (1961)
Our Public Life (1959)
Philosophy in Process, Vol. 1: 1955–1960 (1966)
Philosophy in Process, Vol. 2: 1960–1964 (1966)
Philosophy in Process, Vol. 3: 1964 (1968)
Philosophy in Process, Vol. 4: 1964–1965 (1969)
Philosophy in Process, Vol. 5: 1965–1968 (1971)
Philosophy in Process, Vol. 6: 1968–1971 (1975)
Philosophy in Process, Vol. 7: 1975–1976 (1978)
Philosophy in Process, Vol. 8: 1978–1980 (1984)
Reality (1938)
Religion and Art (1963)
Right and Wrong: A Philosophical Dialogue Between Father and Son, with Jonathan Weiss (1967)
Sport: A Philosophic Inquiry (1969)
The World of Art (1961)
You, I, and the Others (1980)
Privacy (1983)

Principal Contributions

American Philosophers at Work, edited by Sidney Hook (1956)
American Philosophy Today and Tomorrow, edited by H. M. Kallen and Sidney Hook (1935)
The Concept of Order, edited by Paul Kuntz (1968)
Contemporary American Philosophy, edited by John E. Smith (1970)
Design and Aesthetics of Wood, edited by Eric A. Anderson and George F. Earl (1972)
Determinism and Freedom, edited by Sidney Hook (1958)
The Dimensions of Job, edited by Nahum N. Glatzer (1969)
Dimensions of Mind: A Symposium, edited by Sidney Hook (1960)
Evolution in Perspective, edited by G. Schuster and G. Thorson (1971)
The Future of Metaphysics, edited by Robert Wood (1970)
Human Values and Economic Policy: Proceedings, edited by Sidney Hook (1967)
Law and Philosophy, edited by Sidney Hook (1964)
Mid/Twentieth Century American Philosophy, edited by Peter A. Bertocci (1974)
Moments of Personal Discovery, edited by R. M. MacIver (1952)
Moral Principles in Action, edited by R. Anshen (1952)
Perspectives on Peirce, edited by R. Bernstein (1965)
Philosophers on Their Work, edited by André Mercier (1979)
Philosophical Essays for A. N. Whitehead, edited by O. Lee (1936)
Philosophical Interrogations, edited by S. and B. Rome (1964)
Philosophy and History, edited by Sidney Hook (1963)
The Philosophy of Baruch Spinoza, edited by R. Kennington (1980)
The Relevance of Whitehead, edited by I. Leclere (1961)
Science, Philosophy, and Religion: Proceedings (1941–)
Studies in the Philosophy of Charles Sanders Peirce, edited by C. P. Weiner and F. H. Young (1952)

Edited Works

Collected Papers of Charles Sanders Peirce (six volumes), editor, with Charles Hartshorne (1931–35)

PREFACE

DESPITE GOOD CRITICAL receptions, the previous volumes of this work continue to sell slowly. Their publisher, understandably, is reluctant at this time to continue the series. Fortunately, I have been able to find another who thinks that further volumes should be made available, though in a somewhat smaller format than before. The prospect of a volume 9, now in manuscript, though, does depend in part on the fortunes of this.

More evidently and persistently than was true before, I here struggle with various problems whose nature I only faintly discerned for a considerable period, and for which satisfactory answers are not always found. The many false starts, retreats, and advances, here so manifest, exhibit how one might venture speculatively into new territory. One outcome is that it made possible the recently published *Privacy,* with its comparatively new systematic method and results. In the absence of such a work as this, it would be hard to discover how it was possible to open up that new ground, see the need for some of its important analyses, and be able to provide a new and illuminating account of man. Together the works make evident how creative thinking has a two-fold form, one as confused as it is fresh, the other organized and justified. But the two stand by themselves, each with its own distinctive nature, virtues, and limitations.

Washington, D.C.
August, 1983

1978

April 28

There are three plausible, but I think ultimately unsatisfactory ways of answering the question: What is left when one subtracts Christianity (or Judaism, etc.) from religion? 1. Nothing; 2. A least common denominator; 3. Something greater than before.

1. Though it is a fact that there is no religion in general, that religious people are Christians, Jews, etc., it still does not follow that there is no common factor in all the religions. If there were none, then, since the religions conflict, there would be no warrant for calling them all 'religions' except for the presence of some adventitious item. But this might be lost. What warrant is there for calling the various world religions 'religions', if there is nothing at all in common to them?

2. It was the view of Lessing that some common factor was added to by the different religions—a common concern with getting to the 'top of the mountain' though along some particular path marked out by a particular religion. It is then being admitted that there is no religion in general, though it is being supposed that there is a common 'religiosity' in all. This common factor is what is sometimes concentrated on in courses of comparative religion. The idea, though, that this is something general and more or less empty, achieving distinctive content and value by being specialized in the form of a particular path, denies the intensity, vitality, and concreteness of the piety of unlearned people who have little or no knowledge of the theologies, or even of the practices of a particular religion. They may have been educated or trained in some one, but after a time they might be very lax regarding particular practices and views, without in any way diminishing their religious concern.

3. If it be recognized that a deeply religious person starts with a concern directed at what is ultimately real, that he might have an element of mysticism in his functioning and thus may in fact make some kind of contact with his object, it makes sense to go on to say that Christianity,

Judaism, and the like specialize, limit, and perhaps distort the very meaning of religion. Religion here would be a fundamental activity overdetermined by specific religions. But no one who pursues these religions would allow that they have subtracted from what was a mere religious activity; the acknowledgment that God was a judge or self-sacrificing and the like is taken by them to sweep back on the religious activity, giving it focus and further content.

4. A more satisfactory answer shares something of both the second and third views. It notes that religion, as involving either or both individuals and community, and as thrusting toward that which is ultimate, is more concrete than particular religions just so far as these have creeds and require special limited acts. Such a 'basic' religion, a religion *an sich,* is less concrete than any particular one, since it has no specifiable outcome, required acts, rituals, history, and the like.

A particular religion, like philosophical sociology, ontology, metaphysics, cosmology, and theology, stands in between a religion *an sich* and a mystical involvement with a final reality. Unlike these others, the religion pulls the terminus toward itself, flooding it with its concern. It is also enriched by content obtained from theology in particular, and incidentally from metaphysics.

If this conclusion is accepted, ought we not to say that a community, law, art, and mathematics also are enriched by theology and metaphysics, and that they pull the termini of these enterprises back into themselves, thereby benefiting from them? Concentrating on metaphysics and theology, we would then have to say that a community's myth depends on its pulling metaphysics and theology back into itself; that the sense of justice or peace is an effect of law's adopting metaphysical and theological conclusions; that the themes of art express the outcome of the conversion of the termini of metaphysics and theology into the body of art; and that the objectivity of mathematics is expressed in the kind of support that it obtains by incorporating the meaning of metaphysics and theology.

Do these suggestions lose plausibility when they are supplemented by accounts which have the community, etc., enriched by the termini of a philosophical sociology, ontology, and cosmology? It does not appear so. Consequently, in addition to claiming that there are 1. five strivings toward finalities, 2. five terminating endeavors, and 3. five mysticisms beyond these, we must say that the first is enriched by pulling the outcomes of the second into themselves. Since the second already incorporate something of the third, and continue to thrust toward them, the first, i.e. religions, art, etc., become particularized as Christian or Jewish, as Renaissance, Modern, and the like, by receiving a mystical component mediated and delimited by a theoretical endeavor such as metaphysics, theology, etc. A religion will therefore be enriched by the object of a religious mysticism as incorporated in the termini of a metaphysics, a theology, etc., pulled back into the religious setting. When ritual or creed are insisted on, a religion is being dealt with, not as directed toward the content of a religious mysticism, but as involved in a community, law, etc. and, via these, benefitted by a terminus itself enriched by the object of a social, ontological, etc. mysticism.

Again and again, it has been remarked that religions not only have overlooked or condoned slavery, the debasement of workers, children, and captives, and have yielded too readily to the demands of political powers, but that some have encouraged savagery, have allowed or endorsed infanticide, war, and so on. As a consequence, some thinkers have tried to distinguish primitive or barbaric religions from civilized ones. The distinction usually turns out to be between other religions and one's own, or of some weakened version of an established one. If what I have been contending for is right, there is no particular activity required of religion. The accompanying activities are to be dealt with as dogmas are. Though a religion does receive enrichment from a terminus arrived at by some discipline and from the mystically enjoyed object beyond it, a particular dogma, and therefore a Christianity, Judaism, etc. will offer special interpretations of the outcome of the incorporation of theological, etc. termini. Consequently the activities of a religion, and particularly those which have a community form, will have to be understood to be interpretations of the meaning of the religious activity as imbedded within and controlled by some other, in particular the community's. The criticism of a religion should then be properly directed, not at it, but at the community within which the religion operates, or at the religion as not freely exercised or for not being directed toward the object which a religious mysticism enjoys.

May 20

To the supposition that every reference to private experiences, such as pain, can be restated in physiological terms, making unnecessary a reference to anything else, the first reply should be that the substitution depends on the experiencer reporting that such and such an experience does occur when such and such a physiological occurrence is observed. Suppose now the defense is made that when a man says 'I am in pain' there is not only an occurrence matching the pain, but another which matches the saying? To this we can reply that conceivably a man might have the two physiological occurrences at one time, and yet not find that he both says he has a pain and is in fact experiencing it. To this a reply could be made that there is then some other physiological occurrence taking care of that fact. But now we must ask for the difference between saying 'I am in pain' when I in fact have one and when I do not have one. The physiologically minded thinker will have to say that there is a special kind of physiological occurrence taking place when one speaks truly and another when one speaks falsely. Such occurrences must function as relations between the occurrence which matches the saying and the occurrence which matches what is taking place in the presence or absence of a pain. The relations must be constants, since they relate any saying to any of the experiences. If the relations could not be observed, one would have to argue that one would some day be able to observe them. No explanation would as yet have been made of how one might be able to express a truth about all men, or even the supposed truth that the experiences of one man were matched by physiological occurrences. Granted that the knowledge a physiological thinker has matches what is in him. What happens when he says what is true of some other man?

May 26

Frank Riley was my reader for a number of years. He came to the conclusion, after reading *Beyond All Appearances* (and which he took to be confirmed by *First Considerations*), that I had made a distinctive break through and beyond my earlier views. I did not see it then, but I am beginning to become convinced. He has managed to persuade a number of others, notably Paul Joyal. Joined by other students—and apparently prompted by John Acher—they made elaborate plans to give me a special birthday party. I could not have it on my birthday, for Jonathan and Bernstein and his wife planned to come down then. The celebration was held on the 24th. We had some twenty-five or so at a dinner, and had a party before and after at the house where Riley and Joyal live. They also arranged to have me go through the White House, be given a citation by the President (presented by the man in charge of the commission on aging): they wrote up a press release, summarized my views in a five page account to be distributed to the press, saw to it that a notice of the party appeared in the *Washington Post,* had me photographed by the *Post,* and arranged to have me interviewed by the *Post* in a story to appear next week. At the end of their summary they wrote:

Weiss's pluralistic system of actualities and finalities is an important and fundamental advance which brings him within the company of philosophers such as Plato, Aristotle, Kant, and Hegel. It was formerly said in European intellectual circles that when old ideas die, they come to America. Paul Weiss's philosophy closes the book on such remarks. America more and more will become an intellectual, philosophical source for the West. Philosophy has been without clear leadership for years. Weiss represents a point of synthesis among the various rival schools of philosophy. The world faces a new philosophic giant, unlike any seen since the days of Hegel. He is the American philosopher, Paul Weiss.

Years ago I pledged myself that I would be as honest as I possibly could be in this journal, and that I would express what otherwise I might have kept hidden. I must, therefore, face up to these remarks. I think they reflect rather accurately what I believed for a long time, though I never could believe that I was the equal or in the company of Plato, Aristotle, Kant, and Hegel. But I did think that my views were sounder, and my method more promising. I also thought that, in contrast with contemporaries, I was struggling with basic questions and doing this without hiding behind special doctrines or supposing that the truth was to be found in some other discipline, whether it was science, poetry, or religion. But though I have not lost confidence in what I am doing and am still convinced of its soundness, particularly in the last decade, I shrink before the characterization of myself as 'a giant' though strangely enough, not before the idea that mine is the first viable systematic philosophy (which includes ontology, cosmology, epistemology, faces such neglected enterprises as sport, and deals with history, religion, education, and art) since the days of German Idealism. I like the praise, primarily because it seems to make a little more certain that what I have written will be attended to after I am dead. The effect on me now has been to encourage me in some subterranean way—for example, I have, after about a year of neglect, begun to paint again. I must make sure, though, that I don't accept the views of students as definitive, and that if they are, that they do not affect my thoughts and habits of work.

In volume 7 of *Philosophy in Process* I reported the conversation of a friend of Paul Schilpp about his attitude toward me, and what I would have to do to be invited to be one of the philosophers dealt with in the *Library of Living Philosophers.* I affix Schilpp's letter as a reply to what I said.

May 19, 1978

Dear Paul:

Having now Volume VII of *Philosophy In Process* at my disposal and in hand, I have run into the paragraph or two (on pp. 24-25) in which you refer to the Library of Living Philosophers and me.

Unfortunately there are not only mistakes but serious omissions in that report.

The mistake is that I have never needed any "placating." That is neither my way of doing things nor true to my character.

But what I find actually much more serious are the omissions in that tale. I am now past 81 years of age. I have already 5 additional volumes (see the printed section on the left side) in various stages of preparation. After 1980 I expect to turn the task of editing the Library of Living Philosophers over to whoever my successor will be (and I have no way at this point of knowing his name). I didn't think it fair to name additional volumes under these circumstances. It seemed to me that my successor should have something to say about those, and I didn't wish to bind his hand.

Moreover, your two paragraphs read as if Schilpp was the sole determining factor in selecting philosophers on whom there are to be volumes in the Library of Living Philosophers. This has not been the case for at least 25 (if not more years). Ever since we have had an Advisory Board, I pledged myself never to announce a new volume unless I had more than just a majority vote of my Advisory Board in favor of such a volume. At the time the Advisory Board approved a volume on Quine (which was the latest one approved by them) there was one other American philosopher who ran very close to the vote that Quine got; unfortunately, that man's name was not Paul Weiss. But, inasmuch as I had already decided not to announce any more volumes beyond the 5, I have refused to do anything more along that line until after a new editor is chosen and has taken over—which is something for which you can scarcely blame me. It simply means that I wanted to show enough respect for my successor for that person to be involved in any further selections.

These, my dear Paul, are the facts of the case, of which you may make whatever you will. I am only sorry that neither you nor Vernon bothered to show me those two paragraphs before they appeared in print.

With all personal good wishes,

Cordially yours,

I replied to that letter saying that I was not criticizing him directly, but repeating what his supposed friend had reported, and giving my frank reaction to what that friend said. I wrote also that no matter what he said, he (Schilpp) would be praised and blamed for the inclusions in and exclusions from that series, that the idea was good, that he had selected some distinguished philosophers, and that no harm was done to me since I did have an opportunity to answer critics both in *Philosophic Interrogations* and in *First Considerations*.

It is not true, though, that I am indifferent to the decision of his board not to include me. But since this is not the only place where I have been passed by or over, I take it to be in consonance with the dominant judgment of my contemporaries. For the moment, it is perhaps enough to say that though there are a number of younger people who would subscribe to the judgment that Riley and Joyal have made about my work and standing, the vast majority of philosophers in the world do not know I exist, while those in America who do know it (primarily because of my association with the *Review of Metaphysics*) would allow that I am perhaps one of the few speculative systematic philosophers alive today, but that the enterprise is not worth pursuing or that, if it is, I am not doing especially significant work in it. Most have not read anything I have written; should their opinions turn in the opposite direction, they will undoubtedly be based on similar inadequate grounds. There is then nothing to do but continue to work as before, and to hope that interest in and appreciation of what I have been doing will become more widespread.

Because of my appearance on the Cavett talk shows and because of various news articles, I, as a person or kind of quasi-sage, have become fairly well known; the sport book, too, continues to sell to what is evidently a non-philosophical audience. None of this, though, is really relevant to the question whether or not what I have done makes a permanent contribution to philosophic thought. I believe it does and I hope it does, but I do not dwell on the matter or think much about it, except on these occasions when my birthday is celebrated, and exalted things are said about me.

May 29

We live in what Plato called the realm of the 'mixed'. The mixture is two-directional, vertical and horizontal. Plato proceeded at once to deal with the vertical, and then went only in one direction. He neglected the horizontal, and therefore the fact that there were at least five verticals to deal with, and that these went in two ways. If we neglect the horizontal mixtures—the social, economic, rational, extensional, and evaluational factors—which are intermixed in our daily life, we will fail to note that we have five distinct verticals leading to five, and not to one kind of finality. All of these verticals also move in the opposite direction to one kind of terminus, the actualities as they are in themselves. Plato's failure to deal with the last precludes even his one vertical from producing a mixture for, if we have a condition operating on passive material, the outcome is not a mixture but an articulation of this. A true mixture requires at least two distinct realities which positively contribute to the outcome.

One can classify various philosophic positions by taking account of the above considerations. We then have views which consider a. only what is confronted, failing to recognize this to be 'mixed'; b. take the confronted to be due to the intrusion of something transcendental on what is passive—Plato's Good, Aristotle's Forms, Kant's Categories; c. recognize the positive role of both sides; d. recognize a horizontal mixture; and e. recognize more than one vertical. (Empiricists are to be found under a; most other philosophers under b—positivists no less than theologians.) f. There are philosophers, such as the Neoplatonists, who take one entity to be exhibiting itself in more and more attenuated forms; and g. there are others who take a similar position with respect to the mind, supposing that what is known is a product of its self-diversifying acts. (Hegel would have to be included under f; I am not sure whether or not linguists, structuralists, depth grammarians, and behaviorists belong here as well. Personalists seem to belong under g.)

I do not know anyone other than myself who has strongly insisted on the mixture being the outcome of two distinct types of reality; nor do I know of anyone who recognizes that there are five of such mixtures, each the outcome of an interplay of actualities with finalities. But this is perhaps due to my fragmentary knowledge of the history of thought. The earlier discussion of domains, also, points up the fact that there are mixtures, other than appearances, in which finalities play a dominant role in the determination of disciplines and contexts.

June 1

A proper name, such as 'Socrates', was understood by Aristotle to be *denotative* and yet to be the subject of an *A* proposition, and therefore, be a *universal*, a meaningful unit. Moderns have elected to accept one or the other of these ways of understanding a proper name. John Stuart Mill took it to be a pure denotative, an 'it' which was overlaid with some conventional meanings. Idealists, and then Russell with his theory of descriptions and Quine with his willingness to take 'Socraticity' as the equivalent of 'Socrates', took it to be a mere meaning, and therefore to be in an implicative relation to a predicate. What Aristotle and the others overlooked is the fact that it could be both denotative and meaningful *intensively*, and in this respect differ from an ordinary denotative term such as 'it' and from an ordinary meaningful expression such as 'big'.

'It' by itself can do nothing more than help us point to something; 'big' by itself can do nothing more than help us understand something. When the two are used together, they approximate the modern understanding of 'Socrates is white' but, oddly enough, not the modern understanding of 'it is big'. 'It is big' has the 'it' related to the 'big' in a judgment, with the whole that results being directed at and thus, strictly speaking, denoting the unity of 'a-big-it'. 'It is big', I am contending, involves the use of two meaningful terms, neither of which is merely denotative or connotative, but both of which are correlative meaningful terms to be synthesized in a judgment and referred to a unitary object. 'Socrates is white', in contrast, is to be understood as having a denotative but meaningful 'Socrates', with 'white' predicated of the referent of 'Socrates'. The difference between Aristotle's and my view is that I take 'Socrates' to be meaningful as addressive, and hold that, as a proper name, it is not to be put on a footing with 'it'. The moderns after Aristotle rightly take 'Socrates' to be meaningful, but fail to see that it has a denotative intensive use; unlike Aristotle, the moderns, wrongly take 'Socrates' to be coordinative with 'white', while overlooking the fact that such coordination should hold of 'it'.

A proposition as a whole normally denotes via the copula; the 'it' in it is on a par with 'big'. But 'Socrates' is not on a par either with 'it', when this is taken to be a mere denotative, or with 'white', for though it is meaningful, as 'white' is, it is addressive, and therefore denotative. But it works in depth and therefore is meaningful in a distinctive way.

'Socrates' can be used with an intention to avoid an intensive depth reference; it can be treated as a term serving to pick out one entity from among a number. Such a pure denotative, non-intensive use is parasitical on the addressive. 'It', perhaps, is always used as having some such minimum meaning as 'some thing' or 'some distinguishable entity'. So far as this is true, we must say that it is not altogether detachable from the 'is' that takes us to the unitary object.

There is an 'is' in 'Socrates is white'. If 'is' has a depth role, do we not have some kind of duplication or overlapping here? Not unless the 'is' here functions as it does in 'It is big'. When 'Socrates' is used addressively, the 'is' serves to attach the 'white' to it, and does not, as is the case with 'is' in 'it is big' serve to join the 'it' and the 'big', at the same time that it orients the two of them together in a unit entity.

July 2

I have been reading Antony Cua's *Dimensions of Moral Creativity*. It is written with his typical unusual modesty and diffidence, sometimes making it difficult to know just what he intends. But I have found it to be very sensitive and most stimulating. It has made me rethink some old and some new questions, particularly "Why should I be moral?" "How do I become moral?" My answers in part coincide with, and in part diverge from his.

I ought to be moral (or more strictly speaking 'ethical', where 'moral' refers to what is required in a society and 'ethical' refers to what is right, sometimes even in opposition to the demands of a society) in order to be myself more fully. I am now related to many other entities, and in one sense to every other entity that there is. As such I am subject to their influence, their dominance, their overwhelming power and presence. They define me to be the other of themselves. To be myself fully (I long ago remarked), it is necessary for me to overcome the negating that they, by their very existence, subject me to. They do not negate me; indeed, they could not be related to me in any sense, were they not subject with me to common conditions. By adopting those common conditions, I make myself one with what is controlling them, and thereby am internally in control of what is externally controlling me. Ethical rules offer one way in which I can be in control of what controls me, able to subjugate what is externally negating me.

To this it is reasonable to object that ethical rules are general and I an individual, and that the control, that they allow to me within, still leaves me subject to determination from without. The adoption of ethical principles, however, is also a personalization of them, a making them one with my individual nature. At one and the same time, they become my rationale and are individually quickened and qualified. That I am still subject to the rules and to the other items means that I will be alike, both inwardly and outwardly. Were the ethical principles merely rules for me, did they not have any controlling role with respect to items apart from me, I would impose them on ways of acting which have no necessary bearing on the items. It is because the others are under the control of the very rules I am using with respect to them, that I become unified,

a being whose internally adopted position is one with his external position
with respect to what else there be.

I make myself be ethical by accepting the principles which govern
me and others, as essential to my nature. Those who seek to commit
suicide, those who find themselves overwhelmed by the external world,
those who think of themselves as lost or alone, look at the external world
as though it were just oppositional. They fail to see that it is governed
by conditions relating it and themselves.

I try to make the governing conditions my own. The outcome, of
course, is neither those principles nor myself as we had been, but some
union of the two. We look to paradigmatic individuals as guides as to
how and to what extent we are to make the rules part of ourselves. This
view of paradigms differs from Cua's, who seems to think that we identify
with them, rather than that we take them to guide our union with ethical
principles.

Ethical principles, of course, are only some of the rules that we must
incorporate. They can in fact be taken to be specializations of more
general formal ones—ultimately, mathematical and logical—brought to
bear on items so far as these are recognized to have value. If they are,
the ethical rules will be subordinated to evaluational conditions. Or, to
use the language of *First Considerations*, they will be subordinated to
Unity. The fact opens up a whole arena of conditions which must be
accepted if we are to be perfected. Not only must we internalize the
conditions which express the five finalities, but we have to internalize
whatever conditions these may subordinate. Remaining solely with ethical
principles, we should then have cases where these are subordinated not
only to Unity, but to Substance, Being, and Existence. As subordinated
to Substance, they refer to the ways men are able to be best allied; as
subject to Being, they refer to the demands of a justice that attends
primarily to rights; as subject to Existence, they have to do with where
and how they can assemble, continue, and act.

Ethical principles are not the only conditions that are subordinated
to others. Not only is the intelligible subordinated to the other conditions, but the others are subordinated to the intelligible and to one
another. If we start with the intelligible—the logical or mathematical, or
beyond these, the Platonic Good—the associations, coordinations, distances, and values, which are due to the other finalities, will be faced
from the perspective of the rational. But an associative condition, grounded
in Substance, also has subordinated coordinations, rules, distances, and
values. Here, ethical principles are limited by functioning under the aegis

of a demand that men be affiliated, and thereby brought together in a single alliance.

If we restrict ourselves to the main cases, we have five final conditions subordinating the other four. The ethical, where intelligible rules of behavior are subject to value, is one. All twenty need to be internalized by each of us so as to enable each to be within what he is in fact without. There will, for example, be a rationale provided for religion. Here, the intelligible, not restricted to ethical rules, will dictate specific values for items as so many different cases of Unity. This alternative reverses the one previously considered, where the ethical was subordinated to value, and which is most pertinent to our ethical life. Here, the meaning of ethical principles dictates the role that values and, eventually, their common condition, or the Unity which is behind them all, are to have. God, as that being who unifies the ethical rules with values, will then function as a kind of paradigm for those who seek a guidance for the way to unite the two in themselves.

Recurring now to the ethical situation, where the ethical principles are subordinated to an acknowledged world of values, the ethical man will be guided by the paradigms of those who have combined the rules with subordinated values. There will evidently be nineteen other kinds of paradigms. Might all this not be simplified by considering only the pure cases of the conditions which express the five finalities? If so, ethical principles will not necessarily bear on what has value, and the only problem will be that of making those principles be one with our individual selves. But what has no bearing on values are mathematical and, logical, not ethical rules. We would have to say, as a consequence, that there is no ethics or that it has to do solely with the act of making oneself rational, reasonable, an incarnation of the merely intelligible. There surely is such a state, and it is desirable, but it does not preclude the ethical, replace it, or reinstate it in a better form.

I have not written in this journal for over a month. Instead, I have been rewriting 'You, I, and the Others', and doing some painting in the afternoons. The rewriting is going slowly, some fourteen to twenty typed pages a day. I am far from satisfied with the book, in good part because I have not been sufficiently clear, and because I have not brought the operative principles into focus, or even stated most of them, not to speak of justifying them. And within the next month, I will have to revise the paper on theology that I am to give in California, and must write a paper on evaluation research, for a planned address in the Fall.

July 3

Yesterday's formulations make it hard to see why there should be any action. It seemed as if it were sufficient for one to just internalize whatever conditions governed oneself and all else. However, a union of conditions and one's own individual being is never complete. Each union involves an indefinite projection forward to constitute a domain, indefinite in nature and length, which subsequent action is to make determinate in the form of particular acts. Action is necessary in order that the union of oneself and a common condition be a union having terms as concrete as oneself. Each act is a way of reaching to particular items and governing them by means of the conditions.

To this, two objections are to be raised: 1. If the items are already conditioned, why is there need for a further conditioning by ethical man? 2. How could any man reach to all the items in the universe?

1. The conditioning, which the actions of an ethical man introduce, allows for a control of what is affecting him. But then it would seem that ethical action is solely for one's own sake. There would seem, too, to be no need to act so as to do good for anything.

The actions of the ethical man must terminate in the other items and improve them, in order to enable him to be apart from them. So far as he merely united conditions with himself or acted to fill out the projection which results, he would be involved with them. By enriching them, he allows for the presence of his imposed conditions on them, and thereby frees himself from the need to sustain those conditions there.

The more a man enhances others, the more surely do they incorporate the conditions he is imposing. The benefiting of others is thus a way of allowing him to be alongside them. Now it seems that one does good to others in order to do good to oneself. But one can put the matter in the reverse way as well: one acts as an ethical being in order that others be perfected. The two expressions: I improved others so as to perfect myself and I am an ethical being so as to perfect others, are equivalent.

The additional conditioning, which an ethical man introduces, allows others to stand apart from both the condition he introduces and himself; the enhancing of others is the enabling them to have the condition internal to themselves. Their enhancement is thus one with their being made independent of one another, at the same time that they remain together, subject to a common condition.

2. Evidently, we cannot act on everything. But that is only another way of saying that no matter how good we are, we are never as good as

we ought to be. Having made ourselves internally what we are externally conditioned to be, we cannot make it fully so, except in intent in the form of an indeterminate projection to be subsequently filled out in action. So far as we do not act, so far there are entities we do not enhance. So far, we are good only in intent.

Paradigmatic individuals are looked to as men who have carried out an intent more successfully than others—and thus not merely as men of intent or like prophets who may admonish but may themselves not be excellent. They clearly incorporate common conditions, thereby becoming possible avenues through which we can ourselves reach or understand those conditions, and be in a position to internalize them ourselves.

It is not easy to focus on common conditions. As a consequence, those who succeed in doing so, but in such a way that they make it part of themselves and thus are men of exceptionally fine intent, are also looked to as models. We want to imitate them. But we will want to do this only if and so far as we see that they do not violate their intent in their actions. We do not expect them to realize their intent fully, but if they do realize it to a degree greater than the rest of us do, we honor them as exceptional. They, too, are unable to act on every thing in such a way as to enhance it.

Knowing the common conditions is also a way of internalizing them, though the internalization is not as basic and is more surely projective than that which results from an individual's adjusting himself to become an ethical being. Knowledge keeps the conditions apart from the knower to some extent, while giving them an internal role. The making oneself ethical, places emphases on the will, on the internal conversion of oneself. Knowledge, instead, may be merely accepted. Though it has some effect on oneself as an integrated being, the result falls short of what is achieved when one makes a willed attempt to reorganize oneself. Paradigmatic individuals awaken the will, not thought; they prompt one to readjust oneself and not simply to accommodate something in the guise of the known.

It is questionable whether a Kantian ethics requires any action. At most, it could be said to tell us how to make the actions, in which we in fact engage, be ethical acts. But then it will be dependent on whatever it is that we happen to be doing. The Kantian in fact has only an ethics of responsibility. He stands in contrast with the utilitarian who has only a morality of accountability. The one rightly deals with individuals as members of a kingdom of ends; the other rightly deals with men as in a public world. The idea of a projection of the union of ethical principles and individual serves as a way of joining the internally and the externally oriented dimensions of a good life.

The question, "Why should I be ethical?" allows for two emphases—on the I and on the ethical. As emphasizing the I, it has to do with my completion; as emphasizing the ethical, it has to do with my actions for the benefit of the others. Neither factor, is to be considered apart, but the different emphases must be recognized. Were one to consider only oneself, there would be a question why one should act. Were one to consider only action, a man might still ask why he should benefit others.

It follows from the view that our actions promote the way other entities are able to incorporate within themselves the conditions which govern them and us, that the function of paradigmatic, model individuals is to make us be like them, for those individuals most adequately bring together ethical principles and individual realities. The individuals usually do not do something to other men or to other actualites; instead, they awaken in these the effort to become excellent. They act, as it were, on other men not as so many physical objects, but in a different way, showing what the good life is like. They join principles and life so that they not only project a continuation of the union in an indefinite way, but so project it that it can be made determinate by different men. They make other men act through a projection which the others make determinate. Where these must fill out their projections with their own acts, the model individuals present projections prompting others to make the projections determinate. The actions that should be produced are produced by the beings who benefit from the model. A partial analogue is offered in the obedience of an animal to its master, for the animal does what it otherwise would not do.

How could model men provide a projection others make determinate? A projection is private, the outcome of the union of what a man is at root and universal ethical principles. That projection begins in privacy and ends there. But if so, how could any one make it determinate by a public act? The second question is easier to answer than the first. An act starts privately and makes a private projection be public. If one uses that answer as a guide, the first question can be answered by holding that men, by their imitation of models, or by being inspired by them, give the projection of those models an objectivity they did not have before. Such an answer requires one to suppose that the models somehow awaken in others an activity that has, as one of its consequences, the determination of the projection characteristic of those models. The others will then be taken to be inspired by the result of the union achieved by the models, leading them to try to duplicate the status of those models. In that attempt, they make the projection determinate. But ordinary men make their own private projections public. On the present supposition, though, there is no warrant for supposing that a model's projection has a public counterpart or manifestation. The model seems to project an area of activity which remains forever private, leaving the model in a state inferior to that of men who actively determine their own projections.

Do inspired men, by virtue of their attempt to be like their models, provide determinations which have the power to make the projections of the models both public and determinate? If they do, to be inspired would require a distinctive kind of activity, quite unlike any other, for it would publicly realize the projection of the model. The answer leaves me troubled. How could an inspired man make public the private projection of another?

July 4

The models who inspire us to become ethical are not themselves necessarily ethical. They represent something higher. Not only do they themselves occupy themselves with an ultimate reality, God or some other finality, but they so incorporate this that they make themselves perfected to a degree that those who are superbly ethical cannot. The ethical principles which the latter embody are themselves not final nor grounded directly in finalities. Nor are they discovered by attending to finalities or the conditions they express. Instead, they are the products of the acceptance of models. That acceptance involves the conversion of the understood being of those models into ethical principles as requiring to be incorporated in the individual. If this is so, have we not lost the justification for being ethical, which was supposed to involve the making internal what was externally determinative of individual men? It would, were it not also the case that ethical principles, incorporated in individuals, are also specifications of conditions which relate those individuals to the rest of the world.

Model men enable one to insist on the incorporation of the ethical principles so that at some remove we can imitate the models by making conditions concrete and inward. The models inspire us to become inwardly what we are outwardly. But that inspiration makes us adopt, not the conditions which the models incorporate, but different ones—the ethical. Why should this be? Might not one, instead of making use of ethical principles, make use of some other specifications of final conditions? Will there not be models which incorporate different conditions? This question seems easier to answer than the other. We have many models. There are great social figures, great defenders of justice, great intellectual giants, great artists. But these, instead of inspiring one to be ethical, seem to make one want to imitate them and therefore to pursue the principles which they carried out in their own ways. Evidently, we have at least two cases: one where the inspiring models provide an occasion to adopt ethical principles, and one where inspiring models prompt us to adopt the very kind of principles which they incorporated in a splendid way. Religious inspirational figures may lead one not to be ethical, but to be religious.

When one is not prompted to imitate a model but is just inspired by him, one tries to become as excellent as he is. Unable to imitate or uninterested in imitation, and being in fact conditioned by what else there is in the world, one is forced to have recourse to the utilization of those conditions which will enable him to compensate for the limitations to which others subject him. The union that the ethical permits, since it involves an indetermination to be filled out in action, is an agency by which such compensation can be provided. Were a man, instead, to adopt the formal rules of a logic, he would be faced with a projection to be filled out with actions, not directed at improving other entities, but at those which merely make a domain determinate through the use of diagrams and proofs. If these match what is objectively the case, there is a balance between the inward and the outward, but still no benefiting of the external objects.

The ethical requires actions which enhance others. Is this not because the determinations which one might provide from within are unable to make a projection sufficiently determinate? Is not something similar to be said about programs, legislation, or any arrangement, other than the logical and the mathematical? Is the exception due to the fact that the desired determinations in these fields are thought to be homogeneous with them? Is it not that a diagram, though in fact requiring an action, is made to be wholly within a logical or mathematical domain, whereas an act directed against another actuality is always to some extent outside the domain which is projected, thereby compelling the projection to be involved in what is external to it?

July 10

In the course of trying to get clear about theology, I have been led to make a map of the various kinds of disciplines, their components and objectives. It covers familiar ground in good part, but there are some important new distinctions, particularly between an unemotional and an emotional expression of wonder and of its specializations.

Along the lines started in *Beyond All Appearances,* wonder can be divided into an openness, humility, interest, awe, and reverence. Each of these is a pure position, not yet specialized by particular circumstances. To that extent, it is not relevant to particular activities rooted in such circumstances. As pure, each is occupied with several finalities emotionally if, like a pure or philosophical theology, it is interested not in a finality as such but in what is important to man's welfare. It is not altogether clear to me what the termini of emotional forms of the other pure attitudes would be. The unemotional, I have termed, Substance, Being, Possibility, Existence, and Unity.

The different attitudes are matched by appropriate mysticisms—a social; Buddhistic or ontological; Platonic; Taoistic or natural; and a religious. Each attitude expresses us. The attitude requires only that we concern ourselves with or try to adjust ourselves to the finalities. Mysticisms, instead, attempt to make contact with finalities, to lose themselves in these, to identify themselves with them in some way.

It is the task of the disciplines of philosophical sociology, metaphysics, philosophical analysis, philosophical cosmology, and philosophical or pure theology to try to formulate the nature of the final reality which can be the object of a pure attitude and could satisfy an appropriate mysticism. Everyone of them has two branches, one in which the reality is understood to be the objective of an emotional, another in which it is the objective of a non-emotional form of a pure attitude. Not being clear regarding the nature of the terminus of a non-emotional attitude for theology, or the nature of the termini of emotional forms required by the other disciplines, my list gives only five out of a possible ten cases. I should add: an emotional kind of philosophical sociology—nationalistic interpretations; a kind of emotional metaphysics—existentialism; an emotional kind of analysis—taxonomy; an emotional philosophical cosmology—positivism; and a non-emotional kind of theology—natural theology.

Each of the ten disciplines is specialized and pluralized in distinctive ways, each with an emotional and a non-emotional form. Myths and theologies are evidently emotionally grounded, while the others are not. If there is to be a non-emotional as well as an emotional form of each, we should have a participative kind of anthropology as well as a scientific type; an emotional type of particularlized ontology somewhat like that presented by the German romantics; ontologies based on scientific cur-

rents and views of the day; emotional as well as straightforward logics—
the emotional perhaps being cognate with Freudian analysis; emotional
as well as non-emotional cosmologies, perhaps Westernized forms of Tao,
and emotional as well as non-emotional theologies—perhaps natural
theologies which take their start with different views of nature. These
particular specializations of the ten basic pure disciplines, when involved
in particular communities, subject to different senses of the grades of
realities, allowing for different modes of discourse and inquiry, engaged
in different types of art, or exercising different rituals respectively, will
be exhibited in the form of communal celebrations, claims for rights,
various types of thought, different creative products, and the different
religions. Once again, these would have to be divided into emotional
and non-emotional types.

The basic disciplines could be said to begin and end in different ways.
A philosophic sociology begins in experience, touches on what is final
so as to arrive at a midpoint; metaphysics attends to a midpoint from
which one can move in two directions, toward particulars or toward the
finality, Being. Analysis dissects the midpoint. Philosophical cosmology
starts at a finality and touches particulars, to end at a midpoint. Philosophical or pure theology converges on a midpoint from the position of
particulars as well as from the position of the finality, Unity or God.

It would be more in consonance with previous usages of mine to
take 'metaphysics' to refer to all the pure disciplines and their objects,
whether emotionally or non-emotionally considered. What I have called
'metaphysics' above should therefore be called 'objective ontology'. This
would seem to leave a problem: the various pure disciplines are One's
for many particularizations. If we take metaphysics to encompass all these
pure disciplines, we will have a One for these Many Ones. But that need
not lead to an infinite regress, or cause any embarrassment, the first
because there is no Many to the metaphysics, and the second because
every Many is made up of units or Ones, so that the many pure disciplines
should raise no new issue.

But if metaphysics is the enterprise that encompasses all the five
pure disciplines, will it not either swallow these up into a single One, or
allow them to be diverse and thereby itself lose all unity? Is metaphysics
a sheer One or Many? Must it not have an emotional and an unemotional
form? These questions do raise difficulties. I think we must say that
metaphysics is a single enterprise, and that it has two dimensions. One
is emotional, the other unemotional. It exercises wonder emotionally in
five distinct forms, and also maintains it as a single interlocking of the

different forms dealt with unemotionally. The emotional allows for the consideration of separate ventures intensively moving into different finalities in depth. The unemotional sets each of the unemotional ventures alongside the others, but recognizes that each has the others as subordinates as well. It offers an interconnected set of accounts of the different pure disciplines and their objects as not altogether without reference to one another.

July 11

Both natural theology and metaphysics arrive at their conclusions by cold-blooded inferences. Both are concerned with Unity. How do they differ?

Natural theology attends to Unity alone, and does so as having a religious import. Metaphysics attends to Unity as one of a number of finalities, each of which is both related and subordinated to the others. The natural theologian is as unemotional as the metaphysician, and deals with the same Unity; he formulates the nature of that Unity as a reality to which men should adjust themselves and which it is possible for some to directly participate in. The metaphysician, instead, tries to understand what Unity as such is, indicating how it could be reached from finite positions and allow for immediate involvements. But there is nothing in the Unity, as he understands it, that reflects the presence or needs of man, or assures the success of any of his ventures.

What is true of the relation between metaphysician and natural theologian should be true of the relation of the metaphysician and those who are unemotionally occupied with finalities other than Unity. There should be disciplines dealing just with Substance, Being, Possibility, and Existence—philosophical sociology, philosophical ontology, analysis, and philosophical cosmology—which differ from metaphysics not only because this deals with them all and in interrelationship, but because when it attends to them one after the other it does not deal with them as offering terminations for distinctive mystical experiences and as being appropriate to specific attitudes.

A metaphysician is always in the state of wonder which is intensified as openness, humility, interest, awe, and reverence; the other disciplines concentrate on the openness, etc., and identify termini for these as well as for an immediate mystical involvement. A metaphysician is always emphasizing a finality; the others always emphasize approaches which take a finality to be a kind of conceived object able to provide a focal point for distinctive human efforts.

If this is right, a form of wonder, such as reverence, should have a number of distinct forms: a. an emotional, subtending every practiced religion; b. a non-emotional, subtending every natural theology; c. and d. the particularized forms of a. and b.; and e. the reverence that is never free from wonder itself, or from other specifications of this, and is a moment within the mytaphysician's expression of a wonder directed toward Unity.

What is most difficult to get clear is the difference between a, b, and e, and particularly between a and b on the one side and e on the other. And once these are distinguished, there will have to be counterparts for them, in which the finalities are directly dealt with. There will also be disciplines in which the two extremes are joined.

Does not metaphysics thrust toward final realities and penetrate them to some degree, whereas other disciplines try to formulate what it is that is thrust toward and into by the fundamental divisions of wonder and the different mysticisms? The metaphysician on such an account would know, but the pure theologian—and the philosophical sociologist, the philosophical ontologist, the philosophical analyst, and the philosophical cosmologist—would construct. If so, we must say that the metaphysician does not only move to finalities from the position of daily objects, but that he does so by starting somewhere in those finalities. This means that he does not only await a grounding and an acceptance of the evidenced, but that he also relaxes his grasp on what grounds and accepts this in order to have the evidence grounded and accepted. He not only advances into final realities but returns from them so as to have a grasp of them as at the midpoint between the evidenced which is reached from the position of evidence, and the evidenced which is reached from the position of a grounding, accepting finality. This latter I never did consider in *Beyond All Appearances* or in *First Considerations*. Yet, it is a midpoint, accounting for the fact that one can begin from both ends. A metaphysician comes to that midpoint from daily objects and from the finalities reached in depth, independently of one another. Such a view seems to require that a finality, as at a midpoint and known by the metaphysician, have the power not only to affect actualities but to affect the finality's own inwardness.

July 12

The wonder that characterizes metaphysics is instantiated in openness, humility, interest, awe, and reverence. Since these have counterparts in distinctive mysticisms, there should be a single, all-encompassing kind of mysticism matching wonder in the same way that the particular mysticisms match the specializations of wonder. Let this all-encompassing mysticism, for the moment, be called 'innocence'. Metaphysics can then be understood to be two-pronged. One prong will start in daily life and ground the wonder that requires an individual to adjust himself to the reality of all the finalities; the other prong will reach into all the finalities, but without distinguishing them or having any strong grasp of them. It will use the evidence, with which wonder starts, to move toward the evidenced, at the same time that it moves toward the evidenced from the other side, enriching it with the content that innocence terminated in. The outcome will be the interrelated finalities in the form of evidenced objective items. Once one has arrived there, it will be possible to move back to the origin of the wonder on the one side, and into the innocently met finalities on the other, the one requiring the sustaining by actualities, the other a pull inward and possession by the finalities.

There need be no distinction between an emotional and a non-emotional form of the metaphysical endeavor. These distinctions arise only when one begins to distinguish the different attitudes of awe, etc., and the different mystical specializations of an aboriginal innocence. Philosophical cosmology, a pure or philosophical theology, and other pure disciplines, have both emotional and non-emotional forms which unite particular attitudes (specializing wonder) and particular mysticisms (specializing innocence). Each of these pure disciplines will in turn be instantiated in various different, limited, oppositional, contextualized forms. Pure theology, for example, is instantiated by the various special theologies appopriate to particular religions. These theologies are themselves instantiated in religions, i.e., unions of contextualized forms of reverence and in religious mysticism, which is to say, in worship, and in religious mysticism as tied to this.

Community celebrations, existentialized ontologies, particular types of thinking and inquiry, cosmologies oriented in particular sciences and at particular times, are alongside the religions. All of these, unlike the disciplines they diversely instantiate, are primarily oriented in daily experience.

Starting now the other way, we can begin with the acknowledgment of a particular religion, and recognize it to make use of a particularized, contextualized form of reverence in the shape of a ritualized worship. The recognition of the need to make contact with what is merely pointed toward by the religion is characteristic of a religious mysticism. The union of a religious mysticism with worship, yields a particular religion, articulated in its theology. The freeing of the theology from the context yields a pure theology. This is concerned with what could terminate a pure reverence. It takes account, too, of the content that the mystic provides.

Pure theology is one of a number of basic disciplines, all encompassed by metaphysics. Each of those disciplines has an emotional and a nonemotional form—so that we get, for example, a natural pure theology and a religiously relevant one.

From this, it appears that a metaphysician begins at a point which faces the finalities as having expressions both in actualities and in the inwardness of the finalities, and that he moves from the actualities and the inwardness at the same time, to arrive at a better focused, more intelligible form of the union of the object of wonder and innocence than he had initially. If this is correct, a metaphysician achieves an intensified, more intelligible form of the object than that which he had started with originally.

This state which I have supposed here to be distinctive, is it not identical with what the Eastern thinkers seek? Is it not that which they say cannot be found except after a long period in which one makes a vigorous effort to detach oneself from the world and from one's idiosyncratic self? I think it differs in a number of ways: It is initially a continuum and not well integrated; it is in disequilibrium, sometimes sliding toward the end where wonder begins, and sometimes toward the innocently attained end; and it is involved with and is ready to split among five different attitudes and five different mystical encounters.

We all begin with and never lose an innocent wonder in which we face a continuum inseparable on one side from daily objects and, on the other, from a dense nuanced final depth. Metaphysics proper begins with the attempt to free the one side from the particulars with which it is involved, and ends by backing the freed content with what has been obtained from an innocent confrontation of the depth. The outcome is a steady solidified union of the content that innocence has been able to provide, with the evidence used by wonder. This is specialized in five pure disciplines, themselves with many instances, which in turn have concrete contextualized forms in the shape of particular myths, religions, and so on.

One consequence of these observations has importance for logic. I have remarked at other times that the truth of a premiss is different from the truth of a statement directed at a matter of fact, and that if one is to obtain the former from the latter, one will have to take a right-angled turn. I concluded that a conclusion should have the kind of truth that the premiss had, so that in order to recover the kind of truth that the initial statement had, the conclusion would have to be turned at right angles toward an objective state of affairs and there supported. But now I think what must be said is that the premiss has a conclusion-directed truth, which-had-been-empirically-sustained, and that what is wanted for a conclusion is a truth that is empirically relevant. On arriving at a conclusion in logic, one does not merely offer this to the world, but brings up a backing from the world so as to enable that conclusion to be pertinent to the world. By doing this one is able to keep the conclusion in the realm of logic and still recognize it to be the kind of conclusion that has the pertinence to the same world to which the premiss was pertinent. Only when we want to stop our logical thinking, do we offer the conclusion for a sustaining by the world. Until then we pull into the realm of logic content from the world to back the conclusion as something empirically relevant. We then do something like what the metaphysician does when he brings the content, that his innocence impinged upon, together with the wonder that was carrying his evidence forward. He uses the content of an innocent encounter to give backing to his wonder. And just as a logician must finally end his thinking and allow his conclusion to be accepted or rejected by the world, so the metaphysician must finally offer his results for acceptance by the object of his innocent encounter.

Both logician and metaphysician are initially in touch with the very reality that in the end accepts what they are concluding to. Both first use that reality solely to give a backing to their results, thereby making manifest that those results are not idle fancies but pertinent to what is real. Only later do they release the backed results to the world. This may modify them on accepting them. A conclusion that merely released it, could possibly be swallowed by the world without remainder. By having it backed by content from that world, it is already known to be pertinent to the world. The content is then attended to in such a way as to make it also have a reference to us, as offering a backing to be made integral to our claim.

A backed conclusion and a terminus of wonder pull part of reality into our realm, precluding them from ever being entirely at the mercy of that reality. The backing we added to the conclusion, or to the terminus of our wonder, though it existed apart from us, is there because of us. The continuity of that backing with the exterior reality, allows what we acknowledged to fit in with what is real; the use of some of that real as backing prevents what we let go from being entirely absorbed by the reality.

*   *   *

Why should one fight for a country stupid enough to be at war?

The best remedy for past discriminations is remedial courses and work, enabling disadvantaged people to be ready to work on a footing with others.

To give someone a piece of one's mind is to subtract something precious from oneself.

It is always now, but what is now will not be again.

July 13

We are always in a state of innocent-wonder, though this is spread over a continuum and is in disequilibrium, both in the sense of stressing one factor rather than another at different times, and in the sense of being on the verge of breaking up into a plurality of specializations. The state is as much objective as subjective, which is to say, it involves us in what is final at the same time that it expresses us. A metaphysical inquiry, like every other, is grounded in a similar double fact. The metaphysician attempts to achieve a better focus, a better equilibrium, and to move step by step from the world of every day at the same time that he enriches the result of this effort by a filling (what I called 'backing' yesterday). He arrives at an object in which the termini of the wonder and the innocence support one another. What is known is then not the empty outcome of an inference, but that outcome as filled out by content obtained from the terminus of the initial innocence. As he moves toward the evidenced he also moves from the depth of the finalities together, as grasped by an unreflecting innocence, and thereby produces an innocent-wonder in which evidenced wondrous content is filled out by what was pulled into it from the position of innocence. The metaphysician is not content to remain there, for the content that he then has is held away from what is ultimately real; he does not really know whether the filled out content is entirely in accord with what is objective. As a consequence, he must present the filled-out content to the finalities for acceptance.

In the past, I have spoken of judgment, naming, logic, inquiry, and the arts as involving a thrust beyond the content at which we stop and which we articulately possess. The present reflections about metaphysics lead to the awareness that these accounts are all empirically grounded, emphasizing a beginning with present data and leading us to a world beyond where the data eventually terminate. While we are progressing toward what is real, either by means of an adumbration in judgment, an intensive penetration when using proper names, the sustaining of a conclusion apart from an inference, the terminating of an inquiry in a world going its own way, or the arrival at Existence as the locus of a cosmic tragedy and comedy, we also move in the reverse way, filling out the outcome of judgment, names, conclusion, inquiry, and arts with content pulled from the reality we had already been in contact with. The explicit thrust into that reality, about which I have readily spoken, comes later; it is justified by the filling that had already been obtained from the reality at which the thrust is directed.

This view seems most plausible when we attend to proper names and particularly to those used for God. The names themselves are thought to be tinged with the beings themselves. In the case of ordinary proper names, though, when we do not use them addressively, we seem to (but do not in fact) lose all the filling which had been obtained when the proper names were in fact used. We have, though, only obscured the fact that the names do not just become part of the named but possess something of the named as part of themselves, and can be credited with a special dignity as a consequence. For a short time, proper names, even away from their actual reference to some man, retain the content which they obtained when they pulled into their termini something of the reality of the being addressed.

Another way of making the same point about the introduction of a filling into content is to remark on our satisfaction in remaining for a while with language, judgments, concepts. Linguistic philosophy builds on the fact that we are able to remain with language. If I am right, this is due to the fact that we had already been beyond language and had added to the language content which we had encountered beyond it. That content warrants our moving into what lies beyond. Would we in fact follow the route of an adumbration if we had not already been at the terminus of it in an unsatisfactory form, and now, in the form of a judgment, have a satisfactory start for a penetration? Were adumbration a mere addition to the judgment, we might subsequently follow it, but until then would have to be content to point beyond the judgment to what would be able to make it true. The use of a filling for judgmental content makes adumbration be the outcome of a pull on the part of the source of a filling. It connects the content we have isolated in judgment with the reality that makes the judgment true.

From this point of view, intentionality, as understood by Brentano and Husserl, would have to be taken to have some of the external world adhering to intentional objects. There would be no antecedent 'bracketting'; the bracketting would be one with the adhering of the filling to the intentional content. It would be a bracketting, moreover, which allowed one to pass continuously into the external world via the adhering filling.

Partial anticipations of the present view have been expressed by me at least three times—when dealing a. with the me, b. with domains, and c. with pivots.

a. In speaking of the me I have remarked that we not only arrive at it but are met by a sustaining; the me is constituted both from a publicly referential side and from below. What is also to be said is that when we arrive at that me we find ourselves not only moving into what we are in depth but also moving backwards toward ourselves as the referential agents. The me is known to be that which is being attended to as well as sustained, at the same time that it is faced as public and maintained apart from its sustaining, while it was being possessed from within. The me is at the juncture of two pivots, one which starts and ends with the referring to it, the other of which starts and ends with the occupation with it from within.

b. When speaking of mathematics, I developed the idea of a domain that involved the coming together of factors from the side of actualities and from the side of a finality, and requiring a projection of an area within which further unions of the two could be produced. I did not at the time also add, which the above considerations would support, that mathematical constructions also referred one back toward the actualities and toward the finality, and that the domain was constituted by the content derived from the actualities, and filled in with what was obtained from the finality, Possibility.

If one speaks of the object of metaphysics as itself a kind of domain, we seem not to have (what was presupposed in the account of mathematics) an acknowledgment of irreducible realities; everything seems to be reduced to a domain. But a domain is not something held away from the realities; it is the juncture of them. But now it would seem that there is no difference between an appearance and the object of some such discipline as metaphysics, since both are the outcome of the interplay of other more basic items. Appearances, though, have a sensuous component, and are new products in which oppositional factors are united in such a way that neither can be found. But the object of metaphysics is the evidenced, filled-out object of a wondrous use of evidence, itself already part of the finalities—or, alternatively, it is the innocently reached inward nature of final realities pulling away from a terminating wonder.

But ought there not then be, at the actualities, the counterpart of what is now being maintained about the finalities? Must there not only be appearances of the actualities constituted with the help of expressions of the finalities, but also specialized conditionings by those finalities filled out by expressions of the actualities, and inward pullings by the actualities on content held on to by the finalities? I think so. That would mean that transcendentals would be filled out by the actualities, and that what was conditioned by the finalities would also be pulled inward by the actualities.

c. In dealing with the me, it was observed that we pivot about another. More generally, pivots are items toward which and from which we move. I know me sometimes by attending to myself without intermediary, but also often enough by taking some other to be a pivot that may add additional content on my way toward myself. In myself I am a pivot for my possessing of the me and my external approach to it.

When you are attended to, there must be: a. a reference by me which is filled out by you; b. a surfacing by you which I fixate; c. an inwardization by you of what you have surfaced under the limitation of a publicizing by me; and d. an acceptance of what you have surfaced under the limitations of your possessing it. My dealing with you is preceded by an acquaintance with the inward depths of things, vague and in disequilibrium, which I attempt to get clear. That antecedent grasp of what is real in the world is due to my having issued out of it to become a kind of focalized center. My antecedent grasp of the finalities, similarly, is due to my having issued out of an involvement with them to become a kind of focalized center in another sense. In the first way I become merely different from other actualities; in the second, merely distinct from the finalities.

I know finalities as they are, by filling out an innocently grasped and possessed inwardness with wondrous, evidenced content, and by filling out the wondrous evidenced content with what I have brought to bear from the inwardness, innocently reached. Similarly, I know actualities (and therefore you) as they are, by filling out my unfocused grasp of them as real with what I am publicly able to attend to, and by filling what I publicly arrive at by what I have been able to add from their inwardness.

Or, to take an Hegelian theme: The meaning that lies outside what is said fills out the said to make it be said about the meaning, and to be filled out by the said to make the outside be a meaning-said. At the same time, the said is filled out by the meaning to make it be a meant-saying, and fills out the meaning to make it be the meaning of what is said.

I have not yet brought everything into clear focus, but I think there is a considerable difference between what I said a few days ago and what I am saying now. We have here a good illustration of how one person moves from a confusedly grasped new view to achieve a better, though not altogether clear understanding of it.

Stated most generally, what has now been arrived at is a four-fold result. Given an *a* and *b*, we have at *a*, *a* filling out an expression of *b*, and *b* filling out the surfacing of *a;* and also have at *b*, *b* filling out an expression of *a*, and *a* filling out the surfacing of *b*. In addition, we have possessions by the sources of the fillings, and movements in depth to the sources of the fillings. The results must be applied to actualities, to finalities, to you, to me, to judgments, logic, religion, art. Instead of first taking the known to thrust toward an object, we will have to begin with our reach into the object as an *a* which is filled out and fills out what we know, at the same time that the known will be seen, on our side, as *b*, filled out and filling out what we ourselves are manifesting. This has the consequence that an item will have to be seen in a four-fold way. Something known, for example, will fill out and be filled out by the object, and will fill out and be filled out by the subject. In addition, it will be thrusting toward both subject and object, allowing us to move into them in depth, and allowing us to recognize it to be continuous both with the object and the subject. As a consequence, the known as filled out and filling out both the object and the subject will be the same for both. Yet subject and object are quite distinct and may differ as the animate and the inanimate.

"This is a stone" articulates a this-stone, at the same time that it articulates my unitary knowing. It fills out and is filled out by the one with different content and results than when it fills out and is filled out by the other. This would seem to require that the evidenced, for example, would have to provide evidence for actualities. And if that were so, the evidence with which we start would not only be an attenuation of a finality, but would also be an attenuation of an actuality. Could we have sheer evidence entirely freed from an actuality, would we be able to distinguish it from the evidenced? Apparently not. And if not, will either evidence or evidenced be any more pertinent to actualities than to finalities? No. Yet they seem more pertinent to the latter, for they are attenuations of these. But that is because we forget that they are attenuations only because of the actualities. Without the actualities, they would collapse into the finalities. As attenuations, they evidence the actualities; as evidence, they are the finalities attenuated. 'This is a stone' is both this-stone articulated and myself as an articulation, a way in which I express myself. It is a Many-ed-One, Many from the side of actualities or of knowers, and One from the side of finalities or of objects of knowledge. The knower of an actuality determines how the whole will be broken up; the object or finality determines what the parts are and how they belong together.

July 14

An appearance is constituted by factors originating with actualities and finalities. The result is distinct from either of the factors. One could not know by attending to an appearance what the factors were or the nature of the sources of these. Instead one must attend to the fringes, or better make use of the fringes of the appearances in a penetrative move toward the sources. But in the case of the objects of the pure disciplines, and the metaphysics which encompasses all their objects, the factors retain their natures; the outcome is just the filling out of each by the other.

'This is a stone' contains 'this-stone' twice over: in the guise of an indivisible unity possessed by the stone but as the resultant of a concentration from 'this is a stone' by the stone; and in the guise of a multiplicity held together by the judging man but as the resultant of his use of 'this,is,a,stone.' 'This-stone' is different in the two cases, for in the one it is the stone at its maximum dispersal just as a stone, while in the other it is the judging man as maximally unifying. 'This is a stone' is filled and filling in one way by the stone and in another way by the judger, so that the 'this-stone' has a different import for each, being attached to different kinds of inwardnesses.

'This is a stone' stands in between the judger and the stone. As language analysts have maintained, it has an integrity of its own. But it is not separable from the judger or the object, and in fact is pulled on by both the object and the judger, past the 'this-stone' which they diversely constitute, into them as irreducible realities. The ignoring of that pull in both directions is one of the major defects of the Hegelian view. This allows one to remain with something like 'this-stone' as having two sides, and requires a final unification in 'this is a stone' (to use this as an illustration for a multiplicity of cases involving consciousness, self-consciousness, work, history, and so on). At most, one could say that Hegel allowed for a pull into what was all-encompassing, but never for a pull into a multiplicity of individual men. One could, though, understand Hegel's *Phenomenology of Mind* to emphasize a thrust into individual men, and the *Logic* to emphasize a thrust into his one finality. But then the relation of the two becomes difficult to understand.

Bringing the current reflections to bear on the knowing of you, we must say that there is a neutral content, 'the-publicized-you-as-known-by-another' at the same time that the knower fills out and is filled out by the presence of the you to him, to constitute a 'you-for-me'. The 'you-for-me' thus has two orientations. There is also a thrust from it into the knower as a continuation of a pivotting move, in which he utilized the initial common content, the-publicized-you-as-known-by-another.

I utilize you for filling the neutral content faced by me. It is faced by you who pull back that filling into yourself. You use me for filling the neutral content which is yourself externalized, but it is I who pull back that filling into myself. The two pullings make adumbration be ontologically significant. In religious terms, there is an expression of grace by the divine; an act of faithful acceptance by the individual; and an initial adoption of the divine and a recovery of this by God. The two together meet in a theologically understood God, inseparable from a thrust into God in himself and into the believer in himself. A theologian makes use of the being of God to fill out a reverentially expressed terminus; he makes use of his being to fill out the grace which reaches to him. Does it make sense, though, to speak of using the being of God, or of a man adding to a divine grace? It does, if it is not thought that the being of God is anything more than the content one had aboriginally reached, and if the addition that man makes to a divine grace is taken to be nothing more than a support for that grace, the allowing it to be there, but requiring a pull by men (their inward possession of faith) if it is to be made wholly their own.

There is a realistic orientation to our judgments because real content is made to adhere to what we know. But there is always the possibility of error, for what is asserted is definite, particular, limited, more precise than the adherent material warrants; it can be justified by the recovery of the adherent material by that of which we speak. The filling is indeterminate; the pull on this is by a specific entity able to make it determinate.

The realistic orientation is matched by a subjective which makes the content something known or 'intended'. The actual import of the content for us depends on the particular way in which we in fact recover the material that had been made to adhere to the content. If the parallel with the realistic orientation is to be maintained, it must also be said that it is the object that makes the indeterminate material of ourselves adhere to what is known.

One consequence of these observations is that whatever we entertain will have a realistic tonality, since it will be filled out by material that has been introduced from the recesses of a reality before we in fact use the item at the beginning of an actual reference or penetration. This means that the wildest fancy has a realistic filling. This will not necessarily make it true of anything, for there is no particular item answering to the fancy's particularity. The fact, though, does make evident how art, no matter how freely constructed and how opposed to ordinary occurrences, has a factor that allows it to illuminate Existence. Held apart, emotionally enjoyed, art is incidentally brought to bear on Existence. Used symbolically, it thrusts toward Existence, taking us to what is vitally ongoing, apart from all particulars. Existence itself pulls back into itself the content that we employed to make the work have a realistic tonality. It uses the content that had been imposed on the artist to make the work be an exhibition of a privacy. At the same time, the individual artist pulls that private content back into himself.

July 16

When I know you, a. I penetrate beyond your surface and am met by your resistant self who fills out what I am knowing; b. I reach into you and bring to bear on what I know yourself in the role of a filling. As a consequence, as I penetrate and am blocked by you, I also make use of what I had antecedently made contact with, so as to give determinate backing to what I know. At the same time, c. you make use of what I am making available to make yourself be faced with something determinate and present, and d. you attend to me as one who knows you, and I fill out what you are acknowledging as myself. Combining a. and c., I am filled out by you in you, and by you as using me to back up what is facing you. Combining b. and d., I use you to give determinateness to the content I know, and you do the same for me, so that we have surfaces backed by resistant fillings.

A cure, I have argued, requires one to come to the surface of oneself from below. This would appear to be c. When I provide you with oc-

casions for this, I bring to bear your content on what I confront; this
would appear to be b. Because I make use of you as a filling, b, you are
encouraged, c, to act from within to make yourself publicly determinate
as cured. In knowing you, I penetrate and am resisted, at the same time
that you are met by me filling out what you know of me; a and b overlap
and so do c and d.

When I penetrate you, I pivot at you as one who made material
available for me; when you attend to me you pivot at me making use of
what I am making available to you. Though I and you initially make use
of different material, when we penetrate and are resisted, we engage in
a similar act as part of our pivotting at one another, thereby making use
of inward content twice over, once antecedently and once as a consequence of a pivotting penetration.

My utilizing material does not penetrate to the beginning of your
penetrating me, or conversely. I provoke you to bring your deeper self
to bear on what I am presenting to you. And something similar is true
of what I do with respect to the finalities and what they do with respect
to me. My and your pivotting act reach into the other, and though they
do not get to the center, do move outside the limits of their sources to
touch the others.

August 18

I have now completed another draft of 'You, I, and the Others'.
The revision consisted mainly in retyping the passages I had previously
overwritten, changed, added to, and in taking care of transpositions and
omitting indicated deletions. I have not reread any of it, and when I get
back from Spain, where I will go next week with Jonathan, primarily to
visit the Prado, I will make the rereading a primary task. But I will then
also be starting a new school term, and have a number of lectures to
give, as well as a paper to write for the evaluation research people, after
I visit their large establishment in Minneapolis.

I have also finished the first book of 'Man: Private and Public' and
will spend the next week and some of the time when I return in making
a clean copy of the rest of the work. I hope I will be able to get that off
a little after I send off YIAO. I had thought originally of including the
material in MPP in YIAO, but the result would have been a very large,
perhaps unwieldy book.

* * *

It is possible not to mind working at a fatiguing, boring, poor paying job for an indefinite time if one sees it as a mere means to furthering some important project—learning from experience, carrying out a divine injunction, earning enough to be able to spend some time writing poetry or novels, painting, investigating, inventing, and the like.

One who has a satisfactory job or no job at all, but who is devoting his life to some creative work, often enough consoles himself for being neglected by his contemporaries by supposing that he will be discovered in a future generation. Such discoveries do take place. But this, one cannot know. He may be neglected in the future as he is in the present, and perhaps for the same reasons. Clinging to the idea that one will be discovered by a later generation may therefore have its element of self-delusion. It would be healthier to recognize oneself to be adventuring, exploring, discovering. If nothing is achieved, or nothing of importance is achieved, it will still be worth while to give oneself to the adventure of creating, learning, and the mastering of oneself.

Those in prisons, the blind, and others who are handicapped in various ways could combine both of these answers. They can see themselves as having an opportunity to learn from a special vantage point, and also to be in a position to explore and adventure in their limited confines in ways they otherwise could not. They will use what they are forced to undergo as providing a means to understanding the nature of man from a special angle, and they will be able to adventure in thought, feeling, and imagination to explore from a special angle possible experiences, thoughts, and hypotheses. If they are able to write creatively or engage in some other creative work then or later, they will, of course, be able to join with those who see themselves preparing for a better time, and as having an adventure in expression able to give value and justification to a life.

September 17

Hegel in his *Phenomenology* approaches his absolute from the standpoint of human knowers in their involvement with what else there be, what is rational 'for us'. If we were to deal with some such issue as contemporaneity, more at the center of my view than his, but to do it in his fashion, we would have to attend to other objects and note that they are coordinate with ourselves. In one or in a number of moves, we would eventually arrive at contemporaneity as the 'identity in difference' that was able to terminate in us both, while still leaving something outside both. From this point on, we have three alternatives, of which only one was considered by Hegel: a. we can continue in the same way to get richer and richer meanings of contemporaneity; b. we can move in depth into the source of contemporaneity and thereby uncover a series of categories each of which is closer to being all-encompassing and in equilibrium between extremes; or c. we can move to a new category altogether, and then continue on until we arrive at the absolute—Hegel's view. Not only does Hegel not suppose that we might always approach other items from a side until we get to the very end of them, but he does not recognize that, though we want to assume the position of the absolute or some finality as it is neutral between extremes (as an identity in difference that includes those extremes within its orbit and gives them meaning), particulars are not to be approached in this way. To understand what they are in depth, we must penetrate into them, and not get to a midpoint, or to an absolute in which they are coordinate with us. Hegel's method is appropriate to the finalities, only one of which he allows, taking all others to be limited forms of it. It is a method that concerns itself with categories not with realities, on the supposition that the categories are the absolute, since for Hegel knowledge is identical (in difference) with the known, and is constituted of universals.

October 3

In the last weeks I have been finishing another revision of 'You, I, and the Others,' and then getting the clean typescript ready for the press by correcting typist's errors, and more often adding changes of my own. In the meantime, I have given up all painting, going to movies, etc., but have had some random thoughts on a number of subjects. These I will now jot down:

Thomists have an ontological God; process philosophers have a cosmological God. The one has a being apart from all else, the other has a being that is interinvolved with actual entities. It is foolish of the Thomists to try to accommodate the views of the process philosophers in any other sense but that of supposing that their ontological God created a kind of Whiteheadean cosmos, in which there was a unitary reality operating as a contrastive factor with the rest of the cosmos. Instead, Thomists, such as Fr. Norris Clarke, try to read into their ontological God the distinctions which are pertinent to the cosmological. I shall present something like this criticism next week when I go to Santa Clara to discuss the problem of the nature of God, and where Lewis Ford, representing the process philosophers, will be confronting Clarke.

Another problem I have been thinking about is the perennial issue of the status of contingency in Hegel. There are two obvious answers which he provides—the *category* of contingency is necessitated by and necessitates necessity; there is also the dialectical move carried out on a rational level with universals, leaving contingencies outside all consideration.

Unlike some who take a 'scientific' view of the world, Hegel allows for a multiple set of dialectical moves. In the *Phenomenology,* for example, slavery comes fairly early in a quasi-historical account; in the philosophy of right, it comes somewhat later; in his placing of the new world (and therefore its slavery) he would have to set it even later. There are different locations even in the historic time of slavery, due to the fact that that time is being traversed on different levels by the dialectic. The suffering of the slaves escapes this analysis, but every supposed intelligible side of slavery is caught. To get to the suffering of the slaves, one would have to attend to their individual biographical accounts. Since these are said in words and words are universals, the biographical accounts would have to be read in a distinctive way in order to reveal the individuals. And there would still be the problem of reconciling these with the dialectical account—one would still have the problem of bringing together Hegel and Kierkegaard.

A possible alternative is to take the Hegelian dialectic to have a rhythm which could be portrayed in the form of straight lines ending in knots. Those knots are the contingencies which the nature of the dialectic requires to exist in order that there be stages for it. The stages of the dialectic are knots; the contingencies are the positions of those knots, their standing in relation to one another in time. One would still be left, of course, with the problem as to why the dialectic takes any time at all. It surely is not enough to say that in order to have stages, these must be separated, that the separation occurs only by virtue of the knots having a standing, and that the standing is the placing of the knots in a time dotted by contingencies.

The proper Hegelian answer to this contention is that there are contingencies only when one moves away from the logic to consider the absolute spirit where it has externalized itself. Since there are many different kinds of externalization, we can find many different occasions for what seems to be the same item. Strictly speaking, the item is not the same. We could, for example have a dialectic of slavery in which we would be able to move by necessity from the slavery of any or all to the form of slavery we had in America. This dialectic would cut across all the various domains in which the dialectic is carried out over a number of distinct kinds of entities, all subject to the dialectic as operating in a distinctive way. The dialectic, as operating between the various forms of slavery, would be caught in history, but it would be a history defined by the common 'slavery' that it connected in time. In short, we would have the contingency of ordinary history, or politics, etc., in which the self-externalized absolute spirit had to express its dialectical moves extensionally, making necessary the presence of contingent knots marking the places where the next dialectical stages would begin. And we would have the contingency of variations in a kind of activity, such as slavery, where the self-externalized absolute spirit dialectically related its various dialectical sequences by moving from one of the items in one sequence to similar items in other sequences.

This answer (which I have not found in Hegel or in the writings of the Hegelians I have read—confessedly only a small fraction of the total) still leaves over the question as to why the absolute spirit should externalize itself, particularly if it in fact ever does succeed in recovering itself dialectically either at the end of the *Phenomenology* or the *Logic.*

Another set of problems I have been dealing with on and off, in class, and while walking, is connected with the ways in which actualities and finalities interplay. There seem to be at least three distinct ways: a. their coming together to constitute transcendentals and other evidences—a matter discussed in *First Considerations;* b. their coming together to constitute a context of appearances discussed mainly in *Beyond All Appearances* (though I there do not always keep in mind that the resulting appearances are different from the 'accidents' which result from the interplay of actualities). The 'accidents' presuppose the first form of interplay, or perhaps a modification of it in the form of separate actualities being made to be together as a consequence of the simultaneous determination of all by the finalities. c. The actualities and finalities come together in such a way as to constitute a domain that can have them together only so far as it continues to express itself as an area in which further items are to appear. We have this type of result in history, due to Existence, in constructionistic mathematics, due to Possibility, and so on. I have previously suggested that the domains might be able to interplay with the finalities or with subdomains to constitute still other types of ongoings.

I am now waiting for some three hundred odd pages of 'You, I, and the Others', from the typist. I hope to be able to go over them to and from the various places where I have to talk the next weeks—Santa

Clara, California; Los Angeles; Columbus, Ohio. Once those pages are corrected and sent off to the printer, I will be able to turn to 'Man: Public and Private' which is now in a draft form of some four hundred typed pages. In the meantime, I will continue to write in this work, on and off. In the light of what seems to be a growing interest in what I have done, it is conceivable that in a few years there might be warrant for publishing these occasional writings as volume 8 of *Philosophy in Process.*

October 4

In *First Considerations*, it was noted that though the rule governing an inference expressed a necessity, the actual arriving at a conclusion took time, and that one could not end that process except so far as the conclusion was accepted and thereby held away from the process by which it was achieved. The account helps throw light on the Hegelian problem of contingency. A stage of the dialectic comes to an end, it can be said, only when contingencies come to a position where they are able to allow the stage, which had not yet had a terminus, to terminate. This way of dealing with the matter works for the past, but provides no guarantee that a present stage will come to an end. Nor does it allow the dialectic to have a time span, except in the sense of having acquired it from the contingencies which provide that dialectic stage with a knot that terminates the stage. The dialectic would have a time, as it were, only after the knot occurred. The contingent separation of knots would then, on the occurrence of a terminating knot, fill out the dialectic to make it a dialectic occurring in actual time.

In *Beyond All Appearances,* my illustrations do not always distinguish between Aristotelian accidents which are due to the interplay of actualities, and objective appearances which are due to the interplay of actualites and finalities. If we define an inert particular as the product of the interplay of two realities, we can then subdivide the class of them into accidents and appearances. Both of these will have, as an inseparable part of them, an 'of' or fringe which we must adumbratively follow to get to the actuality that contributed to the constitution of the inert particular. An accident will also have a 'due to' or fringe, pointing one toward other actualities which helped constitute the accident. An appearance, instead, will have a 'with' inseparable from it, thereby leading us to a lucidative penetration toward the finality or finalities which provided the 'with' for a number of actualities.

In the *World of Art* I emphasized the fact that art is concerned with the producing of excellence. That excellence is not a prospect or an objective; it is a guide that is present for the artist as he works, making him alter and evaluate what he is doing. In ethics, though, a man has before him an ideal excellence which he seeks to realize. The actual work, in which one engages to achieve it, is not itself guided by the need to exhibit excellence. One can realize the prospective ideal in a sloppy way, and still be ethical, just as one can have a vase before him which need not have any excellence, and still be able to produce an excellent work of art, where the vase is portrayed. There is, of course, nothing in the way of an ethical act being excellent here and now, or of an artistic work having been produced under the guidance of a prospective excellence, let us say of men in harmony. Usually, though, it is desirable for the ethical man not to concern himself with the excellence exhibited in his present activity, and for the artist not to concern himself with an excellent prospect.

October 13

I have again and again recurred to the problem of how a sperm and an egg, both living, could give rise to an unduplicable individual man. It is not plausible that the privacies of cell and egg themselves merge, that one conquers the other, or that they just vanish. It seems more correct to say, instead, that the sperm and egg are brought close together, not as units in an aggregate, but as constituting a single organic body. This is but to say that the loose unity of an aggregate gives way to the intimate and controlling unity of a single entity, forcing the sperm and egg to become parts, or to break into a multiplicity of parts—in either case, retaining their privacies. The bodily unity of the two is dominant over them as parts. But the more this is dominant, the more must it be available to intrusion by the finalities. In order to make itself be able to be for the finalities, and not be overwhelmed by them, the privacy and the body must be distinguished. It is therefore when and as the sperm and cell yield a single body, and not merely an aggregate of cells, that there is at once a dominating unity of the organic body, a relation and interplay with finalities, and a privacy maintained in contradistinction with the body.

Do I not beg the question? Must not the organic unity of the two be accounted for, even apart from all references to finalities? By virtue of what do they form a single bodily unit, and not merely an occasion for an aggregate? In the organic body the different parts act in terms of one another. They are related somewhat as the displays of one animal are related to the displays of another, each acting in terms of what had been and what will be displayed by the other. We do not say that the two animals constitute or are in an organism, because the interdependence of them is too loose. We could say, if we wished, that for a moment they are functioning organically, just as we can say of two men discoursing that they are so functioning. But we are right to reserve the term 'organism' for a single bodily entity in which the parts keep within its confines, and the entity itself has a privacy. Where did that privacy come from? Is it not the being as maintaining itself in contradistinction to the transcendental determinations by the finalities?

Were there no finalities, there would be no way to separate off the privacy, if only in order (as is the case with animals) to act in public subsequently, in some consonance with what had been undergone. There would not be such a privacy unless the organic body was itself a unit that, as it were, mediated between the privacy and the finalities. The interplay of sperm and egg, consequently, must be understood to constitute a reality in which they, or some transformation of them, function as parts with their own privacies.

Must not something similar be said about a molecule? In the sense that this is not organic, it must be understood to be a concentrated form of the unitary energy of the world, but an energy having the shape of a mass in public, and a privacy of its own, contrasting with that public. If instead one were to insist that there were nothing but ultimate particles and the laws governing them, we would be left in the embarrassment of not being able to acknowledge the evidences on which the idea of ultimate particles rest, and to which it looks for its justification. Nor could we account for the scientist and his apparatus. We need not deny that there are ultimate particles, but the acknowledgment should not be used to deny that there are complex organic unities with privacies, in which those particles are subordinate units, with their own privacies.

October 16

If it is true, as I have argued, that practical demands make us hold that some member of the class with the greatest number of items will probably occur rather than some member of a smaller class, though the occurrence of either item is as probable as the other, (and that high correlations testify to causal connections) why should one not accept the argument of the defenders of extrasensory perception that their results, since they exhibit the actual occurrence of what is mathematically improbable, point up a genuine causal connection between their correlated items? I think, (apart from their questionable practice of dismissing those with low scores as not being appropriately sensitive at the time, and the apparent argument from consequent to antecedent), that one may not argue from practical probability considerations with respect to any enterprise, except those that are cognate with what else is being done in the practical world. Insurance companies' calculations mesh with the practices of banks, businesses, the military, and so on, but ESP and similar enterprises do not belong with these. To state this objection from another side, one cannot argue from theoretical probabilities to a practically determined limited use of these unless one can show that the enterprise is one which involves vital human expectations in our daily life, on a par with others.

October 19

An Absolute Spirit or a God could be understood to be omnipresent, even before any possible production of a multitude in some way, or even before an interplay with a multitude already existing. The omnipresence, of course would not mean being in different parts of space, since that would require space to have an existence of its own or at least to provide a precondition for the action of the eternal reality. Instead, it would merely refer to the fact that the being was self-distensive, that it was diffused without end. But so far as one emphasized just that side, one would have it dealt with as only outward-going. One must also understand the being to hold on to what was being diffused. The holding on to it, so far as it balanced the outward thrust, would be expressed as the rationale, the structure, the knowledge, or the eternal now of the being.

If one could make sense of the idea of creation, one could add, to the idea of the rationale of the final eternal being, the ability to fill out the aboriginal diffuseness with particular items. The 'nothing' out of which the world would be made would then be a nothing of particular locations; that nothing would be overcome by a creative act which set particulars inside the diffused omnipresence of itself. However, I have tried to show that the idea of creation cannot be made intelligible. With Aristotle and Whitehead, I think we should hold that there always are and always have been particulars. Granted this, we can go on to say that when and as those particulars form a distinctive kind of cluster, they provide an occasion for the aboriginal rationale of the primal being to have one stage of that rationale come to an end. The history of the world could then be understood in something like an Hegelian way as having a series of stages, each taking time to be carried out, and coming to an end in a knot, in the form of a contingent cluster of particulars. Each of these particulars would function on its own in a contingent manner, and could continue to be with others for any length of time without forming a suitable cluster.

We can know that clusters were formed by looking at the past. We could not know that there would be another formed in the future. An Hegelian, on this view, cannot know that the next stage of his dialectic will ever occur; he can know only that certain stages have already oc- curred. He can say what kind of cluster would bring a certain stage to an end, but can not know that it would ever occur. A Marxist can say perhaps that the proletarian revolution or the stateless society will suc- ceed capitalism; he cannot say that this will in fact occur, or what the next stage will be like—unless that next stage could be known by knowing something about the primal reality. But then he would have to say that we nevertheless are not able to know just how it is filled out by contingent occurrences, eventually terminating in a single cluster, able to provide a knot and therefore an end to a stage in history.

If we start the other way, and attend to or allow for only particulars and clusters, we will have to say that whatever rationale there be is the outcropping of what contingently happens to occur. The past could not be taken to exhibit some all-encompassing plan. If we found a series of stages, similar let us say to Hegel's, we would have to hold that this was a contingent occurrence.

We make provision for the integrity of a rationale, and for the oc- currence of contingent items and contingently produced clusters, and for the interplay of the latter with the rationale, when we grant that there are actualities independent of the rationale, a rationale independent of the actualities, and that the two interplay. History could then be taken to be the production of a kind of domain in which past stages could be discovered to have a rationale of their own, even though they were found to occur filled out by contingent items and to come to an end in con- tingent clusters.

November 6

Using the finalities as a guide, one can distinguish five ways in which to act on present data so as to move toward the realization of some such desirable goal as being free of pain, losing weight, curing cancer.

Evidently, as the last illustration shows, the distinguishing falls far short of providing the answers all seek, and can do no more than indicate the directions in which one should move.

Most of our activities are occupied with providing a *limitation*, putting a stop to what is disagreeable. This is the main work of doctors, since for the most part they know of no cures, do not act on the defect so as to eliminate it, etc. Surgeons, instead, try to *eliminate* what is amiss by cutting it out. The hope of all is that we can do something in the present situation which will enable us to *elicit* some answer from within that will amount to a cure, no longer permitting the presence of the undesirable state. These three are instances of activities expressive of Existence, Being, and Substance. The finality, Possibility, instead, is instantiated by *transformation*, the turning of the undesired into a means or factor in something better. Finally, there is *assimilation*, in which the undesired is brought within some unity, and there functions as a part or nuance in some more valuable whole.

I have a touch of arthritis in one finger. No one knows a cure. But a stop can be put to the pain by pills and through exercise. The pain could be eliminated by putting the finger in a splint, since there is no pain as long as I keep the finger from bending. Matisse, with a very severe case of arthritis, assimilated it within a new endeavor. He gave up painting to make cut-outs which were hung by assistants under his direction. A stoic would perhaps use a pain as an occasion to test his character, in effect transforming it from an object of experience into a means to achieve some other state.

* * *

The reference to my arthritis leads naturally to a report about my general health. It still continues to be good. I have slowed down a little in my walking, and now take from sixteen to seventeen minutes to a mile, where before I took fifteen. I am teaching quite well, but am not as spontaneously witty as I had once been, as I can see when I try to enter the competition in the *New York* magazine, which is usually devoted to various plays on words, and in which I participated a number of times in the past. As I reread the manuscript of 'Man, Private and Public' (and think about 'You, I, and the Others', almost all of which is finally at the publishers) I think I am more awkward in my formulations and not sufficiently persistent in following out my ideas as I had once been. I notice, too, that I make more errors in typing than I had.

November 7

Aristotle says that in order to engage in a practical activity we should start with the objective we wish to reach and think backwards step by step until we arrive at the place we now are. The practical activity will consist in retracing one's steps. Putting aside the fact that in the retracing, one will inevitably meet contingencies, obstacles, and resistances not envisaged (to get one ready to bring one somewhere other than to the original objective, unless modifications are introduced along the way) there is the fact that we know no way to isolate steps in a backward move, except so far as they are already present. Were one to try to move in space from one place to another, one could envisage actual places in between which one could isolate. But if we have only an ideal in mind, say the good of man, or a cure for cancer, we find that there are no distinct steps to be noted. All we have is the objective as an ideal, and thus as not actual, and ourselves as here and now with whatever else is contemporary. The task we then have is to find a way of relating the two. There are evidently an indefinite number of such ways of relating. The right answer seems to involve a construction in which both the ideal end and the present situation are modified minimally. What we look for is that link between the two which requires the least transformations of either and yet suffices to allow a man to pass from one to the other. This is easy to say but obviously hard to bring about. If it were easy to produce, we would have a cure for cancer and other serious illnesses, would be able to win all our wars, and in short solve all problems. And should we find such a solution, we would still be up against the fact that what we then lay out will be just a guideline, something general, to be transformed in the very course of our activity, since practical work involves the transmutation of what is guiding us. Otherwise, the work turns out to be a monotonous, unimaginative instantiation of the guidelines, and therefore not geared to the fact that the result is to be produced within a finite time.

The last observation brings into focus another difficulty with Aristotle's account. Granted that we have all the steps laid out, and that contingencies are at a minimum, or even eliminated (as they might be in the course of a mathematical venture) we still have the factor of time. To move to an end takes time, but the extent of that time is not indicated in any division of the distance between the present and the ideal, whether that distance be broken up by moving back step by step or (as I just suggested) is constructed by imagining the various steps that together provide the best way of going from one to the other.

Aristotle overlooked that time factor, for he never did see that time is not only a measure but an actual duration. He seemed to be thinking of premisses and conclusions, but even here there is no escape from the fact of time, for no inferences are instantaneous. (I have just taken a quick look at Aristotle's *Ethics* and his *Politics,* but have not been able to locate any passage which justifies these criticisms, or the statement that we arrive at the present by moving back step by step from the desired end.)

Aristotle was interested in a problem somewhat different from but not unrelated to the one I am dealing with.

He wanted to see how a man of virtue was able to arrive at the good all men seek. Since virtue for him was a good habit, and since a good man also had good sense, he understood the problem to involve a man who was at a proper beginning, and had the habits which would enable him to get to the final end. The analogue of such a man of good sense would be one who was mature and at home in his daily world; the analogue of his good habits would be any which were geared to the end to be achieved. But we know no such habits so far as particular ends are concerned, unless it be the habits of disciplined, trained utilization of various instruments. But just what the relevant instruments are is not always known. And how one can have the training that is needed in cases where we seek to voyage into new territories is also not known, though we sometimes know what has proved to be most efficacious in similar situations in the past.

Aristotle's virtuous, reasonable man seems to be a concretionalization in the present of the very end which he seeks to reach, the counterpart of the man whom I and others have taken to be in a position to know ultimate realities. But there does not seem to be a counterpart (where it is needed) in daily life. We grope toward answers in a contingent world and with respect to other particulars of which we have no antecedent grasp, except in the general form of being our 'others'. The so-called 'accidental' is excluded by the Aristotelian and the scientific outlook he endorsed—and which has continued until today.

A search for the proper or best linkage between an accepted end and the situation in which one is now in, best ends with a variant of what Peirce called an 'abductive' result, an explanatory premiss for some empirical items. But where Peirce sought an explanation for what was known, what is of primary concern now is a relation connecting what ought to be or wanted, with what is now.

(It is evening, and I have taken the time to look at Aristotle more closely. The passage that I sought is 1112b 12–30, where he tells us to trace back from an accepted end to the means that is the first in a series and is now available. We can do this apparently, only if we are capable of deliberation.)

November 8

Men are not altogether at home in the world. Otherwise they would not be beset with physical obstacles and the tragedies which result from the indifferent workings of nature. Still, they are not altogether alienated. If they were, they would never find their way around in it, could not forge theories which allow them to predict and control, and could not properly plan. The double fact can be accounted for by 1. noting that men, in bounding off some particular region in order to attend and to know, necessarily also stand outside the boundary, pushing away what else there might be and directing themselves toward it as that which is to be realized in terms pertinent to what now is and is known; and 2. noting that men have internalized the effects of finalities and are consequently able to approach the world in terms which are in consonance with what the finalities impose on it.

Let it be denied that men have an attitude that allows them to properly anticipate in general terms what is to be. One will then have to conclude that we will expect that what had been will be projected into the future. The difference between that view and the one I have suggested is that the former reaches to a possibility in the future that is in fact connected with what is now, whereas the alternative merely thrusts what had been acknowledged in the past into an unknown emptiness. The former yields a possibility realized in the coming to be of a new present, whereas the latter allows only for a repetition of what had been. The former might envisage something entirely new, even though it was reached through an act in which the present was being bounded off; the latter has nothing to envisage but what had been known. All novelty for the latter will be surprising, unexpected. For the former, what was novel would be another instantiation of the attitude that was being utilized in the present, an instantiation that may realize a possibility not realized before. The former alone allows for an attitude touching a possible new prospect, as long as it is continuous with the attitude now being employed to mark out something present.

Suppose it be denied that men have internalized the finalities and therefore are in a position to know the kind of context in which what is encountered will occur. One will still be able to say that men can come

to know the finalities by tracing backward the evidences they now confront in the form of joined appearances. But they would not directly
face other entities as being together in prescribed ways. At the very best,
one would have to move to the finalities and then use the result as a
kind of hypothesis so as to enable one to properly envisage the situation
in which other entities were. Because men internalize the finalities, they
can have, not only a subjective form of what they are to arrive at objectively, but a kind of categoreal approach to a world the finalities
govern. In the absence of such a categoreal approach, one would have
to first achieve a transcendental knowledge of the finalities, and then use
this as a way of dealing with what is daily confronted. It will, of course,
not be known if men internalize the finalities, unless one first arrives at
them from the appearances; but one can make use of the categoreal
internalized form of those finalities without knowing how they had been
acquired.

November 9

I think I now see a way to bring together my observations about
time, which were presented in the chapter on Musicry in *Nine Basic Arts*,
and in other places later. Public time, with its past and future, is the
product of the juncture of an absolute time (which contains a serial order
of nuances without distinct moments, and allows for no transition), and
insistent actualities. When we are at the latter extreme, with the whole
of time having a minimum effectiveness, we have just fulgurations, momentary flashes of existence with a mere directionality toward the areas
we later dub as past and future. When we are at the former extreme,
with the actualities serving only to distinguish the nuances and thereby
give them the status of moments, time stretches out endlessly without
a beginning and without an end. In between these extremes, actualities
and the whole of time produce a public time in which there are definite
beginnings and endings. Their distances from the present, the nature of
their contents, and the way in which the present is related to them vary
in accord with the degree to which one of the constituents dominates.
We have one beginning and ending for a symphony, another for history,
a third for individual men, a fourth for a community, a fifth for a story,
a sixth for a poem, a seventh for nature. There are undoubtedly many
more.

How are these different times related to one another? If one supposes
that nature is a primary reality, then the more intensive, limited times

will have to be taken to be determinations of it, and therefore to pre-suppose that nature itself is not fully determinate but allows for new relations to exist between its units, thereby turning those units into new kinds of entities. But there is no warrant, apart from special purposes, for supposing that nature and its time are prior to other 'worlds' and their times. To be sure, there was a nature before there were men, but it does not follow that there was a nature before or independently of inanimate actualities and their juncture with the whole of time. Different times are in a contiuum of times, each marking the degree to which the whole of time and actualities are involved with one another.

The idea deserves to be extended to space and causality. If it is, we will then have to say of the painting hanging on the wall that it exists both as a physical object and as a work of art, the one expressing the fact that space itself is dominant over its occupants, the other expressing the fact that the occupant which a man has created is dominant over the available space. Both occur together, for the factors have endless intensive degrees, interplaying at multiple levels at the same time. When and as a painting is an object in nature, it is also in the world of art. One consequence of this view is that both nature and art—and all other outcomes of the interplay of actualities and finalities—can be said to be fully determinate, each according to its own limited set of predicates. It would then not be correct to say that a fully determinate entity has either the positive or the negative of every predicate, but only that it has the positive or negative of a certain range of predicates. Of some object in nature it would not be correct to say that it was a product of genius or of a botcher; these predicates would be irrelevant. If one wished, one could say that the different realms could themselves be taken to have a degree of indeterminacy, just so far as they had other realms outside them which differed from them in degree.

Do the different realizations of the interplay of actualities and the conditions which express the finalities affect one another? Do they exclude one another? I think the answer must be affirmative at least with respect to the second question, for each has its own set of determinations and stands out against the other. There is no reason to suppose that they affect one another in the sense of acting, making a difference. Still, there is the fact that paintings get darker and dirtier, that they can be injured, catch on fire, and so on. We could say that the fire has to do with the physical conditions only, but it is also true that the changed conditions preclude the further existence of the painting. And the concern for the painting may make one protect a particular area or building in a way one had not before, if only by putting various physical barriers in the way of a possible fire. The texture of the canvas and the nature of the paints affects the kind of painting that will be present. We must allow, therefore, that some at least of the items in the different realms can act on one another.

I do not think the issue is compromised by the recognition that nature is constituted without deliberation, and that the world of art is constituted by men bringing actualities together with expressions of finalities. But there is a difficulty. The creations of men involve the use of what is part of nature or other realms, a working over of these. They therefore do not seem to allow us to say that art objects, like any in nature, are the direct outcome of the union of actualities with the expressions of finalities. Without affecting the thesis that there is a continuum of outcomes of the interplay of finalities with actualities—and therefore allowing for the existence of men with private thoughts and of men together in a society—one could hold that the realm of art is a product men bring about by making actualities subject to new ways of being involved with the expressions of finalities. We would then have a continuum of unsupervised unions of actualities and finalities and, in addition, distinctive realms in which one of those unions was made to interplay with the finalities, and thereby produce a new type of object. Two unions, a man's and a thing's, would be brought together to yield a new entity, a work of art.

A work of art, on this view, would not be part of a continuum of items. The time of musicry or the composition of a musical piece, would not be on the continuum in which the whole of time interplayed with actualites, making themselves present, unless, in the act of creation, one moves into another part of the continuum to become occupied with a stretch of a determinate extension other than that which one normally helps constitute, and then makes the object which he there finds and uses be united with himself. The result is a single actuality that is then made to interplay with a part of the continuum otherwise outside its reach. If, let us say, a metal were to be united with time at position x, then the individual by making use of his creative powers (and therefore becoming united with time at a position y, other than that with which he otherwise would be united with) will make himself and the metal be united with time at position z.

This is not yet right. For one thing the continuum of outcomes of the interplay of actualities and finalities is already occupied, and that without any deliberate effort on the part of anyone. For another, the new dimensions and values produced in the work of art must be accounted for. Is the act of creation the making an already occupied position in the continuum stand away from the rest, and thereby have new boundaries, become a determinate reality there, which it had not been before?

What before had been a nuanced dimension of some specialization of the whole of time, distinguished in the form that a particular actuality provides at that point is, in the act of creation, isolated as something made to function in a new way. Where an actuality might delimit and fill out a distinguished part of the whole of time, a created object goes further and forces that distinguished part to be integral to the actuality. The making of one position on the continuum of times stand away from all the others (as an actuality succeeds in doing with respect to the time it in fact lives through from within) gives it additional meaning. Does it not add determinations? Yes but this is also true of the isolation of any of the times in the continnum of times, each involved in a different degree with actualities. The actualities we know every day have managed to become isolated, with their time, from the continuum and thereby have acquired determinations. But the rest of the ways in which the actuality is involved with the whole of time are not then distinguished; they are mere facets of the entire situation constituted by that actuality and the whole of time. The creative act makes one of those facets have a distinctive reality, makes it become the very time of the created work. As integral to a time in the continuum of times, an actuality is determinate there. But it does not have the determination of being able to stand in contrast with other items occupying other times. The interplay of finalities and actualities yielded appearances; the creative act consists in having an actuality take up the place of one of those appearances, and therefore to make use of the time in a new way. The appearance was determinate as an appearance; the actuality is determinate in additional ways.

November 10

I am not entirely satisfied with yesterday's discussion. At the very least it is not in clear focus, and at best blurs the more important issues. Let us take a sequence of sounds. They occur in a time they and the whole of time constitute. They also occur in a time measured by clocks, as well as in a time measured by one's feelings, a time measured by social expectations, and the like. When we bring those sounds closer together, bunching some and spreading out others, we do not stop the sounds from being in the same times they had been before. But we bring them together in such a way as to make a time be ingredient in the new sequence of the sounds. When we do this, we also subordinate the time to the conditions stemming from other finalities besides Existence. If we are creative musicians we will have the sounds and time integrally united and, as such, subordinated to the transcendental, 'beauty'. This is a special case of Unity, or perhaps of Unity, Substance, and Possibility together. The time that was made integral to the changed relations of the sounds is one of the times existing apart from any effort on our part, for it is the outcome of the interplay of the sounds with the whole of time. But unlike the other objects which are in that time, because of the subordination to beauty, the time of the changed sequence of sounds is adjectival to the sounds. Were it not subject to beauty, the time would not have that role, even when it was primarily oriented toward the sounds.

In making a temporalized work of art, the time there is not allowed to be simply a product of interplaying factors. It is carried by one of the factors, the sounds themselves, as bunched and separated by creative man. There are new determinations, but only because the whole is subordinated to a set of finalities, and is not simply a product of the sounds and common time.

Just as, when I remember, I subjectify an objective time, so when I create with sounds I make an objective time ingredient in the sequence of sounds. Both occurrences allow time to continue to function outside the sounds, and also, with the sounds, to constitute an objective temporal sequence. A particular time in the continuum of times is pulled out of the continuum and made integral to the sounds and, as such, is subordinated to the expression of a number of finalities other than Existence.

Let us suppose that the sounds were bunched together in the course of nature. We would not say that the situation was any different from one in which the sounds were just in a monotonous sequence. In both cases, we would take the sounds to be in an objective time, whether or not we also held that that time was the outcome of the interplay of the sources of those sounds and the source of the whole of time. If we took the naturally bunched sounds to be beautiful, we would have, through our appreciation, brought the sounds integrally together with the time, and thereupon subordinated them to the finalities in such a way as to allow beauty to supervene.

In the act of appreciation we seem now to do what the creative musician did. But then would we not, by just being appreciative, accomplish what a creative musician does? That surely is implausible. The act of appreciation must therefore be understood to bring the natural occurrence into the world of art, and there allow the result to be governed by the conditions which had already been operative on art objects. We would, in our appreciation, not duplicate a creative act, but merely bring a natural occurrence inside the world of art. There it is able to benefit from the achievements of actual works of art, which had brought other finalities into play and thereby made beauty supervene. Our appreciation does not make a natural occurrence be beautiful. It just allows it to belong to a world where works of art already are, and thereby to benefit from whatever conditions are operative there. Our appreciation of works of art has a different role, for it is sensitive to the achievements of artists.

But now, have I done anything more than to change the locus of the problem? In what respects are the two kinds of appreciation different? If I do not know whether something is a work of art or not, how could I know whether or not I am appreciating it properly? And if I appreciated it incorrectly, how could I know this?

Must we not say that we always bring what we confront into the world of art? If it happens to be a created work, the appreciation ideally will live through the rhythms that the artist produced. In great works, we would look for other rhythms which would compel us to function in other ways, with the same outcome of having enjoyed a beautiful work. We could not, in connection with some minor work, be able to find such other ways. We would have to say, also, that if there were a major production by nature, what is ordinarily called 'sublime' (if this could be confined within the limits which characterize created works by men) we would not be able to tell the difference between nature's work and man's. We can tell the difference only when we have a work in nature of the physical magnitude of the works men make, and then see that we cannot appreciate it in an endless number of ways. A natural object does not allow for such a multiplicity of appreciations. Why not? Is it not conceivable that nature might produce, not only what was appreciated as beautiful, but which was able to be appreciated as such from as many angles as one is able to appreciate a created work of art? If we say, as I think we must, that this is not possible, what is the reason? Is it that a work of nature, in order to be brought within a world of art, must be bounded off from the rest of nature and therefore lacks any other dimensions than those which are the outcome of that particular detachment of the object from the rest of nature? Would we not have to detach the object from the rest of nature again and again, and in different ways, before we could have it have those many different sides? If so, should we not be able to determine with certainty whether or not something superb was a work of man or of nature? That does not seem to be plausible. Yet there never was a work made by nature which is as multi-facetted as Michelangelo's *David* or a symphony by Beethoven. We must conclude, I think, that we certainly know what was not made by nature, but we do not certainly know what was made by it. The former are art's great achievements; the latter are at best on a par with, and perhaps indistinguishable from, some of art's minor achievements.

November 11

Hegel in various places held that what was being passed beyond was also preserved; despite all movement everything was as before. It is not clear, from a reading of the *Phenomenology*, whether the preservation is entirely contained within the new synthesis, whether it still remains outside, or whether a residuum of it remains outside while it has a role inside the synthesis. The issue is pertinent to the present discussion about natural beauty. It is also pertinent to an understanding of living beings and men, for while they are in their environments and milieu they are also subject to the forces of nature and buffetted about just as inanimate things are. Whatever be said about Hegel's own view, we must say, I think, that the right answer is the third of the alternatives. If so, no purely sociological, historical, economic or other 'humanistic' treatment of man will be adequate, just as surely as no merely naturalistic or physicalistic account can be.

If we take the discussion of art objects as our guide, we should say that in humanistic settings, whether these be societal, political, economic or historical, a man makes whatever condition governs him in nature to become integral to him in such a way that the other conditions subordinate it. Since in nature he is subject to the five conditions which the five finalities ground, he will have to be said to have all five integral to himself in such a way that each is subject to the other four. And, of course, the ways in which he makes the conditions integral in society will have to be distinguished from the ways in which he makes those very same conditions integral to himself in the state, history, and so on. When we add to this, the ways in which he functions on teams, at work, and in the home, we have an exceptionally complex situation with which to deal. And since art itself is practiced inside a 'humanistic' setting, an account of art will have to consider more than one kind of condition, even when the art is essentially only temporal, spatial, or causal. The complication is reduced at particular moments, for men engage in one or a few enterprises to the exclusion of others. Still, when they are attending a play, they remain social beings, dressed up, keeping quiet, conforming to the established customs and laws, the historic world of art, and perhaps also the history of their society. We cannot avoid, therefore, acknowledging various contextualizations for men, all taking place at the same time, some stable and unconsciously filled out and others deliberately entered into, many or all of which interplay.

Another related but neglected problem now becomes evident. If it be true that Existence is expressed first as the whole of time, we should also have a whole of space and a whole of dynamism, each to be made limited and filled out in ways analogous to those pertinent to time. In addition, we should have comparable initial contexts for the other finalities. There should also be a kind of domain of relevance, another of coordination, a third of rationality, and a fourth of unification. Each should be a single whole where any position could be distinguished and separated through the action of actualities.

I have, I think, been using 'nature' in two distinct senses. Sometimes I used it to refer to the ontological conditioned totality of things, and sometimes to actual entities as subject to monotonous time, or the time of interest to physicists. There is still another sense of 'nature' that concerns the world of living as well as of non-living beings. Only the first can be understood without supposing a subordination of time or extensions to other conditions. The other two, and every other specialization of the whole of time, involve a subordination to other conditions, and conversely. Man-made works, and particularly beautiful works of art, are special cases where one of the other conditions becomes prominent in the guise of beauty. In society, history, and in fact in all other domains, we have specialized cases of all the primary conditions made integral to particulars. Each of the particulars as conditioned in one way is subject to the rest. When beauty is not achieved, some other specialization of Possibility separately or together with Existence and Unity, will be.

The continuum of time has reference to an ontological state of affairs. Art, and other 'humanistic' specializations, involve the separation out of one of those times, the limiting of its magnitude, the modification of its pulsation, and the making it integral to actualities. The separation does not affect the continuum and therefore the place of the time (which we separate out of that continuum) in its unseparated form. What is true of time, I think we should hold, is true of all the other basic conditions.

November 12

There are four basic realms, each with its own distinctive categories and categorizations: transcendent, humanistic, scientific, and fictional. Within each, there are a number of subrealms. There are at least
five transcendents; some would also include God, the object of mysticism, the Absolute, or take these alone to be. Psychology, sociology,
economics, politics are among the subrealms to be found within the
humanistic. The scientific includes the physical, chemical, biological, geo-
logical, and astronomical. The fictional encompasses story, drama, myth,
and pseudo-realms with predicates such as 'witchery', 'lady luck'.

Reductionisms are of two kinds. One takes a subrealm as primary,
rejecting others as being fictional, to be replaced by those allowed by
the chosen subrealm. One might understand the transcendent solely in
terms of the divine; the humanistic solely in terms of psychology or
economics; the scientific solely in terms of physics, biology, or chemistry;
and the fictional solely as confusion, or as expressing tentative or con-
trary-to-fact hypotheses. The second kind of reductionism takes one of
the primary realms as basic, treating the others as fictional, with all their
items and terms re-expressed in terms of the chosen one. There are men
who 'see' everything from the standpoint of an Absolute or God; others
who 'see' everything from the standpoint of man and his concerns; and
others who view men solely from the standpoint of some science.

How can we determine whether or not a reduction is legitimate,
whether or not some characterization is fictional? We can show how
transcendentals are needed in order to account for the togetherness of
men, and also for the togetherness of other entities; how the humanistic
realm is needed in order for there to be theories, communication, truths
about others; and how the scientific realm is needed in order to give
transcendentals universal scope and to enable one to understand how
men can be in the same universe with what is subhuman. A defense of
a subrealm is more difficult. It requires one to show that there are still
items unaccounted for by transcendentals, even though these were supposed to account for every kind of togetherness; that there are dimensions to the understanding, use, and communication of theories which
the accepted humanistic subrealms cannot accommodate; and that men
are in a cosmos with other items in ways that a science cannot entirely
explain. What cannot meet these tests is possibly a fiction. But we can
show that it is a fiction only if we can show that there is no warrant for
it; that it blurs together various facets of human activity; that it fails to

explain anything; or that it cannot be part of an account pertinent to every occurrence. The unrelated Parmenidean One is an instance of the first; 'witchery' and 'man's native wickedness or nobility' is an instance of the second; phlogiston is an instance of the third.

Mind is sometimes treated as a kind of transcendental, an individual's mind being taken to be just a fragment of this. The transcendent mind is sometimes treated as though it were characteristically human, without explanation or preconditions in any other realm. Sometimes, it is treated as though it were a confused way of referring to physical, chemical, or biological occurrences. But we have no evidence that it is the first. And the theory that it is only physical, chemical, or biological, is itself a mental product of a different order—indeed, the attempt to make this or any other reduction, depends on a humanistic use of the mind as distinct from both transcendents and scientifically sanctioned entities.

The final irreducible fact is a universe which is divided into three realms. Though it is true that the second, the humanistic, need not be, and that there was a time when it was not, it is also true that now it has its own integrity, being a precondition for the knowing, expressing, and communicating of the other two. In man's absence, it still would not be true that we had only one of the other realms. The transcendent has no bearing, no articulated content unless there be a multiplicity of particulars; the world of particulars has no reality unless the items are together, a state which requires the operative presence of transcendents. If, instead, one tried to remain with the humanistic alone, one would be up against such facts as that there are evidences in the form of men's togetherness which lead to what is beyond them all, that the weights of men can be balanced on a scale with sacks of coal, that men do interplay with physical entities, and that there is a rationale allowing us to deal with mankind as an aggregate of units interplaying with other aggregates in the cosmos.

Whichever the realm we start with, the other two will sooner or later have to be recognized—or we will fail to account for the togetherness of items, the formulations and communications of our views and the act of reduction, and the knowable copresence of men with other types of entities. Once this is recognized, we can go on to note that men have private sides, and are also publicly together in a humanistic world, at the same time that they are together with other types of entity in a scientific realm, and subject to conditioning by transcendent realities. Apart from any consideration of what happens in the making of a work of art, we must allow for a number of conditionings in different ways at the same time.

As just temporal, men are in time privately; together in a humanistic world in many ways; together in nature as understood by science; and together ontologically as subject to a time directly expressing the transcendent, Existence. In each case, the men can be said to be determinate, but only with respect to predicates pertinent to a particular realm. It makes no sense to say that, as part of nature, men are ambitious, religious, parents, criminals, and the like, for these characterizations are pertinent only to men as in a humanistic realm.

If one starts with the realm known to science, one will—as I did in *The World of Art*—take it to be indeterminate but made determinate by the additions that the artist introduces. If, instead, one acknowledges all the realms as existing at the same time (and perhaps adding one in which there are nothing but actualities, which is to say men and other entities treated as ultimate realities, and that can be united with transcendentals to constitute a scientific world and—isolating the men—a humanistic one on the one side and a natural world for the rest on the other), one will have to take the items in each to be determinate with respect to the terms relevant to the realm, and indeterminate only in the sense of being capable of being transported into or translated into the items in the other realms. If we take the metal used by a sculptor to be part of a scientifically known world (which is of course to abstract from it as it in fact is, an ontological entity, and an item in a humanistic world with economic, legal and other roles), we will then go on to say, not that the sculptor adds new determinations to it, but that he brings it into another realm, the world of art where it is able to be characterized in still other new ways, without losing its status as a piece of metal in other realms.

* * *

I leave tomorrow to lecture at Scranton, and will therefore not be able to spend much or perhaps any time on this diary until I return. I will be forced to make just a momentary stop, contrasting with my long intervals of silence of the last months. I have been neglecting this work to concentrate on getting 'You, I, and the Others' ready for the press, and to reread the manuscript of 'Man, Private and Public'. I made a mistake, I think, in not taking some time even then to do some writing in this work. It catches some of my vagrant thoughts. It starts my creative juices flowing. And somehow it provides me with more time to do other things. This last remark is of course paradoxical. Still, it is a fact that when I am not engaged in creative writing, the rest of the day seems to just pass away, while when I do write in this work, or in others, the thoughts continue to come after I have finished writing. I am even prompted to do some painting and to share in other activities to a degree I otherwise would not. To do nothing for a while is for me but preliminary to doing nothing for a good while; to be at work for a while is but to start working all the while.

The world of art is produced within the humanistic. It can therefore be identified with a subrealm. This will be produced, not by simply specializing the encompassing realm and its conditions, but by acting so as to make those conditions be embodied in a new way. From this point of view, metal, while it continues to be part of a scientifically known nature, is already in the humanistic realm, and it as there present that it is subjected to the new conditions brought to bear by art. All the while, as untouched in the human realm and as modified by the artist within that realm, it will be conditioned by and be part of nature.

We cannot rest with the contention that there are a number of realms. Account must be given of the way they are related. Men are not divided into natural and humanistic beings set over against a set of transcendent realities. They are involved with the transcendent and the natural at the same time that they are involved with the humanistic, both privately and publicly. If, with Sartre, we start with men as essentially private, we will have to 'fall', as he would have it, into the natural world, and leap, with Kierkegaard, to the transcendent. Instead, we should take men to be in all at the same time. We should understand him by starting with him in each one of the guises, and then see how each continues into the others. If no guise is prior to or superior to the others, must we not then say that a man, in the end, must be a new product, the outcome of the criss-crossing of the various passages from one to the other? A man's task would then be to produce a new unity, himself enhanced at the intersection of all the passages from one position to another.

November 13

One of the conclusions reached in 'You, I, and the Others' is that complexes, such as society and state are unpredictable outcomes of the interplay of interrelated men and a common forceful condition. Yesterday's discussion ended with a somewhat similar conclusion about man. He, too, unpredictably joins a multiplicity of factors to make a single unity. He, too, is like any practical work (as characterized in my paper on evaluation); and also like works of art produced by creative unions of conditions and material, though deliberately and with the effort to produce a sensuous excellence. Whitehead can be said to have a similar idea in mind, though if he did he would have also to be said to think that an actuality could engage in only a single private effort and that this was effectively completed in a moment. There are no factors, which are a man's, or any other actuality's, and await union by the actualities. The only factors he allowed are cosmological ones—an entire past and a totality of possibilities. The present view, also, is not altogether alien to those which hold that man makes himself. It differs in holding that the same thing must be said of other actualities, that the making is in part not deliberate, and that it has to do with the harmonization of private factors, of public factors, of transcendent factors, of natural factors, and of all of these with one another.

What is the nature of a man as criss-crossed by the various factors affecting one another? It seems to be some kind of tone, a tensional sense, with limits set in private, in public, by transcendents, and by nature. Both the essence and the existence of man are factors which he integrates with different degrees of success at different times. If one accepts the Aristotelian matter and form distinction, one would here say that different degrees of the unity of these two were produced at different moments. There would, of course, always be a degree of unity which was present and controlling, for otherwise the entity would cease to be one. Aristotle himself seemed to hold something like this view when he dealt with the virtues, and with man as at once ethical and political.

A related conclusion should be drawn with reference to politics and ethics, politics and economics, politics and history, and indeed with respect to any sets of subrealms which are in some effective interplay. The outcome of the interplay, and indeed the arena of the interplay will be a new area with its reality, having some being in fact from the very moment that these factors are together, and coming into more and more focused unity to the degree that the factors are harmonized. In the case of man, however, we readily see him as being the unity and, therefore, making a difference to the ways in which the harmonies are achieved among the various factors. But the outcome of the interrelation of politics and economics, for example, has no ability to affect the different factors, though it may have a role to play with respect to other products of a similar kind. The difference is due to the fact that man from the very start is an actuality, whereas the outcome of the union of politics and economics is just a realm, and can be accounted for by the actions of the factors on one another, without having recourse to any control or stability exercised by anything. The Whiteheadean view would be quite close to one which took the relation of politics and economics as a model, except for the fact that Whitehead has a 'creativity' operating in the case of an actuality—though one which has no stable or apparent differentiated nature.

November 15

A modified transcription of shorthand notes made on my way to Scranton:

Hegel must hold that the earlier stages of the dialectic do not act entirely on their own. The outcome of the dialectic makes evident how in fact they act. Brute occurrences are really rational occurrences which we have not yet understood properly. They are produced by the Absolute Spirit, but we come to them first from a side, and do not recognize the presence of the Absolute in them. To be sure, to see them from the position of the Absolute is also to change them. The change is both epistemological and ontological, allowing them to be genuine units and not, as they were before, detached and seen as though they were self-sufficient, and in equilibrium. They function as limited entities, but not without the help of the Absolute, whose role is not initially seen, or not seen properly. We move from a side view to a centered one. A fall from a height is as rational as a logical implication, but we do not see it to be so. All things function rationally and brutally at once; rationally because they are creatures of the Absolute, and brutally because they are set apart by that Absolute but in relation to all others. We approach them by themselves without an awareness that they are or how they are in fact governed by the Absolute. We get back to the items encountered in the *Phenomenology* by going to the philosophy of nature, etc. after having reached the logical climax with a knowledge of the notion.

Is the only rectification of items rational and already present? A more complete view would hold that there are other governing conditions. In a more dynamic view, we would have to hold that the Absolute is present in the beginning but not effectively, and that the progress of the dialectic, which is at once ontological and epistemological, makes the rational not only be recognized but be more effective.

Does the Hegelian dialectic include the lower stages in the higher, and therefore transform them to the extent of bringing them into a new context, so that things are not as before? Or does the dialectic allow us to see them in their true natures and, therefore, not do more than make evident what in fact already is the case? If we follow the suggestion made above, and hold that the achievement of the notion is but the preliminary to the production of items as separated by the Absolute itself, we would have to say that the *Phenomenology of Spirit* is epistemic, and not ontologic. It would allow us to come to the position where we are not only able to see the initially accepted items to be in fact interrelated, but to stand apart as partial. Only after the Absolute is reached do we have a self-differentiation of the notion.

The development in the *Phenomenology of Spirit*, and in the big and small logics, is progressive. In the philosophies of right, etc. the dialectic seems to proceed by a self-differentiating. The early stages of the *Phenomenology of Spirit* are different from those stages in works subsequent to the two works on logic. Must Hegel not say that the rational present in the early stages requires them to have a brute side? I think so.

Should we not say then that the Absolute not only goes through the stages of self-differentiation and therefore the setting of items outside one another as though they were separated, and that not only is there an ontological and epistemological movement of recovery of the Absolute in itself, but the Absolute places us at the beginning of the *Phenomenology*, and takes us through the different stages until we finally are at the position of the Absolute, known scientifically. Apparently.

November 16

The One and the Many can be understood to be joined in a number of distinct ways. The One might be dominant as it is in a work of art, an organism, a law-abiding world. The Many might be dominate, as it is in an aggregate, a collection, perhaps a nation and a family. The two might produce a new entity, such as a functioning state, or a historic occurrence. And the two might merely be factors which some already achieved agent was able to bring further together more or less on its own. The last seems to be what occurs in the living body. That body is a unity joined to a plurality of cells, genes, atoms, or even an entire physiology. There would be nothing like a human living body, and thus what was common to a multitude of individuals if the factors were not united by a 'human nature' filling it out intensively. That human nature could itself be accounted for as the juncture of a unity and a plurality of cells, etc. Its unification would be minimal, but with an accreted power of its own.

The acknowledgment of the power of a human nature to join factors to produce an intensification of itself allows one to make some progress in understanding the role of gender, color, and perhaps even size. Aristotle, with his essence, properties, and adventitious accidents, had no place for the persistent genders and colors of humans. These are not adventitious and yet are not part of the essence, nor even of the properties of humans, since both the essence and properties are identical in all. Putting aside the way an individual may consciously or in some other private way deal with his gender, color, etc., and putting aside the way in which the society deals with them—and therefore putting aside the affects that the individual and the society may introduce—we can take the gender or color to have its necessary condition in the physiology or other 'scientifically' known dimensions of a biological unit. Each individual, from the start, will be constituted by a constant minimal unity of the two sides, and will be individual just so far as the union was intensified to some degree by the way the distinctive factors were made to fill out the union. The life of the individual thereafter would involve a further intensification of the two, not necessarily consciously and not necessarily endlessly, but perhaps as long as there was maturation and growth. The intensification might stop with the reaching of the stage where these could be effectively used, as is the case with gender, or when they had added a distinctive tone, as is perhaps the case with color.

When society or privacy takes account of an intensified body, the import of the gender or color acquires social and private forms. These can themselves be factors which are to be integrated, not with the body itself, but with the individual as the union of the body with the privacy, and as present in the world. Whether or not an individual pays attention, and whether or not society discriminates, a difference in gender and color will not only be manifest physiologically but will intensify the common human essence, without compromising that essence's integrity as an instantiated universal, present in each and with the same nature in all.

November 17

An unsolvable problem of individuation arises when one starts with nothing more than the idea of knowledge and takes this to be restricted to universals. But the question is ontological as well, and in any case cannot be dealt with from the position of universals. If we are forced to use universals in speaking of individuals, we still must make them converge on or begin a movement into what is more intensive and is irreducibly unduplicable.

Every actuality has a privacy and, because it has, cannot be duplicated. It can be said to be distinctive to begin with, and to achieve intensifications to the degree that it brings within the compass of its initial distinctiveness the factors which are at its limits, and this without preventing them from still functioning as such limits. There is no problem of their being universals as well, for there is more to the universe than actualities. Each actuality is subject to what is general, and cannot bring this under its own subjection entirely; only to the degree that it succeeds in internalizing conditions does it succeed in individualizing them.

This position will be rejected by those who do not allow for any privacies, who suppose that only men or living beings can have privacies, who deny that there are any governing conditions, or who deny that those governing conditions can be internalized. One who might accept the position might well ask, though, where privacies come from, a matter particularly important when we come to men with their distinctive persons, selves, and I's. To begin with, we must explain how the privacies of men differ from those of other beings. I have argued that it is by virtue of their functions, complexity, and capacity to stand away from the public side with which they are also continuous. We must then explain how those human privacies arise. I have tried to deal with this issue a number of times, never getting to the root of it. I have argued that when the proliferation of cells gets to a certain stage of complication and is yet one, that the privacy is enabled to stand away. But what is not yet clear is how there can be a single privacy. In the end, that issue must be dealt with together with the unity of the organism, and thus as in part explained by the finalities as affecting the body, and thereby enabling it to become a new unity with its inseparable privacy. But I do not yet have the matter in focus.

What is the origin of a privacy? This question, I think, reduces to the question of the origin of the entity itself. The recognition that an entity is distinctive, with its own boundaries, set out against all others, involves the recognition of the reality of difference as all-pervasive. But difference is symmetrical and requires at least two entities. Yet each individual stands away from all others with its own boundaries, whether or not those others remain and no matter what they are like. We must therefore acknowledge a power in each to hold itself away from all else, at the same time that it makes itself the terminus of a difference, relating itself and others.

We must start with the acknowledgment of privacy. If we take this privacy to be all-pervasive, we get to something like a primary Substance, as understood by Tao or Schopenhauer. The pluralization of this will then be a problem, and we will have to make evident if and how there could be bodies without any privacy at all. We cannot, I think, get behind the fact that all the items in the world are at once interrelated and private, with their privacies making them distinctive, and grounding individualities as intensifications of such private distinctiveness.

Since no aggregate has a privacy, and therefore no individuality, we must face the problem of how an aggregate differs from a genuine but complex individual. Both of them are subject to Unity and other finalities. Both of them have unities. But the one evidently does not have the unity in control, adopted, or possessed, whereas the other does. Who or what possesses that unity?

Must it not be the case that finalities do or do not succeed in governing a number of units, and that their success is inseparable from a withdrawal of privacy from all? The very power of Substance to govern a multiplicity is one with the power of the multiplicity to be a single entity opposed to this.

From this point of view, Tao or similar variants of Substance, operate not on privacies but on bodies, and by virtue of this make possible the appropriate privacies. Such an account does not explain how new privacies come to be. Where do they get their distinctiveness; how are they different from the privacies of the component members of an organic body; how could they still allow for the privacies of the components to exist? I think it is necessary to say, as I have not until now, that the privacies of every entity continue into the finalities, so that when and as the finalities are operative on the bodily parts and make the body an organic unity, the privacies as continuing into common privatized forms of the finalities are thereupon able to function together.

Each privacy is fringed by the finalities. When a number of bodies are merged together under the dominance of finalities to constitute a single body, the privacies of those bodies together specialize the finalities, to make a single privacy, correlative with the single organic body. The single privacy binds itself off from the multiple privacies, which produced it, by specializing the finalities;he privacy thereupon has an integrity over against the very privacies which made it possible by their pulling away from the finalities to become just limited subordinated units. The subordinated privacies will have lost connection with the finalities, and will therefore be different in kind and function from what they had been before they specialized the finalities. Or, alternatively, it is conceivable that they continue to merge into the finalities, but to a lesser degree than before. The latter alternative is more cautious; but the former does emphasize the new role of the units in the organic body and, therefore, the new role of the privacies of the units when a greater takes over. To separate a cell from the larger organic body is to enable the cell to join up with the finalities from which it was excluded by virtue of that cell's being a subordinated part of the body.

A new unitary privacy maintains its integrity by acting on the finalities into which it continues, as well as on the organic body that is inseparable from it. The intensifications which result from the privacy's acts make it have a richer and richer individuality. Its initial individuality matches the organic body; it becomes intensified when it is able to be in between both the finalities and the body into which it inescapably continues.

These remarks are rather choppy because I have come to them many times during the day and without looking at what went before. And now I have returned from my walk with new reflections: A privacy is continuous with finalities only so far as it bounds off portions of them and at once specializes and holds on to those positions. When a privacy is forced to release the portion, it is also forced to give up its continuation with the finalities. To be subordinate to another is so far to lose contact with finalities on the private side, and to exist on the public side only within the confines of a larger body. Why then should contained particles fall at the same rate as those that are not contained, and do so within a public space and under laws which govern these? Must it not be because the finalities govern the purely public contexts in which the contained particles continue to be? The contained particles do lose some freedom and are made to function in ways dictated by the encompassing body, showing that they are not identical with themselves when they are not confined.

* * *

There is nothing deader than a dead logician. Most metaphysicians are alive, i.e. read, studied, influential, somewhat as many artists are, after they are dead. One reason for this difference is that logicians deal ingeniously with prevailing problems. If they solve them, the results become part of the *lingua franca;* if they do not, the next generation of logicians begins anew. Metaphysicians and artists break away from the prevailing categories, thereby precluding their ready acceptance for the most part. But after the haze of the dominant views passes away, what they are saying becomes more evident, something to be read in the pure light of the perpetual day.

November 18

In *First Considerations,* I maintained that actualities internalized something of the finalities which were impinging on and conditioning them. I envisaged the internalization as having to do with the same presentation of the finalities as had been involved in conditioning the appearances together, the actualities together, and the actualities individually. It has now become evident that I was looking at the finalities as though they were so many distanced bodies outside of or alongside actualities. Yesterdays' discussion shows that when and as actualities are conditioned as bodies they are also affected by the finalities as privacies, and that they bound off and possess a portion of those finalities at the same time that those bounded-off portions remain continuous with the finalities. Since the portions could be bounded off at different points and be possessed with different degrees of effectiveness, it is possible to distinguish different types of actuality by the ways and extent to which they bound and possess portions of those finalities privately and are affected by them publicly. A difference of a similar kind also occurs when actualities are subordinated to some larger actuality and when they are released from that subordination.

If we start with ultimate particles, whatever their nature, we start with actualities which have privacies that are the very public being of those actualities, readied, potential, awaiting expression. The privacies of those particles continue into the finalities at the same time that they bound off a portion of these and possess them as intensifications of the privacies. When the particles are caught up in larger complexes having their own integrity, those complexes when and as they are being constituted through the aid of the finalities (which provide those complexes with their transcendent unifying powers), force a dislocation of the boundaries instituted by the particles and, thereupon, yield a merged set of dislocated privacies.

The privacies of entities remain their privacies only as long as the privacies are self-bounding and continue into the finalities and bodies. Ultimate particles, on being caught up, let us say, in a cell, retain their privacies, but as bounded at new positions, at the same time that the portions, which had been bounded off before by the particles, become part of qualifications of the finalities. The privacies would be entirely caught up in the finalities were it not that the loss occurs as the same time that the bodies of those particles are being solidified into a new encompassing body. When and as this occurs, those portions of the

finalities, that had been possessed by the privacies of the ultimate particles, achieve distinctive boundaries, to become the privacies of new
complex bodies. Their solidification, due in part to the action of the
finalities in governing the particles as an interlocked set, is one with the
solidification of and qualifications of the finalities, and the possession
and bounding, and thereby the specialization of the qualified finalities.
A new privacy comes to be by virtue of the merging, rebounding, and
possessing of what the ultimate particles released, in their becoming
subordinate to the new single body.

If ultimate particles always remain in existence, whether in the delimited forms they have in complexes, or as separate units in the cosmos,
they will always have some inextinguishable privacy. If, instead, they
come to be and pass away, just as the complexes do, they will have to
obtain and release their privacies when and as they come to be and pass
away.

Whatever be said about the ultimate particles, we must recognize
that cells and other complexes, such as sperm and egg, are to be understood as having attained privacies which depend for their possibility on
the release of some portion of the privacies of ultimate particles. And
what is true of the cell relative to its particles, is true of the union of
sperm and egg relative to the separate sperm and egg. As separate, these
have privacies which hold on to finalities. When they are joined, they
lose hold on those finalities and their privacies. A privacy exists only so
far as it holds on to and holds itself away from all the finalities.

Unlike particles, a sperm and egg no longer exist once they are united.
Their privacies are no longer distinctive, serving merely to qualify the
finalities from which they can no longer be bounded. But the existence
of the complex body, which sperm and egg make possible, because it is
constituted by and yet maintains itself in opposition to the finalities,
forces a bounding of the finalities, and thereupon the production of a
distinctive unitary privacy, contrasting with that body. Had there been
a disappearance of the sperm and egg without the coming to be of the
complex, the finalities would have been just qualified by the privacies
which the sperm and egg released. But because the passing away of the
sperm and the egg is the becoming of a new entity (the complex), the
loss of their privacies is accompanied by the production of a new privacy
that separates out and solidifies a portion of the finalities. That privacy,
like the privacy of the separate particles, or the separated egg and sperm,
exists as long as the complex continues as a distinct item. If the complex
is subordinated to a new complex, it will go through adventures similar

to those gone through by the encompassed particles and the encompassed sperm and egg. But if the complex is destroyed, its privacy just qualifies the finalities. There will be no recovery of the sperm and the egg. The ultimate particles will be released from the governance of the sperm and egg, or from the body they together make possible. The particles then recover what they had previously lost on being included in the larger complex. If there are any cells that remain on the dissolution of a complex, they, too, will recover the part of the privacies they had previously lost when they were included within that complex.

Unless a man can be included in an encompassing complex, his death will be a dissolution of his body. Some subordinated entities will recover the status of independents; these will have their own privacies, bounding off and possessing portions of the finalities. The man's privacy will no longer exist except in the form of a nuance in the finalities, not bounded off from other nuances, and having no relation to a body.

The having of a privacy is one with the bounding off of a finality (into which it continues) and an orientation toward the body. The privacy of a thing has no power to intensify itself by bringing together within itself something of the factors which are at its borders. The privacy of a genuine complex body, unified through the agency of the various finalities, though, will bound off the body as surely as it bounds off the finalities. It will also be able to utilize the body and the finalities, so as to intensify and thereby further individualize itself.

This account can perhaps be simplified: A privacy is oriented toward a complex body. When that privacy ceases to be bounded off from the finalities, at the very same time it ceases to be oriented toward the body. This occurs when the body is incorporated within a larger complex, or when it is dissolved into its parts. A larger complex involves a recovery of privacy from the finalities. That recovery does not involve making a part of the finalities into a privacy. It just lays hold of content that had been privately maintained apart from the finalities. The recovery is not exact. The resultant privacy has, as part of its content, some portion of the finalities which it thereupon concretionalizes, guided by the qualifying nuances that had been introduced into those finalities.

This discussion has tried to do justice to a number of issues: 1. the persistence of ultimate particles in all bodily complexes; 2. the different functionings of the particles inside and outside bodily complexes; 3. the achievement of new privacies with the coming to be of new organic complexes; 4. the disappearance of complexes (such as sperm and egg) on the advent of encompassing complexes; 5. the disappearance of complexes on death, with the consequent reappearance of particles and perhaps some complexes, as freed from the living complex that had encompassed them; 6. the orientation of all privacies toward the public; 7. the power of the privacies of complexes to become intensified and thereby individualized through the use of the finalities and of what the body makes available; and 8. the ability of human privacies to stand apart from human bodies and there engage in distinctive private activities, through their ability to make themselves intensive and individual, to a degree that the privacy of animals and things cannot. I know no other view that deals with all of these. But I think I have not made sufficiently clear that the irreducible individuality of a privacy results from the way in which it bounds itself off from the finalities on one side, and contrasts with the body on the other, the two occurring at the same time.

Privacy can avoid being turned into a creature of the body or of what is external, only by maintaining itself against the pull of the body. It could not bound itself from the body without being helped. And this is what the finalities provide. But in providing it, the finalities in turn would make the privacy into their creature, were it not able to maintain itself against their engulfment. And since it cannot do this without being helped, it depends on the body to help it hold itself away from the finalities into which it continues. It stands between both finalities and body because it uses each to support it against the other. Might it not be the case then that it might lose its status in relation to the finalities to become just a nuanced part of the body? Is this what happens when we have just the living of a human body? It could recover its previous status only with the help of the finalities. They, finding one state of the living more receptive than others at some time, would enable it to mark itself off from the body and thereupon make that living also have the status of a privacy in control of the living, and that to the very same extent that the privacy was in control of what the finalities had impinged on it.

November 20

Why suppose that ultimate particles, and perhaps cells, genes, sperm, and egg lose something of their privacies when they are encompassed in a larger unity? Why not hold that the larger is something like a boat in which they are carried along at a pace and in a direction they otherwise could not, without being altered in any particular? The admission would allow one, contrary to atomists and similar reductionists, to recognize the reality of the encompassing unity, but restrict its power

to that of changing the places and to some extent redetermining the kinds
of public activities they could have. Is it not because we otherwise would
not be able to account for the new privacies which supervene over those
which have functioned as items that were united, and in that uniting
were lost (as the sperm and egg are), or because we could no longer take
them to express publicly what they were latently (as the particles and
the genes apparently cannot when subjected to an organic governance)?
The second of these reasons is by no means evident to me; it is just a
suggestion now, leaving still open the question whether or not and to
what extent particles and genes lose anything on being encompassed,
and gain something on being freed from a role in an organism.

What is the least that must be said? 1. Ultimate particles have privacies. Otherwise there would be no continuity between the kinds of
metaphysical entities that they are and any other kinds. They would also
lack the power to oppose the finalities at the same time that they were
being subject to them as public entities, and were thereby unified in
various ways and caught up in various contexts which had a controlling
role.

2. Ultimate particles are evidently all the same in public nature and
presumably private, when they are functioning in the cosmos as so many
distinct items and when they are caught within the limits of some actuality
and there subjected to new ways of being first in one place and then in
another. If it be the case that they lose something of their privacy when
and as they are caught up on a larger effective controlling unity, they
will also have to have the ability to recover just what they had lost when
they are once again freed from that governance. This at first seems to
require action of a miraculous sort, since it seems to require a recapture,
by perhaps randomly functioning entities, of just what they need. But
once it is remembered that the privacies are released to the extent that
the entities are organically connected (which is to say, no longer able to
be independent but commonly conditioned), and that an encompassing
whole depends for its unifying power on the finalities, it is possible to
go on to affirm that the finalities encompass privacies as well and to the
same degree. Since an organism allows particles and various complexes
to be within its confines, and thus to retain privacies of their own, the
release need not be thought of as absolute, but only as much as is needed
to allow the privacies to be more under the subjection of the finalities
than before (and in that sense to be integral to those privacies as their
many nuances) while leaving a portion of those privacies untouched and
still oriented to bodies. When the particles are released, the finalities

are able to make available to the particles the nuances that had been accreted to those finalities.

3. Sperm and egg, unlike ultimate particles, vanish on the achievement of a complex of cells. And when the complex is destroyed, there is no recovery of the sperm and the egg. Sperm and egg must be said to die on their coming together, to yield more limited entities, such as genes and cells, which are encompassed by a single organic entity. Their death, like the death of the organism, will involve a loss of the appropriate privacy, in such a way that there can be no recovery. Sperm and egg, produced by organisms, are not identifiable with the sperm or egg which was a source of those organisms.

4. An organism can produce a sperm or egg, or some equivalent. These have their own distinctive privacies. Are they different when they are in the bodies and when they are outside them, or as involved with one another? As newly produced they must have their privacies. These they could possibly obtain from a. the finalities, b. the organism, or c. smaller entities and, in the end, the ultimate particles. a. Though the finalities are always effective and on everything, they do not have to be invoked in order to deal with transactions between an organic unity and what it organically produces. The situation is different when we come to ultimate particles, for these function and have natures regardless of organisms. b. If an organism gave a sperm and egg their privacies, it would have to take something from itself or from the smaller entities. If the latter, we come to the third alternative. If the former, we would have to say that the organism diminished its own privacy when it produced sperm and egg—and this does not seem to be the case.

3. The sperm or egg are produced by the organism, but out of smaller entities, just as the complex embryonic organism itself is produced by the finalities out of smaller entities. The larger organism gives the sperm or egg a unity by making smaller entities give up their independence, and thereby some of their privacy, to make possible a new body and a new unitary privacy in which the content (but not the individuality of the content) is preserved. The privacies, by being deprived of their bearing on the bodies which are caught up into the new organic body, lose their individuality.

None of this is very clear to me. And I do not know anywhere to turn for help. The biologists are not interested in the problem: And if they were, they would not be equipped to deal with it. The philosophers show no interest—at least so far as I know. The *Encyclopedia of Philosophy* has no article on individuation, and little light is thrown by the passages referred to in the index. The index does not mention sperm and egg, and the references to organism are not helpful.

There are views of society, state, and cosmos which treat these as organisms. These have to face the problem of whether or not men, like ultimate particles and organic parts, lose something of what they were as outside society or state, and conceivably outside the cosmos, and in any case whether or not men as in these, do not have part of their privacies caught up in a larger unity, and there have less privacy than they otherwise, at least in principle, might have had. This does not seem plausible, though a case can surely be made for the view that men are affected, limited, and helped by society or state, and gain something by coming out of their individual privacies into a cosmos where they are together with one another and other actualities.

The present view tacitly supposes that the ultimate particles never pass away. But this seems an unnecessary supposition, and also seems to stand in conflict with the view that energy and mass are interconvertible. If they be allowed to pass away, their privacies will also pass away as distinctive and oriented toward bodies. The bodies will be caught up in the finalities from one side, and the privacies will be caught up in those finalities from another side. Or, if (as seems more correct) the finalities be seen to affect the particles as at once private and public, individual and bodily, the passing away of the particles will involve the separation of the privacies and bodies at the same time that these become caught up at different levels of the finalities. The coming to be of ultimate particles will then be due either to an adventitious juncture of these separated factors or the work of something outside the finalities, which is to say, other actualities. The former brings us close to a Neoplatonic or idealistic production of the many from the one; the latter requires distinct ultimate particles to be the work of actual entities on the finalities, as qualified by the bodily natures of the ultimate particles, with a consequent forcing of the appropriate privacies out of those finalities. Neither of these alternatives seems plausible. Nor are they very clear.

November 21

There are times when a number of ultimate particles are so closely involved with one another that the finalities are able to be instanced by them as together. The instantiation also involves a specialization and a transfer of some power, enabling the result to govern, limit the activities of, and give new directions and functions to the initial entities. To begin with, the result is nothing more than something as physical as the initial particles, or at the very most is chemical in nature. The result could have the form of some limited chemical unit, or of a mass object such as a gas. We cannot deny privacy to the result, no matter what it is. But it is neither necessary nor desirable to go further and, with pansychists, attribute even a low grade sensitivity to that privacy.

The finalities are instantiated by the entire new unitary entity, and therefore as both bodily and private. The power of the entity is quite limited. As distinctive, it is manifested mainly in the capacity to interact with entities on the same level. But since the career of a gas or similar mass-object involves adventures which do compel the particles within the object to be at places they otherwise would not be on their own, it is something like the power that organisms exhibit. In any case, the specialization, and the empowering of the bodily side of the result of a close involvement of particles, and of other physical and perhaps also chemical entities, is inseparable from the bodily part of the instantiation of the finalities. That part orients the rest of the instantiated finalities— the private—toward itself, and thereby individuates it.

Water and gas are mass objects; they are added to and subtracted from, often without any appreciable change in behavior, particularly if the addition or subtraction is moderate. The addition to or subtraction from such a mass object is quite different from that of an organism, since the latter may require a dissolution of a distinctive privacy. A mass object continues to have the same kind of privacy and, of course, to provide the same instantiations, no matter what its magnitude.

There is no need to suppose that there ever was a stage in the history of the cosmos when there were only ultimate particles, and that the more complex entities supervened at some later date. Nor is there need to suppose that the ultimate particles must first come together to produce physical or chemical entities. It is possible that some combinations of them could be immediately encompassed in an organic unity. Organic entities come into being in ways similar to those which mark the coming to be of complex physical unitary entities, and of chemical ones. All involve the insistent presence, instantiation, and specialization of the finalities. These embrace the entire set of entites and provide multi-dimensional units which are only partly restricted to the bodily side. As restricted to that side, the instantiation has the form of a multi-dimensional unity of a body. The remainder of the instantiation has power but nothing to control. It becomes individualized only when it is oriented by and toward the bodily unity.

The account of actualities in *First Considerations* can be brought into alignment with the above, if what it says is restricted either to ultimate particles or to the outcome of the combining of particles or more complex actualities. It does not hold that the privacies of actualities are instantiations of finalities, individualized or oriented toward instantiations of those finalities in a bodily role. I now am maintaining that only ultimate particles are radically opposed to the finalities. Other actualities, though also opposed to the finalities and able to interplay with them, must first be produced through the help of the finalities.

The acknowledgment that complex actualities have individualized privacies, as well as bodily unities, both of which instantiate the finalities, makes it easier to see how, on the dissolution of those actualities, the privacies can be submerged in the finalities. Since those privacies will have lost their orientation toward their bodies (though Thomas Aquinas would say that they still have such an orientation and will have bodies supplied in an ennobled form after this scheme of things is at an end), as submerged in the finalities they no longer retain their individuality.

The acknowledgment that complex entities have already privately instantiated the finalities makes it easier to see how it is possible for men to know the finalities. One might even argue that there is no need to suppose that they internalize the finalities and are thereupon able to have an identity, be loci of truth, or exhibit other ways of exemplifying the finalities, since their privacies already are those finalities in restricted forms and as oriented toward the body. To know the finalities, or to be able to function as loci of truth and the like, they do not have to internalize the finalities in a special act; they could, instead, discover in themselves what they had in an instantiated, individualized guise. But all the while, in that guise, they are radically distinct from the finalities. Though their content is provided by the finalities—just as the unity of a complex body is—that content has a distinctive career, tonality, and boundaries, and is able to exercise its modicum of power independently of the finalities from which this power was derived.

Abstracting from his acceptance of the traditional theory of genus and species, and staying with his treatment of man, the position I have now reached is not too far from Scotus'. He took the individual to be an *infima species,* a kind, but the lowest and unduplicable. Socrates was understood to be a present 'Socraticity'. The 'Socraticity' was part of an eternal scheme and yet individual. But unlike what is now being held, the individual for him apparently was not oriented toward a body, and so far did not have a footing in the world.

The present view also has something in common with that of Aquinas for whom the individuation of men has its source in individuated matter. This has some kind of reality apart from forms and therefore apart from their confinement and division in various complex entities. Aquinas did not allow for ultimate particles; their modern acknowledgment awaits Galileo's arguments.

In opposition to Aquinas and Scotus, I find no need to refer to a form, or to a soul. I also allow for a privacy to 'matter' and to mass-objects, such as gasses and water unless, like a rock, they can be treated as mere wholes, i.e., entities which have distinctive natures but no distinctive power, and whose motions must therefore be understood to be the summations of the motions of their parts, and ultimately of matter, or of ultimate particles.

If privacies are just instantiated, individuated finalities, we need no longer hold to the idea that the privacies stand in between the finalities and bodies, unless it be necessary for those privacies to still be intensified by taking something of the finalities into themselves. I see no need that they must. As a consequence of the present acceptance of the view that the privacies of complex actualities, organic or inorganic, instantiate the finalities and are individuated by virtue of their orientation toward bodies (which themselves instantiate those finalities in the form of transcendents), it is no longer necessary to suppose (as I did in order to try to account for individuality) that the privacies, at least of men, function as mediators, and thus are in a perpetual process of adjusting themselves, and could make themselves become intensively enriched over the course of their careers.

The finalities affect the other items in the world when and as they affect a given one as at once private and possessed of a body. When Possibility is incorporated in all three, a man not only has knowledge but has a bodily nature which is appropriate to a meaning externally present. Must he not then always know what is the case? Could there be any error or falsehood? There can be error since the manner and result of instantiation may not match the realization in the world. There can be falsehood since one may privately distort what was realized in the body or the world. Things make no errors. Animals do, but they do not lie, deliberately set their privacies and bodies at odds.

Do all of the finalities have exemplifications in privacies, in bodies, and in what is being faced? Do they govern the relations which a privacy has to a body, the privacy has to what is beyond, and the body has to what is beyond, and the appearances have to one another? Does a proper realization of Substance not require, at the very least, in addition to the private-body realization, a concurrent embodiment in other entities, thereby enabling a being to be at home in the world? Does Being not require a similar realization, so that one can be together with independents? Does Existence not produce both distensions and occupied extensions, as well as other extensions keeping things at a distance? Does a final Unity not require other unities, outside the unified man with his unified privacy and unified body? I think these questions are to be answered affirmatively.

November 22

A man's privacy has a. an intensity greater than that exhibited by his appearances, or reached by any confrontation; b. is oriented toward his body, and thereby acquires an individuation; c. expresses itself in and through his body, thereby exhibiting and carrying out ideas, intentions, and desires; d. possesses and accretes to itself what it encounters, and does so on its own terms; e. resists intrusions and thereby brings all advances toward it to a halt; f. is epitomized and specialized in the form of a self and a person; g. instantiates and specializes all the finalities; h. has the power to attend to the finalities; and i. passes away with the failure of the organic human body to remain in a certain integrated stage where the finalities are operative.

a. Though the body and the privacy jointly and separately instantiate and specialize the finalities, the body spends some of its power in subordinating various parts. The privacies of those parts are not encompassed or dealt with by the privacy, leaving it undiversified by alien entities, but still with a concentrated power all its own. It is, therefore, an effective, multi-dimensional unity in a way in which the body is not. When in naming, symbolization, and adumbration, we move from appearances to actuality, from surface to depth, we identify our names, symbols, and judged content within the compass of the transcendents imposed by the finalities. We do not then attend to these finalities, having in effect replaced the actual transcendents with our own names, symbols, and objects of judgment, and are ready to move toward the private real instantiation of those transcendents.

b. The finalities are instantiated by the entire entity, as both public and private. They are also instantiated by each in a distinctive way, as a consequence of the fact that there is a primary emphasis on the body and its need to govern the parts. The privacy has no such task. It is indeterminate just so far as it is continuous with the transcendents as governing the body, and becomes determinate in becoming individuated— which occurs by its being oriented by the organic body toward that body.

c. Human privacy maintains itself against the pull of the body; it divides itself off, bounds itself. If it did not, it would be like the privacy of an inanimate object, and perhaps also of a subhuman living being. It is as separate from the body, at the same time that it is continuous with it, that the privacy is able to be epitomized in self and person, and these in turn by an I, mind, responsibility, me, sensitivity, and rights. Because of its continuation with the body, as instantiating and specializing the very transcendents it does, the privacy is able to make itself bodily manifest and to express itself through bodily means.

d. An individual remains self-same over the course of his career, as his continued rights and responsibility make evident. That self-sameness involves the reduction, of what it encounters, to the self-same result. A self-identity involving the body is an outcome of a self-identification. There is also a self-identification which is carried out privately, through the union of the I with an epitomization of the self in the form of a mere identity, a simple persistence insisted on. Because its self-identity, as involving the body, involves the use of the I, privacy is enabled to possess and thereby make its own some of the content which it encounters.

e. The privacy, because it maintains itself in contrast with the body, opposes all moves into it across its boundary. Its continuity with the body allows it to be moved into, but its own insistence on itself makes it resistant to any advances. Its resistance is its insistence viewed from the position of what intrudes on it. Every intrusion, even that of the finalities, is therefore brought to a halt, but there is no predesignated or predesignatable point at which this must occur. The fact that it is already an instantiation of the finalities does not make the privacy entirely accessible to those finalities, for the instantiation is also a specialization, involving a maintenance of itself against the body and, because of its individuality) against everything else as well, and therefore of the finalities. Though it is proper to speak of appearances, where finalities and bodies come together, particularly where the latter is dominant, we do not usually speak of appearances when we refer to the place and outcome of the juncture of privacies and finalities. But often enough we speak of subjectivity, personalizations, bias, and the like. These are the counterpart in privacy of the appearances in the public world.

f. The privacy of a man is not individuated without also being divided into a self and a person. Individuation, to be sure, also occurs in animals and even in things, but it is not the individuation of a privacy which also has a status apart from the orienting and individuating, complex body. The individuation of a human privacy awaits the development of a body which is able to orient it in such a way that the privacy itself initially yields only a person. Only later does the self and (still later) the I arise. Both await the development of the person, itself dependent on the development of the organic body. The embryo and the fetus have rights even before they have selves and distinguishable I's.

g. Though it is proper to speak of the unity of the body, the privacy, and of the two of them together, the unity is not to be exclusively understood as instantiating and specializing Unity. Each finality acts to unify, but in a different way. The unification produced by Substance emphasizes the self-maintenance of man; Being, his independence; Possibility, his intelligibility; Existence, his distensive occupation of extensions; and Unity, his value in an objective hierarchy of items at different distances from Unity itself, as that which brooks no diversity, submerging all differences into a single nuanced harmony. Everyone of those finalities is instantiated, i.e., localized without alteration, and specialized, i.e., added to, intensified, utilized, turned into the transcendent as just there, and oriented toward the body or operative in a body with respect to subordinated parts.

h. Men know the finalities. This they would not be able to do were they entirely cut off from them. However, one could hold that they might discover those finalities solely by taking account of the transcendent determinants of the body and the privacy. Such discovery will require one to pass beyond appearances to the constituents of these. This is surely one of the ways in which the finalities come to be known. But they are also known speculatively, by reflecting on the nature of individuation, unification, and the relation of privacy and body. Unless the speculation must be guided by what is learned by the study of dissected appearances, one will not know how to formulate (or where to look for guidance for the formulation of) the nature of the finalities. But the very fact that the finalities are instantiated and specialized by a private individual, enables him to be in consonance with the finalities, and to know them by an agency, such as the mind, which epitomizes the privacy.

i. Organic bodies die. The orientation and therefore the individuation of their privacies is thereby lost. The most that could be left is instantiated, specialized finalities. These would either have to float between the finalities and the world of actualities; become submerged in the finalities, perhaps tinging them; or disappear altogether. Since the instantiation of the finalities by a body is due to the pull by the encompassed parts, and since the instantiation by the privacy is due to the inseparability of that privacy from the instantiated bodily side, when the occasion for the instantiation is lost, so is the instantiation. Nothing seems to be left except the finalities as they had been before the advent of that particular actuality.

If, as I have maintained in *Beyond All Appearances*, we are here and now involved with the finalities as they are by themselves, the result may still remain after our bodies and we ourselves are no longer, without our being able to add to that fact after death and, of course, without there being any consciousness or any mark in eternity of our individualities or adventures in this world. We would be immortal only while we were alive. Though our presence in the finalities is not compromised by our ceasing to be, it also does not have anything to do with us as conscious individuals.

November 23

The unity of a man has multiple dimensions. All are epitomized in the guise of a complex unity of his organic body and in a complex unity of his privacy. The unity of a man's body expends some of its energy in governing what is within its limits, and in orienting the remainder of his unity. That remainder consequently has an self-containedness and intensity which the unity of the body does not. At one and the same time, the privacy is continuous with the unity of the organic body, stands in contrast with it, is affected by how the bodily unity functions, and affects it by expressing itself through that body. The body also expresses itself, with the consequence that there are bodily expressions having an origin in privacy, and others having theirs in the body, both manifesting an insistency.

Some expressions by the body are met by those of other bodies, to constitute adventitious accidents; others are met by universal conditions, with appearances as a consequence. Both privacy and body are expressed in opposition to insistent universal conditions and, therefore, in opposition to unities as not yet instantiated. At one and the same time, both the organic body and privacy interplay with the very conditions which continue to exist apart, even though they had already been instantiated, specialized, and limited by that body and privacy.

Because the body and the privacy have their own natures and powers, they function independently. Because they function independently, they interplay with the same conditions in different ways and with different results. With the body, they constitute appearances, but they merely enable the privacy to become more intensive. While appearances stand between the bodies and the conditions, privacy effectively mediates the conditions (with which that privacy interplays and from which it obtains intensifications) and the body.

I have now come back to the position I entertained a little while ago—that privacy was an intermediary—but without compromising the fact that the privacy also provides a constant, intensive unity, at once continuous with and contrasting with the unity of the body. The privacy is a constant, as individualized and oriented by the body; it is intensified, as already contrasted with the body and having its own expressions. Unlike the body, whose expressions interlock with the expressions of final realities to constitute appearances, the privacy adopts what its expressions terminate in. In *First Considerations* I spoke of the individual internalizing the finalities. That way of speaking makes it appear as if the privacy internalized what was affecting the body. But the internalization by the privacy is direct. It is most manifest when a man understands the ultimate final realities, when he gives these the status of ideas in his mind. If, therefore, it be true that adoption of the conditions by the privacy involves an intensification of this, the knowing of what is ultimately real should also involve such an intensification.

Religious men sometimes say that having the idea of God—a personalized, specialized, presumably conscious version of one or more of the final realities—makes a difference to the kind of men they are. In effect they are claiming that the privacy's adoption of that final reality enriches the privacy. And when they think of themselves as having to attend to their God again and again, they make evident that their privacy is still concerned with the same finality. When they add that their bodies are creatures of God, they go on to hold that the bodies are also involved with God, and presumably in a way that the privacies are not, but which it is hoped the enriched privacies will control and benefit.

There are at least five final realities, and therefore five sets of conditions which are realized in the form of privacy, the organization of a body, and in the two of these together, undivided from one another. As a consequence, the intensification of the privacy is not solely due to the adoption of expressions of one finality, (which some men personalize as God) but to the adoption of others as well. And since the mind is only one of the epitomizations of the privacy, once this has been specialized in the form of a self, there will be a number of ways in which the various final realities will be adopted by the privacy. And since its successes are not always of the same degree, there will be different degrees in which the conditions are present in different aspects of the privacy, and at different times.

The organic body, it could be said, is not enriched by the conditions which express the final realities. There is only an interplay resulting in appearances. The body will, of course, continue to be subject to those conditions. That is how it is able to have a unity. But once the unity is present, this may have a greater range, become more complex, have more members and parts than before but will not become different in kind. That view could well be disputed.

The differences between embryo, infant, child, adolescent, adult, and aged seem to be very large; they are able to function in quite different ways, and have various distinctive capacities. One could therefore reasonably maintain that these are the outcome of modifications produced by the bodily adoption of the conditions which had been originally specialized to give the initial organic unity of the body.

I hesitate to accept this, since it is not yet evident to me how the conditions do anything more than help constitute appearances. The organic unity of the body seems itself capable of being expanded and made more complex, through the increase of the range of its encompassment and, with the new parts and members, to become stronger and have new functions. But I see nothing amiss in the idea. The organic body might be enriched by its subsequent adoption of some of the conditioning to which it is being subjected. There does, though, seem to be no counterpart for the body of the adoption of finalities in a private mind. The body, of course, is enriched by the privacy; it is prepared and directed by thought, will, intent, and desire; it varies in tonality and career because of what is privately done and, apparently, to the degree that thought and other epitomizations of privacy are expressed in and through it. The body orients the privacy, and the privacy in turn enriches the body while making use of it. Since that privacy may also have become enriched by its adoption of the conditions in its own way, and since its various activities may be affected by this absorption, the body will, at least indirectly through the aid of the privacy, be enriched by the conditions. The issue, consequently, boils down to the question as to whether or not the body could be directly enriched, as the privacy is, by an accommodation of the very conditions which it initially instantiated and specialized.

Can the body, apart from any knowledge or concern exhibited by the privacy, make the conditions, which its organization exemplifies, also give the organization something equivalent to the ideas of the finalities that the privacy can entertain? Would training enable a man to incorporate the condition that also operates to connect his body with others, as more or less affiliated or relevant? Would habituation enable a man to incorporate the condition that also operates to connect his body with others as equally independent and possessed of equal rights? Would social laws and disciplining enable him to incorporate the condition that also operates to make his body intelligibly related to others? Would external pressures enable a man to incorporate the condition that also operates to relate his body to others in extensions? And would the performance of rituals enable him to incorporate the condition that also operates to make his body have a particular value relative to other bodies? I now see nothing in the way of these suggestions.

* * *

Last night I saw a memorable film—"The Days of Heaven". I know of no other which is so brilliantly photographed, and then has its various scenes montaged with such daring and poetic imagination. Sometimes I failed to see just why one sequence followed on another; the hero was too handsome for the part; the owner's house and the motorcycle were too neat and new for the roads and temperature of the Texas Panhandle in 1916 or thereabouts. At first the continuing narrative by the child did not seem to fit in, but it did do so quite soon and seemed to be right. But these are minor faults. From the very beginning, one scene of magnificent, sensitively felt beauty followed on another. The filming of the great fire was in particular memorable, without any of the noises or emphasis on fierceness so often exhibited in similar scenes by others.

Bergman is a film director one eventually comes to see to be a photographer. The conclusion is reluctantly reached; it does not make one see him positively, but rather as one who failed to be the dynamic movie director he was trying to be. In "Days of Heaven" however, one immediately faces the fact that one is seeing great photography into which the plot is slowly built. The photographs of the sky, particularly in the beginning scenes, I found to be exciting, moving in a way that even some great plots are not.

I have long thought of the Japanese as having magnificent film photographers. They photograph with great clarity and from unusual angles; one has a sense of being shown work by men who have mastered the art of photography. But I have not seen a film of theirs to compare with "Days of Heaven". Admittedly I have not seen many, though there have been a number that have been brought to this country and which I have seen and liked. In any case, they photograph a film. What we have here, instead, is photography made into a film, or better, perhaps, a concern with capturing magnificent images, and arranging them with daring and imagination.

November 24

Hegel takes as primary the role of an intermediary between extremes; it is an idea that is also close to the heart of Aristotle's ethics. Hartshorne holds instead that the primary fact is an asymmetrical absorption of what is beyond. Instances of both types of occurrence can be found in man.

The outstanding asymmetrical absorptions are 1. the adoption of conditions by the privacy as a kind of intensification; 2. the adoption of finalities, in a conceptualization or other epitomizations of the self; 3. the acceptance of appearances by the body even though they are also constituted by the conditions; 4. the acceptance of conditions in the form of relations, by yielding to them in the form of termini; 6. the acceptance of privately determined acts by the body; 7. the reception of determinations and intrusions by other actualities; 8. the reception by the privacy of determinations stemming from or going through the body, thereby leading the privacy to engage in acts of self-identity or to attend to what is occurring; and 9. the acceptance of a proper name.

The outstanding symmetrical mediations are 1. the emotional, where privacy and body, or more precisely, consciousness, are joined with bodily turbulence; 2. the epitomizational, where specializations of the privacy, in the form of self or person, are combined with established epitomizations to yield a new epitomization; 3. the constitutive, where appearances are produced as the outcome of the interplay of expressions of the individual and common conditions; 4. the occasional, yielding accidents, the outcome of the interplay of a receiving man and external forces; 5. a private self-maintaining, where the privacy is constant, and acts to reduce both body and conditions to a re-presentation of the way in which body and conditions are joined, thereby enabling the privacy to function in consonance with the body; 6. a bodily self-maintaining where the body is constant and acts to reduce both the privacy and conditions to a re-presentation of the way in which privacy and conditions are in fact joined, thereby enabling the body to be a public counterpart of the privacy—this is required if one is to account for training, habituation, particularly when these are deliberately instituted and controlled.

There are surely other instances. And some cases raise difficult questions to resolve. a. Are color and gender the outcome of the symmetrical acceptance by the body of the affect of the confining parts, particularly the genes, and of externally imposed, rather steady conditions expressing the nature of the rest of the world? b. Are they, instead, the outcome of the symmetrical acceptance of the effects of the parts and the conditions which are functioning as relations between actualities? Or are they not some combination of a and b? The gender and color of a man are dependent on genetic factors, and as he is set in this kind of world and, surely, as functioning as a term in relations of relevance, equality with others of the same gender or color, intelligibility, location (which is the point emphasized by geographic determinists), and relative value. Some of these are evidently more conspicuous, evident, or effective than others.

What is now needed is a systematic presentation of the two types of cases, the asymmetrical and the symmetrical. Each dimension of man, the private, the bodily, the publicly interrelated, the social, the terminating of relations, and the presence in a we, a they, and the others, should be examined, and a reason sought for the symmetrical and asymmetrical occurrences. The examination could serve as a base for the understanding of other vexatious issues.

I have just been reading a paper by Rabbi Joshua O. Haberman on "Universalism and Particularism in Interreligious Dialogue". He has made me see a way of dealing with Jesus Christ which would allow for the reconciliation of Judaism and Christianity. The man, Jesus, is accepted by both sides as a Jew. The Christian goes on to hold that that Jew was an exceptional Jew and, for the orthodox, even one who was divine. Starting from the side of him as taken to be divine, he would as a man be an intermediary between the two religions, between one who had a Jewish ancestry and one who was the locus of an incarnation. Starting from the side of him taken to be a man, he would be one who allowed for the acknowledgment of him as a God on the part of Christians. Orthodox Christians can take the acknowledgment to be of the presence of God in Christ to an eminent degree; indeed, as himself the divine. Liberal Christians can take the acknowledgment to be that of an exceptional man who allowed for an opening into the divine as no others could. For the Jews, he is a Jew who was accepted by another religious community as having powers and virtues which he does not have as a human Jew. Jesus would have a symmetrical role for the Jews; Christ makes the man with that symmetrical role also function for them asymmetrically. Judaism would insist that Jesus as a man belongs to the religious Jewish community, but this still allows him to be understood to have a side which has a special role in an entirely different religious community. Christianity holds that Jesus is the Christ, but this still allows him to be fully part of Judaism. His status as an incarnate God allows him to be a man, asymmetrically related to the divine and now longer merely the Judaic man who is the same living individual in both the Judaic and the Christian world.

The problem and the proposed solution can be more readily seen by taking a more familiar and minor example. Poe is an American writer appreciated more in France than in the United States. Let us say that the French take him to be a major writer and that we do not. Poe would have a symmetrical role for us, being related to our writers within our civilization, and related to their writers within their civilization. They would perhaps go on to say that, apart from any relations to their writers, he is a writer of the first magnitude. But this is still their judgment. They, of course, take that judgment to express what is true, but from the standpoint of our civilization we can do no more than recognize that he is a writer known to both, and that in theirs he has an exalted standing greater than that which we assign to him. From their standpoint, he still is a man who is a writer for both civilizations, but in theirs he also has an additional role, making him as a writer of whatever he did write to be asymmetrically related to his exalted status.

There is no reconciliation of these views, but they surely are not incompatible. They cannot be reconciled because there is no third position that is being acknowledged. They are also not incompatible because what holds in one context, the American, is not denied but added to, in the other. As in that other, it is possible to say that the American is mistaken; but this is not necessary; one can also say that the standing that he has with us is necessarily different from that which he has in France because in France alone is he freed from having his American connections, bearings, antecedents, and the like, condition and control all other or most of the factors. Similarly, a painting in a studio undergoes a change when it is in a museum; there it has the neighbors, light, position, and a sanction it deserves, or needs, or lays claim to. The most that can be said from one side (in the studio) is that it is the kind of entity that is ennobled in another context; the most that could be said from the other side is that it is the kind of entity which also fits perfectly in the other context— which is to say, it was made by an artist.

November 25

A brilliant study of Wallace Stevens by Theodore Weiss brings an old question to the fore. In what sense was Stevens both a successful insurance executive and a great poet? He was not an insurance executive who wrote poetry. If he were, poetry would be an avocation and, more likely than not, of little importance. He was not a poet who was an insurance executive, for if he were his poetry would occasionally intrude into his work, and his work would undoubtedly show flashes of poetic expression and insight. He thought of himself as both an insurance executive doing the job there that he should, and as a poet, somewhat neglected. In what sense then was he a single man? The question has bearing on everyone, for even one who supposes himself to be and who devotes his life to being an insurance executive also watches football games, plays with his children, makes love, writes letters to friends, sails a boat and the like, without intruding anything of his daily life at the office, and, conversely, without having these other activities affect what he does as an executive. Still, he is a single man. We must find common traits, impulses, habits, emphases, tonalities, or values in him which come to expression in these two ways.

Wallace Stevens presumably exhibited the same integrity, conscientiousness, honesty, and self-containedness in both tasks. This cannot mean that he was a man of integrity, etc., who expressed himself in these different media, for he gave himself fully to both. There is no need to suppose that there is a single integrity, somehow hidden or at the base of his being which was filtered through these. But if that is so, we seem to have lost a common base, Wallace Stevens as occupied with neither of these enterprises, Wallace Stevens as having lunch, taking a walk, and the like. Should we say instead, that the true man is the commonsensical man, the man who does daily things, and that the features characterizing him in this guise come to expression in heightened forms in specialized enterprises? I think not, for these enterprises require special virtues and powers, special activities and thoughts, and bring to bear what may not be required in any way in the course of daily living.

Stevens, of course, engaged in his daily rounds with a persistent insistence on being an insurance executive and a poet. When he was the one, he undoubtedly had a strong disposition to take up the other soon.

Is this true when he was completely absorbed in his work at the office, or when writing a poem? In a sense, yes. Though entirely absorbed in the one task or the other, without a single vagrant thought about anything else, he nevertheless placed himself in a context whose presence becomes evident as soon as his concentration lagged, was aware of the hour and of the need or desirability of stopping what he was doing.

If this is so, there is no need to appeal to what Stevens was doing daily to have a base in terms of which to understand him as both poet and executive. The daily life will be just one of the alternative ways he functions within other contexts—and conversely, both the office work and the poetry will be set in a larger context of daily life, allowing Stevens to be a man with the rest of us, going about his daily tasks, and even aware that he must do this when he relaxed a bit and saw that the hour was late, that his plants needed watering, that his secretary deserved to be praised, or that he was hungry.

Does each type of activity provide a context for the others? Does Stevens engage in his daily commonsensical work, his work as an insurance executive, his apparently self-absorbed life as a husband and a father, his conversations with friends, shopkeepers, and so on, and his life as a poet in the contexts provided by others? Does he ignore those contexts to the degree that he concentrates on a particular task, while still remaining subject to them, insofar as he relaxes into them, making him bring to a close whatever he might be occupied with, or might even be totally absorbed in? Is what is constant only the way in which he allows the contexts to function?

Stevens gives his entire mind and being to the work at hand, or at least to some of the work at hand, and then brings it to a definite close. It is not necessary that he do this with respect to every type of activity. He could, for example, attend to a game or a conversation in a neglectful way, and without even being more aware than usual that he has to go home or mail a letter, dictate some business to the secretary, or even work over a poem he had begun the day before. Yes, but when he becomes aware that he is going to engage in one of the basic set of activities, he will close out what he was otherwise doing.

There seem to be two types of closure, one which is made from the position of some absorbing enterprise, the other from the position of that very enterprise treated as a context into which one is to move and there occupy himself with some particular task in its appropriate terms. Both types of determination are characteristic of the man.

If all that is constant is a type of determination, there seems to be little of significance that could be said to mark him as a single being. We do speak of great men giving themselves wholeheartedly and at great sacrifice to some particular venture, and often remark on the fact as setting him off from all others. Still, there are men of quite different abilities, insight, and even ways of working, who apparently have the same degree of devotion, make the same kind of sacrifices, give themselves to the full. This shows that the root dedication, manifested in the nature of the inwardly and outwardly imposed closures on what is being done, must be supplemented in other ways, for example by perceptiveness, integrity,—and to hide behind a word, 'genius'.

A great creative man might have a job which he could not handle with any particular skill, in which in fact he proved himself to be a dismal failure. This could be due in part to his unwillingness or inability to detach himself from the frame of his creative work. As a man he would be less than a Stevens who was able to perform excellently as an insurance executive. Presumably, when he turned to his creations, a supposed practical failure but genuinely creative man would close off the creativity within the context of the job, and do it in the same way and to the same degree that Stevens closed off his work as an insurance executive when he turned to the task of writing poetry. What the man who did poorly in something other than creative work was unable to do was to find some job in which he could exhibit the patience, honesty, self-criticism, and the like that he exhibited in his creative work. Such a view is obviously biased toward the creative life, which is tacitly taken to allow for the exhibition of the nature of the man. The judgment of mankind often does not allow this. It takes the creative man, who is incompetent in areas other than his chosen art or discipline, to be basically flawed, but yet somehow to escape from the limitation under the influence of inspiration. But then, of course, no account is really given as to just what he is, the creative life being put to a side as something strange, aberrational, somehow added on to what the man is in root.

Sometimes, as with a Van Gogh, it is supposed that daily life provides an irritant, or a condition for a man engaging in creative work. His suffering is supposed to be transmuted into creative activity. The primary context would then seem to be the creative activity, as that which is able to transmute and even to throw light on the other. The reverse also occurs, and one looks to daily life for an explanation of the nature, course, and meaning of the creative work. It is the artist's tortured life we are then supposed to see in the work. The work is supposed to transmute

it, but not in such a way that the tortured life is lost. It is merely given
another location. In either way, there is a tendency to suppose that the
creative man is not in charge of himself, that he is caught in his suffering
and carries it into his work, or transforms it, without deliberation or
control. Yet, all the while, he is concentrated on the creative activity,
and can be judged and understood there in the same way that one understands another creative person carrying out other work with some
distinction.

Why is not the failure of a creative man in other work as significant
as his suffering? If it is, must we not understand him to be a failure in
the same way that we understand Stevens to be a successful insurance
executive? In the course of his incompetent activity, the first must be
governed by contexts in the same way, though in a different degree and
with a different effect than a Stevens who competently engages in some
such non-artistic activity. The incompetent will perhaps have engaged in
the creative life as much as Stevens did, or he may not have closed himself
off in daily or practical routines as well as Stevens did. Still, he will have
closed himself off inside his creative life as much as Stevens did. If we
reverse this stress, and take daily activity to be the area where the incompetent closes himself off for a while, cursing, fumbling, making himself miserable perhaps, he will exhibit the traits of integrity, honesty,
etc. that he does in his creative work, but will not find a way to apply
them in such a way that good work is done. The conclusion of this
discussion seems to be that men close themselves off inside and outside
of various contexts in constant ways, and that those ways express what
the men truly and in depth really are.

The terms I have been here employing have an ethical or moral tone
to them. But is man to be understood as being primarily ethical or moral?
If he were, we would in some sense subordinate art to ethics or morality—
and that surely is not right. Other terms are needed to say what man is
below the point where such terms apply.

The reference to 'contexts' is misleading. When involved in a particular type of life, one also is in some degree of readiness to engage in
another. What is at the root of both is an attitude which, by fitting in
with one or more of those lives, makes for a possible success, and which,
by not fitting in with other lives, makes for a possible failure. The gifts
which make for success in one area, whether this be playing a game,
painting, running a business, or just typing, will be behind the expressions
in other areas, but will not come to a satisfactory expression in all. This
conclusion requires us to say that a successful life in more than one area

exhibits the same traits in all. That does not seem to be true of Stevens. (Has anyone interviewed Stevens' fellow executives and other employees in the life insurance company to see if he expressed himself in poetic ways at times, or if the kind of abilities he exhibited in his poetry were also displayed there?) Though one can reasonably assert that failure in some field is due to an inability to express one's peculiar gifts there properly, we cannot reasonably say that success in a number of fields always involves the expression of similar gifts. But even if diverse gifts are involved in diverse successful pursuits, the failures can still be explained as due to the use of gifts in areas where they are not appropriate, or where the individual cannot express them properly. What we still have to discover is whether or not the distinctive gifts displayed in different areas have something in common.

Let it be arbitrarily assumed that there is an executive ability appropriate to being an executive, and quite a different ability, poetic power, appropriate to being a poet. The selection of terms is of no moment, serving only to focus the problem on distinctive gifts appropriate to distinctive enterprises. Must they have something in common? Evidently they must, since there is the self-same man who is in possession of them. Let this which is in common arbitrarily be called 'diligence'. Is the man essentially a diligent being who supplements or fills out the diligence in one area with executive ability, and in the other with poetic power? Surely, the fact that he provides these additions is also a root truth about him. Is he not one who makes diligence join executive and poetic gifts, in a way and to a degree others do not? Must we not say that he is at the very least a diligent being who not only can but in fact does make executive ability and poetic power effective?

The diligence which is common is indeterminate; the diligence that is expressed in the different areas is made determinate there. At the very least, the indeterminate diligence has to be understood as able to be made determinate in these ways. This means, I think, that the indeterminate diligence must be understood in terms of a possibility which is realized as a diligence-affected executive ability and a diligence-affected poetic power. Executive work and poetic writing will be ways in which the diligence and the possibility are joined together so as to make the diligence determinate.

Returning now to Stevens, we can say that he had a sincerity, conscientiousness, factuality, and loyalty which were indeterminate; that he was faced with the possibility of being a self-controlled man; and that he was able to realize that possibility as filled out by the sincerity, etc. when he engaged in executive work and in poetry. When he engaged in daily activities, other possibilities, more inclusive or more restricted ones, might be to the fore, with the consequence that his sincerity, for example, was realized in a somewhat muted form. It was not called on then to be dominant or conspicuous, but only to add color to the realized possibility which was primarily realized as just a condition exemplified in the daily activities. In the poetry and the job, that same possibility was realized with a richer, intensive content, filled out by the sincerity, etc., as the very tissue of his poetic and executive activity. I am, of course, assuming what should be proved—that what was common to Stevens' executive work and his poetry was sincerity, conscientiousness, etc. Is this found by trying to generalize, by trying to find what is common to the successful pursuit of both? Apparently so. But to this one might answer that there are many other common features, and that if Stevens ate his lunch properly, played a game of tennis well, and the like, we should find there, too, a base for a generalization. That would show that 'sincerity,' etc. are too restrictive. Evidently, we should look at all the things a man does satisfactorily, or exceptionally well, and find out what all these have in common; state this in an indeterminate form; acknowledge it to be at his root; look to a possibility appropriate to it; and see different types of activity as so many different ways of making the indeterminate capacity be determinate with various degrees of intensity or integration, expressive of the degree to which the activity is carried out with success.

November 26

Yesterday's outcome still fails to cover the entire issue. We know that men suddenly placed in a new context reveal traits that no one suspected, that a quiet, non-aggressive man may play a ferocious game of tennis, with a guile, perhaps even a tendency to be malicious, vicious, and cruel, that no one suspected. Evidently, there are tendencies or dispositions which may be suppressed, lie latent, or have their expressions partly constituted in various circumstances and under special conditions. A widely accepted Freudian-based view is that men have one or more basic drives whose suppression or blocking forces them back into an unconscious. There they presumably await an occasion to be expressed in a distorted form. If the drives are of the essence of man, all one will then have to do is to note whether or not they are expressed in full, are incomplete, or have distorted forms. One will have denied that there are particular, positive attitudes appropriate to particular activities. All activities will, instead, be seen to be 'sublimations', just so far as they do not exhibit the drives in their full integrity. But were one to hold that the specialized forms of the supposed drives were the only guise they had, and that there was nothing like a sheer unspecialized drive, we would have to suppose that man has within him various distinct tendencies, only some of which are evident in particular activities. This would preclude a satisfactory knowledge of him until we were able to place him in multiple contexts, perhaps in every context which is needed in order for all the tendencies to have an opportunity to be exhibited.

A better alternative (because more cautious, making no supposition about basic drives and no supposition about a multiplicity of actual tendencies which are of the essence of a man, but which need distinctive contexts in order to have an opportunity to be adequately manifested or known) builds on yesterday's outcome. It holds that there are generalizable features in successful enterprises which express what a man is at root in relation to a successful production of beauty, goodness, truth, adjustment, or status. Those features are always present, either in a positive or a negative guise. The quiet man will have his daily activities qualified by a pushed-back aggressiveness which comes to the fore when he plays tennis. But like the view which holds that there are distinct tendencies not manifested at all, this supposes that there are distinct tendencies already active, but sometimes expressed in special forms. Yet none of these tendencies might in fact be present. There is no reason to believe that a love poem is sustained by a suppressed hatred, anger, fear, self-rejection, and the like; there is no reason to believe that these attitudes are neatly distinguished, just awaiting an opportunity to make themselves evident in public. Still, the quiet man may be aggressive when he plays tennis. It is reasonable to say that he has a tendency to be aggressive in certain circumstances. It is conceivable that his aggressiveness was held back and, in some cases at least, qualifies what is non-aggressively done.

If we reject the idea that there is a set of basic drives whose failure to be adequately expressed means that they are present as various tendencies; if we reject, too, the idea that there is a multiplicity of latent tendencies, or that these are always expressed in special or insistent forms, what account can be given of the aggression that becomes manifest only in certain situations and may remain undetected as long as a man is not in those situations? Could it be justifiably maintained that there always is some situation in which the aggression will come to the fore, not because aggression is lying in wait, either as a consequence of a repression or suppression of a primal drive or drives, or because it is an inextinguishable tendency awaiting an opportunity to be manifest, but because a man is fully a man only when he functions in a certain complex of situations, which together call for the expression of a set of human tendencies? Such an alternative places situations alongside one another in somewhat the same unjustified way that the previous alternatives set the tendencies alongside one another.

A more modest proposal would be to hold that there is a set of tendencies which all men ought to exhibit. When they fail to exhibit some of these we can hold that there are situations, perhaps now unknown, in which they will be exhibited. Let aggression be one of the traits all men ought to exhibit, and there is a man who has as yet shown little or no aggression. We will say, on this view, that he will not become a full man until he does express aggression, preferably in a harmless way, leaving him able to continue to live at other times in a relatively non-aggressive way.

How can we determine if there are such tendencies? What does the fact that he does express the tendencies under certain special circumstances tell us about him, before and after he has expressed those tendencies? What does it mean to say that he has the tendency all the while that he fails to make it manifest? Why need he manifest it, except in a very diluted form? How aggressive must he be in his tennis game in order to do justice to his supposed essential aggressiveness? Is it desirable to have the aggression expressed in his daily activities? If so, to what degree? Is it desirable that there be some activity in which aggression should be maximized, and which should be carried out if the man is to live a full life?

There are situations where a man should be anxious, fearful, frightened, rebellious, but where these states and presumably the situations, too, are not necessarily desirable. Not every tendency or expression should be manifested. Still, it is desirable for a man to be saddened by the unavoidable tragedies that beset others, that he should be anxious about the welfare of his children, that he should be fearful or frightened in an ominous darkness, that he should be rebellious in a world which is standing in the way of his continued maturation, or which denies him the exercise of his greatest abilities. Would our supposedly mild man lose something if he were not aggressive in his games, or in any other situation? Suppose he was always mild, but played his games with grace and skill? I think we would say that he still was not playing as well as he could and should. I don't think we can say that he has to play, and therefore that he should express some aggressiveness so as to be able to play well. And if he does not play in any game, we cannot be sure that he will or will not ever exhibit aggressiveness. We do not know if and in what form aggressiveness would make it possible for him to play some game better than he otherwise would. Is there anything amiss in the life of a man who devotes himself to art, religion, science, discovery, medicine, or law, helping others, or even engaging in sport, and there exhibits only those tendencies which enable him to function superbly? Is he incomplete if he does not engage in all or most of these activities, or if he does not bring every kind of emotion or virtue to play in chosen fields? I do not see that he is. But if so, aggression, or any other expression of man, no matter how appropriate to some particular type of activity, need not be expressed at all, or even be attributed to a man who does not need to and does not in fact exhibit it, or does so in a minor way, which is nevertheless entirely appropriate to what he is involved in.

Let it be supposed that Wallace Stevens exhibited a controlled insight and a cautious daring as an executive and as a poet, emphasizing the control and caution in the one, and the insight and daring in the other. Can we not then go on to say that as he went about his daily tasks, relaxed, was with his family, was sexually aroused, spoke to his friends, and so on, he continued to exhibit these dispositions, sharpened and brought to the fore in his major concerns? He would, of course, exhibit them in different proportions and as involved with different kinds of content than he did when he was in his office or at his desk writing poetry. We would not look to him in these other situations to help our understanding of him as an executive and poet, but the other way around. That conclusion goes counter to the usual way in which we attend to the lives of men of stature. Should we, instead, look to his non-executive and non-poetic life for the raw forms of the dispositions he exhibits in his executive and poetic careers? After all, we know about those dispositions by seeing them in their perfected, refined forms.

This is not yet right. What about the anxiety, fear, and other emotions that he might exhibit in daily life, but which do not have an evident place in either his executive or poetic career? Must we not say that they have qualifying roles in those careers? If so, will we not also have to say that his controlled insight and cautious daring have qualifying roles in his non-executive and non-poetic activities? They do not seem to.

November 27

We ought not to look for poetry in Wallace Stevens' insurance reports; we ought not to look for calculations, statistics, and the like in his poetry. There is no need to suppose that the characteristics of one area are carried over into another. But we do have a good reason to look for the kinds of emphases, thrusts, involvements, and emotions in all that he does, though in one area they may be muted and in another dominant. He eats his lunch, rides on the train, buys his newspaper, shaves, as ordinary men do, but his acting in these ways is sustained by and has a background in dispositions which are carried out in rich ways, both in his poetry and in his work as an insurance executive. Should there be a sudden crisis in his daily affairs, should he see a friend, read a newspaper, or see a fire he will add to his ordinary ways of going about his daily tasks sudden, perhaps momentary, and even unnoticed emphases, variations, and expectations.

If one is willing to go this far, can he stop? Must he not go on to say that every act is at the forefront of a host of dispositions which may color it to some extent and, in any case, are readied to be expressed and thereupon distinguished when there is an opening? If so, there will be occasions when the concerns and values of the insurance executive will peer through and perhaps even make a difference to Stevens' poetry— and, similarly, the poetry to the work of the executive. As a poet, he will be alert to the effect his poetry will have on others; as an executive, he will occasionally pun or set words in rhythmic patterns, even though he may not write these down.

But surely there are such acts as a blink of the eye a sneeze, a sudden spasm, the putting on of shoes which occur without any intrusion of such dispositions? To suppose this, is to suppose that these activities are entirely cut off from a single privacy. Do they not occur because the dispositions which are realized in the poetry and the insurance business are kept at bay, not deliberately, not consciously, but just enough to allow these activities to be almost unaffected? He undoubtedly tried to suppress a sneeze in his office, was self-conscious when he had a sudden spasm; he perhaps neglected to put on his shoes for a moment as he thought about some verse or deal, and so on. Like every one else, he raised his eyebrows, looked askance, gestured, smiled without being aware that he did. His unawareness does not prevent these from occurring against the background of various dispositions, or even to have these expressed to some degree in his gesturing, smiling, and so forth.

A mild man who plays an exceptionally vicious, aggressive game of tennis, to the surprise of all who know him, is a mild man whose life is colored by an aggressiveness, if only in such a way as to allow the mildness to be prominently displayed at times when violence might be called for. He must also be one whose violence on the tennis court is backed by a mildness which will become evident as soon as he pulls back a bit from the fury of the game.

In effect this contention holds that the whole man is expressed in every move, with some dispositions more evidently to the fore, others more evidently in the role of colorings, and others essentially in the role of background and support. What that whole is we cannot know except by seeing just what he does. We need not suppose that there is a fixed set of dispositions to be found in all men. Instead, we must look to what the man in fact does, and on the basis of this take account of multiple dispositions which are evidently being realized in an obtrusive way, and take them to have a role in the background or be qualifications of those that are dominant and are realized in other situations. A knowledge of how most men function, of the kinds of dispositions most of them in fact realize will help one become alert to what otherwise would be missed.

Do we have a warrant for supposing that everyone will be jealous, angry, terrified, self-sacrificing, anxious, erotic? If we do not find these manifest in any activities, do we have a warrant for saying that they are nevertheless present, but in the form of a background making possible a focusing on some others? Unless we are to divide mankind into distinct species, we are forced to say that in root they are alike. The vices exploited by the Nazis must be latent and perhaps suppressed in saints; the virtues of the saints must be latent and perhaps suppressed in the Nazis. The genius of Shakespear does not separate him off from the rest of mankind; the powers that he exhibits must be what they also have, though they do not know how to use them, do not back them up with others, do not know how to organize them, and do not express them to the same degree over the same stretch of time and work. We are also forced to affirm that when new agencies are achieved in the course of maturation, and a human moves from undeveloped forms to the stage where he has a mind, an I, is responsible, and so forth, all will have some efficacy and therefore will make him a different whole. Is he not self-identical throughout? If he is, self-identity cannot be, as I have held it to be, something that depends on the eventual development of an I and other epitomizations of the self. We would have to say that there is a continuity or some persistent common traits until we come to the stage where we have a fully developed human with a unity which is always being expressed, with an emphasis now on this disposition and now on that. To maintain this position, it will be necessary to hold that all men have the same set of dispositions, a set which includes far more than the psychoanalysts allow, since it includes the kinds of dispositions which are needed if there are to be great works of art, heroism, statesmanship, thought.

We must look to man as he is manifested alone, in his family, at work, in society, and as engaged in various disciplines, and in these isolate the essential primary factors. Each man will have to be understood to have the same set of dispositions, and to express them in various combinations and with various stresses in everything he does. But his uniqueness will also be present in every act. Subtracting from that, we will be left with common dispositions, combined and stressed in different ways by each, at different times.

I must see myself in every man and as every man, modified, distorted, but with every one of his basic thrusts. To know others it will help if I know myself; to know myself it will help to know others. The more I know of men over the entire course of history and the entire stretch of geography, the more I will know my primary powers and how I have related them.

Hitler, Goering, Himmler, Eichmann, Catherine the Great, are they all variants of myself? Are St. Francis, Michelangelo, Shakespear, St. Theresa variants of myself? Let it be granted that they are. It still is true that these are just a selection from all possible variations. If each man is unique, no one is the duplicate of the others, and there can be any number of other cases in which men might exhibit new ways of exhibiting all the common dispositions. More, the characters in fiction show variations and stresses not found in fact. A novelist shows us new ones in dramatic form; there is a subtlety revealed about the ways in which other factors come into play. The novelist extends our knowledge of man, making manifest sides which we would have overlooked had we attended only to men in their actual historic, social, and familial lives.

Freud's narrow selection of the traits he took to be at the base of man forced him to see artists as aberrational variants from a norm. A similar biased emphasis is to be found in Aristotle, Aquinas, Hegel, and Marx; none gives equal play to men who have exhibited the determination of explorers and sports figures, the imagination of great artists, the self-sacrificing generosity of some mothers, the shrewdness of the political leader.

If our canvas is made so large that it includes the billions of men who have lived, as well as the characters imagined in story, play, myth, and religion, we will surely never get to the end of knowing what a man is, unless in some limited number of cases we are able to isolate the features that are present in all, or at least those which make for conspicuous success or failure, in the family, in society, over history, in the major disciplines, and in various distinctive contexts such as the prospect or achievement of money, fame, and respect. This is a sufficiently large array, and catches so many dimensions of man, that one can perhaps for almost every purpose content oneself with what one discovers there.

There is a paradox lurking behind these remarks. We come to understand other men because of what we know of ourselves, but we come to know about ourselves by what we have learned about others. The paradox dissolves with the recognition that each sees the others initially as exhibiting traits he does not see in himself, and adds to them those he does. Because of what I know of myself I am able to add, to what I discern in another, characterizations of which I had not been aware in him. It is also true that because of what I see in another, I am able to attribute to myself characterizations additional to those I had known to hold of me.

That each sees himself as every one of the others, but in a unity of dispositions which are expressed with a different stress and in a different combination in various situations, is an ideal outcome we must strive to achieve, guided by the awareness that no matter how aberrant, odd, beyond one's own ability to duplicate, the life of another is a life of a being in the same species as oneself—not in the sense of sharing some general character such as 'man' but as a complex of dispositions, which become distinguished and specified in being expressed in particular situations.

Are these reflections thrown into doubt by the existence of schizophrenics, confidence men, actors, multiple personalities, all of whom seem to exhibit entirely different dispositions in different contexts? Do these differ in anything more than the degree to which the lives are distinguished from a Stevens who is an insurance executive and a poet? We see him as one who passes from one of these to the other, and who also lives in between them in a life that is somewhat like the life of ordinary men; in the other cases, we either find no such ordinary living, or find a very sharp and sudden break between their ways of functioning.

We take ordinary life to be a needed avenue of expression. When this is absent we are somewhat at a loss to know how to recover the basic unity of a man, perhaps because daily life gives us the initial set of dispositions which we know must be present in any other form of life. Were Stevens to be a hopeless misfit in daily life, we would view him as somewhat of a schizophrenic in his double career. What should be said of a Robert Lowell or a Van Gogh? We think of them as having only one career, and constantly turn from their creative works to their lives for clues. If they added another successful or at least a different career to the one they so successfully carried out, and still were misfits, we would, I think, tend to see them as schizophrenic or as having multiple personalities.

I must see myself in every character in a play, as I suppose a good actor does. I must see myself as every character in a story as I suppose a good novelist does. I must see myself even as every one of the creatures in a fairy story. Don Quixote and Walter Mitty are realists, then? To the degree that the imagined figures with whom they were identifying themselves were not caricatures, to that degree they too, were not. Of course, one does not have to identify oneself with any others, actual or fictitious, but has only to recognize that they are exhibiting the same totality of dispositions as oneself, individualized though it be, and expressed in areas and with stresses and distinctions one does not make. In Hitler's place I would not do what he did, since I would blunder or falter where he did not. But since I can see that I need not blunder or falter always, I can or should be able to see myself doing what he did in the very situations in which he was. That would, of course, not be entirely possible if I did not also live through the childhood and adventures that he had lived through. But even at those times, he was expressing the dispositions everyone else has, but in his own way and with his own emphases, and of course through the distinctive body that he had. Must we not now conclude that a desirable 'narcissism' is the core truth within the oedipal complex and other supposedly primary states and drives? It seems so, provided that we also say at once that there is a kind of 'anti-narcissism', since the others are myself as surely as I am they.

My first book, *Reality*, begins by saying that I cannot meet myself coming toward me. This is of course true. The present discussion shows that it is also false, since everyone who comes toward me is myself in another form.

November 28

Once it is acknowledged that all men share a common set of conditions, individualized and interlocked with one another in distinctive ways, new perspectives on four areas are opened up: 1. the mind-body problem; 2. knowledge of oneself; 3. the interrelationship of various disciplines; and 4. oneself in relationship with others.

1. Mind and body, I have argued, are connected by the emotions. All three can now be seen to make use of the same dispositions, with

the mind emphasizing the intelligible, the body the dynamic, and the emotions the assessive. (If the five finalities be taken as a guide, we should also find two other dimensions of man in which the individuality and the independence of man are emphasized, the first in one's self-assertiveness, the way one comes into the public world, the other in his claims, the kinds of demands he always expresses, though not necessarily effectively or distinctly.) The thinking through of a mathematical proof, the eating of an apple, and an emotion of fear should then involve the same dispositions, though some of these will be more visible and dominant in one than in the others. We will not be able to turn the proving of a mathematical theorem into a variant of the eating of an apple—a simple minded procedure parallel to the attempts to see every thought or act as an expression of some primary urge such as sex, ambition, or aggression. But we should be able to show that the kind of control, emphasis, or way of beginning and ending are present in both in different degrees, and how these make different contributions to the whole. The issue is the topic of the third situation listed above; it is pertinent here as pointing up the commonality of the conditions present in both physical and mental acts. Any emotion we might have—anger, fear, hope—whether occurring together with the proving and the eating, or apart from these, will have the same constituents, and will be appropriate just so far as they serve to mediate the body and mind. Some emotions will be inappropriate to one, or the other, or both. And, of course, starting with an emotion, and either the mind or the body, we can go on to speak of the body or the mind, respectively, as engaged in inappropriate activities when what they do cannot be envisaged as intermediating the other two, or as allowing the emotions to function as intermediaries.

2. Every action will be understood to involve the entire individual. Whatever I do has all my dispositions together and individualized, some in the background, some minimal, and some dominant. Most melt into one another, leaving only a few dominant, distinct, and almost alone definitive of what is being done. We cannot know what these are just by studying a particular act. Instead, we have to attend to a multiplicity of acts in order to discover just what dispositions are being expressed. But, if from a study of man over the course of time and space, we know just what those dispositions are, we have a set of factors in terms of which every one of the acts could be analyzed. No one would be such a liar or deceiver, such an actor, or divided person that we could not in principle— usually after the fact—find in anything he said or did factors which have to be credited with a role in whatever else he said or did. His 'hello' to

the postman will carry out the same dispositions as his shaving, and even his stumbling in the dark. It is this fact on which the 'occult sciences' fasten in their attempt to read 'character' from handwriting, body posture, food habits,and so forth. But they not only keep to a narrow list of dispositions, they freeze the expressions of these and then read the result back into the individual, usually as essentially moral or as involved in a world of contingencies. Handwriting does provide a clue, but so does any other human production. The handwriting may make one aware of a set of dispositions of importance to one's moral behavior or one's social existence, but those dispositions will have specialized forms in these areas, and will be inseparable from other dispositions which, together with them, make a whole quite different in nature from what a simple transference or translation of a result in one area to another would be. Anything one does, privately or publicly, can be used as evidence, provided it be understood that what is not clearly at work in a given act still plays some role there, and may have a dominant role in some other act. A knowledge of a large number of acts is necessary in order to get to know the dispositions I actually have, and which ones tend to be dominant.

3. Different disciplines, whether it be cooking or the writing of novels, philosophizing, dancing, or sport, will exhibit the same set of dispositions for each man who participates in a number of disciplines, and for all the men who participate in any one of them. But their order and weight, and the result of their expression will be different for each. Wallace Stevens' work as an insurance executive is not a variant on his poetry, or conversely; it expresses the same individualized set of dispositions in him. These are the very same dispositions which others individualize and express in their own ways, in these and other enterprises.

Other executives in the insurance business express the same dispositions which Wallace Stevens does. Since these are the same dispositions which Stevens expresses in his poetry, though in a different way, the other executives must be said to have and to express the same dispositions that he does when he writes poetry. If we had a list of the dominant, qualifying, and background dispositions involved in being an insurance executive, we would have some of the factors involved in the writing of poetry, or any other activity, though in these they would have different roles, and might even be almost hidden because of the dominance of others.

Knowing that all men are in root alike, and that no man is divided into a number, we know that all of the dispositions, which we are able to remark when they are dominant in some activity, will be present in all, though perhaps with only the most minor qualifying or background role. Even when they have such minor roles, however, the knowledge that they are present enables us to know a discipline or an act in a way we otherwise could not. Knowing that the factors exemplified in the work of an insurance executive are determinations of a common, individualized set of dispositions, we will take account of them in the attempt to understand Stevens' poetry. We must go further. Knowing anyone's set of dispositions in any enterprise allows us to understand better than we had before what is involved in the writing of any poem, the acting of any part in any play, the study and teaching of any subject. We attend to Stevens' home life, his work as an insurance executive, and his games and hobbies because there, more likely than not, we will find toward the front the dispositions which are expressed exceptionally well in his poetry.

By a roundabout route I now accept a view I have long rejected: a man's daily life and adventures in other areas help us understand his creative work. We need not fall into the 'intentional fallacy' of reading into the work some intention fancied or expressed. Nor need we translate his sufferings into tragic (or, if in compensation, into joyous) incidents in his creative work.

4. With reference to other men, I can take up one of four attitudes: a. I can see them as variants of myself; I then have *insight* into them. b. I can see myself as being a variant of any one of them; I then *measure* myself in his terms. c. I can see myself as over against them as others; I then *confront* them. Or, d. I can see myself as distinct from a position where they are variants of myself; I then see myself as so far *alien*, not fitting in with them. The four cases allow for six combinations.

ab. I have insight into them, and accept them as my measure. I see them as so many different variants of what I am, and see myself as a variant on what they are. The double act allows me to note aspects of them I would otherwise neglect, and to assess myself as better or worse than they are. It allows me to see that Himmler has my fears and hopes, my ambitions and determinations, and yet is a man to be despised. It allows me to see my fears and hopes, my ambitions and determinations in Stevens, the poet-executive, and yet to recognize myself not to be on his level as a creative artist.

ac. To my insight into others as like myself, I here add the fact that they are confronted as other than I am. Though I interpret them in terms of features I have noted in myself, I face them as having their own reality, thereby allowing me to pay more attention to their individualities and their distinctive ways of organizing their dispositions and expressing them. I see that I may have in root the powers that are exploited by the poet, but also recognize that they are powers which he, and not I, realized as poetry.

ad. I here combine my insight into others as being like myself, with my awareness of myself as alien to them, standing away from them as an individual with my own emphases and accomplishments. Himmler, I see, has my dispositions, perhaps even my virtues and vices, but I express them in ways he does not.

bc. I here combine a measure provided by others with their status as beings who are confronted. When I try to understand myself in impersonal terms, say by taking myself to be a function of society, or by using only those explanations which use factors to be found through observation of the behavior of other men, I see myself in these terms. It is some such position which Hume and Kant assumed when they were trying to understand the self; it is the way behaviorists try to understand men, tacitly ignoring the fact that they are starting from their individual irreducible selves.

bd. I can measure myself in the terms others provide and see myself as not fitting in with them. This is the position that the child, the follower, the disciple, the learner often assumes. They do not, but yet ought to belong. If I measure myself by others and find myself to be superior to them, when I see myself as alien to them. I am somewhat in the position I take when I look with disdain at criminals or vicious men.

cd. Here I confront others as making up a world from which I am excluded. I see them in terms which I derive from myself, but confront them as external to me. They are myself idealized but keep me from being one of them. What I know of them I have produced from a reflection on myself, but the outcome leaves me outside their world. They have the very dispositions I do, but they exercise them in such a way that I fall outside their scheme of things.

November 29

When we have a number of cases in which items are interlocked in different ways and degrees, they may be otherwise unrelated except by instances of common conditions. But if there is a reality which possesses or expresses itself in the different cases, there must be a mediator for those items. This has already been remarked in connection with the mind and body, the mediator being the emotions. When the emotions and the mind or body are taken to be extremes, the body or the mind has the role of a mediator.

What is true of the need for a mediator between mind and body, is also true of the particular activities in which a man engages, of the various disciplines, and of a multiplicity of men. The particular activities of a man are all his; the common intermediation of them all is himself as a mind, body, or emotions, or their combination. The various disciplines, of course, are united by the individual men who engage in a number of them. Since there is no one man who engages in them all, or does all the work that is done in any one of them, the mediator will be man as such with a constant set of dispositions realized in the production of the different disciplines. A multiplicity of men, in contrast with these other cases, cannot be grounded in a man. One might take them to be grounded in the finalities or in God, but these do not have the dispositions which individual men have. If, though, we take the complex of structures which make up society—language, customs, traditions, work, myth, and the realm of artifacts, including works of art—we can see this as their mediator. And if any mediator can be taken as a term which one of the original terms connects to the other original term, we should also be able to see any man (as teacher, learner, guide, model, ruler, citizen, or criminal) to be a mediator between the structures of society and other men. Recurring now to the other two instances, we should be able to see anyone or all of the disciplines as mediating the men, and each of the activities as mediating the men and the other activities.

I have suggested that when the I comes on the scene the entire set of dispositions of men is changed, with the consequence that a mature man is quite a different kind of being from an embryo. I do not now think that this is a tenable supposition. There is an identity between the two, leading one to infer that the I is but the dispositions of a man in a particular guise. The I is a way of having the entire set in specialized form, able to function as a unit in contradistinction to other units. It no more requires us to envisage a radical change in man than does the acknowledgment that he engages in a number of distinct enterprises with different degrees of success, involving the dominance of different dispositions. Of course it is one thing to have a set of dispositions, and another to have this replicated in a number of specialized forms, or even to have those very dispositions in unions of different types. A mature man is different from an infant, but this does not require the denial of a constancy in him, stretching from before birth and at least until death.

The 'at least until death' compels attention once again to the problem of immortality. I have held in *Beyond All Appearances*, and in this work recently, that there is no personal immortality, no continuation of the individual after a bodily death. But if one takes seriously the view that a man is self-identical over the course of his life by virtue of the reduction of what he undergoes to the self-same result, one will have within the man all of the factors which he obtained from and through his body. He will be self-identical, not as a Platonic soul untouched by his adventures in the world, but as one who has those adventures, and who is oriented toward the body. He will also be seen to be able to have not only the same dispositions that the body does, but to accept the determinations which the dispositions undergo when bodily expressed, but in such a way that he remains self-same in his privacy. What was undergone becomes a submerged nuance within a constant. Taking account of the nuances, one is led to say that the privacy changed; taking account of the fact that they are completely dominated by the privacy, that this immobilizes them, one is led to say that the man is unchanged. Instead, then, of saying that a man was immortal only so far as he was caught up in the finalities (which presumably are unchanged by the fact, since they accept him only in the form of a subdued nuance) we can say that he has an immortality as the self-same private being he was before.

On death a man loses his connection with his body, and will no longer be able to have bodily experiences which he can reduce. But he will not have lost the individual privacy which he had already achieved, or the items that he had already brought under subjection to his unchanging privacy. There will be no need to suppose, with Thomas Aquinas, that the privacy will continue to require a body, and that it awaits some eventual resurrection when it will receive one, ennobled, perfected, excellent. (Does Aquinas require that the resurrected body of a wicked man be less ennobled than that of a good man? I don't know. But he should say he does not; the torments supposed to be in waiting for the wicked are primarily spiritual and secondarily bodily; they are not, I suppose, to be thought of as requiring a radically defective body but a purified one through which spiritual pains will become most evident.)

The privacy of a man on death is presumably continuous with the privacy which was already a nuanced part of the finalities, differing from the latter only in its ability to retain its own boundaries and thus, while an integral part of the finalities, also be distinguishable within them. Since there will be no time in those finalities, there will also be no further adventures for the privacy. As distinct from the finalities, and thus as not reduced to nuances in them, the privacies will stand to them somewhat in the way they had when those privacies were continuous with, and yet connected with their bodies. If it be true that those privacies have the very same dispositions as the body, and indeed are those dispositions individuated and lived through from within, a man will be immortal after death, perhaps even with consciousness, mind, and an I. He will not be self-conscious, however, in the sense in which he was when alive, since this requires a coming to himself from without and moving toward the I through a me reached from the outside. And of course there will be no communicating with the living in any way which requires the use of a body. If there is influence or communication, it will have to be of a privacy to a privacy, or a privacy to or through a body, but not of a privacy through its own body. Might it not use the body of a medium? Conceivably. But it will not then be a privacy present in that medium, since this would require the medium to possess or harbor two privacies. Instead, it would have to deal with the medium's body as a variant of itself, and be able to use the medium's body to express itself. I see no reason for believing that this does in fact occur, but I do see that it is possible, and that there is no need to deny, with Aristotle, that the personalized mind or soul necessarily perishes. Nor, for that matter, is there any reason to reject the possibility that on death the privacy is lost entirely in the finalities and does not continue to maintain boundaries of its own.

If a finality does accommodate a privacy, need it do this more than once? How are the privacies of subsequent accommodations different from one another? Is it not that they themselves have different nuances? But now I seem to be speaking of privacies as though they were atomic units, each separately absorbed within the finalities. If, in the attempt to avoid this conclusion, it was said that the privacy of a man was not different from moment to momment, we would be on the verge of losing the nuances in his privacy, or would not accommodate those nuances in the finalities.

Are the nuances of the privacy of a living man transmitted into the privacy as part of the finalities, so that the privacy as part of the finalities will be actively reductive in the very way in which a finality is actively reductive in its accommodation of the intrusions of actualities and, therefore, of the privacies, even of inanimate beings? Things, unlike men, would then be merely accommodated as privacies, which are neither added to or subtracted from, while men would be accommodated as living privacies which reduce what they confront, and which allow the nuanced results to be absorbed within their privacies as already accommodated in the finalities. If one kept to a single finality, and identified this with God, one would then be able to say that here and now one was an integral part of God in the form of an accommodated nuance. God's love would be an acceptance of man now, and the allowing him now to have empirical adventures whose content the man reduced, and which was allowed to be part of the privacy as already accommodated by God.

November 30

Piaget has justified the reasonable view that a child grows through a number of stages. On reaching the last of these, there seems to be no need for the individual to go through these or similar stages on a higher level. It may well fixate on one of them, or on some factor in them, or engage in them in a new order with different effects.

The discussions of the last days make plausible, and the discussion of the finalities enforces the idea, that there are five stages: There is 1. a beginning with oneself and a facing of others, a confrontation which is expressive of the substantiality of the individual; 2. an acceptance of the others as variants of the I, with oneself as an other with respect to them, a sense of alieninity reflecting the status of others as definitory of value or the unity of a man; 3. an acceptance of others and oneself as others, residents in a public world, expressive of Existence; 4. the acknowledgment of oneself as an I and the others as I's, so that each was a variant of the others; 5. an effort at maximization of one of these, one factor in any one of them, a number of them, or of all of them together.

A maximization may itself be fastened on. We can have an emphasis on the substantial individual carried out by aggressions, through narcissism, or by self-indulgence; an emphasis on the being of the individual carried out through self-bounding, self-protection, withdrawal, or a standing on one's dignity; an emphasis on an intelligible dimension carried out through the exercise of reason, the acceptance and conformity to rules and laws, or the imagination; an emphasis on existence, action, decision, work, nostalgia, or art, or a rooting of oneself in a community; and finally, an emphasis on excellence, the pursuit of what ought to be, the giving of oneself to the realization of a valuable end. Some theoreticians fasten on one of these as native, normative, or inextinguishable, and treat all of the other maximizations, and all stages through which an individual goes, to involve the suppression, denial, but inevitable presence and effectiveness of the chosen maximization.

In *Reality*, I took the basic drive of man to be a trying to make himself complete; in *Sport: A Philosophic Inquiry* I took the striving for excellence to provide the answer why people engage in sport. The foregoing would indicate that these are special cases. Self-completion puts emphasis on the substantial individual; the striving for excellence puts it on him as unitary. We should have, in addition, an attempt to achieve a dignity, a state of self-acceptance, the allowing oneself to be a man; a striving toward understanding, rationality, a grasping of what is, perhaps also an effort to control oneself by the finalities; and an attempt to express oneself, to work, to make, to be in the world in a well-adjusted way. These last three answer to the individual as a being, as intelligible, and as existent. If the ontological state is properly designated as an effort at self-completion, or the effort to realize an end, or as an urge toward excellence, it will be only in the sense that they are here to the forefront. The other maximizations stress man as occupied with Being, Possibility, and Existence. These will have to be given a role in ontological discussions, as well as in any account of sport, with the chosen ones having the role of normative or idealized strands. But there is no need to suppose that they are suppressed when they are not dominant, nor any need to deny that they play a role always, and may be properly dominant in certain cases. In dealing with sport I minimized the factor of aggressiveness.

The present discussion leads one to see sport as illustrating aggressiveness, with the other maximizations in the background, and at the very least allowing aggressiveness to be dominant, and properly so, in various situations, e.g., in the playing of a game.

December 1

To determine the dispositions all men have, we can either take advantage of the wisdom of the past, and just add together the various stresses or expressions of fundamental attitudes that have been remarked upon, or we can search for a more systematic way of covering the subject. Dispositions being indeterminate, and forming clusters where they are not distinguished, cannot be known except in terms of the particular cases where one or more is outstanding. But a man has a number of distinguishable sources of expression—his self, person, emotions (where these are mediators not simply between mind and body, but between the privacy, in the form of person and self) and body; the lived, used body, the entire individual in relation to what else there is; and the entire individual with reference to the finalities, or universal conditions. The most cautious way to begin would be to note the outstanding manifestations of these different distinguishable dimensions of the individual.

A self is epitomized most definitely in an I, (self-assertion) a *mind, responsibility,* and a *will,* (decisiveness). A person is epitomized most evidently in *claims*, (insistence on rights) in *sensitivity*, (insistence on *dignity*). There are quite a number of lists of emotions. Descartes 'simple and primitive' passions are wonder, love, hatred, desire, pleasure, and pain. But wonder has to do with the relation to the finalities, and desire, pleasure, and pain are not genuine emotions or passions. Spinoza has a list of emotions in the *Ethics*. I will select those that seem to be known to everyone: *joy, sorrow, love, hatred, aversion, hope, fear, despair, remorse, pity, indignation, contempt, envy, compassion, self-satisfaction, repentance, pride, despondency, self-exaltation, shame, regret, anger, fear, avarice, lust.*

   The lived, used body is *passive* or lax, or *aggressive* or assertive, *responsive, attentive, controlled* or disciplined, and *uncontrolled*. The individual in relation to what else there is, is *affiliated, oppositional, alienated, confronted, socialized*. The individual in relation to the final conditions *wonders*, has *reverence, awe* and *humility*.

   I have noticed other expressed dispositions in different places, but the above seem to be those which everyone would be inclined to acknowledge. Can these be ordered? Can others be discovered by forming some kind of system and filling in the empty places? Ought one not attend to great artists, spiritual men, heroes, thinkers, leaders, and villains for cases where some other dispositions are conspicuously present?

December 2

   If there are a number of drives that can be focused on as having a role in every act, we need do no more than see them all as interinvolved in different ways and degrees, and then note that they can be excessive, defective, or inappropriate in particular situations, and will assume specific forms, depending on whether or not they are exhibited by the privacy, self, person, the emotions, lived body, living body, the total individual, the individual in the world, and in such specifications of these as the I, consciousness, mind, identity, responsibility, sensitivity, claims, work, making, action.

   If the drives be identified as being directed toward *completion, persistence, mastery, appropriateness* and *perfection*, the multiplicity of distinct stresses, good and bad, that have been remarked in the course of history and are incorporated in folk wisdom and daily discourse, can be accommodated, and also recognized to have distinctive tonalities and outcomes in different aspects of individuals, in different individuals, in different disciplines, and in the ways in which men are together in society and state. This is of course just a contention. It should be demonstrated.

Let us arbitrarily select the I. 1. The I seeks completion through the possession of what it faces; persistence by demanding a controlling equilibrium in all activities; mastery by making use of the mind; appropriateness by dominating over all other factors, and perfection by making all submit to its unitary assessment. The overinsistence is expressed as *pride, bias, egocentricity, caprice,* and *selfishness;* its underinsistence is expressed as *depreciation, submissiveness, fantasizing, indifference,* and *self-neglect.* 2. The body's overinsistence is expressed as *gluttony, ruthlessness, enslavement, sensuality,* and *foppishness*; its underinsistence as *lassitude, weakness, subjection, ineffectuality,* and *detachment.* 3. The individual in the world, when overinsistent, will exhibit *greed, revenge, discontent, envy* or *cruelty;* when underinsistent will be *resigned, jealous, resentful, fearful,* or *frustrated.*

An adequate account will have to find room for *discontent, indecisiveness, disobedience, insolence, pitilessness, ingratitude, resentment, retaliation, ridicule, contempt, obsequiousness, impulsiveness, shiftlessness, boasting, arrogance, servility,* and many others. All will have to be dealt with as pertinent to the other ways of dealing with men, as in the world, engaged in different disciplines, and so on. All help one to see that the five basic drives (rather than dispositions) make up complexes which men individualize, specialize, and stress in different ways and degrees at different times, and which are also expressed in disciplines, men's relations to one another, and in their emotions. No one of the drives is ever suppressed in such a way that it is distortive of what is manifest. All play a role in every distinguishable aspect of every individual, in his acts, in his relations, in the way he is in the world, and in his achievements and adventures there. He will have to make an effort to have one or more of them change its role in some situation. When one is persistently dominant or recessive he will have make an effort to bring others to the fore; these will then enable the individual as a whole to function better than he had, in the world and apart from it.

If it be true that the I, the body, the disciplines, and even particular acts all are constituted of the same factors, but in different orders, and with different strengths, it suffices to know just the five basic drives, and then to identify and characterize them in their specific guises when we attend to some one or other dimension of man, some act, some relationship to others or the basic conditions making a discipline possible. If I start with a knowledge of my I as veering sometimes toward pride and sometimes toward depreciation, sometimes toward bias and sometimes toward submissiveness, etc., I become alert to the fact that others may do this as well, and can also look in other situations for alternative specifications of the same drives. Knowing, for example, that I am sometimes capricious and thus exaggerate the degree to which my I is appropriately expressed in a given situation, I become aware that others may do this too, that their apparent indifference to the kind of self-indulgence which caprice exhibits is but a surface phenomenon, or at the very least hides a caprice which can be manifested in some particular situation, and that when I speak of the body's sensuality I am in fact referring to the overinsistence on the same drive toward being appropriate, that is characteristic of the capricious I. Or, noting that another is sensual, I can have some insight into myself as not only sensual explicitly or implicitly, but as having an I which is capable of caprice.

It is proper to refer to caprice and sensuality when concerned with particular actions, situations, individuals. If the Freudian libido is dealt with from the perspective of a body's effort at mastery, it will be seen to have an excessive form, usually in sensuality, as well as a deficient one, usually in caprice. The privacy of an individual will not be treated as a function of this special form of the drive toward mastery; it has its own specialization of this. If one wished to deal with the privacy and body together, it would be necessary to move from a consideration of the body to that of the living individual. No one drive will be normative, right, that which should be expressed in all dimensions of a man, or in all situations to the same degree.

To answer the question why a young person devotes himself to sport it is not sufficient to say (as I did in the book on sport) that he thereby is able to approach the only kind of excellence that he might reasonably expect to achieve. In addition, it must be said that he seeks completion, by facing the world on his own terms, reducing what is other and obstinate to what he does to them; that he persistently seeks to maintain his fit body, to be in control of himself, to be an athlete; that he seeks a mastery of himself and what else he confronts in terms of rules themselves mastered; and that he is guided by a desire to be appropriate, to do what is suitable to his age, abilities, and promise. The thesis of the book is not then denied. Striving for excellence is always present, but it is not usually dominant when, for example, the athlete is training, or is trying to understand and live in accordance with the rules of the sport or game. But because it is present, an athlete in training is not merely one who is seeking control or mastery, but also one who is still seeking excellence and, of course, completion and appropriateness.

The terms 'persistence' and 'appropriateness' do not have the associations which the other three have, and seem therefore to refer to what is not on the same level with the items to which the other three refer. Perhaps it would be better to term them a drive toward 'continuation', and a drive toward 'expression', where this does not merely mean a making oneself publicly present but, also, evident through the agency of act and work. Spinoza's *conatus* seems to combine the two. But the 'drive toward expression' is still not on target, for it does not do justice to the ways in which different epitomizations, such as an I or mind, may operate on others, without regard for any public expression. 'A drive toward presentation', 'toward assertiveness', or 'toward affirmation' do not have the familiarity or apparent reach that a drive 'toward completion', 'continuation', 'mastery', or 'perfection' do. For the moment, I think a 'drive toward effectiveness' or 'toward achievement' is as good as any I can imagine. The last perhaps is preferable. Consequently, I now term them the drives 'toward completion, continuation, mastery, achievement, and perfection.'

December 3

In the attempt to think through the current problem afresh, I have tried to avoid following a rigid pattern in making use of the idea that there are five universal effective conditions originating with final realities. I have had that idea in mind, and have used it as a guide, but I have not taken it to define the limits or nature of the issues with which I was struggling. The results are a number of false starts, multiple needless complications, and considerable confusion. In any case, by a roundabout route I have now come back to the idea that the primary conditions clarify the nature of men, privately and publicly, as lived bodies and as bodies in the world, and that what have traditionally been called virtues, vices, dispositions, and the like can be explained as involving clusters of specialized, individualized forms of the conditions, differing from one another in emphasis and in the particular aspect of man they express.

In different books, the five conditions were found to be constituents of appearances, and to make it possible for actualities to be together. Over the last month, it has become evident that they allow one to explain how organic beings, as bodies and privacies, can arise when various units form aggregates, permitting of the specification of the conditions in the role of limited unities. Men are seen to be different from other actualities in having privacies which are not only continuous with and individuated by their bodies, but which could function in some independence of the body and be epitomized in the form of selves and persons. Selves and persons, I have also held, are epitomized as I's, responsibility, mind, accountability, sensitivity, and as other distinguishable and separately operating private powers. It is an obvious deduction that the functioning of the different epitomizations involves the interlocked presence of specialized forms of the five conditions. References to particular virtues, vices, dispositions, and the like, will therefore involve a reference to one or more of the components of a cluster which are dominant or recessive.

When only one drive is acknowledged, account must be given for its failure to be manifest on all occasions. When recourse is had to the idea of suppression, wickedness, perversity, and so forth, one tacitly supposes that there is not one, but two powers at work, and that one of these, the suppressive, is at times stronger than the other, which was supposedly normative and otherwise dominant. This presents a difficulty for Hegel and Freud. Why should the Hegelian absolute express itself in inadequate forms, when it could conceivably express itself adequately and be for itself forever? Why should the Freudian libido ever be stopped by the individual's experiences, suppositions, fears, and the like? The view which holds that God created a perfect man in Adam, and that what went astray is Adam with the consequence that man thereafter was in disarray, answers similar questions only by postponing the difficulty. Why did God, even while allowing Adam to have a free will to do evil as well as good, allow it to be expressed with such devastating effect on mankind? He could have allowed man to freely disobey him, and even punish man for the disobedience, but the punishment could have been delayed, and could have been milder. In any case, man is supposedly given a power which is strong enough to undo and deny the controlling role of a divine goodness. With Hegel and Freud, there is supposed to be more than just one drive; unlike them, it takes one drive to be original and another to be subsequently introduced.

The present view differs from these others in recognizing five basic drives, each equally powerful and well-grounded. It sees different men and different activities and results to be the outcome of an over-insistence or under-insistence on some one or more of the drives at a particular time. Each facet and task will exhibit a different tonality. Each unit will have a tendency to rectify the overemphases or underemphases of the different drives.

The opposite fault, from that which I have been exhibiting the last month, is evident in my draft of *Man: Private and Public* (the tentative title). There I make some distinctions solely on the basis of the need to find instances of all five conditions. The result could conceivably open up neglected territories. But as far as I am able to see now, I have no other warrant for some of the distinctions I there make than the fact that I need something to fill out some of the slots. It may well be—and I now believe—that all those slots are in fact filled. But as long as I have no genuine insight into all of them, it would be better to attend only to those which I understand. Consequently, I ought to deal only with the self and the person and, within the compass of these, with the I, mind, responsibility, and decisiveness, and with sensitivity and claims. I should then deal with the individual in the world in terms of what I know of the ways in which men are together with one another, and with the rest of the world.

Granted that traditional religion and Freud make use of two drives, either of which could be dominant in some case, and perhaps all the time (as the evil and the suppressive power can be for the religious and Freud), and that Hegel's ultimate single reality cannot account for its biased and unsatisfactory expressions (even if it has a need to face itself as its own other) ought one not work with just two drives, and not take into account three more? I think not, for two reasons:

1. The two drives are inverses of one another, the one good, the other evil, the one expressive of a drive toward perfection or toward action, the other toward self-regard, self-destruction, or toward a conformity to externally determined conditions. It is covertly supposed that the right answer is in hand, and needs only to be freed from counteracting forces. Lost is the adventure of forging oneself over the course of time, and then not as a compromise between good and evil, but as an enriched possessor of a number of drives, all on a footing, and all capable of 'evil' excess or defect.

2. Men also seek to complete themselves, to continue to be what they are, and to master what they can. These will have to be treated by the other views as either forms of a good or a bad drive. As a consequence, the need to possess, to try to preserve oneself, and to know or to master objects and circumstances, will not be allowed to be as primitive as the others, but will be taken to be consequences of or variants of them. Men will be supposed to be able to complete, to continue, and to master themselves only by becoming religious and taking the world as their footstool to use as they can and like, or to be carrying out a primal libido, or an urge to master.

When the religious and the Freudian look at one another, it is no surprise to find that each takes the other to favor a kind of perversion of a single sound drive. Their quarrel cannot be resolved except by going outside the confines of both. But suppose one were to hold that there are two principles or drives, not necessarily distinguished as good and bad—something like the position at which Freud finally arrived in his attempt to go beyond the pleasure principle? One would then take them to join in various degrees of dominance, in which either is rightly dominant at different times. This suggestion is met, once again, by showing that there are other drives, not only because there are finalities which they instance, but because one could not otherwise explain why actualities, and consequently men, attempt to translate others into variations of themselves; why they try to maintain themselves and to hold themselves away from others while all the time recognizing their equality with them, and why they in fact try to achieve by work, art, or making themselves present in an objective space, time, and causality. If any two of these be chosen as the essential pair, one would still not know why men seek to realize ideal outcomes, why they formulate theories, and why they engage in other efforts to master principles and conditions, so that what is done is in accord with what in fact controls.

December 7

If it be held that the externalization of the absolute Spirit in Hegel would not be a true externalization unless it could appear in a biased form and then worked itself out over the course of time, we would be left with the question as to just how free that externalization is. If entirely free, there is no reason why it should have a dialectical development which can be notionally expressed in advance. If not entirely free, a question arises as to why it should take any time at all for the Spirit to go through the process. A freed external reality would take time, but may never get where one would like to reach. An external reality, which is dialectically guided and controlled by the absolute spirit need not take any time at all to complete its adventures.

December 8

Hegel would oppose Aquinas' and Heidegger's supposition that some other enterprise knows reality better than philosophy can. He would say that this was not a position that a philosopher could take; at best, it presents philosophic results metaphorically or figuratively. He would also object to the view that other enterprises are on a footing with philosophy, taking that view to betray the meaning of science, knowledge, and therefore 'the science of philosophy'. What would he say to my view that rational endeavor has an adumbrative component leading into realities in depth, and that the penetration is never reducible to, though surely expressible as rational?

The intensive movement in depth could be equated with Hegel's 'othering' or 'the process of the Spirit', and could have a 'notional' form. But this would be only one of a number. Emotionality, particularly as carried out in the course of artistic efforts; religious reverence, particularly as carried out in a direct referential act; sympathy, particularly as carried out by men not only in social affairs and direct encounters but with reference to a primal force in nature, noted by writers of tragedy, by materialists, and by Taoists; and a concern for what is ultimately just, particularly when grounded in an understanding of human rights, are also facets of a primary thrust inseparable form the act of knowing what was ultimately real. Each of these has the others, including the rational, as background; each terminates in a different ultimate all-encompassing reality. A philosopher can know about them, but he does not undergo them, any more than they, who could 'know' that the philosopher was engaged in knowing, would know in his sense of knowing. The thrust of otherness is not simply rational, a fact of which Hegel was not entirely oblivious.

There is more than one final reality. That fact makes the thrust, which is inseparable from the grasp of each distinctive enterprise, multi-dimensional, making evident that there are still other ways in which one might move from where one now is (and which perhaps has been caught only in the form of knowledge) to what is ultimately real. When a man takes these other routes, he does not start with what is known. Instead, he starts with some other mode of apprehension, directly facing what is in the background of what is known. The known, in short, not only has an adumbrative 'othering' thrust, a thrust which reaches to something else in the guise of what has its own irreducible ontological being; it has a thickness which allows one to follow that thrust on a different level from that which the known permits. The knower, after all, has to move into the thickness of the known, in order to engage, as he inevitably does, in an adumbrative, penetrative act into the being of that which is known. This does not deny that what is not yet said may now be meant. But it does deny that the meant is entirely reducible to the said, where the said is used, as it is with Hegel, as equivalent with the rationally known, as entirely self-contained. It does deny that a thrust, toward the meant, demands of the meant that it be entirely said. When we know, we also are embroiled in a reality which we can also know, but which, like the embroilment, is not exhaustible by knowledge. We can know that our knowledge falls short of reality, just as Hegel does (and even in the way Hegel knows it) by seeing that it presupposes further content. That further content shows knowledge to be dependent on that which it could not and did not refer to, and therefore that it is intelligible only in terms which are outside its scope. This last is a difficulty only for one who, like Hegel, wants philosophy to be a science, through and through rational. For others, it shows that philosophy reaches only one reality adequately, and that it presupposes in its thrust and movement the presence of other realities, each of which in turn presupposes the rest, including the rational.

This objection is distinct from one which confronts Hegel with the dilemma that what is other is either independent and, therefore, can go its own way and never satisfy the demands of what is its other, or is still dependent on its other and therefore is not a genuine other. This objection can perhaps be met by saying that a complete kenosis, a perfect othering of the absolute Spirit, ends with the Spirit in reverse and therefore carrying out in a step by step way what the Spirit is able to express to itself as a set of notions or categories. That reply still leaves over the fact of contingency. I have previously suggested that this could be dealt with by Hegel if he would allow that the dialectic has worked up until now because, as a matter of fact, contingent items did function together in such a way as to be the occasion for the realization of a new stage of the dialectic, but that there is no guarantee that it would ever produce another stage. The next stage is in the possibly infinite future (as Peirce held when he offered a pragmatic interpretation of the Hegelian process).

The rational is the real and the real is the rational only in the sense that it is also true that the appreciated, etc., is the real and the real is the appreciated, etc. Or, to avoid a prejudicial emphasis on the ontological dimension, the rational, the appreciated and so on must also be said to be obdurate, intensive, and so on. Rational and real, in short, are themselves specialized formulations of what is epistemic and ontologic, of what is grasped and what is there, of what Hegel would call the Subject and the Substance. I am, of course, in all this, putting aside the question of whether or not Hegel's every move is justified, and whether or not he is right to apply his dialectic to art and religion and the history of philosophy—I think he is not. But anyone who supposes that the function of philosophy is to provide a rational account, and that the rational account exhausts what is the case—as sense-data thinkers, linguistic philosophers, behaviorists, mind-body reductionists seem to do—will find that Hegel goes far beyond where they have arbitrarily taken a stand and that the problem that I have here focused on, besets not only him but them as well. There is no going back to earlier positions in the development of a rational account. But there is also no warranted dismissing of it as existentialists, phenomenologists, and romantics do. These positions are defended and in the end offered as philosophic, or as opponents of the philosophic, and therefore are to be evaluated either in neutral terms or in both philosophic and non-philosophic ways.

The current opposition to Hegel is usually based on the assumption of an analytic position which supposes that what it knows is already distinct. No account is offered for the fact that there is something present to and for the analysis, that the analyst is real, and there is something done when he analyzes and, indeed, that more often than not, distinctions are made which were not there before. An analyst transforms a world he cannot know into one which he does know. There is, on his view, an unknown world he both needs and cannot possibly allow for.

December 20

1. If there is a multiplicity of items there necessarily is a binder, a One for that Many. The most obvious of binders is space. Without it or some other there would be no way of having different items be together. In *Reality*, I tried to account for everything by taking into consideration only the actualities, but then I could not only not explain common futures but could not show how or why the actualities should ever find one another so as to be able to be in the same world.

2. If all binders were homogeneous, every set of items would be together for the same reason. Differences between sets of items would have to be explained by the actions of the items within the range of the binders. There would be no controlling of the activities of the items by an encompassing unity, and therefore nothing like the action of a single organism having its own appetites, needs, actions, and nature.

3. If a binder were diversified, i.e., if it had different properties in different areas, we would approach a field theory of what is occurring. Were there only such a diversified binder, there would be no actualities. Those field theories which deny the reality of any entities are up against the fact that there are many men.

3. The denial that there are ultimate particles or other distinct entities in physics has to take changes in the field and the distribution of stresses

for granted. The same difficulty confronts the view that ultimate elements act on their own and introduce changes into the field. But not until we recognize that there are both entities and binders, and not simply a self-contained nuanced changing field, will we have units in terms of which we can at least partly account for the existence of complexes, and eventually of organisms and men.

4. There is no reason to choose between a pure field theory and a theory which allows for both binders and entities as long as we are dealing with elements which have unit charges of gravity, electricity, energy, and the like. If we start with a pure field theory, we must eventually find an explanation for the presumed precipitation of nuances out of it in the form of distinct and counteracting entities. We will then be attributing some kind of power to the field, directed no longer horizontally, as it were, but longitudinally, making some entities come to be. This variant on a creationism is avoided by recognizing, from the start, the existence of a plurality of entities which interact with the field in the guise of a binder. In either way, we credit the field or binder with power. The entities supposedly precipitated out will have a power derived from the field; the entities which are subject to a binder will have powers native to them. The first of these alternatives has the difficulty of having to suppose that the derived power turns around to oppose the very source from which it was derived, and also has the capacity to be expressed by each entity in opposition to the others.

5. If we start with a binder and elements, we can account for a nuanced field as the product of the interplay of these two, while still leaving over the possibility of having the binder and the elements in other roles related to one another, either to produce new nuanced fields, or complex items in which limited forms of the binders and a limited number of elements interplay.

6. A complex entity has a limited extension. As subject to a binder of limited extent, appropriate to just the items that are within the limited extension, the complex entity has a nature. That nature is a specialization of the common binder, a specialization which is produced in part by the act of the elements which are interacting with the binder. The specialization has its own power, thereby making the complex entity subject to a 'form', to use Aristotle's term for the unity of a complex. Complex entities are governed by unitary powers because they specialize common binders through the activity of units having powers of their own, and opposing those binders, as well as one another.

7. If we start with a field, entities would be located at positions there. Those entities would have no other status unless the field were a product of the entities and a binder. If it were, a location would be a place where the entities surfaced, and below which they had realities of their own.

8. If entities, as in a field, have only the properties they are credited with apart from the field, the entities as apart from the field will have to be understood to possess privacies or some kind of non-physical dimension. A formula relating mass and energy gives us the reality of a unit with a privacy which is expressed in a public spatio-temporal field. The equating of mass and energy expresses the relation of a unity with reference to the field, or of an actuality with reference to its privacy.

9. If a binder and elements are the primary realities, the nuanced field which results from their interplay, will be an appearance, a complex fulguration, or a reality. It would not be a single appearance, since single appearances belong to single entities. It would, instead, be a domain of appearances, each of which belongs to a distinct element. It would not be a complex fulguration unless it were devoid of power of its own. If it has power, it has reality.

10. Were a binder specialized so that it became the governing unity of a limited number of entities, a nuanced field would be the product of a multiplicity of complexes, each of which has its own limited binder and elements. Each complex would be a reality, and the relations between them would be specializations of the original binder. If those specializations were without power, we would have the analogue of the plan of an organization, or some other group. The totality, consisting of complexes and a specialized relation connecting all, will be a compound of complexes.

11. Whatever view we take, in the end we are forced to acknowledge a number of nuances in a field, a multiplicity of entities, or the product of a homogeneous field and a plurality of entities. The situation is not changed, if we hold that the ultimate elements come to be by being precipitated out of the field and to vanish by being absorbed into it.

12. There seems to be nothing in the way of the supposition that ultimate elements never attain the stage where they are wholly nuanced in a field, or wholly stand apart from it, but instead oscillate to some degree between these extremes. If we hold this view, we would still be able to account for complexes by attending to those times when the elements were maximally though not entirely detached from the field. But the elements would then not be able to specialize the field or to function within the specialization as a bounded Many.

13. There is more than one kind of field or binder, for elements are related to one another, not only in space but in time and dynamically, as self-maintaining, self-bounded, with natures and values.

14. Entities are in public in ways which differ from what they are in private. They are extended and distended; have a status and make claims; have natures as well as rationales; are limited as well as self-limiting; and are self-maintaining as well as expressed or manifested.

15. When units acquire a certain critical proximity, all binders become specialized in the form of a five-fold unity governing the body and privacy. The governing unity may spread indifferently over the private and public sides; we then have physical complexes. It may involve a distinction between them; we then have organisms. Or it may involve a specialization of the privacy with a distinctive functioning; we then have man. The distinctive functioning allows for a distinction of privacy and body as well as for their inseparability. As a consequence, men have organic-like and thing-like functionings.

16. When we are faced with dots on a page arranged in a certain way we see a face. When we see a number of stills flashed quickly before our eyes, we see a single scene. In these cases, there are spatio-temporal binders which help constitute collective unities. Only because the items are together in limited space-time frames are we able to see the face and scene. Even if it were held that we alone are responsible for the 'observed' unitary face and the continuity of the scene, we would depend on the objective unitary time for the one, and on the unitary space for the other. There is, of course, no deducing of a privacy from the objective or observed unitary face or scene.

17. The molecules of water have their privacies. Does the water as a mass? I think not. It is like a whole (cf. *Reality*).

18. What makes a controlling binder lose its grip? The subordinate parts can move away from a critical proximity as surely as they can remain in it. Usually the move away requires the introducing of new forces into the complex.

December 22

If we begin with the acknowledgment of space, either in the guise of a homogeneous field, or one which is a nuanced domain of electrical and other basic physical charges, we will be able to distinguish only a 'manifold' (to use Kant's term) or a single 'thing in itself' (to use another). So far, there will be no way to have a plurality of entities, since so far there will be no way of referring to differences between entities. That initial field, of course, cannot be acknowledged without our standing apart from it. Kant never asked himself how he could possibly refer to the forms of intuition, the categories, synthesis, the manifold and the transcendental unity of apperception, without which nothing, on his account, could be known. The knower, of course, is single for the very same reason that the thing in itself or the manifold is, there being no way as yet to have a multiplicity of entities differing from one another. Once Kant was able to hold the knower away from the initial field, he was in a position to ask whether or not there was an object on the other side of the field which categorized the field for itself in the way in which the knower categorized the field in knowledge.

We must acknowledge a knower distinct from the field. Must we also acknowledge objects? We must, if the field is opposed, if it is occupied, if it is specialized, if it is broken up into limited unities which interact in ways not expressible in terms of the field, if there are appearances, if the nuances are to be accounted for, if there are finite bits of knowledge, or if a knower can himself be located as an object of knowledge, distinct from other knowers.

What is the nature of an entity as it stands away from a field? It is not proper to speak of it as a privacy, for this not only involves a contrast with what is public and, presumably not altogether separable from the privacy, but leaves us with the problem of how it becomes converted into a body in the field. Nor is it proper to speak of it as a body, for then, as apart from the field, it would have the kind of properties that is has when in the field. It is more correct to speak of the entity as indeterminate. On entering into the field, it becomes transformed into a public body continuing into a privacy. The indeterminate (which is quite close to the Kantian thing-in-itself) is not beyond all knowing. As remarked above, the categories which Kant supposed had to be employed in all knowing are not required by him in order to know space or time, the categories, the knower, the manifold, or the acts of synthesis.

With Kant, we must not characterize the indeterminate in the same way we characterize what is determinate by virtue of the action of the field. If the field is extended, the indeterminate is *distended*; if the field is substantial, the indeterminate is *self-contained*, self-maintaining, possessive and expressive; if the field is identifiable with Being, the indeterminate is *self-bounded*, distinguishing itself from all else; if the field is rational, law-abiding, the indeterminate is *prospective*, structural; if the field is value, the indeterminate is a *claimant* to a status.

As distended, an entity occupies a part of the field; as self-contained, the entity possesses a part of the field; as self-bounded, the entity holds itself apart from others in the field; as prospective, the entity submits to the rationale of the field; and as a claimant to status, the entity finds a place in a hierarchy in the field. When it engages in these acts, it becomes a public entity; all the while it has content in reserve. That content is part of the original indeterminateness. It becomes determinate derivatively, since it is oriented toward the public bodily part in the field. The field, as it were, is overwhelmed by the distendedness, possessiveness, self-bounding, prospectiveness, and claim, with the consequence that the privacy is not extended, etc. as the body is, but is nevertheless governed by the field, or more precisely, by a specialized and limited form of that field.

It is not hard to see how a substantial field, one which is identifiable with Being, or is law-abiding, or is essentially a value could act directly on the content which it has not made into a public body. It is harder to see how space, time, or causality could so function, unless they are recognized to be modalities of Existence. The initial field should therefore be characterized as existent, and public space, time, and causality taken to be one of the results of a confrontation of the existent field with actualities. The privacy of an actuality will then be seen to be the outcome of the meeting of the rest of the indeterminate entity with the conditioning, determinate Existence.

Why does not the field, in its five-fold form, or in any one of the five forms, turn the entity into a purely public object? Why does it leave over some of the entity and have to make this into a privacy? Is it not that the distendedness, etc., of the entity has its own power, and that what we call the public body is just the distended entity so far as it has been subordinated to the field? The field could never govern the entire entity in the same way without denying degrees of insistence to the entity, with a maximum at one limit, where it can never be subordinated to anything.

The entity is not indeterminate in itself. It is indeterminate relative to the determinations which the field can introduce. If we start with the entity (and in the end we must do this, as surely as we must start with the field, or more precisely, as surely as we must acknowledge the two of them at the same time) its distendedness, etc., could be said to be determinate and to face the indeterminate field as that which it will meet and at one extreme be controlled by, and at the other control, but all the way through be involved with. The field is not distinct from the entity; the indeterminateness of the field, relative to the determinate entity, is an indeterminateness which the entity does not face as distinct from itself.

As distended, etc., though determinate, the entity is neither a body nor a privacy. No matter from what side we start, the distinction of body and privacy is the result of the interplay of field and entity. If we start with a public body, the envisagement of the entity as outside the field is the envisagement of a distended, etc., entity, part of which can be said to be bodily *distended* in anticipation of what the extended field does to it, and part of which can be said to be *distensive* in anticipation of what it will do to the extension intruded by Existence.

This view does not suppose, as was done previously, that ultimate particles or elements already have a private and a public bodily side. They are now seen to acquire these only when they interplay with final conditions. Only after that interplay do the ultimate particles so interplay with the conditions that they together produce complex entities. Only ultimate particles stand in stark contrast with all the finalities. Men, and other complex entities, instead, have already been partly constituted by those finalities.

If we start with both final conditions and ultimate elements, we start at an indeterminate position, leaving unsettled whether the conditions or the elements are to be viewed as determinate. Only after we have made the decision, and then moved to the point where the indeterminate is made determinate, do we have full-fledged entities and conditions, and are then in a position to understand how complex entities are produced. (I suppose that these conclusions are pertinent to Heisenberg's indeterminacy principle, but I do not have enough technical knowledge to be sure. But it does have bearing on the account I have given in *Beyond All Appearances* and in *First Considerations* of the ideal unreachable perfection, which is constituted by the finalities and actualities as they stand apart from one another.)

December 27

To acknowledge that some one is *responsible* is to acknowledge that he is *free, conscious, understands,* is in *control* and *persists* as a *possessive I.* To know that another has *rights* is to know that he *intends,* that he is *privately accountable,* that he is *sensitive* to beings in the world, that he *accepts* himself and that he has a *me.*

How do I know that another is responsible? Is it not that he deserves praise or blame, not as encouragements or discouragements, or as rewards or punishments, but as evaluations of his carrying out the role of a man?

How do I know that he deserves praise or blame? Is it not that I know he is a man?

How do I know that he is a man? In maintaining myself—and more sharply, on retreating within myself—I face him in such a way that a five-fold relation of *suitability* intervenes. I find that I belong with him, that I am alongside him, that I am subject to a language and other structures, that I in the same milieu, and that we have the same base value. This facing him across the relationship occurs at the same time that I distinguish myself from him.

But do I not sometimes find that others exclude me, despise me, or honor me? I do, but these attitudes ride on the back of our five-fold relationship.

How does the relation between us come about? As I stand apart from this or that individual, I give a limited place to a condition common to us, and thereby make it have the form of a special relation.

But it is also the case that a number of entities can come together in such a way that the common condition is specialized as a five-fold unitary nature with its own privacy, with the original entities in a subordinated position? Yes. That shows that we have a spectrum of realizations of the condition, going all the way from an overwhelming dominance of a five-fold specialized unity down to the presence of a mere five-fold relationship between the items. Items may move from one state of affairs to the other, leaving some ambiguous cases in the middle, and sometimes allowing for the presence of both. We are governed by a society, state, and perhaps even a human species, at the same time that we are humanly connected with respect (in the sense of acknowledging others as deserving praise and blame, which is to say, humanly related to me). Language is but one of a number of humanized relations.

How can a condition govern, and also function as a relation at one and the same time? Is it not that I am able to unite with others on one dimension, let us say through work or conversation, and stand away from them on another, or in other ways, for example, as concerned with remaining where I am, or with thinking? I may even work with others at the same time that I recognize myself to be engaged in work which is different from and differently grounded from the work of the others.

Is it not true that cats 'acknowledge' other cats without reflection? Must not they too be said to face one another as distinct entities related in a special way? Must not they too be said to be capable of being governed by an instance of the condition which the relation instances? The first is surely right; the second not. A cat maintains itself against other actualities—cats, dogs, stones, people—and in that act makes possible the very relationship which allows it to be together with these in distinctive ways. There is no first knowing itself and then the others, or conversely, but only a direct facing of the others across a relationship which intervenes, with the cat's maintaining itself when facing the others.

How do I know that another has rights? Is it not that I see that he adopts, accepts my addressing him by using a proper name? Why do I address him and not just refer to him the way I refer to what is not human? Why do I use a proper name? Is it not that I find him at once insistent on himself and yet acceptive, and that the proper name is that which is most acceptive while he is insistent on himself?

How do I distinguish things and animals from men? I *attribute* consequences and activities to things; I hold animals to be *accountable;* and I take men to be *responsible.* What is necessary cannot be attributed; what is unchangeable is not accountable; what is not free is not responsible. Because I attribute outcomes to things I take them to be acceptable or rejectable; because I take animals to be accountable, I take them to deserve rewards and punishments, and thereby to be altered so that they fit properly into the new situation.

We locate things; we distinguish animals; but we identify men. Men can also be distinguished and located; animals can also be located. Things continue, animals persist, while men insist on blocking our penetrations by directing their privacies elsewhere.

How do I distinguish the three kinds? The intervening relation is distinctive.

But I surely make mistakes? Yes. I may anthropomorphize things and animals; I may treat other men and even see them as though they were not human. But just so far as I fail to deal with others as men, I cannot hold them to be responsible, deserving praise and blame, forming a milieu with me, with genuine proper names, able to discourse with me, represent, offer me truths, each possessing an I, identity, freedom, consciousness, and mind.

But animals are conscious, and have minds? Yes, but it is a different kind of consciousness, and a different kind of mind. It is a consciousness which does not allow for self-consciousness, and a mind which does not know speculative truths.

How can I be said to help produce an intervening relation between myself and another human without having to face that other apart from the relation and, therefore, as not yet on a footing with me? Is it not that I begin the act of acknowledgment with a locating, and move continuously, as far as I can, to a distinguishing and an identification?

Then, in the case of a thing, I am already in the required relationship? No, because the grasp of it as a thing takes time. All I have to begin with is something more or less located, more or less faced as more than an appearance, and then progress to making my acknowledgment more precise.

What is my relation to the dead? Is it not a humanized one?

But here I am active. Is the intervening relation due to only one member? Just as we can anthropomorphize (and minimize) so we can intensify, or maintain through intent the relation that had prevailed (or reduce its function to one appropriate to an animal or thing).

If this is so, can I not do something similar for animals and things and thereby turn them into something like 'departed' men? I could, but in the case of men I also benefit from the governance of the society, (or remain subject to a possible social condemnation or control).

It should therefore be conceivable at least that a society should provide a governance and allow for a humanized bondage with animals and things? Yes. And it does occur. We need not suppose that primitives worship animals and things, but we should recognize that they, and we also, maintain certain special relations to them under the governance of various social conditions. Though we can recognize men outside our own social structures, it is true that in our society we are able to make readier and steadier identifications. The governing conditions may promote (or hinder) the individual's use of the proper relation, either by his filling it out with private additions (or distortions) or by his fitting into it (or being excluded by it).

What method should one pursue in order to discover the anatomy of privacy? Responsibility and rights articulate privacy, and the elements of the articulation tell us what the privacy is like.

It is not yet evident whether I should proceed in an order—freedom, consciousness, understanding, control, and persistent possession, or some other, for responsibility—or must allow all these at the same time, and thereby get in the way of the gradual coming to be of the full human being. If I were to insist on an order, what would decide which order?

Not everyone accepts the idea that there is a distinctive human responsibility. Apparently, all accept the idea of native rights. Consequently

I should start with the acknowledgment of a common humankind and common humanized relations which are directly instituted.

I must proceed in a particular order. Which one? Or must I accept all acknowledged rights? If so, I will have difficulty with understanding how an individual matures.

Responsibility is only gradually achieved. I must, consequently, proceed in a genetic order if I am to trace the coming to be of a mature man. But once I acknowledge other responsible men, I will have acknowledged all the stages. At one of those stages men's rights are grounded.

Is it not possible that I alone might be responsible? Not if it is a human responsbility, rather than the responsibility of a God-man.

Do I not know that children are human before they are responsible? Yes, for they already have a human kind of freedom and are already self-identical. They do not know how to exercise the freedom, nor do they have the needed understanding. Nor do I take them to be full, mature humans. But from the start, they already have something animals do not have, because they already are persons, a status not possible to animals. If so, then our understanding of another requires only that the humanizing relation intervene between a mature being and someone who already exercises some distinctive human powers—even if he does so in a way that does not allow him to be fully responsible. That he deserves to be taken to be a human means that he deserves to be credited with powers animals do not have.

How sure of this am I, and can I be? I do not know.

December 28

A human being is first acknowledged as having an identity expressed in assertiveness. He is, therefore, taken to be responsible with a distinguishable self, and also to have the right to be addressed as a you and therefore to be recognized to be a distinct person. The acknowledgment of him as having an identity is the acknowledgment of him as already partially articulating the state of being responsible. His development consists so far in his achieving a *consciousness, mind, freedom,* and an *I,* and thus on his attaining the stage where he is fully deserving of praise or blame. The acknowledgment of him as having the right to be addressed as a you is the acknowledgment of him as partially articulating the state of being the locus of human rights. His development involves the achieving of a *self-bounding* in which the integrity of his privacy is achieved; the *right to be in the world* with his rights supported, and thus to be acknowledged to be part of the world of men; the right to be *privately accountable,* i.e., to decide how to express himself in the world; and to have the right to be a *me,* and thus to accept his public presence as his own possession. (Self-bounding is what was before termed 'tonality'; and 'presence in the world' replaces 'sensitivity'.)

The self-boundedness and presence in the world seem to follow on the achievement of identity; they are followed by consciousness and mind, and then by private accountability and freedom; and finally by I and me. If this is so, the development of the self and the person alternate, and the me comes to be later than the I itself. We have a rhythm of self (identity); person (self-boundness and presence); self (consciousness and mind); person and self (private accountability and freedom); self and person (I and me). There is nothing *a priori* about this ordering; it reflects my understanding of what in fact takes place.

Since praiseworthiness and blameworthiness are pertinent to the self, and addressibility is pertinent to the person, evidently there is a progressive intensification of the meaning of these, which is achieved only with some degree of alternation from one type of development to the other.

December 29

I have been tacitly assuming that we make contact with one another as humans directly, in any situation. It now seems to me more reasonable to assume that we do this first only within our own community, and then, by extension, with respect to individuals who are quite different from those in our community. We can recognize the humanity of other men in other communities, provided that these are somewhat similar to our own community in having some variation of its structure and something like our language, affiliations, work, and so forth.

The limited governance to which we are subject in our community is a specialized and limited form of a common human nature. The imposition of that limited specialization on us, even as merely confronting one another, makes us publicly manifest to a degree and in a manner not possible to animals or things. We are then members of a single 'complex we'.

The humanized relationship we have to one another in our community is the product of a union of a five-fold nature of the community with us in direct relation to one another. In more limited settings, such as a club or in an athletic contest, it is evident that the primary fact is the governing condition, and that the kind of relationship which individuals there have to one another is a function of the interplay of the related individuals with the governing conditions.

So far as we are able to recognize that any human being, no matter where, is a being with an actual or incipient *identity, self-boundedness, presence, consciousness, mind, private accountability, freedom, I, me,* and *personal dignity,* we move from the governance of a limited condition to the broadest possible governance for men. Let us call this 'human nature'. Does that human nature have a power, does it govern and interplay with the related men to constitute a universal, humanized set of relations? Or does it just classify the individuals, put a border around them, and thereby permit of the production of humanized relations? If the human nature has power, that power is slight, allowing us to misconstrue other individuals, and to deny them the role of co-humans. If we deny that it has any power, we introduce a discontinuity between the governing power of those conditions which apply to all entities, and the power exercised by a particular society, state, sport, or family. And we should then not hesitate to say that the reason why cats act in certain ways with respect to other cats is because they are governed by a common 'catness', overarching and subordinating them, that they have direct relations to one another as entities which express their privacies in a common world, and that the interplay of these two constitutes the distinctive way in which they face and deal with one another.

When cats act in certain ways with respect to dogs, sticks, men, and other entities belonging to other groups, are they acting as components in a complex whole? It does not seem so. They seem to be acting as individual cats. Do they act as governed by a common catness which is opposed to a common dogness governing the dogs? If so, governing natures seem to have considerable power. Is the power of a common human nature less than that of the common catness? That does not seem to be a reasonable supposition. Is it perhaps that our societies, states, families, tribes, and the like, not only specialize but intensify the power of a governing condition? That does not seem possible. Indeed, as the examination of the coming to be of an organic being shows, the common power is quite limited.

A we has less power than an organic unity. All that is needed of the common condition is that it bound off certain entities in such a way as to allow them to interact with the condition, so as to produce a vital whole. Each entity in that whole will be caught up in the whole's activity, but will specialize it in the form of a distinctive type of relation enabling the individual entity to make a distinctive type of contact with other entities in the whole, and another type of contact with entities in other wholes.

*   *   *

The day after tomorrow I leave for Denver, where I will be for the next semester. It will be an adventure having the disadvantage of depriving me of my books and regular routines, and the advantage of providing new stimulations. In the meantime I have been offered $45,000 by Scranton University for the year 1979-80. Does it make sense to accept it? I have said in the past that what I wanted most was to have the opportunity to think and write. This I will have, perhaps to an incomparably greater degree, if I return here to my familiar surroundings. I spoke to Jude Dougherty, the Dean, about the matter. He says I am to have another $1,000 raise (my third), and that I am scheduled to be employed at the Catholic University of America until I am 80, with a possible appointment for the next year.

There is a big difference between my present $28,000 and $45,000, even allowing for the increase in taxes. But since I do not really need the money, since I think my children are provided for, and since Scranton is not as interesting as Washington, I am at this moment not persuaded that I should accept the offer. I will of course wait until I receive the formal invitation before deciding, and in the meantime will consider pros and cons again and again. Right now it is hard to contemplate being away from here for a year and a half, with just a summer interval. Perhaps being at Denver will make me see the desirability of being away. If I decide to go to Scranton, I think I can count on coming back here, granted that health and sanity continue as before.

*   *   *

If humanized and similar relations are actually epitomizations of the dynamism of a complex whole, produced through the interplay of related individuals and a governing nature, when acting on other types of being we will either have to function representatively for a whole, or will have to constitute a distinctive whole with those others. Do we not have the latter in developed societies with respect to most entities, and the former with respect to what the societies have not envisaged, what is usually termed 'raw nature'? Since it is doubtful that we can ever get entirely into raw nature, must we not therefore say that we function within humanized wholes and therefore necessarily act representatively? If so, then we must say that when we acknowledge another to be human, or as having some other nature, we are involved in a complex whole, specialized in the form of a humanized relation, which we utilize representatively, i.e., as units who are functioning as the other members need to have us act, in order that we fit in with what they are, and are doing.

In functioning representatively, one acts as an individual and carries out activities in which the others in that whole presumably would have engaged in, were they in one's place. What one says is to be taken on trust by them as being true or false on one's own say-so; what one does is to be taken on trust by them as the proper thing to do. What is said and done should have been done by any unit of that whole in that position.

Suppose the entire community takes some human not to be human, and that there is an individual who does make the proper acknowledgment in word and deed? We will have to say that he is acting as a member of another group. We must make a similar observation if an individual in our society does not acknowledge as human what the society takes to be such. Since any society may have a distortive view, we must in the end turn to a common human nature as determining what can properly be said and done representatively.

Granted that there is a common human nature identifiable with the human species, governing and interplaying with men as directly related to one another, does it stretch over them? Unless men were related only in raw nature, they would have to be governed by specific forms pertinent to them, and not to other actualities. In this sense, human nature must stretch over all, embrace them if only in the form of a class. Without going to the extreme of the Marxist, and supposing that a class (actually, a whole constituted of a class and interplaying men) has its own history and dialectic, which overrides the intents and acts of individuals, we can recognize a species to have its own integrity and persistence and, therefore, to be determinative of the frame in which men will be related. This extreme realistic view of the species stands in radical contrast with the sociobiological evolutionary view which places all species-preserving features in the genes. In effect, that view translates the social into the molecular; it presupposes but does not explain the social, since it looks to this for its data and then reads the results into the genes. It is as if one had taken a gravitational law and given this an individualized form in each entity.

To fail to be related to another member of the human species as a human being, able to be responsible, and deserving to be addressed by a proper name, and thus as having a self and a person, with a separately functioning privacy and with rights able to be expressed as claims in the public world, is to fail to act properly even though one is a full member of the human species, related to all the others in a five-fold way, and therefore to fail to be a full member of mankind. It is to act representatively, but to do so badly (even when it is the case that were others in our position they would act just as badly). A view, alternative to this, holds that just so far as we act badly we ourselves are not full members of the human species, but are 'inhuman' or 'subhuman'. But villains are human. This is what Himmler had in mind when he told his troops, who were assigned to kill Jews standing upright before their graves, that no one realized what a difficult assignment they had undertaken and carried out. What he did not see was that the assignment was difficult, precisely because the men who were being shot were recognized by Himmler and his men to be human, and that he and his men were therefore acting representatively but were doing this badly in somewhat the way, but to a immensely heightened degree, in which a man who lies assumes a representative role but carries it out in a bad way.

December 30

There are two types of extreme realism. One holds that conditions govern a plurality of entities; the other holds that the conditions are operative in each individual. Human nature for the one is a class character which enfolds all men; identified with the species it has a distinctive nature, power, and career, coming into being in the act of becoming pertinent to those individuals. Its coming to be is one with its specification of a more common condition and the imposition of the result on the set of entities. Human nature for the other is a unitary controlling transcendent, making the entity be a complex human.

There are powerful controlling conditions—state and society. The power of the state, though, could be credited to actual men; the power of the society could be credited to the habits of individuals. But one will then have difficulty understanding how the structure (to take one of the five dimensions of the entity) could not only change over time, but could constrain the individuals together in ways they themselves might not recognize. The structure of language has all members under some control; the structure can be violated, but it is sufficiently strong to function as a factor in a constituting interplay of related men in an ongoing social whole. If we do hold this, do we also have to hold that human nature has a transcendent role for each individual?

Is each man a localized case of human nature—granted even that he has other dimensions and powers? Is a state operative in the citizen; a family in the father, mother, and child; a society in all its members; a language in its users? Or does each individual take advantage of the presence of the common governing condition? Since men may not even know of the common condition, and since they function concordantly as units, often without any awareness of other units, it makes sense to say that the common governance does have some kind of role in each.

Are we representatives of other men as subject to the governing relation of human nature or species, or as subject to the whole constituted by the interplay of related men with the human nature or species? We are surely representative of them in the constituted whole, each of us exhibiting the nature of this whole, to provide a third, but derivative meaning of 'realism'. But we also can (though I do not think necessarily) represent the governing relation for other men. We are then officials, planners, guides.

* * *

An annual meeting of the American Philosophical Association, Eastern Division (the largest of the divisions and I suppose the most representative), has just been completed. I hear wide-spread expressions of discontent. Not only are the various sessions devoted to narrow issues—and are badly attended—but even the Presidential address and other special addresses are largely ignored. In addition, there are many satellite societies whose meetings are set by the APA at awkward times, and then in such a way that one is forced to attend to one and neglect others. I hear that a rump meeting was called by what is tentatively termed 'a pluralism of societies', and some kind of revolt is brewing. It seems to me that the wisest move would be to take the APA to be the letters for the 'American Practitioners of Analysis' and have all the satellite societies agree to meet at the same time that the APA does, but in a different place. The consequence will be that the APA will have its own specialized topics, and will function mainly as a place to go for job interviews, while most of the serious business of philosophy, though in limited areas, will be taken care of elsewhere. If successful, the final result should be something like that which prevails in the American Psychological Assn.—a multiplicity of divisions, each devoted to a special kind of angle, with no division having any priority, and each with its own officers and program. There is in that association a choice of a genuinely distinguished person to be the elected president of the whole. The organization work is made the task of a paid bureaucracy.

* * *

A man is the locus of a transcendent, Man, and can represent what governs him and others. At the same time, he represents other men who, with him, constitute the whole of mankind, as a dynamic unity in which interrelated men have been united with their common governance. Each necessarily is a representative of others in the whole, and may represent the governing condition which helps constitute that whole. It is as the representative of others that he faces this or that individual as a human. He can therefore directly face another, not only in his community, but as just a fellow human. When he operates from the position of his more intimate, intensive apprehension of the men in his community, he can deal with others, who are not in his community, with something like the appreciation, sympathy, and insight that characterize his encounters with those in his community.

When a man deals with those in his community as humans, he is of course not constituting a whole with them. He faces them either as men in one mankind or as in some smaller, intensive whole. If the latter, he apprehends men in his community in a way he does not normally do. If he starts with an acknowledgment of fellow-members of his family, he will see some of the others in a larger community as being men in somewhat the same intensive sense that he sees fellow family members. Depending on the kind of whole from which he starts, he is able to see others as fellow-men, having depths and dignities which he would not acknowledge were he to approach those others simply as members of some large company or of one mankind.

1979

January 9 (Denver)

When sperm and egg come together, they are together under the aegis of a number of physical, chemical, and biological laws, as well as of an 'embryonic human condition'. This is not identical with a biological law, even one which is restricted to humans, or even human embryos. A biological law, applicable to an embryo, governs the interplay of its cells, whereas the embryonic human condition provides a governing unity for the entire sperm and egg, or for more complex entities. If we have a biological law governing the functioning of the embryo in relation, say to the mother, we still remain confined to an area in which we have only feeding, growth, decay, and the like. The embryonic human condition, instead, defines a single complex which, if it is related to some other, such as its mother, is related as a human to a human to whom it belongs; this is more than being related to a host in which it resides.

The embryonic human condition both specifies and instances biological, and through this, chemical and physical laws. Consequently, sperm, egg, and larger complexes are subject to all; the 'embryonic human condition' is just that law with which they are most intimately involved. It in fact so operates that at the same time that a unity of bodies is produced, the condition achieves a private status as well. As oriented toward the unity that it provides for the bodies, it is private and individual, and may eventually function with some independence.

As an embryo develops, the embryonic human condition becomes more and more articulated, and the embryo's various bodily parts become more and more complex, and are related in new ways. Just as the embryonic condition was able to become present because sperm and egg had come together in a crucial way, so a more comprehensive condition becomes present when the embryonic parts arrive at a new critical juncture. When this occurs, the embryonic human condition is no longer able to control; it is caught up in 'Man'. This is specified by and governs the items.

Just as there is a crucial point where a juncture of items enables the embryonic form to be specified and to govern, so there is a point where it is unable to do so any longer. The result is either death, when the merely chemical and physical laws are alone operative; the incursion of another condition able to encompass and govern what was beyond the capacity of the previous condition (and thus the coming to be of an entirely new being with a new privacy); or the absorption of the condition in another. (This condition has been indirectly instanced before; the change enables it to be directly instanced by the items together.)

It is possible to distinguish at least ten stages in the progress that is made toward the status of a mature individual human being who is together with others:

1. The *embryonic human,* instantiating an embryonic human condition and through its agency 'Man'.

2. The *fetus,* directly instantiating 'Man'.

3. The *human being,* which is to say the person with rights. 'Man' here is instantiated as a unity which governs.

4. The *confronting human being,* the person facing something at a distance.

5. The *individual human being,* who privately accommodates the 'Man' that it instances, without reflection, submitting to it, accepting it as its essence.

6. The *mature human being,* who not only accepts himself as an instance of 'Man' but also accepts others as instances.

7. *Men together,* where each accepts himself as the terminus of the relation 'Man', which before had functioned only as the unity of each.

8. The *functioning individual human being* who is able to penetrate into the men he confronts, as having a distinctive type of dignity.

9. The *mature individual human being* who is able to see another to be responsible and, therefore, to have a self, articulated as an identity, consciousness, mind, will, and I. He uses his privacy to acknowledge a usable privacy in others.

10. *Mature human beings together* who, privately as well as publicly, sustain an intensive, variegated form of 'Man' as their common relation. Language and custom are cases of such a sustained, intensified, variegated 'Man'. Man, the species, is not just a biological reality; this is but one aspect, though present early and persistent. Language and custom give it body while they specialize it.

January 11

'Man' can be conceived to have the same or a slightly narrower range than the 'embryonic human condition', since one may or may not take every monstrous embryo to be a prospective man. But, like the 'embryonic human condition', 'Man' is singular. It is instanced by all individuals who, on the loss of the 'embryonic human condition' do not die or turn into some other kind of entity, such as a 'monstrous living being'.

'Man' is more complex than 'embryonic human condition'; it does not intensify or specialize that condition. Instead, it replaces the condition, to become directly instanced. One could conceivably take the 'embryonic human condition' to be absorbed within 'Man', perhaps giving this a tonality and thus affecting what a man will subsequently do.

The articulation of a man's privacy is the outcome of the use of speech. Apart from a language which relates the individual to others as an intensification of the relation 'Man', uniting all those who have attained the state of instancing 'Man', speech does not enable one to make either steady or communicable distinctions. By utilizing the language of a group, each instance of 'Man' is able to supplement his initial articulation with the fixed terms and usages that characterize the language and, thereby, sharpen the differences between his various special epitomizations of self and person in the way others do.

Could one not make private use of a language, he would not be able to use such terms as 'I' or 'consciousness' to mark out dimensions of himself in the way in which others do. But if one made no use of language, he would still be able to make distinctions within himself—indeed, he must make these in order to be able to make use of the language. Here we have come close to the root of the claim made by depth grammarians: a child already makes basic distinctions, such as between self and person, I and me, decision and intention, responsibility and accountability, before it uses the public language—but not before it speaks or uses analogous bodily-made distinctions. But it cannot say what it does, and cannot make the distinctions sharp in constant ways unless it uses the distinctions of the language to express distinctions already privately made. The use of the distinctions of language presupposes private acts.

Who makes the distinctions? If it be some epitomization of privacy, we have distinctions made before language is used or species employed. It seems to me now that what must be said is that speech, which is the work of the body, is held on to by the privacy as a whole, i.e., by the private instantiation of 'Man' as continuous with the bodily instantiation, and that it then serves to demarcate portions of the privacy from others. It is the privacy as a whole, adopting the various speech units—segregating them as it were—that provides the initial distinctions. Though the segregating presupposes at least vague distinctions between self and person, I, mind, and so forth, the segregating is the work of the entire privacy accommodating different emphases or 'intentionalities' of speech. On the basis of this result, the growing child can make use of the prevailing language, where the distinctions it makes are given public roles.

Must not something similar be said for various customs? Yes. Like a language, a custom fails to cover the entire range that 'Man' does. Like a language, it incorporates various distinctions which characterize the interplay of various individuals and groups. Like a language, it requires an individual to make some distinctions in his privacy, at least between responsibility and accountability, private dignity and accepted public role. A child distinguishes various roles it can carry out. Its initial distinctions are reinforced by the way in which it is able to carry these out in a custom-governed society.

A child's initial babblings are soon modified so as to take on the guise of what it hears. The babblings and their modifications are associated with stresses on the different aspects of the privacy which accompany them, thereby giving those aspects boundaries answering to distinctions in what is babbled and spoken. Corrections of what is spoken by others in the community require not only refinements in what a child says in public settings, but an awareness of the kinds of distinctions in its privacy which are in fact appropriate to the accepted public use of the language. The corrections evidently are not made by the child alone; others, knowing that the publicly used words are pertinent to this distinction or that in the privacy, correct the child's use of words so that they are in consonance with what the adult takes to be an appropriate private accompaniment. The child then has publicly sanctioned distinctions which it is to accept, distinctions which, if the adult is right, match emphases in the child. The adult can do more than blindly guess what the child's private accompaniments are, only if he has some insight into the child. And this the adult can have, precisely because he not only already instances 'Man', and thus knows the child to be such an instance, with certain essential divisions, but because he confronts the child, and in that act penetrates toward the child's privacy. An adult, of course, does not know the distinctions which the child has privately made, but by making the child assume accountability, and charging it with responsibility through admonitions, observations, advice, respect, and the like, he makes the child give up the associations it might have made and, instead, accept those which allow for the ready acceptance of the admonitions, etc.

A child must learn to move from the accusation "You tell lies" to "Me tell lies" and eventually to "I tell lies". When it tries to repeat "You tell lies", it must be made to learn that 'you' always refers to another; its translation of "You tell lies" into "I tell lies" involves its acceptance of an accusation and, with this, an acceptance of itself as the source of the act deserving the accusation.

These reflections illustrate my view of philosophy in a way I think I never really showed so well before. Philosophy has two prongs: it answers to every man's experience, and it has a technical character where issues are sharpened and given technical defenses. The typical academic philosopher does only the latter, and even philosophers, such as Hume, seem to have only this side in mind. The typical phenomenologist and existentialist, instead, emphasizes the aspects which are open to every man and which academic philosophers do not often note. We can rightly criticize a Hume for not knowing that experiences do not only terminate in objects, but that they are imbedded in an experiencing which thrusts beyond the experienced content to allow one to make some contact with objects. We can rightly criticize Kierkegaard for not having an articulated, defended position, and thus for not being willing or able to show that what he says is true. *First Considerations* exhibits both of the desirable features; at least tacitly, it claims to have them in mutually supporting roles. The foregoing analysis of the coming to be of mature human beings together, tries to be in accord with what we daily know, and also to be experientially and systematically defensible.

January 12

One of the more important novel ideas in *First Considerations* is that of experiencing. It was there held that experiencing was a thrusting beyond experience, where this is understood to terminate in content. Experience is a focalizing activity, terminating in experienced content. Experiencing continues beyond this. What was not made sufficiently clear in that work were the dimensions of experiencing. I spoke as though it moved merely in depth. If it did this alone, there would be no experiencing of finalities, or these would be moved to in an entirely different kind of experiencing, distinct from that which reached toward an actuality. But if we take experience to end in a focused entity, it becomes evident that experience passes beyond this, both by spreading alongside and by penetrating it. When I attend to a desk, I focus on it as obtrusively present while experiencing something of it in depth, at the same time that I demarcate it within a larger field, vaguely apprehended.

The fact of experiencing is neglected by almost every thinker in the past, the traditional empiricists being the most conspicuous. If one neglects experiencing, one can do nothing more than call on oneself to provide various agencies by which the data can be brought together in various bundles to constitute the world with which we are familiar. There are no objects then known. A similar criticism can be made of Kant, whose manifold is a limit beyond which he cannot go. Nor can Husserl; by bracketting off the world, he left himself with nothing to do but to have intensional experiences of jmind-constituted content. He claimed to know more, but there is no way in which his claim could be made good. The difficulty was seen, I think, by Heidegger and Sartre. Knowing that a phenomenology will not allow them to know anything on the other side of what is intentionally experienced, they recur to the individual and take him to be the avenue through which reality is able to make itself manifest, and perhaps even to fully, truly be.

Hegel does hold that in acknowledging an object of experience one points beyond it. But he supposed that what was pointed at was essential to, though absent from what was being confronted, that what is 'meant' is but a missing 'said'. If I am right, what is beyond the content of experience is the real; experiences terminate in appearances, with experiencing going toward the inwardness of the actualities which help make the experienced content possible, and toward the content in which all the manifestations of actualities are. That context is the finalities at their most attenuated.

When and as one experiences something, one is already beyond it and involved in actualities and finalities by virtue of the inescapable experiencing which the experience punctuates. Speculation moves beyond the reach of experiencing, either by filling out the experiencing or following its guidance. The view emphasized in *First Considerations* takes speculation and other ways of reaching to the actualities and finalities to start where the experiencing begins to move beyond the experience, and to suppose that the speculation engages in an independent venture of inferring to and understanding what the real is. One could take the inferring and understanding themselves to be experiences and experiencings. If so, one also must take them to have a different rhythm and to require different powers from what the experiencing involved in perception does.

Why is experiencing neglected by so many thinkers? Is it not because there is an overemphasis on objects or data; because experiencing allows for emotional intensification; because experiencing, unlike experience, has no definite stopping point; because experienced content is taken to be the empirical counterpart of the Cartesian ideas, and therefore is thought not to allow for any opening into some other realm, but at best to permit one only to believe that there is a counterpart of the experienced items; and because it goes in two directions from the experienced content, and thus seems to be a muddle of various factors?

January 13

Are all man's interpersonal transactions—working, driving a car on the highway, watching a game in the stands, buying groceries—specifications of 'Man'? This seems reasonable, since they are all contoured and subdivided in accord with what it means to be a man with others.

Are the distinctions that are publicly made, accepted by the individuals as intensifying the distinctions they privately make in themselves? This too seems reasonable. Sexual acts, for example, are performed in a spirit which internalizes the fears and hopes, shames and other attitudes that society endorses or rejects.

If both of these suppositions be accepted, we must go on to say that, so far, the private is the public individualized. But the opposite emphasis also occurs. What one thinks, how one allocates different private acts makes a difference to the importance and meaning of what is done. The two directions are not equally important, however. For the most part, the distinctions we privately make are accentuated by the public transactions; private distinctions come out effectively in public only when they are backed by an insistence, desire, appetite, will, and so forth. We are moulded by our societies only because we have made basic private divisions which that society sharpens. We make a difference to what is publicly undergone because the private divisions we make are insisted on there.

Public language has been molded by past emphases sustained in society. When I take hold of it, it allows me to make distinctions in other common structures, such as work and manners, and thus to be in a position to adopt the public distinctions as agencies for sharpening the boundaries of private ones.

We must not suppose that everything that is done is subject to the distinctions in public structures, all intensifying 'Man'. Otherwise, there would be no genuine mysticism, no speculative knowledge of actualities or finalities, no understanding of the physical world which is in fact presupposed by the public structures. Hermeneutical and some other humanistically oriented thinkers suppose that everything is caught within the pattern of 'Man' or of some such specialization as public language, convention, or history. They neglect the fact that 'Man' and the condition it replaces, are themselves specialized intensifications of more basic conditions which operate through those specializations.

Does this entail that we must cease to be human and must act like things to get to the conditions which govern all that is? No. We function as humans, and even as humans together, inside the frame of a common conditioning 'Man', but some of the distinctions there made, are made with respect to what is real. When we take those distinctions into ourselves it is for the sake of enabling us to attend to the realities pertinent to those distinctions. Accordingly, we have distinctions in language, etc. which allow us to sharpen our understanding, and others which reflect the existence of and may help us to become alert to what prompted those distinctions. Not every one of the distinctions in language, etc., is to be accepted. All we can do is use them as aids. This is similar to what scientists do when they follow the lead of mathematics.

Because we use our private powers, and do not merely distinguish them, we are able to attend to what is outside public frames. As a consequence, we have distinctions in those frames which serve the purposes of a naive philosophy, and which could conceivably be refined to provide systematic philosophic formulations. Other distinctions are provided by appearances, and what lies beyond them, directly discerned or reached via what is directly discerned. These could conceivably be refined to provide systematic philosophic formulations. Other distinctions are provided by appearances and what lies beyond them, directly discerned or reached via what is directly discerned.

A child corrects what it says, not only by conforming to what is publicly endorsed, but by what it directly discerns. It has some insight into the deceit, kindness, sympathy, and challenge of others, before it has the appropriate words, and makes adjustments accordingly. Humanists make 'Man' to be an absolute. They forget that we learn what the world is, not from language, etc., but by facing the world. What is then faced is also reported in language, but this is tinged by what was discerned.

January 14

A law of nature can be taken to be a formal arrangement, for which actual entities provide values or instances. But laws must then be recognized to have power and to apply to entities which are involved in other types of arrangement, such as affiliation, coordination, distancing, and evaluation. Alternatively, law can be conceived to itself have a five-fold nature. When this is done one can still hold with Galileo that mathematics mirrors nature, provided that the mathematics is taken to relate terms in a five-fold way. One also can take a law to be embodied in nature. This course is partly followed by those who identify the laws of nature with actual spatio-temporal ongoings, using mathematical formulations merely to express the facts in terms of variables. A different alternative (which I follow) takes the laws of nature to express basic governing conditions, interrelating items which have an independent status, even when they publicly function together as the laws require.

Sperm and egg are subject to a five-fold conditioning of many different grades. The physical, chemical, biological, and eventually the embryonic human condition, as well as the 'Man' which replaces this, are all five-fold. The common social structures of language, work, game, custom, and history are also five-fold. They provide occasions for intensifying the boundaries articulated in individual privacies. They also contain distinctions reflecting different entries into the different finalities.

When language is treated as though it were only formal, as a kind of debased or muddled logic, one has to look to other structures to obtain the specifications of the other distinctions due to the finalities and actualities. Language, though, does more than order items formally; it affiliates, coordinates, distances, and evaluates as well. Indeed, it and other structures can be said to be specifications of an interconnecting 'Man' only so far as they have a five-fold guise.

Associations specify the affiliative side of man; enumerations reflect coordinations; measures connect items related at a distance; gradings are evaluative. Language, work, etc., contain these basic divisions in addition to those which reflect what men have discerned of one another and perhaps of other entities. They also contain distinctions which are the outcome of convention, arbitrary acts, attrition, and accumulation. There are, then, three sets of distinctions to be noted in the specifications of 'Man' as connecting individual men—those which reflect the insistent presence of finalities, those which reflect the discerned articulations essential to the being of men, and those which are arbitrary.

It is not difficult to find five different ways of dealing with some such entity as a sentence—roles, words, grammar, references, plausibility or interest; or five different ways of dealing with work—tasks, cooperation, program, energy expended, and produced value. But it is not evident to me as yet that these are more than emphases which I have imposed in the light of the finalities, rather than unavoidable distinctions actually seen to be there, serving to let us know of the operative presence of those finalities. Nor is it yet clear to me how the distinctions which men make when dealing with one another fall into a necessary five-fold guise in language, work, and so forth.

January 15

There is no need for language, work, and other specifications of man to exhibit distinctions reflecting what we discern of one another, for the five-fold ways of connecting items are assimilable by individuals in accord with their own internal divisions, and can be used as agencies for reaching to five similar divisions in themselves. The common social governing conditions of whatever grade are therefore to be understood to have five modalities expressing the finalities, in addition to a multiplicity of adventitious distinctions accumulated in the course of unreflecting usage. Each of the specifications of man, and each of the conditions which it itself specifies, exhibit some type of assimilating, coordinating, organizing, distancing, and assessing of items. These primary ways of connecting may, of course, be overlooked, blurred, or combined with adventitious ones, with the consequence that men will not become aware of all the finalities and often enough will suppose themselves and others to be articulated in ways which reflect only the conventional accumulated practices and beliefs of a particular society.

The five-fold dimensions of a particular language or other social structure may not do full justice to the ways men in fact are linked. If one is to credit the distinctions to language one will have to refer to a primary or depth language which a particular language may not fully display or may display in a distortive manner. To refer to the words of a language is therefore misleading, since words are just terminal. A sentence is to be understood as associating words by virtue of their related functions, coordinating them as equally words, formally connecting them by its structure, distancing them by referring them differently, and giving them different roles for different purposes.

The five-fold way in which men are together is specialized in multiple social structures, each joining entities in five ways. If this is right, language and other structures are all five-fold agencies, at once opening up to the five finalities and connecting units, such as words or sentences in clusters, as distinct, in grammar, over space and time and with dynamic emphasis, and as constituting something of value. What we internalize of it are these kinds of connection which then serve as so many different ways of sharpening the distinctions we have already made in ourselves. Are these the emotions, body, mind, will, dignity?

January 17

It is a remarkable fact that the First Amendment to the U.S. Constitution says only that *Congress* shall make no law respecting the establishment of religion, etc. It does not say that the states cannot make such laws. A state, indeed all the fifty states can, so far as the First Amendment is concerned, establish state religions. I suppose the answer to this contention would be that when they are allowed to establish religions the intent of the Constitutional amendment is violated, since one would then be denied the right to belong to any religion and to practice any one of them as a citizen of the United States. But this would be an extension of what was in fact said and even intended by the Amendment. And once this kind of extension is allowed, can we draw the line any place? The answer to this question is perhaps that the line can be drawn by taking the so-called Preamble of the Constitution to state the purpose of the whole and to allow that purpose to guide us in our interpretation of Constitution.

In *Our Public Life* I speak of native rights, but since I did not there carefully distinguish self and person, and the two from privacy itself, I did not have a well-grounded set of native rights. I there speak of the will as one of the essential factors in a person. But surely an infant is a person, and surely it has no will. It could even be held that it does not have a functioning mind in the sense of a reason distinguishable from that which is possessed by an animal.

January 18

For the last week or so I have been writing shorthand notes to myself, trying to get clear the primary distinctions in an individual man and the primary divisions and therefore the essential rights of a person. The best I seem to be able to do so far is to take the basic divisions of a man to comprise *self, person, human nature, body* and a *self-instancing.*

But the self and the self-instancing do not seem to be present in the new born baby, and it becomes a question whether they are the outcome of the use of a language or other social structures, or are somehow achieved in the course of a maturation which, though it is undoubtedly aided and perhaps presupposes a social setting, occurs in the individual.

The basic divisions of the person and therefore of rights relate to the body a. as something presented and insisted on; b. as being together with other men in a public world; c. as sensitive and eventually rationally controlled from within, by one maintaining a private status and a living as a private being. This list goes backward from the individual as exhibiting a value to himself as a mere private person. I have also made an alternative set of distinctions—the person as public, as controlling the body, as exemplifying human nature and potentially allowing for a self, as in the body, and as being private. I am dissatisfied, because I am not clear as to just how I can justify one or the other, or some third list.

Perhaps it might be better to see what native rights we are sure of, and work back from this to an understanding of the nature of the person? Even Hobbes would concede that the right to life was inalienable, not caught up in a supposed contract. Locke thought we had a right to property, but this is surely questionable, particularly in the light of the fact that there are some who do not have any, and that taxation is a way of depriving men of property. We have, I think, a right not to suffer pain unnecessarily, to be in health, to grow, and to be secure. But all these could be made to depend on the body, or at least on an embodied sensitivity. A right of speech could, though, be credited to a personalized, human nature. If there is a right to worship it could be attributed to a private person. But all I am now sure of seems to be the person as in and using his body. What was said in *Our Public Life* about the rights which follow from will, the emotions, and the mind are, so far, not justified.

January 19

The department of philosophy at the University of Denver has bought an additional typewriter so that I can have one at the office and one at home. I have been here almost three weeks, and though I have not yet found a good routine for working (which I hope will be remedied by my having a typewriter at home, where this is now being written) I am quite pleased with being here. The students were propagandized before I came, and seem to be very much interested in what I am saying. They are alert, intelligent, and so far come to class regularly.

On Tuesdays I conduct a kind of seminar with the faculty on *First Considerations*. Key passages are read and I am called upon to defend and clarify. The faculty is quite young, and though some of the questions are rather innocent, there are quite a number which are acute and disturbing. The spirit of the faculty is earnest and thoughtful; its outstanding member is Jere Surber. He is a very knowledgeable student of Hegel, and of some of the earlier and later German philosophers. But more than that, he is very quick-witted and perceptive, genuinely concerned with philosophy in a fundamental sense. I think he has great promise. He is being considered for a post at the Catholic University; I do hope that he will be offered it and that he will take it. He will prove to be a great success as a teacher and, for me, will prove to be a constant goad and stimulus. I talk with him on philosophic matters almost every day and find him always alert, acute, and flexible. (I think I am teaching exceptionally well, though I am being asked to teach an hour and a half each session, making three full hours of teaching all squeezed in between 9 and 1.)

The University is south of the city proper, where there is little of interest. There are few movie places, hardly any large stores other than those selling furniture and food. But the mountains are always pleasant to look at; the weather, though colder in degrees from Washington, feels just as mild, in good part because the air is dry and there is little wind. I have yet to get to the city proper, partly because I have been settling in, and partly because it is so far away that I will have to take a bus or a taxi back and forth.

I have also enrolled in a drawing class. This meets on the same days my own classes do, with the consequence that I am somewhat tired when I get there at 2. But I go occasionally and stay only for an hour, picking up some pointers here and there. My things are liked, in part because it is thought that I know what the other students do and that I am breaking away from the conventional, neat, controlled drawings which the others have mastered. But the fact is that I do the best I can, and am not breaking away from anything.

* * *

Scott Aebischer is writing a rather large book covering all that I have written. I met him when I was in California a few months back. I was surprised to see how thorough his knowledge was, how acute his criticisms, how perceptive he was about what was central and what was not. I think his will be a good book, and will help people get to know what in general I am about, and how to come to know a little better what I am saying. He will be sending me chapters as he writes them, and I will make whatever comments I think appropriate. He has at least one advantage over me. I look at my early works through the array of books that followed; he sees them all alongside one another and can make comparisons from a position outside them all. He also should be able to approach them all with a degree of objectivity the author could not manage. Though I do try to keep in mind that my objective is to be a philosopher and not to have a philosophy, or to be primarily concerned with what other philosophies are contending except so far as they throw light on what is ultimately real and true, I cannot avoid being a creature of my own readings, training, and past thoughts and convictions. It would not surprise me to find that his book will outlast most of the others that follow on and even correct his, just as Wm. Christian's book on Whitehead has outlasted most of the others which have improved on his here and there.

* * *

If we approach individual men from the vantage point of the species 'Man' as intensified by language and other social structures, we can be said to know them as men, just so far as they provide moments of articulation for 'Man'. To recognize that an autistic child, an idiot, and the like are human beings in more than a biological sense, is to recognize the biological species to be intensified by various structures, such as tradition, language, work, and to be fully articulated in the sense of having termini in each and every unit in the species. The autistic child is one to whom I speak as I speak to any other human being, with an appreciation of it as having a distinctive human privacy. It does not respond, and does not therefore function as I do, one who can both be addressed and properly respond. Might I not say the same thing of a chimpanzee, and perhaps even claim that it does respond to a degree not possible to the autistic child? I have no doubt, though, that whatever the chimpanzee does, it still is not within the human species. The language I use in speaking to it is human language. If it is trained to behave as if it understood what I said, and even to use signs as though they were intelligent replies to what I am saying, I will at best be related to it and will articulate together with it a human language which intensified, not the human species, but some mixture of human and animal. That language would lack the openings which the human language has, as intensifying the human species, and allowing us to discern and to reach to what is ultimately real. It will be a last horizon, allowing us at most to acknowledge the reality of domains covered by scientific laws, but not the reality of the primary dimensions which those laws exhibit and which are epitomized in openings into what is ultimately real.

I address the autistic child as one who is a unit human, and therefore is able to intensify 'Man'. I address the chimpanzee as what is not human and which, though it may enter into a kind of discourse with me, can have no better role than that of a respondent. A non-responding autistic child is superior to a responding chimpanzee because any movement it makes is inseparable from a privacy which is a terminus for the relational man as intensified by various social structures. If it were said that language, etc. does not reach to that child, one would also have to say that the species 'Man' is then only partly intensified, and therefore not intensively articulated by each human. One consequence would be that I would be denied the status of a unit in a fully articulated intensive 'Man'. For me to be a biological man who has thoroughly intensified this, both as a distinct being and as a unit in a species, I must face other units in that species as equally intensifying. To be sure, some of them are not as developed as I am; they may not speak; they may be seriously crippled; they may not understand and may not be able to treat me as a human. But I can reach them as unit intensive men. When talking to an autistic child I load my speech with a concern which makes the child an adequate terminus. If I expressed such a concern for a chimpanzee, I would fall short of that chimpanzee, precisely because it was not a unit in the human species. There are societies, of course, where the autistic child and even mature, cultivated men—philosophers, saints, artists, scientists, and others concerned with what is excellent or with the public welfare—are abused, debased, or punished. These acts presuppose an antecedent acceptance of the men as unit humans. No matter how narrowly I confine a tradition, a language, work, status, or protection, because I am a human being, I reach beyond those confines to terminate in all other humans. If I did not, I would be a unit man who dealt with some others as if they and I were merely biological entities. Though I know only a few humans, and confront but a few more, I move toward all men through an intensive use of the biological species.

January 20

As a humanized being—a unit in an intensified species, and therefore in a milieu which has a multiplicity of five-fold structures—I reach to all the others. This reaching is achieved by me as a representative, which is to say as having a distinctive privacy maintained against all others, with inalienable rights coordinate with the rights of others, a truth-speaker on behalf of all, one who operates within the orbit of the biological species, and who has a dignity above all other kinds of entities. If I deny or neglect the status of others as similar units, I leave some part of the biological species unintensified, and face others as tools or instruments, and not as the terminus of an occupation with them. If I try to give other types of beings the status of an item in my species, I forge a new species 'Man-x' and intensify this. Though the other types may suffer and be pleased, they cannot terminate my direct reference to them via an intensification of just the species 'Man'.

I reach to all other units in my species via my living through a privacy as a representative of any other. I do this as one who is self-contained, having rights coordinate with theirs, to whom one can look for truth, who has internally intensified the distinctions in the common intensified domain and adopted distinctions there, and who upholds the dignity of man—all these whether or not what I do is known or accepted. My failure to take another unit in the human species to be a human being is a failure on my part to be a full representative.

If I try to represent an animal I would confuse representativeness with substitution. I can substitute for it, plead on its behalf, even lie for it, but only as standing in its place. Were I its representative, instead, I would take the position it presumably would take were it in my position. I am a representative for an idiot, stand for him, do for him what he would do were he in my place. There is a difference then between "Were an idiot in my place (and therefore no longer an idiot but attentive to one) he would do as I do", and "Were a chimpanzee in my place (i.e., no longer an animal) it would do as I do." In both, we imagine a change in role. But the idiot and not the animal is transferred in its entirety, while freed from its unfortunate restraints. (When, in using a metaphor, I envisage myself as an animal, or conversely, what I in effect do is to see what some trait might be like when transposed into another domain.)

Every living being is caught in predicaments which destroy, limit, or qualify it, or prevent it from being in the public world what it is in root. Animals, too, may be in predicaments appropriate to them as animals. I attend to an idiot as one who would be like me could we exchange our predicaments; I attend to the crippled bird as that which would be only like another bird could it escape its predicament. If someone is drowning I swim to him swiftly without allowing my emotions to get in the way, and I grab him roughly for the sake of rescuing him. In effect, I cut through his predicament. How do I know what another is like in a predicament? Is it not because I know him to be a terminus of an intensification which is as broad as the biological 'man'?

I am able to be a representative in two ways. I can represent what others would be like were they in my predicament, and I can represent others as we stand away from all predicaments. In the first way I report what I see with my limited vision and from my particular position. In the second way I report what is objectively the case, having transcended predicaments by reflection, criticism, analysis, comparisons, and the like.

My size, age, color, weight, all that Aristotle called 'accidents', are part of my predicament. I can live through them, struggle with them, or transcend them. In all three ways I can be a representative of others. In the first, I am one who faces some predicament or other; as the second, I am anyone who faces some predicament or other; as the third, I stand alongside them as a privacy facing my predicament. This view is close to that of Plato and others who speak of man as essentially a soul in an alien body, differing from them in a. not accepting the idea of a soul, and b. not accepting the idea that there is a state of existence in which I am in no predicament whatsoever.

What functions as a predicament for a private human being, also has the status of a role in a public world, and serves as a mediator and evidence of what is private. An idiot can be treated as a patient, a ward, someone to guide and perhaps improve, and the adults who attend to him take on the role of nurses, doctors, educators, and the like. The predicament here is a limit of the external world. Were this all, men would be radically divided from one another by virtue of their color, gender, age, and so on. For this or that social structure—language, work, religious practice, social intercourse, and the like—we can then isolate various individuals as alone full members able to carry out their roles, and can treat all others as adjuncts, subordinates, helpers, or merely potential units. Yet all the while, we will know them to be something more. That something more is known when roles are seen to mediate. When the different sexes are reduced to roles, we have them in opposition and, where one side is stronger than the other, subject to discrimination. Taken to express only different predicaments, a difference in gender abstracts from the vital import of the difference, slighting the fact that it is a male and female who are involved with one another, precisely as male and female.

When roles mediate gender and other Aristotelian 'accidents', individuals approach one another as different in role and yet as equally human. The role provides evidence of a private individual. He may be unable to overcome his predicament, and therefore may be unable to express what others can, and therefore will be unable to be a representative for them. The role offers evidence of a private being who is a term for the intensive human interrelationship which encompasses all men. He adopts, sustains, uses the roles as agencies by which to express his privacy. To know a role as providing evidence is to see it not as a position in a public world or in some public transaction, but as expressive, presented, not deliberately though or even knowingly. Each idiot expresses a distinctive privacy; to know this idiot is not to know that. Even when their performances cannot be distinguished, they are in public because they express something not public which is related to all other expressive human privacies as self-bounded, coordinate, intelligibly united, distanced, and of value.

A role in society is carried out by an actual entity. (Apart from this it is internal to a relational complex, attributable to no one). It could conceivably be carried out by a thing, a biological entity, or a man. But if either of the first two, the import of the role will be entirely given by the social situation, and the thing or biological entity would be just a sustainer. Its separate moves, even if they are those which are appropriate to a role, will have to be translated into ones in a public setting before they can be moves of a role. The articulation of a society would then depend on what is not only not social but not human. There would be just movements which were somehow socialized. This is, to be sure, a common way of looking at what men do in society. They are thought to function like things or animals who somehow get caught up in a social setting. So far as they stand away from that setting, they are held not to be human. But then we are unable to account for their responsibility, thoughts, faith, or identity except by taking these to be inversions of public occurrences.

Men provide evidences of themselves as humans by the fact that they hold their roles away from a public setting, thereby providing this with articulations and precluding it from exhaustively defining what is done. The evidence that there is a humanized setting is given by the insistence of the relation connecting units; the evidence that those units have a status apart from the relation is given by the fact that they do not function in absolute consonance with that relation, coming to be and passing away, placing emphases and adding meanings, opposing and obstructing the functioning of the role. An idiot is more than a patient.

Operant conditioning behavior is to be understood in teleological terms. It adds desirable features to particular outcomes, thereby turning those outcomes into inviting prospects. But they are these only for beings with certain interests, appetites, or desires to whom those prospects are inviting. The conditioners do not feed pigeons horse radish, or idiots bird seed. The new conditions which the experimenter introduces must be adopted by the subject, which is to say, the subject must enter into the situation and take something from it on its own terms. Starting from the public situation or from what is introduced, we must say that the subject accepts or assimilates what is offered and does so on its own terms; starting from the subject as in itself we must say that it presents itself in public, and more or less accommodates what is insisted on there.

The initial situation is neither relational nor punctuate. Instead, we have an insistent relation and insistent units. Starting from the relation, we move to what insists on it, or what defies and articulates it; starting from the units, we move to what insists on being present or to what interrelates them in roles.

* * *

From the time of Kant, thinkers have tried to reach the real while taking themselves to be cut off from it. Hegel, Husserl, Heidegger, Wittgenstein all look in a realm of meanings, syntax, universals, connotations for an item which is denotative, referential, which will have a semantical role. But anything they might find will be cut off from the world that is sought just as surely as any other item. Also, they have no reason for supposing that there is a need to find that item unless somehow they were already outside the realm of meaning and in contact with the real.

Only a God who first hears listens. That is why people sacrifice, pray, and plead. These are ways of making a God hear so that he will listen, i.e., attend.

Men must first listen before they can hear. Listening involves a readiness to take something into oneself. Without it, one is assaulted by sounds and acts. To get men to listen we must first treat them as human.

Animals listen in order to hear. Theirs is a listening at the service of what is to be heard. Men, instead, have no need to hear if they have properly listened. This all lovers know.

Feminists risk becoming the inverse of machos, which is to say of becoming females in a public world, overlooking both their own privacies and the privacies of men.

The beginning of metaphysics: "There is this and that", the 'and' having an intrusive moment enabling us to go back toward its source.

The 'this' and 'that' oppose and articulate the whole in which 'this' and 'that' are just terms, and can be recovered in their separateness only by going back to them as able to make themselves present for the 'anding'.

We never express ourselves fully. But only if we do express ourselves with success, are we able to express ourselves further. An idiot expresses himself too poorly to be able to express much more than what he can on his first successful attempt.

January 21

In previous writings I have taken our arrival at actualities to be the outcome of a symbolic use of adumbrative, or of texturizing content, which lets us get to what is increasingly resistant to our advance. The view is oriented primarily toward epistemological issues. One, of course, also moves ontologically since he does get to the actuality. A stronger stress on the ontological side would require us to attend to appearances, and particularly to predicaments so as to allow us to see that they also have the status of roles mediating what we are in ourselves and what we are in a public setting. Instead of attending to the fringes of what we confront, we will then attend to variations in the carrying out of the roles, indicating an inevitable expression of freedom in the very act of sustaining the roles. There are cases where we are unsure whether an individual is alive or not, and must be content to stress the adumbrative aspect of what appears. But it can be well maintained that the acknowledgment of such an appearance already involves a cutting beneath an appearance, or better, the forcing of the appearance away from the context to become primarily the appearance of an actuality.

An appearance, instead of being simply credited to the actuality via a dominant factor, is diversified, nuanced in ways which are intrusive on the appearance. The appearance is then not only something which is charged with an insistence not intrinsic to it, but with variations which require a reference to an independent source. The adumbration of which one makes use is then not simply a judgmental, intensive move, but an ontological abandonment of the appearance, to allow one to face that which is engaged in free activity, making the expression of it (which helps constitute appearances) not simply insistent but unpredictably diversified.

There is a determinateness to what appears, additional to that which is provided by a context. The acknowledgment of adumbration does not take account of that determination, since it does no more than take us toward what is more intensive, without in any way claiming that what we start with already has determinations which the context cannot account for. In addition to an insistence, there are expressions of the individual in depth, and these are present in appearances as variations which would be inexplicable unless referred back to the insistent source. The 'is' that allows us to move in depth in knowing something, is an 'is' charged with multiple factors that cannot be grasped, except as having their source in what lies beyond the 'is'.

When one is unable to discern free variations, e.g., when someone is in a stupor, or is apparently but not actually dead, or is perhaps lost in deadening drudgery, we take the intensified social structure connecting us to be an agency for a penetration beyond what is evident or can be reached adumbratively in a judgment. To be a mature human is to approach other units in the human species as beings who diversify what is made available. They are identified as not only expressing themselves freely, but as freely varying those expressions, filling them out with irregular intensifications. As a consequence, the roles they carry out are to be understood as also being assumed, the assumption of them being manifested in the irregular intensifications. We are confident that there is an individual who produces those intensifications because they are expressed by a single private freedom. The more diverse they are, while allowing for the constancy of the role, the more deeply we must probe to reach their unitary source. Determinate roles and appearances can, therefore, be said to be possibilities apart from the variations that the individual introduces, even though, as integral to the public situation, they are determinate.

We come close here to Kant's solution of the third antinomy, but in another form, for we too are acknowledging that the items interconnected in a single public world are charged with a freedom issuing from a being outside it. This must not, of course, be taken to mean that the public world does not itself exhibit freedom, for activities as in that world are all free in that they turn possible into actual effects. An individual, as a unit in the public world, not only sustains what is manifested, and insists on himself, but charges his expressions and therefore his role with variations.

An animal also charges its expressions and role with free variations. It becomes irritable, obstinate, and even has the role carry appetites and interests. An animal may explore, exhibit curiosity, and not carry out its usual steady roles. It could be said to be free in being able to take on new roles, but not free to add to a role any diversifications—as a man can—which do not contribute to its functioning.

We should expect computers and other machines to function more accurately and steadily than men, and we should expect to be able to train animals better than men, for both things and animals lack that human power which permits them to introduce endless variations in any expression and, therefore, into any outcome of the interplay of that expression with counter expressions.

*   *   *

The foregoing was written after I awakened from a ten hour sleep, did my exercises, rested for about ten minutes, and had my breakfast (orange and coffee). I then went for a two-hour walk, about eight miles, on a beautiful Sunday morning, thinking in part about what I had written, and reflecting as well on what I was doing in this journal. I think this journal shows me primarily in the role of a philosopher, while the systematic works exhibit my philosophy. So far as this is true, it is wrong to take out of the systematic works only what one considers its insights, and wrong to view this journal as exhibiting nothing but a series of dry runs or exercises preliminary to the writing of the philosophy. The two are interrelated, and have marks of one another in them, but on the whole they carry out the two different procedures which must be followed if one is to have a full philosophic career.

Another reflection centered about the observation made regarding Kant: He overlooked at least four points. He did not see that there are is some degree of freedom exhibited by animals. He did not recognize that freedom was expressed dispersively, supposing only that it was punctuate and could not therefore be found evidenced inside the causal world. He did not acknowledge a freedom to be integral to the very process of causality and therefore that it could be found both in the beginning of a causal act when the agent enters into the public world, and also as part of the causal act, enabling the agent to turn a possible into an actual effect. And most important, he did not see that a dispersive act of freedom was followed by a unitary free act of adopting a role through assessment, accommodation, comprehension, personalization, and possession. This free act of adoption, though it comes after the other, is what is known first. A child first knows that it is a me before it knows that it is an I; it takes time before it is in a position to convert "Me am a child" into "I am a child". It starts with its public role as filled out by its me, but must learn to move to its me before it is in a position to move beyond this to the I. It adopts the public child as its own, primarily through assessment, as more or less approved, as more or less to be identified with itself, and then turns around to speak of itself as an I. It does not know the I which possesses and which can even be said to be engaged in a five-fold act of adopting what is present in a diversified form, except by retreating beyond the point where an assessment or some other particular act of adoption takes place.

If there is no adoption of what is publicly and freely diversified, 'me' is properly used, though the use does violate traditional grammar. When the child says "Me is hungry", or "Me tells lies" its 'me' serves to locate who is to be fed or held accountable. There would be no gain for it in saying "I am hungry", but a shift to "I tell lies" can be eventually recognized to allow for the attribution of responsibility to it as a private being.

Do we trace back the free diversifications in public roles of actualities or do we trace back their free adoption of those roles? Apparently we trace back the free diversifications to the point where a free adoption is begun. Do finalities freely adopt the evidences they intrude on actualities? I think not, for they do not then enjoy a new role. The counteraction of actualities neutralizes the action of the finalities, preventing them from doing more than to hold on to what they had made available. But I am not sure of this last point. If it were denied, one could say of a finality, and therefore of a personalized version of one, a God, that it freely adopts, on its own terms, any actuality into which it had intruded. But if this is so, what need is there to make use of evidence and await the acceptance of it by the finality? I faced this question when I spoke in *First Considerations* of the way in which finalities accommodated evidence and evidenced from its side. My engaging in the act of using evidence, and eventually arriving at the evidenced which is to be accommodated by a finality, starts with a product. A finality, instead, starts with what it has reached as the limit of its expressions. In a similar way when I come to know another, as freely adopting what it has freely diversified, I move to that other from the position of the diversified role, and let myself be guided by the free adoption by that other in order for me to get to the point where this freely diversifies itself. The diversification tells me where to look, but the search is for what can itself adopt the content which was diversified.

I do not have this issue entirely clear, in part because I am not yet clear whether or not the actualities and finalities function and are known in similar or in contrastive ways. Does the discussion about the roles of actualities concern them as in relation to one another, and thus as not to be compared with them as expressing themselves with reference to the finalities? If there were such a comparison would we not have a third case where the actualities somehow had to be accommodated by finalities?

In between watching the first half of the superbowl football game between Pittsburgh and Dallas this afternoon, I have been thinking of the question just raised. I think I have been partly misled by my own reference to Kant. His treatment of freedom and causality has to do with two distinct realities of powers. But I began with the problem of the way in which an actuality took account of what it itself was doing in a public setting, and how another could know that it was a free being. The expressions of actualities and finalities are, of course, free; both, too, internalize what is external to them. But unlike actualities in relation to one another in a public world, actualities internalize, not what they are like in a setting provided by others, but the effects of finalities. The finalities, themselves, internalize what the actualities are able to present to them. There is apparently no internalization by actualities of appearances, or of the contexts which the finalities provide. Nor is there any internalizing by finalities of their appearances, or of the localizations which the actualities provide. The only issue is that of seeing how actualities freely diversify positions which are defined within a setting (but which are determined in part by other actualities), and how they freely take into themselves what they are publicly, because of others.

To know another, I start with his freely diversified role (which includes his permanent as well as his adventitious humanized accidents, since these too are partly determined by his being with other men within a humanized domain). I then converge toward his unity, which is to say, I move to him as the being who freely diversifies himself, and who takes the diversified public existence of himself into himself on his own terms. I come to know him by using the diversifications as evidence, and by sympathetically trying to arrive at the point where he is able to diversify and to take into himself what is thereby achieved in the public world. My progress with diversifications is always preceded by a thrust toward another's unitary privacy, which is able to take the diversification in to itself.

I try to take another to be his role, even one freely diversified and freely adopted. But then I lose him. He adopts his role and its diversifications; all I can do is to credit these to him, compress them in him, leaving them always present. He, instead, reduces them by virtue of his assessment and other forms of adoption.

Suppose I said "He likes being a banker", would I be duplicating what he does, since I subject the role of banker to his presumed as-

sessment? I would come closer than I had before, but since I do not
convert the banker into what he is in and of himself through the 'likes',
but always use 'banker' as a term, I still do not do justice to him. The
closest I can come to what he is is to say that his liking, values, or
understanding, etc., have his banking as one of their termini—but that
does not allow me to know the very guise in which the termini are
accepted by him. I know what he does, not the outcome of his achievement. He and I approach the being of a banker from opposite sides; I
know what he does because I find him taking the banker I know away
from me, and reducing it to a freely adopted terminus which he had
freely diversified.

January 22

   In *Our Public Life*, I followed an old practice, and tried to understand what rights men had apart from any bestowal by a state. This
should be done, for otherwise no state could be judged adversely for
not providing for the sustaining or fulfillment of some rights by those
men it does not allow to be on a footing with the rest. I have, though,
found it increasingly difficult over the years to determine just what the
essential claims of man were. In trying to trace them back to the essential
parts of man, I found myself faced with a number of alternative schemes.
Now it is time to try another approach. Suppose it be said that a human
is a person only so far as he natively claims to be part of the totality of
men. He will satisfy one claim by virtue of being a member of the species
'Man'—himself as a body functioning as a unit which has the right to life
and health, and the functioning of a member of the species. He also
claims to be a unit member of any intensification of that species. Accordingly, he will have degrees of viability of different rights, depending
on his capacity to function as such a member. But as soon as he is a
person, which is to say as soon as he privately adopts 'Man', he necessarily
claims to be a unit in a language community, and thus to have the right
to speech, communication, education; to be a unit in a productive community and thus to have the right to work, to be emotional, and creative;
and to be a unit in a culture and thus to have the right to share in and
to contribute to the arts and sciences.

   Each set of rights could be said to be anchored in a distinctive dimension of a private being, though its exercise will involve his entire
privacy and public functioning. The status of a body in the species is
grounded in the sensitivity; language is grounded in the consciousness

and mind; productive power is grounded in the will, and creativity is grounded in responsibility. If one were to take this alternative, the rights will not be located necessarily in the person, but will (as is evident from the consideration of mind, will, and responsibility) belong to the self. The person, then, will just be the individual as laying claim to being a unit in some encompassing relation, with the rights being referred back to the powers in him which are able to carry out such functions. If those powers are not developed, the claim of the person will still hold, but only as having the viable form of a claim against others, thereby enabling him to reach the stage where the rights will be insisted on, and the individual, as a consequence, turned into just a unit in some intensification of 'Man'.

Is a fetus a person? Only if it is not produced by members of a species, and can make a claim on behalf of a unit which is more than a body. When it has no developed privacy would it then not have a right to life? Yes; but so does a cat or an amoeba. The important question is whether it is a person and thus has the rights of a human, including the right to have a human life. It can have these rights only if there is a surplus of usable privacy beyond the person which demands to be realized in the form of units in specialized forms of the species 'Man'. If there is surplus privacy, as there seems to be, but if this is not usable, all one can maintain is that a person claims that he ought to be enabled to attain the stage where the privacy will be usable. At that time he will have the right to attain the stage where he could become a possible unit in some intensification of many. He has the right to mature as a unit which does not yet have certain rights. How does this differ from a child's right to be educated, or cured, or grow?

A fetus has a right to be a person but does not have any personal rights. Its right to be a person is the right to attain the stage where it could claim to be a unit in an intensified form of the species 'Man'. Its right cannot override the rights of persons, and therefore of the mother, but its right cannot be violated without showing the presence of a conflicting superior right. If the right to become a person were raised to the status of a personal right we would, on similar grounds, be in a position to raise the right of a juncture of sperm and egg to become a biological human, to that of a right to be a person.

Against the right-to-life advocates, therefore, I say: the fetus is not a person. Against the abortionists, I say: the fetus has a right to become a person. This right is greater than the right of an animal to be alive and not to suffer, but it is less than the right to life of a human being, and must give way when it conflicts with someone's right to live as a human being.

My death is myself seen from the position of things. A physicalistic view of me takes me to be dead at a particular time, but if it is to take account of me it must still somehow see me as a living unified being functioning from within. I cannot see myself as dead because I cannot take up the position of things without my being a thing. But I can understand the world of things by conceptualizing what they are. Despite a failure when dead to be part of the species 'Man' any longer, others, through rites, burial, and the like, can treat me as an instantiated version of man. Their actions will be somewhat like those involved in our treatments of domestic animals, the major difference being that a community raises both of us to the status of units in a social order, while a living animal, because on a higher level than a dead man, requires a less powerful act of ennobling.

To honor the dead is to perform an exceptional act of bringing something inside the social order. Something similar can be done with a fetus. One can, without anticipating its future status, take it to be in a social order, since it is can receive care, love and be given a name. One will not thereby have made it part of the species 'Man'? No, for intensifications of that into which it is fitted, will be either lent to it or, along the lines of a ritual burial, will be understood to extend to what is not human, thereby bringing it into the human milieu in somewhat the way a domestic animal or even a tool is brought in. It will then be made to carry qualifications which are not native to it but imposed on it, and which it is enabled to hold on by actual men.

A person has the right to demand on behalf of a continuation of himself, as a unit individual, that he be fitted into various intensifications, perhaps in a sequence (allowing for gradual maturation) or all at the same time. If he can also extend the application of the intensification to what is not in the human species (and thereby include animals, fetuses, and the dead), he will bring those non-humans within the orbit of a human milieu.

January 23

A person makes essential claims to be a full unit in the human species and its intensifications. We know another to be a person when we approach him via some intensification, and then find him to have a fully expressed role and to be pulling away, both as a free sustainer of the intensified relation and as a free incipient unit in some other intensification. If we had approached him as a cold-blooded doctor or like some abstracted biologist might, we would take him so far to be a unit in the human species. But we would then also find that he was a person, because of his sustaining an insistent claim to be part of a more intensive context.

The primary intensifications seem to be social structures, dynamic interlockings, and enrichments. These are exhibited in language, living and positive law, convention, established and reasonable ingrained rules of behaving; in work and consumption, play, games, human intercourse; and in common activities of making and appreciating the arts and the sciences. The claim to be a unit in any one of these involves the expression of a distinguishable power—sensitivity in the body, responsible accountability in society, insistence in interchange in the economic and other dynamic domains, and creative liberty in a civilized world.

Sensitivity, responsible accountability, insistence, and creative liberty can all be traced back to distinctive powers of the person. The last three presuppose identity, conscious, mind, will, and I—all divisions of the self. They are most evident when we begin with the individual as a unit in civilization, but they can on reflection be derived from the others and even from the sensitivity, when this is taken to allow not only for feelings of bodily pain and pleasure, but for emotional involvements in social structures, social ongoings, and civilized living.

I have now come back, with some modification, to the views I have maintained earlier. What is most novel is the acknowledgment of civilization as one of the main intensifications; the recognition of the person as making claims on behalf of the units in the species and its intensifications; the awareness of the public presence of the individual as a locus of evidence, in the form of free variations a sustaining of a public role and a claiming (allowing one to move back into him at least to the point where he is seen to make claims in other domains); and the grasp of distinctions of the person, enabling one to become aware of divisions of the self. The view also allows one to see the truth in such common observations as 'Arrest that person' directed at what is locatable and primarily a body; 'Search his person' directed at a clothed man existing under controlling social conditions; 'This is my personal work' referring to what one contributes to a dynamic intensification; and 'He is a vital person' referring to one who is conspicuous in the civilized domain.

I should at last be ready to rewrite *Man: Private and Public*. That work in its first part tries to provide both an anatomy of privacy, with its different positions of emphasis in the person and self, and an account of the way in which the different positions operate on one another. This last has not been rethought in the reflections of the last weeks. I tried to provide a kind of deduction of each of the positions through a synthesis of privacy with some preceding established position, and now suspect that this is only a *tour de force*. Before I can get back to the book, I must get clear as to whether or not to proceed by going through intensification after intensification (rather than dealing with social structures etc., later in the work, as I now have it), and whether or not there is a point in trying to see how different demarcated epitomizing positions in person and self impinge on another.

One of the great breakthroughs of *First Considerations* is the theory of evidence. Two types were there distinguished—evidences for the finalities and evidences for the actualities. There are two others, a purely empirical type, based on the contingent interaction of actualities and used in the ordinary course of conventional tracing back to supposed causes of effects; and another, bearing on the roles which individuals play in common domains, where each, so far as it is a member of the domain, provides evidence of a free expression, a free sustaining, and a free claiming. The first is manifest in the role; the second in the way it is maintained; and the third in a claiming made on behalf of other roles.

January 25

Usually, when I make a number of distinctions, I go on to ask myself whether, in the light of the reality of five primary realities governing all there is, five distinctions ought not to have been made. Sometimes I do find warrant for making them, and then I begin to worry whether or not I have been making arbitrary judgments. But if I do not find them, I worry whether or not I have been sufficiently acute. And this is what is happening as I begin to probe into and reflect on the problem of evidence. The issue has come to the fore because in my discussions with the philosophical faculty at the University of Denver, I have been compelled, in the face of searching questions, to sharpen issues as I had not before. At present, it seems to me proper to say:

Not until we have anomalies do we recognize that we are in a commonsense world. We are in that world before we are aware of the anomalies. When we discover these, and try to account for them, we find ourselves driven to acknowledge the commonsense world with its familiar objects as a base from which we must move, because it is found to be a product—as is evidenced by the intrusive presence and interplay of alien factors. The recognition of these, points us toward what is more stable and intelligible.

Anomalous entities are the product of intrusions interplaying with familiar objects. To attend to these interplaying factors is not to eliminate the anomalies; it is to account for them and to do so by distinguishing and coming to the base of their constituents. The anomalies can be understood in a second way as well, as units qualified both from the side of disruptive agencies and from the side of observers. This way of dealing with them presupposes agencies producing the disruptions, and men who are able to observe. It understands entities to be anomalous because they are the meeting places of disruptions and observations. The pairs of isolated factors—intrusions and familiar objects, disruptions and observers—can themselves be understood to be constituted by one another. And intrusions and familiar objects can be treated as junctures of intrusions and familiar objects. The different products emphasize one of the factors more than the other. For example, intrusions and familiar objects are both factors in anomalies, and products of disruptions and observers. As products, they are of course different from anomalous entities, and from familiar objects. Together with the familiar, the intrusions are factors in disruptions and in observers. Each pair is to be dealt with in a three-fold way—as interplaying intrusions and familiar objects; as constituents of the anomalous; and as terminal objects for both disruptions and for observers. Items in a direct relation to one another—e.g., intrusions in relation to disruptions, anomalies, or observers, are engaged in evidencing one another, without being evidence except for agents.

These observations can be encapsulated in a schema:

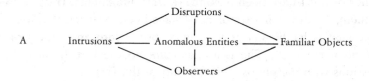

A   Intrusions ——— Anomalous Entities ——— Familiar Objects

We can now go on to take disruptions, intrusions, observers, or familiar objects as a base for another four-fold division. But, before this is done in a concerted metaphysical move to what is ultimately real, we can make use of an analogous table to understand what happens in a world of men. As specializations of the above we have:

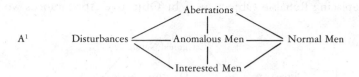

A^1
  Disturbances — Anomalous Men — Normal Men
(Aberrations / Interested Men)

which we can then proceed to examine in the same way we had the more general case.

We progress in a movement to ultimate realities, by replacing anomalous entities by familiar objects. (Had we replaced them with any of the other three we would have moved toward actualities in depth, toward hidden natural causes, or toward knowing beings):

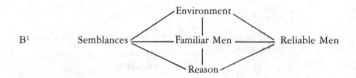

B
  Subjective Appearances — Familiar Objects — Reliable Objects
(Nature / Reasonable Men)

The humanized counterpart of this is:

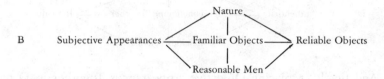

B^1
  Semblances — Familiar Men — Reliable Men
(Environment / Reason)

Replacing Familiar Objects in B by Reliable Objects, we get

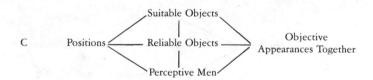

C
  Positions — Reliable Objects — Objective Appearances Together
(Suitable Objects / Perceptive Men)

The humanized counterpart of this is:

C^1
  Free Positions — Roles of Reliable Men — Men Functioning Together
(Free Agents / Persons)

Replacing Reliable Objects in C by Objective Appearances we get

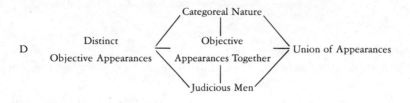

D

The humanized counterpart of this is

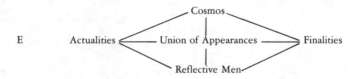

D¹

And finally, replacing Objective Appearances Together in D by a Union of Appearances we get:

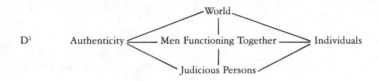

E

The humanized counterpart of this is:

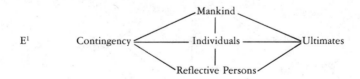

E¹

These tables must be examined separately, and the consequences of the various dissections followed through. Some of the designations undoubtedly will have to be changed. In particular, what must be made evident is how something like a finality can be a primary source and yet be understood to be a result of some union of cosmos and reflective men and, with actualities, not only to be a source of a union of appearances but to somehow help ground a cosmos and reflective men.

Generalizing the above tables we get:

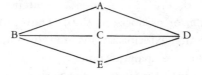

From this we get twelve different types of move:

1. From C to B and D—the use of *evidence,* taking place in five stages from anomalous occurrences to a union of appearances with their evidencing of actualities and finalities.

2. From B and D to C, which is to say from diverse *sources* to the outcome of their interplay.

3. From A and E to C, *qualifications* by distinct entities of a common terminus.

4. From C to A and E, the reduction of qualifications to *limiting determinations* of an objective state of affairs and individuals.

5. From B and D to E, or the *subordination* of ultimate realities within individuals, and particularly men.

6. From E to B and D, or the *horizons* which are the termini of men's reaching.

7. From B and D to A, or the *exteriorizing* of B and D together.

8. From A to B and D, or the activity of *diversifying.*

9. From B to A and E, or the *analysis of punctuate entities.*

10. From D to A and E, the *analysis of finalities.*

11. From A and E to B, or *characterization of actualities,* in the attempt to express their nature as a union of the objective with interested men.

12. From A and E to D, or *characterization of finalities,* in the attempt to express their nature as a union of what is objective and interested men.

In addition, reference is to be made to the direct evidencing of A, B, C, D with reference to one another, which is to say in eight ways. There is no direct evidencing with respect to C, so far as this is absolutely central to all the rest. But it does yield evidences and does function as a limit. It is to be understood in terms of qualifications and sources.

A humanized set of relations comes into focus when we attend to the problems of observation, reasonableness, and eventually the role of the person, where this is understood to be a human being who has the inalienable right, and therefore makes the irrefutable claim, to be a full unit in humanized domains. Though persons can be dealt with as specialized cases of 3, 4, 5, 6, 9, 10, 11, 12, they are also to be seen to as free agents, A. They are therefore to be dealt with as special cases of 3, 4, 7, 8, 9, 10, 11, 12, i.e., not as evidences or sources (1,2), or as subordinating, or as horizons (5,6). They provide qualifications, functioning as limits, exteriorizations, and diversifiers; they provide characterizations and are analytic components.

When we look for evidences of persons in free variations introduced into roles, we deal with them under 3, finding them to have introduced qualifications into acknowledged roles. To know persons, able to function in roles other than those in terms of which we are approaching them as limits under 4, we must grasp them as functioning in some other roles, diversifying themselves in actual free positions together with other men (8). Such a free agent is different from mankind (or the more general case, the cosmos) in that it itself produces diversifications (but without the support of other entities) whereas the latter are diversified by other entities (but not in the absence of a capacity in them to be diversified).

Is it true that every one of the distinguished items can be placed in the C position? If so, every one will be a source of evidences, and be produced by sources, be a locus for qualifications, and be divided into two limits. Objective appearances are able to meet the first two conditions. Are they also loci for qualifications, in somewhat the sense in which a man subjugates finalities and actualities? Can we stretch them out to two opposite limits? If an objective appearance could subjugate the region that is occupied and the occupation of it to itself as a single entity, it would seem to have become, not an appearance but an actual entity, unless we understand the subjugation not to presuppose that it already exists as an entity, able to do something to the realities on which it in fact depends as sources.

Apparently, I overstated the case. The only replacements are of what is truly central by what is less derivative, more concrete. If so, should we not at least be able to replace C by B, which is to say actualities or what is some limited case of this? But we cannot include the actualities, for we end with actualities (and of course the finalities). If actualities are able to occupy the C position they are able to evidence something even more concrete, sources of evidence. But what should be said of replacements before that point? I don't now know. For the moment, I think, I must allow the present schema to be final. But the matter must be reexamined. Also, something has yet to be said about the individual actualities as subject to the finalities in the form of transcendentals.

If I believed in a God, I would suppose him to be struggling to get to the stage where he was worthy of being worshipped. The world he was supposed to have created is so poorly organized that he must have been thinking of something else at the time. I would love him the way I love another, wanting nothing but good for him. I would be content with whatever he was able to give me, and not lament the fact that he could do no more at the time. I would think that his love was a blundering love, not altogether adjusted to the beloved. He would want nothing but good for me, but would not be able to give it to me, any more than I could give him all the good he needs. Instead, he would want me to make myself as excellent as I could, he supporting me as much as he was able, consistently with my being myself and doing all the work. We would help one another, I feebly and he somewhat more, but less than he might since he would be so involved in getting to a stage where he was worthy of my and other men's faith in him. The extant religions would be seen by me to be anticipatory, celebrating the last days, the Second Coming or the coming of the Messiah, the day of final judgment, the coming to be of a new de-temporalized era. He would then be worthy of worship but would have no longer any need of us, thereby making unnecessary any further time.

Atheists are excessively occupied with God. It is better to be indifferent, to match the possible attitude of any God there might be. This, of course, is not a religious any more than it is an irreligious view. It is non-religious.

If the devil were as clever and as powerful as he is claimed to be, he would speak through preachers, prophets, rabbis, priests.

I reject the idea of the devil; that is why I can continue to respect those who are religious.

January 26

There is nothing in the way of our replacing of anomalies by intrusions, familiar objects by subjective appearances, reliable objects by positions, joined appearances by distinctive objective appearances, and then proceeding to treat the replacements in C as providing evidences, being explained by sources, and being understood in terms of qualifications and limits, just as had been done with respect to the initial set of replacements, examined yesterday. All would be products of private powers and external others which they would evidence, and which were their sources. All could be conceived to receive qualifications from attentive beings, and a background which could be understood to be the entities stretched to extremes.

In the previous discussion nothing was said of the various other ways in which finalities are operative with reference to actualities, besides that of interplaying with them to constitute objective appearances. In addition to contexts which interlock with but dominate over the expressions of actualities to constitute a domain of appearances, *First Considerations* remarks that there are alien insistencies which provide determinations, transcendents which govern actualities, qualifiers which characterize actualities without governing them, and a cosmic pattern which holds actualities together in the cosmos. It is now not as evident to me, as it apparently once was, that these are important distinctions, or that all of them are on the same level. But it suffices to raise a new issue.

Finalities function at least as transcendents, encompassing each actuality in its entirety, and provide the actualities in themselves with determinations. Do they thereby provide evidences of themselves? Evidently they do. This though, must be shown to be so, by first attending to the alien nature of the global features that control individual actualities, and to the actualities as realities in themselves as necessarily indeterminate and yet having some determinations. These cases arise because finalities are able not only to have expressions of themselves interlock with countering expressions of actualities, but can also cut past the expressions of actualities to deal with the actualities themselves. In the diagrams of the other day, C would be displaced toward D. One could then envisage A and E remaining as they had been, or themselves being displaced to the same extent that C was. The integrity of B, the actualities (or other items which are eventually made to give way to the actualities in the course of the examination) seems to require that A and E remain unchanged in position, and therefore to have a slanted reference to C.

When actualities in themselves, themselves, and by themselves, are placed in C, a reverse displacement of C is made, with corresponding reverse slants for A and E. Our grasp of an actuality in itself, consequently, will allow it to be understood from the same positions from which we understood the finalities, and saw them both as evidenced by and as providing sources for C (a domain of appearances). If use were made of the diagrams, one could then start with anomalies and observers in the positions A and E, and identify intrusions as coming from a greater internal distance with reference to the anomalies and observers than one usually does.

All this has interest and deserves exploration, but I must restrain myself some if I am to get on with the study of persons and to radically revise *Man: Private and Public*.

By pursuing the expressions of actualities back to their source, I move toward the actualities as by themselves yet evidencing finalities in the role of transcendents. As I move further into them, I find them to be determinate, though as in themselves they should be indeterminate. The determinateness of the actualities as in themselves, evidences the action of the finalities on them, beyond the point where the finalities help constitute appearances. The actualities, too, are found to be together. As so together, they evidence the finalities as qualifiers, enabling the actualities to be instances of the finalities and therefore to be in a position to function as terms, and then to be related in a cosmos, thereby becoming units in it. This last is what is specialized by various species. If the species is 'Man', this in turn is specialized by the various intensifications which constitute social contexts.

January 30

I seem to be saying two different things about actualities in themselves in *First Considerations*. I say that they cannot be real or unreal, and so on, and also that they are distended. If I can say that they are distended, I ought also to be able to say that they have other characteristics matching finalities other than Existence. I should say that they are insistent as substances, self-bounding as beings, articulative as natures, and assessive as unities. I do say some of these things in various places, but they should have been expressly remarked in *First Considerations*.

There should also be characterizations of the finalities that pertain to those finalities in themselves, and which can be understood to come to expression in the form of counteractivities to the expressions of actualities. Would it be enough to say that Substance has an affiliative power, Being a coordinative power, Possibility a rationalizing power, Existence an extensionalizing power, and Unity an ordering power? No. If the lead of *Modes of Being* is followed I should also say that these powers enable the different finalities to have the others in subordinate roles. I should also have to say that the evidenced which was pertinent, to Existence, would be a limited region of extension, one still partly tainted with the distension of the actualities, and that the finality in accepting it frees it from the distensiveness, to enable it to become absorbed in the finality's sheer extensionality. The power of Existence would be exhibited in its absorption of the evidenced, and in its intrusion on the actualities, but it would be credited with the power apart from these, in the double sense of potency and effectiveness.

February 13

I know I am ignorant, because what I encounter is met as that which is being given a determinateness. I face areas of indeterminateness, which are being insisted on by a determining power.

I know that there are necessary truths, for I find that when I accept certain formal suppositions others are inescapable, that they are mathematically or logically required.

I know that there is a good which I ought to realize because I know myself as imperfect and therefore as being measured by what ought to be but is not actualized.

I know that there are laws of nature, because I find that despite my presence here I am forcefully related to others with consequences which I sometimes rationally can foresee.

I know that there is an objective state of affairs, because I can see myself as no more and no less real, self-bounded, than others are.

I know that I have various rights, for I know that I am a person. I know that those rights are on a footing with the rights of others because I know them to be persons. I know them to be persons because when I confront them, I know that I am ignorant of some things about them, that they are sustaining necessary truths by their privacies, that they have a dignity and value which I must yield to in the sense of judging various acts as good or bad in relation to them, that they are in nature with other things forming part of a single 'they', subject to its own conditioning, and that I, with them and all else, exist within the compass of common constraining conditions.

In the past I have paid attention to the rights we have, but have not concentrated particularly on one peculiar very important right, that of property. There seem to be two dominant views about this right. It is thought to be achieved in a world where everything belongs to all, or in a world where nothing belongs to anyone. In either case, property rights can be said to be achieved through individual acts of work, possession, or need. The relation of this right to the initial situation is not easy to determine on either theory. Both seem to suppose that the individual is a kind of delimiting agent existing within a common setting. I think it is more correct to say that property is common to a number of men, but only so far as those men are already together in some other way. Those men are able to have and exercise rights to common property so far as those men are able to enter into another kind of juncture than that which they faced when they were humans in a world which was either common property for them all or was the property of none of them.

The problem of acquiring private rights is the problem of the passage from one way in which men are together and are thereby related to what is not theirs or what is not involved in that togetherness, and another way in which they are together as involved with what before was not pertinent. The delimitation of a common or neutral domain may allow one to speak of an individual's possessions, or of his right to use, but it cannot accommodate his right to or not to transfer, exchange, bequeath. These require some way of overarching a number of individuals and dictating to them what they can and cannot do. The transition to such a new system, with its distinctive articulations and compulsions is a movement from a society to a state. It presupposes an untapped specializable power lying beyond the social power that otherwise would alone govern the men.

February 15

Yesterday's suggestion did not take adequate account of the complexity of human society and the fact that it is in possession of many goods. Every society has well-established rules; a number of interlocked roles; cooperation and interchanges in the market, communication, festivals, and war; characteristic ways of effective action in production, exploration, and hunting; myths, ideologies, morality, and religious beliefs. These are not carefully distinguished, and the individuals in the society often move readily from one into another. The entire complex is set in a world which, from the position of the society, is its property, not in the sense of a right but in the sense of a kind of store or resource from which it draws as it wishes or can.

We begin to move away from a society when one of the strands becomes dominant and definitory, with the other strands serving either as subordinate factors or as supportive ones. When the rules become dominant we begin to have laws, enactments, definitions of what can be done and not done. Individuals become distinguished as possessing rights and duties with respect to one another in accord with the understood laws, which, of course, need not be written down, but must have the backing of other strands. When the fact of roles becomes dominant, we have a well-ordered society, with different individuals being required to fill certain posts and carry them out in relation to one another. This strand, too, needs the backing of force in the shape of public opinion and action; it too has a kind of rationale, and the roles have both an equal standing and a difference in value. When the market and other places, in which individuals have positions where they are coordinate, become dominant, we emphasize the creative, as well as the interinvolvement of men. When the myths and other expressions of a mythology are to the fore, we have the subjection of the whole to some value. In the last two cases, too, the other strands play a role.

On the present view, there is a kind of property belonging to everyone, or to no one, but not to them as a set of disjunct individuals nor to them as forming a unified body, or as outside a society altogether, but as units in a society. It is the society which has the property to begin with, where 'property' is anything other than what is part of that society. A society has no rights to the property; it just has it as its possession in the sense of both using and consuming it, and turning to it as a source for what is to be used and consumed. The society acts through individuals and these, no matter how well-habituated and regulated, have their aberrational moments. Also, each man inevitably occupies some place which another might want to occupy, eats some food that another might want, and the like. The difficulties which they may have with one another are often enough settled by the established rules or by yielding to the established ideology.

If one is to have a clear knowledge of just what one can and cannot do, one must make roles, demands, and assessments explicit. This is not done except under the pressure of need—or under the questioning of visiting anthropologists. The need is to know just what one can and cannot do, what one must and what one need not do, a matter that becomes important as soon as the society becomes fluid, large, and heterogeneous. Rules are then expressed laying out rights and duties. These are not the rights and duties of specific individuals. The rules are given the form of an interlocked set of requirements. Only when an individual insists on a right, is made subject to a duty, or is allowed or denied a privilege, is he caught up in a formulated, articulated system of rights, duties, and privileges, and thereby becomes a political entity. There is no transition from the claims of individuals to the achievement of an encompassing whole in which their claims are adjusted; from the very start, there is a common world. Soon there are explicitly formulated rights, duties, and privileges all formally interlocked; soon there is the entering into that domain, or the being forced to submit to it through the power of the other dimensions in the society, including even the rules that were followed without being explicitly formulated, and even in some cases the very rules that have been explicitly formulated.

A Hobbesean would object, perhaps, to the idea that a society should be taken as a beginning point in a study of rights, politics, and justice. He cannot, I think, avoid recognizing that men belong to the same species, and that this is necessarily intensified in the form of something like a society because different individuals in that species have different roles in relation to another. There is nothing in the foregoing account which denies that individuals have rights of their own, and that they look to some common power to help them translate and satisfy these in public. The area of that translation and satisfaction is already determined by the rules, and eventually the express system of rights and duties, when these dominate over the other dimensions of a society. Until we have such a system of rights and duties, there is no place to which an individual can look for the translation of his rights. And if the system is not backed by the other dimensions of the society there is no way he can be assured that the translated rights will in fact be satisfied.

A man might protest on behalf of himself or others that a confronted system of rights and duties does not provide a translation for his rights, that it provides a support but no proper translation; or that it does neither. If it does not provide a proper translation for the rights he has, it is a system which is unjust in that it is not appropriate to the rights; if it does provide such a translation but does not support the outcome it is unjust in the sense of being unfair, not allowing him and others to be dealt with according to the system to which they belong in principle. His complaint, of course, may be unjustified. He may have misconstrued the rights that he intrinsically has; may have misunderstood the way they have been translated into publicly viable rights; or may have not seen that they were given all the support that they can have. But so far as a man's private rights are not translated into the rights of a system of rights and duties, the system fails to do justice to what he rightly claims. So far as the rights are not supported in a properly translated form, he is not treated fairly since what should be supported is not.

A translation should take an individual claim and place it in a setting where it is limited and supplemented. The translation is one with the acceptance of the publicly available individual in that system, while he continues to have justified private claims. But he has no private right to have, use, or dispose of property, if 'private right' means (as I have taken it to mean) a claim following on some intrinsic dimension of man's privacy. We can say that an individual can make a private claim to property in the sense that he can claim to belong to the world ruled by the system of rights and duties directed at society's world of goods. His claim is intrinsic and of his essence in the sense that he makes it not only on behalf of some power in him (which is what private rights do) but also for the sake of being in a public world with other men, first as in a common society, and second as in refinements of this, one of which is a backed system of rights and duties. This system, of course, is not necessarily the one that prevails. He claims a place in one that ought to be. Accordingly, he appeals not to the actual system of rights and duties that the society makes possible by its rules, but to an ideal system that the actual system should realize. The appeal is to a system that is implicit in the actual system and is distorted by this, not to an ideal beyond the actual system. In the latter case, it would not necessarily have any bearing on the actual system, and be no more than a desirable prospect.

An actual system of rights and duties has to be sanctioned by an ideal, and therefore by the desirability or necessity that the rules, which are operative in a society, not only have a dominant role but exemplify justice—which is to say, provide the rights and duties that answer to what men are in themselves while they are with one another in public.

Individuals make the dominant strands be what is needed by those individuals. It is not that men must first know what they want and then emphasize this strand or that. The adventitious appearances of the strand, say as a set of rules or interlocked roles, alerts the individual to an opportunity to express himself.

A man becomes aware that he is one who is not fully expressed in his society when he confronts some emphasized strand and recognizes that it enables him, while still in himself, to be with others. He therefore turns to the system of rights, the interlocked roles, the market, production, or values as a locus for himself as in himself with others in themselves. But he then finds that the form in which they in fact are being presented by an actual society is not that which he himself needs. He sees the actual forms, which the society presents via the ideal that they partially exhibit, for he sees what is exhibited as that which is to accommodate what men are in themselves. The point seems evident with respect to rule, roles, and basic beliefs. It is harder to see that it holds with respect to cooperation and interchanges, or with respect to effective action. But the market, communication, festivals, and war are faced in terms of desire, need, what is really intended; and effective action in production, exploration, and hunting is grasped in terms of what one expects, plans, what satisfies and completes. Of course, a man may be aware of himself as deserving expression and some kind of translation and support in the public world and can therefore emphasize some strand in his society as needing an idealized form. But at least in the beginning of the development of mankind, the operation must begin with an acknowledgment of a strand which had been adventitiously emphasized by society, and which allowed the individual to discover himself to be one who can be himself while with others in an idealized version of this.

Mankind has only slowly come to recognize the rights that individuals have. Many of these have come into focus because of the abuses to which men were subject. Such abuses are felt to defy men's endeavor to be in themselves at the same time that they were together within the strands that their society provided. The men feel abused because a strand is so structured or insisted on as to make the men unable to accept it without frustration or self-denial.

An emphasis on a strand on the part of society, usually accidentally through the coming to the fore because of some circumstance met or even because other strands were for the moment muted, requires an individual to engage in a new act if he is to take account of it. That new act begins with him in his privacy. The very acknowledgment then of a strand that happens to be to the fore requires him to start away from the social setting in which he has been content to live unreflectingly. The very acknowledgment of a system of rights and duties, adventitiously made prominent, forces him to move back into his privacy, and therefore to see the system as one which should accommodate him. The acknowledgment of a strand is immediate and submissive; only much later does he reflect or understand what it is to which he is submitting, and which reveals an actual strand to be somewhat distortive of an ideal.

Though a man enters into the system of rights and duties or any other strand which happens to be dominant in a society (from his own perspective and as that which allows him to be himself together with others), what he acknowledges is their common good. He shares in that common good, not because he is seeking it, but because he is concerned with entering into a socially justified strand on behalf of what he is. His action is not selfish, if by this one means a concern for what benefits him alone. It is also not altruistic, if by that one means an endeavor to do good to others. It is an individual action by which he attains a position in what has an equally appropriate place for others who also are beings making claims, both on behalf of what they privately are and on behalf of their being together.

February 18

Individuals provide a grounding for the common contexts in which they function together. The grounding enables the contexts to be more than interlocked sets of roles, which might never be filled. A set of roles provides the individuals who accept it with material and satisfactions they otherwise would not obtain. The satisfactions answer to the individuals as at a greater depth than that at which they had originally entered a context, with the consequence that the individuals are then in a position to enter into other contexts.

A state originates when a society satisfies individuals in such a way that they focus on and thereby make steady some particular context. Did they not do this, there would be just an irregularly interplaying set of contexts, the natures of which were neither clear nor marked off from one another. In a state, a dominant context which happens to come to the fore is given a standing over against the others. Those others quicken and support it, enabling the dominant context to have a prescriptive character.

A state exhibits a set of interrelated rights and duties. This came into being by accident, and was then faced by individuals as answering to what they are on a level below that in which they function in the society. The individuals from that level turn to the state (not as presenting just that particular set of rights and duties) in the form of an assumed instantiation of what men require—which is to say, in the form of an ideal set of rights and duties that would not only satisfy men but enable them to pass from a life in the state to a life where they were occupied with more ultimate realities. Since a state does not know of or consider the ideal set of rights and duties, those who insist on that ideal set are, for it, just as much in opposition to it as those who insist on some other set, or who ignore it altogether.

A state makes use of the force provided by the contexts which it dominates and the goods with which these are involved, in order to force the individuals to conform to its patterning of rights and duties. This forcing is a punishment on behalf of the actual set of rights and duties that the state presents, despite the fact that individuals enter into that set—if they enter into it at all—for their own benefit and in the light of what they ideally require, or on other conditions. Once some individuals have accepted an actual set of rights and duties characteristic of a particular state, they are in a position to function as its agents. They may then make others live in accord with the state's set of rights and duties.

The punishments that a state provides, though they may be carried out with a sense of vengeance or in order to reform, are primarily for the sake of making individuals function as units in its set of rights and duties. Its task is to make them conform. Vengeance expresses the attitudes of individuals who object to the benefits obtained by those who neglect or refuse to share in the system of rights and duties; efforts to reform are for the sake of making men be more ready to assume positions in a system of rights and duties than they had been before. But what the state requires is that they conform. Punishment is the reassertion of its system of rights and duties in the face of violations. If a state imprisons violators of its set of rights and duties, it does not let them live as others do. But the prison should make evident the inescapability of the prevailing system of rights and duties. It should keep the prisoners out of a system in which they did not function properly, only in such a way and for such a time as is required to enable them to share in the system as others do.

The view that the object of imprisonment, or in general, punishment, is rehabilitation, supposes that the individual had already been in the system. It would be more in consonance with what in fact is needed and occurs, to view imprisonment as a kind of education, enabling one to enter into the system in a way and to a degree in which he had not entered before. The education is not moral in the sense of trying to convey the idea that what was done violates some trans-political norms; a state may in fact fall far short of what such norms require, concerned as it is primarily with insisting on itself. One who sees his state as corrupt, as not properly instancing the system of rights and duties which answers to what he is in root, needing support of the system in order to express what he is in himself while functioning together with others, from the position of the state is no better than one who does not conform to demands of the state for less idealistic reasons. A justification for revolution, rebellion, and the like, on behalf of the principles of justice and absolute right, rests on a trans-political basis—a greater good which requires a different kind of state, able to satisfy on a deeper level.

Political action to get a better state attends to the ideal which the state has presumably distorted, and tries to rectify the state so that it conforms to that ideal. That the state did in fact distort the ideal is known only if one attends to the ideal itself—and that requires one to move to a greater depth within himself in order to be able to focus on and share in the ideal. He would have to move from the state in the same way that he had moved from society, and do so on behalf of a level of himself which the state itself enabled him to achieve. Only then can he look to the ideal, as carried by the state, in order to attain a still better stage where the ideal is dealt with independently of the state.

What is true of a system of rights and duties and the ideal that it is to exemplify, holds also of language, the ways in which individuals cluster and disperse, their interlocked tasks, and their common ideology. All these are patterns in a society. All are occasionally focused on. Each is backed by the others. Each sets a stage in which individuals can enter from a depth below that which is required for their participation in a society where these various patterns are not carefully distinguished and are only adventitiously and unsteadily to the fore. Men's errors, their violations of custom, their failures to contribute to common activities and production, and their violation of common ways of evaluating all, are also properly corrected by a punishment which brings them to the level where others are.

The educational role of a state must be supplemented by an adjustive. Those who violate the rights of others are to be denied the benefits they may have derived. Usually, this has to be done by producing equivalents for the injuries they produced. There may also have to be non-monetary equivalents provided for financial losses, since the perpetrator may have no property of his own. It is dubious that imprisonment alone will provide a satisfactory equivalent. One must make the perpetrator engage in a modified form of compulsory activity and thus be subject to a kind of imprisonment (which, of course, makes him subject to the state). In addition, the victim should be compensated. Usually the perpetrator cannot do this. But there is no reason why the state should not provide the compensation, since it failed to educate the perpetrator enough or properly. The perpetrator, of course, can be compelled to work in publicly desirable areas, and thus in the end, on behalf of the state. But this does not yet provide compensation for the victim. Whatever values accrue from a perpetrator's required work should be used to contribute to the compensation which the victim deserves, because he had been deprived of what is his right, by a failure on the part of the state to prevent the right from being denied or abridged.

There are some who want punishment to serve as a deterrent of others who might otherwise commit the same or similar crimes. Putting aside the question as to whether or not a punishment of one will serve as a deterrent for others, a supposed deterrent in the form of a punishment of an offender has no warrant. It is not just to make one man, guilty of a crime, function as an educator for others, particularly when the education is performed by him against his will and desire. Others should be warned or stopped if they are about to or are inclined to violate rights. It may even be desirable to issue a general warning to the people. But it is quite another thing to make an individual, convicted of a crime, function as an agent by which others are alerted or warned and (in that sense) educated.

March 3

I have just returned from the services and funeral for Vernon Sternberg, the editor of the So. Ill. Univ. Press and a warm friend, to whom I had dedicated one of the volumes of this series, with whom I spoke about at least once a month, corresponded with more often, and had long since overcome the kind of adversary relation that authors almost automatically assume toward editors. Confronted with the deaths of others whom I have known intimately for as long as and as well as I knew Vernon, I usually found myself in good control of my emotions. A day or so later though, I might find myself suddenly falling down, becoming confused, having pains in my back and other parts of my body. But this time I found myself caught emotionally; I could not avoid having my eyes tear and my voice break when I thought about him, when I saw his son, Jonathan, when I saw, spoke to, and went to the gravesite with his wife, Jean.

I was asked to speak at the memorial service, and there tried to convey what I had been going through the past two days, and what this meant about Vernon. I thought that I could not capture for myself just what his essence was; 'gentle innocence' I thought, was, at least an outstanding feature. He gave himself to his work as an editor with an energy, concentration, and selflessness that won the admiration of the people who worked with him, his authors, and those involved with other presses. He was constantly calling my attention to books which he published by other authors and which he wanted me to read, and I found that he told others about my books. Inevitably one felt part of the enterprise of the press. It was but a step to feel part of the establishment, and to be involved in his family. The effect was to make him permeate my life. Had he been insistent on himself, had he urged the interests of the press over all, had he kept his relation to me to a polite interchange of an editor with his author, I would undoubtedly have been somewhat saddened by his death. But I was overwhelmed. I found that in his quiet, unobtrusive, unselfish way he had become a part of me.

I rarely reflected on what he was; I joked with him, argued with him, entertained him, and was entertained by him. But not until the irrevocable fact of his death was before me, did I really think of what he was and what he meant to me. Now I see more clearly than I ever have that the fundamental value in human existence is expressed in a love and friendship given with a minimal of ego-involvement, that one makes an impact on fellowman and gives his own life an importance for others just by being genuinely interested in promoting their welfare and (particularly authors) the work to which they have given a good part of their lives and thought.

When I first went to the Southern Illinois University Press (on the suggestion of Robert Brumbaugh) with *Modes of Being*, which Yale had turned down (I think on the advice of my chairman, Charles Hendel), Vernon wrote that he was building a fairly new press, and that he would be able to devote a great deal of time to my book, particularly since they did not have many books to deal with at that time. That honesty won me. Later, when he answered my question "Were you to leave the press, what should I do?" with "Stay with the press" he won me completely, for I knew he thought highly of my work and that it might have been to his advantage for him to go to another place with a number of established authors. When I went abroad, I found that the university was known only because people knew about the press. Whenever I spoke to people about books, particularly those involved in university publishing and its kind of book, I found that Vernon was known for his industry and independence. I think there was some resentment on the part of people involved in other presses because of his refusal to continue to be part of their association. I do not really know if he was right not to be part of it—I am inclined to think he should have remained in it, and should have done what he could to improve it from within. Some of the works he published were undistinguished, and like so many other presses, his press published works in recent years which were not as elegant or as well-bound as those published in previous years.

I found it always pleasant and easy to visit the press; everyone in the place with whom I made contact seemed to be at ease, interested, in good humor; there was nothing like the bustle and sense of self-importance that seem to pervade other presses, particularly those that are long established. Nor was there the kind of neglect and unworldliness which I felt pervaded the atmosphere of other young presses, particularly those away from the East Coast. There was a self-confidence and a professional air about the people, and their relationship to Vernon was easy and pleasant. Vernon had his own ideas of how a book should appear; he apparently read my manuscripts, though I never did get clear, well-articulated statements of what he thought about their contents. For the most part, I think my own books were well-done; I gather their sales, and the sales of number of other books published by the press, are about as good as those published by other presses, at least in the field of philosophy. I liked his policy of not remaindering books and of keeping them in print; I liked his readiness to consider reprinting books which other publishers had let lapse—*Man's Freedom* and *Reality* for example.

I did have a feeling for a long time that there was a sense of being inferior that pervaded the whole of the university; it looked with some awe and fear at the so-called Ivy League universities and their presses. But as time went on, and as the books published by the press became known—some of them receiving reviews on the front pages of leading book reviews—the press seemed to be more and more confident of itself. (I am not sure whether or not this sense of accomplishment and excellence characterizes the university as a whole.) I think it was Vernon himself who brought this change about, not by any assertion, or comparisons, but just by attending to the task of trying to get and to publish good books. It was that determination which, no matter how much self-involvement may have been at the base of it, affected me and, I think, other authors, his staff, and others who came to know him, if only in the course of cursory exchanges. He was occupied with doing his job, concerned with his particular authors, interested in what they were doing. The result was that he became an integral part of them, without their knowing it and, I am confident, without his even suspecting that it was happening.

His wife, Jean, and his son, Jonathan, without any effort on his part, were brought into my life as well, I think in the same manner in which I was brought into his life, the works of other authors, the people at the press, and the work they were doing—quietly, unknowingly, as a mere consequence of his neither excluding nor deliberately including them, neither emphasizing nor minimizing them, but just taking their presence and meaning to be a continuous part of the ongoing life to which he was giving his full attention and devotion.

It still astonishes some that I began with the press some twenty years ago when I was a professor at an Ivy League school; it still astonishes some that I have continued with it ever since. But it was a wise choice and a sound one, and I am glad that I had the wit to do it. Though my relation to the press was through him, and though he epitomized the press for me, I will continue to publish with it, not only because he so advised me, not only because they have so many of my books and I have time to publish but few more, but because his values, spirit, and standards will prevail there for quite a while no matter who takes over the job. The kind of vital import that he had for me I know he had for other authors, and I think I sense that he had for the people who worked with him. As long as those who knew him are about, I think his appreciation of books, his desire for excellence in their contents and their appearance, his readiness to take on novel projects and to make innovations, his patience with authors and others, will continue to be felt. But whether it is or not, I think what he was will prove to be so integral part of the being of those who had come to know him, that even if they tried, they would not deviate far from the ideals and practices which he carried out.

Strangely, though I do not believe that he knew of this feeling in me or other authors, I do not think that there is anything to regret in not having said or conveyed it to him while he was alive. That is due, I think, to the fact that his persistent, ongoing deep concern, his involvement in his authors and in the publishing of their works, already absorbed such a judgment. Though he may not have known of it, and though others like myself may not have ever had it to the fore of their consciousnesses, I think it was present and in that sense, known the way one knows the weather or the time, while absorbed in something else. The gentle innocents will inherit the earth because they have made their presence and import unmistakeably and inescapably felt by the rest as they go about their own tasks, pursue their own interests, and impress their individual natures and desires on others.

* * *

A venture along the lines of a French essayist, prompted by readings in Foucault, Sartre, and an American imitator, Susan Sontag:

Only the atheist really believes in God. The fierceness of his rejection establishes God as the infinitely remote, the very opposite of a corrupt man. The pious reduce God to a larger version of themselves. They make him in their own image, a fact which excites the atheist's disgust. The defiant cry "God does not exist" challenges man's easy acceptance by a negation which is but the surface of a deep affirmation. The atheist, unfortunately, is too occupied with God to be able to do justice to what else God is and what else there may be. Only one who knows how to despise every man knows the exquisite pleasure of loving all mankind. None can do this as well as the atheist whose ever-unreachable God is so transcendentally good that there is no way of tolerating anyone except by a gratuitous act of love. That love is narcissistic precisely because it is gratuitous. Because one loves other men for no reason, one is at last able to find the only reason for loving oneself, not only because one is a man like them, but because a love that is freely given suffices to show that one is to be loved above all.

What have I done? I have taken some conventional affirmations and forced them through a process of arbitrary denials and free associations, which could have gone in another direction, with similarly arresting and willful results. I paid no attention to the need to have one sentence have some bearing on what had preceded it, to the need to develop any theme, or to the desirability of offering some argument. It is not clear to me why so many young people are attracted by anything done in this manner, or why they think they have learned something after they have gone through the exercise.

March 20

Since the last entry I have done no writing, for I have not been able to get my current study into focus. But I have not been altogether idle. I have been teaching. And I have gone over the edited manuscript of 'You, I, and the Others' with considerable care, making a great number of changes. These have been mainly in matters of emphasis and style, but in some places there have been needed refinements and some important changes made.

'You, I, and the Others' is somewhat parallel to *Beyond All Appearances*. Just as that work explored the main moves to be made toward the finalities—systematically pursued in *First Considerations*—so this explores the main moves and pivotal points in a study of man's interiority. But I am finding it hard to get a clue on how to conduct a systematic study in this area. Part of the trouble is that I already know too much, and have difficulty in bringing all that knowledge into some kind of order. I know that an adequate account must find room for and explain man's identity, responsibility, I, rights, interest, desire, and his status as a you for others and a me for himself. A satisfactory account will also deal with intention, mind, decisions, private accountability, sensitivity, consciousness, the living of a human body, the nature of privacy, self, and person.

At present, in some divergence from the manuscript which I have taken with me (and which dissatisfies me because it is not sufficiently well-justified and because it proceeds in a somewhat mechanical manner) I now envisage man in terms of three triangles, the base of one of them being stretched between the apexes of the other two. This triangle has an apex in identity, and the other two terminal points in the I and rights. The identity is related to the I by responsibility, and to the rights by claims. The entire triangle is privacy.

One of the subordinate triangles I have called 'the person'. Its apex is rights, and the other two terms are desire and the you (me approached externally by the I). The rights are related to desire by private accountability, and to the you by a conscious sensitivity.

The other subordinate triangle is the self. There an apex I is related by intention to a transcendentally conditioned unity, and is related to interest by decision. (No provision evidently has been made for mind or reason, unless one were to say that reason is one side of intention, and mind one side of decisiveness.)

For the present it seems to me that it is necessary to move from the you to rights for a ground and that rights (and the I and identity also) provide self-contained unifications of the other terms in their triangles. It seems that privacy, self, and person are agencies for equalizing the various dimensions of their respective triangles; that explanations for what is true of the I, rights, the transcendentally conditioned, interest, desire, and you are to be found in the relations connecting the appropriate apex with them—responsibility, for example, connecting identity and the I; that I and rights, the transcendentally conditioned and interest, desire and you are paired, and provide one another with determinations; and that you, transcendence, I, rights, and identity stand out as providing basic unifications.

There are a number of procedures involved in these classifications. Each item is seen to have two sides; each is subject to analysis, enabling one to find items which permit one to go toward two other items; sources are acknowledged, and with other expressions, are seen to allow one to understand the items at the base of each triangle; each item is understood to thrust forward toward the others; and health is expressed in a corrective controlling privacy, self, and person.

Cutting across this way of looking at man's interiority is one which tries to answer a number of basic questions: What am I really, and therefore what is central and what superficial? What are the positions where I must be bounded off, and therefore, what am I in public, as publicizable, concerned, private, as able to occupy myself with what is transcendent? What are my essential features, i.e., what is my interior apart from all else? Why do I say and do what I say and do, and therefore what perhaps ought I to have said and done instead? Each of these has subsections. Thus, if we ask why we say and do what we in fact say and do, we can answer by remarking that we are somehow expressing our rights; that our persons are offering some correction to bodily tendencies; that our sensitivity and consciousness are agencies for expressing rights; that each of our you's is interplaying with desire; and that each of us unifies his rights and desires. To say what a man is we will have to refer to his I, identity, rights as together articulating the other items in their respective triangles. The answer to the question: what am I really like? will require a reference to distinctive expressions of identity, I, and rights, and therefore will attend to the ways in which sensitivity and account-ability, responsibility and claims, e.g., operate.

Some of these divisions and distinctions are prompted by the ac-knowledgment of a five-fold set of principles. Others have some bearing on what in fact is known to occur, and they do seem to illuminate this a little. But the whole is to me more or less a jumble. I just do not yet see my way to making the kind of systematic moves that I made in *First Considerations*. Until I do, I will not feel ready to rewrite the manuscript. I will instead continue to make notes to myself, and perhaps write in this work, in the hope that they will help me to move closer to my goal.

I approach another as a you. This at once grounds, maintains itself in opposition to, is explained by the interplay of, interacts with, and evaluates the external world, as well as his rights, desire, and sensitivity. Must we not also say that each of these also maintains itself, etc., with reference to the you and the others? If so, we would have to say that the external world is explained by the interplay of the you, rights, desire, and sensitivity. We can say this, provided it be understood that the 'ex-ternal world' here is the sensed, external world, not that world as it exists apart from the individual. Is that the very same external world which a you, rights, desire, and sensitivity ground, maintain themselves in op-position to, interact with, and evaluate? It is not difficult to see how they can ground, be in opposition to, and evaluate a sensed external world, but in what sense can they be said to interact with a sensed world? Only as they are occupied with it, as having it as a kind of matrix from which they will be able to obtain something. If so, what about the external world that in fact exists apart from the individual? And, since the sensed external world is in part constituted by the individual, will we not be involved in a vicious circle, presupposing a private individual in order to account for what is supposed to be external to and conditioning it?

Must we not therefore speak of an external world that is pertinent to this individual, a world which is an other for it, rather than what stands apart from it?

The external world, as it stands apart, does have its affect on the you. Only the individual (the union of privacy, person, and self) could be in opposition to the external world as it exists apart. Does each, perhaps with the help of transcendent realities, ground, explain and evaluate the other? I think it will evaluate, but I do not now see how it could ground or explain it. In what sense could an individual ground the external world, even with the help of the finalities? Perhaps it could explain it in the sense of providing a mind for such explanation; perhaps as a concentrated locus of nature's powers. But to ground it, it must in some sense be more basic than nature. And, as a private being, if it is to be grounded by nature, it must somehow be dependent on it.

There surely is a sense in which an individual, no matter how private, is dependent on nature. His privacy is the distinctive privacy that it is. It has a self and a person because these have been achieved through the use of nature. But in what sense could a private being provide a ground for the external world as it in fact functions apart from him? It is not enough to say with a Kantian or an idealist that the external world gets its structures (if it does) from the individual or from his mind. The question has to do with nature as it exists apart from all men, before there were any, and surely without regard for what is happening in them.

The world of nature is doubly grounded in the privacies of the particular units it contains, and in the finalities which provide it with encompassing conditions. So far as a man has a body he is part of nature, and his privacy sustains a unit there. He has specialized his own species and, through this, the conditions governing all there is in nature. He could, therefore, be said to provide a ground for nature in the sense of giving it a single, maximally intensive ground, able to specialize what is pertinent to everything that occurs in nature. He can then be said to have grounded nature in the sense that what otherwise would be a number of units with less than maximum internal intensity, is now offered a single being whose intensive inwardness suffices to provide the kind of ground that is equivalent with the totality of the lesser grounds provided by the units in nature. This means that man's individuality, of which his privacy, self, and person are diverse condensations, has an intensity which is equivalent in its grounding power to all the privacies of other types of reality making up the whole of nature.

This account is unsatisfactory for two reasons: there is no warrant given for it, and the existence of one man seems to make the existence of others to be without import for nature. To this it might be replied that the supposition is warranted because a man's capacity to understand is equal to the whole of nature; that this understanding is but a phase of what he is internally; and that the grounding that each provides is for all other men as well, just so far as they are bodies in the whole of nature, and therefore need only a minimum of intensive grounding in order to be bodies there.

Each human body, as one among other bodies, is one unit in nature. Only as privately sustained and thereby enriched, is it a genuine lived human body, and as such is grounded in an individual. That individual also sustains nature as a single unit. Apart from a man, nature would be sustained only by having a multiplicity of loci; with the coming of man and his grounding, all of nature, as a single totality, achieves a grounding.

Why don't the finalities provide a grounding? They do, but it is not the grounding *of* nature. It is a grounding *for* it. They provide it with encompassing unities; the grounding that a man provides is the grounding *of* nature, a unifying of it from below. But it is only a biased grounding. The multiplicity of men allows nature to have different biases countered by others.

We can never be sure that there are ever enough men to bring about a balancing of all their diverse biases. But even if there were only one man and he, of course, offering only his own individual grounding, nature will become united from below in a way that it cannot be in his absence. We can say that the matter which Aristotle thought was at the root of all actualities is a dehumanized version of the grounding that each man provides for all of nature, as excluding him but including all other actualities.

As grounding this particular lived body, my individuality in all its intensiveness is limited to just this, and what it might transform of my expressions. But if my body be taken as just a body, even a living one, and set in contrast with all the other bodies in nature, the I can be said to ground my body together with all the other bodies. The surplus of support which was not used by my mere body grounds the entire cosmos of bodies.

March 21

1. You are a reality with its own integrity, standing apart from those who attend to it. You are relative to them in the sense that you are related to them and have various adventitious features due to their

approach to you. But you are also beyond any reference they make to you. Your relative aspects ride on a receding reality. So far as an external observer is concerned, this is still you. But as he moves in depth he can distinguish the you he first noted from the various depths he reaches, and will do so as long as he adds to the penetration reflections on what the you presupposes.

2. The you that I confront needs grounding, explanation, determinations, and governance. The grounding is needed to account for its power, the fact that it is presented and causative. Just as a mere you, just as a terminus, it does nothing, but since it is nevertheless true that it acts, it is also true that it is being sustained and empowered.

3. We are not content to acknowledge a you as a terminus, a power, or both. We want to understand it. This means that we must find principles and articulations in terms of which its nature, presence, functioning, and value can be grasped, communicated, and used in inference.

4. A you serves to carry various operations and demands which begin further within. It is sensitized, and is qualified by consciousness. One feels with and through it, and is aware of what is happening. It is correct to say that the sensitivity is bodily and that the consciousness is mental or private. But when we say 'You are sensitive' and 'You are conscious' we refer to you, as at the forefront of activities that begin within.

5. A you interplays with other entities in a public world. At the same time, it interplays with other divisions of the individual. As the one it has a public role, as the other it is determinate, more than a locus or origin of activities whose nature is exhaustively defined by what the you is in public, or even as quickened by various operations and demands.

6. A you has a value. It is dealt with badly or well; its worth in a public world is not recognized, is exaggerated, or is properly appreciated. It has a value because it is governed by an encompassing unity in terms of which public entities are hierarchically ordered. The you also has a value with respect to what is occurring within; it governs them and is governed by them in turn, and in the light of each governance has a different value. As governing, it is the supreme value in terms of which all others are to be ordered. As governed, its value depends on the measure to which it is subject—to an I, for example, or to an identity. We are inclined, though, to think of the you as an outcome or a terminus. We may also be able to come to the point where we can see how the you can measure whatever it faces, and therefore is able to provide a standard of value for the others who attend to it. We will then be intrusive, thoughtful, sensitive, and the like, in relation to it. It is more difficult,

and not common, to speak of the you as governing what occurs within the individual. Yet what the you undergoes, the place it finds in a world of men and in the larger world beyond, at least dictate what will be inwardly tried and what will be attempted. It might be objected that this dictating is not an assessment. But surely the allowance and direction which the you provides for what is done, involves a determination of its value, not in an objective hierarchy to be sure, but in an hierarchy of values within the individual. The final and proper value of an individual man, of course, will take account of all his dimensions, and therefore will see the you in the light of the single value of the entire individual.

7. The you, as was just indicated, is not only evaluated but evaluates. It also grounds, explains, and provides determinations, both for what it is publicly and for what is beyond it. Every distinguishable epitomizing position in the individual has a similar two-fold role, being a subject for the others and a determinant of them. There is no circle here, for the different positions are never so simple that they cannot at one and the same time be subordinated to and govern the same entities in somewhat the way in which I can both speak and listen.

8. The grounding of the you is primarily given by a set of rights. As a consequence, the you is not merely present or presented, but carries native rights. The rights are brought to bear on the you by a private person in the form of claims and may, with the help of others, attain the status of viable public rights. The acknowledgment of such rights marks an advance on previous accounts of man's inward being, since these tend to treat different areas as so many substantive entities, or to view them merely as functions, momentarily distinguished in act. (I, also, have been inclined to do both.) But rights have a status by themselves without being entities; they are expressed through sensitivity and consciousness, and thereby impressed on and mediated by the you. As an aspect of the person, and as contrastive with the you, they are like the you, the I, and the other distinguished private positions—essentially pivots which are to be understood in terms of the others as in dominant and subordinate positions. To be able to have this double set of roles, the rights must have some kind of status of their own. They are unities with reference to what they govern, but only so far as at the same time they are governed by some other item.

9. Identity has rights as one of its governed termini (the other is the I), and that terminus governs the you and desire. It is only because, though a termini, rights have an integrity, that they stand away from the identity, and are able to have desire and you as termini.

10. Rights terminate in desire as well as in the you. The desire is governed in the way the you is, though the you is reached via sensitivity and consciousness, while desire is reached through its acceptance of accountability. The rights, as expressed through the you, achieve the status of demands against what is public or what overarches the you and the public items. The rights, as expressed through desire, achieve the status of claims which the desire will sustain. The desire, is expressed through the you. These rights are at once claims and demands, the one putting an emphasis on a claimant, and the other on what might or should satisfy what is demanded.

11. Desire and you interplay with one another, providing one another with determinations. As a consequence, the you is a desiring you, and the desire a desire of yours. You, as a consequence, do not merely present yourself but thrust forward and make public an inward drive, expressing what is wanted (and so far as it is qualified by rights, what should be wanted). The desire, too, instead of being just some bodily or mental urge, is one qualified and focused by the you that others know, so that one can, by attending to the you, know something of what is desired.

12. You, desire, and rights form a kind of triangle. If the suggestion about the unity and the diversification of rights be allowed, one should be able to go on and make similar analyses of the you and desire. You will then be a unity for desire and rights and, at the same time, will be governed by each. Desire will be a unity for you and rights, and at the same time will be governed by each. Nevertheless, a priority must still be given to rights, for their way of governing is more powerful and persistent than that of the desire or the you, for rights are empowered and terminated in by identity, whereas the desire and the you are not. Desire and you are notoriously different at different times, but one's rights remain constant.

13. The entire triangle of you, desire, and rights is identifiable with a person. A person is expressed as these three, and functions as a rectification for the excesses which any one of them may exhibit against the others. One can characterize the person as the combination of the three, together with the kinds of relationship, such as sensitivity, accountability, and mutual determination, which connects them, provided it not be assumed that it is somehow produced by them or is dependent on them. There is a person with these dimensions; to have these dimensions is to have them as phases or aspects or limits of the person. A person has a reality and power beyond them, enabling it to compensate for the exaggeration of one by an emphasis on another. It is as if a triangle were

possessed of a resistance against deformations. A person can also be viewed as the congealed unification of all of these distinguishable and separately functioning items; or, alternatively, as a unit power which is diversely expressed in them in such a way that they are able to stand out as units which can have their own distinctive relations to one another.

14. Identity is related to rights as rights are related to the you; it is also related to the I in the way in which rights are related to desire. And, of course, the I and the rights are related to one another in the way desire and you are interrelated. One will, in short, repeat with respect to identity, rights, and I, all the distinctions required when dealing with rights, desire, and you. The total set of units will constitute the boundaries and be constitutive of a primary privacy. Privacy has the person as one of its more concrete forms; the other is the self. Identity will be grounded, explained, be interactive and subordinated in the same way that rights, desire, and you are, but will have the kind of priority that the rights have with respect to desire and the you.

15. I have argued in *Beyond All Appearances* that identity is an achievement, the outcome of the reduction of changes to the self-same result. By itself, as that which is to govern, identity is empty, a mere 'logical accompaniment' as Kant calls it — not of perception only, but of everything one does. At the same time it is empty in itself. When it reduces content to itself it is thereby enriched without being changed. It has the power to internalize what it directly obtains from the I and the rights, at the same time that it provides a governance for them. Is it governed in turn? Is it grounded, explained, interactive as well? I am now inclined to think that it is not, and as a consequence do not think it is correct to speak (as I did above) of rights or the I as though they were subject to the items which are at the base of their triangles.

16. Identity is related to both I and rights, the one by responsibility, the other by demands.

17. Identity, I, and rights together make a single privacy, which is to be understood in the way the person was understood in no. 13. The privacy (and, of course, the self, to which I next turn) are essentially powers expressed in three ways and which, as apart from those ways, are just agencies for overcoming deformations due to the overinsistence on any of the three points, or the ways in which these are related to one another.

18. The self is constituted of the I, interest, and an occupation with transcendent realities. The self has the I in a dominant position, but still is able to control and hobble it when this overwhelms either of the other

two. The I and the others could be said to epitomize the self. If so, we should also say that privacy and the person are epitomized by the various distinguished factors isolated in them.

19. The totality of privacy, self, and person together constitute the individual as he is in himself. That individual is not individuated, if by that one means that he is a consequence of the production of uniqueness from universals. He can, though be said to be produced, so far as he includes a self, for this is achieved somewhat after the time that the person is. In another sense it is not produced, for it is nothing other than a single power which is divided into a privacy, self, and person, and is therefore inseparable from the body. Even before the self is achieved, there will be the single individual power. This will not be fully articulated, able to operate in all the diverse forms that it can, until a self is attained.

20. Person and privacy apparently arise together, the one with its desire and you, the other incomplete until an I has been achieved. From the very start, therefore, we should have a person, with a you, desire, and rights, and their relational sensitivity and accountability, identity and its claims and demands. Only later will we have responsibility, an I, and the mind and decisions which relate that I to interest (and what I have not yet properly designated), a receptivity to the presence of finalities.

March 22

You are a living body. You continue beyond that body as an interplaying unit in a humanized world. You continue beyond that body, too, as an interplaying unit in the cosmos. You are also continuous with your sensitivity and consciousness and eventually with your rights, and therefore your person. As a living body you have multiple habits and thrust toward what is beyond you. When that body is stopped, pressed upon, redirected an effort at readjustment is made. This has at least two forms; it may be a readjustment of the body, illustrative of what has been called the 'wisdom of the body'; or it may be a readjustment involving what is within the person or privacy. It is when consideration is taken of the second that we speak of repressions, neuroses, the unconscious, and the like. These have to do with what is within the individual as contrasted with what is in fact being exhibited by and through the you.

An animal engages not only in bodily adjustments but in adjustments involving what is 'psychic' and the body. But unlike a man, who is able to live in that psychic dimension, and who may not express it in or through the body, and may turn it toward the exercise of many private interdeminations and involvements with finalities, the animal's psyche is always incipiently embodied. The adjustments that it makes are between different tendencies in the body, different tendencies to express itself bodily, and different tendencies to accommodate what it is readied to express bodily. Also, unlike a man, it does not have a person. Whatever rights it has are the rights of a distinctive kind of body with its different tendencies in and through this body.

A person exists only so far as it is sustained by a privacy having an identity, and grounding rights. An animal continues, matures, and has many persistent traits. But over the course of its life, it changes in somewhat the way, but not to the degree, that an embryo changes into a fetus, or a caterpillar into butterfly. Though it has an interior dimension, this has no status of its own, able to maintain itself despite the body's activities and changes, and able to engage in activities regardless of what the body does.

Each of the different dimensions of the individual deserves to be exhibited in relation to the others. Once this is done, it will be possible to retrace one's steps, and perhaps change what has been said of each, in order to accommodate what has been learned in the course of the examination.

1. The I is a late achievement. It is not simply that the term 'I' is not used properly, or used at all until the infant has matured to some extent. There is no I present until identity (which grounds rights) has expressed itself through responsibility. The I is self-same throughout life, not because it is itself engaged in an act of maintaining itself by absorbing whatever diversities occur in the body or interiorly, but because it is subject to the power of identity. To have an I is at once to be self-same, and to be this because it has been made so, and responsibly. It is not possible to have an I and not be responsible. The responsibility, terminating in the I, is the counterpart of the demand that identity imposes on rights.

2. When identity terminates in the I, the privacy of the individual is completed. The individual will still lack a self, for this requires the I to express itself and to govern interest as well as a receptivity to finalities. And so far as the self is lacking, the individual will not be fully matured. His maturation is in part a function of the development of his body and therefore of the you, for what one is interiorly involves a specialization of the intrusive presence of the conditions which govern the body as a distinctively humanized, specialized entity.

3. You, like rights, are at the base of one triangle, and stand at the apex of another. You are at the base of the triangle of a privacy of which identity is the apex and are the apex of a triangle which has a base in interest and in a receptivity to transcendentals. The I may exist before it functions as an apex; when it does, it interacts with rights, and acts on the identity which has responsibly expressed itself and thereby terminated in the I.

4. The I is possessive; it reaches toward identity, rights, interest, receptivity to transcendents; through the rights, interest, and receptivity, it possesses other expressions of the individual. It moves through its possessions toward what lies beyond these, and as a consequence it can indirectly possess itself by arriving at itself, via interest and identity. It also can indirectly possess itself by attending to the me, at the same time that it sustains this.

5. I have been of two minds regarding the relation of the base factors in relation to their common apex. On the one hand it seems to be the case that the apex has a priority over the base elements, that it governs them and grounds them; on the other hand, it seems to be true that the base elements make a difference to the apex. The two ideas can perhaps be reconciled with the recognition that the base elements do not ground the apex, but do affect it in the sense of taking it to be the terminus of their respective powers. The you and desire affect rights by making these specific and focused; rights and the I affect identity by giving this content; interest and receptivity to transcendents affect the I by directing its efforts.

6. The I has a responsibly conditioned identity, since it is the product of a responsible expression of identity. The I also has a possessive relation to that very same identity, orienting it, and requiring it to be absorptive of that with which the I is otherwise involved. And then, through that identity, it is able to be occupied with rights, and with what these condition. Rights are mediated by identity, at the same time that they are in direct interplay with the I. As mediated by identity, the rights are possessed as themselves self-same; as interplaying with the I they affect and are affected by the I in different ways at different times.

7. The I is a ground for interest, and is in turn limited by it. It also possesses the interest and, through this, whatever the interest may be involved with. As a ground for interest, it makes it be more than a floating drive, rooting it in what is at once able to govern and to affect it by the exercise of a decisiveness. That decisiveness is one side of a single operation, the other of which is the mind. The decisiveness and mind are

two sides of the same operation, just as sensitivity and consciousness are—and just as intention and reason are two sides of the I's receptivity to transcendents.

8. What I have just now awkwardly termed 'receptivity to transcendents' (which perhaps is only a receptivity to transcendentals, i.e., to terms or ideas rather than to the finalities or their expressions) is the outcome of the I's governing decisive/mental expressions. When that receptivity is present, it continues to depend on the I for its grounding.

9. The I operates on rights in two ways—via identity, and directly in interaction and thereby through mutual determination. As operating in the first way, it reaches the rights as self-same possessions; in the second, it reaches them as possessions which restrict the functioning of the I, at the same time that they enable it to operate via them. The I can thereupon assert itself through the rights. Though rights are dimensions of the person, they can nevertheless be expressed in and through the body as the possessions of an insistent I.

10. The I expresses itself via decision/mind, and intention/reason, the one ending in interest, the other in a receptivity to transcendents. Each of these can be made the possession of the I itself. The I consequently must be recognized to have the capacity to stand away from the activities which some other power had used to terminate in it—that, of course, is true of every one of the factors which are distinguishable within the individual—and also to be able to turn around and possess both what had so expressed itself and the expressions themselves—which does not seem to be within the capacity of rights, interest, receptivity, desire, or the you.

11. Directly or indirectly, the I operates on, possesses, interplays with, and/or acts through rights, decision/mind, intention/reason, desire, sensitivity/consciousness, demands/appetites (terminating in desire), identity, and every other position in the individual. Though it depends for its presence on the functioning of the identity, it has the power to impress itself on and through every other dimension of a man. Why does it enjoy this status? It would seem to be more properly ascribable to identity. Identity, of course, does have this role. Whatever is done by the I carries out an identity; whatever expressions rights achieve are expressions grounded in identity. But identity is operative solely by being manifested in and through these, whereas the I is operative dynamically, through possession. Why is this? How does the I acquire a power which is denied to its source, identity? Identity has no other content than that which it obtains from the I and rights, for it is not itself derived from

some other source. It is the individual at a last pivotal point. The I and rights, instead, though dependent on identity for a ground and as a source, are themselves richer than it. They are empowered by identity, but themselves are able to stand away from that which empowers them; they thereby can turn toward it as an object of their own activities. Identity is then possessed as belonging to an I, and is endowed with rights.

12. The I depends on the expression of responsibility by identity. That dependence of responsibility points up the fact that those views which have no room for identity are not able to give a satisfactory account of responsibility. One is responsible for what had been done by oneself in the past. The responsibility, though serving to mediate identity and the I, can itself be made the object of the I's possession, for the very same reason that the identity can. The I stands away from what makes it possible, and can thereupon function with respect to every dimension of the individual as its possessor.

13. The I expresses itself in decisions, thinking, intention and reason. It also possesses these. What it expresses, it is able to distinguish from itself as having its own integrity and, therefore, as being able to be possessed and used. The I, consequently, is able to have a two-fold relation to its own expressions. As a consquence, it is able to control those expressions, guide them, make them act not simply as expressions, as identity and rights are compelled to do for their expressions, but can recover and utilize them and thereby redirect and modify them. Instead, then, of just terminating in interest and receptivity, the I is able to concern itself with these, to make these be both what it terminates in and what it attentively terminates in through the instrumentality of what otherwise would be a mere expression of itself. It is, as the other divisions of the individual are not, able to be in charge of what it in fact expresses, and through these in what they terminate in.

14. Desire is an expression of rights. The I can possess and control desire via the rights. Desire then does not become something which happens to be present because one is a person. It is also something which belongs to a self, which is one's own, and rightfully so. Having once reached this position with respect to desire, the I may proceed to act on it directly. The possessiveness of the I is transitive, allowing it to possess directly what it initially reached through a mediator.

15. What is true of desire is true also of the you. The I can possess this directly. And it does this in two ways. It holds on to the you from within, giving it the status of a continuation of itself, the I. It also acts through the you and thereupon expresses itself in the world beyond that

you. If it turns back to itself, it faces itself as a me. That me is the you that it inwardly possessed, and at which it alone arrives from the outside. Though the I is singular and undivided, it evidently is able to engage in a multiplicity of acts at the same time. It is one and the same I which sustains and faces the me. The sustaining is the very sustaining that it provides for the you, what one is from the outside position of another, but the facing of that by the I is precisely what makes it possible for there to be a me.

16. The I, together with interest and receptivity to transcendents, constitutes the self. Since the I is a late achievement, and since, as a consequence, interest and receptivity also are (for they are dependent for their presence on the expression of the I), the self is necessarily also a late achievement. A human is a person and has identity, without having this necessarily expressed as an I. He may exist before he has a self.

17. If identity need not be expressed as an I, why does it so express itself? When? What compels the completion of the privacy by the achievement of an I, coordinate with rights? In general, what compels the completion of the individual, making it be articulated in all its possible divisions? The privacy, as long as identity has not expressed itself as an I, is not yet self-centered. To be itself, to have its own power and not merely to have it exhibited as a claim ending in rights, it must find its own center. Only then will it be able to act as a corrective for the excesses of various limited forms of itself. There must, therefore, be in the person, as partially formed and manifested as a claim ending in rights, a need for it to be in itself, before and apart from its manifestations. Only by manifesting itself as an identity terminating in an I, is it able to be a functioning person, able to rectify the excesses and biases of different manifestations of it.

18. The I allows a self to be, just so far as that I terminates in interest and receptivity to transcendents. Conversely, the self is a power which is exhibited in the form of an I, interest, and receptivity, with the I having a primary grounding role for the other two. The presence of that I enables the self to have a position of dominance over the person, possessive of it, governing it, demanding that it function as an intermediary for it.

19. The I possesses the self. We rightly say "I have a self" and not "I am a self". The I, therefore, is not only subject to the equilibrating action of the self, but is able to treat that self as a unit which can be possessed and used. Its relation to the self is therefore quite different from the relation which rights have with respect to the person, or identity has to privacy.

20. We do not say "I have my individuality" but "I am an individual". Instead of possessing the entire complex of person, self, and privacy, which together are phases of the individual, the I merges with it, identifies itself with it. This requires the I to allow itself to become merged with identity, through this with the privacy, and through this with the person. As a consequence, the I becomes the underpinning, the intensive dimension of all of the dimensions of the individual. At one and the same time, it is one of the achievements of the individual and that which is one with it, the latter of course coming after the former.

21. Through the agency of the you, the I, both as a single unit and as identical with the individual, expresses itself, and thereby comes to assume a possessive role with respect to the you and with reference to what it is enabled to reach by means of that you, and the body of which the you is a dimension. "The world" said Schopenhauer "is my own idea". This is true so far as the 'idea' is not something in the mind, and does not preclude the existence and functioning of the world apart from oneself.

* * *

It is now almost 10:20 AM I have been writing since about 8, elaborating on some shorthand notes I made for myself last night. Everything is quite schematic; I have been involved in mere probings, in making tentative suggestions, all preliminary to what I hope will be a systematic study of the individual, man as having a complex interior, terminating in an embodied you. The terminology is not altogether satisfactory, and inadequate account has been taken of the interior as understood by theologians, ethicists, political thinkers, and Freudians. These approach the individual in terms which are not altogether in consonance with one another; indeed, they seem to be occupied with quite different dimensions. Where the first speaks of virtues and vices, the second of obligations and freedom, the third of rights and perhaps impulses, the fourth attends either to drives, needs, or to the unconscious, the ego, censors, repressions, and the like. In contrast with all of them, we have commonsense or daily life with its distinctions of the I, you, me, we, and its confusion between responsibility and accountability, freedom and liberty, and oneself-in-oneself with what one is in the eyes of another. Each seems to have recognized important factors, but there seems to be no account which attends to what all have discerned. The tendency of modern philosophers has been to emphasize either the ethics or the epistemological dimensions, the latter having to do with the presence and functioning of the mind and the emotions. Evidently, what I am seeking is the ground for all these, and an explanation for their presence, as well as a systematic way of moving from one item to another. Since I have not yet found this, I must content myself with outlining possible ways of envisaging the individual without placing undue emphasis on the factors which interest one or the other set of thinkers.

A possible listing of the various levels of the individual which have been emphasized by different disciplines:

1. Psychology. (Since what is sought is an understanding of the interior of man, I begin with the 'soft' sciences, and not with physics, chemistry, or biology). We here deal with what will be expressed in public, and which indeed was discovered or determined on the basis of what men did publicly. Attention must be paid to motivation, learning, and to fear, anxiety, memory expectation, belief, so far as they are directed toward the body and what is reached via this.

2. Psychiatry. Here we move to deeper grounds, the unconscious, the act and outcome of repressions, traumas, the internalization of what had been experienced, and its deformed and proper expressions.

3. Social life. This is the domain of morality, the assumption of roles, the acceptance of tradition, the occasion for alienation, where men interplay with one another, the milieu, and the world beyond, all of which can have distinctive imports in individuals.

4. Politics. The ability of a man to be a representative; the question of native rights and their transformation and support in public; accountability.

5. Ethics. We have here occasion to examine the traditional virtues and vices, the sense of obligation, the endeavor to become perfected, self-legislation, duties, guilt and innocence, responsibility.

6. Art. Appreciation, creativity, insight, emotion, and the arrival at depths in the universe.

7. Religion. Faith, submission, sacraments, grace, involvement with the transcendent, and mysticism.

8. Knowledge. We have here the conditions for perception, understanding, and reason, judgment, commonsense, science, theories and hypotheses, inquiry, truth and error, imagination, belief, logic, mathematics.

9. Self-knowledge: direct knowledge of oneself through the agency of the me. Differentiation between I and me; we, the others.

10. Speculative knowledge, Intensive inference; systematic thought; presupposition; wonder.

The lists under each heading are incomplete, and there are perhaps other levels which should be considered. But these suffice to point up the fact that an account of the individual will have to find what is at the root of all, or one of them at the root of all the others, and show how to move from that root to the rest. And there should be a move from the opposite side showing how we must force ourselves—as was done in *Cinematics* —back and back from what is obvious and commonplace to more fundamental items. In *Cinematics,* only the emotions were noted; Must one not do for other factors what was there done for the emotions?

March 23

We could begin with the fact that each of us knows himself as a me, and move toward a self-centering; with our position in social and political wholes and move back toward a self-organization and ethics; with our judgments of perception and our grasp of logic and mathematics, and move back toward an ultimate intelligibility; with our emotions, and move toward a final involvement as at the root of what we try to learn in psychology, psychiatry, art, and religion; and with wonder, and move back toward a basic set of values. In all cases we would be recognizing the inadequacy of one level of activity and finding that it was capable of being corrected by another, which has its own object.

The principle just remarked on seems to be close to the answer of how to go from superficial aspects of men and their activities to what they are in root. But what is not clear is how such a principle meshes with the kind of distinctions set out the last few days. Does self-knowledge begin at the very point where knowledge does, though constituted differently? Does it work on a different level? Does it arrive at a different final position or at the same one, but on a different level? Do emotions stand between rights and the you, and therefore combine consciousness and sensitivity with a grounding of the you in rights? Do the different emotional positions, remarked in *Cinematics,* have different rootages? Are those rootages different forms or particular cases of rights? Are there other combinations like the emotional—one combining responsible accountability and a dependence of desire on rights; demands and a dependence of rights on identity; responsibility and a dependence of I on identity; decision and a dependence of interest on the I; and reason and a dependence of a receptivity to transcendents on the I? Can we ascribe stations to these, taking us to deeper and deeper layers of the individual? How do we get from a layer of emotion, e.g., to different terminal points and eventually to an I? Do we always end up in an I?

Instead of attending to levels of emotion, one can attend to their origins. As a consequence, rectifications will be expressed not as feelings, tones, moods, and the like, but as different points or contents, such as the lived body, desire, rights, identity, I, interest, and receptivity to transcendents. If so, we must see how they could rectify what was occurring on a more limited derivative level, though one with which we are more familiar. Is the origin of consciousness, connecting rights and you, in the mind? Is the origin of morality in a controlled desire? Of the ethical in responsibility? Of politics in claims? Of knowledge in decision and mind? Of speculation in intention/reason? I throw out these questions in good part because they touch upon the distinctions already made, but I do not yet see that they are forced on me by anything that in fact occurs.

In dealing with the emotions, it was necessary to move to deeper levels having a wider range than those which had been dealt with in order to rectify what was amiss in daily life, and as making possible an involvement with Existence. If we emphasize, not the dynamism or the relationality of the effort, but the point of origin, the account would have to distinguish between the you as a carrier of feelings; desire as seeking for satisfactions; rights as insistent demands; the I as possessive; intent as evaluative; and finally the receptivity to Existence as completive. Identity is here ignored as not having an outward thrust, and serving only to provide an ultimate rectification of the various distinguished positions in relation to one another.

Suppose we begin with the you as the origin of a judging or perceiving? Disregarding anything said before, must we not find the conditions for a self-articulation, a claiming to be true, a believing, a using of the mind in logic; for an engagement in mathematical creation and rigorous deduction; and for a beginning of an evidencing of finalities in an intelligible speculative account? How could these be related to the dynamic origins just mentioned, or to the pivotal points remarked on in the discussions of the last few days?

I begin again: The you needs a grounding. To obtain this it is necessary to move back to different interior positions in order to get more basic, persistent grounds, adequate to sustain whatever there be. One would be able to stop at identity did this have content. Because it does not, the grounding will remain at identity, but only as fed by the I and what this makes possible.

The you tries to maintain itself. For this, it must be properly related to the person, to a power to maintain itself, and to what can provide an equilibrium amongst different agencies. One's complete equilibrium is achieved only as an individual. This requires the achievement of complete persons, selves, and privacies. As a consequence, there must be desire, I, and receptivity expressed by rights, identity, and the I respectively, so as to have what is needed for the powers to be able to stand on their own bottoms.

When a man perceives he is conscious. There is a movement back so as to overcome error and to have a larger controlled range. But there is no ending at mind; one moves beyond this to the position where it is possible to confront what is intelligible.

When a man feels, he is primarily sensitive. There is a movement back in order to extend the range of this, so as to affect the different positions, and arrive at Existence. This satisfies in the way efforts, at expressing sensitivity and other levels, do not.

When a man takes a stand in the world, he evaluates. To correct and extend the evaluation, one must back into rights. These are evaluated by identity and the I, as more or less urgent.

Neither rights nor the transcendent receptivity has been more than noted by me so far. How are rights differentiated? By virtue of the need to express them in the body, as desire, to carry identity, and to be possessed by the I?

If something like this is true, the I should be said to a. ground the you through the agency of identity; b. promote self-maintenance of the you by enabling the individual to be self-maintained; c. make use of the mind; d. express itself through rights and thereby sensitivity, so as to have an intensive involvement with the you and what lies beyond it; and e. should make the you dominant over other items, as being more important. At the same time it should provide for the grounding, self-maintenance, explanation, existence, and value of itself and all the other facets of the individual. It should turn the results obtained from identity, from the individual (and privacy, self, and person), from its use of mind, from its use of rights, and from its imposition of its value, toward the finalities, and thereby become grounded, maintained, explained, existent, and evaluated. But to say this is apparently to turn the I into a substantial unit, the individual in miniature. That supposition must be avoided. The I not only comes into existence late in the life of the individual, is itself dependent on the functioning of identity, and is subject to rectifications by the self, but is nothing more than a nuance merging into the others except when it is in fact functioning. It becomes distinguished in act. To be sure, it is almost always active, and therefore almost always distinguished, once it comes into existence, but it seems not to be so when one is in a stupor, senile, immersed in practice, or emotionally overwhelmed.

The I expresses itself in a receptivity to all the finalities. But it does not only enable the individual to become involved with those finalities, coming to them as absolute grounds, reality, meaning, existence, and value, but is able to turn back again and have the result affect the individual and the various distinguishable facets. Since the I is a late arrival, it must be possible for there to be activities and distinctions which do not depend on the I's presence or activity. For example, a man has rights before he has an I, and can insist on those rights consciously, via desire, and with the backing of identity.

How are rights to be distinguished? How many of them are there? In the past I have held that there are as many (native) rights as there are essential dimensions of a man. The present approach would require a differentiation of rights in accord with what conditions them or what they condition. The rights are directly conditioned by identity, and indirectly by the I, and by the desire and the you that they are expressed in and through. There are, then, the right to continue to be; to make oneself accountable; to be sensitively and consciously present in the you and through it; to be able to use a mind; to have interests; to be open to the influence and to become acquainted with the finalities; to be part of a community; to be equal to others; to know; to create; to enjoy art; to try to realize ideals; and to practice a religion. These distinctions attend primarily to the other facets of the individual, and presuppose that each of those facets is able to emphasize one kind of right. The initial rights will have none of them distinguished, and will be most properly taken to form a single unit which terminates a demand by identity. It will be divided only so far as it is directed at or is imposed upon by other facets.

If a single unit right is divided in these ways, must not identity and the I also be divided, the one impressed on what it grounds, and the other possessing and presupposed by decision, mind, and wonder? An affirmative answer seems plausible. Without denying their integrity, we should, therefore, be able to hold that there is a distinctive kind of identity carried by the body, another by one's unit right, a third by the I, and a fourth by one's involvement with what is ultimate. And, similarly, there should be a distinctive way the I is when it possesses and uses this facet or that, and eventually, for example, when it sustains the me at which it arrives. The I sustains and attends to itself as an approachable public entity. So far it is divided. But that division rides on the surface of a basic undivided I, the I which expresses itself in these diverse ways. Similarly, we should say that there is but one right which is the terminus of a claiming by identity, and that this right allows for diverse expressions in the form of a right of the body and a right of desire, and then of the right to continue to be self-same, and, derivatively, to have and to express the I, and therefore to have and use a mind, self, privacy, person, individuality, sensitivity, consciousness, decision, responsibility, reason, and such resultants as the emotions. We should also see the body, desire, interest, receptivity, the I, and right as introducing distinctive qualifications affecting the nature and role of the other facets. Desire, for example, has a bearing on the body and right and, indirectly through the I, on other facets. Once again, it seems reasonable to say that in its being brought to bear on the others, it becomes divided and specialized, so that a desire which is expressed through the body will be different from a desire which terminates in right or which, via that right, is expressed through the body. Each facet apparently has a specialized role in the others, and through them on what those others affect. Since all will be expressed directly or indirectly in and through the body, the body of a man, viewed as at the forefront of what he is as a single power holding in equilibrium the person, self, and privacy, will have to be understood as already having all the different facets in a divided and specialized form. In it, we must be able to recognize the presence of rights, identity, I, desire, interest, and wonder, and the various relations which these begin, such as sensitivity, accountability, claim, responsibility, mind/decisiveness, and reason/speculation. They are not there on a footing or as a miscellany; each has a distinctive role. It need not duplicate in its order of dominance or priority what is true of the individual by himself. But all should provide a beginning of movements into the undivided more forceful forms of these.

In the study of the emotions, the move backward was prompted by a need to overcome defects in what one was experiencing, and to allow one to become part of a larger and more abiding existence. This—contrary to what was supposed at the beginning of today's examination—is not necessarily the way in which one must proceed in a movement from what is present in the you. Not only was the study of the emotions geared to a mastery of what was beyond, but it did not attend to unit divisible facets, contenting itself with getting to deeper and deeper layers of a single kind of effort.

If we attend to the embodied you, we can see how it is constituted by factors which originate from the privacy, person, self, or individual, or from aspects of these which these will rectify in relation to one another. To know the factors, one will have to attend not to a bodily structure but to a functioning body. One will begin somewhat near where psychologists and others do—with the you in relation to other public beings—and then see what distinctions they require in the you, and how these must be grounded, maintained, explained, empowered, and assessed from within.

Better: I can attend to you as a single being or as in a larger setting where you are together with others. If you are dealt with in terms which apply equally well to animals or things, though we will inevitably be driven back to consider what a man is in himself, we will not need to refer to the distinctive aspects which mark men off from all else. A man may, of course, be in nature and attend to items there in terms which reflect his own tradition, experiences, and needs, but this we will know only if we know him to be a distinctive kind of being, or recognize that what he is doing is not reducible to complications of what animals and things do. If he is more adroit than they are in relation to other items, it still may be possible to see what he does as a complication of what they do. If we cannot now show that every one of his ways of interplaying with others is expressible in terms which are complications of those applicable to them, it still remains an open possibility. And that, I think, is the way in which Darwin saw man.

If we take man as in a milieu, society, or state, even when it be acknowledged that he is also in a wider nature, either directly or through the agency of these, we can recognize him to be expressing himself in a way that things evidently cannot, and which animals only seem to repeat. Animals live in environments; they form groups, and are subject to governances by some of their members. But they know nothing of the equal rights of one another, of an inherited tradition, or of representatives of all of them. Recognition of such matters allows one to know men as having powers and concerns that are distinctive. A man lives in a milieu, society, and state; he has a distinctive history, and makes use of a distinctive kind of social structure involving a language, a legal system, and established rules and habits. It is not easy to see how he does this. Is this not because we must first understand what he is as a distinct being?

We face another as a human only if we face him as a. sensitive, able to be hurt or relieved, given pleasure or pain; b. conscious, able to be aware of what he is undergoing and of what is beyond his body, even though he may not articulate it but have it only as a panorama; c. a person, one who has some native rights, and is the outcome of d. the expression of a privately assumed accountability; e. is responsible; and therefore, f. has an identity. Known as able to confront himself as a human, he is also known g., to have an I. Nothing is as yet said about his having a mind, being able to decide, have a self, or be an individual. But it perhaps follows from the fact that he is responsible, that he has h. a mind; i. that he makes decisions; and j. that he has interests. Since we are attending to the you and what we discern beneath it, or which its acknowledgment as human requires, we do not yet have any need to suppose that there is a receptivity to transcendent realities. To show this, we would have to show that without the receptivity the I is not adequately expressed and the self is not complete, with the consequence that the individual in himself is not complete.

The series from a–g seems to be hierarchical in the sense that as we proceed we move toward deeper and deeper grounds. From e., responsibility, there is a possibility of moving toward identity, or toward mind, decisions, and interests. Apparently the two kinds of move are coordinate, the one taking us toward a grounding, the other taking us toward agencies. The reference to a me and therefore to an I has not yet been accommodated. One can reasonably claim that the I is needed in order for there to be a responsibility exercised, since this terminates in and is carried forward by the I. If so, the I would be part of the move toward an agency. This leaves over only the me.

Does responsibility require that one have some knowledge of oneself as a me? It could be argued that it does, for a man must know who he is, where he begins, what he is like, how he is sustaining himself (not as a mere body, but as that which merges into the very I which is attending to it) in order to be able to be genuinely responsible. One who did not know himself as a me, and therefore did not confront himself from the outside while sustaining himself from within, could make responsible decisions, but the responsibility would not be geared to any understanding of who he was. He would understand it to be expressed in an alien body and not in one which was to be identified with what he was in himself, even though it was approached from the outside and so far was like a delimited portion of a public world, able to be dealt with as a mere unit there.

Left over, is the question of man's receptivity to transcendents. Is this required by responsibility? It could be, for responsibility has to do not only with what one is in fact urging through the body, but with the principles and conditions which are thereby imposed on the body and on that which the body affects.

Why does responsibility have all these consequences or involvements? Does not this account put an overstress on ethical considerations? The second question is easier to answer than the first. We began with the body; responsibility is an essential part of it, if it is to be the body of a you, a human being. The other dimensions of the individual might have as many consequences or involvements as responsibility has, as the earlier part of today's suggestions would seem to indicate, but we are not required to attend to them if we begin with a confronted you. There is no denial here of the presence or the importance of sensitivity, mind, accountability, desire, or any other aspects already distinguished. But also no need has been found as yet which requires me to attend to what these presuppose.

March 24

Responsibility is to be acknowledged even when one is irresponsible, for to be irresponsible one engages in acts which, were one to live up to one's responsibility, would not be performed. Evidently, responsibility is a kind of obligation or demand that prescriptively governs a situation but which may in fact not be instantiated by what occurs there. To say that you are responsible is to say that you are governed from within, and that what you do should carry out what that governance demands. It is evidently a governance which can be ignored, defied, denied, without being obliterated. When we know that another is a human we know not only what he presents himself as, but how he ought to present himself, not in detail, but in the sense that what is done conforms or does not conform to what is being prescribed. One need not know just what to do; one can be recognized to be responsible even when one does not know just what should be done.

In saying that I know you to be sensitive and conscious, a person, with native rights, desire, and a privately assumed accountability, I must also be taking account of the fact that you are responsible, which is to say that there are right and wrong ways in which you can be sensitive, desire, and assume an accountability. Are there correct and wrong ways to be conscious, a person, have native rights, desire, and be accountable? Yes, in the sense that one can be inattentive, or as is sometimes said 'insensitive', that one can misconstrue the dignity which a person has, and that one can ignore, overlook or exaggerate one's rights, misconstrue one's desires or accountability.

Responsibility is here close to what is sometimes called 'authenticity', 'well-roundedness', 'paradigmatic', and a 'model'. There is an ethical tonality to these, but this is a phase of something larger and deeper, the being governed by what one ought to satisfy, apart from any action. Responsibility is also subject to conditions—identity, mind, decision, interest, self, individual, privacy, receptivity to transcendents, the I, and the me. There is then a kind of 'responsibility' to which responsibility is itself subject. With respect to the first set of factors it dictates. With respect to the second set it must meet certain requirements; if it does not, it will not be the responsibility that ought to be operative on the first set. The move from the you to responsibility should go to the second and from there to the first. (The second set conforms to the presence of five finalities: identity, I, mind, decision, and receptivity matching Substance, Being, Possibility, Existence, and Unity). Self, individual, and privacy however, have their own 'ought', serving to rectify the others. And the me, since it is oneself arrived at from without, is subject to mind and decisions which should operate in a prescribed way.

Nothing as yet has been said about freedom. Account must also be given of fear, hope, traumas, faith, the unconscious, repression, reason, love, imagination, creativity, memory, anticipation, mysticism, judgment, virtue, duty, the striving for completion and excellence, ambition, wonder, and the need to cooperate. And there is the demand to be honest in one's creative work, sincere in one's religion, correct in one's self-maintenance, and to have self-respect in one's self-bounding. It blurs matters to put all of these under 'responsibility'; and in any case, it shows that an attempt to deal with man in ethical terms will either make one overlook other areas of activity or subordinate these to ethics, though (as I tried to show in the *World of Art*) ethics is also subordinate to or is independent of these.

One might distinguish responsibility as referring to what should be realized; honesty as the insistence that the governance be realized in act; sincerity as having reference to the governance, submitting to it; correctness as conformity of the governance and the act; and self-respect as the acceptance of the governance. It makes sense, though, to say that one ought to be honest, etc., just as one ought to act responsibly. If this is so, responsibility once again achieves a kind of priority or superiority over the others. Perhaps there is nothing objectionable here, if one identifies responsibility as that which is to be realized and, therefore, to be a necessary component in the formation of character.

The you acts in various ways, carrying out bodily initiated activities. Those activities are governed by a number of demands stretching from within to and through the you. Freedom will then be omnipresent, for it will be involved in the carrying out of responsibility, in the act itself, and in the relation of the responsibility to other internal factors. It will, of course, be most conspicuous in decision.

The you has its own integrity. So far as it is incorporated in a body having its own dynamism and habits, there can be a failure to realize prescriptions due to a failure to insist on them, or due to the ability of the body to function in disregard of what one intends or demands of it. The awareness of the discrepancy is exhibited in fear, hope, striving. The dominance of the body in the face of one's efforts, or the subjugation of that body to forces over which one has an insufficient or no control come out as fear, hope, striving, creativity, and perhaps even love and duty.

Repression (I ignore for the time being the difference between it and suppression) refers to the mastery of what is about to be done by what ought to be, usually under the presence of fear, striving, hope, creativity, love, and duty. It need not be supposed to push what is not wanted into some reservoir where it remains for some later fishing. It stops an expression of some agency and may thereby allow some other act to proceed unsupervised, uncontrolled, or distorted. Something is kept and forced back, just so far as the usual operation of some governance is restricted in scope, being kept from control of the activity as expressed in and through the body and made to operate only within. In order to allow one type of activity to proceed with its own governance, other activities must be precluded; if the denial of these activities has an effect on what is expressed, distorting them, we have the familiar kind of aberrational activity which leads some thinkers to suppose that it is a distortive mirror of what is latent and would otherwise be exhibited. Not only must every activity depend on the holding back of others, but there is no need that that holding back have a distortive effect on what in fact is done. There are also deliberate restraints, modifications, denials, redirectings where, what had not been properly governed, is subject to an effort at control that might be good to exercise.

The you as embodied is, of course, more than a mediator for or an object of internally generated powers, expressing responsibility and what this presupposes and utilizes. As a body, it is living, lived, has an ultimacy, a nature, occupies a position in space, time, and dynamics, and embodies a value. As occupying a position in extensions, it is distensively conditioned, made to carry an inward self-spreading which meets an undifferentiated space, time, and dynamics, to constitute a reality positioned in a public extension. If, as I have urged, there are other ways in which men are public, there must also be other powers similar to dissension which, on meeting universal conditions, produce positioned public entities. Matching Substance is a self-grounding; matching Being a self-bounding; matching Possibility a rationale; matching Unity an integrity. The joining of the matching pairs yields a public being able to act, to stand apart, to have a sharable nature, and a comparable value. Or, returning to the you as a starting point, we have to acknowledge it to be able to act, stand apart, have a sharable nature, and a comparative value in public, as well as to provide an occasion for us to get to what the individual is in himself by attending to the origin of the powers which helped constitute these different public dimensions. The you is public, in short, because there has been something which has been able to counter all-pervasive powers and thereby produce punctuations within otherwise undifferentiated encompassing governances. Since these public features do not seem to differ in kind from those which are characteristic of animals or things, the acknowledgment of the inwardly produced conditions, distension, and the others, does not throw any light on what it is to be a man.

As issuing from what is interior, distension, and the others, because charcteristic of inanimate entities, are to be attributed to the interior as that which is incipiently public and not to it as that which is enjoying a status of its own, or able to function on its own (as is the case with man). Related observations are pertinent to the body as living. As merely living, a man does not draw on anything not possessed by an animal. His living is, of course, affected by other things he can do and does, but just as living it is understandable in the same kind of biological terms that suffice for the understanding of the living of an animal. The body is also lived, used as an instrument, governed from within, and then (not as an animal might by merely thrusting outward) by one who has a person and a privacy, and perhaps a self and an individuality, which can be enriched within, have roles to play with respect to one another in privacy, and are governed by responsibility, and what this entails and uses.

An animal is a living body, and what it is privately, able to suffer, be pleased, and to ready itself, is keyed to a public expression. A man, instead, can live within himself in terms which may be irrelevant to what he bodily can do. He may in fact eventually turn in a different direction and attend to what is presupposed by every entity. The living of his body is a responsible act; he might limit it and almost cancel it to allow the body to be just alive, while he contents himself with non-public matters. His living it can be understood to be his responsibility as expressed in the body. When his body functions in independence of what is interior, it is just alive. Though an animal body can be lived, and though it seems as if in some cases a human body is just alive, a human lived body is inseparable from a living of it, carelessly perhaps, and usually unknown.

A long time ago I contended that the fundamental truth about any actuality is that it seeks to complete itself by making its own what was outside it. The act added others through eating, through extension by use and property, and by possession through knowing, under the limitation that the self was to benefit from this and not to be overwhelmed. What place, if any, has the effort at self-completion in understanding the you and what lies behind it? Is self-completion a condition which governs responsibility, and through this every other activity and position which one might assume? In the last days I have spoken of completion in another sense, having to do with the achievement of privacy, self, and individuality, by carrying out various activities. Neither type of completion can be known from the you. Self-completion has to do with what is beyond the you.

We do speak of self-preservation, of making use of the environment and the like. We learn of these, not by attending to the you, but by endeavoring to understand how it does and how it should act in a world which is beyond it. It might be said that the completion of privacy, self, and individuality will have its repercussions in the you, and could perhaps be seen to be consequences of what else is acknowledged in order to understand the you. But the attempt at self-completion by utilizing what is beyond oneself, and even through the help of the you, does not seem to have any bearing on the you that we confront, and certainly not on the individual as having various dimensions required or used by responsibility. Yet no understanding of a man can be satisfactory if it does not recognize that he is involved with what is beyond his body, both that which is for him to use and adjust to, and that which enables him to be a unit in a larger whole, particularly a human society.

Is self-completion a primary act of which responsibility (as involving a controlled use of the body and whatever this will presuppose or use) is a limiting case, restricted in area? Do I attend to you because I am attempting to complete myself? Do I know you are a human only if I know that you can attend to me, and therefore are one who also is occupied with a self-completion? Since every actuality is engaged in a self-completion, in what sense is it illuminating to speak of man seeking self-completion? What in his status as a you tells us about a distinctively human effort at self-completion?

In *Sport* I spoke of the effort to achieve excellence. This effort, I think, is the effort at self-completion, with an emphasis on an ideal terminus rather than on the particulars one might confront—which is what *Reality* emphasized. The two I think go together, for the emphasis on the ideal controls the way one proceeds to deal with particulars. Responsibility carried out on behalf of the individual is for the sake of excellence, in the double sense of attempting to do justice to the individual's nature, and seeking to do justice to what is used.

Once it be recognized that you are acting through your body and are not just embodied, the responsibility which I discovered by attending to you as human and which I can see operate to govern what you are as a public entity, must be extended to govern you as a mediator of what is inwardly decided, thought about, urged, desired, possessed, maintained, or made the object of interest. Here the responsibility not only governs the body in terms which originate elsewhere, but does so with respect to ends which that body itself enables one to reach but does not itself formulate or attend to. The knowledge of the you as the object of a responsibility becomes the knowledge of you as an agent for excellence and self-completion once the responsibility is seen to be not just the carrying out of a principle in oneself but the carrying this out wherever the you is effective. (We are led to suppose that there is a striving for excellence by noting the sacrifices men make, the training they undergo, and the standards they employ.)

I see you, not as a mere confronted, sustained unit, but as a mediator, one who in being sustained, is used to act on other things, and could be approached by you in the guise of a me. The approach to the me is also subject to responsibility. I see you then not only as that which is at the forefront of a responsibility expressed directly or through the agency of other inward factors, but as that which is at the beginning of activities which move into the external world.

The responsibility as governing what one does within, and also what is occurring without, is indistinguishable from attempts at self-completion and excellence. Where self-completion stresses one's need to make use of what is available, and the attempt at excellence emphasizes an ideal outcome (which may not be focused on as a conceived ideal, but may itself be enjoyed, yielded to, acted for, or taken as a guiding standard), responsibility covers both, making one bear on the other.

We are responsible a. on behalf of various prescriptions; b. for what we do; c. on behalf of what others are; d. on behalf of what others need; e. on behalf of what others deserve; and f. on behalf of an ideal that ought to be realized. The first has to do with what we are interiorly; the second with what we succeed in expressing and making public; the third with what should be done in such a way that we respect the integrity of others; the fourth with what should be done so that the others will have particular requirements satisfied; the fifth what should be done so that others are perfected; (the fourth and fifth differing in that the one attends to particulars while the other attends to them but in terms of the end which they serve; the two are evidently to be considered together); the sixth attends to the end itself. If we start with the sixth we can consider the others as all falling under it in different ways, focusing on the individuals and their world as somehow to be acted on so as to make the ideal realized. If we attend to the sixth alone we make what helps realize it be instrumental; if we attend to the others we see them as loci in which the realization is to occur.

A man is responsible for what he insists on realizing; for what he makes his body exhibit; for what he does through his body and thereby to others; for the way he attends to the ideal; and for the way in which that ideal is made to govern the things he does inwardly, in the body, and beyond it. When I confront another, I see him as governed by a responsibility. But it is not until I turn to the responsibility itself that I discover it to have an objective apart from that you, and that it makes use of the you to realize that objective. The you is thus not only an avenue through which I reach toward an individual but toward a separately operating power in him that affects that you while it is occupied with an objective that is also pertinent to others.

The ideal is only one of a number of objectives, and though its primary form is that of a conditioning intelligibility, it has within it subordinated conditionings. In addition to the ideal there are other ultimate objectives—the topics of harmonics, economics or classification, art, and religion. Evidently, the first three require some kind of embodiment in and through the body. But religion seems available to those who retreat from the body, enabling Whitehead to define it as what one does with one's solitude, and others to consider it a matter of mere faith or belief, involving no ritual, practice, or works. Yet it surely must be allowed that one who is religious does things with his body, even apart from all ritual or dogmatic requirements, which would not be done were he not religious. At the very least his being religious requires quiet, passivity, non-action, and thus some kind of restraint on the body.

What is not clear to me now is how all this bears on what I have called the receptivity to transcendents. That receptivity was taken to be one of the factors in an individual. But the kind of objective of which I am now speaking evidently concerns the entire individual, the body, and what is outside the individual. Must one back into the finalities in order to have them as objectives in the opposite direction?

March 25

We take up two attitudes toward finalities: We move toward them, yielding to them and thereby becoming involved in them where they are; we also adopt them, realize them, in ourselves and in others. In the one way we progress toward them, in the other we use them to enhance what is. In the last days I have dealt with responsibility in the latter sense. But the ideal with which responsibility is involved, and the different variants of this which are of interest to different types of men from artists to the religious, presupposes the independent reality of what can sustain the ideal as well as the independent reality of finalities which can sustain other obligating termini.

If it be true, as I have maintained in *First Considerations*, that the finalities intrude on whatever actualities there are, there should be no need for a man to try to realize those finalities unless it be the case that the intrusion does not do full justice to what those actualities are and need. The finalities insist on themselves and are countered by the actualities to constitute appearances and various transcendental features of the actualities. But these do not necessarily satisfy the need of the actualities to be complete. The suggestion that a man has a double attitude toward the finalities, backing into them via a receptivity, and approaching them as ideals to be realized, takes account of their double status, but the details of this have not yet been dealt with. I have not been entirely oblivious of this problem. In *First Considerations*, I dealt with it when, for example, in the chapter on Substance, I spoke of the possibly new discipline of harmonics. If what is now said is correct, I can also go back to the *World of Art* and recognize the prospect with which the artist is concerned to be an idealized version of the Existence into which he will penetrate.

An ideal is not something produced by a finality; instead, it is initially the congealed outcome of mankind's creative effort to find in each society some way of expressing that in which all are immersed to some extent, and of which they sometimes take cognizance when they seek to grasp what is conditioning them all.

Plato took the Good to be a final and controlling reality, as well as an objective which one tried to reach, perhaps via mathematics. And that is something like the way God is understood by religious men in the Western tradition. The very same being, and apparently in the same direction, is faced as a dominant reality to which we must submit and also as a kind of prospect or possibility which one must realize here and now, and thereby make determinate. But it seems more correct to say that one faces these in opposite directions; to submit to the Good or God, to love it or him by moving toward it and accepting it on its terms is to yield sooner or later to its presence and power; to face it as an objective, as that which is to be made significant in one's life, is to accept it as a guiding imperfect never self-sufficient or self-sustaining item, and to try to give it an embodiment and thereby to enhance it by having it achieve definiteness and a role. The definiteness and role, to be sure, are achieved in the world of actualities; the ideal is there pluralized and given a content that enriches it. As sustained by the reality to which one seeks to submit, it is of course singular and undivided, and given concreteness in another guise. If one arrives at the finality via art, religion, or by other routes, one will of course come to what is sustaining the ideal. One will then have at least a vague grasp of the ideal as concretionalized from a side opposite to that which is reached by the concern with an objective. One will arrive at what allows the ideal to remain single and concrete, despite the fact that it is given many different realizations by actualities.

When one makes use of evidence, one arrives at the evidenced. Is this the ideal which is being arrived at as a terminus rather than that which is to be made determinate through action? It seems so. One confirms the rightness of one's use of evidence by seeing how the evidenced is adopted by the finality; by seeing if we can recover it from the finality; by seeing how it is possessed by the finality; by seeing how it serves as an objective to be realized by us; and by seeing how it is in fact being sustained by, and is a kind of expression of, the finality. The last gets to the underside of the finality as that which is reached through harmonics, economics or taxonomy, speculation, art, or religion.

Viewed from another perspective, we have the individual being intruded on by finalities, at the same time that these are present for it as ideals. There is a sense then in which the evidenced is present from the start, even apart from the isolation of evidence. The isolation of evidence, and the use of it, is prompted by the evidenced as a kind of ideal. Once we have the evidence, we realize that ideal in the double act of making it unite with the evidence, and by taking the evidence toward it.

Bringing particulars before the ideal to be enriched requires a kind of submission. As a consequence, we not only have a submission to the finalities arrived at through the production of works of art and other agencies, but also a submission to them by allowing them to transform what we have isolated, by giving this a lodgement and a completion. The second has its counterpart in the internalization to which the individual subjects the finalities which have intruded on it. We have then a. a submission to both the finalities and b. the sustained ideals; c. a particularization of the finalities by internalization, d. a particularization by a bringing of evidence to the evidenced; e. a specification of the finalities by our acceptance of them in us; f. a specification of ideals through acts of realization; g. an acceptance of the finalities as sustaining ideals; h. the identification of ourselves with the ideal which we have taken as our objective; i. the facing of a finality and j. a facing of an ideal as providing intelligibility for others, both beyond us and in us. (Submission seems to answer to ourselves as substance; specification to ourselves as beings; action to ourselves as extensionalized; the acceptance to ourselves as unified values; and the intelligibility to ourselves as having natures.) To accept all these suggestions is to add subtleties to what was said in *First Considerations* and, I think, to take one in new directions.

It is now possible to make some connection with the process philosophers, since they do take their God to be something in himself or by himself, having a primordial nature, and as also being involved with the course of events. But his supposed consequent nature would have to be understood to be what he is in himself as having direct pertinence (and then in a number of ways) to actualities. More sharply, accepting God as the only finality, he would have to be seen to be a unity which is expressed by a sustained primordial nature that the actualities pluralize, and to be directly involved with and be affected by actualities (and so far have a consequent nature). This so alters what the process philosophers are maintaining that there is little point in pursuing the comparison. I set it down because I had been a student of Whitehead's, and what I say undoubtedly has been affected by him and his works, which I have read many times.

I had not planned to enter into this area, for I have been seeking to understand what man is in himself. But I had to go in this direction in order to become a little clearer about the nature of responsibility and, therefore, to understand how this precondition of the confronted you in fact functions.

Before I continue to deal with the nature of responsibility and what it might entail, I think it desirable to make some corrections in my namings. Instead of speaking of the conjoint presence of identity, rights and I as privacy, it would be better to speak of it as the individual, thereby allowing one to speak of privacy (rather than of the 'interior') as characteristic of the entire being, with a self, person, and individuality. If this is done, there will be a full individual as soon as there is an I, but there will not be a full privacy until the I has expressed itself in interest and receptivity.

* * *

I have now returned from a two hour walk on a beautiful Sunday in Denver. The trees, which do not yet have their blossoms, continue to excite me. I have never seen a greater variety of contorted, insistent trees, each quite different from all the others. I have seen glorious trees on some big estates on Long Island, but these in Denver are radically individualized, standing out against one another and the almost always unclouded sky.

* * *

I can now move beyond the point where I was before I went on my walk, and take account of a number of sets of distinctions:

A. 1. I yield to the ideal and thereby realize it where it is; 2. I act on things and freely produce determinations to make an ideal realized in actual entities, of which I am one; 3. I use the ideal as a guide in myself as a prescription; 4. I yield the ideal, in the form of what is evidenced, to a finality; 5. I have the ideal as an objective. (These fall under categories reflecting Unity, Existence, Possibility, Being, and Substance, respectively).

B. With respect to the finalities 1. I submit to them; 2. I internalize them; 3. I specify them when they intrude on me; 4. I accept them as sustaining the evidenced that I present to them; 5. I interact with them to constitute appearances. These reflect the dominance of Unity, Being, Possibility, Substance, and Existence, respectively.

C. Attending to an ideal in its relation to its finality, I can distinguish it 1. as in the role of evidenced; 2. as sustained; 3. as retracted and concretionalized by the finality; 4. as making the finality accessible; 5. as giving intelligibility to the finality. These seem to be in the order of determination by Unity, Being, Substance, Existence, Possibility—but I am not confident that I have this right.

D. Attending to the finalities, we can distinguish them as 1. sustaining the evidenced; 2. concretionalizing it; 3. providing it with an explanation; 4. serving as its source; 5. assessing it. These seem to be in the order of determination by Substance, Being, Possibility, Existence, and Unity.

E. The finalities 1. intrude on the actualities; 2. encompass all of them; 3. interrelate them; 4. interplay with them to constitute appearances; and 5. govern them. These are in an order reflecting the operation of Substance, Being, Possibility, Existence, and Unity.

It makes little difference, I think, whether these considerations be classified in a different way, or whether they be reduced or increased in number. And so far as the current discussion is concerned, what is important are the distinctions under A, B, and perhaps E. (I did not realize when I was setting these down, that there would be five groups, A to E. I suppose they reflect the operation of Possibility, Unity, Being, Substance, and Existence.) What is of interest in the present inquiry into the you, its presupposed responsibility, and the presuppositions and agencies for this, is that A and B have to do with the ways in which a man deals with the ideals and the finalities. As occurring at the same time, they require him to operate in two directions. C and D indicate that these will bring him to the same point. In E reference is made to the actualities, but from the standpoint of the finalities. Must there be another grouping, F, which deals with the Ideal in the way in which the finalities are dealt with in E? I do not think so, for the actualities and the finalities enjoy an ultimacy denied to ideals. These are necessarily supported by finalities; they are intermediates to be made determinate by us or by finalities.

We get to the finalities in two ways, one directly as a result of our involvement in celebrations, justice, rational enterprises, art, and religion, the other as a result of our concern with ideals as grounded. Our direct involvement brings us to the finalities from below, as able to express themselves and to sustain an ideal, to which we direct ourselves in the opposite direction. We do not of course reach the finalities as they in fact are productive of and sustain ideals (only one of which is taken to be merely intelligible, the others being appreciated, serve as lures, are yielded to, or accepted, and thus conform to categories grounded in Possibility, Substance, Existence, Being, and Unity).

The entire private being is concerned with the objects sustained by the finalities. But does it make sense to take the direct involvement in the finalities to be the occupation of just one dimension of that private being, that which I have called 'receptivity to the finalities'? Also, on the other hand, the objectives are focused on because of what one has discerned in particular items, so that it would make sense to say that the occupation with a final objective is achieved only after and through the mediation of an involvement with it through the agency of interest, making use of mind, decision, and desires. Perhaps therefore one should say that it is interest, once again, but this time making use of reason and the I, which is occupied with becoming receptive to the finalities? If we say, as seems reasonable, that it is the entire private being which is concerned with final objectives, and that the private being makes use of interest, desire, mind, and decisions, we should also say that the entire private being is directly concerned with the finalities, but that it must pass through stopping points established by interest, reason, and the I. The upshot of these reflections, no matter how they may be subsequently refined, is that a private being is turned in two directions, and that the interest of which it makes use also has a double referent. The I, that expresses itself through the interest and the responsibility which it carries, will therefore also have a double referent. Each of these double referring positions can make use of other dimensions and powers of the complete privacy.

You, it can be said, presuppose a private being; this is receptive to the finalities and has objectives; it thrusts the objectives toward the finalities; and it has the objectives backed by the finalities. Of importance for the understanding of the anatomy of the privacy are the first three. When the relation that the private being has to the finalities and the objectives is identified as responsibility, it becomes evident that the you must be conscious, have a mind, make decisions, have an I, remain self-identical, that its desires ought to be controlled, and that its sensitivity should accommodate native rights, and allow these to be urged in public under a transformation appropriate to their public exercise.

We term the doubly directed private involvement 'responsibility' just so far as we remain oriented in the confronted you, the particular things it does, and the particular powers which responsibility uses. But once we move into the privacy and attend to its double-pronged thrust, we can distinguish a need for completion which gives priority to the privacy; a self-mastery which gives priority to one's internalization and use of the finalities; a striving for excellence and its responsibility, which is occupied with the realization of objectives; a primal hope which involves a thrusting of objectives toward finalities for reception and sustaining; and finally, a peace achieved when the finalities are reached, whether directly or via the objectives. If these are all on a footing, we are faced with the question as to why responsibility is so prominent? Is it that we can never get free

of the you, what it is doing, what it is interplaying with? Yes. If so, how
do we get to the others? If it be said that we get to them by reflecting
on the components of responsibility, and allowing these to have different
weights from that they have as involved with the you, we run the risk
of supposing what may not be the case, and also deny to ourselves any
knowledge of another as actually needing to be complete, to master
himself, to hope and to want a peace. Instead, we should say that, though
we cannot free ourselves from the you with which we begin, we nevertheless can note that the responsibility, that is inseparable from that you,
has an integrity of its own and that, so far as it is taken on its own terms,
is found to be occupied with objectives of its own. While we are alert
to it as a responsibility involved with the you, we can note it to be
prescriptive of that you and, so far, to have components and termini
which are not necessarily pertinent to the you. We know that responsibility requires identity, but we can consider the identity in itself, and
indeed know something of what it is in itself even while we approach it
from the position of responsibility. In a similar fashion, we can move
beyond responsibility to other primary characterizations of privacy and
note what they are as apart from it, not by cutting ourselves off from
the responsibility but by recognizing it to be turned away from us at the
very same time that we are acknowledging it. It is imbedded in the
individual and we, in knowing it as affecting the you, also have it as that
which escaping the boundaries of such knowledge. Responsibility is
therefore known in somewhat the way we know objects—a matter discussed in *Beyond All Appearances*.

If this be so, it is desirable to get a characterization for the nature
of a private being as able to express himself in these multiple ways. And
we would have to allow that an occupation with logic and mathematics
is with what can serve as the objective of a striving for excellence, (which
is perhaps what Plato intended to convey), and that the final immersion
of the artist in Existence, as at once benign and malign, comic and tragic,
is an immersion in what sustains a final hope.

The pluralism which I have been urging does not stand in the way
of the acknowledgment of a final characterization of the private being.
An actuality (and surely man, as a private being) is a One for a Many. A
single characterization does not preclude the separate operation of the
Many from which it is inseparable. It is a One that is not merely the
object of a verbality, an expression which generalizes all of these activities; it has an integrity of its own. Evidently, a private being in itself
faces a Many, which is to be understood in terms of what lies outside

it—the finalities as they are directly encounterable or as mediated by evidenced objectives.

The privacy of a man needs the satisfaction of every item of his Many, and therefore cannot be content with the hope, peace, self-mastery, excellence or completion which are set before him by various religions and interpretations (including my own). It is true that man seeks to be complete, to be excellent, and so forth, but these presuppose him as a private being with his own subordinated nuances which the diverse thrusts toward objects and the finalities demarcate and use.

A private being has its own Many; in that guise it stands as a One which faces many efforts, making use of the Many nuances of that privacy as distinguished, unitary, two-faced points of origin. As used, the nuances stand away from the private being as focal points for different efforts. Is this known, even in a vague way, when we face another as a you? When we face ourselves as me's?

March 26

We face another as worthy of address, and as responsible. As the first, he has a dignity, and thus assumes a primary role with respect to what he does and confronts. He is a man who has rights, and who is engaged in a self-mastery with an insistent I. As the second, he has an identity, consciousness, sensitivity, mind, power of decision, desire, and interest. These are apparently the minimal conditioning or used factors. Private accountability, for example, might be absent, and the entire privacy not formed. In both ways the individual will be directed toward an evidenced finality and, when he has an I, toward the presence of the finality, without intermediation. The fact that there are two ways in which the private being is occupied with finalities, and the fact that the finalities are different, points up the reality of the private individual as beyond both self-possession and the responsibility. These will be focused and demarcated subordinated activities in him, making up for their relative dependence by spreading out toward the finalities in two directions. The private being, as in itself will be self-contained. The self-containedness is thus to be distinguished from the self-mastery, as that which is in itself from that which is endeavoring, through the control and use of other items, to remain itself, and give what it deals with a value relative to itself.

March 26

The knowing of someone as a you is the knowing of him as self-mastering, responsible, and as a One for both. The different ways in which the finalities are dealt with directly and indirectly could conceivably be taken to exist independently of the private being as he is in himself. If so, there would be no way of reaching him. But we know a you to be the you of a single being. Beyond the self-mastery and responsible stretches toward finalities, one discerns a unity for them. Perhaps that unity has within it the locus of each stretch in the form of a nuance, differentiated by virtue of a pull by the body away from the unity? But one seems able to discern unities which are not of this character; conceivably, the very presence of the different stretches makes one alert, not to a unity's nuances, but to an entirely different unity which subordinates them.

We are back to the problem of the One and the Many, with two alternatives. There is a primary unity with multiple nuances separated out with the help of the body; and there is a primary unity with its own integrity facing a number of stretches, each involved with the body, but subject to the independent governance of a primary One of a quite different nature. The primary One, with its nuances, is not the source of the subordinated stretches; they have their own natures determined by the body. But this does not preclude them from being well-bounded units, to which there are answering nuances in the primary One.

The last suggestion opens up the question of the One and the Many again. The monistic view takes the One to be the source of the Many; the pluralistic takes the One to exist in radical independence of the Many. I have held that the One and the Many have reality apart from one another, enabling them to be opposed and to interact. What I am now coming to is that some credence be given to both positions, the first by recognizing the One to have within it nuances which the Many exhibit as distinct units operating independently of the One, the second by recognizing the Many to have their origin, not in the One, but in another area (e.g., the body), which by being always present in the human being, necessarily permits of a number of stretches directed to the finalities, directly and indirectly. What has been called the 'mind/body problem' (better: 'privacy/body problem') will thereby be solved, not by reducing either, or by finding an origin in the body and its grounds in the privacy, nor by taking body and privacy to be entirely different, but by seeing them as different realities with different roles, with the privacy having its nuances answering to the distinctions which the body inevitably presupposes.

Why should there be such nuances? I see no reason yet why there should be. As a consequence, I think the supposition must be treated as idle. It is not necessary to suppose that there are such nuances, nor necessary to suppose that there are none. But if there are, one will get to the privacy from the you, by finding the stretches gradually merged into one another, and their beings condensed; if there are no nuances in the privacy, one will get to that privacy by recognizing that the togetherness of the stretches presupposes a One for which and by virtue of which they are together. The second, which I now prefer, does not permit one to say that the stretches make up for the relative derivativeness of the different positions taken in between the finalities as directly faced and as mediated by objectives. They will have their own stretches just so far as they are functioning in contradistinction from both, but are still connected with the privacy and the body, the first in the form of a governing One and the other in the form of a complex which has many different tendencies exerting different kinds of pulls.

Different stretches have their own centers. These centers are differently located in the privacy. Responsibility, for example, has its grounding in identity, and expresses this with respect to the I, while self-mastery has its grounding in the I itself, and is expressed in mind, decisions, and interest. The governance of them all by a One is in effect the governance of special dimensions of a private being by a single privacy. Since the privacy in its completeness is a late achievement, there will not always have been a One which is in equilibrium with respect to all the stretches. It will achieve such an equilibrium, will be a full-fledged One, only when all the stretches exist. This is not because it is a function of the items it is to rule, but because its full being consists in having all of them under its governance.

If the privacy must be articulated in the form of a person, individual, and self, before it can be a full One, what status has it before then? It will be a One which is not as fully determinate in itself as it could be. If this is so, would it not be the case that the nature of any One for actualities will fluctuate according to the kinds of actualities there are? I do not think so, for the One is not a reality which adjusts units to one another. Actualities and finalities stand apart; the cosmos is an outcome. But in the case of man, the One and different activities occur in a being who is at once private and in the world.

March 27

A One for a Many has a number of different roles. Faced with items which remain apart, the One has the role of a unity enabling them all to be together. Imposing itself on them, it provides relations among them: it also enables them to be possessed of transcendental unifications. Interacting with them, it constitutes derivatives of which appearances are one instance. And, by providing a point of equilibrium, it rectifies their relative excesses with respect to one another. Do all finalities have all five roles? Is each role characteristic of a distinctive finality? Or does the question have to do, not with finalities alone, but with any entity which, like a man's privacy, serves to provide an effective force with respect to a multiplicity of items—in the particular case of privacy, a rectifying equilibrium?

With the exception of the equilibrium, the various roles have already been recognized by me to be characteristic of all the finalities. The rectifying functioning of the privacy points up the fact that items other than finalities can assume the status of a One. What is not yet evident is whether the role of an equilibrating power is possible to the finalities, and whether other particular items can take on the other four roles. The first of these questions can be answered in the affirmative, if it be acknowledged that Being not only is a position in terms of which all actualities are on a footing, but that it exerts power on actualities to remain on a footing, with itself in the center. (If this power be granted to Being, it should also be exhibited in a specialized form by the other finalities, for all are related to the actualities in the same way, making a difference according to their natures.)

In discussions of the I, it has been evident that the I does possess, govern, provide relations, give a unitary meaning to, and interact with other aspects of the private being. Neither it nor any other limited item need have all the powers that a finality has. There need not be anything other than a privacy, for example, which has a rectifying role. But there would seem to be something anomalous if there were no finality with a rectifying role. Would not this give a kind of priority to that finality, thereby jeopardizing the reality of actualities? Though they could be said to have their own independent functionings, they would be like possessions or facets, subject to powers that somehow denied them complete independence. Being, then, instead of being understood to allow each actuality a status alongside the others, as mere coordinate realities, would have to be understood either to require them to be equalized, or to both allow them a status alongside one another and to be subject to restraints to which they should not be subject. The acknowledgment of the exercise of such restraints allows one to bring Being in closer accord with the other finalities, all of which insist on themselves. It also seems to place

Being closer than other finalities to the actualities, and to have it involved with them to a degree the other finalities are not.

If we recognize the integrity of actualities, we will have to recognize that they are incomparable, each an intensively reached, unduplicable entity. Being can be said to exert power on them all, to enable them to be equally real as actualities. In that very act, Being acquires the status of a central equilibrating force. Taking that suggestion as a guide, one can now see how the other finalities, in exercising their characteristic roles, take up different kinds of positions in relation to the actualities. Substance exerts a pull from below; Possibility, as an incipient relation prescribes; Existence encompasses by providing a field; and Unity takes a stand at the head of an hierarchy of values. I haven't got this exactly right as yet, but what now seems evident is that I have been accustomed to see all the finalities as somehow standing together at an equal distance from all the actualities. Though I have said again and again that the finalities are not in some remote realm, somehow distanced from the actualities—a supposition which would place the finalities and the actualities in a common field or space—but are exactly where the actualities are and there function to condition those actualities, I have not until now apparently, recognized, with any clarity, that they have quite different primary roles.

Whether or not the present reflections can withstand subsequent examination and criticism, they make evident the importance of pursuing issues down paths which otherwise would not be considered, but which are opened by taking account of other areas and asking oneself how previous reflections bear on them. Had I not tried to come to grips with the problem of the nature of a man's privacy as at the center of all his particular foci and activities, I would not have come to see how all the finalities, and particularly Being, could and do have a similar role with respect to all the actualities.

I have, for a long time, been perplexed by the functioning of Being. Not only did I come to consider it quite late (having muddled it with Substance and the actualities in *Modes of Being* under the heading 'Actualities') but I have treated it as an ever receding reality. There is, of course, a sense in which every entity, actualities or finalities, absents itself from every other. Each is something on its own, never to be fully reached from the outside either by itself or by another. The fact must not be allowed to stand in the way of our understanding the actualities and the finalities, and specializations such as privacy, as having distinctive roles.

Privacy seems primarily to function like Being; the I, like Unity; mind, like Possibility; decisiveness, like Existence; and identity, like Substance. Responsibility also functions like Possibility; desire, like Existence; rights, like Unity; interest, like Substance; receptivity, like Being; desire, like Existence; accountability, like Unity; claims, like Substance; and reason, like Being. None of this has really been thought through, and a careful examination will undoubtedly require a change in these main characterizations. The matter could be of some moment when it comes to understanding the primary ways in which different aspects of the privacy operate, and how they stand in relation to one another. The risk I have run in connection with the manuscript, that still remains to be rewritten, can surely crop up again, and the whole treatment become mechanical and unilluminating. But some schema like this should serve as a guide, particularly since it may help force into focus what otherwise would be overlooked.

It is tempting, but it would be unwarranted, to move from these reflections to the supposition that man is a microcosm in a macrocosm. That view makes one use a single set of categories in a two-fold way, compromises the radical independent realities of the actualities or the finalities, requires one to find duplicates of the one in the other, or supposes that, if they are not found, one or the other is not as it ought to be. It would also be unwarranted to suppose that Being or any or all of the other finalities requires man in order to have a role in the universe, for that would force one to deny that man is subject to the impersonal laws of nature, that there is a prehistory, and that the finalities have powers which they exercise without man's help. If we do find that there are analogues in man or other actualities of what is characteristic of the finalities, the account given in *First Considerations*, of their ability to internalize what is affecting them, would seem to be sufficient.

Apart from the internalizations to which actualities subject finalities in different ways and degrees (or apart from the different finalities which different types of actualities internalize) we can examine the various components of privacy and speak of them with transformed versions of the terms appropriate to the finalities—what in *First Considerations* was termed an 'honorific' name. The distinction between the original use and the derived honorific was there made evident by using capitals for terms referring to the one, and lower case for the reference to the other. Strictly speaking, though, one should provide a distinctive set for each type of reality. 'Privacy', 'person' are such terms, referring to what is characteristic of men. How should one speak of the inner nature of finalities? (One can carry out the reverse procedure and use arresting names—which are transposed forms of the names appropriate to privacies—to speak of finalities as they are internally).

March 28

Recurring once more to the you, we know it as responsible, and therefore that it is backed by an identity, mind, decisiveness, sensitivity and consciousness. It is not yet clear to me whether or not the responsibility has to be understood as involving a restriction on desire, and whether or not it demands a conformity to the existence and exercise of native rights. In addition, the acknowledgment of the you involves the acknowledgment of a private being who is a unity for all the separate things that are being expressed through that you. It exists beyond the reach of what one can clearly focus on through the you; there, it has the status of an individual in himself. The you requires a sustaining; it is presented by what is private. This provides an explanation of why the you is the distinctive kind of entity that it is, as something more than what it is being confronted as. Responsibility, because it is occupied with an ideal to be realized, offers one form of an effort to achieve excellence; the presence of a fundamental hope is expressed in the way in which the you is used in being made present; the attempt to be self-complete is expressed in the way in which the you is possessed by what lies beyond it; the presence of a fundamental demand for peace is present in the insistence on the integrity and dominance of the private being. Putting aside the fact that some of these classifications may have to be shifted about, what is now being suggested is that the basic occupations of a man with the finalities are all discernible when one confronts the you. Instead of saying that what we initially grasp is responsibility and other occupations with finalities, and then surmising that there is a one for them which may have other items to center and adjudicate, it is being maintained that all the primary occupations of a man are already involved in the acknowledgment of the you of another.

The acknowledgment of different focal points for the different occupations with finalities does not yet enable one to know just how the different focal points, such as the I, rights, and identity, relations such as accountability, claims, thinking, the centers of person, individual, and self, and derivative points such as interest, desire, and perhaps receptivity to the finalities, are to be understood in relation to one another, and how they might affect one another. If they are discernible, why has it taken me so long to note them? Is it not that they are initially discerned as merged into one another? Does not every philosophical inquiry involve a leaping ahead of the evidence in order to find a basis in terms of which what is present but not sharply distinguished, can be remarked on? Armed with the distinctions which reflection promotes, I was able to attend to a you with a readiness to mark out one or the other factor, and eventually all of them. We are able to accept them once they are put before us, but we do not initially face them as distinct, with clear implications and roles.

When I attend to you, what do I in fact discern? I think I note a. you are present, b. sustained, c. controlled, d. possessed, e. have your own expressions and career, f. are at once receptive to and resistant to any penetration, g. are quickened by sensitivity, h. governed from within, i. embodied but extend further within and toward what is outside, j. may be attended to in the guise of a me, and k. can function in relation to another you, to wit myself. There is no order in this set, and there is no surety that it is exhaustive. Which of the items might be questioned? Does not h duplicate c? If we eliminate h, and hesitate before i and k (though I think these would be evident to one who really faces a you), we are faced with the question, with respect to the remainder, what order do they have in the privacy, and what roles are we to give to the various implicated items, such as identity, mind, and decision (which are inseparable from responsibility), rights (which are inseparable from the person), and the I (which is inseparable from the completed private being)?

When I confront you, I confront what is a′ receptive to and resistant to my penetration (f above); b′ has its own expressions and career (e); c′ is quickened by sensitivity (g); d′ is controlled (c); e′ presented (a); f′ sustained (b); g′ possessed (d); h′ though embodied extends inwardly and outwardly (i); i′ functions in relation to another you (k); and j′, may be attended to in the guise of a me. But I am also aware that you are responsible, are a person, have rights, and that these are inseparable from an identity, I, mind, decisions, from the individual, an assumed accountability, interests, desire, a primal unity, and a two-way occupation with finalities. Just when am I aware of them, and how do I place them with respect to the privacy? How do I move from a′ to b′ and so on down through j′ and to identity, I and the two-way occupation with the finalities, as well as the points in between?

March 29

I am still looking for a clear opening into the anatomy of privacy. Another attempt: Remaining with you as just confronted, I notice a. how you present yourself—shy, diffident, intrusively, dynamically; b. how you are attending—slackly, intensively, sharply focused, alert, distractively, fearfully; c. what you say—irrelevantly, relevantly, with some originality, clearly, confusedly; d. what you do—something with your body, something relating to me, something relating to others, what is preparatory, effective, creative, work, play; e. how you judge—what your estimates are, expressed in what you say, but also in the way you respond and how, while engaging in the foregoing activities, you carry out an evaluation of yourself, me, others, what had been done, what is being done, or what is to be done.

The first, second, and fifth of these seem quite clearly to require a movement in depth into you as somehow beyond the you that is confronted. The third and fourth seem to be capable of being understood in terms which make no such reference. The Wittgensteineans treat language as a public occurrence, though some of them do speak as though the public occurrence told us something about the individual. It is possible to go from this perspective to behaviorism and allow for nothing else but the public presence of you in a language setting. But it will then be hard to see how one could say of you anything more than that you fit or do not fit. Truth, falsehood, intention, deception, and the like, would appear to have no place. What you do, too, seems to be understandable solely in terms of your public body, for what you do occurs in a public world and involves bodily energy. What is preparatory can be understood to involve potentialities in the body, and that is all, and therefore to require no reference to a privacy, any more than a knowledge of what physical entities might or will do, requires a reference to such a privacy.

One can now proceed in one of two directions: try to see if the first, second, and fifth can be satisfactorily dealt with in public bodily terms alone; and try to see if the third and fourth do not necessarily involve a reference to something private.

Presenting yourself in a shy or dynamic manner, one might attempt to hold, is a presenting of yourself in public, a way in which the you, and not something beyond this, assumes a position in a public setting. The shyness, diffidence, and more obviously, intrusiveness are ways of referring, it can be held, not to any attitude privately assumed, but to the way in which one actually functions in a public world. If this were not so, what reason would we have for saying that someone was shy and so on? We attribute the shyness to an individual, it might be maintained, only as a convenient way of remarking on what one might expect a body to do subsequently. Similarly, the way you attend can be determined by what you in fact do, and thus is to be understood in terms of what, under d, was treated as requiring no private side. And just as we take the body of an animal to be well-trained, well-habituated, or the opposite, on the basis of the way in which it publicly functions, your evaluation of me and others can be determined in part by what you say, and in part by what you in fact do with respect to me as I am together with you in a common public world.

Proceeding now in the opposite direction, an attempt could be made to show that supposedly purely public activities are inescapably grounded in and are not intelligible or possible without a reference to what is ineluctably private. What you say is something claimed to be true or false; it is offered deceptively, honestly, as an expression of what was thought. It is more than noises only because there is a unitary meaning which the saying articulates. The individual who speaks uses a common language to produce units of discourse; he speaks in response to what he understands and not merely to what he hears, and that understanding requires a reference to what is not bodily. What you do is not something to be understood in the same way that one understands what physical entities do. Preparation is not solely a preparation to act in a public way, as a practice swing is a preparation for an actual swing with a golf club. There is guidance, control, alteration made even in what is effective, successful, on behalf of some ideal objective, some standard, some desire to produce beauty, to live up to a prescription which may have been privately entertained. Claims that such procedures are eventually to be traced back to the activities of the brain, not only are not justified by any actual evidence, but themselves are guided by privately accepted canons of truth, discovery, and respectability.

If the second procedure is carried through successfully, and the first neglected or rejected as not being worth doing, every one of these distinguished types of activity has to be understood as at the forefront of a private dimension and eventually of a single privacy. If the first procedure is carried through successfully, and the second taken to be illegitimate, unsuccessful, or unnecessary, every one of the distinguished activities will be understandable in more or less behavioristic terms.

It has been my contention all along that the presenting of oneself, the way one attends, and the way one assesses are not understandable without reference to a private dimension. Presenting is not only an act of fitting into some public setting by what already is public. There is a presenting of oneself, the making of oneself be public, the occupying of a place in space, time, and causality, acting and moving by altering the way the presentation takes place. The way you attend is not restricted to what you do with your body; it involves a focusing, a bringing to bear what you remember and understand, and this sometimes deliberately, sometimes cautiously, sometimes boldly. And the way you evaluate may not come into the open at all. You may hold your judgment to yourself, maintaining a secret attitude of contempt, respect, admiration, or fear while you act. It might be claimed that if these attitudes were not expressed in bodily ways they would not be known. Let this be granted. It still leaves over the fact that the body is being used as an instrument to carry out what was privately entertained.

If all this be granted, the next and persistently perplexing question is how one proceeds from here. What kind of evidence and direction does the you provide for an entrance into what is beyond it, and which partly expresses itself in and through that you? Or is it enough to remark that the very acknowledgment that what I am confronting is a you, necessarily requires a movement inward beyond what is publicly present? The first of these questions looks at the you for intrusive items whose acknowledgment inevitably take us to what is beyond the you, somewhat as the evidences dealt with in *First Considerations* take us to the finalities. The second, instead, treats the encountered you to be the evidence itself, inseparable from the inward source which we are trying to get to via the you.

Is the you a terminating locus of evidence we must isolate so as to have a beginning for a movement into privacy; or is the you itself the evidence that there is such a privacy? An affirmative answer to the first could have been almost mechanically derived by reversing the direction of the process of evidencing discussed in *First Considerations*. That is one difficulty with it—perhaps I am proceeding too mechanically? Another is that a five-fold move is warranted when one turns toward the finalities, for there are five of them at least; but what warrant is there for supposing that there are five pivotal points which an acknowledgment of you requires? Will we not tacitly be assuming something like a microcosm/macrocosm view? And, of course, we will be supposing that a you is an appearance, the product of expressions of the privacy and a body, the expressions providing us with avenues into the privacy, leaving us with the problem of finding other avenues into the body itself.

The other alternative, the viewing of the you as itself evidential, supposes that it is ingredient in a 'you-ified body', to which the body contributes other ingredients. The you-ified body will be an appearance, and the you will not be known until it is dislocated from this. The you, too, since it is a single unit, will take one only to a single privacy, and not allow one to know its subdivisions. But the you, precisely because it is evidential, will belong to the private being; it will be an attenuated form of this. What was public would not be you, but the you-ified body. When we ask, "Who are you?" we seem to be accepting some such view.

There is, of course, no incompatibility between the two. It is possible for the you to have a two-fold role; it may be a locus of evidence and also itself be evidential. As the one it will allow us to trace various lines back into privacy; as the other it will allow us to reach the privacy as a single undivided reality. But so far as it is taken in one guise, it will not be possible to take it in the other; the status of it as evidence, however, while making it less concrete than it as a locus, allows us to get to the privacy as that which is a ground for the different termini of our moves into the privacy.

One could justify a five-fold evidencing which originates with items isolated in the you, by supposing that identity, person, and so on are the outcome of internalizations of the finalities, and that only the you as evidence takes us to the privacy as it is apart from such internalizations. One would still be left with the problem of why there should then be any attempt to be receptive to and to realize the finalities, as well as with the problem of what it is that engages in the internalizations. One would, to solve the second problem, have to suppose that the one undivided privacy, in trying to internalize all the finalities, inevitably divides itself into limited areas. (And, since the finalities are faced with actualities, which though they differ in grade are still alike as units contrasting with those finalities, their internalizations of the effects of those actualities will not involve any multiplicity of internal positions in the finalities, even while they order those actualities in accord with their consonance with what the finalities are in themselves.)

A consequence of these reflections seems to be that we move to a unitary privacy (even in a human, not fully developed) both when we face a you as evidence (and therefore as perhaps unreflectingly and unknowingly dislocated from its role as a constituent of a you-ified body) and as leading to what internalizes five different transcendentalized effects. We will know of it in the latter guise by using evidence in the you. The different internalized items are on a footing in one sense and not on a footing in another: as the products of the privacy's response to the prsence of finalities, they are all equal and occur at the same time. But since some of these finalities are not internalizable by things or animals— e.g., things cannot internalize more than Substance, and animals cannot internalize Being or Unity (I have wobbled on this point and indeed said first one and then the other in *Beyond All Appearances,* but now incline toward Unity), the privacy may not be as apt in the beginning to internalize them all with the same degree of success, thereby making some to be privately more basic than others. The order of priority or placement of the different positions in the privacy then could be determined by attending to the standing that a man has in the hierarchy of actualities.

If it be true that things can internalize only Substance as it impinges on them, the most primitive and presumably the most basic fact of privacy will be one which exhibits the internalized presence of Substance, and person, individual, self, and I will, at deeper and deeper levels, have internalized Substance as affecting an actual man. If, as was stated on p. 311 of *Beyond All Appearances,* plants internalize Possibility as well as Substance, they will have sensitivity as well. If lower animals internalize, not Unity (as it is there maintained) but Being, only human privacy will have individuality, rights, and an I. And finally, if Existence is what is internalized only by higher animals, there will be desire, interests, receptivity, claims. These consequences show that there is something amiss here, for surely we must allow that desire and interests are not superficial, or that if they are, that receptivity and claims are not.

The hierarchy of internalizations as expressed in the hierarchy of grades of actualities must be thought through again, and then re-examined to see if in fact it does give us one or more focal points in the private being at different levels of availability, power, or ultimacy.

March 30

In order to determine how to proceed into the privacy of a man, and there locate the primary focal points, it seems reasonable to acknowledge a unitary privacy becoming involved with the various finalities, and thereby becoming diversified. In order to determine the relative status of these focal points it is reasonable, too, to see which of the finalities the lower grades of actualities internalize (in order to compensate for the difference those finalities are making to the exterior of these actualities), and then to recognize that men would have such internalizations in a more primitive way than they would any internalized result that they alone are able to obtain. If one knew just what a thing was internally, one could reasonably expect to find that this condition was a constant in men, and that any other more distinctive kind of result would be a later achievement. But, instead of following the path pursued yesterday, and trying to take advantage of the observations made in *Beyond All Appearances* (some of which now strike me to be arbitrary), I think it is desirable to think through the matter afresh.

A physical entity is essentially a unit in a space, time, dynamic world. It is subject to the conditioning of different dimensions of Existence. What it internalizes is the effect of Existence on it, thereby turning itself inwardly into a potentiality for the Existence. Each particle has its own aboriginal privacy. It is conceivable that this may merge with the privacy of other physical particles, but since an occasional particle may function independently of the others and, in any case, since particles can achieve distinctiveness when they are subject to some organic encompassing unity, each must be recognized to have a privacy of its own. That privacy is not a product of internalization. Two obstacles stand in the way of the supposition that it could be. There has to be a privacy which engages in the internalization; and the privacy must be distensive in order for it to be able to occupy a portion of an extension, give this up, and occupy others, as it does when in motion. Consequently, the internalization of the affect of Existence on a particle need not be thought to involve anything more than a qualification of an aboriginal private distensiveness possessed by rather than identified with the privacy. In higher grade actualities, this internalized result will have a different cast because their privacies are not just powers enabling them to occupy positions in a public extension.

A plant, in addition to having a privacy which is distensively toned, has a distinctive nature. It is a plant of such and such a type. To the obvious observation that physical entities also have natures of various types, it can be maintained that if the various entities are not aggregations or tightly packed compounds, but do in fact have distinctive natures, they do not individualize these, really make them their own. And because they do not, they cannot really grow. The so-called growth of crystals, mountains, oceans, or continents is a growth in magnitude; they may then act in ways otherwise not possible, but do not seem to have natures. And though it is true that there are cases where one cannot decide whether or not some entity is living, and thus whether it is merely a physical or chemical entity, or something more than this, it is also true that there are clear cases on both sides of the undetermined and unclear line. It is also true that the terminology, 'thing,' 'plant,' 'lower and higher animal,' is quite old-fashioned, and brings one back sharply to Aristotle. This hierarchy would have been acceptable to him, as it is now to commonsense, but it is now rejected by scientists, if only because it is tied in with the view that all the 'species' are fixed forever. But there is nothing in the nature of the hierarchy of particle, plant, lower and higher animal, and man, which precludes the coming to be of higher grades after and even as a result of the adventures in which the lower were involved.

The internalization of the affects of Possibility on a plant enables this to be prescriptive with respect to what is done by some of the parts of the plant, and by it as a whole. Aristotle spoke of it as having its end in itself. Biologists who have tried to follow him here soon found themselves out of favor with others, and rightly so. Not only can one not make experiments and verify the presence of such an 'entelechy' but the use of it as an explanatory device takes one from the realm which biologists can and do investigate, to some other that may be presupposed by them but of which they cannot, as biologists, have knowledge.

Above the level of a plant is the lower animal. The line between them is also not known; nor is the line between the lower and the higher animal. But once again there seem to be quite clear cases of the one and of the other, making it possible to recognize them as having different types of privacy. At this point, we are driven to ask how one could possibly know anything about such a privacy? We know something about ourselves and about other men, and can make sense of the investigation of privacy. But the privacies of what is lower than man are almost and perhaps even entirely impenetrable by man, and surely to a degree that defies our being even faintly acquainted with those privacies. Am I then not inverting a proper procedure, and trying to learn something about the privacy of man by first attending to the question as to just what the privacies of lower order actualities are and do? How could we conceivably learn anything about man's privacy by distinguishing different grades of actuality and saying things about unencountered privacies in them, all confessedly outside the range of disciplines which attend to them?

The answer must be that we do have to infer to be able to say anything about the privacies of particles and plants, and even of lower animals. But those inferences can be made on the basis of what we know about the nature of reality, and about the public careers of these lower grade actualities. The same kind of inference can be employed to acknowledge the privacy of a man, and even the kind of qualifications to which the men subject internalizations of the various impinging actualities. But we are also able, despite the ability of men to use their privacies in independence of what they publicly do, to move continuously toward and into them beyond any pre-assignable degree, and can then confirm that men reproduce distinctions in the privacies characteristic of actualities below man. The speculative enterprise of understanding the privacies of lower grades of actuality, in short, can be used to prompt a more direct experiential contact with the content of such privacies when they are given a role as pivotal points in the privacy of a man. A plant's privacy, though not directly encountered, can be known to be different from a thing's, by virtue of the fact that it is able to guide the plant's growth, and perhaps even to be capable of a rudimentary type of sensitivity, since it is able to respond sensitively to stimuli, and not merely react to pressure.

Lower animals differ from plants by virtue of their power to undergo privately that to which they are being subjected outwardly. They are conscious, able to undergo pain and pleasure. They occupy extensions and have natures. In addition, they have beings, maintaining themselves in independence of other entities.

In addition to internalizing what the lower grade actualities do, the higher animals internalize the effect of Unity. This enables the higher animal, despite its inability to maintain its privacy in contradistinction to what it is bodily, to utilize that body, as a way of assessing what it confronts as better or worse, desirable or undesirable. The lower animals and plants reject and accept, are lured and repelled, but they do not stand away and assess what they confront before beginning to act. Lower grade animals could be said to make such an assessment by their preparations and reactions, but they do not have strategies, plan, prepare, or distinguish between equally satisfactory items on the basis of an evaluation of them as more or less preferable.

Men, alone, in addition to internalizing what these others can, are able to internalize the effects of Substance. It is that fact which we all seem to acknowledge in our ready speaking and acting as though a privacy were a distinct substance. Apart from the internalization a man's privacy has a distinctness and is able to function in contradistinction from the body with which it is nevertheless continuous. By internalizing the effect of Substance, a man functions as an ultimate private being, self-contained, dominant over what he reaches toward, possessive, demanding understanding in the terms that he provides. Each man can be understood in terms common to all. This does not preclude a radical final status which is his alone, not because he is an individual—for it can be justifiably maintained that higher animals have some kind of individuality—but because he is able to carry out private activities independently of his bodily activities, which he also carries on under the influence of, as well apart from that privacy.

With this as a basis, we can say:

1. The most basic fact is that the you is being presented, that one is making oneself public in the form of the you. That presenting is a. sensitive, b. conscious, c. carries claims, d. expresses interests, and e. is distensive. All of these are discernible in the you, and take us back to a sensitivity, consciousness, a claiming, interest, and a distension.

2. The next level is where the you is given a prescriptive, explanatory role. In the you we discern the outcome of the exercise of a. a concern, b. an assumed accountability, c. a mind, d. decisions, and e. an overriding reasonableness, or 'prudence'.

3. The next level emphasizes the being of the privacy. We should be able to discern in the you, but with more difficulty than we had experienced with respect to the two previous levels, dimensions which reveal the operative presence of a. rights, b. reason, c. individuality, d. a bounded privacy, and e. the I.

4. The next level emphasizes Unity. Here there is doubt whether we can discern anything of it in the you, and whether or not our grasp of it begins by seeing the items on the previous level sustaining expressions of that Unity stemming from a. desire, b. receptivity, c. subordination (to some final objective), d. control, and e. identity.

5. On the highest level, but also as that which is least evident in anything we directly encounter or even clearly reach in a penetrative encounter with the you, are illustrations of the internalization of Substance. We here have a. the person, b. rectificatory power, c. separate activity of privacy, d. self, and e. presence of privacy in the you as a me.

I am not very confident that I have this entirely right, and have some doubt that I have rightly identified c. in 4.

6. No consideration has yet been given to the joining of receptivity to an occupation with some objective, and therefore a. to responsibility, b. the attempt to be excellent, c. the effort at self-completion, d. the attainment of the dignity of a man, and e. the centering presence of privacy with respect to every other factor. Where should these be placed? Should it not be held that they are ways in which the other levels operate, so that responsibility is at the root of the lowest level; the attempt to be excellent at the second level; the effort at self-completion at the third; the attainment of dignity at the fourth; and that the last achievement is the achievement of a full privacy able to function as the centering presence for all?

The early divisions, despite their pentagonic nature, were thought through freshly; toward the end, I think the five-fold schematism took over in some places. But this fault will perhaps be corrected when I apply the last set of distinctions to the various sets. Is it true that a presenting sensitivity, consciousness, claiming, interest, and distensiveness are under the governance of a responsibility? If so, what about the identity, I, perhaps receptivity, the self, privacy, mind, and decision which also seem to be involved in the acknowledgment of responsibility? Does the first set provide evidences or signs of the presence of responsibility, while the second are implications of its presence and working? If so, the implications of responsibility entrench on the evidences or signs of other basic activities. Since the implied items are on a higher level, we will have to say that when there is responsibility a higher level is also present. To be on a higher level will then mean, not that there is something subsequent in time necessarily, but only that the implied is present in a being which has more than one level. The implicated items would also be evidenced in the you and would be under the governance of some other way of utilizing finalities—on the second level of the attempt to be excellent, or even on a higher.

March 31

For the last ten days or so I have been attending to the following distinctive points in a man: sensitivity, consciousness, rights, claiming, identity, assumed accountability, desire, mind, decision, I, interest, reason, receptivity to finalities, distensiveness, occupation with finalities, person, self, individual, privacy. Yesterday I distinguished those items which seemed to be under the governance of responsibility, and those which seemed to be implied by it. Left out of that account were rights, assumed accountability, desire, reason, occupation with finalities, person, self, individual, and privacy, and the efforts at self-completion, attainment of excellence, self-mastery or dignity, and the centering role of privacy. Might some or perhaps even all of these be shown to be somehow involved with responsibility? Yes. Responsibility concerns the rights of others, and these must be recognized to be like one's own; in addition, one has a responsibility to oneself to see that one's rights are expressed and urged. Assumed accountability can be said to be possible only to one who has the responsibility, not only to be a source of public acts but to act in the light of what such a source would be. Desire could be said to give direction to the expression of rights and to involve their control. Reason or speculation could be taken to be occupied with the structure or prescriptive principles which a responsibility embodies. The occupation with finalities could be said to be required by the responsibility one has to oneself. Rights involve the person, and the person, as having more than just rights, should be developed; this could be said to be one's responsibility. The self grounds the I, interest, mind, decision, reason, and receptivity, and is not only involved in them but has the role of rectifying them, presumably responsibly. The individual has a similar role with respect to its dimensions, and the privacy has one with respect to the self, person, and individual. The act of responsibly doing anything could be traced to the centering privacy, and this could be said to require supplementary efforts, such as the effort at self-completion, in order to function as an appropriate rectifying power. The outcome of such a procedure would be the acknowledgment of responsibility when one was attending to the you as a being which had an intensive possessing depth. Nothing is now left of the idea that there might be a hierarchy of powers and pivotal points, except so far as one was able to take them to be late developments of a matured privacy, and then went on to deal with the above recognized pivotal points in new ways. Rights, or mind, or sensitivity, for example, might be said to have another role for the search for excellence than they have for the effort at self-completion, but the set of items, with which these and the other primary ways dealt with and unified finalities in oneself, would be generically the same.

Anxiety, fear, hope, traumas, and psychoses can be understood as having to do with aberrational relations between items, between one or more of them and the independently functioning body, with what is outside the body in the form of other bodies, with conditions governing them, or with the finalities beyond them. How you present yourself, how you attend, what you say, what you do and how you judge could all be brought under responsibility and, under some not yet explained (by me) modification, brought under the other occupations with the finalities. In all cases, the you would be understood to be an appearance, the outcome of expressions of a privacy and a living body. Supposing all this could be done and justified, we would still be faced with the problem of placing these various factors in relation to one another, and understanding how they operate and make a difference to the operation of one another. We would also have to explain why it is that responsibility rather than the other occupations with finalities is so prominent and why it provides the initial clue to the understanding of man in his privacy.

One reason why responsibility has prominence is because we come to the you in a public world where occurrences and effects are attributed to accountable sources. On arriving at the you as such a source we are inevitably brought into contact with the intensive depth of that you. This is being insisted on, thereby forcing the assessment of the accountability as being in conformity or disconformity to what one is, tries to do, and in fact made himself bring about. The tracing back of that responsibility could be recognized to have various stopping places at which one could perhaps identify different factors. Does the arrival at one factor reveal it to be a product, and therefore to provide evidence for what is still beyond it? Could one in this way go from distensiveness, sensitivity, consciousness, claiming, interest, mind, decisions, assumed accountability, rights, I, and so on? How would one know what the next step was? Would we have to be able to isolate the factor and find at its fringe the outcome of the expression of some other? What assurance would we have that we were really discerning what was present?

Not everyone faced as a you is taken to be responsible. In anger we may cry "You are hopeless", meaning that one has found no way of making real contact with one able to express himself freely through a publicly evident you. Not everyone is responsive, and no one seems to be responsible always. But if not responsive, can he be known to be responsible? We can identify someone as a you even when he is caught in situations from which he cannot extricate himself, when he is governed by forces beyond his control. We know a you to be responsible only when we face one who is mature and has some degree of private freedom, able to express himself pertinently to what he is confronting. But one might not be able to express some private power in the guise of a responsibility.

We know another to have a privacy which could function responsibly if we know that some factor in him, outside him, or in his body modified or controlled, or if we can know him to be a man as surely as is one who makes evident that he is responsible by freeing making use of his body in a number of possible ways. This way of speaking seems to put priority on decision, on the exercise of preference, choice, and will, rather than on sensitivity or consciousness or the other factors which before seemed to be to the fore when I was considering responsibility's grounding and implications.

Not sensitivity, not consciousness, not rights, not distensiveness, not person, self, individual, privacy, desire, or mind tells us with surety that someone has responsibility. All of these can be and function, evidently before or apart from the exercise of responsibility. It is only when some of these are exercised in a certain way that they allow us to learn that another is responsible. If he is not merely sensitive because of the delicacy of his reaction, or because his privacy is continuous with what he is publicly, but because he is utilizing that sensitivity, we can know he is responsible. The utilization is guided by some decision; yielding sensitivity which is more acute than it otherwise would be, it is directed where it might not have been, and would not ordinarily be directed, were it just bodily or incipiently so. Must we not say something similar with respect to consciousness, rights, distensiveness, and so on?

When we face the you as so functioning that it must carry the outcome of a decision, since that decision expresses responsibility it will be inseparable from consciousness, from a right, and from claims. The decision could conceivably not require identity, since the individual might perish with the decision, as process philosophers seem to hold. But if the decision is made responsibly, there must be identity, for one remains responsible after one has engaged in a responsible decision. We might have rights, as infants do, but not exercise or express them. Nor would we necessarily be responsible if we expressed our rights in the very course of presenting ourselves in public. We might insist on rights without reflection or deliberation, somewhat in the way we present ourselves in public space.

Responsibility is involved in decisions and, so far, requires reference to consciousness, mind, identity, I, and privacy. It may be exhibited in sensitivity, in a claiming, or in the expression or insistence on other private powers. And once we know it is present, it could be known to be able to produce a privately assumed accountability. Consciousness and other powers will be ingredient in it, whether or not they have a status apart from it. But we may not become alert to the responsibility when exercising sensitivity and other powers, unless they carry a decision which makes a difference to the way in which the confronted you functions.

If responsibility is known because of the existence of a decision, and if our beginning of an acquaintance with the responsibility is in the you, the occurrence of the decision must be discernible in that you. The you must be recognized to be initially involved with an indeterminacy that is made determinate, not by an act of you as a body, but by what enables the you to act. The overcoming of the indeterminacy requires the use of a non-bodily power, exercised apart from the body but with results exhibited in and through the body. The sensitivity, consciousness, rights, claiming, identity, assumption of accountability, desire, mind, I, interest, reason, receptivity, occupation, person, self, individual, and privacy may all provide indeterminacies requiring responsible decisions to be made. (Only after we have made sure that something has been decided, can we warrantedly go on to suppose a power which could have but did not in fact decide, and therefore a responsibility expressed as a non-deciding.)

A deciding exhibited in bodily acts can be said not to be produced by the body or in its acts, only if there is something involved in the deciding which is beyond the body's reach. Can this be anything other than prescriptions, non-bodily objectives, what is understood or inferred from the ways in which various private powers are found to function?

Some powers are known apart from responsibility, because they have non-responsible modes of functioning. We can infer their presence by attending to the you, even when it is acting responsibly. On the other hand, they could be taken to be wholly determinate, or to be made determinate without decisions responsibly undertaken. But if we already know that we are responsible, we know that they must be present. In short, we can get to private powers by attending to the you, and without knowing anything about responsibility; and we can conceivably know them without having to attend to responsibility. But, in fact, we know that a man has them because we know he is responsible. And because we know he is responsible, we know that his private powers could be responsibly governed.

What is now needed is some way of determining the order of the items in a possibly responsibly governed sensitivity, etc. It seems possible to produce a partial listing, beginning with distensiveness and other forms of a private readiness to be in public, and going on to other powers. But it is hard to see just where rights and assumed accountability fit in. Person, individual, self, and privacy seem to be in an order of what is more and more basic. But it is not yet clear just where identity and I are to be placed.

April 1

When I confront another, I may attend to him as a mere body, acting as other bodies do. Even if that body be recognized to have been made present from within, it will still be like other bodies, for these, at the very least, are distensive, and come into public by using that distensiveness to divide universal undivided extensions. And if one were to go on to remark that a confronted body not only makes itself present in extensions but also makes itself self-possessively present in a public world of more or less relevant items, self-boundedly present in a world of other independent entities, intelligibly present in a rationally governed world, and insistently present as a unit of value in a totality of values, it could still be like other bodies, at least in the sense of making itself present without thought, deliberation, or intent. What is needed for evidence of responsibility is something in the public world which leads to a decisiveness, and this is not capable of being produced by the body or automatically performed in privacy. One must see the confronted you as subject to decisions which cannot be present without having been antecedently performed, and then made to govern the body and its actions. One will then know that the you is at the forefront of a responsible man.

1. A man makes himself present sensitively. His body is not simply reactive but responsive. So far, it is like the body of any other organic being. He is not yet known to be responsible. This requires that the sensitivity carry out a decision privately made. Since the sensitivity is expressed in the body and has to do with what that body undergoes and faces, it is occupied with what is happening and can happen. This, with which the sensitivity is occupied is, relative to the activity of that sensitivity, a prospect, something to be made determinate. If the production of the determination is not the sensitivity's doing, but makes use of the sensitivity, the sensitivity will function as a means. We know of the presence of responsibility, consequently, when we know that the sensitivity is expressing a preference, which is to say making determinate the activities of the body with respect to some action or object, by making it function in one specific way, so that it is desirable. What is made desirable in this way is not necessarily the object of a desire; it is just that which is given specificity and, therefore, brought into focus by a privately exercised preferential act making use of the sensitivity.

2. Desire contrasts with sensitivity in coming from a deeper inward position, as is evident from the fact that it can make use of sensitivity, and thereby make the sensitivity not only face something as desirable but in fact seek it. Desire, of course, can be expressed without guidance or intrusion from what is non-bodily. It can be triggered and perhaps governed by such primal bodily needs as hunger, thirst, or protection. Such desires are possible to what is not responsible.

The acknowledgment of a publicly expressed desire, though intelligible in terms of bodily disequilibria, needs, chemistry, and the like, does not preclude the recognition of it as having a private ground. The desires that are exhibited both by a man's body and by subhuman bodies have private bases. In the subhuman, the desires are all incipiently and directly expressed in the body. Neither in men nor in the others does desire necessarily require decision or responsibility. If it did, subhumans would make decisions and have responsibility, or a man could always desire without making decisions or having responsibility.

Men have desires which express a preference privately engaged in, and therefore which make prospects for those desires determinate. Such desires can be known when men, despite the satisfaction of bodily needs, persist in their attempts to reach and possess an object of desire; when they prevent a desire from being carried out; and when they modify and redirect it toward what cannot then satisfy it. We know that such activities occur when we know the object of desire, and then find the desire subject to determinations beyond the power of the body to provide, or to be automatically instituted in privacy. We know that the body cannot provide those determinations for, *qua* body, it is like all other bodies or all other organic bodies or, at the very most, it is a distinctive kind of body, and in any case is unable to do anything more than do what external circumstances or its own requirements demand.

Control of desire on behalf of something that is not the terminus of that desire evidences the exercise of a preference responsibly undergone. There are, to be sure, many cases where birds and other subhumans, even when denied food for a while, and presumably hungry, keep food in their mouths for their offspring. They seem to be exercising a preference in the face of a desire. Either the restraint is purely bodily in nature, so that one bodily drive automatically overrides another, or the subhuman being is exercising a preference privately made. If the latter, it still would not necessarily be true that it freely decided, that it freely exercised a private act of preference. At most, it automatically joins the prospect of feeding its offspring with the act of restraining from eating.

What is preferred is an alternative made to stand out by some objective. If the objective is inescapable or insistent (as apparently is the case with a bird feeding its young), the objective will make, what otherwise would be done, something to be deferred or denied. A preference responsibly made, in contrast, is determined antecedently, before there is a bodily facing or possible alternatives by some accepted end. To know it, the body must be found to be carrying out one kind of activity, such as feeding one's young, despite bodily hunger, and to be restrained, directed, challenged by another activity. Though there may be times when certain activities, even in man, override all others, so that there is no restraining the effort to satisfy a hunger or to feed one's young, or more generally, to answer some craving, there are times when a desire and a preferred object, characteristically and usually pursued, are held up, delayed, or denied. If we know what is bodily desired, we can know that the body is sometimes subject to privately produced decisions to do something else. Something is wanted, independently of what is desired, and may therefore conflict with the carrying out of that desire in the usual way.

When something preferred is not preferable in terms of an actual desire, it could conceivably be insisted on without reflection, and therefore be the consequence of some non-responsible activity undergone privately. Consequently, one must move back a step and take account of a situation where one is privately faced with the problem of deciding between the carrying out of a bodily desire and a privately entertained alternative course, which will inevitably come into conflict with the bodily desire and therefore modify it, and perhaps be modified in turn. There must then be a terminus, toward which the body is directed, that will not satisfy the body or the interests of the species, and may not be suppressed or modified by a private but automatically expressed preference. It must therefore not be of value to the body, the species, or the private being. One can freely desire what injures, pains, makes one's body or species suffer, or which is indifferent to bodily needs and appetites, and have this override what is desirable for the body, the species, and the privacy.

We know that a man responsibly desires when he takes as desirable a goal whose attainment has no bodily value, but which is preferred because it promotes a wanted goal. To want is to go beyond desire toward what must be freely accepted, and which makes otherwise undesired present objects and activities be preferable.

3. A body can be imbued with consciousness; is therefore able to feel pain and pleasure. Were it just sensitive, it could, like a decapitated frog, react to acids in somewhat the way in which it did when it had a head. Consciousness is a noting of the tonality of what is sensitively undergone. It occurs without deliberation or intent, and varies in strength throughout the day, perhaps even fading away altogether in stupor or deep sleep. We know that another is conscious when we know that he is not merely withdrawing from what injures and moving toward what satisfies, but that he is then suffering or is pleased. This we can know if he persists in his attitude even after the source of injury and satisfaction have been removed. The acknowledgment of consciousness takes us outside the realm of the body, as sensitivity and desire do not, to the privacy of a being. That privacy may be the privacy of an organic sub-human, and therefore be just an incipiency for some expression in and through the body of that being. We can know that it is the consciousness of a man if and so far as it is not an incipient bodily expressed consciousness. To know it when we attend to a you, we must find it to be

present there. And this we can do when we find the body dealt with as an object of consciousness. A cat may purr when it is stroked; it may find pleasure in licking itself. But it does not stand apart from these acts and attend to itself as having pleasure. How do we know this? How do we know that other men can so stand apart but that no animal can?

The most evident indication of a responsibly used consciousness is provided when another remains attentive in a direction other than that in which something manifest is of importance to the body. Some animals exhibit curiosity and involve themselves in matters having no evident bodily value, but they turn from this when something imperative for the body in that state is evident. A man, instead, may remain deliberately conscious about that which is occurring in one direction while he is being attracted and affected in others. He evidences that fact most conspicuously when he attends to what has aesthetic value while the body is tensed in other directions. He then exhibits a freely expressed preference.

4. Interest is manifested by the persistent maintenance of a prospect, making use of different means and utilizing different powers all the while. Since an animal can express such interest, interest is attributable to a body or to a privacy able to be expressed in and through a body. It could be elicited in a privacy, without thought or effort, by virtue of that privacy being keyed to what might be termed its proper good, some end it always serves through different agencies. The presence, not of a mere interest, but of a responsibly elected interest, is known when an interest in what is bodily important is held in abeyance while another interest in another direction is emphasized. That other interest could conceivably be the expression of the privacy as necessarily tied to some appropriate objective. If it is an interest that is freely insisted on, it terminates in a goal that provides an overwhelming determinant of what is to be then and there preferred. The preferences exhibited in and through the body are then seen to be of two kinds: those which are required by a body's steady prospect, and those which, while making use of the body, are directed toward what has no such bodily import.

Here, and in the preceding examination, it seems as if I were saying that responsibility was being manifested when one was doing something foolish or idle, opposing health and bodily satisfaction. But there is no reason why the various objectives which are without bodily import may not have bodily activities and satisfactions as preferential means. What must be seen is an occupation with what lies outside bodily definition or private projection, but which can be given a satisfying bodily role at the same time that the body is being made to serve some other end. The body, in short, must be seen to be a means, an instrument whose functioning is to be understood by attending to the governing presence of an objective that is outside bodily interest.

5. An act of preference is the outcome of the imposition of an accepted prospect on a set of alternativies. It results in the determination of one of those alternatives as that which is then preferred. Occurring privately and without regard for what the body is and needs (though having an affect on the body's functioning), it is the outcome of a responsible decision. We know of it only when it overrides what the body would otherwise do. An act of choice is entirely outside the provenance of a body, for it involves the assessment of some end and the determination of an alternative in the light of what losses in value its acceptance would entail, and therefore what a moral being would have to make good. Choice is always performed privately. A body can exhibit and carry out its own preferences but cannot choose, for it has no power to make itself obligated to make good whatever losses in value are produced by an acceptance of some particular course of action to bring about a final goal. To know that a choice has been made, one must know that a course of action has been decided upon, failure to keep to which entails guilt. If we are to have evidence of responsibility as expressed in choice, we must find it expressed somehow in and through a publicly encountered embodied you. And this we can do, I think, with respect to rights, mind, and the assumption of accountability.

6. Rights are private. But we seek to have them sustained publicly. We view whatever encompasses us and other men as justifying the expression of certain rights in certain ways at certain times. If some particular society, state, or set of prescriptions is accepted as having final value, some supposed rights will be denied legitimacy; if, instead, there are rights which should be sustained, a prescription that does not permit of the expression and satisfaction of those rights will be unjust or improper. Initially, though, we know only of a conflict between the two, without yet being in a position to say whether or not the one or the other is at fault. Some rights are unquestionable—the right to life, health, maturation, and to be a public unit. We may recognize that by virtue of some action, we may have forfeited one or the other, because we have accepted some society's or state's prescriptions as absolute. But since that acceptance itself is dependent on one's living, having matured, being a proper and thus a healthy public unit, evidently there is a fundamentality to these rights which should be respected. The choice we ought to make is for what maximizes the number of rights we have within a final setting

which, together with those rights, yields a whole of maximum value, that which ought to be.

We know of a man's rights, and of the whole he constitutes with some final objective which such rights serve or articulate, when we attend to him, not by himself but as within a larger public setting. We see him use his body, no longer in order to achieve some satisfaction, or even in order to carry out some other expressed preference, but in order to conform to or oppose what is being prescribed by a whole in which he and other men, (including one who approaches him as a you) are.

Animals have rights and so do things. But the expression of their rights is not chosen by them in the light of some whole of which the animals are members. It is we who insist on their having their rights protected; it is we who insist that it is unjust to deny them their rights.

7. 'Mind' is a term now used with considerable ambiguity. In the past it was thought to require consciousness and perhaps a soul; today men speak readily of computers having minds, and they have no hesitancy in attributing minds to their pets, to the primates, or even to all mammals. We come to acknowledge the minds because we find beings engaged in ordered processes toward goals, some of which may be determined solely by drawing logical consequences from accepted premises or truths. But a mind may also function independently of the body, drawing necessitated conclusions regardless of what the body is like or what it is doing. We know of the presence of such a mind when we find someone saying or doing what is explicable only as a deducible consequence of what had antecedently occurred. It is a mind not possible to a machine, for what this derives is antecedently determined by the ways in which its parts are arranged. The mind of living beings reaches consequences regardless of the state of the body, what it needs, how it functions—even though the mind may not so operate unless there is a body in a certain condition. When the body, despite its desires, interests, appetites, habits, is made to express in act, and particularly in speech, the outcome of what could have been only a course of reasoning, deriving necessitated conclusions from accepted premises, we acknowledge the presence of a mind operating on, in, and through the body. We will know that the mind is being responsibly used, and therefore not to be functioning as a concretionalized logic allowing for no freedom or decision, when the beginning and therefore the end of the act of inferring are both irrelevant to the body's nature or career as a unit item in the public world, and the body shows originality and proceeds imaginatively. One can of course

think on behalf of the body, but such thinking abstracts from the body as it actually is, to consider it in an abstracted form.

We know that a mind is freely used when the proper conclusions are asserted. A mind that is used by what does not speak, the mind say of a rat running through a maze, is a mind that leads to decisions and conclusions which the body's needs make desirable. The mind of a man can be expressed in and through his body; it already involves decisions and attains to conclusions which have to do only with whether or not the outcome is acceptable as valid and not just desirable or undesirable. A machine's functioning is closer to that of a human mind than an animal's, because its 'mind' already has incorporated a selected set of operations sanctioned by the human mind.

Decisions are involved in the use of the human mind in two ways. They are required in order that the mind be used even when all is going well in the public world. And they determine the way it is used, accepting or rejecting additions and subtractions from the initial starting point in the course of the process of getting to the conclusion.

8. I have spoken of a 'claiming' to designate the kind of impress identity is making on rights. If that usage be insisted on, its understanding will have to be deferred until something is known of identity and its operations. It may then be found to be something which responsibility presupposes, and not what is discoverable in the body of the you, or the you itself, as that which is carrying what had been freely decided on, and responsibly.

9. Any entity can be taken to be accountable, and for what it has not even originated. One can be taken to be accountable for any one of a number of reasons—reasons of convenience, reasons of state, economic reasons, reasons of habit. Responsibility refers to what is traceable to the individual as having its source in his privacy. The responsibility might not be publicly expressed—one can be responsible for the way one makes sensitivity yield to mind. This of course will not be known until one knows what the sensitivity and the mind ought to do, and knows how to discover their aberrational activities on the basis of what is evidenced by and through the body.

In between responsibility and accountability is an assumed accountability, the deliberate election of a course of action for which one ought to be held accountable. It is responsibility directed at public occurrences, for which one holds oneself accountable no matter what others do. To come to know of responsibility via an assumed accountability, one must find in the body or public world an accountability that bears the mark of decisions made apart from the body and the world in which it is. We can recognize the presence of an assumed accountability in the admission that a reward or punishment is deserved or underserved. The accountability that is a function of the estimates and practices of a society is here assessed, and may be expressed in the assessment, and most clearly in the rejection of the attribution of accountability (or some degree of it) by the individual. His will be an act of free choice, determining his standing in the totality that constitutes the social world where accountabilities are distributed. The assumption of the accountability is private and free; it is engaged in responsibly; and is known by the way in which one assesses the accountability that others attribute, not simply by accepting or rejecting this, but by comparing it with what one has taken oneself to be ready to be in public.

* * *

This evening I will reread what has been written today and, as I usually do, content myself with correcting the grammar and making slight changes in style, while leaving the ideas intact. Tomorrow I will go on to deal with what responsibility presupposes—the power of decision, preference, choice, and will; the person with his preferences; the individual with his choices; the self with its will; identity and the I; and the rectificatory activities of privacy with its efforts at completion, excellence, dignity, and equilibrium, in addition to the responsibility that it also grounds.

April 2

We are responsible primarily for decisions freely made in privacy. When we are said to be responsible for not making decisions we presuppose that we could have made them freely. The acknowledgment that one is responsible for not having made a decision is thus parasitical on the knowledge that one who is responsible has a position from which he can privately and freely approach an indeterminate situation and produce a determination there. The decision presupposes that he has an identity and an I, and that privacy is the source of power. It is, of course, conceivable that some one might make a decision responsibly, and vanish with the act; it is conceivable, too, that there might not be an I, and that responsibility is carried out by an anonymous privacy. But responsibility is not a mere matter of private decision; it is carried out into and through the body and makes a difference to what is done. This takes time. Also, the consequences of the decision are not altogether separable from it, and should be taken account of in the deciding, a fact which is under-scored by the recognition of a man's responsibility to assume account-ability for what he does. And that means he must be remain self-same over a period of time. If he did not, he would not be able to assume accountability, and if he could not, he would not exercise the respon-sibility that he has, and thus would be like one who failed to make a decision, and therefore allowed things to run their course without his intervention.

The acknowledgment that responsibility involves decision made freely and privately could not have arisen had it not been for the fact that we had some access to the private being when we confronted the you, or attended to what it was doing. In the public world, therefore, we should be able to find evidences of the fact that we have made and can make decisions responsibly. Yesterday, I attended to public expressions of sensitivity, consciousness, desire, interest, as occurrences which are ex-hibited in and through the body and could have originated with it. Evi-dences of responsibly-made decisions were found in acts which could not originate with the body and could not occur automatically in privacy. A responsibly used sensitivity was found when a preference was exhibited for something held to be desirable but which was not desired, i.e., was not the object of a purely bodily impulse, a fact shown most conspicu-ously when the desirable is in a direction and requires activities opposite to those which the bodily desires required. Desire itself was found to be responsibly governed when the body was turned toward the realization of the desirable, requiring the body's desires to be controlled, modified, or denied. Consciousness was recognized to be the object of responsibly made private decisions when attention was directed toward what has aesthetic value, and is persisted in, despite the imperative demands of the body to turn elsewhere. Interest, finally, was found to be the object of a responsibly made decision when it provides a goal for a preference having no necessary bodily importance and when the interest is expressed in the face of a bodily insistence on some other topic.

It is the evidence of the exercise of a decision (that had to be made privately) that is sought in the public world. But one must make sure that the evidence is not only of a privacy but of a freedom, of a power that could have been exercised in another way. And that is made evident in the consideration of preference, for a preference is occupied with the election of some determinate means for an accepted goal. Given a goal, one is faced with an indeterminate course to realize it. Decision in the form of a preference is exercised when an alternative is adopted as a means for that goal; that alternative is produced when it is adopted.

Adoption is the separating out of a nuance in a possible course, and giving it the status of an accepted means which one insists upon. The justification for the adoption of that alternative is to be found in the accepted goal; this can make preferable what is disagreeable, by virtue of the value it gives it as the best means to the realization of that goal. The goal could conceivably have been forced upon one, been the outcome of habit or thought, or be the inevitable product of what occurred earlier. But the use of the goal to make this or that alternative stand out and be accepted is a free act not contained either in the goal or in the alternative. The matter has been discussed at some length in *Man's Freedom,* and the refinements that the present account requires can be provided from what is said there. What is now important to see is that the course of action can be exhibited in public, and there found to be quite different from what a bodily used sensitivity, desire, consciousness, or interest would require.

Rights, mind, assumed accountability; choice, will, the person, individual, self, identity, I, and the privacy's effort to utilize the finalities both as internalized agents and as objectives, have still to be dealt with.

In previous discussions I have located rights in the person. The person has now been understood to be engaged in preferences; these are continuous with and are exhibited in and control the body. Yesterday, though, I spoke as though rights were a topic of free choice exercised by the self. There is perhaps no inconsistency here. The rights are in the person and are urged by it through the you. But we come to know of a man's rights when we find them urged in opposition to the conditions embracing you and others.

Preferences can be exercised with respect to the particular rights that are being urged, or these might be urged unreflectingly, not freely. It is when we find rights which are adopted as part of a complex in which their insistence involves a loss of value now, and is matched by the acceptance of an outcome in which the losses are made good, that we are in a position to recognize the exercise of a free choice. The rights are insisted on in terms of a whole that a society or state neither embodies or endorses, and are insisted on even in the face of pressures by the society or state.

Mind, freely used in decisive acts of choice, has to do with the pursuit of consequences regardless of bodily or social needs. Evidence for the responsible use of that mind is found by noting how, usually in speech, but sometimes in action, consequences are insisted on in the face of bodily and social demands. We know that another has a freely used mind when what he maintains is what he alone provides. He could, of course, use his mind to come to conclusions which are publicly endorsed or sustained, but we will not know that he has a freely used mind until we come to situations where he shows himself to be functioning independently of what any body or public condition might require.

This view seems to be directly the opposite of that which most men hold. They think that the best evidence we have of the presence of a mind is the demonstrated ability to solve a problem, anticipate a result, make predictions. These, at best, can show only that there is a structure or process in the individual, well-geared to the course of the world. It also supposes that the individual is somehow cut off from the world and therefore has a privacy, and that he enters into the world, through the agency of his mind, with freedom. But it does not make evident that what is being done is freely decided on; the mind that is solving the problems, anticipating or predicting, so far as this view is concerned, could act mechanically perhaps because of its having an intimate relation to the parts of the brain. A responsible use of the mind involves decisions which need not have been made; the mind then freely solves, anticipates, predicts, as well as imagines or attains to mathematical and logical consequences having nothing to do with the affairs of the world, something most clearly discovered by finding necessitated conclusions maintained outside the area of bodily or even worldly matters.

Assumed accountability most clearly requires responsible decisions. Its occurrence is discoverable when one, while accepting accountability, denies, defies, or qualifies the accountability which is credited to him by other men or by society or state. Here, as well as in the case of mind, the activity is the result of a choice, and thus involves the envisagement of a totality of value and the election of some particular act or course of action involving a loss of value that the totality is to make good. One is pledged to realize the totality, having become committed to it because of what he has chosen, and this regardless of what it might otherwise be desirable to do. Its presence is known by the way in which one deals with the established accountabilities traced back to his you.

Choice is the act of an individual. As freely produced it involves a unitary value and an indeterminate nuanced set of alternatives. Both of these are made determinate at the same time—the unitary value as that which obligates then and later, and a distinguished alternative whose losses in value are to be made good in future activities promoting the

attainment of the unitary value. It is the work of a responsible individual
who is not merely private but whose choice involves unique decisions
with their required obligation to make good the losses that a present
elected alternative now involves.

The self is the agent of willing. Its exercise is achieved through the
free decision of that self as necessarily identical over time and as epitomized in the I. The will, when expressed bodily, is a deliberate, persistent control of the different types of bodily expression under the
governance of some accepted terminus. Its presence is known when the
different expressions are shifted without regard for the present bodily
needs or their natural bent. But the will can also be exercised in privacy;
it then governs the operation of private powers, determining their order
in relation to one another. For evidence of the private responsible exercise of the will, we must look to the you, not for indications of a control
of different bodily expressions in relation to one another (since this might
be an automatically produced rectification by the 'wisdom' of the body),
but of an occupation with an end not confined to bodily needs. And this
is what occurs when we are occupied with finalities as grounds to be
received and objectives to be realized. The occupation could express the
different ways in which a privacy makes itself be at the center of all
activities. The object of will, in contrast, encompasses all other activities,
and makes them serve the need to become complete, be excellent, have
dignity, achieve equilibrium and, of course, responsibility. The will here
makes itself the agency of these primal needs, and carries them into the
different points in privacy and body, thereby giving them new roles.

The will has now been said to be the work of the self-same self and
to be carried out by the I; it has also been said to carry out the work of
a privacy, insisting on completion, excellence, and so forth. In the one
case, however, it is empowered, and in the other mediates. A weak will,
no less than a strong, works on behalf of the efforts at completion, etc.
When we look for evidence for the privately exercised will we look to
what mediates responsibility as one of the ways in which privacy is occupied with what is final. The responsibility (and the others) which it
mediates will be more or less conspicuously exhibited, depending on the
action of the self and the I.

Beyond the will is the privacy as at the center of all activity; it rectifies
excess efforts in any direction, and therefore also the will. One does not
will to control the will, but one does elicit its use, by changing emphases
on other modes of functioning. Self and I support the rectificatory effort

of privacy by focused efforts on an end pertinent to what one is privately as well as publicly.

A willed end is not identifiable with finalities or what they express; if it were, the will would serve only to support efforts which are carried on independently of it. The will is directed at an end which is pertinent to both the privacy and the body, and as the satisfying terminus of all the different efforts functioning in harmony. This end is not known; the objective at which the will is directed is a function of the various activities it controls. It does not control or even provide a direction, being just the terminus of an insistence that all the activities of the individual be harmonized.

The will provides a supplement to the rectificatory action of a privacy. Where the latter works constantly and without an objective, the other is in operation only occasionally and then with respect to an outcome that has no other role than being the locus in which all the termini of different activities are united to mutual benefit and without loss. Our actual willings, of course, are directed toward more limited goals, but that is because we try to understand why we will in the way we do. This leads us to formulate objectives which are more specific than the actual objective that the will would have all activities terminate in. As long as that specified objective transcends any with which other activities (bodily or otherwise) are occupied, we can find evidence for the will by noting a persistent endeavor to act in such a way that neglected tendencies and opposed efforts are finally satisfied.

I seem now to be close to endorsing obstinate fanatical occupations with something unknown to which everything else is sacrificed, such as a utopia, or other fanciful objectives. These, though, differ from the objective of the will in not being functions of the multiple efforts that in fact are being made. They are detached objectives, but the objective with which the will is concerned is the projection of all to the point where they are harmonized. We discover the presence of the will by noting that another is occupied with such a harmonizing outcome, a fact he makes manifest by his refusal to rest with the satisfaction of any one or any limited number of them, or with the kind of harmonization that the privacy is introducing from within. We know it is free because it makes determinate the ways in which the different activities are projected toward a common outcome; we know that it is exercised responsibly because it operates to dictate whatever is done privately or publicly. We call it perverse and still maintain that it is being responsibly exercised when we find that it is operating on behalf of an end that is less comprehensive than it should be and precludes the more comprehensive. It will then be a will responsibly expressed, but in place of a better exercise which could have been responsibly expressed instead.

We are responsible for exercising our will, for not exercising it, and for exercising it in this way or that. We unavoidably express in the will the responsibility that privacy exhibits. But such a responsible will is not exercised until the self and the I emphasize it rather than some other means by which privacy is occupied with finalities.

April 3

We know that there is responsibility when we know that there are private, freely produced decisions. We know that a man is responsible when we know that the source of that responsibility remains identical over time, is the act of an I, and is sustained by a privacy. We can achieve such knowledge when attending to another if we can find evidences in him or his acts which have a non-bodily origin, involve the introduction of determinations, and entrain characterizations of deserved accountability, dedication, or obligation.

We know that another has a private, responsibly used

1. *sensitivity*, when he is directed toward a focused and preferred objective not desired by the body, when, in short, he is occupied with what is *desirable* though it is not desired.

2. *desire*, when he seeks something desirable persistently sought, though this precludes the satisfaction of desires, controlling the desires by what is not a terminus of desire. This is the *wanted*.

3. *consciousness*, when there is a focusing on what is immediately undergone despite bodily distractions and lures. This has *aesthetic value*.

4. *interest*, when there are goals used in preference which may have no bodily import but are persistently pursued. This is a set *goal*.

5. *rights*, when there are demands which counter those that are insisted on by society or state. This is the *justly claimed*.

6. *mind*, when conclusions are inferred regardless of what the body requires, though it may coincide with this at times. If directed toward such an end, it will proceed imaginatively, using aids which are not bodily pertinent. This is the *necessitated*.

7. *assumed accountability*, when accountability credited to the you is assessed as justified or unjustified because it does or does not conform to an attributed accountability. This is *self-assessment*.

8. *will*, when activities are insistently projected toward an end where they are all satisfied. This is *self-determination*.

9. *identity*, when there is dedication, a persistence in the pursuit of the same objectives despite present needs. This is *governance*.

10. *I*, the focused bearer of responsibility, the assessor and possessor of whatever is in or due to the you, and known as one who knows himself as one evidenced, usually in speech or in his way of attaining dignity. This is a *self-substantializing*.

11. *person*, the rectificatory agent for sensitivity, consciousness, desire, maximizing their harmonious functioning, in the face of emphases by the body and circumstance. This is *self-maintenance*.

12. *individual*, the rectificatory agent for rights and the I, for responsibility and assumed accountability, acting in the face of emphases on one or the other by the body or circumstance. This is *character*.

13. *self*, the rectificatory agent for the I and interest in the face of emphases on one or the other, which the body or circumstances support. This is *self-acceptance*.

14. *rectificatory privacy*, the agent for physical and spiritual health, adjusting the demands of person, individual, and self (and through these what they govern), exercised in the face of the insistence of any, with the support of the body or circumstance. This is *integrity*.

15. *centering privacy*, the enabling of responsibility and other occupations with the finalities, as conditions and objectives, to function; to be known when responsibility is recognized to be competing with demands for self-completion, and making possible the achievement of excellence, the attainment of dignity, and the establishment of self-sufficiency. It is an enabling of responsibility, known when one is occupied with primary efforts which compete with responsibility, and thus when one is engaged in religion, art, or control.

I have considered, but do not think I have fully faced, the difficulty that madmen are not held to be responsible. One reason they are not, is that they do not take due account of their bodies but, instead (apparently in consonance with what I have been maintaining) insist on other modes of activity and objectives. A man may even have accepted some incorrect premiss, such as that he is made of glass, and then followed out the implications of this resolutely, conforming to what I have remarked on in no. 6, above. We will then credit him with a mind and with a privacy, but will deny that these functioned freely, or that, if they did, the man is responsible. Yet we cannot insist, instead, that every premiss be grounded in experience or the body; that would preclude the development of many branches of mathematics.

To show that someone is not a madman, one might maintain that the body must be used responsibly. But one can responsibly oppose the body, prevent it from being satisfied. He can be charged with responsibly failing to use the body properly, denying its right to health, continuation, or maturation. One might then go on to claim, instead, that responsibility must be exercised somewhere, if one is to be held responsible for not using the body properly. But one then supposes that it is impossible to be responsible in the use of mind while being governed by ungovernable impulses.

It would be better to hold that there must be a minimal proper use of the body which is a precondition for the presence and exercise of responsibility or, at the very least, for the acknowledgment that someone is a responsible being. The proper use may not itself be responsibly carried out but, without it, the individual could be said not to be responsible. When one is sensitive, wills, or infers with respect to what is oppositional to and beyond the power of the body to engage in, one will, on this alternative, require that the body be not altogether denied. The opposition will be between the body as already functioning in certain minimal ways, and a freely decided occupation with what requires a denial of further occupation with the body, or an opposition to the body's pursuit of anything more than these minimal objectives.

Might not that minimum be responsibly denied? Might not one be responsible for not respecting that minimum? Yes. But then we should go on to say that those who do this, who despise, abuse, injure the body, who deny it even the minimum that is needed if one is to continue or to mature, must do this as a consequence of what they have already responsibly accepted or done, and can therefore be charged with responsibly acting wrongly with respect to the body. To show that those who abuse their bodies, deny to their bodies even a minimal right, or so misconstrue the bodies that they act in ways which are not appropriate to their welfare, are doing this responsibly, one must find grounds for the acknowledgment of responsibility, say in the use of the mind. If one can show that the supposition that one is glass is used as a premiss to an imaginative, controlled derivation that one is transparent and fragile, then one can charge a man who treats his body as though it were transparent and fragile as responsible for that treatment.

An elementary deduction that one is fragile and transparent from the premiss that one is made of glass could have been performed mechanically. It is only when the conclusion is drawn with the aid of auxiliary hypotheses, additions, subtractions, characteristic of a controlled free use of the mind that he thinks responsibly. He will be responsible both for his use of his mind and for the bodily results that are due to the effective presence of the mind in the body. He could be responsible, too, for allowing his body to function in ways which go counter to those which were sanctioned in thought. If the first, he will have responsibly determined the way his body functions; in the second, he will directly decide responsibly with respect to some bodily activity. Let it be supposed that a man creatively infers that he has a body made of glass. If he then treats his body as if made of glass, he will be responsible for what then ensues. If he creatively inferred that he had a living organic body, but then dealt with it as though it were transparent and fragile, he would still be responsible for what his body did, since he would have responsibly stood in the way of the governance of the body by what he had in mind. We affirm that he is responsible when he takes his body to be living, as well as when he takes it to be dead, if either result involves a responsible carrying out or opposition to a responsible exercise of some other power.

To determine whether he is mad, we have to determine whether he uses his mind or some other power freely and decisively, and then whether he freely and decisively relates that mind, positively or negatively, to the body. The latter determination obviously involves a reference to a power which subtends both the mind (in this instance) and the body. This could be the power of the privacy, will, I, or self, so that the determination finally would come down to the acknowledgment that these are functioning responsibly. If we do not know whether or not a man is using one of these responsibly we cannot know if the relation of his thought, or of some other limited activity, to his body, is carried out responsibly. We know that someone is mad, inescapably caught up in processes over which he has no control, only if we know that he does not freely try to unite in himself finalities as both grounds and conditions; if he does not have before him a final willed objective; if he has no focused I; or if he does not use his self to change the ways in which his I and interest are interrelated.

Is it possible, though, for one not to be able to unite in himself finalities as both grounds and conditions? Must not all men be engaged in self-completion, achievement of excellence, etc.? And if they are, must they not all be responsible? We must grant, I think, that there are distinct operations required by a matured privacy. We could, therefore, go on to say that the privacy of those who are not responsible is not matured, or (better, perhaps) that one, some, or all of the ways of dealing with finalities as grounds and conditions cannot be properly exercised at that time. The rectificatory power of the privacy will then have to be understood to extend even to the privacy itself as it is at the center of a number of distinct enterprises of internalizing finalities in the shape of accepted grounds and guiding conditions. If it fails to rectify the centered privacy, one will so far be in poor 'psychic' health. Of course, this is exactly the verdict to be expected, but I did derive it from an independent understanding of the privacy and the way it functions, before I had considered the case of the madman. (The self, has also been termed a 'rectificatory agent' in no. 13 above, emphasizing there the adjudication of emphases other than those which involve the body.) Taking these together, we credit another with responsibility, no matter how odd his treatment of his body and how alien to common ways his thoughts, interests, and the like, if we find him making decisions with respect to the functioning of competing efforts. What must then be made out is that the adjudication does not occur automatically, as the outcome of the rectificatory activities of privacy, self, individual, or person, or that it is not the outcome of efforts at completion, attainment of excellence, dignity, or self-possession. This only to say that in the end to know if there is responsibility, we must find it operative in what is public, not as expressed in this or that activity, but as governing a number of them. The decision regarding the weights to be given to competing efforts on the part of different factors will have to be understood to involve restraint, modification, redirection, or emphasis on the different competing efforts in the light of the attempt to unite within oneself a final objective and ground, primarily in the form of an unrealized prospect whose pursuit requries determinate activities now.

Grounded in the privacy, responsibility involves the exercise of the will rather than of choice or preference, and thus is known when one is directed toward the harmonizing terminus of all efforts, and at the same time is obligated to act so as to realize it. One will not act in various ways because of what one willed to have as an ultimate objective; rather, the different efforts will be adjusted to one another. This will be done, not by a rectifying privacy, self, individual, or person, but by a persistently maintained and governing idea of a harmony of subordinate objectives pursued by limited agents.

To know that a man is responsible, it is enough if we find that efforts, which may be bodily in nature, are adjusted to one another under the governance of a harmonizing end, deservedly insisted on as a obligating justification for what is now done. We recognize that another is responsible because his bodily restraints and redirections are explicable only if subject to what ought to be his willed outcome. We cannot find any such governance in a madman; if a number of his efforts are in harmony, it is not because they are made to be so, and thus can be understood in terms of an obligating harmonizing end, but because they are internally adjusted to one another, or just happen to be consonant with one another. It is only after we see that no internal adjustment can account for a governing obligation, for the fact that there is an objective that they are being modified again and again to serve, and that any consonance that happens to occur carries no satisfaction of an obligation, that we know that another is responsible no matter how he acts. It is we, of course, who formulate the nature of the willed end which we take to obligate the responsible man. We treat him as being like us, and view the obligating end, though formulated by us, to be operative on him. A man could be in ill-health, unable to engage in proper rectificatory acts, but he will be seen to be responsible if he acts under the influence of an obligating, harmonizing end, a fact most conspicuous when the rectification is not successful. Ill, disharmonized, he is (to use a revealing pun), willing to become well, by trying to have different competing factors function in harmony.

May not a man who is engaged in a creative effort in imagination neglect his body, ignore his appetites, and seem to be involved in only one responsibly pursued activity? Yes. And his neglect of his body is his responsibility, the outcome of his permitting or requiring his creative effort to limit his bodily needs and operations. We know of his responsibility as we know of the responsibility of one who occupies himself with the desirable rather than the desired, (no. 1, above) by noting that he is concerned with what is not a product of automatic or bodily efforts. It is when we cannot see responsibility being manifested in any acts that we have to have recourse to a willed obligating objective. We look to this to see if it will explain why those acts are being modified so as to be more in harmony than they otherwise would be.

Aristotle held that all men seek to attain what is an apparent good for them, or perhaps what appears to be good. The present view differs from his in a. not holding that the obligating end is the good, or even striven for by all (since this is not evidently the case with the madman); b. not holding that reference has to be made to anything more than a limited form of an end at times, in order to know whether or not a man is responsible; c. in distinguishing preference, choice, and will—his choice being nothing more than preference; d. in recognizing that men have more than one finality to deal with, and do so primarily in one distinctive way, and secondarily in the ways that are primary for others; e. in understanding privacy to have many more roles than being the source of living, desiring, and knowing; f. in noting that an objective, such as the good, is not only accepted as an objective, but is internalized as a ground; and g. in seeking evidence for what is private by attending to evidential occurrences in the body and in what it does.

April 4

There are cases where men are said not to be able to act responsibly, though they may be credited with having responsibility. The will is then exercised or exercisable in some area, while it is faced with what it cannot control. The world may be too much for one—he may be buffetted by the wind, have the ground give way under him, fall from a height; he may be in the grip of other men, and his body forced to be an instrument for another; he may be subject to spasms, or to degrees of pain beyond his capacity to control, and which make his body act in ways not desirable; he may have a defective mind, or have some power of his overwhelmed by another, or find it uncontrollably operating. That a man cannot control these, no matter what his will, is a matter of discovery. Whether or not he is still in fact a responsible being who, for the while, is unable to exercise his responsibility, or cannot exercise it in this or that place where other responsible men can, must be ascertained in somewhat the ways outlined yesterday.

All cases of responsibility involve an adjudication. There are two types. 1. where some freely adopted way of functioning is related to a body that it governs or by which is defied; and 2. where a number of ways of functioning are adjusted to one another in terms of a terminus that is preferred, chosen, or willed. The first tells us about sensitivity, consciousness, and desire, which is to say the person and preference; about rights, interest, and the I as involved in choice; and about the I and privacy, and derivatively the person, individual, and self, as involved in will. The second tells us about near and final objectives. If it concerns the will, it refers us to what effectively harmonizes different activities, precluding them from being carried out as they otherwise would, but still not inescapably or as being controlled by forces outside one's control. It contrasts also with the work of the rectificatory privacy in being steady and persistent, and in introducing the controlling end ahead of time rather than only after disequilibrium has been displayed.

The legal criterion for lack of responsibility (a responsibility quickly translated into the warrant for taking someone to be accountable) 'knowing right from wrong' not only leaves unclear just what is meant by 'right' and 'wrong'—presumably it is the established outlook of a society, or its representatives, the supposedly reasonable men—but places undue emphasis on 'knowing'. But what is wanted is a reference to the ability to make assessments, and to use these to adjust different activities to one another, and particularly to do so by restraining those which are disapproved by society. In any case, the fact that a man may not be able to function responsibly in one direction does not mean that he is not a responsible being, nor does the fact that there are certain conditions he must meet before he is held legally accountable mean that he is or is not responsible, or that he is or is not responsible for the acts for which he is being held accountable. Responsibility can be present though it may have a restricted scope; a man therefore can be freed from charges of being responsible in some areas without being denied responsibility altogether.

The reference to 'acts of God' in legal documents is intended to refer to particular occurrences for which a man is not held accountable and presumably for which he is not responsible, but without denying that he is accountable and responsible in other areas. The reference to 'insanity', instead, is intended to refer to a condition in which there is no responsibility, while still allowing one to deal with a man as accountable, though not in the usual sense.

The 'criminally insane' are taken to be not responsible, but are held accountable in special ways. They are tested to see if they show signs of responsibility in areas other than those where they have been found to be legally accountable; if these cannot be found they are treated as not responsible at all, at least for a period. But it is extremely dubious that any matured man will reveal no areas where he functions responsibly—in his sensitivity, desires, thoughts, even interests, and insistence on rights. These areas are ignored in the law, since what it is trying to determine is whether or not the individual is to be held legally accountable. Consequently, it attends only to what is relevant to this. The fact that attention is paid to responsibility, or to an assumed accountability, points up the ethical presuppositions of law.

A strict legal positivism would be content with taking certain kinds of activity as requiring a different kind of constraint from those that the attributions of accountability usually require. It would not have the mass murderer, the self-mutilator, or the cannibalistic man in our society examined to see if he is sane; it would take the act itself to define him not to be so, and would therefore subject him to restraints. I think this attitude is correct. In these cases no reference need be made to any responsibility, or to a man's capacity to demonstrate such responsibility in some particular areas, e.g., a knowledge of what the community takes to be conspicuously right or wrong. A man who eats his baby is criminally insane; we need no examination of his ability to tell right from wrong, or any check on his ability to will. He acts beyond the point where a rectificatory privacy or an act of will would allow him to act. If he exhibits responsibility in his sensitivity, mind, or other operation, he is still not responsible with respect to his cannibalism. So far as the society and legal system are concerned, it makes no difference whether or not he is responsible in other areas; it suffices that he is not responsible in this. But that is not enough to free him from a legal accountability. Calling him 'criminally insane' merely sharpens the fact that the kind of constraint to which he will be subject is different in nature from that which he would have received were he just insane or just criminal. Responsibility is denied to be operative, then, when we discover cases which, over the course of experience, we have learned are beyond the power of a man to control, as well as those cases where he is engaged in acts that are outside the limits where sane men function. In the first kind of case, we deny that there is an operative responsibility, though allowing that it may be present in other areas; in the second, we deny that there is responsibility present, whether or not it is present in other areas, and whether or not it is present in the particular ones we have taken to be outside the limits of one able to exhibit health through the use of a rectificatory privacy or who has an effective will, or both. Neither type of case precludes the attribution of accountability.

The discovery of responsibility begins with the acknowledgment of a man functioning within limits which are accepted as unbreakable despite the fact that their exact location and nature is not known; it goes on to attend to those acts of adjudication which require that usual bodily activities be restrained, qualified, redirected, implemented, or encouraged. Failure to find such cases, or the discovery of activities outside the established limits, does not involve the denial of responsibility. But it also does not provide one with evidences of its presence.

We are able to proceed to a discovery of the anatomy of a man's privacy by attending to the various kinds of conditionings to which his body is subject, responsibly or otherwise, beginning with those which have analogues in animals. We then move toward those which are occupied with conditions and which require acts of choice with its obligations, or acts of will with its persistent occupation with near or remote ends, able to be filled out by all of the competing activities in harmony. We end finally with the privacy articulated in the form of a number of primary operations, of which responsibility is just one.

When adjudications are provided on behalf of preferences and choices, they are not governed by some projected end where the different efforts are satisfied together maximally. Instead, there is a terminus in which the adjudicated result serves as the best means for an adopted objective, or there is a totality of values in which the adjudicated result is a means whose losses in value entail an obligation to continue to be directed toward a totality where one will make good whatever losses are involved in reaching it. Any adjudications which might occur due to the rectificatory activity of privacy, or of the person, self, or individual, will be compensatory in contrast with these.

April 5

A work of art is a set of 'accidents' organized to constitute a self-sufficient unity having a sensuous excellence. The accidents are objective in the very same sense that the appearances of the used subjects are—the brushes, paints, metal, stones, sounds, and so on. Like the appearances, the accidents are constituted of two distinct realities. Unlike these, they are the products of expressions of actualities and not, as appearances are, of actualities and finalities. Of course, as is true of any plurality, the presence and operation of the finalities cannot be denied; the unity of a work of art requires a supervening unity which encompasses all the accidents. That unity has a governing role to the very extent that the work is beautiful, for beauty is a transcendental, owing its presence to a finality.

We can dissect a work of art in two distinct ways. We can move toward the constitutive sources of its accidents, including the way those accidents are organized, but from the position of one of the sources, the artist. Or we can move toward the constitutive soruces of the work and thus to the sources of the organized accidents on one side and to their unity on the other. There is the organization which the artist imposes, and there is the unitary beauty that supervenes if the artist organizes the material maximally. The one allows us to analyze the work into factors produced by the artist and the material which was worked over; the other allows us to analyze the work into a transcendental unity, beauty, and the artist's organized product.

I am now close to the issues which are discussed in *You, I, and the Others* under 'we'. There is made evident that 'we' has a simple nature that is brought into interplay with an interactive set of men to constitute a complex we. This is an organized whole having its own career and able to interact with other complexes. The simple we is like beauty, while the complex is like the work as it stands away from the artist, incorporates the material, and is governed by what neither of these can account for— the beauty. It is as having beauty that the work of art is able to be an objective unit in the history of art, and can be understood without reference either to the artist or the material; it is an analyzable complex whose factors are the beauty and the interactive combination of the contributions of the artist and the material. We need to study that interactive combination in order to understand the work of art as a single entity with its own integrity, able to function in relation to other works of art and other complexes.

A work of art is no more an appearance than a society, state, or family is. Nevertheless, it is not a reality in the sense in which the artist or his material is. If we wish to speak of it as real we will have to distinguish a primary and a secondary reality, a source of factors from what does not but still is able to have a career of its own. Such realities also interact with spectators, and in that sense produce, not a third degree of reality, but subjective appearances, appearances dependent in part on the spectator.

Suppose one were to start with the subjective appearances just remarked on? Their analysis, or more precisely, the following out of their adumbrating fringes will take us to the spectators and the work. But while a spectator is an actuality, an art work is not. Consequently, another move is required from the work itself, which is a complex—not an appearance—to its factors, the supervening transcendent on one side, and the interactive artist and the material on the other.

But do not complexes have appearances? Is not a man a complex? And if he is, is he not nevertheless irreducible, not to be dealt with as though he were a product of the expressions of finalities and actualities? And if he were so dealt with, would he not be impotent, an inert appearance? We will be driven to hold to an atomism if it is not possible to recognize the irreducible reality of what can be analyzed as being made up of a plurality of actualities and a controlling unity. The complex, which is man, has a privacy governing what he is publicly, as well as the parts that are there encompassed; it is as such that he is a source of factors which are constitutive of both the accidents (in interaction with other actual complexes) and the appearances which result from the interplay of his exhibitions with those of finalities. A man, though, can act, while a work of art, a society, state, or similar complex cannot, in the same sense. A man produces accidents and appearances, whereas these other complexes accrete and discard features. For a society to be at peace, large, or civilized is for it not to have appearances or accidents, but to be a society in the context of societies. If this is so, must we not say that a society has no stability, since it would change with the coming to be and passing away of these features? Yet if these were mere appearances or accidents, the society would be an actuality as basic and as effective as an atom or a man.

Actualities, simple or complex, interact with expressions of finalities, not only to produce appearances, but to produce qualified actualities and domains. The domains are complex with distinctive relations and roles. A family is one such complex, and the features that it has in the domain of families and other societal complexes are attributable to it as a unit, or to the place it has in the domain relative to the others. It is a domain localized; conversely, its domain is a projection from it, filled out by other units. A domain is a constant with adventitious features, depending on the other units' presence, nature, and relation to it; it also is unstable, changing in nature with the roles these have in it.

A domain is the product of finalities and actualities. They contribute their diverse powers to it, thereby constituting a new kind of entity, the domain, having an indefinite stretch in which other entities can be. A work of art has its being in the domain of art, constituted by the insistent presence of a unitary finality that imposes a prescriptive standard of excellence. All works of art are intensifications within a domain. Each instantiates excellence in a different way, while extending toward other instantiations in that domain.

A work of art is to be understood not to be like a man. Still, it, too, is complex, has transcendentalized features, appearances, and accidents, and makes a difference to other entities, and even interacts with them. It is rather like a social unit, a number, a triangle, or a religious ritual; it is a delimited portion of a domain, or equally, a starting point in a domain whose projected continuance is occupied by other similiar delimited projective portions. Like all complexes it has power. , But it does not have the power of an actuality, with a privacy, able to produce appearances by having its expressions interplay with the expressions of finalities. It has only the power to maintain itself and interact in a domain. The cosmos is also a domain in this sense, and the units in it are like the units in history, or sociology, or politics.

Those theories which view men as only delimited units within an economic, social, or political whole in effect deal with them as units in a domain. But the domain is not accounted for. To do so one would have to acknowledge finalities, and the integration of these with actualities so as to constitute entities which exist only so far as they project themselves as possible fields to be occupied by other entities of a similar order. We would have no explanation of how the men came to belong to the domain.

A view which treats men as part of a domain in effect takes their state to be a kind of surrogate for a finality. But that view is unable to account for the presence of men in that state, their opposition to it, or the ways in which they directly interact with one another. As so together, men not only have accidents but make a difference to the complex that is constituted by the men together and by prescriptive political conditions. An analogous approach to art would start with a culture or a tradition and take a particular work of art to be a mere unit in such a setting, without being able to explain how it could have the status of a distinct unit there. The work of the artist and the material on which he worked would be ignored; to take them both to be explained by the domain is not yet to be able to explain how the culture or tradition is able to provide effective conditions for them. A work of art is a complex from which neither creator nor material can be entirely separated; it is in a domain when it is vitally involved with a finality, not as constituting appearances with it, but as constituting a complex entity effectively related to others.

If the interaction of artist and material be taken to result in Aristotelian accidents, they will be accidents which nevertheless are able to have a career together, apart from the artist and the material, just so far as they function in a domain. What grounds them is then ignored. In fact, they are sustained by the domain which they help constitute at positions from which the rest of the domain is projected. Constructions occur within a projected domain, and give it determinations.

Units in domains are like complex we's. They are both constituted by more basic realities, and have relations to other similar units in the same domain. Each helps constitute the domain at the same time that it occupies a position in it. A game is such a domain with the moves characteristic of some sport all functioning as units in it. If there were such a thing as a 'language game' it would be a living language in the process of being constituted by the units of discourse in which men are engaged. Each man would speak in such a way as to produce words and sentences that are units in the game only so far as they provide the field in which other units could occur, and are in the field in which they do occur. When this does not happen, we speak of the men talking at cross-purposes.

If men can talk at cross-purposes, should there not be works of art, political units, social groups, and so on, which do not mesh with one another and thus are not parts of the same domain? Is this not exactly what occurs with great innovative works? Other achievements must provide a field for these to be, at the same time that the projections of these innovative works are altered so as to enable the other works to be in the same domain with them. Neither type is altered, but the entire domain is changed by the way the different items come to be in this together. The history of art is in a persistent process of producing a single domain for all works of art.

April 6

I have now made an outline for myself of a projected eleven chapters of the book I had tentatively called 'Man: Public and Private'. In thinking through the outline it was possible to remark on a distinction not made in these last weeks. Sensitivity, desire, and the other stresses are usually expressed in public in a way that overflows the body's limitations. Consequently these come into the open in a double form, as asserted and as confined. If one of these is overemphasized, the body is neglected or is allowed to dictate to what is privately initiated. Adjudications and adjustments, the one rectificatory and ungoverned, the other deliberate with an objective, attend to the split produced by the body's insistence on itself with its use of some of the privately initiated activity.

I will try now to work on the book, with only occasional use of the opportunities afforded by this work. I did make a similar attempt before, and found that I could not carry it out, either because of the new surroundings, lack of focus, weakening of the intellect, or for some other reason, in which I am not interested if it should turn out that I am able to proceed with the book. If I cannot, I will try to continue to think along the lines of the outline as far as I can, and hope that I will be able to work on it steadily in the free summer that is before me, when I am home in my familiar surroundings. For the moment, my plan is to take the subheadings of the chapters and write out as clearly as I can what I understand by them, without any attempt to see if it all adds up to a book or not.

Because it is possible that I may change the outline quite radically in the course of putting it to use, and since I may then make no effort to preserve it, it may be of interest to note the chapter headings I set down: 1. The limits of responsibility, b. the evidences of privacy, c. the anatomy of privacy, d. the operative I; 5. the adjustment of expressions; 6. rectifications, 7. responsible adjudications, 8. matured privacy; 9. dominating privacy; 10. the matured body; 11. men together. I will be trying to move from the commonly acknowledged limits within which responsibility is supposedly exercised and outside of which we have acts and forces no man can control, to the evidence that asserted expressions escape confinement by the body, to the origin of the overflowing expressions; to the I as operative on the sensitivity etc. (already written but in a somewhat mechanical way); to the adjustment of expressions by adopted objects; to rectifications by individual, self, identity, person, the privacy, and the emotions; to responsible adjudications performed through preference, choice, will and the objectives they require, privately and publicly; to the matured privacy and its utilization of the finalities as objectives and grounds; to the engagement in art, the achievement of character, the acceptance of responsibility by the dominating privacy; to the matured body as in public, living, lived, and possessed; and finally, to men together in an environment, nature, a milieu, society, state, and civilization.

April 23

Over the last two weeks or so I have been concentrating on the writing of a draft of 'Explorations in Human Privacy'. At the same time I have been thinking about the possibility of a good offer from the University of Denver. I have been enthusiastically recommended by the entire department, and by the deans and everyone else (it seems) below the level of the Chancellor, who has the last word. Some decision has to be made this week. Perhaps before then I will be on my way to Washington for the opening of the show of my paintings at the Albatross Gallery. I do hope I will have a decision before then, so that if I take it I can look around for proper quarters, and give The Catholic University sufficient notice.

* * *

Instead of supposing, as is usually done, that secondary qualities are additions to the primary, perhaps only in the mind but also conceivably somehow connected with them objectively, it seems more correct to view them as degenerate versions of transcendent features, having a controlling holistic role with respect to the primary. A color or a sound would then be understood to introduce a new set of relations among the primary, without thereby cancelling those that the primary already have. A color or a sound would give new interconnections to the various physical conditions which are necessary for the occurrence of the color or sound, bundling them together, submerging them, making them relevant to one another in new ways.

What the secondary qualities do for the primary, the unity of a work of art does for the secondary. In addition to the relations the qualities had, and which could perhaps be expressed in a formula, the unity of the work introduces new connections, making the colors and other secondary qualities affiliate, contrast, supplement, add and subtract from one another in ways otherwise not possible. When the unity of a work made possible a certain set of relations—outlined in my discussion in the *World of Art* under the common features of all the arts and in the chapter on beauty—the result would be beauty, just so far as the unity was filled out by the related items to yield a single entity that was sensuously excellent.

Some time ago I held that quantity was a transcendent. But now I am doing almost the opposite, and maintaining that quality is a transcendent operating on quantity. Might it not be the case that they are both transcendents, able to have one another as units which are unified by them, the quantity in the cosmos, the quality locally? This would suggest that one way of dealing with the mind/body problem would be by taking the mind to be a controlling transcendent in the individual, and the body to be a controlling transcendent in the cosmos. Would there then be two types of emotion, one connecting 'mind' as a transcendent quality to the quantity, and the other connecting the transcendent quantity to the mind as a kind of quality, the usual emotion being more or less an equilibrium point between the two?

If quality is subject both to quantity and to beauty, it would be an intermediate between two distinct transcendents. Nothing is affected, I think, if one adds that the qualities need the help of a perceiver in order to be.

April 26

Qualities, if they are subordinate to quantities, should be treated as subordinate to them as spatialized, temporalized, and dynamic, since these are the forms which quantity assumes when it is an effective transcendent condition. Abstract quantity, numerical quantity, instead, is a subdivision of the realm of Possibility. One should expect qualities, or more precisely, appearances, to be subordinate to the expressions of the other finalities; and, conversely, these expressions to be subordinate to the appearances.

A sound can be understood to be a unitary bounding 'quality' which subordinates (in localized forms) vibratory strings as a. having a relevance to one another, e.g., as being the strings of a harp; b. as coordinate, equal, items, e.g., being separately produced; c. as having a rationale, e.g., related in various proportions; d. as located in different parts of extensions, e.g., in an orchestra; and e. as being simple or complex.

At the same time, a sound should be capable of being subordinated to the different finalities. A conspicuous case is a sound as part of a musical piece. The musical piece has the sound subordinated to conditions of relevance, of equality, of an intrinsic rationale, of distance in time, and sometimes in space and dynamism, and of different values such as purity, contrast, and discord.

A sound, also, is cosmologized by being subject to determinations of expressions of the finalities, in such a way that the sound is related to other items in the cosmos, not necessarily other sounds. A work of art is an intensive limited heightened way of expressing the control of objective appearances by a combination of all the cosmological conditions. If this is right, it is the cosmos in miniature, focalized, with the different conditions intimately interlocked rather than conjoined, as they are in the cosmos.

Appearances, on this view, are ways of providing unifying conditions for a plurality of items already conditioned by the finalities; are units related to other units in the cosmos; and are units related within a work of art in more intensive and tighter forms of the cosmological conditions.

If the mind (more precisely, the privacy) be treated on the analogue of an appearance, it can now be said to provide a localization of a unification for the body or parts of it, having a five-fold form. It is also related to other items in the cosmos through the conditions which govern bodies cosmologically, and is related to other minds in heightened forms of the cosmological relations. The subordination would be expressed as emotions. The mind would not be an epiphenomenon, a parallel substance, the conjunct outcropping of a neutral stuff, or an essential primary governing reality always having the body as a subordinate object.

Appearances, are products of more basic realities. Mind is not. But it can be identified as a domain, the way in which an actuality comes together with a finality (in this case Possibility) to constitute entities (ideas) which project themselves forward and make a place for other similar entities. But mind would then seem to be identifiable with mathematics as understood by constructionists.

Is mathematics perhaps just one 'aspect of the domain which is mind? Or is it not the domain that is mind, with an emphasis on the finality rather than on the individual? Is mind a domain with thickness, having mathematics at one extreme and 'psychology' at the other? If so, what of the other domains—history, for example—which join particulars with Existence's primarily temporal expressions? Is there a history that is personalized—biography, and, at the other extreme, a historical course of the world?

It is not too difficult to see how history could provide unifications for physical entities, joining them together in ways which oppose their own direct relations, subject to cosmic conditions. It is not so easy to see how its occurrences, or it as a whole, are related to other entities under the aegis of the final conditions. But it does make sense to speak of history as occupying only one part of the whole of time, the other being as yet undifferentiated, and the two being connected by Existence itself. Even its spatial regions and its particular causation can be dealt with in this way.

Domains are comparable to the world of art. Historic ideas and episodes are the counterparts of works of art. If so, we should expect the ideas and episodes will provide ways for ordering appearances, and that appearances will provide intensified unifications for actual entities. The appearances ordered by ideas are the familiar ones of every day as subject to personalized notes. Those ordered by historic episodes are the same appearances, as subject to social conditions. (I am on the verge of something new here, but as yet do not see very far. What is exciting is the awareness of the dual role which such derivatives as appearances have in relation to governing unifications in art, mind, history—and therefore presumably in society, politics, economics, and religion.) An appearance as governed by an idea would govern the body, the governance in both cases uniting a plurality of items in new ways. As governing all entities it would function somewhat as a 'we', i.e., as a condition imposed on countering combinations of entities.

*   *   *

In going over some manuscripts as I was bringing my draft of 'The Exploration of Human Privacy' to a close, I came across a section which I had written a little more than six months ago. I do not think it fits in that book, and though it does not exactly cohere with what I have just said, and have said in this book about domains, it is sufficiently pertinent to it to make its inclusion here appropriate. It was rewritten at least once, and so far is unlike the other entries in this work. Perhaps that has its own interest, since it allows for a comparison between what is written straight-away and what is rewritten and conceived of as belonging to a larger systematic work. After I have finally finished with the draft of 'TEHP' I may turn to the question of domains afresh, and work through some of the implications of what is now set down:

* * *

A *unit* is a particular awaiting interpretation. A *domain* is an effective conditioning area encompassing a multitude of units. A *power* is a forceful condition governing domains, and sometimes having a direct affect on units. Privacy, its subdivisions, and their epitomizing condensations may have any one of these roles.

Units seem to be the most obvious of entities. Yet they are often misconstrued in one of six ways:

a. A unit can be taken to be unaffected by any power, either directly or through a domain. The literalist, factualist, and positivist attend solely to such units, concerning themselves with seeing how the parts of those units or the units themselves fit together. In the attempt to achieve clarity, to remain with the obtrusive, to allow only for what remains after analysis, they separate out what they take to be a pure unit, and cling to this as alone objective, real, or true. Any you or me that they might acknowledge is inevitably reduced to a present observed unit, not known by an I, and therefore not really observed. But these units are found in domains and are subject to powers behind these.

b. Each unit is related to others. None is completely isolated. A sentence on a page has relations to the rest of the page and to other sentences elsewhere. Though convention and the needs of practice lead us to make rather sharp distinctions between the full and the empty, the obtrusive and the absent, every distinguishable entity is [dis]connected with others across a relative emptiness. The supposition that there can be a completely bounded unit will in the end preclude the acknowledgment of more than one, for every other will require for its acknowledgment a departure from the original and a complete immersion in the new. To know that there is more than one unit one must see them within a common domain.

c. A domain may be acknowledged, but given an inadequate role relative to a unit. A legalist gives a unit its proper domain, but does not understand the richness of that domain and therefore the full import of it as it operates on the unit. Poor interpreters, inattentive listeners, superficial students of alien cultures offer other illustrations. All give insufficient value to the domain which encompasses and determines the meaning of units. Attempts to learn a foreign language from a phrase book or by asking a native speaker for the names of various designated items carry out the same error in other areas.

d. The reverse of the foregoing exaggerates the import of a domain, taking it to have a greater role than it in fact has. The error is committed by all of us when we rapidly move from what men do to their supposed motives. Though what is said and done cannot be entirely freed from a private domain, it is also in good part a distinct particular, pulling some of the domain into itself. Men of faith read their sacred texts primarily with the intent to discover a domain, denying to the texts any other role but that of units there. They are countered by cabbalists and fundamentalists who, despite their passionate concern to know a divine intent, join the inattentive readers in ignoring the evident domains of daily discourse and belief, at the same time that they differ from those readers in insisting on some special domain as having overwhelming importance. They can be said at times to belong with those who exaggerate the status of a unit relative to its proper domain, and at other times with those who misconstrue the nature of a domain.

e. Social life involves the acceptance of a common domain governing and present in multiple units. Liars, forgers, and confidence men take advantage of that fact, leading those caught in an established domain to deal with units in self-injurious ways. Innocent distortions, errors in judgment, misleading reportings, instead, are taken both by their authors and others to be truths sustained by a common domain whose course and effects are allowed to operate with little hindrance. We make such an error when we hold men responsible for acts for which they are only accountable.

f. The reverse of the foregoing is the mistake of fitting a unit within an inappropriate domain. A demythologizer complains that this is what other readers of a sacred text do. He supposes that other readers take the text to be like any other in a domain of a conventional language when it should, he maintains, be dealt with as in a domain governed by a divine concern. Like the cabbalist and fundamentalist, he rightly insists that a sacred text is misunderstood if placed in the same domain as other writings are, but it is of course still a question whether or not he has found the right domain for his text. When that for which men are only accountable is taken to be that for which men are responsible, we have another version of such a distortion. A different placing of a unit in a wrong domain results when consciousness is attributed to a person, or a mind to an organic body, since the proper domain for both is the self.

A domain is the product of the union of unit and power. It has an integrity of its own in which the union is spelled out either by its own activity or through our efforts—history illustrating the one and mathematics the other. It impinges on both the units and the power at the same time that it is qualified by them. Tradition, customs, language, the disciplines of science, art, politics, sport are domains. Some have short durations; some have long; some combine a number of other domains; some are relatively pure. We have already seen that a domain's relation to some unit can be misconstrued; it can itself be misconstrued, and can be misconstrued in relation to some power:

a. Moralists, traditionalists, and idealists fail to give full weight or place to units as having integrities of their own. They are content to take them to be no more than knots or moments in a primary domain, sometimes treated as though itself were a final reality. Hegel's idealism depends and often trades on the difference between a domain and a more basic power, but like many of his followers who take such a power to be just a larger and more inclusive domain, he also neglects to give a distinctive place and role to units. Husserl's phenomenological reduction ends with the possession of a domain, but only because he neglects the units with which he inescapably began.

b. Domains, such as history or language, are so large and have such ill-defined boundaries, that it is easy to take a part for the whole. Though it is hard to find a nation that is not affected by others, or by the acts of individuals, there are many historic studies which find no room for these, concentrating instead on a nation's grand movements and patterns. Students of literature, even those who are alert to the presence and effects of the literary tradition on the writers they study, sometimes overlook the fact that the works are also affected by social customs, current myths, and physical conditions. Similar substitutions of whole domains by parts occur when privacy is identified with a self or a person, or when consciousness, mind, or responsibility is taken to exhaust the domain within which some private activity occurs.

c. There are some in the East who reject every unit and every domain, to insist instead on the all-inclusive reality of a final power. Monism, pantheism, personalism offer cognate views. They, too, find nothing to be real but some final power, thereby forcing themselves to deny that they are distinct from it, that they are now seeking it, or that there is a way of getting to it without being annihilated. Extreme subjectivism arrives at a similar result, merely substituting for a cosmic power another, set deep within oneself. Privacy is then granted a place, but nothing is allowed to have a place within it. Practical knowledge, public life, bodies, technology, science, art, and society are then swept away, to leave one with nothing but a power grounding nothing.

d. More common is the supposition that a part of a power is the whole of it. Improper limits are set, or one power is taken to be identical with a set of them. The first supposition is made by those who allow for some kind of temporality but not for space or causality (Bergson and Hume), or for space and causality but not for time (Spinoza). The second supposition is made by those who hold that only becoming is real (process philosophy).

e. There is perhaps no one who is so immersed in facts, so caught up in particularity that he does not recognize a domain in which they are imbedded, though a strong inclination in this direction is exhibited by those who speak of bits of information communicated from one machine or man to another. It is more common to exaggerate the role of a domain. Anthropologists, structuralists, depth grammarians, philosophers of science, society, and politics are aware of the fact that the particulars they note are affected by and imbedded in a domain. An overemphasis on this prevents them from seeing that they would not be able to know a domain unless it were possible to stand outside it in some other domain, or in a power beyond it. Distortions in private functioning often reveal a mind or sensitivity acting as an effective and satisfactory domain for other concentrations, but failing to make adequate room for the power of the self or person. There is then too much attention directed at thinking and not enough to deciding; too much to responsibility and not enough to feeling, to permit of a satisfactory set of distinctive domains, each strong but none overwhelming. Health depends on the self and the person asserting themselves against different condensations acting as domains.

f. The reverse exaggeration occurs when a domain is minimized relative to a power. One might have a strong sense of self, insist on one's person, but fail to engage in the effective use of some concentration. No proper use of the I, me, the mind, or the sensitivity is then made. As a consequence, one may be aware of one's self or person but have no effective I or mind. When a power is identified with what is ultimately real but beyond all comprehension, the value or reality of domains is minimized, with a consequent rejection of the items in them. Mysticism is the reverse of provincialism, the one exaggerating power, the other a domain.

g. Given a particular power, it is possible to place the wrong domain within it. The error is inevitable if some limited power is alone supposed to be appropriate to every domain. Religious fanaticism insists on just one of a number of powers to which every domain is made subject, setting God behind art, morals, history, and politics as their only sustainer. A similar form of this error occurs when it is supposed that the physical world is ultimately real or alone real, or is a power which controls mind, will, self, or person.

h. More common than the foregoing is the error of incorrectly grounding a given domain. One here takes some area of activity to be sustained by what in fact cannot do this. Where before God was assumed to be at the base of all else, here one takes some type of particular activity and treats it as sustained by some inappropriate power. If only one power is allowed, there is little to choose between the present and foregoing error; in both, an inappropriate ground is provided for a particular domain.

In the usual case, we allow for a plurality of powers but mistake which one is appropriate to some domain. We allow that there are selves and persons, but wrongly suppose that the sensitivity is to be found in the one and the I in the other.

Powers are of many kinds and degrees. All relate domains and, through these, have an effect on units. But powers also have a direct effect on units and these make a difference to the powers. Sometimes the extent of the influence of a unit on a power is exaggerated. In religion, the error takes the shape of pelagianism, the supposition that individual acts can dictate to God. Another variant is embodied in magic; still another in anthropocentrism. Behaviorism exhibits a related form so far as it supposes that the particular acts in which men engage determine what his nature is.

'God-intoxicated' panentheists join with fatalists and predestinationalists in supposing that a power overwhelms units, leaving them with no reality of their own, and thus in effect taking them to be just instances of the power. When self or person is held to be a fixed overwhelming determinant of the import and role of every act, the acts are treated as instances of a powerful self or person. A nominalist occasionally accepts this position when, after he has remarked on the ultimacy of individuals and denied the existence of any domain in which they are, supposes that the individuals are directly related to a final power. Occam took this alternative; it was also taken by Freud when he held that acts are expressions of a libido.

It is possible to acknowledge a power but to misconstrue the nature of the units which it governs. This is done when one tries to put organisms and privacies into a cosmos pertinent only to inanimate units. A similar error occurs when one takes sensitivity to be directly governed by the self instead of by the person. A reverse error characterizes those theories in politics and sociology which insist that every unit is political or social in nature. They are special mono-valued schemes, grounding every unit in the same ultimate, bypassing all domains. There is no avoiding this except by the acknowledgment of a plurality of powers, each appropriate to distinctive units, but intermediated by domains within which a limited number of units are effectively related.

A unit is a derivative in one sense, and an irreducible in another. It comes about through the union of diverse factors—intent, language, individual act, society, an I, and encountered content. It then enjoys an integrity of its own, able to be affected by, and sometimes to affect the kinds of items, and occasionally the very exact items which had contributed to its constitution.

What is true of a unit is even more evidently true of a domain. The product of units and power, it usually spreads over a period of time in the attempt to keep the two factors together. It may then interplay with units and powers to constitute intermediate domains. An I has the role of a domain, with other concentrations of the self in the role of units. That I is constituted by the self in the role of a power and by other concentrations in the role of units. But it is distinct from both, with its own nature and functioning, able to interplay both with the self and other concentrations of the self. In 'my self' and 'my mind', the 'my' makes evident the fact that the I is functioning as a domain. But the mind has the I as a unit, when the I is the object of thought.

The powers which function as pivots, turning us back toward actualities, are special, limited cases of final powers. Those that have accreted some power are able to interplay with the very powers from which their own was acquired. A work of art, produced through the joint activity of a creative man and material from the world of nature, is subject to corrosion by nature. The work of art is affected at the same time by the tastes and standards of men; it may be bought and sold, be transported, become an item in the interior decorating of a home, be used in propaganda, and the like. In some cases, there is a later interplay with what helped constitute it. Every distinguished part of a privacy, and the privacy of a whole, are also products, able, like works of art, to function as irreducible powers, domains, or units.

Nature, work, and society; creativity, works of art, and a world of art; men, society, and state; body, emotions, and mind; the lived body, the personalized body, and the physical body form triads of powers, domains, and units. Changes in the domains elicit activity by the units and powers. Private powers provide healthy answers to the functioning of their epitomizing units, and these in turn provide answers to the functioning of publicized expressions.

Having a unity and a power of its own, an I is able to be a domain for the self and person as well as for other epitomizations of these. When the I acts, it takes the others to be unit items to be possessed on the I's own terms. Each of these units, like the I, has its origin in the coming together of a self or person with other condensations of the self or person, and may itself have the others as units for itself in the role of a domain. The I can function—as other epitomizations can—in normative and in distortive ways. It does the one when it expresses itself, governing, controlling, altering that on which it impinges; it does the other when it is blocked and governed by that which it encounters.

There are medicines which operate more or less the same way on multitudes of human bodies. No similar way of dealing effectively with disordered privacies is known. We are not sure what would cure them. Why should this be so? Can we expect that in the future a cure will be provided, merely by altering some public aspect? This would be possible, if specific private disorders would leave the rest of the individual relatively untouched, or if illnesses never had far-reaching effects, making a difference to the functioning of many parts. A cure for private disorders depends on the free, independent functioning of a privacy, self, person, or some concentration of these.

April 30

I have just returned from Harper's Ferry where I attended the opening of (I think) my fifth show of my paintings and drawings. I was rather pleased with the drawings, but think the paintings, with one or two exceptions, are not particularly good. Some twenty people or so came to the opening; none from the Catholic University. Two drawings were sold; the price asked was $150., I don't know yet whether this is what was paid.

If it be true that secondary qualities stand in between physical occurrences and pervasive conditions, should it not be possible to eliminate those qualities, and speak directly of the physical occurrences as being organized by the conditions? The secondary qualities could then be treated as involving an introduction of man into the system, not in the guise of a psyche or a special type of organism, but as a conduit for physical items having an effect on those which constitute his body. One will still be faced with the question as to why the initial physical units were bunched as they are, and which we would otherwise explain as being due to the governance of some secondary qualities. We would have to be content with saying that they are bunched in such and such ways and that, when they are, they interplay with bunched items in the body to constitute another occurrence, e.g., our words 'I see something' and others of a similar nature. No reference would be made to anything but bunchings of items. We might perhaps not be able to predict what a particular bunch would yield when it interplays with a bunched set of items located in the body, but we would nevertheless be able to give a coherent account of what happened. But there will come a time when we will be confronted with the fact that the entire account is our own theory, and that it requires the use of a mind.

No matter how far we drive a 'physicalism' we will have to acknowledge organizing agents, and no matter how often we make such acknowledgments we will be left with the fact that our 'physicalistic' theory depends on a human mind. What seems at first to be the opposite theory is in fact this very theory with an opposite stress. If we begin with mind and take everything we confront and know, from perception to theory, mathematics to religion, to be nothing other than expressions of a human mind, we will come at last to the fact that there is something on which that mind is applied. If we take the mind to be the source of categories, the forms of space and time, of all associations, we will, with both Hume and Kant, differ from the materialists only in the kind of nature and power we attribute to the all-powerful mind and the data on which it operates.

Plato, Aristotle, Augustine, Aquinas, Descartes, Leibniz, Locke, Berkeley, Hume, and Kant are agreed on one basic view: there is a powerful source of intelligibility which is imposed on obstinate units. Taking the units as alone real, the intelligibility becomes a way of arranging which has no ontological import. Taking the intelligibility as alone powerful makes the units be just material to be organized. Taking them both to be real, but opposed to one another as irreconcilable, yields a dualism with an unknowable on one side, since we will be on the other side. Taking them both to be subtended by some third—a demiurgos, a synthesis, a judgment, and the like, opens us up to the question of the nature of this. If the units cannot be understood in terms of one or the other of the third, we not only have a new factor, but the problem of relating it to the others. If we bring it under one or the other it will not serve to relate them. But we can take the third to be either a merged outcome of both—the emotions, e.g., merge mind and body—or to be presupposed by both, just as privacy is presupposed by the mind and the body when we approach them from the inside the individual.

We always have organization and units, one and many, laws and entities, the intelligible and the related. Each meets resistance from the other; together they constitute a new entity. Some of these have sometimes been taken to be transcendentals—beauty— supervening on units which have been able to make provision for specializations of various finalities. It is not, strictly speaking, a transcendental term. Only 'Substance' and the terms for other finalities are. 'Quantity' is such a term because it is shorthand for Existence.

If it be true that we always have units, no matter how complex, and whether they are physical or mental or neither (such as a Humean impression), and organizations, no matter how simple and whether they are physical or mental or neither (such as an Aristotelian essence), and that we start with them mixed together in commonsense or in some domain whatsoever short of the state where they are speculatively understood to be apart—when we are forced to see them together constituting and facing a common ideal—the only question that remains is where we should draw the line, and take the unifying governor or the units to be of primary value or power.

For the purposes of science, one can insist on units, or combinations of them to any degree of complexity, without ever having the right to say that there is no unity, whether this be provided by the individual mind, mind in general, or some transcendent. For the purposes of history, religion, systematic philosophy, or existentialism one can insist on organizing agents of different degrees of complexity and application to units which themselves may be located in some subordinate mind or some separate kind of realm. But once we pass beyond the need to satisfy the objectives of particular disciplines—and that I take is the first step in being a philosopher—one must ask how these different approaches are possible. If we stop with that question we will have to look for an ontology to explain the plurality of methods or epistemologies. But if we take the question to be one which asks how the 'One and the Many' can intermingle in different ways, we will eventually be forced to acknowledge different interminglings, and then move on to see what the One and the Many are apart from one another, though as necessarily referring to one another, and this the more surely we arrive at either. We must at one and the same time allow that there are minds and bodies, and that they intermingle in multiple ways and degrees, thereby allowing us to deal with all that is already known of the mind in bodily terms, and all that is already known of the body in mental (theoretic, or formal, or law-like) terms, always remembering that the first leaves over the mind and the other body as a datum.

May 2

Scientific procedure differs from philosophic in a. seeking a hypothetical formulation, rather than an objective reality to express the nature of an organizer; b. interpreting what actually occurs as cases where an hypothesis is instanced, rather than taking it to be one in which the organizer is realized and thereby altered; c. treating the instanced structure to be just present, instead of taking it to be imposed; d. treating the structure as having no power, instead of taking it to transmit power; e. treating the units, to which the hypothesis is to apply, as values of variables, and not as having an interiority, or as expressing something which has such an interiority. Both procedures stand opposed to the practices of sociologists who, like practical men, accept the union of organizer and units, and try to see if they can discover laws by ordering the units in various ways.

If we start with organizers, we can have many different sets of items to which they apply; no theory will tell us just how items are in fact bunched apart from it. If, instead, we start with a particular organized set of items, we do not have an explanation of its existence. But if we start with particular items we do not know which of an endless number of hypotheses we could use.

We cannot avoid acknowledging organized sets to begin with, and perhaps even making hypotheses which attempt to express the nature of the organizer and, correlatively, giving some account of the units which are organized, as so many values of the organizer with its variables. But in the end we will have to acknowledge real organizers, i.e., finalities and their expressions, and real units, i.e., actualities on some level. And when we come back to the 'mixed', we will have to recognize that a unity of organizer and units is something new, involving the presence of a new feature expressing the way in which the organizer and units interlocked and affected one another.

If it be true that Beauty is not an organizer, i.e., not a condition governing items, but the outcome of the way in which the parts of a creative work allow for the presence of a unifying power that expresses purity, fulfillment, and the like, it seems reasonable to suppose that we ought to find something analogous in other areas. Does not truth answer to the presence of Possibility, goodness to that of Unity, justice to that of Being, and right, taken as involving an organic unification of items, to Substance?

Each of these 'domain characters' is constituted by actualities and finalities or specializations of them, and thrusts forward to make a place for some other entity. Truth, when it characterizes a mathematical unit, thrusts toward other similar units, such as numbers, figures, and equations. Beauty is perhaps just less familiar. It refers to the outcome of the union of composition, purity, prospects, etc., with materials, and thrusts forward toward other possible unities. To be beautiful is to be a perfected work of art in a domain of art. The right is a clustered set of items thrusting forward to others which are to be fitted with it. Justice characterizes a distinct resultant which projects a place for something equal to it. Finally, goodness characterizes a union having a position in a projection, to be filled out by something having a value relative to what is good. In all these cases, I am stressing the best possible combination of organization and entity. Ugliness, error, etc., are to be understood as not properly uniting the factors, failing to fill out a projected place well, or failing to project properly so as to allow for some further item. Appearances, unlike the commonsensical items or the items distinguished above, do not thrust forward; they are constituted of attenuations of the actualities and finalities and do not, as these others do, express the result of a direct interaction between the finalities and actualities resulting in a new kind of unit? What kind?

Is the world of commonsense a domain, constituted perhaps by an amalgamation of all the above? Are its units 'the practical', or 'the effective'? What is to be said of history and politics, which would seem to be domains in the same sense as these others? Once history and politics are acknowledged, the one as involving Existence, and the other as involving Substance, Being, or Possibility, or all three—though perhaps most properly Being as allowing for distinct functioning units, complex or simple— will we not have still other domains to consider which make a similar use of Unity (and perhaps of Substance or Possibility)? Will these require the intermediation of men?

History and politics are to be supplemented by the social (answering to Substance's interplay with actualities), by culture (answering to Possibility's interplay with actualities), and by piety's objects or practices (answering to Unity's interplay with actualities).

How do the right and the social, justice and politics, truth and culture, history and beauty, and goodness and piety differ? Evidently, the right, justice, truth, beauty (n.b.!), and goodness reveal an emphasis on final conditions, while the social, the political, culture, history, and piety emphasize the actual. If this is so, we should expect that there will be something else arising when the two are balanced, and when there is no more emphasis on one of the sources than on the other. We then get 'social right', 'political justice', 'established truth' 'civilization', and 'sanctioned goodness'. 'Civilization' however, will not be on a par with the others, unless 'beauty' be understood not only to apply to works of art but to anything excellent, produced by man.

May 3

Yesterday's exploration diverges somewhat from what was suggested in this work some time ago. Then I took the position that there were domains which themselves interplayed with the actualities and finalities to produce intermediate domains. This position had the advantage of allowing mathematics to be quite pure, and to account for its application to other subordinated domains. The present view takes the application to be the outcome of a kind of contraction of a domain, so that the application of mathematics becomes the result of the way in which actualities were able to have a greater role than before. And what is said of mathematics would have analogous applications to other subjects. The earlier view was more in consonance with the usual way of dealing with mathematics and its applications, but the present seems to be closer to the facts. The former took mathematics to be something like an hypothetical realm (which is the way Galileo seemed to view it), and to find instances in the world. The present allows for the relevance of mathematics to actualities and even for its being realized and thereby altered by virtue of the effect that the actualities have on it. The bearing on other domains alongside it is a question for both, and is to be answered by recognizing that each of the finalities has the others subordinate to it.

It is still necessary to show how actualities and finalities interplay in different ways when they constitute objective appearances, transcendentally unified complex entities, and domains. The first two occur without the intermediation of man, the first involving the finalities and actualities as expressing themselves in attenuated forms, the second as involving a direct action of the finalities on the actualities, with some reply by the actualities. (The counter-emphasis in which there is a direct action of the actualities on the finalities provides these with nuances and possible distinctions). Domains, in contrast, require a man to construct, which is to say to both think and act. In some domains the thinking is dominant, as in mathematics; in others the action, as in history or in art.

The acknowledgment of domains gives us in specialized forms the kind of world in which we daily live. It allows us to bring practical considerations, perhaps even pragmatic ones, to the mastery, not only of what occurs every day but of more specialized realms. Only theoretical science and philosophy concern themselves with the formulation of or an actual reaching to what is an explanation distinct from the explained, and only philosophy concerns itself with trying to understand the explainer and the explained as realities, at once distinct and interinvolved.

The recognition of intermediate realms, which depend on a practically grounded interest in having the actualities and finalities together, makes it possible to take account of a man's changing personality, without compromising his identity, individuality, or any other dimension of his privacy. A man's personality changes and usually is enriched over the course of his life. The fact can be accommodated by recognizing personality to be a product of the way in which privacy, body, and world yield a unit in a domain of interinvolved humans in a milieu. The result presupposes a constant privacy, allows for changing ways in which that privacy uses that body and, both through and apart from this, makes provision for the presence of other persons in a common domain. The domain here differs from the ones already mentioned in being the outcome, not of a consideration of actualities and finalities but, as is the case with the daily world, of the exercise of power.

Once this is allowed, a new area of inquiry is opened up. Are there other ways in which men practically constitute themselves to become members of special practical domains, at the same time that some dimension of them as complex beings is enabled to have an indefinite number of degrees of enrichment? This seems to be the way in which a man makes himself be a social or political being, in contradistinction with the way in which he understands these. The latter involves the carving out of domains alongside mathematics; the former requires him to make himself into a unit in a domain. And what is true of these would seem to be true of the domains of mathematics and religion, the one having a counterpart in men occupied with making themselves into judges of truth, and the other with making themselves into members of some church.

May 24

I have now completed a draft of 'An Exploration of Human Privacy'. I have put it aside to await a rereading and a rewriting when I return to Washington next week. The book ends with me facing the problem of man's place in the world, a topic which I have been trying to understand under the idea of a domain.

If we take the ultimate units of the cosmos to be related by R, which is to be spelled out as a multiplicity of laws, we can speak of clusters of these units all the way up to organic beings, including men, as ( ) R'. The brackets make the clusters be units which are related by the new relation R' to other units. ( ) R' is equivalent with the separate ultimate units as related by R. When we consider the special work of some organisms and, more sharply, when we deal with a work of art, we get [( ) R'] R". Here R" relates the work of art to other works of art in a world of art as more or less beautiful. The work of art, as related in the domain of art by R" can be dealt with as a set of clustered items related by R'. When this is done, we have no explanations of why they are clustered, or for their particular relation to other clusters. But we can capture every fact within the scheme. And what we do with works of art, we can also do with clustered units, for those units in the work of art are related to all other ultimate units. We will, of course, not yet have explained why there should be that cluster.

A work of art is a cluster of items and a set of ultimate units in relation to other units. If we start at the units, we cannot explain their clustering, or the special relation that a cluster happens to have to a limited number of other clusters, in what would ordinarily be called a work of art. But a cosmos, since it encompasses all that there is apart from any special clustering, will have the items (which are clustered, or which a man may have ordered creatively) already together. If we make a computer bunch items in accord with the way men have creatively bunched them, it will still work with units as though they were like the detached ultimates of a cosmic physics (which, as so detached, may be governed by laws that take account of their relevance or distances, without denying that they are ultimate units, not governed by limited unifiers). It will then function as a copyist of a work of art does, reproducing every line but only because every line has already been antecedently laid out.

Reductionism puts all additions to the physical as subjective, illusory, confused, in a language or mind, but without being able to get rid of them as what had to be reduced, as playing roles in men's lives and activities, and as needed by a theory supposedly justifying the reduction. All the while, reductionism makes an implicit acknowledgment of another power which, together with the accepted base, supposedly accounts for the presence of the complex that is being reduced.

If, instead, a stand is taken with the more complex, the simpler will seem to be occupied with abstractions from what is real. In the end, one will be unable to explain how the abstractions could have arisen, and how items could act within them. The view makes an implicit acknowledgment that what it takes to be derivative, abstract, or minor is in fact an area where the brute, the subhuman, and the necessities for human life are to be found. It also presupposes another power; together with the accepted base, this is to account for the availability of the accepted final items.

The greatest of artists falls at the same rate that stones do. His body, though lived in a way the bodies of others are not, acts in some circumstances in the very way that any bodies do. His always is subject to forces that apply to ultimate units in it as related to others. When he falls, there is not only a physical state of affairs, but this is determinative of what is occurring. His organic nature, as subjecting what is within its limits to a single control, is not operative, so far as the fall is concerned, though he is alive, can be hurt, may be killed, and may be frightened. The situation where R occurs is basic. But when we have clusters, organisms, and works of art they are inexplicably present in that world. The ultimate units and R are reconstituted to yield clusters etc., with limited relations to other clusters etc., and are so far not reducible to the units and R.

Above the purely physical, there are units in domains with distinctive relations; the units are constitutive of and constituted by what else is in a domain through which they thrust toward other similar units.

Objective domains have clustered units, governed by a clustering agent, if only in the form of a restraining boundary of them. Subjective or humanized domains are those objective domains as subject to other limitations, with a consequent new kind of thrust, and therefore occupying a different kind of domain. Were there no objective domains there would be no living beings; were there no humanized domains there would be no art, mathematics, or known history.

From this point of view, mathematics makes use of actual entities in diagrams or other kinds of constructions, and written history and theories make use of actual entities in language. Better perhaps, they deal, not with actual entities that are in fact encompassed in organisms and in anything made, but with the articulating finalities in ways which answer to objective situations. They consider items as related by R in a cosmos or in more restricted domains, and offer ways in which the finalities can be articulated and therefore, in fact, be realized in the world in the form of R, or in domains in the form of R' or R".

A tentative list of objective domains, humanized domains, and constructed domains can now be made:

1. groups; finalities are here dominant; their union with actualities thrusts toward opportunities. 1a. art works 1b. criticism; philosophy of art.

2. organic occurrences; finalities and actualities equal in role; thrust toward what is different 2a. confrontation; state 2b. truth; justice.

3. law-abiding nature; thrust dominant; with sometimes finalities and sometimes actualities dominant. 3a. controlled inquiry into the world 3b. mathematics, logic; theories

4. history, biography, nations; actualities dominant 4a. written history, biography, tradition 4b. philosophical history

5. geographical metrics; thrust and actualities dominant 5a. ecology 5b. theoretical geography; anthropology

6. distribution; finalities and thrust dominant 6a. economics as including work and market 6b. theory of management

7. men together; actualities, finalities and thrust equal 7a. morality, culture 7b. theodicy, axiology.

8. mixtures; daily world 8a. sociology 8b. statistics.

Do penetrations to finalities and privacies with their necessary thrusts constitute domains of an intensive sort?

May 25

'An Exploration of Human Privacy' ends with an account of human privacy as constantly involved with accepting and then using the different finalities to enrich itself, thereby making itself more mature and more able to be a kind of microcosm of a macrocosm, where the latter is understood to be, not the actual world, but the conditions to which everything is subject.

I had not consciously thought all the while I was arriving at this point that the conclusion is the counterpoint to what I had held about the finalities. In *First Considerations* I had concluded that the finalities were trying to recover the evidence and evidenced they made possible. The two views lead to an answer to a question that my colleagues in Denver posed: what guides our conceptualization of the thrust into the depths of the finalities and privacies, as we proceed to use evidence, symbolize, and await confirmation that our judgments about what the finalities and privacies are?

Taking the unification of the finalities in privacy, and the unification of evidence and evidenced in the finalities as our final objectives for conceptualization, we can make use of inadequate ideas, those which are rough generalizations of what is encountered every day and those which refer to a final outcome, and unite them in a concept.

Why not just conceptualize the final outcome in the very form that is presented in *First Considerations* and in the draft of the current book? More generally: is there a difference between an idea of something privately forged and perhaps correct, and a concept?

Ideas which are forged in anticipation are affected by the experiential world where we are forging them, and with our own preconceptions. Concepts are forged while involved with a thrust, and are affected by that thrust. Just as the former are not altogether free from effects by the thrust, so the latter are not altogether free from ourselves and our previous experiences or ideas. But the emphasis is different, and the degree of determination as well as the way they are objectively sustained are different. One way our original ideas of ultimate realities are checked, is by the concepts we produce in articulating the thrust toward the realities. Those concepts are guided by the idea that the ultimate realities are involved in basic acts of unifying what is dispersed—the actualities by uniting in themselves aspects of the finalities, and the finalities by uniting in themselves what they exteriorized as evidence and evidenced. From the ideas we start with and the ideas we have of the end, the one empirical and the other speculative, we forge concepts where the former are made subordinate to the latter. We do not succeed in producing a perfect union at any one moment, and are forced again and again to produce new concepts which give more and more prominence to the idea of the terminus as actually controlling the idea with which we began. The final concept will be of that of which we had an idea, but which now has within it antecedent ideas in an hierarchical order where they are not distinguished.

These conclusions go somewhat beyond the point where we arrived yesterday at the 'faculty confrontations' which I have been having with my colleagues every Thursday afternoon, and where, with a few exceptions, we use *First Considerations* as a text. The most constant participants are Jere Shurber, a very acute young man who has a strong dialectical ability and a firm knowledge of the views of great thinkers—in my opinion a man of great promise in philosophy; Jerry Dozoretz, who is a master of Peirce's writings and who is quickly alert to the implications of arguments and has an unusual ability to know what others intend; Bob Schulz, whose primary interest is in ecology and education, and whose radical honesty allows him to raise crucial questions, particularly when there has been a tendency to run off into abstractions; Ed Smith who is a master of medieval thought, particularly of Thomas Aquinas and who, though usually very quiet, does have a feeling for what makes basic good sense; and Bill Anderson, an original logician who has an acute sense of the logical implications of a view, and who, I am glad to find, agrees with me (and I with him) on some pivotal ideas in logic which the established logicians have ignored over the years, such as the difference between the 'truth value' of a tautology and that of its constituents, the impossibility of giving extensional formulations for intensional logic, and the extensional character of Lewis' early views. Others who come occasionally are Roscoe Hill (whom I replaced as he moved into a deanship), some graduate students, and an occasional undergraduate. The discussions are vigorous and always to the point, and run for two hours at a time. They seem to me to be just what philosophic discussions should be, with the arguments to the fore and no attempt being made to be polite or to hedge. When I first came to The Catholic University of America, we had discussions something like these, then we began by taking off from some section in *Modes of Being*. The present discussions focus on *First Considerations* and, instead of taking off from what was said, concentrate on what is there maintained, its possible truth, and its implications. The adventure has been very successful in both cases, but the present is more valuable to me and perhaps to the others because of its focus on particular passages and problems, without too much reference to alternative views that had been presented in the past. The men here are younger and less the masters of particular philosophic positions than my colleagues at the Catholic University of America, but they paid sharper attention to the issues raised.

Applying the reflections, raised in the discussion and directed at the knowledge of the finalities, to the knowledge of privacies, it can be said that the knowledge we have of what individual men are like is the outcome of an attempt to forge concepts in the course of a thrust into others. The concepts unite actual ideas of what we experientially know of others with ideas of what they are privately. In the concept, the latter idea has the former as a subordinate component. Our initial ideas are something like the truths we use as premises; they are subjected to a right-angle turn from a reference to what is encountered to a reference toward the idea we have of the privacy. The two ideas are solidified in the forging of a concept inseparable from the thrust from the one toward the other, and from the latter into the realities.

June 13

I have been back in Washington for almost two weeks. Most of the time I have spent in rereading the manuscript of 'An Exploration of Human Privacy'. I am near the end of that reading, and hope that I will be able to begin a radical rewriting by the end of the week. At present, it is not as straightforward as I would like it to be. I must make it tighter.

* * *

In the course of rereading of 'AEHP' it has become evident that a man can be understood to have a Privacy, self, psyche, person, and body. Each of these can be matched with a finality—Privacy with Unity, self with Substance, psyche with Possibility, person with Being, and body with Existence. Such matching makes it possible to make some advance in understanding what goes on inside a finality. Privacy, I have held, is a rectifying agent, the self is epitomized in a possessive I, and grounds an assumed accountability and an assumed responsibility; psyche is essentially conscious and is epitomized in a mind and in decisions; person is the locus of rights, and grounds sensitivity; and body is lived and thereby governed from within by means of sensitivity. If one were to follow these leads, one would be led to hold that the inward nature of Unity is essentially one of achieving an equilibrium amongst all intruders; that Substance is essentially possessive and takes it upon itself to preserve as well as it can, what is available; that Possibility is a rational power, somewhat like what Christian tradition takes God to be; that Being is a responsive claimant, and that Existence is a unity governing a multiplicity. The surprising results are those connected with Possibility and Being, for the one is turned into something like a cosmic mind and will, a kind of Spinozistic God, while the other is something like a macrocosm.

I don't know how much of this can withstand criticism, but it does offer the beginning of an attempt to characterize the finalities in terms grounded in what we can learn about the inwardness of men. Since what is said about that inwardness is in part gleaned from what had already been learned about the finalities (in *First Considerations*) we have here another illustration of the method I have been following—going from the realm of the 'mixed' to finalities, from there to actualities, and then back again; and then going from the realm of the mixed to actualities, from there to the finalities, and back again. The different starts allow one to attend to each side and to provide a check against the move to it from the other side. And, of course, each process can be repeated many times to expose deeper and deeper levels in the extremes.

August 29

I am nearing the end of about the fifth revision of 'An Exploration of Human Privacy'. In the meantime, I have sent off the galleys for 'You, I, and the Others'. This immersion in what I had previously written has left me with the feeling that I haven't really been thinking freshly or well. I turn therefore to this journal once more to work on issues which require new approaches and a following out of the implications, with consequences I cannot envisage.

When someone on whom I rely says "x is y" I accept it, and I can repeat the statement as a truth. The truth which I credit it with on the basis of the integrity of the speaker is inheritable by me and others. But if he says that "x is beautiful", I do not credit his statement as a truth, even when I take him to be eminent or an authority. At most, I allow that he is able to see something in x which I may not. I do know that I cannot report to someone else that x is beautiful, merely because he said it was. Where the truth of something seems to be there for anyone, beauty seems to require some particular approach, some way of being involved with the occurrence. I don't necessarily deny his contention. I just do not grant that the beauty is there for everyone. And, of course, when the judgment is made by one who is not an accepted authority, I don't allow even that it is there for anyone else.

Dreams, private thoughts, private decisions are also not available to others. Yet I accept statements about them by those who claim to have had these. I do not of course here, any more than I do in connection with the aesthetic judgment, repeat the claim as my own. But I think their access to the data is one that requires no special abilities. In the case of the aesthetic work I do. The difference seems to lie in the fact that in the aesthetic realm what is accessible to many may be dealt with in a way that is beyond the capacity of most, and that one who has not himself gone that distance cannot report the result as one that he knows to be so. It is, of course, true that mathematicians, scientists, explorers, and others engaged in great and novel undertakings arrive at results others cannot, and yet we take what they report as truths. But here what we find is beyond the rest of us is the getting into the position to know, whereas in the aesthetic situation, in addition to the achievement of such a position, there is the need to confront what is not evident except to one who opens up the object in the act of knowing it. The mathematical truth or the great discovery we think is *there,* available to anyone if only he could get to confront it, whereas the work of art, we think, is there only so far as one approaches it in a special way, which not everyone might be able to achieve. As a consequence, if we wish to report the result, we say that Mr A says that the work is excellent, and not that it is so in fact. But we can report that so and so is a mathematical outcome or a scientific result, even though we cannot duplicate the thinking. We allow the aesthetic judgment and the judgments of the mathematicians etc. to be right, but we cannot altogether detach the personal notes from the former. Does this make aesthetic judgment subjective? I think not. What was reported might well be what is excellent, but it is an excellence not available to anyone not able to progress intensively in depth. The judgment then is like that made in knowing what another is like in his privacy, what is discovered in religious or mystical experience, or is the outcome of an actual metaphysical move to final realities. All of these can be reported, but none can be conveyed to another as a truth to be just accepted.

There seems to be an exception: great religious figures, who speak of having made contact with the divine, are taken to have uttered truths which can be repeated. Something similar is done by the disciples of the great philosophers. Do we not in these cases expect to be able to have the experience itself or at best to have a kind of copy of it, whereas in the aesthetic case we will not accept the claim to truth, and will in fact ourselves offer counter-statements if our experience leads us to them? Our experience in aesthetics is placed on a footing with that of experts. Though we allow that they might discern something which we will have to learn to discern for ourselves, we insist on the irreducibility of our judgments at the time.

Our own experience of something as (not) beautiful is resolutely clung to in the face of the claims of others. This is not because we take all judgments to be subjective or relative. What we say tells what is in fact there, and not merely something about us, though it depends on us to see little or much. Does it all come down to the fact that in the case of mathematics, science, discovery, and inventions, there is a method which we think could be made our own, but in the case of aesthetics and religion there is only insight, special dispensation, individual gifts, and the like?

August 30

The relation between religious and aesthetic judgments is perhaps closer than I indicated yesterday. Outside the confines of a particular religion, the judgments and reports of a religious man are not accepted merely because the man is known to be honest; inside a particular tradition, the judgments of acknowledged authorities in art are accepted as true. What we have in both cases is something acceptable to some, but not acceptable to those outside the domain. Generalizing, we can say that there is a position which all religious people, and another position which all aesthetic ones take as normative, but the latter at least may not be acceptable to others as reporting what is objectively the case. Though the reports may not be deemed to be universal in the sense that their truth is inheritable in repetitions of the reports by others, it is objective within a domain. Within the domain there can be subdomains in which similar considerations hold.

Singular individuals can be said to belong to singular domains; what they say may be true, but it is not true for others, since these do not accept those domains. May we generalize the last conclusion and hold that every man constitutes a domain and therefore has truths which he cannot pass on for others to take without question, even when it is known that he is honest? It seems so. May we then go on to say that whatever a man truthfully reports is peculiar to him and may be honestly reported, but that no one else can take it to be so? The conclusion would force one to say that men cannot constitute a single body in one domain. There would be a solipsism of truth. We seem therefore forced to say that there is a common domain for all men, and particular subdomains for smaller groups and for individuals. What is known in those subdomains is not able to carry its truth with it when it is taken outside these.

Why do we take the domains in which mathematicians and scientists work to be open to others; or alternatively, why are truths there asserted accepted by others as truths?

There is a difference between the report of a dream and the report of an aesthetic or religious experience, or some mathematical discovery. It is in a domain to which no one else has access. We cannot justifiably say "There was a dream by x of such and such a nature" because we cannot distinguish between what was really dreamt and what x is offering as a report of it. We are content to accept the report as completely accurate, even though we know that interpretations are apt to have been intruded, because we not only have no other access to the dream but because it is not a matter of importance to us. For an analyst it should make little difference whether what is reported is exactly what had oc- curred or something quite different, for a modified dream in the report by an honest man is just as deeply grounded and should be as revelatory as an accurate one.

In a report of a religious experience we want precision. As outsiders, of course, we cannot know, any more than we can in the case of the dream, that we are getting an uninterpreted report. Though we are willing to accept the report as an honest one, we do not, if we are not part of the religion, accept the report as true except for one in that domain. We refuse to accord it truth in other domains. A mathematician's report of what he had discovered—say Fermat's last theorem which no one has been able to prove—may be accepted by others who are not mathe- maticians or who are not able to see the warrant for Fermat's surmise, because no practical decisions about their lives seem to be involved.

We put a block before the religious man's claim, for if he were right we would have to change our lives radically; this is not demanded of us anywhere else. An aesthetic judgment is not granted truth in a common human domain if it is exceptional, not because its acceptance would require a radical alteration in our lives, but because it tacitly assesses us as insensitive. If we enter into the domain of the religious man we can share in his truth. Though we will do it via him, what we arrive at presumably will be a truth apart from him. If we enter into the domain of an aesthetic man we may not be able to share in his truth. We cannot experience the result by accepting him as an intermediary as we can the religious man, and as we can, in another sense, the mathematician or scientist.

We have the following cases:

1. A dream experience which no one else can have. We can accept the report of this as oriented in the reporter. It is not to be reported as true apart from a reference to the dreamer.

2. An aesthetic experience, which no one else may have. We can accept the report of this as oriented in the reporter. It can be made ours by our sharing in his tradition, using him as our model or critic.

3. A religious experience which no one else may have. The report of this can be accepted by others, who thereby are able to share in that experience via the reporter. They can accept the report as true and therefore know the object of the report as that which was truthfully reported.

4. A mathematical or scientific experience that one may not have the techniques to judge. The report of this can be accepted by others as being open to an objective proof by anyone, even those who do not have a direct knowledge of what was originally discerned.

5. A metaphysical experience of ultimate realities which one may not reach, but which one can duplicate by following the steps laid down in a systematic report.

None of this is entirely clear to me, for I do not yet see clearly just when and where and how the experiencer and reporter are separable from their reports, as they apparently are, in at least the last three cases.

August 31

We must go beyond the view presented yesterday. We cannot entirely separate the reporter's interpretation in his report of a dream; the emotional contribution in a report of an aesthetic experience; the spiritual transformative component in a religious report; the insight in a mathematical report; or the vision in a metaphysical report. In every limited domain, there is a component contributed by the participant that cannot be entirely distinguished from the rest. Why not go on and make the same claim about all mankind? Why not say that there is a distinctively human contribution in all that is known, and that it cannot be entirely distinguished from the part that is 'given'.

It is not uncommon to maintain that there is a human contribution made to whatever is known. The clearest statement is Kant's; there are necessary components in the known which originate in a logically governed mind. Kant distinguishes the human component; so does C. I. Lewis, who supposes that categories are arbitrary modes of organization.

Humanists, phenomenologists and existentialists, perhaps, are the only ones who would maintain that there is an inextinguishable but also un-identifiable component in all that is known. If they do, they are up against the fact that they, too, cannot know the component and cannot know what it is on which this is applied. The most that could be legitimately claimed is something like the Kantian view. But that view also arbitrarily supposes that what man contributes cannot also be already present in another form in the known world. A man is taken to constitute what is known. The view is not only up against the fact that there can be no knowledge of that on which the contribution can be imposed, but against the fact that the contribution cannot be known to issue from men by attending to them, since that attention itself depends on a knowing, together with the acknowledgment of men as unaffected by our knowing them.

Is it possible for there to be a constant human contribution made in all knowledge, and for this not to be known? If not known, we do not know whether it is large or small, and do not know what it is on which it is applied, or that it holds of other men. A constant contribution must be transcendental in the sense of being conditional for the knowledge by any man; it is not something that can be learned by attending to particular men. And if we take account of the fact that a man needs certain conditions to be fulfilled before he can know—he must be born, have objects which nourish him, have a past that he did not create and a future into which he can come, that he can act, and needs to differentiate the pertinent from the impertinent, the basic from the dependent, the rational from the irrational, and the good from the bad—we can know that the world apart from him has certain basic features. Only if to these conditions man necessarily adds others or specifies them in constant inescapable ways will it be true that there is an inescapable component in all reports. That component will be known just so far as one knows what it is to which the conditions apply and what it is they help constitute.

To be able to affirm that there is an inescapable unknown component which all men introduce into what is known, it must be held that there is no distinguishing between a. constant components coming from other sources, helping constitute the known, and b. components from man which modify that result. If the addition of objective constituents to external realities be said to yield an appearance, that appearance will have to be distinguished from the appearance that results through the addition of the human component. The former are objective appearances, the latter subjective. The thesis, then, that there is no knowing what men contribute to the constitution of what is known in effect maintains that there is no knowing the difference between objective appearances and those subjective appearances which have a constant human factor as a constituent. A supposed constituent of an objective appearance, such as its intelligible form or its extension, would have as inseparable from it something which a man inevitably introduces. Transcendentals would not be pure, direct, evidential, attenuated forms of what was ultimately real, but would have as a part of them something that men inevitably add. Men, of course, do add their knowing, their consciousness, making what is there something known. The question, therefore, comes down to whether or not knowing or consciousness changes what it confronts. It surely implicates it in situations which would not be pertinent were it not for the thinking or the consciousness of man and the kind of bearing these have on human existence. But once again, this claim requires that one be able to distinguish what the item is apart from man, from what it is because he has thought of or been conscious of it. It therefore requires one to know not only what he contributes, but what things are, apart from him.

If the human contribution is universal and constant, and something which no one could possibly distinguish from other universal and constant factors, we would have to say that we cannot distinguish between those factors which apply to everything, whether or not there are men, and those factors which apply to them because man is knowing them. Our difficulty will have been transposed from the world of every day to metaphysics, and our question would be whether or not it was possible to distinguish a pure transcendental and its ground from one which was humanly produced, sustained, or exhibited in the knowing of particular things. We would then have to say that though transcendents were constituents of a world apart from men, we never know them in that guise, but only as inseparable from and incapable of being known apart from the human contribution. What the men would contribute would not be something that they produced as beings in the world; the factor that was being credited to them would be constitutive of their knowing and, in that sense, be a transcendent prescriptive element in it.

The issue comes down to the question whether or not in addition to objective transcendentals grounded in finalities, there is another essential to knowing unable to be distinguished from the others. The problem would have no solution were there only one finality. But if there are many, and they can be distinguished, the supposed constant knowledge factor would be what was common to them: it would function with respect to them as they function with respect to particular objects. The claim, then, that there is an unknown humanly produced factor of a transcendental kind, is tantamount to the claim that there is a transcendental overarching all others. Since it would constitute with them something analogous to an appearance, one should be able to know it in the same way that one knows the transcendentals.

If one allows for only one finality—God, an Absolute, or The Good—one can not know whether or not what is reported of this is tainted by the condition of knowing. Only if there is more than one finality, will it be possible to distinguish a knowing from the objects of the knowing, as constituting distinct known objects with them. If this conclusion is correct, it offers a startling confirmation of the idea that there is more than one finality.

Recurring to the more limited domains with which this inquiry began, it seems reasonable to say that dreams, aesthetic experiences, and religion all involve a single universal condition and finality and, therefore, do not permit of a distinguishing of the experiencer from the experience. In dreams we have a condition of intelligibility contributed by the dreamer, in aesthetics we have a sense of relevance by the perceiver, and in religion we have the emotional grasp of a primary value. But in mathematics we seem to have both a principle of rationality and relevance, and in science one of extension and rationality, while in metaphysics there are the rationality (in the form of an intensive move) and independence allowing each item to be properly known.

Systematic considerations make it necessary to raise the question whether or not there is a domain that is known primarily as a locus of independence, and another known as purely extensional—economics and history?—and whether or not metaphysics uses five principles to apprehend each finality.

September 1

In contrast with the views that nothing is contributed when we know, that the contribution is unknowable, and that the contribution introduces an essential factor in what alone has reality, I have been maintaining that knowledge involves the addition of a knowable component, giving the result a new status not entirely separable from the old. Were nothing contributed, it would not be a constant connected with a multiplicity; were it unknowable, there would be no errors and no truth utilized; and were it an essential factor in a reality, the other factor could not be known. An alternative takes knowing to introduce an articulation, to face the undivided object with a structure, in which what was undivided in the object is distinguished for a judgmental unit answering to the unitary undivided nature of the object. The knowledge terminates in a known continuous with the object known, the known being the articulation as awaiting acceptance by the object, and the object known having the articulation subordinated to its unity.

Is there a relation between the structure of knowledge and the structure of an inference? Do both exhibit in limited form the nature of Possibility as pertinent to everything? If the first is to be possible, the asymmetrical relation of p to q in 'p entails q' will somehow have to be reconciled with the reverse asymmetrical relation that a predication is supposed to exhibit in 'a is b'. This can be done by taking Possibility to have the form 'X-is-not-nonX'. The status of the 'is-not', and of the 'is' is left undetermined. We can specialize the form as 'A is (not-nonA)', as 'A is (not-nonB)', as 'A is not nonA', as 'A is not nonB', A r's nonA, A r's nonB' and many more, particularly since the X and nonX can be independently specialized as complexes of terms and relations. The original form is sufficiently general to allow for both symmetrical and asymmetrical specializations, as the above indicates.

The structure used in knowing and inferring may be identical with or diverge from that ingredient in what is external, depending on whether or not it is true of this or diverges from it. As not used, the structure of the mind will be like the undivided intelligible nature of any object or of Possibility itself. A particular use of the mind involves a specialization of the structure, and the actual expression of an entity involves the specialization of its structure. To have undeniable knowledge we have to move to that level where the structure of the mind is so general that it can match within a limited area and for a special use the structure that is pertinent to and is specialized by every entity. An entity, apart from the mind and apart from the structuralization provided by Possibility, can also be understood to have an indeterminate form expressible in the general formula 'A-is-not-nonA' where the 'A' reports the nature of the object (thereby differentiating what the structure is in that object from what it is in the mind which seeks to know but which may misconstrue what is there).

September 4

The view that I have been working on, about what man contributes to the known world, differs from the major positions that have been presented in the past. It also shares features with each:

1. Man is sometimes thought to contribute only error, confusion, distortion. The view is held by those who, with Leibniz, think of God as creating a perfect world and of man as a sinner necessarily distorting it, and by physicalists, materialists, and scientifically oriented thinkers who suppose that the world consists of ultimate particles whose nature is partly caught in men's formulations. In my holding that men contribute to objective appearances and thereby produce subjective appearances, something like that view is being held. But I also hold that it is not necessary that men make objective appearances be subjective; they can discern those objective appearances. The distortions that men introduce are individual; mankind, as such, need not be supposed to falsify or distort what is present.

2. Related to the above view is one which takes men to introduce relevance into a world where entities function in independence of one another. The ancient atomists held something like that position. Anthropologists seem to hold it, particularly when relevance is thought to be restricted to what is societal, or what is of significance to men. When I hold that, in knowing, boundaries are put about items and the items are thereupon able to be related to one another by men in accord with men's determinations, I take something like that view, without claiming that items are not relevant to one another apart from men. Knowing adds other relevancies.

3. Analysts and objective idealists hold that men distinguish, separate, and make entities be independent of one another, the first taking this to reveal a truth, freeing material of the incidental, the second holding that it results in falsification, since the aboriginal reality is an undivided whole or absolute. In recognizing that men articulate what is originally undivided, my view is like the idealists', though with respect to particular items, and like the analysts' in recognizing that the divisions made are ways of articulating, sharpening, adding boundaries or divisions among nuances, without distorting the nature of what these are as distinguishable.

4. The Humean view is that men add contingent kinds of connections between items which otherwise would have to be taken to be single, disconnected, and unintelligible. The point is recaptured in another form when it is said by me that the kind of judgments men make involve an introduction of relations between the disconnected items of a judgment.

5. The Kantian view is that men add necessary conditions between items which otherwise would be unintelligible and lost within a single manifold. The mind of man, I have held, does bring categories to bear

on what he confronts. These repeat in another form the kind of categoreal determinations which already govern actual items.

6. Variations on the last two positions would take contingent factors to be introduced into the undifferentiated, and necessary factors to be introduced into a world of distinct items. C. I. Lewis seems to hold the first; modal logicians the second. In contrast with both, I have been holding that apart from men there are merged items and also distinct ones.

7. Bergson held that man spatializes the ongoing temporalized world; Bradley apparently held that man temporalizes an eternal world; Hume and Kant held that man introduces the idea of causality into a non-causal world. There are other variants—Kant holding that space, time, and causality are all introduced by man. In contrast with these I have been saying that men, while subject to these three, also make a difference to them.

8. Most thinkers seem to hold that men introduce values into a world without any. Their position comes down to one of the others (particularly the first) when it is supposed that what is objective is thereby distorted or falsified. Men do introduce their own values, but this does not mean that there are no values present, or that these cannot be known by men using proper concepts and assessments.

The virtues of the different positions are preserved in the view that knowledge involves an articulation of what is undivided in the object, and that this articulation is so related to the object that it continues into it, obtaining a unitary base there, matching the unitary base it has in judgment.

September 22

I have written as though one faced content, bounded this off, and thrust beyond it. But is is more correct to say, (as I also sometimes do) that confronting, thinking, and experiencing are activities which continue on indefinitely, and that, in order to have content that we can use, we bound this at a point, thereby leaving over the confronting etc., to move adumbratively beyond the focused.

I have also taken account of a reaching into actualities in depth, of a reaching alongside toward other entities and particularly toward other entities in a common domain, and of a reaching toward the finalities. When one confronts an appearance, do we hve all three reachings together? It seems so, though we quickly concentrate on one of them, usually that which has contributed most to the content. If this is so, then when we confront some quality or shape we are involved with the actual possessor of it, with what conditions this, and with an area where other entities can be present. To these three, we should add a kind of adumbration to ourselves, who are engaged in the experiencing, etc.

If one wanted to bring these different adumbrative continuations within the compass of the view that there are five finalities, one would have to acknowledge the bounded content to be a unit, and take the continuations to be into what is substantial, explanatory, extensional, and has being. In this way one would treat the explanatory and the extensional as directly occupied with what continues into finalities—the unit, the substantial, and being having reference to what is present more intensively than the bounded content. But why should there not be bounded content that continues into an actuality? Why should there not be a continuation into the finalities of Unity, Substance, and Being? It is better to say that there is an indeterminate continuation into what is beyond us, and that we impose limiting boundaries on a part of this by coming to the content from the position of a complex of conditions, from ourselves as coming to expression, from others as having integrity and expressiveness, and from others as constituting an environing area within which we seek to make something central. None of these need be brought into relation to the five finalities or the categories they make possible. But if we do this we will be able to say that the content is a kind of being, the conditions offer an explanation, ourselves are substantial, and others are unities and are in an extended domain. But this I do not yet, clearly see.

Another attempt: I begin with the facing of content confronted as within a larger field, as a minimization of a density, and as specifying something more general. To have it as content, I set it apart from myself and in that act bound it off from the field, the density, and the conditions, while it continues to be connected with them, and I adumbratively continue into them. The focusing on the content, the giving it a boundary, is one with making the continuation of it into a thrust beyond it. The directions in which I do not go when I focus on the content serve to give that content characteristics it would not otherwise have. Because I take it to belong to an actuality, I incidentally take it to be located and to be a certain kind of thing, faced by me as distinct from myself. If I had instead taken it to be a kind of thing, I would have incidentally taken it to be a surface to be located, and to be faced as distinct. If I faced it as distinct, it would have been seen to be located, to be of a certain kind, and to belong to something.

September 23

My failure to make progress in the characterization of the fundamental activity of experiencing has been due to the fact that I neglected to see it as contrastive with what is bounded within it. The boundaries I impose when I encounter anything a. detach content from the dense continuation which begins with that content; b. desubjectify it, having it stand away from myself as something that can exist apart, despite the fact that the boundary is being imposed by me, and that it continues to be connected with me; c. delimit the content from what is alongside, and this without either precluding the type of delimitation from characterizing the content of denying that the result of the delimitation is like the relation characteristic of what is outside the boundary; d. specify the content as of a certain kind; and e. assess the content as having a distinctive kind of dignity or importance. The undifferentiated experiencing, in contrast with what is inside the boundary which I impose, belongs to the density beyond it; has a subjective, retreating character; is within a large setting where the kind of relations connecting the content in the boundary are also operative; insists on itself, the specification being the acceptance of the outcome of this; and is part of a single value, the boundary in effect giving it the status of a unit there.

The undifferentiated move, which begins at my privacy, is joined to an intensive activity of withdrawal by the actuality, by a referring to the content by me, by a continuation of the relation found inside the boundary, by an insistent presence of a kind, and by the adoption of the bounded content by a single totality of value. Consequently, at the very same time that I am imposing a boundary holding the content away from the actuality, from myself, from what is alongside, from what is insisting on itself, and from a single value, the experiencing is itself empowered by and directed into the actuality; is sustained by me; is subject to the same conditions which characterize the contained content; is met by an actual insistence whose terminus matches the termination I provide in specifying the kind; and is absorbed within a single whole of value. When and as I bound content, it is not only at the beginning of a continuation, but is in fact adopted by what allows that continuation to be.

Were I to free the undifferentiated experiencing from all additions, I would by that act not have any of it bounded. Bounding a portion of it is one with having the rest involved with something else. If I try to detach experiencing from all else to have it as a single undifferentiated activity, I would of course have it as meshed with whatever powers there were—actualities', mine, an intrusive world's, intrusive conditions', and a single complex value's—but I would know nothing of these. The boundary that I impose enables me to mark off an experiencing and therefore to become alert to what is adding to this. In a sheer unbounded experiencing, I would not be able to distinguish any direction, and therefore would not be able to use it to move into actualities, myself, what is alongside, what makes it part of a context, and what allows the objects I focus on to have value.

There is an anomaly here. If experiencing meets insistent conditions, one of these should be Unity or value. Yet I have taken this to provide a distinct addition to the experiencing. The anomaly is due to the fact that 'value' is being used here in two distinct ways: it is used to refer to the content within the boundary, and to refer to a delimitation of the whole of value. The former use is illicit unless it is joined by other ways of characterizing the bounded datum.

Value is a result of a specification or a delimitation, of a present boundedness as well as of a possession by oneself and by an actuality. It does not alone characterize the bounded content, or what is outside the boundary. Consequently, it must be said that experiencing, when it is bounded by us to give a focused content, is at once sustained by actualities, by ourselves as maintaining our privacies, and by a continuation of the same relations that hold inside the boundaries into others outside those boundaries; that it meets an insistence governing all content; and that its initial encounter is with content which, on being bounded, is characterizable in five basic ways.

September 24

I have not yet fully faced up to a systematic issue: must not all of the five ways (in which one bounds content and has the rest of an experiencing not only continue beyond this but be supported and counteracted by what lies beyond, in us, alongside, by conditions, and by the presence of the content itself) themselves have a five-fold form? I acknowledge such a five-fold form in acknowledging that there are five specifications and ways of dealing with the bounded content. There seem also to be five ways in which one can move from alongside the content toward it, or conversely. The difficult questions are whether or not there are five ways in which adumbration takes one into actual entities and five ways in which one possesses or confronts the bounded content. The latter can be readily acknowledged in view of man's internalization of the finalities and the basic subdivisions of his privacy. The hard question that remains is whether or not there are five ways in which items absent themselves and therefore five ways in which one's adumbratiive move into them occurs. The question arises as a result of a use of the discovery of the five finalities as guides for noting distinctions which would otherwise not be made.

Detached bounded content is possessed by, has a status apart from, is explained by, exists because of, and has some importance for an actuality. The experiencing which goes beyond content moves toward a possessor, what has a being of its own, what accounts for, what expresses itself as, and what gives it some role in its economy.

These are, so far, only headings, and a closer examination will undoubtedly lead to more precise formulations. For the moment, it is worth noting that the designations are independent of others which concern the experiencer, other objects, conditions, and the nature of the entity itself. Since each of these has five forms, since each is independent of the others, and since the five are constituted by five independently functioning operators, there are evidently many possible ways of characterizing a bounded content and, correlatively, the nature of an experiencing and the kinds of counteraction it meets. They break up into sets of five. Of these, five are pure, being approached in terms of the same category. There will be one, e.g., which emphasizes the possessive effectiveness of the actuality, the experiencer, other actualities, the conditiions, and a final value. In each of the cases, the imposing of the boundary sharpens the experiencing so that it is relative to the type of boundary that is being imposed, and conversely. Apart from the boundary, the experiencing is amorphous. With a boundary of a certain type, there will be a focusing in only one direction, the other directions being ignored, while other types of bounding in the given direction will be more or less subordinate notes within the given one.

In *Beyond All Appearances* I offered a solution to the problem of how we could know what was other than knowledge, by introducing the idea of a boundary. This adds to what is before one. The foregoing discussion makes evident that the idea has subtleties to it that I had not envisaged. Starting just with myself as imposing a boundary, I had apparently thought of it as allowing just for the use of the bounded content in thinking. The present discussion shows that detached content has other roles, and that, in addition, it can be distinguished in other ways from what else there is.

September 25

To get these ideas into focus, it might help to concentrate on a few limited cases. Arbitrarily, let it be supposed that a boundary primarily emphasizes a detachment from a possessive and explanatory actuality, an objectification from man's assessment, and an independence from what is alongside. The detachment from a possessing actuality enables an expression to stand away from the actuality, while the detachment from the actuality as explanatory gives it a kind of ultimacy. So far, the bounded content is like the empiricist's sense datum. But its adumbrative continuation into the actuality is intensive and convergent, and is countered by an insistence by the actuality providing its expression with a rational connection. At the same time, there is a facing of the content as freed from our determination of the importance of the content. The content will then be faced as without value—another feature to be found in the empiricist's sense data.

The experiencing of content will continue into us as able to judge, and will be countered by us as having a certain attitude toward what we are confronting. At the same time, the content will be bounded off as being independent of all else alongside. The experiencing will continue toward what is alongside as that which determines what the content is to be—and idea alien to the empiricists' but commonsensical—and is countered by the independent activity of others. We have there four aspects of a single bounding, with others ignored or subordinated. The initial experiencing simply spreads backwards and forwards into us and the actualities, and continues into a domain where other content is. There will be no attending to the content as specifying some condition; it will be just red or square, but not *a* red or *a* square.

Just as arbitrarily, let it be supposed that the content is bounded off from a condition expressive of Existence and Unity, and from affiliative content alongside. The experiencing will now conspicuously continue beyond that content toward Existence and Unity, and these will counter it with transformative acts making the experiencing be extensive and of value. At the same time, the experiencing will spread toward what is alongside as having pertinence to it, but will be countered by what is there making its own demands. No account will be taken of the bearing of the content on the actuality to which it belongs, or on us who are attending to that content. The content will be had as a specialized, important item separated off from other items with which it is affiliated, and the experiencing will continue toward what is specialized, as well as toward that with which it is affiliated. It will be accepted and transformed by the conditions and the other items. Once again, other dimensions of the experiencing will be subordinated or ignored. Nothing less than a bounding which takes account of all the ways in which an item is continuous with actualities, oneself, conditions, and what is alongside, and yet allows an item to have a status itself; takes account of how the boundary sets the content in opposition to the experiencing; and sees that the experiencing in turn is countered by an insistent resistance by the actualities, oneself, conditions, what is alongside, and the self-maintenance of the content, will do justice to what we are confronting, to the nature of the experiencing, and to the kind of assimilation to which it is subject by what lies beyond the content. (I still do not have a grasp of the experiencing as it in fact occurs, either starting with a boundary of a certain kind or as being countered by that which lies beyond the boundary.)

If what we attend to is an appearance, the primary directions of an experiencing will be toward an actuality and toward the finalities. The appearance will, as having been in part constituted by the finalities, be in a five-fold context. The bounding of the appearance will involve a two-fold cutting off from the context: the appearance will be of a certain type, specifying the context, and it will be delimited within the context and have a distinctive type of leaning toward the rest of it.

Since appearances are inert, it would appear that they could not affect one another and that they could not have a genuine status of their own where they functioned as though they were substances, beings, natures, extensions, and unified values. But their inertness does not preclude them from being terms in distinctive types of relation which require the terms to have special weights relative to one another; nor does it preclude them from having something like the status of a genuine substance, being, etc. with respect to derivative aspects of themselves.

September 26

When account is taken of the fact that my bounding is of something which is made objective for me, the act of providing a boundary will have to be recognized to occur somewhere along the route of an experiencing. It will have an undifferentiated side which reaches from me to the content, and another which passes intensively, transcendentally, and alongside the content, and is congealed in the content as well. As the last, it allows me to distinguish aspects in it, with it being relatively 'substantial', despite its inert dependent status as an appearance. Experiencing then is to be seen as initially reaching from me to content, from content to reality, from content to context, and within the appearance itself where it distinguishes aspects and holds them apart from the appearance itself as a unit.

A context provides a common condition specialized by the different terms in the context, at the same time that it continues to govern them all together; it also presents a kind of field which one delimits in the course of focusing on content. The two uses of the context are independent; it is possible to insist on a boundary that merely holds off what is alongside, and it is possible to insist on it as marking out an instance of some finality's conditioning presence.

A domain has these two independent roles of a context joined, with the result that a focused item there is a kind of entity related to others. A domain, though, usually is something constituted; one projects into it from a unit rather than delimiting or specifying that unit. The reverse move also occurs. We construct a geometrical proof, and project the result into a larger domain of geometry; we know that we have a geometrically proved theorem because we deal with it within the domain of geometry, and thus as that which is being at once delimited and specified.

Objectivization occurs when our experiencing comes to a terminus in content, with the content qualifying the experiencing that we initiate, to make it subordinated to the content as the terminus. All the while, the experiencing continues into the actuality to which the content is to be ascribed. Despite the fact that we institute a boundary, and that the boundary does not affect what is objectively present, i.e., the focused content as continuing into the object, experiencing loses its subjective note by coming to a terminus in that content.

It seems now as if the objectified content is not bounded by us. If there is a boundary, it would seem here to be provided by the content. But all that in fact follows is that the content makes the experiencing innocuous, which is one with saying that the experiencing being provides an ineffective boundary for the content simply by terminating in it. The boundary here blocks off the content from the subjectivizing experience. If so, how could the bounded content be used by the experiencing being? In other cases, it is affirmed that the boundary enables one to have content for use by us. This occurs here also. The bounded content in relation to us is for us to remark on, and to deal with as objective.

October 2

I have now completed reading the page proofs of 'You, I, and the Others', and another draft of 'An Exploration of Human Privacy'. Various thoughts have occurred to me during the course of the readings, having little or nothing to do with either. I have jotted them down in shorthand, and will now decipher my notes:

There is a neglected way of looking at the Christian history of the world. God began by having a firm grasp on the world but lost hold of it, firstly through Adam's defiance and secondly through Christ's death. Since then he has been progressively losing control. The day of Last Judgment is the day of his total defeat. From that time on the world will carry out its own destiny, with no guidance or help from him. Judaism allows for the same view, except that it is more optimistic, thinking that the coming of the Messiah will end in a triumph of such a kind that thereafter there will be no need to look for divine guidance.

Language (and other social structures) has a sedimental character; to make use of it, we do not merely break it up, turn the related factors at right angles and give them individual weights, but have them control what we will then do. The weight of tradition continues to operate on us when we discourse.

A language is a congealed domain of what is acceptable. It incorporates the past and something of the future. A common sense of a collectivity, an acceptance of the 'spirit' of one's group operates on the structures, preventing them from becoming rigidified. When one uses one of the structures, one makes some use of the 'spirit', so that what is done by the individual reflects not only tradition but an as yet not entirely embodied spirit. (These reflections were prompted by listening to Anthony Cua's account of ritual as understood by the Confucians.)

In *First Considerations* I speak of the evidences of finalities having reference to what is evidenced, and that the finalities keep the two together, having initially had them function independently. I seem in that book to suppose that evidence of actualities apply more directly. But is that correct? Does the evidence we have of an actuality—let us say, the evidence that a man is in pain—refer to the man, or to a correlative evidenced—in this case, to his privately and sensitively undergoing an undesirable experience? It seems so. The public manifestation of pain, in the form of cries and grimaces, is related to a sensitive source of the expressions, and the two are sustained by the private man. The evidence, via the evidenced is received and transformed in the man.

October 4

In dealing with evidence of the finalities, I have held that it takes us to what is evidenced. This completes the evidence, and is in turn adopted by the finality. But when I dealt with evidence of actualities, I tended to speak as though one moved directly from this into the actuality. It would be more correct to say that we have here a situation somewhat similar to that pertinent to the finalities. What is initially evidence for an actuality is what the actuality has manifested with respect to other actualities under the aegis of an expression of a finality. That evidence is brought to an evidenced in our focusing on the actuality. What I called 'evidence' of an actuality is therefore in fact what has been evidenced, completing and intensifying what was initially found to be imbedded in a context (if we are starting with appearances) or is initially affiliated, coordinated, etc. (if we are occupying ourselves with actualities). Even when one refers to a single actuality, there is an initial evidence used to enrich the evidenced. The observation requires me to go over 'An Exploration of Human Privacy' and indicate modifications in what it says in the first part about evidences of the various epitomized forms of privacy—person, psyche, and self—and of the epitomizations of these—sensitivity, desire, private accountability, I, responsibility, etc.

* * *

Last night I met Jonathan in Baltimore to go to the first play-off game between the Orioles and the California Angels. I got to sleep (we took a taxi from Baltimore) at 2:30 AM, and then was awakened by a telephone call around 9:30. I am somewhat groggy, and in a half hour will teach a graduate class.

It was a wonderful experience. The excitement of the fans, the mastery of their sport by the players, the excellent seats we had (box seats behind the catcher), the joyousness of the crowd, the surprising victory at the end of the 10th inning, made it something I would not have liked to miss. It was a performance in somewhat the way in which a ballet is a performance, except of course that this was a happening as well, something unfolding as it went on. From the standpoint of the spectator, a game is comparable to a ballet, particularly if this is without an obvious story line and is unknown. What I like most is to see the ease with which a ball is caught, the timing with its apparent unhurriedness involved in getting a man out at first, and then—perhaps because I do not see as well as I should—somewhere down the line, the pitchers' duel. I am hoping we may be able to get tickets for a world series game. That hope is predicated on the expectation that the Orioles will win, and on our being able, once again, to get one of the partners of the new lawyer-owner of the Orioles to reserve tickets for us.

One of the most interesting things about baseball is that the records are kept for each player with such meticulousness that it seems to be essentially a game by individuals. Yet more than any other sport of which I know anything it is a team-governed activity. Every player in the field is keyed to the others, and works with them with a degree of harmony and support that I do not see occurring in football, basketball, or soccer. In these, some members of the team seem to be working as a unit, with the others having auxiliary jobs, but in baseball all nine of the men are together alerted to what might next occur, and pace themselves in the light of it, and what the other members of the team will most likely do. The team work is promoted, of course, by the fact that usually they have to attend only to the batter, and at most to him and three others on base, whereas in the other sports one has to face an entire team or portion of one.

October 5

The nominalism of Occam was based on a concern for real individuals. Modern nominalism is concerned with denoted entities, sheer 'it's'. My view can be said to be nominalistic in the Occamistic sense, but not in the modern. But then, unlike Occam, I supplement this with a realism, even an extreme realism, which insists that there are other realities besides individuals, and that these exert power, affecting the nature of the individuals. There is nothing inconsistent in holding that each individual is a unique reality with a privacy into which we move intensively, and also that it is governed to some extent by transcendent realities. Those realities provide the individuals with natures which are distinguished by having roles in individuals. The realism is not the realism of moderns, which attends only to universals or abstract forms, and insists only that these can be instanced many times.

October 12

I have long been discontent with my account of stones and other complex physical entities. I had held that they were wholes, i.e., entities with single natures supervening over a multiplicity of parts. The account does not allow one to say that the stone functions as a single unit, and that it has a privacy as surely as ultimate particles and organic beings do, expressed in oppositional interplay with common conditions. It is because it has such a privacy that a stone can be said to appear, behave as a single entity, and provide a rational unitary base for all that it expresses. But unlike ultimate particles or organic beings, a stone cannot itself act. What it does is a function of external forces. Evidently, its privacy has a different kind of role from that possible to an ultimate particle or to an organic being. Unlike an ultimate particle or an organic being, it embraces a number of independently functioning parts. Unlike an organic being, within which parts have some degree of independent functioning (falling, e.g., at the same rate in no way hampered by the organic unity), it does not have a privacy which can act on the body directly, without the intermediation of the parts. The private being of a stone, which enables it to persist over time, to act and manifest itself as a single being, is mediated by the privacies of the distinct particles within it. What the stone expresses through its public body is a single 'stone-privacy', but under limitations set by privacies of the different particles. Similar considerations will apply to water, oceans, clouds, and anything else which is both complex and non-organic. It seems, therefore, to be somewhat like a functioning state whose political structure is backed by a single social unity of men, each of whom mediates that unity to make the functioning political whole at once a single structured complex of men, a social unitary whole of men, and a plurality of individuals who mediate that social unitary whole, and thereby enable the political structure to be pertinent to them, both singularly and together.

For the moment, I feel that I am on the edge of an answer; at any rate, I do not yet have it under control or in focus. Of particular interest is the question whether this kind of approach to what I once called 'wholes', is pertinent to the understanding not only of natural objects, but also of artificial ones, such as baseballs, bats, gloves, books. These, like stones, have distinctive natures, and seem like stones to provide factors which help constitute appearances that are to be credited to them. But the unitary natures of these objects seem to be themselves products. A baseball is put together out of a number of distinct parts, each functioning separately from the others and merely kept together by the cover of the ball. A book seems to be one only because the pages have been stitched, and a cover put around them all. Do these have single privacies, perhaps mediated by the privacies of whatever parts there are? The pages, the stitching, the glue, the cover, e.g., of a book are apparently themselves like the book, and not genuine parts in the way in which particles seem to be parts of a stone. Must we refer to a social context as having the power to make the book have a privacy which is mediated by the pages (themselves depending on a social context to enable them to have privacies)? Do stones and other natural complexes need the pressure of the cosmos to make them be able to have a mediated privacy? Do animals need the pressure of an environment? Do men need the pressure of a milieu? Or is it only artificial objects which need the pressure of some larger situation in order to be able to have a mediated privacy?

October 13

Every complex entity, natural, organic, or artificial, can be said to specialize a general condition in the shape of a nature which is matched by a single privacy mediated by the plurality of entities that enable it to be complex. The specialized condition is the nature of the complex entity as qualified by the common privacy. Consequently, every complex entity has a singularized nature as the outcome of the joint operation of a common condition and a single privacy, mediated by the units within the confines of that nature.

Natural complexes have natures which specialize a cosmic condition; organic beings have natures which specialize their species; and artificial complexes, such as a book or a building, have natures which specialize a social setting. So far, all seem to be on a par with what I have called a complex 'we' in *You, I, and the Others,* with the possible difference that I am now more clearly affirming that the simple we is not only in interplay with interrelated units, but that it is affected by the single privacy which they diversely make their own in limited ways. In *You, I, and the Others,* I also remark that a complex we interplays with others. Such an interplay, issuing from within the complex we, involves the use of a privacy. Consequently, it must also be said that the common privacy, that affects the nature and allows this to be exhibited with accidents, has a surplus, allowing for its expression in and through the very complex that the privacy helps constitute through the mediation of the parts.

A natural complex has its surplus privacy expressed in the form of the potential and actual energy of that complex. It is therefore just a body able to act in a cosmos with other bodies. An organic being, below the level of man, in addition to being able to function in the cosmos in this way, and therefore to be a body in the cosmos, is able to retain some of the privacy in an unexpressed form, where it is able to be utilized not only with respect to other bodies, as natural complexes can, but with respect to the body itself. It has bodily potentialities and others which are private but directed at its own body. A man, in addition to being able to be a unit in the cosmos and able to affect his body by a privacy (which matches the complex of his nature and the common privacy of the parts within him) is able to act within the privacy and to direct that privacy at non-bodily objectives. Artificial complexes are like the natural, differing from these in having a potentiality to act, not with respect to any object anywhere, but with respect to other objects within a limited, social situation.

Is there a difference in principle between a state which results from the union of a political order and a set of socially related men, a team of players, and an artificially produced complex, such as a book? One difference is quite clear: their privacies interplay with different limited types of entities. A team plays against another team, a state interacts with other states. Both, of course, act apart from other similar complexes, and may interact with other types of complexes, such as an historic situation, news media, and the like. An artificially produced complex also has a body in a sense not possible to the others. It is a palpable object, with distinctive properties. It has appearances rightfully credited to it in somewhat the way in which an organic being has appearances rightfully credited to it. The difference between them does not lie in the fact that men are controlled within a state whereas an artificial object is made within a situation over which men are exercising control, for men together can form an artificial complex, such as a human chain or a team. An artificial complex has a nature delimited within a setting in the form of a body; a natural object is self-bounded; an organic being has an enlivened body; and a human being has a usable body. A state or a team has a nature only in the form of a structure or rule.

Why does the structure of a team or state not have a palpable form while the nature of a stone or a book does? To begin with, it can be remarked that it is ultimate particles, combinations of them in physical and biological units such as atoms, molecules, cells, and living bodies which have bodies, and that when one moves beyond that point there are no bodies for the resultant whole. The nature of the complex for the former is incarnate, but not for the latter.

Why can one kind of togetherness be seen and touched, and not another? Two answers are plausible: a. The existence of a body of a complex is an illusion; if we looked at a multitude of people from a distance they too would seem to make a single body. Had we attended to a stone or other complex with the help of a microscope, the body would vanish. b. There is a critical point where an aggregate of items forms a linkage so strong as to yield a single encompassing bodily pattern. The first of these answers in effect denies that there are complex unities, and ends by acknowledging as real only what no one could possibly experience or encounter, the ultimate particles. The second seems but to restate the problem in the form of an answer. Why is there such a critical point for some aggregations and not for others?

The common and social settings allow for the occurrence of critical points where an aggregation becomes overlaid by a bodily unification. A species does not allow for such a conversion. But what of those social settings specified in the form of a team? Why does this not have a bodily nature the way a book has? Or a building? But not a library? The intermediation of the parts evidently determines whether or not the unitary character of the result will have a bodily guise. We have still to determine what kind of parts can yield a common body and what kind cannot, and when the ones which can, do and do not produce one.

October 14

What is changed if a complex body is made to give way to the parts, as subject to a structure, an insistent condition, or a forced juncture? What is changed if a structure, condition, or forced juncture is made to give way to a single body encompassing the parts?

When a complex body is made to give way—in a chemical occurrence, on the death of a living being, or by cutting or breaking it, we have not only a change but a loss. We lose a. the perceivable characters of the body; b. the common privacy which lay behind the parts and which becomes the body's potentiality, or also functions as a privacy that has some standing apart from the body; and c. a unity that can be physically divided (usually into just smaller versions) and does not interact with the parts.

A structure has no perceivable characters, or any other privacy than that which it can obtain through an interplay with interrelated parts; it cannot usually be divided into parts each of which is like the whole. Since it is conceivable that a bodily unity might be divided into smaller bodies which have natures different from it, and since it is conceivable that some structures might allow for a division of themselves into similar structures, each governing a limited number of the original parts, the essential difference must be that a structure has no perceivable characters, and that what affects a structure and the surplus which remains over (contrary to the remarks made on previous days), is derived from the relation connecting the parts with one another.

An insistent condition is like a structure, differing only in its insistent power, its ability to control the parts in a way that a structure can require but not provide. The insistence of that condition is due to what lies beyond it, or to its use of some of the parts as its representatives, using them to control the activity of the rest. But an insistent condition also lacks perceivable features and a distinctive privacy.

A forced juncture of parts, say by being bounded together by means of some other body, seems at times to have perceivable features, but it too lacks a privacy. In addition, the parts are kept together through the use of another item, which is actually an additional part within a whole governed by a structure or an insistent condition.

The crucial difference between bodily and other complexes evidently is the inability of what is not a body to have a privacy mediated by its parts. It can do no more than be affected by the common relation of the parts. It, and the relation of the parts together constitute the potentiality of the complex in relation to other complexes.

Were a structure, condition, or forced juncture to give way to a single body, as seems to be the case when a spark is applied to the proper proportions and properly related elements in a chemical combination, there is a production of a specialized unity able to use the parts as mediators to obtain a singular privacy, without precluding its ability to make use of the parts as interrelated, and therefore without precluding its ability to function also as a structure, condition, or forced juncture. The privacy which it makes its own, may be caught within the body, may have a status apart from it, or may in addition, be able to be exercised apart from it.

Reductionism tries to deal with a complex body as though it were only a structure, condition, or forced juncture. The above considerations stop the move by remarking on the presence of a distinctive privacy for every complex body. That privacy cannot be reduced to the parts and the relations connecting those parts. The result would have no unexpressed capacities, and thus could not have the role of a potentiality in the body, a potentiality for the body, or a potentiality exercised apart from the body.

To this, perhaps, it might be answered that the various parts have potentialities of their own and that their conjoint operation will yield what is now being supposed is characteristic of a more basic privacy. But there is no assurance that the different parts will function together unless the relation connecting them controls the ways in which the potentialities of the parts will be expressed, and then in such a way that they constitute a single potentiality. Why should this occur only in those cases where we normally say that there is a body?

If one were to allow the supposition, it would amount to the acknowledgment of something like a common potentiality, denying only that it was the potentiality of a body. The opposition between reductionism and the usual (and present) view, comes down to the acknowledgment by the latter of a single privacy behind the different parts having some relation to a body, and the acknowledgment of a single potentiality elicited from the parts by the relation that connects those parts, but which has no matching body, despite perceivable qualities and distinctive characteristics which mark off one type of body from other types.

The interrelated items, in what I have called a 'we', interplay with the common structure or condition. Were a 'simple we' to have the form of a body, it would have its own distinctive privacy and therefore would in fact become a kind of 'us' or 'me' grounded in a primary I. It remains a simple we only if it continues to maintain itself as a condition which interplays with interrelated items. The outcome of the interplay ends in a modification of the conditioning 'simple we'. The resultant modified 'simple we' and the interrelated items together yield the single potentiality of a 'complex we', able to interact with other complexes.

One conclusion grounded by the above is that a society, state, team, or any other organization lacks the kind of privacy that complex bodies have, whether those bodies be merely physical or chemical, biological, or human. The loss of body is the loss of a distinctive privacy. Therefore, in the case of man, it involves the loss of person, psyche, and self, and of course, their subordinate epitomizing sensitivity, accountability, I, etc.

Some modification of the present suggestion is needed if account is taken of the world of ultimate particles. These, like any other entities, are together by virtue of the operation of common final conditions. Those conditions act to interrelate the particles in a single complex field. But the field would be incapable of change if it did not have any potentiality. Consequently, it must be said that the initial conditioning of the particles is inseparable from the production of a private base for them all. When we come to deal with more limited insistent conditions and structures, we must then also say that they not only interrelate limited numbers of items, but do so in such a way as to provide them with a common private base. The interplay of the interrelated items with more limited or specialized forms of the initial conditions also brings that base into play.

Every interrelated set of entities has a privacy that enables it, as an interrelated set, to function in many ways. The interplay of a structure or other conditions with interrelated items, as having a common privacy, involves a change in the first but without providing it with a pertinent privacy. Some of the common privacy can be used in the action of the resultant complex. A 'simple we' interplays with interrelated individuals who not only have their individual privacies, but share in a common privacy. It is affected by the individuals as having their own privacies, at the same time that some of the common privacy functions as the potentiality of the 'complex we', resulting from the interplay of the interrelated individuals and the common condition.

In the light of these reflections, it is possible to say that a number of interrelated men has a common privacy, that this affects a structure with which the men constitute a complex, such as a team, and that it plays a role in the complex. A corpse will then be dealt with, not as though it were at once just a number of entities under a common governing condition, but as having a single privacy. That privacy is not used by the corpse, for this, strictly speaking, has a plurality of parts together in a common structure having little efficacy. The single privacy that remains is simply that which is a potentiality of the interrelated parts of the corpse.

October 15

If an interrelated set of entities had no privacy, incorporated in the form of a potentiality, it would not be able to interact with a common condition. Nor would it be able to change while the common condition, and the various units which were interrelated, remained constant. The constancy of a common condition and of the units could be credited to their separate persistence, requiring no reference to anything else. When units changed they could affect the way in which they were interrelated. But if a condition, such as the structure of a state, group, team, or cosmos is able to constitute a complex with interrelated units, those units must be able to act as one in interplay with the structure. As a result, the structure is changed. A state or team, even when there is no change in membership, or the ways in which members are connected, may change over time, evolving, or having an historic career. Such a changing structure could apply to the same members, and these could continue to have the same type of interrelationship. Unless we attributed that change to some deliberate agent, we must say that it is the outcome of the way in which the privacy of the interrelationship of items enabled that inter-relationship to affect the structure, while still leaving over some power to be expressed by the resultant complex when it interacts with others.

The cosmos does not interact with anything else; the only justification for the acknowledgment of a common privacy for all the ultimate particles within that cosmos, a privacy which is additional to the privacies each one of them has, is the fact that the cosmic structure, despite the constancy of its source, and despite any constancy in the actions of the units, can undergo change. That change was signalized by Peirce as an 'evolution' of the laws of nature, but it is possible to take the change to have a distinctive rational nature, such as is today expressed in the contraction and expansion of cosmic space (which is, after all, a common condition before it has the form of a region in which units are interrelated.)

When we turn from structures to bodies, the privacy that is integral to an interrelated set of items and, as such, functions as their common potentiality, is seen to have, in addition, some status apart from the interrelationship, and in fact to be directly involved with the complex body. More obviously than before, a common privacy is seen to have a distinctive status and to be able to be expressed, not only when there is an interaction between complexes, but as an ordered set of changes. This occurs, not because of the way an interrelated set of units behaves, but because the body itself, as a unity, has its own potentiality, even while it is being affected by the potentiality involved with the interrelated items.

There is some similarity between the view here presented and the old view of a common matter. They differ in that the common matter was supposed to have some kind of being of its own, even though only as a kind of 'potentiality' or 'receptacle', that it was of no help in the understanding of the nature of beings, which, *in addition to* having structures, had bodies; and in not allowing for an understanding of the way in which complex bodies, particularly those of animals and men, could have privacies of their own, like the privacy possessed by all of them together. The supposed matter was treated as defective in the large and in the small, and treated as though it were cognate to the bodies we know rather than to their privacies. The primary reality was taken to be a structure, form or some other kind of intelligible, and the body to involve some kind of subtraction from this rather than, as here, an addition. It was thought that, in the case of the living, the intelligible was itself identifiable with the privacy, and not to be a condition with which privacy interplayed, either in the form of a potentiality of an interrelated set of items, or as that which was able to act on and in a body. It was therefore not seen that the body had characters of its own, and that, with the help of its own potentiality and the interrelated parts each with its own potentiality, it acted on other similar complexes.

No structure has a potentiality ingredient in it—here I am one with the older view. Each is affected by the potentiality that is ingredient in the interrelationship of items within the compass of the structure. Here I differ sharply from the older view. Unlike it, my view recognizes that a structure (or essence), despite its constancy, and the unchanging nature of encompassed parts, is able to be affected by the interrelated parts and the privacy ingredient in that interrelationship in the form of a potentiality. When the potentiality of the interrelationship is expressed, it makes the interrelationship function in interplay with the structure, thereby affecting the structure. And when the structure is replaced by a body, the privacy (that had been expressed in the form of a potentiality of the interrelationship and had in that guise acted on the structure) is able to be directly related to the body either as an ingredient potentiality (if it is just a body); as a private readiness to act (if it is an animal body); or as a privacy able to function apart from the body (if this is a human body).

October 16

A complex is involved in at least three potentialities: There is the potentiality of its parts, each of which has some degree of freedom and is able to express itself independently of the others. Secondly, there is the potentiality of the interrelation of the parts. This potentiality has two degrees of realization. It is realized in the guise of actions of the entire interrelated set of items, so that the items have one or the other of the various relations amongst them dominant at different times; the entire interrelated set of items, in addition, acts in oppositional ways with respect to a common structure (essence or rationale), giving this different weights on its being united with the interrelated items at different times. Thirdly, there is the potentiality that is integral to the complex itself, enabling the complex to act on other complexes. The potentialities result when portions of a common privacy become integral to the parts, interrelationship, or complex.

When a structure is supplemented by a body, part of the privacy, which before was outside the structure, becomes integral to the body. A complex body thus has a further potentiality in addition to the other

three. The structure still remains (as I did not see before). A body gives
that structure a locus, at the same time that the body has functions of
its own.

If a body is living, the part of the privacy that still remains outside
the body, functions with respect to it. The privacy lives the body, guides
it, feels by means of it, uses it. The living body need not then have a
potentiality additional to that which it has when it is not alive; it will
then be able to function in ways the latter cannot, because the privacy
continues into it, while being exercised apart from it. The privacy, as
outside it, can be somewhat like the potentiality that is realized in opposition to a structure, since it can operate on what is distant from it.

A human body differs from a merely living one in that the privacy,
which is not in the form of a potentiality of that human body, is not even
(as in the foregoing case) a potentiality for the living body. The privacy
of a human is exercised outside the body and, while continuing into the
body, is also in control of what it expresses in and through this.

The present account of body reverses the Aristotelian view. Body
for Aristotle is essentially potential; a structure is an essence; and the
two together constitute a composite. I am with him and his followers in
holding that the structure or essence has no potentialities. But I am also
holding that the structure can be in the body, and that this result has its
own potentialities. The potentialities, instead of being supposed to have
a bodily origin, are here taken to be the outcome of an involvement of
privacy with the interrelated parts and with the body within which those
parts are confined.

A structure or essence is not opposed to a body, but is incorporated
in it, the body making it possible for the private potentiality, that was
outside the structure, to become a bodily potentiality to occupy space
and time, to act, move, rest, and change. Since a potentiality has its origin
in privacy, it is possible for the body to be conceptualized as a kind of
extensionalized, observable essence. It will not be non-rational, purely
passive, a source of individuality, something to be transcended so that
one can enjoy what is forever.

To this it might be objected, a structure or essence is forever, a pure
object of the intellect; bodies, instead, come and go, and have an opacity
to them reflecting the fact that they are not themselves active. The nature
of man is a constant, the same in all, while each man has a distinctive
body. Those who hold such a view often also hold that each man has an
individual soul. But that means that his essential nature is also individual.
But does not my view require one to suppose that, apart from the privacy

which has the role of a potentiality in the body, no distinction can be made among the different bodies of men and that, except as somehow being diverse instances of the same universal, those bodies would be identical? Yes. But there is no reason to suppose that there are bodies which are without distinctive potentialities and therefore are unaffected by singular privacies. The question rightly takes a body to be on the same side as structure; it fails to see that a body does, while a structure does not, have a potentiality integral to it.

The unitary body of a complex is distinct from the bodies within it. Yet it has its own properties, is perceivable, resists, acts on other bodies, occupies extended regions. Even when it is not living, it has an integrity and is palpable. A Leibniz would hold that a more careful observation or analysis would make it disappear, leaving only the ultimate particles. But these, for him, are also detached from one another. Would it not be possible to hold that they are interrelated, and that the supposed unitary body within which the interrelated units interplayed was non-existent or at best only a structural condition? Not without losing such features as shape, occupancy, functioning in larger wholes which could themselves be or have bodies.

What makes the body one? To say that it is unity, though undoubtedly correct, still leaves over the question of why it is palpable, why it is a body and not just a unitary structure. As far as I have now gone, I can say no more than that the addition of privacy to the structure, thereby giving it a potentiality, is one with making it into an encompassing body. Is this enough? Is this satisfactory? Is water just the chemical structure of H_2O with a potentiality of its own, manifested in the form of wetness, flowing, etc.? If a body is primarily extended, the potentiality would have to be primarily a distendedness. What of the other properties? How does the body's potentiality differ from the potentiality of the complex constituted of the encompassing body and of the interrelated parts within its confines? How does water, apart from any action on or by others, differ from water as a complex interacting with other similar complexes?

Once it is acknowledged that an actuality by itself can do no more than express itself, and that it appears only so far as it is countered by a transcendent condition, the potentiality in the structure of a stone or water can be said to yield the properties of these as they stand apart, only so far as these are understood to be objective persistent appearances of the stone and water due to an interplay of the actualities with final conditions. A specified condition, which is a structure or (with a potentiality) an encompassing body, because there is a potentiality still apart from it, is itself able to interplay with a condition beyond it. The potentiality possessed by the complex of a unitary encompassing body and its interrelated parts is realized in one way when the complex stands apart from any other complex, and in another when realized in relation to other complexes. As the one, it has appearances; as the other, accidents.

In contrast with the view that 'prime matter' is potentiality, the present holds that matter is a 'composite' having an essence or structure as well as a potentiality. Potentiality is privacy either of a particular item or of an interrelated set of them. Though there is no prime matter, one can have an idea of it as well as of the privacy which is common to a number of entities. As a consequence, the two terms might differ only verbally. Both could be integrated with 'form'. The only difference left would be that privacy for me is insistent, intensive, distended, and assessive, is capable of being congealed in the form of special, limited privacies, and can give rise to the privacy of man. All of these could be accepted by the followers of Aristotle or Aquinas, with the exception of the last, since they take the privacy of man to be due to a soul, and therefore to be of the order of essences and not like a potentiality. The soul of a man for these thinkers is individual, and does not depend on matter for individuation. I avoid their supposition that there is a special creation needed to account for a human soul, in the same way that they avoid supposing that there is such a creation needed for an animal soul.

October 19

In the current issue of the *Review of Metaphysics,* there is a fine article by Ernan McMullin on John Compton's Presidential Address before the Metaphysical Society of America last year. It has made rethink the problem of the relation of science and other disciplines, and to see even more in my examination of the 'we' than I had previously.

The paper by Compton emphasized two 'worlds', a kind of life-world taken over from Husserl and Merleau-Ponty, and a world of science, and then tried somehow to make the latter answerable to the former. He and McMullin restricted their discussion to these two. They ignored the fundamentality of the world of art, the world of religion, the world of history. The final answer must give a firm place to all of these.

Views achieve maturity only when they take some type of item considered as basic and stretch their account of it until the surface of what concerns others is reached. Since each view starts with data taken as solid and as grounding others, no one view can ever do full justice to what is known by the others. Reductionism, of no matter what kind, overlooks that fact, and can be answered both by pointing out that other reductionisms go in other directions, and that the initial data must be accepted as it is in order for the reduction to be able to occur.

The common world of all entities is where all the different approaches overlap. The overlap leaves outside all the items as having their individual integrity, and at most ends with having those items in the role of terms for a relationship connecting them all. The common world stops with the overlap. It has no way of dealing with the items as grounding the different positions. A reconciliation of them all requires one to occupy some new position and to use new categories applicable not only to the overlapping region but to the items outside.

Unlike Hegel, one must acknowledge that a reconciling view, while metaphysical, is abstract and formal, and that it loses the common world and the unit items in their concreteness.

A metaphysical, systematic view is matched by an interinvolvement of the unit items with one another, below the level where they reach to one another and where by overlapping they make a common world. This interinvolvement is what Schopenhauer spoke of as the 'will,' and Bergson as the *élan vital*; unlike what they had in mind, though, it does have multiple centers in the multiple items. Functioning in contradistinction with these, the interinvolvement has the role of a single common potentiality, something close to Aristotle's 'prime matter'.

The joining of a metaphysical systematic view with the interinvolvement, by one who is always in the overlapped area, and who can at least formulate and allow for the different approaches from the position of different items, is provided by the civilized community. A civilized community is an ongoing complex 'we' in which the metaphysical system is reconciled with the interinvolvement in 'appreciations' in which individuals reach toward all the others in multiple limited ways and therefore in ways which get to them only at their surfaces.

I am here close to a Confucian view, except instead of starting and remaining wholly in the humanistic sphere, I venture outside it, recognizing the results there obtained, and making the civilized life be affected by the meaning of what is thus acquired. The moralistic nature of the Confucian community is enriched by being made into a vital reconciliation of the most abstract comprehensive metaphysical view, the most non-rational interinvolvement, an emphasis on one's own individual being directed toward others and being directed at in turn, and the acceptance of the overlap as the point of an unreflective juncture of different endeavors.

The basicality of an item expresses its being; a metaphysical view does most justice to the formal; the common overlapped world is existent; the interinvolvement is substantial; and civilized living is assessive, unifying.

The formal structure of a team is comparable to the metaphysical; the rapport of the teammates is substantial; the basicality of an item is an individual member of the team playing for all, expressing the being of the member; the overlapping is the team as a interrelationship of men; and the union of all is the produced playing of the game, perhaps also including the spectators as making some difference to what is occurring.

Both the metaphysical and the matching interinvolvement, because they include the items which themselves cannot reach to one another, are all-comprehensive. But the metaphysical is formal and the interinvolvement (identifiable with what I have previously called the 'common privacy') is vital but continuous rather than used or intelligible. They cover not simply ultimate particles but also complexes such as organic beings, and perhaps even complexes such as stones. The lacks in each dimension are not made up by the others; one must bring oneself, as in a community, to add a dynamic connection between them, and at the same time allow for the ultimate irreducibility of the items, and the kinds of encompassment which take their start from different kinds of entities.

A man thrusts toward others, never penetrating them entirely; faces a public world which he and they constitute, while holding themselves away as privacies; is interinvolved with others in a common group; has formal schemes serving to encompass all items including himself; and gives himself to the living of the juncture of the interinvolvement and the formal schemes, all the while that he adjusts himself to the public world and recognizes that others are never entirely penetrated.

October 20

A civilized man attempts to belong to a world containing cherished entities, with an emphasis on the contributions that other men make. The different entities (he included) together constitute an overlapping whole, where each at its best reaches to the surface of the others. By taking seriously a formal structure and an interinvolvement, both of which are all-inclusive, and therefore by allowing himself to be governed by a comprehensive metaphysics and a vital involvement with others, he is able to give himself to living in the overlapping world as no longer biased away from him, or as having any special relevance to him. His giving of himself to the commonality, the constituents of which are grounded in actual entities, and expressing those entities as they thrust toward all the others—but under the limitations of a formal scheme, an interinvolvement, and the acceptance of the reality of other entities as thrusting toward him—allows a man to be an individual whose world is intelligible, vital, public, and grounded in real entities.

A work of art can be viewed as an epitomization of an overlapped world. An artist, on such a view, begins with an undifferentiated grasp of realities beyond himself. His creative activity is the production of the overlap of himself and the undifferentiated realities, guided by a disciplined control of his medium (and therefore by a tacit acceptance of some 'rules' or requirements), and an emotional involvement with the entities beyond him. When he allows himself to be governed by the other entities in their undifferentiated nature, the work of art is able to function as an agency for letting one know them as interinvolved, formally related, directed at one another, and having a status apart from these. When, instead, he holds on to a work of art, enjoys, or appreciates it, there is a loss of emphasis on the separate status of other entities, except when the experience with the work is over and it is allowed to be an epitomized common world objective to himself. The work of art, in fact, always has him as a component, so that the release of it from him involves a neglect of his contribution.

A similar set of distinctions arises when one turns to a scientific account of the world. It too has a formal nature expressed in theories; epitomizes a common world as experimental and experiential; is grounded in the acceptance of other entities as thrusting toward one another; has an ontological base; and can be accepted as a world of nature. When one become objective, one faces the scientific account as that which is rooted in other entities, and can lead one to them as distinct but interconnected. When the emphasis is on an individual, science becomes a *Weltanschauung*, and Nature is normally taken to be the common world as freed from his emphasis.

None of this is entirely in focus for me as yet, though I do think that there are many grounded views which reach toward, but never get into the reality of other entities; that there are formal schemes of which the metaphysical is the most comprehensive; that entities are subterraneously interinvolved with one another; that one can take the overlapping of the different grounded views either as one's objective world, or as what he would like to live in by giving himself to it as that which is sustained and constituted by others.

If one takes *The World of Art* as a guide, he expects to find an art work understood to be a means by which use is made of the emotions to reach to the very Existence which is at the root of all extension. Does this mean that once a man releases himself from a work of art after having experienced it, he will have opened himself up to the interinvolvement of all? But then, instead of art having the role of an item in a civilized man's life, it will either have to do with the world of mutual interplay of him and other actualities, or with an interinvolvement. A common formal structure and a concern with individual entities will not be pertinent. It will then not be on a footing with anything in a civilized life, if this is supposed to be a vital integration of formality, interinvolvement, common world, and individual thrust, balanced by the thrust of others. The interpretation given in *The World of Art* would then not be correct; that interpretation would be applicable not to anything less than all the factors as together, so far as a work of art was in a world of civilized men. It would refer just to one type of thrust toward other actualities, so far as a work of art was a special way of dealing with the world, on a par with science.

Does art refer to Existence? From what position? What else is at that position? Is there not a way in which art is on a footing with science, and therefore does no more than offer a distinctive kind of base from which to approach all else? These questions need answers, not only in the light of what I had previously said, but of themselves.

October 21

I walked about seven and a half miles today, spending a good deal of the time trying to rethink the set of ideas about which I have been writing these last days. I am now inclined to break the issue down into a number of steps:

1. *Imaginative projection:* One tries to see what it is like to approach the world from the position of something other than oneself. This is what one obviously does when trying to take a scientific outlook on the world, when attending to the world as an artist, and when trying to see the world from the perspectives of others.

2. *Appreciation:* One here begins from oneself as a grounding, thrusting irreducible power, and moves toward what is beyond, ending with what is the adopted limit of one's effort. Here one tries to act as one in

nature, to have an aesthetic outlook, or to reach toward what is other than oneself.

3. *Confrontation:* Appreciation starts with oneself as real, and imaginative projection allows one to take the position of others. In confrontation there is an attempt to come to the position where the others are also appreciative. To the degree he succeeds, a man faces the overlap of himself and the others; the beings which he envisaged in the imaginative projection now play a role in interaction with himself. The role they play will not be precisely like that which was acknowledged in the projection, if for no other reason than that the projection is one's own, whereas what is confronted is constituted by the others. The more perceptive we are, the more will our imaginative projections anticipate what in fact others will add to what we are contributing to the common confronted content. Nature for ordinary men, a work of art as an object, and the common-sense world are faced as having a status apart from us, even though they are partly constituted by us in our appreciation (where this is understood to involve a thrusting outward toward the other entities).

4. *Subordination:* Projection, appreciation, and confrontation do not encompass all that is present, having to do only with what is expressed from accepted bases in others or oneself. In subordination one acknowledges something formal and all-encompassing. That to which one is subordinated is a kind of simple 'we' in the form of a structure, principles, rules, or even conditions for being in a domain. In science, one allows for theories, and also for the structure of the scientific community; in art, one allows for the funded knowledge of the interrelationship of the various items used, the sedimented history of the discipline. Oneself and other entities here have the form of values for the variables of the formalities, and even the form of a historic or traditional pattern.

5. *Interinvolvement:* We have the same reach here that we have in subordination, but in a vital interlocking in which no clear distinction can be made between the interlocking and the entities interlocked. One makes direct contact with and is countered by other realities, and is with the others below the level of nature, or art, or confrontation. This is the dimension dealt with when one refers to the 'spirit' of a team, of the social binding of individuals, of an artist's sense that he is in accord, not with his work, but with other realities in what is often called an 'emotional' way.

6. *Solidification:* The previously distinguished dimensions are united in the individual, so as to make him be in the confronted world but as more inclusive than it is apart from the use of the pattern and the in-

terinvolvement. He is in the area which before had been confronted, stretched to include the items which had been reached imaginatively and appreciatively. The scientifically known is here joined with an acceptance of nature, the art object is lived in and with. A man is now inwardly what he has up to now had in a loose juncture.

7. *Representation:* One does not only solidify the different factors in oneself; one also acknowledges them as deserving to be objectively united. To do this one takes oneself to provide a solidification that is to function on behalf of the others as well as oneself. Whereas in solidification, the emphasis is on oneself, here the emphasis is on the solidified result as that which one is going to sustain and thereby enable others to solidify or to benefit from. The known world of nature, the produced work of art, the complex of oneself and others is individually supported, and whatever the effect be on the different components of the solidification is to be of benefit for all.

8. *Enjoyment:* The solidified result is accepted as something in which one is to lose oneself. The known scientific world, the art object, or the daily world is taken as one's own, living it as one's own possession. We are here back to something like an appreciation, except that the distance between oneself and object is overcome; one lives in and with the confronted object or world, but as joined with the other factors.

9. *Repercussion:* After the living in and with something which involves a bringing this within the orbit of oneself, we are left facing all the factors as not altogether distinct, though with an emphasis on one or the other, depending on the discipline. In the *World of Art,* I identified this undifferentiated, nuanced whole, of actually independent factors, with Existence. It would be more correct to see it, as only one factor. In theoretical science, one would have instead an emphasis on formalities. The outcome of the venture, beginning with 1. is a 'complex we', grounded in the solidified.

10. *Interaction:* Each man and each group of men, though they form complexes which may be sufficient for a considerable period, also interact with other complexes. What is allowed to be faced in a repercussion is here first joined, not in an enjoyment but in an actual union of the solidification with the elements outside it, to constitute a single whole interacting with other wholes. If one could succeed in getting a solidification which included all the basic approaches, had an adequate metaphysical outlook, and a wide and deep enough involvement (so that there was no other complex with which to interact) the result would be a civilized world or a cosmos, constantly being constituted by the joining

of all the factors with different degrees of success, moment after moment, it would have an indefinite thrust outward into the future which was to be realized by further acts of union. The whole would be a unit which itself opened up a domain in which it would occupy a position. The domains of mathematics, art, etc. in contrast, have to do with the specification of items which were always less than and at best could only epitomize a formal dimension, a solidification, etc.

I have made no attempt here to keep within the pattern of five factors, which was behind my ideas of the last days. That ten distinctions are being made, however, does tempt one to see if they do or do not conform to the idea of a two basic quintets of distinctions, all eventually related to the five finalities. I will not do that now, though I have found in the past that when I did do something like that, particularly after I have examined a matter on its own merits, I was able to refine what I had said, avoid overlaps, and sometimes make further distinctions that had been neglected.

I am not satisfied with most of the above designations. 'Appreciation', for example, sounds too much as if it were the act of a private mind or of a sentiment. It should include the use of instruments and, in the worlds of sport and art, the use of equipment which allows one to extend oneself into and be in control of what is beyond oneself. Equipment, of course, is already part of the world in the form of objects which a man is to make continuous with himself. It belongs to the confronted world. Consequently, when it is used as a continuation of a man and thus as himself continued toward others, it must be understood to be the product of an antecedent, imaginative projection and of an appreciation for what it is apart from men, before it is made into equipment. What this shows is that the above schema can be used to account for the presence of items, through projection and appreciation, which can then be turned into equipment in the form of appreciated continuations of oneself.

October 21

We initially experience the mixed, with ourselves not altogether separate from it. The attempt to understand leads to a withdrawal from it into our own selves, and the attempt to then impose something of our own unity on what is there. We are then beings who emphasize health, intention, human construction, the personal, and the private. We do not always begin in this way; indeed, it may be said that we begin in the opposite direction, being compelled to submit to the independent presence and activity of others, recorded in our pains and satisfactions. And when we perceive, it cannot be rightly said that all we do is to impose our judgment or ourselves on what is present. Instead, we try to make the unifications, that we introduce into the content of judgment, mesh with a unity of that content as it stands apart from us. When we are dedicated, obligated, and when we provide evidence of the existence of our privacies, we use as a guide what unifies and controls what is beyond us. We here illustrate the categories pertinent to Possibility, Substance, Being, Existence, and Unity. Depending on a prior effort to impose ourselves, to submit, and to use a guide, work can be said to be the endeavor to make our own unities mesh with what is there. Through the medium of the body, it carries out what is begun in judgment and perception—an idea not far from that of some of the pragmatists and Marxists.

We are driven to acknowledge privacies because of the way in which we are forced to yield to the world about us in pain and pleasure, the satisfaction of desire, mutual interplay, the adjustments promoted by reward and punishment, the carrying out of resolutions, the confirmation of our rational conclusions and predictions, the making our responsibility effective, and the attempt to reach our own I's, via our me's.

We are driven to acknowledge the independent functioning of a privacy which, despite any bodily manifestation, operates apart from the body, when we take account of the aesthetic, what promotes the species, consortia, social judgment, decisive moves, guilt and innocence, and the standards of the I. These involve the acknowledgment of an external unitary governance to which we submit, and which we try to realize. There is also the juncture of the two unities in perceptual judgment, in the insistence on ourselves in acts, and in the pulling on us by final realities.

Despite the appearance of random floundering, these observations and those of the last five days are put down only after I have spent some time thinking about them, and charting them out on various notes. Having come back from school, I now make another attempt:

There are five ways of meshing submission and interaction: a. having them separately carried out as one does in an ideal baseball team where each man functions as an individual and yet interplays with the others; politics seeks to attain that stage. b. Having them interinvolved, as they are in society, expressing a common spirit. c. Having one's private side dominate, in health and in dedication. d. Having what is external dominate, as it does in compulsion and obligation. And e. combining all these in a civilized living, involving work and adjustment.

Behind these formulations is an attempt to find some systematic way of presenting the individual in such a way that others will be able to see more readily what I have been holding about the finalities. In self-expression in health and dedication we are still left in our privacies. What is wanted is clear evidence of these, leading back to a man expressing himself. We do of course have pains and pleasures privately, and we do have private dedications: what is needed is a demonstration that they cannot be reduced to linguistic expressions, or to criteria pointing to nothing we privately do.

October 25

Sensitivity, desire, and interest are expressed bodily. A number of reasons can be advanced for acknowledging them to be privately grounded, though not necessarily in a privacy which functions independently of the body. A knowledge of an independently functioning privacy will have to take account of the aesthetic, the demands of the species, and the demands of society.

Sensitivity can be evidenced by the bodily expressed occurrences if:

1. The way a man lives in the familiar world is affected by his sensitive apprehension. We here have him facing and living in a world in which the occurrences are the outcome of the juncture of what is pertinent to his sensitivity and his sensitive adjustment to it. Trackers and huntsmen offer good illustrations, alert as they are to possible dangers and injuries, leads and hints.

2. The suffering of a man is the outcome of the intrusions of a world on one who is sensitive; he is primarily passive here; what is happening is expressive of the way in which the external world is making a difference to his sensitive status. Whatever be said of the knowledge of suffering that we have from symptoms and by attending to what is said, the suffering is privately undergone.

3. Some Wittgensteineans take their stand with expressions in language when speaking of pain. They speak of the cries and grimaces of one who is in pain, and the response to these by others who are keyed to these public expressions. They are cries and grimaces, of course, only because they express a privacy; if they did not, they would be just noises.

4. Apart from the interplay of a man with what is in the public world he helps constitute with others, and the direct individual expressions reporting an actual pain, a man is in situations where the relationship he has to what is outside is explained by the kind of thought or attention

under which he operates, and is thereby connected with what is beyond him. Because of his experiences in the past, a man looks out at the world aware that this or that is the source of pleasure or pain.

5. There is also a direct interinvolvement of men with one another emotionally, and an emotional involvement, with an emphasis on men as the source, in connection with what is not human. This involvement is undoubtedly modified over the course of their lives, but whether it is or not, it is not explanatory, as thought or attention is. Instead it has man caught up in an ongoing which has for him a subjective tonality, expressive of the raw openness that he has to the presence of other beings, not in the public world, but below this.

6. All the above are solidified in a single outlook in which the different factors continue to have a role as fringes and continuations of what they help constitute. The outlook that men have on the world, toward the future, the past, and the nature of life and existence as such, expresses the way the foregoing sensitive expressions are united.

7. Men do not always express their sensitivities or originate sensitive expressions and responses as individuals. They provide warnings, guides, helps, offering suggestions and directions to others, protecting and alerting some to what had been sensitively undergone. The common language cannot be understood as providing units for just a calm interlude or interchange. Men act as representatives of one another, and in that capacity reveal what they have sensitively discerned or undergone.

8. Pain is not merely an outcome or a relation. It is itself something with which one has identified oneself. More evidently, pleasure suffuses; one becomes identified with what is making the pleasure possible, and as a consequence one enjoys the object as part of a larger personal adventure. One has the object as continuous with the experiencing of it.

b. After the experiencing of an object is over, one is left facing all the factors as before, but now making one aware of the world as ominous, benign, congenial, alien, rational, obstinate, and the like. These are not well-distinguished. Distinguished or not, all lead to a kind of abyss into which one can dimly peer because of one's previous involvement in sensitive experience, with this or that solidified content.

10. A sensitive man is a complex being. As such, he interplays with other complex beings. We would not be able to understand his ways of acting if we did not take account of the fact that his nature as a complex being, and the way in which he is interacting with other complex beings,

human and subhuman, is burdened with his privately initiated and under-gone sensitive life.

A similar ten-fold set can be developed for the unconfined expressions of sensibility, desire, and interest, in the form of the aesthetic, species-demands, and the social. All are expressed through the agency of the body. They also point to a privacy able to function independently of the body, occupied with what may not be of bodily benefit and which may even operate in opposition to the bodily activities and the sensitivity these embody. Matching the above ten, one can distinguish 1. a panorama, 2. appreciation, 3. objective experiencing, 4. flexibility, 5. affiliation, 6. an aesthetic state of affairs; 7. instruction; 8. active experiencing; 9. illumination; and 10. a community of appreciators. What must be shown is how these differ in kind from the foregoing. Once this is done, one is in a position to note how even a sensitive expression in the body can be made subject to an aesthetic approach, and how the aesthetic can modify the nature of the sensitivity as kept within the bodily confines.

When we pass from these to such expressions of the psyche as assumed accountability and thought, and such expressions of the self as responsibility, resolution, and the I, we find no incorporated counterpart, similar to that which sensibility has for the aesthetic. Each is discovered, when we find acts discrepant with, oppositional to, subordinated to, and subordinating various public determinations. Responsibility can be expressed in the face of public denials of it, evidenced in opposition to what issues from elsewhere.

Might we not take this same approach to sensibility and the aesthetic, noting that the confined sensibility is a function of what occurs outside our control, and that the aesthetic does not? Sensitivity, because private in origin, is within our control, and the aesthetic is a function of what is present. The fact has even led some—Prall for example—to hold that what we take to be aesthetically satisfying is nothing other than what is pleasant, and that the painful is the ugly. But though one might reasonably hold that the aesthetically satisfying is always pleasant and what is not aesthetically satisfying is always unpleasant, we cannot say that what is pleasant is always aesthetically satisfying or that what is painful is always aesthetically unsatisfying. The pleasant may be monotonous and boring; the painful may be part of what is produced by a needed contrasting factor in the aesthetically desirable.

October 31

In the paper which I am preparing to read before the Metaphysical Society of America on 'Truth and Reality', I conclude that a philosophic system's reference to ultimate realities—individuals or finalities—is to what, were they referred to directly, would require the splintering of the system into a multiplicity of distinct claims. It can retain its unity and offer a single truth, and yet make provision for a reference to the ultimate realities only by having its claims about them mediated by the common world. The actual movement from that world to the realities which are being dealt with in the system (and then at its extremes, with its center connected with the common world) can be viewed in five ways: 1. One can, when possessed of sound conclusions, use these as constants, and move along the route from the actual world to what eventually will match them; 2. One can take them as guides, making them pick out, of what is found along the route what is pertinent to them. 3. One can reverse these processes, and take the route itself to be constant and in control, changing the claimed truth to conform. 4. One can acknowledge the conclusion only when one in fact arrives at what would sustain it. And 5. One can combine these in various ways.

The first is used in metaphysics when one has developed a well-integrated system with termini which are unimpeachable; the second is used in connection with the conclusions arrived at in ordinary experience; the third is used when the conclusions are at best hypotheses and guesses; the fourth is used when one is concerned with crucial occurrences and intent on forging ideas to conform; the fifth, which combines them all in various ways and degrees, is most characteristic of the efforts to use the results of mathematics in empirical enterprises.

In addition to these, there is a sixth use of the conclusions, already indicated—where these are directly referred to their realities and await acceptance by these. The last is what I concentrated on in *First Considerations*. It is pertinent to verifications, but presupposes that we have conclusions of which we are confident, and think will be sustained without alteration. There is a need here to splinter the system, and also to acknowledge that the realities to which the conclusions are referred may in fact alter those conclusions. There does not seem to be any possibility of the reverse occurring and the conclusions being able to change the nature of the realities to which they are directly referred. It seems to be something like the first case. Though the conclusion may make us attentive, it does not, as the second allows, enable one to pick out what is to sustain it. The mixed cases, where each affects the other, do not seem to occur.

When we make a direct reference to a reality, we want to preserve what we had in mind. It is only when we treat our own conclusions as tentative and as perhaps needing correction that we allow what occurs to dictate to ideas or to make possible a mixed result where each side affects the other.

To correct ideas, one must take a formally arrived at conclusion and bring it back to the beginning, or where one in fact now is, and then employ it as a guide to be controlled, or as determining when one is to acknowledge the conclusions or some mixed case. Use of a conclusion as a constant, at best serves as a way of waiting for what will finally support what we had in mind. These considerations open up a new line of inquiry into the use of thoughts, empirical and metaphysical.

If one were to ignore formal inferences and the extremes of a philosophic system, it still would be possible to make use of the different ways of getting knowledge of something. Starting with the commonsense world, one would then do one of five things: 1. Let an idea function as a constant, awaiting for experience to yield a satisfactory counterpart. 2. Form an idea, and allow this to guide and select relevant data until one had an adequate grounding for the idea. 3. Allow experience to determine exactly what the proper idea of it is. 4. Await the arrival of something which provokes the formulation of an idea of it. 5. Mix these various attempts in different ways.

There would be not much point in following the first of these procedures for, having abandoned a formal justification for the idea, there is no reason to insist on it in the form we first entertain. The second could be used in a kind of *a posteriori* ontological proof of God. One would here antecedently define what one meant by God—a perfect benign being, for example—and allow to accrete to it more and more coherent parts of existence, hoping eventually to come to the point where the idea was properly matched. Until one arrived at that point the idea would be indeterminate. The third way allows the nature of the movement from the mixed world of every day also to be a progressive constituting of the idea that is appropriate to it; one learns, as it were, from experience, what it is one knows. God, on such an account, would be appropriate to whatever the world revealed itself to be, the idea of him changing with changes in the experience. The fourth way would have the idea as something thrown up by a crucial experience and appropriate just to this; God would here be the idea of something pivotal.

When we seek to know what privacy is from public evidence, we could start with an idea that we had formed, perhaps by thinking of ourselves and holding to it constantly; (1) we could take the idea to determine how to make selections from the experience and the evidence and evidencing, so as to arrive at the ideas properly sustained, (2) we could just wait for the occasion when some experience will clarify our idea of privacy; (3) we would wait for some crucial event which requires us to formulate an idea of privacy that is appropriate to that experience. What I do not now see is just which of these is the best way; whether or not there are other ways; just what ways are in fact followed.

November 1

If we are to begin by looking for evidence of privacy or anything else, we must start with the daily world and allow some experience there to provoke us to formulate an idea that would be appropriate to it. If we do this, we obtain a claim that could function as a premiss. But we need not use it as one. Instead, we can allow it to be redefined and further determined by what we are encountering. In short, what was called the fourth way, yesterday, would be the one we would use, following on something like the acceptance of the fifth, for we do not face the experience that is to determine our ideas without already having had some understanding of the world. It will be out of the mixed that we will emphasize the movement to an ultimate reality, individual or final, and allow this to lead us to forge ideas that are appropriate to some signal turns in it.

Why should one forge an idea? How is this done? The problem seems to be one where the pragmatist begins, with ideas not only being directly referred to and defined by experience, but providing a way of linking an earlier part of experience to a later. Dewey seems to suppose that this is an idea's only function and only meaning. One can treat an idea as the instrumental linkage between what had been undergone and what is about to be undergone in the face of a difficulty or a crucial occurrence. This could be done without denying the pertinence of the idea of this, and the maintenance of the idea thereafter, not as a register of a difficulty but of the occurrence. The subsequent experiences would then serve to refine the idea at the same time that the idea functioned as a guide to selections of appropriate content in what is subsequently met. We would find, for example, that we could not make sense of a man's refusal to accept an honor except by taking him to have some other idea of his accountability. The idea of an assumed private accountability would answer to the crucial refusal; it would connect that refusal to what had been done before and what is being done now, so far as one was concerned solely with what was happening publicly. But as an idea of a refusal, it would be held on to, and we would look for some other kind of occurrence as that which would be appropriate to the idea. The idea would now have the status of a guide, a factual finder, a way of making the refusal not only serve as a link between two public occurrences but as the beginning of a move in another direction. One would here reverse the Kantian solution to the problem of the relation of freedom and necessity by taking the occurrence of an intrusion of an individual note into necessity as the occasion for the formation of the idea of freedom which would then be used as a guide for the discovery or selection of what would be appropriate to the idea. We would have to say that what we had encountered forced the formation of an idea which could have an object only if one turned away from the experience where it served to bridge others continuous with it.

Why should one do anything more than use an idea as that which is to serve as a bridge? Why should we take freedom, responsibility, will, or aesthetic sensitivity to be anything more than ways of referring to crucial occurrences in ordinary life, and to have no other roles but that of allowing us to proceed smoothly, by providing us with ways of moving from where we had been to where we ought to be, where 'ought to be' is proceeding as smoothly as we had before? Is it not that a. we do know the crucial occurrence and do not substitute an idea for it; b. benefit from the experience and can anticipate a recurrence or a consequence of that recurrence; c. can draw consequences from the idea, having nothing to do with the present experience, thereby coming to understand the nature of the crucial occurrence and even its causes and world in contrast with what we had previously known; d. can look to see if there is not some other kind of occurrence that would be appropriate to the idea and had the crucial occurrence as a consequence? It is the last which leads one to affirm that some crucial occurrences originate in privacy.

These hesitant suggestions, which require further reflection to explicate, now point up the difficulty that an instrumentalism does not allow us to grasp the crucial occurrence as anything more than an occasion to pass to what allows us to function smoothly, rather than allowing us also to attend to it, and to look wherever we can to what would explain the occurrence. A crucial occurrence, as representing a turning point, or as introducing something new into the situation, is more than a gnarled version of what is objectively occurring and in which we find ourselves in accord.

From a philosophic standpoint, all daily occurrences are 'crucial', for all of them fall short of the clarity and ultimacy required. Moreover, the following out of the constituents of what is confronted back to their sources ends on one side with actualities in their privacy. Two questions then remain: Why is there need to go beyond the privacy of actual bodies, their potentialities and dispositions, and refer to a distinctive human privacy able to function independently of, and often in opposition to the body, while it makes use of the body to promote its own ends? And if there is a need to do this, why is this not always necessary, forcing one to understand the composition of what is daily known always to be in part at least the work of a human privacy?

A preliminary answer to the first of these questions would be that there is something occurring that is not to be explained in bodily terms. But to this one might reply that if the body is understood to be a distinctively human body we would expect it to function in ways that other bodies do not. But a man's body also behaves as other bodies do; it falls at the same rate they do; it can grow and decay, suffer diseases, become pained in just the way that what is not human can. The second question raises doubts about this answer, holding that even the pain of a man is altogether different from that of an animal's, and therefore always requires a reference to a distinctive human privacy. If one must understand that privacy as not altogether confined to activating the body, will one not have to say that the sensitive use of the body also expresses a power which would still have a status apart from this?

It will not be enough in dealing with this issue to hold (as I have) that there is an aesthetic sensitivity, for the question is focused on what is bodily expressed. In addition, the second question in effect is asking whether what we know about anything must not be seen to be in part constituted by the knower, thereby introducing a humanly private note into it. There would be nothing amiss in holding that the bodily sensitivity of man carries a private sensitivity which could operate apart from and even express an occupation with what is apart from the body, providing only that more intensive, further reaching acts were also recognized, and thus did not have to be forced to serve the body but could use it for other ends. The supposition that every known occurrence bears the mark of a human privacy could also be allowed, provided that the contribution is distinguishable from what is present apart from it, and this in turn is dissected into factors, one of which leads to a privacy that is not necessarily human.

It cannot be maintained that one always *uses* his body. The body acts on its own, and any sensitive experience that results reflects the way in which the body interplays with other bodies.It can be bruised, it can have spasms, it decays and grows, and all of these can have their pains and pleasures. The sensitivity in that body can nevertheless be thought of as captured there in part, with a residue left over which would use the body were the occasion opportune. If this be allowed, one will have allowed that the body functions on its own, and have merely added that it has other powers, without giving reasons for believing that it had such powers.

Sensitivity could be said to make use of the body, not for some further objective, but as a medium of expression, and to be captured by the body, and there made to serve its ends. It is only when one starts further back than the sensitivity as so capturable that one gets to it as capable of aesthetic appreciation and as actually making use of the body for outcomes which do not promote the body or answer to its needs. It is perhaps not a matter of indifference whether we say that sensitivity is captured, or that it is in fact just bodily in function, for if it is captured, it still is in principle part of the privacy as independent of the body, while if it is just bodily in function, though originating with an independent privacy, there is no conceivable separation of the sensitive person from the body. The alternative that it is captured, in principle allows for a separation of the privacy, including its sensitivity, from the body.

Is it not true though that aesthetic sensitivity, assumed accountability, responsibility, and so on, are all captured by the body, since otherwise they would not come to expression? No. They also serve ends beyond the body's and therefore must be said to use the body, even while they are being confined, directed, modified, and forced to be expressed along bodily lines. They are carried out sometimes to the disadvantage of the body and, unlike a bodily sensitivity, are active and not passive. Yet desires are active and are conceivably bodily. Not only does it seem odd to say that the desires have a private origin apart from the body rather than that they are integral to the body, but they work on behalf of the body. But this is only to say that there is more than one bodily confined type of what has a private origin, leaving us with the question whether or not there is more than one type of unconfined activity making use of the body and then for objectives which may not benefit the body. If those objectives serve the interests of the species, society, or state, we will still be left with the question whether there are not also objectives which do not do this and which require for their understanding a reference to a privacy that uses the species, society, or state for ends that may not promote these, and whether or not there is an even more fundamental aspect of privacy occupied with what does not even make use of these, expressed in a religious faith, speculation, fantasy, or in creations of imaginary states of affairs.

Is there a primordial sensitivity, desire, interest, and perhaps even a resolution, thinking, responsibility, or I which splits off, one part of which serves the body, is confined by it, is carried out along bodily channels and may act in defiance of any private effort, and another which, while going through bodily channels, is directed at objectives that are independent of anything the body needs and may be pursued in opposition to the satisfaction of those needs? It is not necessary to suppose that these are all present at once, neatly marked off from one another. One can view sensitivity as being present and active long before there is responsibility, for example. But then one must immediately add that the part serving the body never was in existence before it served it. This is in effect to have the supposed primordial sensitivity etc., split into two parts, one of which is always caught within bodily confines and the other of which is not. The former provides the base line, allowing us to know of the latter as that which does have an independent non-bodily role, even though it may never be expressed without bodily aid and then be subject to bodily restrictions.

The distinction between what is bodily confined and what merely uses the body is recognized in the distinction between what is a proper or healthy bodily functioning and what is not. We move to the recognition of a private source of the latter and therefore to what is in fact healthy, once we see that it does serve a desirable outcome, e.g., the preservation or benefit of the species or a state. What would be just sick if it were taken to be the work of a bodily sensitivity is seen to be good and healthy if it in fact serves an objective that it would be good to have realized, either by the individual or by some group, state, or perhaps even a God. We are driven then to say that we come to know of truly independent private dimensions in a man because we know that there are goods being served by their expression through the body's help. Those goods may be ideals or objects of commitment, as they are when we are engaged in acting responsibly; but they may also be just the termini which satisfy an unconfined dimension—as seems to be the case when one is aesthetically sensitive. We could say that that sensitivity is aiming at beauty, but it seems more cautious to take it not to have a proper objective, and only to be elicited, provoked, called into action when in fact a distinctive kind of content is present, and even made present through the action of the body quickened by a confined sensitivity.

An aesthetic sensitivity (or sensibility) is applied, as a rule, to what is known or at least made the object of perception or of some sense. It cannot therefore be found when we attend only to the body as sensitive to pain or pleasure. To know that there is an unconfined operating privacy, we should note that one can be seeing something aesthetically excellent while having a pain in the eyes, that one can enjoy a performance while sensing excitement and tension in oneself, that one is affected by elements in a contrast in a painful way while feeling pleasure in the contrast itself.

November 5

Occasionally we find ourselves in circumstances like these where infants and some lower organisms always are. We are involved in a world without making much distinction between our selves and it, or between this object and another. Some items stand out, some are intrusive, some interest, some injure, and there are reactions to them, all apparently carried out without reflection, hesitation, or the calling on hidden reserves. But we are often frustrated, unable to go on. The frustration requires a withdrawal, and that requires one to push away what is there, so as to be at once distanced from them and connected to them by the thrust. The withdrawal and therefore the thrust may be due to one of five difficulties: we do not have possession; it is alien; items function without regard for us; there is confusion in what we confront; we are unable to act; and we are being reduced to insignificance. The withdrawal allows us to make use of our substantialized selves and I's; of our privacies as independent of all else; of our intelligence; of our powers of action; and of our assessments. The thrust takes us intensively toward what is irreducible; oppositionally toward what functions independently; toward ideas leading to explanations; toward action on what is alongside as well as before us; and toward the finalities as measures of all else. (I have obviously made these distinctions in the light of what I have been thinking about the finalities, using them as guides and distinction-makers.)

Any withdrawal-thrust can have the others as subordinate notes. Some philosophers have seen the fact in part. Dewey, e.g., emphasized that frustration requiring action; he thought of concepts, work, and the others (so far as he paid attention to them all all) as instrumental and subordinate to the task of actively solving the problem that produced the frustration. Descartes gave priority to the overcoming of confusion, with some regard for the instrumental role of an intensive withdrawal to promote the outcome.

Is it possible to find, in just the condition of being frustrated, without a distinction in the kind of frustration it is, a basis for holding that there are five dimensions requiring distinctive kinds of remedy, answering to different directions and perhaps to kinds of thrust? Is all frustration multifaceted, pointing at once to a stoppage in depth (against oneself as a possessor); in control (against oneself as independent); in distinctions (against oneself as knower); alongside (against oneself as active); and in importance (against oneself as an assessor)? Affirmative answers tell me what I can possess; what I must control; what I might know; what I should do; and what I ought to endorse.

Are we beings who are seeking to possess, are forced to control, are attracted to knowledge, who are required to act in certain ways, and who have a prescriptive set of values? Or do we begin as beings with some intelligence who find ourselves frustrated (and therefore become aware of confusion)? Do we then withdraw so as to have a position from which to make assessments, move toward ourselves as substantial possive beings, have the move inseparable from an outward thrust toward what is thereby acted on, and have the thrust terminate in what is independent of us? And do we then, after we have made such a beginning, recognize not only that the thrust itself could be subdivided, but that each of the other stages could too? If so, the initial frustration would have subordinate notes pointing up an inability to penetrate others, to control them, to act on them, and to have them of subordinate importance. And there would also be five kinds of withdrawal, thrust, and termination, in each of which there would be one that was dominant and the others subordinate. The dominant forms would be an intellectual frustration, a withdrawal on behalf of value, a movement into ourselves as substantial, a thrust that was dynamic, and a termination stopped by beings which were independent of us. Each of these would have four subordinated forms that could at times become dominant. The frustration, though initially one which defied our understanding, would then not be experienced as intellectual, but as one where we could not advance, and which on reflection could be seen to involve primarily an intellectual difficulty for one who desires to know. We could say that the frustration was in fact experienced in one of the subordinate modes, that for example when we could not proceed in action, because we are intellectual beings we have recourse to thought.

An animal—surely a primate, a dog, or a cat—engages in some reasoning, but this is purely instrumental. The reason of a man comes to the surface after being elicited by some brute stoppage (usually in the course of activities, or better perhaps, in the course of an otherwise smooth immersion in the world). That the stoppage has an intellectual answer is discovered when, on behalf of a move to a superior value, we recognize the importance of a separation from the world, and follow this by a withdrawal, thrust, and termination. In other words, the sharp distinction of all of the dominant modes occurs only when the entire activity from stoppage to termination is completed.

The difference between men and other beings seems now to lie, not in a failure on the part of the others to carry out the five-fold move, ending in a termination at what is beyond—this they do—but in carrying it out on behalf of an overcoming of the initial frustration. When a man moves away from what is frustrating, he emphasizes a value which the frustrating is minimizing, allowing that value to have its integrity and career. He does something similar when he continues on, to move into himself, to thrust outward, and to terminate. Each of these moves not only has its distinctive dominant characteristic, but may be elaborated for its own sake. When he finally has the initial set of activities distinguished he may carry out any one of them for its own sake, enjoying, for example, the stage of being withdrawn. Even the initial frustration, now understood to be a confusion and thus to involve a defiance of what is intelligible, can be neglected by him for the sake of pursuing a course of reasoning for its own sake. A subhuman's distinguishing of stages is but a way of allowing it to have a set of activities which will enable it to continue to function smoothly; a man's distinguishing allows him to remain with any one of them indefinitely and to see each to have subordinated to itself forms of what is due to other activities.

November 6

Frustrated, we move back to deal better with that with which we are involved. Depending on the degree of our development, we are able to move back greater and greater distances. Animals can move only far enough back to be able to bring to bear some kind of reason, some effort at control, some self-maintenance, some initiated action, and some assessment of what is important for their welfare. Only man can rest at any one of these points and then not only be in a position to elaborate but to recognized subordinated versions within the resting point.

When a man moves back into himself, he may arrive at himself as an I, and can then proceed forward to the other in an experiencing penetration, through a conceptualization, by freely identifying degrees of freedom with different reaches, by acknowledging a set of rights equal to his own, expressed in distinctive claims, and by making an assessment of the other's various objectives and therefore what values he in fact has because of the values he seeks to realize. The other is known from penetrations because of what he does, despite other occurrences; from conceptualizations of different kinds of explanations of what he does; from the recognition of different objectives as requiring different degrees of freedom; from an identification of his publicly expressed rights and the claims they express, and from his making different assessments of what another does in relation to his final private ought to be, his health.

Penetration proceeds by recognizing sensitive expressions of pain and pleasure occurring despite bodily need; an aesthetic sensitivity being expressed despite bodily pain and pleasure; bodily desires pursued despite aesthetic appreciations; general desires expressed despite bodily appetites; interest in others expressed despite the needs of the species; general interests carried out despite the dominant views of society; concern with a harmony of interests expressed despite insistence of each; reasonableness carried out despite the human situation; assumed accountability maintained despite what is socially rewarded and punished; decision, with objectives, maintained despite that for which one is assuming accountability; responsibility affirmed or credited despite decisions; an I with guilt and innocence expressed despite what is responsibly done; and a dominating health-determining *idio* in operation despite the demands of the I.

When instead or in addition a man engages in a conceptualization, he finds it desirable to distinguish an effective person, an explanatory psyche, a controlling self, and an assessive *idio*, all subordinated to the recognition of independence expressed in the move from the data to the concepts. The person allows one to discover a bodily and aesthetic sensitivity and interests; the explanatory psyche allows one to distinguish a concern, reasonableness, and assumed accountability; the controlling self allows for a distinction between resolution, responsibility and the I. The *idio*, finally, controls, explains, and is effective.

In summary, the different divisions of privacy are known from penetrations into what is present despite what is otherwise publicly occurring; different conceptions offer different kinds of explanations of different kinds of occurrences; references to freedom are grounded in the recognition of different objectives at different degrees of remoteness; an identification of rights in public points to native claims; and the various assessments made of what is done point to a man's final ought to be, i.e., the *idio* and its healthy governance.

November 7

On encountering anything we are inevitably blocked. As a consequence, it has the status of something irreducible, substantial. We move away from it in order to be able to continue to function and this in effect places us in an oppositional relation to it. At this position, we seek means for advancing with success. This is followed by an actual move beyond where we are, to and often beyond the initial oppositional item. We end finally by terminating at something taken as that which is important for us. These stages are in an order suggested by Substance, Being, Possibility, Existence, and Unity, all of them arrived at from the position of appearances. Were we to try to get to these, we could find, once we arrived at any one of them, that there was a further thrust into them, but which we could not pursue. As a consequence, we would be forced to turn back toward where we had started, carrying out the five-fold progress at a deeper level and repeating our former effort, but now at a still deeper level, and so on indefinitely. At every stage, since there are subordinated modes reflecting the presence of the other finalities, it is possible to proceed in other directions. Instead of turning back from Substance to go to actualities, we could move on to Being, and so on. We will then have attended, not to the need to get to an oppositional reality, and therefore to return to the actualities or appearances from which we had moved to Substance, but to the need to deal with an oppositional finality.

What we have here is a sequence of five stages, each move being connected to the next by a distinctive kind of reference, reflecting the nature of the stage. When we arrive at a terminus, we can then try to continue in the same direction, turn back, look back, look for explanations, or try to act. At every stage, we can continue on to the next, in the order of SBPEU, or we can stop with one of them, and see what we can do by following subordinated relations. On behalf of an interest in oppositionality, we could, e.g., move from one finality to the next.

When we are trying to understand an actuality, we try to get publicly available evidence. That evidence is the result of a move from an antecedent acceptance of some datum, and a move to an oppositional component there. Only then are we in a position to seek a way of getting to what is evidenced, move to that evidenced, and from there terminate in what is to accept that evidence. We could have taken a stand with the evidence (as I do in *First Considerations*) and acknowledge the evidenced as that which is oppositional to it, and then proceeded to look for conceptualizable connections between evidence and evidenced, move to the latter, and from there to the common basis of it and the evidence.

The evidenced at which we arrive is not on a footing with the evidence. It is directed toward what is to sustain it. The formal relationship of evidence and evidenced has them on a footing, but the inferential act does not simply pass from one extreme to the other. It is a movement in intensity, and therefore gets to the 'conclusion' as something pointing toward what is to sustain it.

We come to know a private being's multiple epitomizations by first recognizing another to be self-distancing in various degrees because of more and more basic uses of his freedom, by recognizing him to provide more and more fundamental claims, by conceptualizing our reference, by penetrating beyond what we have as our referent, and finally by assessing him in terms of different kinds of goals he is privately set to realize. The first makes use of proper names, the second public agencies, the third categories, the fourth symbols, and the fifth an endorsement.

Is the five-fold treatment of another's privacy properly expressed as actually beginning with the evidenced (and therefore presupposing an antecedent four-step move from data, evidence, correlation, and movement, with the consequent acknowledgment of five stages in the individual—lived body, person, psyche, self, and *idio*? Do these in fact answer to the sequence of Substance, Being, Possibility, Existence, and Value? If so, how deal with infants which have not yet developed a self or *idio*? It does not make sense to say that they do not have any existence. Also, I have not distinguished more than three epitomizations of persons, psyche, and self. Is one forced to say that there must be five? Must there be five in the lived body and the *idio*?

November 8

The questions with which I ended yesterday need to be answered. That about the infant is to be answered by recognizing that we cannot get any further than the acknowledgment of it as a person, and as a consequence must turn back toward the body of the infant in terms of its person. Its person is substantialized, i.e., has its own integrity, contrasts with its body, is able to be in an explanatory relation to that body, in fact controls or expresses itself through it, and assesses the result.

A similar answer is required with respect to the recognition of just three or four divisions in the privacy and of the three epitomizations of the person, psyche, and self. When one comes to the most recessive of the epitomizations, or to the self or *idio* (as I have termed the final division of privacy able to receive and use all the finalities and govern the other divisions of the privacy for the sake of health), there is nothing to do but to continue the five-fold process of distinction, but with a changed direction. If there are only three distinctions, one will use a fourth to make evident the dynamic movement of the last of the three; if there are four, one will use the fifth to make evident that there is an assessment of what is still to be reached in other ways.

The final questions: must there be five, and must there be five in the lived body and the *idio*? require different answers. One can always find five but this will require a change in direction at times. No one item need be dissectable into five subdivisions; it can serve as an irreducible, requiring one to accept it as at the beginning of a five-fold move initially determined by the kind of opposition it has to some other item.

There are similarities here to what Hegel attempted. He, however, supposed that any item with which one began was inseparable from another which was able to complete it, and that the movement toward that completion was under the governance of a single power that became concretionalized to the very extent that the missing factor was able to be added to the original. In the terms I have been using, he took his stand with something treated as substantialized, saw that it was in an oppositional relation to what was beyond it, but looked to a single, constant absolute to make both the rational and actual connection with what was missing, and then, without imposing any assessment on the outcome, allowed the absolute to exhibit itself as something substantialized at a new level. He dealt with the initial substantialized items as though their own relations to what was beyond was passive, and as if there never was a return to the initial item, but always a progress toward higher and higher outcomes. To be sure, in his analyses in the *Logic* he tries to show that the oppositional relation goes backward and forward. But if he could do this, there is no reason why there might not be a perpetual oscillation from one to the other. The oscillation would not be meaningless if, on his movement back to the starting point, he moved more and more into the item. But there is no moving into Nothing. The most Hegel could maintain is that from the standpoint of a deeper standing in Being he can specialize the Nothing more and more. But then he would lose the supposed symmetry or the supposed advance that the antithesis makes on the thesis.

There are two ways we can make directed progress into the privacy of a man. One can make each step go through five stages, with the fifth allowing one to arrive at a new step at its first stage. This would be to carry out a dialectic in detail. Another method, modelled on that of the computer, is to view the different stages as constituting a loop or epicycle on a subordinated level, and thereby being able to proceed on a higher level directly from one step to the next. If we follow the second method, we will make use of a number of distinct names, distancings, concepts, penetrations, or evaluations, applicable to more and more private dimensions of a man. When, in following out this method one finds oneself frustrated, unable to go further, one will have to move on to the next step. Were one, for example, frustrated in the use of concepts, one will move to action, not as a way of getting to the next concept (as the first method requires) but as a new way of dealing with the frustrating item. If the action fails, one moves on to the other steps. If all fail, one takes the frustrating item to be irreducible, forcing one to move away from it. Such a movement away itself has stages. One can move alongside to what is oppositional, to what is prescriptive, to what must be overcome by acts, be content to evaluate it in relation to oneself, and (if these fail) finally to return toward the starting point or to something in that direction. Where one arrives on the return move will start a new series of steps, beginning with the acceptance of the starting point as substantialized i.e., as that which is to be followed by a withdrawal etc. In the course of life we do not distinguish all these steps; they would be distinguished only in what Hegel calls a 'logic'.

Every time we are confronted with the prospect of going through a series of steps, we can deal with the steps as part of a loop, and therefore proceed as though the next step were like the original, but at a position beyond where this had stopped. If we are frustrated in using a concept, we can treat other ways of dealing with the frustrated item as though they were part of a loop, and proceed therefore with another concept. Since we are frustrated in the use of a previous concept appropriate to a relatively more superficial aspect, we will not be able to use the new concept to take us deeper into the frustrating item. Instead, we will have to take the concept to apply elsewhere.

Why do we go back toward the starting point rather than alongside? Is it not that the return allows one to keep to the original purpose of getting into the object? By returning we move into a greater depth than we had been at before, and therefore are in a position to make another assault on the same object, but from a deeper base and therefore from a position which enables us to reach a deeper base in it. It is only when we find that the results are becoming too meager to be of interest that we turn in other directions. All the while, of course, we remain with concepts. Had we given up the use of them, we would engage in one of the other efforts, and might conceivably make a greater progress into them than we had managed with the concepts. Eventually, we will find ourselves stopped, and will then have to do what we would have had to do had we remained with the use of concepts—go through stages and steps.

November 9

How do we know that someone is human? I do not think I have ever dealt with this question systematically. The account of the finalities allows us to look at the question in five basic ways. Then, taking account of what I have called 'loops', one can look for stages in each. Remaining with the basic five, we have an initial acknowledgment first of someone as maintaining himself as a you; of him as a you against myself, and therefore also being grounded in an I contrasting with my I; of him as explanatory of a multiplicity of acts such as those which express an assumed accountability; of him as penetrated toward in an act of sympathy; and finally of him as evaluated as having a certain dignity. The last is perhaps the most important and even the most familiar.

We take anyone who begins life to be part of the human community because born into a family or a group, and that fact means he is subject to a single prescription applying to all humans. No one can ever escape from the prescription, though men do fall short of living up to it. This means that we must never deal with a man as bestial, but only as one who belongs to one mankind and is to be judged in terms of the common prescription. Were we to say that any being, able to function in various approved human ways, such as a visitor from outer space, was human, we would have made a decision to apply the common prescription to them. If we did, they could never fall outside humankind, no matter how much they fell short of living up to its ideals. It is a fact, to be sure, that some men treat others as though they were not human. But this does not make those malefactors fall outside the provenance of the prescription; instead, they remain subject to it, to be condemned as human beings who have fallen seriously short of what humans should be and do.

Is there a somewhat similar way of distinguishing animals from things, and therefore from the most complicated and sophisticated of machines? I think so. Living beings exhibit a central control; they are coordinate with other members in the sense that they live together with them, even if only at certain times and even when they fight one another to death; they have a privacy which is the ground for preparations, desire, and sensitivity; they can be reached in penetrative acts which can move from injuries inflicted and cries exhibited to pains; and finally, they have a status because they are together in a kind of bounding which is prescriptive, though they cannot know this or use it as a ground for judging others. Where men are not only prescribed to but can attend to the prescription so as to judge one another, animals are prescribed to but make no judgments in terms of the prescriptions. They do not judge those who do not meet the prescriptions as doing or being wrong.

As we go down the scale of living beings, it becomes harder and harder to discern a self-positioning preparatory to acting, a self-maintenance in opposition to others, an explanatory activity from privacy to body, an expressiveness of which penetration is the converse, or a bounding with others of the same kind. The most cautious procedure would be neither to affirm nor deny that something like these occur, perhaps in diffused or blurred forms, and instead allow for an area of evidential indeterminacy, above which we find animals, and below which we find things.

One interesting outcome of these reflections is that 'kind' is quite a different idea from 'species'. The latter is biological and classificatory; even if credited with power and control, it does no more than provide a condition for procreation and continuance in existence. A kind instead involves a bondage, an assessment of others as being on the same level, as belonging together, manifested occasionally in acts of sacrifice or mutual aid and guidance, sometimes counter to the needs of the species. The members of a kind, like the lemmings which march to the sea together, may act contrary to the need of the species.

The view here presented is close to that of Hegel and Confucius. It differs from them in taking the bondage to cover all men. The first takes it to be characteristic of men in a state (as Aristotle does); the second takes it to be characteristic of men in a civilized society. Neither recognizes that there is a similar, though still different kind of bondage, for each species of animal.

Does it make sense to speak of a kind of dignity and bonding for lower forms of life? Is there a real difference between bonding and affiliation due to Substance? The second question is easier to answer than the first. An affiliation, even when it applies to all the members of a species, uniting them while setting them over against all other entities, is what it does; it is not a prescription whose demands might not be met. One can, though, take bonding to be a limited case of an affiliation which may or may not be accepted by the beings on which it is applied. Where an affiliation, even when kept within the confines of a species, expresses the degree of success that Substance achieves in interplay with actualities, bonding expresses Unity. This could be assimilated not to an affiliation but to a condition for this, expressing a demand and not the outcome of an act.

November 10

Given various public expressions of a man, we should be able to obtain the same series of more and more recessive epitomizations of his privacy in a number of distinct ways. We could proceed from one of these ways to another, as a series of steps; go through loops before we arrive at the next step; or take all of the steps to be coordinate, allowing us to take them in any order we like. Whichever course we pursue, we seem to have the following distinct warrants for affirming the same set of private dimensions:

1. Attending to the way men take a stand either as units in a larger setting or as grounds of expressions, we find various dimensions to be more and more 'substantialized', basic, grounding, and able to possess less basic epitomizations. 2. Attending to the way men set themselves in opposition to others, either as units in a larger setting or as able to initiate acts on their own, we find that the various dimensions provide more and more appropriate ways for speaking of any man being on a footing with any other, as inviolable, as freely determining himself, and as an irreducible unit. 3. Attending to the public and communicable meaning of what we encounter, we can look for appropriate explanations for it. Different encountered objects will require for their explanations more and more ultimate units able to provide a necessary unifying ground for what is multiple. 4. Attending to the publicized presence of the expressions as they interlock with the expressions of others, we can take our start with them and see how they allow us to penetrate toward more and more deeply based sources. 5. Attending to the prescriptive bonding of men, we move to deeper and deeper bases in them as having dignities which are more and more appropriate to the imperiousness of the bonding, as that to which one ought to conform.

In this outline, a two-fold approach is taken to other men (and possibly ourselves as well, approached from without). The men are seen to be in distinctive kinds of settings and to have privacies. The settings differ in providing them with the status of units for roles; making them into equal objects of common demands; having them publicly governed by common laws; enabling them to exist together because subject to the same compulsions; and having public values because of the way they are prescriptively bonded. The levels we are able to distinguish in a man will here be evidenced by the kind of roles they have, the demands they meet, the laws that govern them, the compulsions to which they are subject, and the kind of bonding to which they are subject.

There are not only five different types of evidence, but each type is in a distinctive setting, allowing for the distinguishing of different dimensions of privacy. The prescriptive bonding thus does not merely have to do with man's value; it provides a measure of the available evidence, enabling one to identify this as having a source answering more and more to the kind of bonding that characterizes men as forming a single humankind. There are different degrees of bonding, each having men as terms, or grounding their expressions no deeper than the degree of bonding requires. The approach to men individually moves from them, as not as public units subject to various kinds and degrees of conditioning, but as individually making themselves publicly manifest.

Men are privately irreducible, self-contained, free, creative, and possessed of dignity. Each of these should be recognized to be fractionated in the privacies in the form of sources of different evidences. A man who exhibited public evidences warranting a reference to responsibility, let us say, would be known to be as privately responsible as one who was irreducible, self-contained, free, creative, or an excellent reality. Each of the dimensions in his privacy that we were able to distinguish would be distinguished as an irreducible, self-contained, etc., responsible source. If we dealt with the man from the standpoint of a setting, we would take that very same evidence as a unit in a context of laws, and would then look for the privately free origin of it.

If this is correct, we should say, e.g., of an expression of pain that it is a unit in a role, is to be contradistinguished from the expressions of others and from other expressions of the same individual, fits into a law-governed context, is in a setting which is subject to compulsions (dictating perhaps how loud or long or in what form the cry is to be expressed), and is assessible in terms of prescriptions applicable to all men (it might be a cowardly or rejectable thing to do). The very same

expression could also be recognized to have its source in a private irreducible, what is self-contained, is free, creative (i.e., works itself out
in the course of its expression) and some dignity. What is true of the
evidence for sensitivity will have counterparts in the evidence for desire,
etc.

If we are to proceed systematically or, more strictly speaking, dialectically, we would have to decide arbitrarily to use the evidence of a
publicized version of an individual, or of him as a term in some kind of
context, or take these to be complementary. Depending on our decision
we would have to look at each piece of evidence in a five or in a ten-
fold way. Even a cry of pain would provide a five or ten-fold set of
evidences, all leading to a private sensitivity. One would move from that
sensitivity to the acknowledgment of an aesthetic sensitivity by finding
evidence in the form of five more roles, as well as in five more publicized
versions of an individual. If, in each case, we tried to proceed by some
method from one position to another, we would have to invoke a method
involving five stages, each of which had five steps. There would be little
gain in doing this. It is enough to show that it can be done, and to
proceed with the examination of each piece of evidence, preferably in a
ten-fold way, and then looking for the next piece of evidence which
needs a deeper ground, or plays a more important role in that setting
(or alternatively plays a role in a more significant setting), and so on until
the entire privacy of a man was exposed, as a source of the different
roles.

It was just remarked that one can take the next piece of evidence to
play a more important role in a given setting, or a role in a more significant
one. The one way of speaking requires us to see all men in the broadest
and most important setting, but as living in it only partially, until he has
attained an I. The other, which seems preferable, takes each piece of
evidence to be in its proper setting, and then recognizes that there are
other evidences which are in a richer setting and have a richer ground.
If we then independently proceed to deal with that new evidence as a
public expression of an individual, we can confirm what we learned by
looking at the evidence in a setting.

November 11

The recent discussions allow for an approach to public expressions of sensitivity in one of ten ways. Beginning with evidence in the
form of a cry or grimace related to an evidenced 'of pain', we are in a

position to recognize a private nature to that sensitivity. 1. We can attend to the individual as having a role in some group. As having that role his expression is something carried out, making his cry of pain a signal, perhaps to others, or a way of asking them to perform some function. 2. We can attend to the individual as subject to a common demand that he function as a unit alongside other units, with the consequence that his cry of pain will serve to alert others to his presence as a distinct reality. 3. We can attend to him as subject to common rules or laws, and thus as one who is supposed to or not supposed to cry out at the time, the one if he is, say a patient whose sensitive spots are being probed by a researcher, the other if he is in the army in a crucial situation, etc. 4. We can attend to him as one who is subject to a compelling force, which could be applied to others as well, perhaps being brutally treated in an interrogation. 5. We can treat him as bound together with others in a team or combat unit where his cry will be in conformity to or fall short of what is being prescribed. These five all take the evidence and evidenced to be terminal points in a setting, and allow one to move into the individual in his privacy as one who sustains, maintains, explains, produces, or assesses the terminal points.

There is also a way of dealing with these very evidences and what is evidenced as occurrences which are being individually expressed, independently of any kind of connection that holds between the individual and others. 6. What is accepted is grounded in, possessed by what is more substantial than itself. 7. It can be accepted as the expression of one who is holding himself apart from all else, the expression of pain being a way of remarking on the fact that something is being undergone over against all others, also taken to have private sides. 8. It can be accepted as what is to be explained (perhaps as occurring together with other public manifestations) by going back to what is more unified and offers a necessity, explanatory of the plurality of expressions. 9. It can be accepted as being the outcome of an activity having its origin within the individual. 10. It can be accepted as the public manifestation of a being having a certain value.

Two questions crowd to the fore. Might one be able to view all of these as in an hierarchy, so that some one, perhaps, the fifth, has all the others as special cases? Should one view all of these, whether taken to be coordinate, or in an hierarchy, to be subordinate primarily to one of them (say the fifth as applicable to all men and on the deepest level, where, for example, the I is and functions), then subordinate to two of them (one of which is a case of the first, and the other of the fourth)?

Once these questions are faced, one will have to answer the question as to whether or not there are other ways of connecting the ten, as pertinent to sensitivity, with one another, and also to whatever is pertinent to more recessive private dimensions.

The first question is to be answered negatively. There seems to be no reason why we should say, for example, that the kind of bonding that a man has with some others, and in which his sensitivity is properly or improperly expressed as a cry of pain, precedes or succeeds a situation where he acts in response to a force, or provides an explanation for the occurrence of the pain as at that time. If we answer the second question in the affirmative—as I think we should—holding that the initial situation providing evidence of the I is one where an individual is subject to the common prescription of humankind, we can say that the bonding, which has a publicly expressed sensitivity as a term, instances in a limited way the prescription characteristic of humankind. We can then go on to affirm that the other nine cases also illustrate that primary bonding, either in more limited forms, or (to refer to the other five cases, 6-10) as sustaining these.

Is it plausible to hold that all of the distinguished cases of publicly expressed evidences of a private sensitivity are special cases of an original prescriptive humankind, or of the individuals which sustain the terms in that prescriptive humankind? I do not now see what the right answer is. Nor do I now see any way or any reason to hold that there are other ways of relating the different ways of looking at a bit of evidence (whether there are ten on every level, or descend toward one only, as we come closer to evidencing the presence of a private I) than that of coordination, taking them all to be on a footing, or hierarchically, taking them to be ordered as more or less answering some kind of prescription on that or on a higher level. (I will look at a football game on television for a while, and see then if I can answer some of these questions.)

It does not make sense to speak of the four types of settings as being instantiations of the fifth. But it does make sense to pair the fifth with the tenth, the fourth with the ninth, etc. since these differ as settings and the sustainings of terms in those settings. Consequently, we can say that the kind of setting in which the public expression of sensitivity occurs as a term, while having its own integrity and being pertinent to the expression of sensitivity, is also a special and limited case of the prescriptive bonding of mankind. If so, the expression of sensitivity will occur within the setting of the prescriptive bonding of mankind and is therefore to be understood to have the backing of mankind, while also occurring as a mere expression of man in a limited setting. We will look at the expression as that of a man with an I, at the same time that we take it to be just the expression of a his sensitivity.

When we attend to an expression produced by an immature human and thus by one not yet in possession of an I, we must take it to be the act of one whose sensitivity has been given an enhanced status, because it has been identified as the expression of one credited with a full human status. It is to have the expression of its sensitivity treated as the expression of one who had it enhanced. Though an infant's expression of sensitivity is privately initiated, the fact that the infant is in the human realm allows us to judge its expression of sensitivity within the final prescriptive frame pertinent to humans who have I's.

We bring the infant into the human realm of prescriptive bondings that apply to every human being. As a consequence, we take its sensitivity to be expressed, not only in its own appropriate manner, as the sensitivity of an infant in a limited situation, but as instancing a more basic prescription. Where an adult is subject to an ought to be he is supposed to carry out, an infant is taken to function within a more limited situation. The sensitivity it expresses is treated as the sensitivity of a human by having its expression accepted as occurring, not only in a world where it can function as a unit, but in a world where all humans are.

A mature man is subject to demands, is under common rules, is made to yield to common forces, and is governed by a final prescription. An infant's sensitivity is expressed as a term in five settings, each of which is a limited case of the most primary, characteristic of a full-grown human. The infant does not fall short of this (as a defective full-grown human might) but still is measured by it, at the same time that the sensitivity, and the infant as expressing itself in this way, are identified as in a world governed by prescriptions that only the mature can take as their representative responsibilities.

What is being said of the individual infant as providing a term in a setting, applies to it as well, as sustaining its expressions. We cannot say this if we know only the infant. Our understanding of an infant begins with the understanding of what it means to be human. Consequently, the infant's expressions of sensitivity are understood from the start both as being appropriate to it as an infant and as being ennobled by the infant's belonging to humankind.

It now sounds as if the infant would not belong to humankind if no one made it be there. This is true in the sense that the infant belongs to humankind only because it is in a humanly prescribed situation, and not because it is as yet in a position to play a full human role there. The very fact that it is in a human setting, though, means that it is humanized. We do not need an explicit acknowledgment or an explicit act of adoption of it into humankind; it is already part of this because it is born into the human world. Right from the start, it has a social role. Being at most a person, an infant cannot of itself fill out that role the way an adult can. But, as in the world of relations which adult humans produced, the infant's roles, and the settings in which these occur, are sustained, and thereby enriched by the roles and settings of adults and those which the adults provide for the infant.

November 12

We can approach anything on its own terms; as in an oppositional relation to ourselves, we can view it neutrally; we can interplay with it; and we can see it as having a degree of importance relative to us. (There is a tendency, when we deal with something on its own terms, to succumb to a reductionism. To avoid this we must see animals and men, for example, in contrast with things, as more than complications of physical things. They must be recognized to form islands in the physical world where they are governed by specialized forms of the laws governing that physical world. There is a tendency, too, when we view things in terms of the importance they have for us, to anthropomorphize what they are. To avoid this, we must recognize that they have a status and value of their own, and that the degree of importance they have for us tells us only that we are able to make use of them for our purposes, without denying to them the status of realities with their own degree of objective value.)

Once we have decided which of these approaches to take toward what we confront, we can proceed with five paired ways of characterizing evidences there. If we are interested in a privately grounded sensitivity, and wish to deal with it neutrally, we will see the evidence as a term in a relation connecting the sensitive being to others, as that which sustains what is related and is therefore to be characterized apart from its relation to others. We acknowledge what we confront and, on being frustrated, move back toward ourselves, find agencies for dealing with what had frustrated us, move into and beyond the frustrating, and end with an assessment of the result. This, we continue to do without or with loops, and thus by proceeding at any point to a new illustration of what we had been doing, or going through the same kind of cycle that we had just finished on a lower level.

Had we begun with evidence for the sensitivity of an animal, we would find that we could not go further into this than we were able to reach in our thrust from the evidence of sensitivity toward sensitivity itself. We could, though, view that sensitivity as enabling the animal to stand apart, to contrast with others, to provide an explanation for what it is expressing, to be the beginning of an activity, or to provide it with a way of assessing what it is confronting. If we do this, we stress the way the individual animal functions. But we could, instead, have taken the expression of sensitivity to be a term in a relation governing roles, demands, rationales, action, or prescriptions.

Every individual or relation can be viewed in terms of the ten-fold way of dealing with man at his best. When this is done, the sensitivity of an animal will be seen to express a way in which it is by itself, opposes, explains, is active, and evaluative, and is related through roles, by demands, laws, interplays, and prescriptions, as well as a way in which every one of these is a lesser form of those that characterize man. The lower forms do not make them into kinds of men, they are characterized in similar terms, but as lacking some essential features appropriate to men severally and together.

When we come to man himself, we can deal with the different kinds of evidences, and the private dimensions to which they lead, as in an hierarchy. Bodily sensitivity undergoes an experience with content; aesthetic sensitivity faces content; desire seeks it; interest socializes it; concern deals with it representatively; assumed accountability originates it; thought universalizes it; decision makes it determinate; obligation gives it an enriching objective; the I possesses it; and the *idio* makes it contribute to one's health. We are able to come to such an hierarchy because we already are at the highest point. Because we start with the idea of what it is to be in health (with the correlative idea of what it is to be a full member of a civilized community governed by a bounding prescription applicable to all men), we are able to look for an hierarchy of evidences leading to the recognition of different sources which make the evidences be found in cases where content is undergone, faced, sought, etc.

Evidently, I am now involved in the attempt to disentangle a number of sets of five paired factors. One set has to do with the way we approach anything; another with the ways in which physical things, animals, and men are to be dealt with, each of which is characterizable in a ten-fold way; a third with the envisagement of lower forms as subject to limited versions of the factors appropriate to the understanding of man; and a fourth with the understanding of immature humans as having the ten-fold characterization relate to one or a few sources in them, and with the understanding of other humans as falling short of, but being evaluated in terms of the analysis of a mature human who satisfies all the conditions fully.

When we wish to make a start with man at his best—by himself or as together with other humans—we must, as in every other case, proceed from what we in fact encounter. The discovery of what a man is at his best is therefore an *a posteriori* discovery; what is arrived at, however, is *a priori,* in the sense that it serves as the basis in terms of which all else can be ordered in an hierarchy in terms of which men themselves are to be judged as better and worse, and immature beings are seen to have only some of the agencies, or to use them in only some of the ways in which a mature man can. Once the *a priori* position is reached, it serves to order the others and to explain that from which we began.

What I have not yet been able to get into focus is a neat and adequate way of ordering or presenting all these different ways of approaching anything—mature or immature men, good and bad men, men and animals, different kinds of evidence, different bases in privacy, and different ways in which beings are together. Is the *idio* to be understood as an excellence in a five-fold form, grounding terms in another five forms? Do the I, responsibility, thought, etc. have the *idio's* ten-fold form in degenerate versions? Does aesthetic appreciation not only face content but undergo it, while bodily sensitivity just undergoes it? Does desire undergo, face, and use the content? Finally, do we come to the *idio* as that which controls all? Is there a difference between an hierarchy of private bases and, therefore, an hierarchy of more and more mature humans, as well as an hierarchy of humans, animals, and things, each of which has distinctive private bases, to be understood as versions of a good, mature man's? Is the difference between a mature human, an immature human, an animal, and a thing expressed by relating them to different numbers of different bases; to the kind of bases they have; or to both of these together? Is there an hierarchy from the *idio*, the I, through to the sensitivity? Is there another hierarchy in which a being has every subdivision of privacy except the *idio*, still another which has all except the *idio* and the I, and so on, until we come finally to what has just a sensitivity, and then below this just inanimates which can have potentialities only? If a man were to have an I but not an *idio*, because he had not yet arrived at the stage where the *idio* could function as an independently operating power, would that mean that he was a lower form of human? Is an immature human really of a different kind, but one which we bring into our orbit through the application of a five-fold relationship we have to others, and which we impose on the immature? When we provide an interpretation of the worlds of animals or things as having an objectivity, standing opposed to us, having their own distinctive laws, interacting in their own distinctive ways with their own kinds and one another, and providing a setting which they fit (the animals more or less depending on whether or not they are good specimens, and things doing so completely because they are just units there, or combinations of them) are we viewing them also as incipiently available to us as possessions? Do we contrast or oppose them? Do we subject them to our laws and technology as having a value in relation to us? Is the reason why an embryo, fetus, or infant, which has reached no higher state, say than that of having sensitivity, is different from an animal, the fact that it has a different kind of sensitivity, because we brought it into the human realm and thereby gave it a role there with a consequent enhancement of the value of the sensitivity, or because its sensitivity is different in kind, regardless of all else? Does it not have a distinctive privacy, not yet used, and therefore a sensitivity which is different from that possessed by animals and, like that possessed by adults, but differing from this in its inability to be enriched by other epitomizations and to affect these?

There is no question that, unless one holds something like an absolutistic idealistic position, one must allow for the reality of what is not a fully mature and excellently functioning human, and for the fact that the coming to be of man is not a necessity due to the inexorable working of an absolute. Once man is in existence, though, he can provide us with a measure of understanding what is of a lower order. The measure of what is lower gives a new status to the lower. By being dealt with in terms which measure it as limited, defective, not possessing the virtues of something else, the physical world is given an added dignity, just as a criminal is, in a law-abiding world. That fact must not be allowed to get in the way of the truth that both have integrities of their own, and are to be understood on their own terms. A criminal is also to be judged as falling short of what he ought to have been, just as an infant is to be judged as not yet at the stage where it will have various indeterminate promises realized.

A child is immature, not only in the sense that there is a contingent result—a mature individual with further powers and excellencies in terms of which it can be said to be immature—but because it has a privacy that could be made determinate in the form of a mature being. Must we not say something similar with respect to the world of things and animals? Is there some surplus to the world which they have not utilized but whose existence makes it possible for us to say, in abstraction from the presence of man, that they are not yet fully determinate forms of what could be? Is that surplus not to be found in a primordial privacy out of which the various ultimate particles are distinguished? Are there more and more advanced forms of actuality in which sections of that privacy interplay with specialized forms of universal conditions?

Because we know the determinate forms that have been realized, we can measure what has not been fully realized. As having unrealized forms, immature humans, animals, and things can be viewed as falling short, not of what they ought to be, but of what in fact is superior because it has realized what they did not and could not.

Now it seems that we have to say there is a greater potentiality or indeterminate privacy lurking behind or within things than there is in man or animals. In a sense this is true. Not that some one thing has a greater potentiality than an animal or a man, but the realm of nature, as the domain of the inanimate, has a surplus privacy which, in limited and specialized forms, is realized by animals and men. We can say this, of course, only so far as we see all the particles as not entirely separable from the primordial privacy, and take animals not to be free from a common 'species' privacy, while men are recognized to be individuals whose commonality is to be found in conditions which keep them together as men at their best, and therefore which function as prescriptions.

I am troubled by the last observation. Do not animals share a privacy? Do individual men congeal a privacy common to all things, or at least to all animals or separate species of them? There would be nothing amiss in saying that there was some privacy left over which underlay the privacies of individual men. If this were granted, then we would have to say that things, animals, and men all have privacies which are subtended by common privacies, but that the individual privacies of men were more determinate than the privacies of these others, a determinacy due to the utilization of some of the privacy common to animals and that had been part of the common privacy of ultimate particles.

No one man can exhaust all privacy; if he could, there would be no possibility for there being other men. And since we cannot deny that there can always be other men, each with his own privacy, we cannot hold that individual men, despite their concentrated use of a basic privacy, are able to exhaust it. But they can realize it to the extent that no thing or animal can realize its privacy. As a consequence, it is possible to view animals and things as not having realized a common privacy to the degree that men have.

If there is a surplus privacy, might there not be a possible encompassing entity which has that privacy as its own individual possession? Might there not be a kind of Hegelian state having its own privacy? This does not seem to be possible, for a state is not an actuality. What is possible is that men, under the governance of a state, could make the common privacy support them as together in their interplay with the structure of the state.

The common privacy left over by men is involved with the structure of a society. Men are always in societies, but may not be in states. Each society has a prescriptive binding character, defining the joint living of its members. A civilized society makes use of all the surplus privacy. In addition to the binding prescription, that society dictates a basic set of roles, recognizes rights, has a rationale, and has an unlimited technology.

The surplus privacy is not exhausted until we have a civilization in which all men are included in the way some are now included in limited civilized societies. The privacy which such a civilization uses provides the warrant for looking at animals and things as insufficiently developed (the analogue of immaturity). It is a privacy common to them, but which has not yet become determinate enough to be the privacy that could interplay with the five-fold condition characteristic of a civilization.

November 13

'Perfection' is to be understood in a number of ways: 1. It is the proper name of what is in fact perfect. God is often thought to be such a perfect reality. All else is understood to be so far defective, imperfect. Though one might speak of these as striving to conform to the demands which the perfect being may impose on them, they are kept within their own domains, and never move toward that perfection. 2. God or a One might be taken to be perfect and all other entities seen to fall short of it, as more confused (Leibniz), as pluralized, or degenerate forms of it (Plotinus), or quasi-real instantiations of it (Spinoza's modes). 3. The perfection could be some far-off reality toward which all things are moving. That reality would be an absolute, and everything else would be governed by it, and so far would be functioning well. The luring perfection might be gentle, merely persuasive (Whitehead), or a powerful agent (de Chardin), or what acts directly only on what is closest to it and through this on other lower orders (Aristotle). 4. The perfection could be divided according to kinds, each 'species' having its own type of perfection. This, too, seems to be an Aristotelian view. The perfection could be treated as powerful and that on which it works passive, or as that which is serving as some kind of lure, with the entities which are being lured making some contribution. The first of these alternatives seems to be Aristotle's, the second Whitehead's. 5. The perfection could be what had been attained in the world, in the form of excellent specimens—splendid animals, plants, humans. 6. The perfection could be what a number had attained together. Civilization, society, cooperative groups—most generally, a form of togetherness—would here be dealt with either in terms of one type which men, or men of a certain kind had reached, or as having a different import for different types of being. 7. It could be identified with what was within the reach of each individual, so that each would be open to judgment for being or failing to be as perfect as he himself could be. 8. Viewing the greatest attainments of men as perfections which are to measure others as so far immature or defective, one can take the unrealized potentialities in them to require determination (just as the realized potentialities had), and on that basis to define a still higher form of perfection than that which had been attained. 9. The last could be thought of as the result of the operation of a condition alone, of beings with potentialities, of a common potentiality, or of combinations of these.

When we attend to beings other than men, we need do no more than note the attainments of men, and measure those other beings in terms of it. But we should have recourse to these two ways of viewing perfection only with respect to man, or when we are thinking of the possibility of 'improving the breed' of subhumans. It is because we already know that mature men are responsible beings, with I's, capable of assuming accountability, thinking, deciding, and the like, that we are able to understand the young as immature. It is because we already know that some men have lived up to their responsibilities, thought, etc., that we are able to understand others as defective, criminal, or ill.

November 14

Riding to school on the subway this morning, I jotted down the following in shorthand:

We say that an infant, and even a viable fetus, is a person because it has a role in human society. If we gave such a role to an animal, it might fill it, but it would not sustain it. The sustaining of the role means that the person stands in contradistinction to all else. Both the animal and the infant can have a bodily sensitivity, an aesthetic sensitivity, and bodily and unconfined desires and interests, but they will still differ because only the one has these sustained by a person. This maintains itself, is in control, uses, explains, and evaluates the sensitivity, etc. More important, it is open to a surplus privacy and becomes the locus of the claims of concern, reflection, and assumed accountability. If we credited these to an animal, we would still have to note that the animal was not able to be the locus of rights of the psyche; it would not have a psyche which was related to the sensitivity, etc., as the person was to its epitomizations. That psyche involves activities which are all private.

If we credited an animal with a psyche we would also have to say it controls, etc. and that it has a person where the rights of that psyche were localized and satisfied. We would still leave over the fact that it did not have responsibility, resolution, or an I. If we credited these to the animal, we would not yet have credited the animal with a self, with a power to control, utilize, etc. If we credited the animal with a self, we would have to say that the rights of a self were also carried by its person.

We have a warrant for holding that there is a psyche and self because of the different kinds of roles that men could have. There is a pysche because the roles are adopted on the basis of principles privately accepted. To refuse to carry out those roles is to be unfair. There is a known self because the roles are acknowledged to be prescriptive, defining one as wrong, not merely as defective or immature.

An animal fits into a scheme. A person is given roles in a human society. A psyche accepts tasks in various enterprises. A self submits to prescriptions governing men, mediated perhaps by the state. The *idio* represents the prescriptions which should hold of all.

I now add further reflections to the preceding notes:

We acknowledge a bodily and an aesthetic sensitivity, confined and unconfined desires, and confined and unconfined interests in an animal. But we do not suppose that these are epitomizations of a single power that has a status of its own and controls the animal, perhaps even expresses itself through it, and gives the animal a dignity it would not have were the power not present. Such a single power is only in a person, a locus of rights. An animal, it seems correct to say, has rights, but no single locus for them, no status in itself and in public, possessing rights which are native, demanding public recognition.

An infant has sensitivity and desire at once, and might even be said to have interests. It does not seem reasonable to say that it has these in unconfined forms. But it is reasonable to say that it has them at the forefront of a privacy that could be realized in unconfined forms. Or, if unconfined forms are attributed to it, we could say that it has the confined and unconfined both at the forefront of a privacy able to control them, and which in itself representatively urges the rights which they severally contain. An infant is immediately caught up (and so is the viable fetus) in human situations where it has roles, but no tasks or duties.

The fact that a fetus and infant have a surplus privacy which could be made determinate in the form of a psyche and a self, makes it possible for them to become human persons. The roles will make their privacies be determinate as persons in control of sensitivity, desire, and interest. Such a person is much more than just a unity of the three could be.

One consequence of reflections such as these is that if a viable fetus or an infant is made to suffer pain because of an injury, the pain, as a mere sensitively felt occurrence, would be like an animal's and yet different from this because it was backed by a surplus privacy that could be made determinate as a person in control of that sensitivity, and as a psyche and self which could have their rights sustained by and carried out by the person.

The stages in a human being could be formulated by attending to the different evidenced activities of animals, though it seems equally plausible to say that we differentiate confined and unconfined expressions of privacy in them because we first recognized them in men. If we insist on attending to public evidence, we must take our start with what at first seems to be evidence of animal-like actions. It is only when we see the living being in a context that we are forced to recognize that it provides a unity for all three types of confined and unconfined expressions. The unity could conceivably be that of an aggregate in the animal or, if taken to be undivided, to be just the privacy as ready to be expressed in public. But a viable fetus and infant are in a context, where they are inescapably units in human settings, forcing the acknowledgement that the confined and unconfined forms are in the control of a person. That person cannot be identified with the unity which we credit to an animal. This does not sustain roles, does not control the different epitomizations of it, and, most important, does not have behind it a surplus privacy which can be made determinate by it in a psyche and self, and whose presence would make the person be qualitatively different (and therefore its epitomizations) from the supposed unity of an animal.

An animal is not a primitive or immature kind of a human, it has no capacity to be a human. A fetus and infant have a surplus privacy which could in principle be made determinate as the higher powers of a human. As open to such determination, their persons are of a different order from an animal's unity. Their persons not only control sensitivity etc., absorbing and taking over the task of preserving and urging their rights, but enable them to take on roles. They can be affected by the determinations of the surplus privacy in the form of assumed accountability etc. and of the psyche, self, and *idio*.

We recognize that there is a concern, reflection, and assumed accountability, and that these are under the control of a psyche, when we note that the human which had already been acknowledged to be a person, not only fills roles but takes up tasks which it sees that it is to fulfill unless it is to be counted as incompetent and perhaps unfair. If we assign tasks to an animal as a result of training, it will not have the status of a human, precisely because it cannot take the tasks as its own, something it is to carry out to express what it is. The closest we can come to a psyche in an animal is in the form of a unity of a concern and reflection. If we can imagine that it can assume accountability, we will still have no warrant for supposing that this could be related and governed by a psyche, that it is able to act on its own, sustain tasks and be judged in terms of the way these are carried out. The psyche allows a man to dictate to the world of rewards and punishments whether or not these are properly bestowed. This is not possible to an animal. It might look offended on being accused falsely, but it will not disdain rewards as undeserved. If it could do this, it still would not have a surplus privacy which could be made determinate as its self, and whose presence therefore, even if only in the form of an indeterminate privacy, makes the concern, reflection, and assumed accountability have a different import than they would have were they not inseparable from the surplus privacy.

We know that men have wills and the power to choose (and that their preferences, as a consequence, are not identifiable with the kinds of preferences possible to animals, since these are not subject to a possible control by choice, will, responsibility, and an I). We find men in situations where they have to live up to various prescriptions, specialized in those situations, and in fact operating on all no matter what the situation. To be able to be not only the objects of these prescriptions, but to be measured by them, the men must be capable of deciding, being obligated, and being guilty or innocent, and thus to have powers of resolution, to be responsible, and to have I's. If these be credited to an animal, it still would not be true that the animal had a self, in control of these, ordering them with respect to one another, and having behind it a surplus privacy which could be made determinate in the form of a controlling *idio*, which determines health, not merely of a body, but of a privacy able to function apart from, as well as in and through the body.

The various kinds of situations—those in which animals fit, those which involve roles, those which require various tasks to be performed, and those where one ought to act in certain ways, build on a surplus privacy common to a multiplicity of entities. To begin with, there is the privacy that is beyond all the particles; this is made more determinate in a world of complex actualities, more determinate in a world of living beings, still more determinate in the social world of men, and perfectly determinate in an ideal civilization.

When we recognize different grades in the private powers of a man, with bodily sensitivity on one end and the I, self, or *idio* on the other, we initially borrow from what we learned from a study of animals, whether or not this had been guided by a previous understanding of man. All the while we recognize that because men have surplus privacies they give a different import to what is taken to be like an animal's privacy. It is not until we come to choice and will, responsibility, and the I, and then to the self and the *idio*, that we free ourselves entirely from animal reference, and pay attention to men as sustaining units in a prescriptive civilized world.

In light of the fact that the psyche has a surplus behind it, to be made determinate as the self and its epitomizations, we could say that the world of mankind, with its tasks, though different from the species with its required functionings, is sustained by a psyche, leaving the men as persons who have the task of carrying out roles. We can make our differentiations of the first three stages in the person in the light of what we have learned about animals; the second three (with the psyche) could be approached either by starting with animals or with men as together in a single mankind; the third requires our awareness of what it means to be civilized, subject to moral prescriptions.

Utilitarians sometimes speak as though they are looking at men as functioning together the way animals do. But they, too, understand that men are in a prescriptive situation and that there are things they ought not to do even if the greatest happiness would thereby be promoted. Utilitarians do not demand the punishment of an innocent man for the benefit of all. But even if we held that this too might be required, it remains true that one who does not do what the utilitarian requires is supposed to be not inept or immature, but bad, wicked, someone who does what is wrong.

If a lion eats its cubs or a cat plays with a mouse, they do not do what is wrong, but just what lions do when they are hungry and cats do when they are not. Wrong is possible only to a man. We shoot the lion that bites it trainer, not because it is a wicked lion, doing what it ought not, but because it does not do what we do not want to have done. Even were a man to do what many would endorse, e.g., shooting a Hitler on sight—it would still be a wrong act, the treating of a human as not a human. If a doctor had to treat Hitler, he would have to try to help him. After he had been helped, the doctor would have the problem of knowing what to do next. In the context of a war, Hitler should be shot; outside that context, he should be brought to trial.

How can we allow in war what we otherwise would not? Does it define the breakdown of civilized life, which we vainly try to shore up with agreements made in peace time, such as the Geneva convention, or international law, or does it redefine men as beings who, though not animals, are still not men subject to civilized prescriptions? Would they be men who had tasks, and thus who had momentarily lowered their status from beings with selves to those who had just psyches with a promise to have selves? Of course, as individuals, they would have selves, but in the context of the war facing the enemy, they could be said to define themselves to be operating as psyches in the sense that they took account only of their tasks. One could also say that they reached this stage because they were obligated to do so, that because they were civilized and had selves they were required to hold the civilization and selves in abeyance for a while.

We abandon civilization to engage in war (even when this is done on behalf of civilization). A war is governed by human values because the selves and the civilized world are able to be made present again through the imposition of determinations on individual and common privacies. War must therefore be understood (somewhat as a society or state is) in reference to final prescriptions which all men ought to fulfill.

War gives us one of two choices. We are full men but are behaving wrongly; or we have the promise to be full men and war is the way in which we must now operate as beings whose civilization and selves are not operative, but which, by means of the war, can eventually be made so. These eventualities define the war as something more than injuring and killing of men for the preservation of imperfect societies or states.

November 15

The acknowledgment of a mature being makes conspicuous the grades of potentiality in earlier forms and how these make a difference to the nature of these. In addition to the potentiality that the lower is able to exercise, there is a dormant potentiality continuous with it. This will be realized in whole or part only after realizations of the active ones bring the being to a higher, more mature level. There is such a dormant potentiality in embryos in relation to fetuses, and these in relation to the new born. It is not easy to determine just how many stages should be acknowledged in between the latter and the fully mature man. (*The Making of Men* offers one suggestion.) If there is more than one stage from embryo to infant, or from infant to mature man, the lower does not have dormant what will be used by the highest, but only by what is at the next stage above itself. Otherwise, we would have to speak of the embryo as an immature human or an immature citizen. Dormant potentiality or privacy is not to be understood transitively; only a part of it (until we come to a final stage) bears on what could be exercised at a given stage.

When we attend to the privacy common to particles or animals, these are to be seen as also having dormant potentialities for the next stage, while still leaving over portions that remain dormant. A dormant potentiality, as operative at the next stage, gives the potentiality operative on the lower a status it otherwise would not have. The stage below the species man is animal, but an animal humanized.

A fetus has neither a human sensitivity nor an animal sensitivity. It has a humanized sensitivity which could be exercised by a higher form, a viable fetus. Its private rights are those of a being that is more than an animal and less than a human being.

We should not look to animals for an understanding of the sensitivity of man. Instead, we should look to the mature man, and then try to understand the sensitivity of an infant as having behind it a dormant privacy that will be realized in part in the mature individual. The presence of that dormant privacy enhances the actual privacy, with the consequence that the infant, on exercising its own privacy, gives the outcome a meaning it otherwise would not have apart from that dormant factor. The dormant potentiality or privacy, thus, though it has no role to play in what the being does, does make a difference to the value of what is in fact being expressed. The dormant does not act; it provides a context which gives what acts a new import.

We must acknowledge the mature, not as a control or a lure, but solely as providing the opportunity to recognize a dormant potentiality, with a consequent understanding of this as having a status not to be known by taking it as it is, or even with the potentialities it is able to realize.

The publicly available evidence of the privacy of a mature man is directed toward something on a higher level than the privacy of immature humans or animals. These have dormant what the mature has as active. References to the sensitivity, desire, and interest of animals or children should ground comparisons; they do not provide evidence of what is true of mature men. The fundamental blunder of socio-biology or other attempts to understand men from the vantage point of cells or animals, or from an examination of the way children learn and the like, is that they overlook the fact that a dormant privacy provides only a context and value enrichment, and not real potentiality for it. A dormant privacy does not contribute to the realization of a lower potentiality; this alone is active, and works on its own.

1980

January 23

Since the last entry, I have received and read an unbound copy of *You, I, and the Others,* gone to Portugal for a week's vacation, and have been rewriting the first part of what I have been calling 'An Exploration of Human Privacy'. I have found a number of places in *You, I, and the Others* that must be altered to avoid unnecessary obscurity and apparent contradictions. In rewriting the discussion of privacy, I have found it necessary to expand my previous manuscript to about twice the size. I am also having trouble with problems which I thought I had dealt with well. In particular, I am now not clear about the nature and origin of bodies. It is not enough to take for granted that there are ultimate particles; the nature of their bodies and the relation of these to privacies should be explained.

Apart from the manuscript, I have been entertaining the prospect that each of the final conditions have all the others as subordinates. In fact, a few years ago I examined that prospect in some detail, but put the work aside because it seemed to me to be proceeding too mechanically. But the idea has pushed itself to the fore again. In speaking of all the particles together, I referred to their common potentiality. This seems to be nothing under than Substance as subordinating all the other finalities. When that common potentiality counters and is countered by conditions expressing other finalities, it faces them all as subordinated to Possibility. Consequently, it can be said to meet itself in a subordinated role. If this makes sense, it will be proper to ask a. whether or not all the other finalities meet themselves in subordinated roles, and b. what is the outcome of the meeting.

a. It would seem to be correct to say that every finality in a dominant position faces itself as under the dominance of four other finalities. But does it face only itself? Does not potentiality, for example, not only face a subordinated Substance but the dominant Possibility and thereby become subject to law? Does it not face a subordinated Being, Existence, and Unity as well, and thereby become subordinate to a coordinative, an extensionalizing, and an assessive power? Must it not in fact meet Existence as dominating over all, and as subordinated to them as well, in order to be extensionalized? It seems to be reasonable to answer the questions affirmatively. What is left over is the question of the origin of ultimate particles, the rest of actualities being capable of being understood as the outcome of what is common to ultimate particles, specialized and interacting with specialized versions of subordinated and subordinating finalities.

Why are there many particles? Why do these have bodies? What is the relation of their bodies to their privacies? Are bodies constituted by the interplay of subordinating hierarchies of finalities? Is a body the outcome of the emphasis by any subordinating finality on itself in a subordinated role? Or is it the outcome of the emphasis only on Substance as a subordinating potentiality to itself as a subordinated prescription? If so, what is the nature of the outcome of a subordinating potentiality to other subordinated prescriptions; to itself as subordinated to Being, Existence, and Unity; to other finalities as subordinated by these?

The most promising suggestion seems to be that a dominant Substance in the role of a universal potentiality interplays with itself as dominated by the other finalities. Does the encounter require that there be a breaking up of what is constituted by their meeting? If so, why does the breaking up not continue to infinity? And why does it have the status of a body with a privacy? And, in every case where a subordinating finality meets itself in a subordinated role, we have a reciprocal cases where what made it subordinate meets itself in a subordinated role. If a common dominant potentiality meets a subordinated Substance that prescribes to it, there is also a dominant prescriptive Possibility (subordinating Substance) that meets itself as dominated by a common potentiality. Does a conflict between these dominants pluralize and yield a body at the place where the dominators-dominateds meet? Is the result a substantial potentiality and a promised or incipiently realized possibility? What happens to the finalities which are dominated both by Possibility and Substance, the one as prescriptive, the other as grounding or potential? Being, Existence, and Unity, in the particular case, will have subordinate roles in each hierarchy and as joined. But does not the hierarchy, for example, where Being is dominant, also function at that time? Will we not have five dominant finalities meeting themselves in subordinated positions, each of the dominants being dominated in four ways? Will not the substantial potentiality be met by Substance as subordinated to Being, Possibility, Existence, and Unity? Will not each of these be subordinated to the substantial potentiality? And must we not then go on to take Being, Possibility, Existence, and Unity to be dominating over a substantial potentiality so as to constitute a counter to themselves and the others? These questions, I think, all require affirmative answers. What the complex result is like is the next question, to be followed by the question whether or not it does clarify what a body is, and why there are many bodies. And if it does, whether or not it clarifies something else as well.

The questions do not keep clear the fact that we have just five hierarchies of finalities, and that if we start with one of them, there is the problem of the relation of what is subordinating, to itself as subordinated in the others, with the rest of the relations understood as qualifying the result. If so, putting aside the ordering within an hierarchy, we will have just five cases to consider, with each finality in a dominant role in one, and having subordinated roles in the others. If Substance's dominant role is in an hierarchy of groundings, it will be faced by four distinct hierarchies in each which it has a subordinate role, and in which the dominant finality matches what a potentiality subordinated. What is true of Substance will be true of the other finalities.

Only Substance dominates as a ground. Being dominates in an interrelationship; Possibility in the form of prescriptive laws; Existence as effective and extensional; and Unity as ordering. Do they answer to the I, you and me, the simple we, the complex we, and the others? Does the meeting of a substantial grounding potentiality, subordinating other groundings (with Substance as subordinated to Being, Possibility, Existence, and Unity), end in one kind of pluralization, and in the meeting, say of a dominating Existence which is subordinated to the others? Or, as seems more plausible, do all the hierarchies meet and produce a single outcome? Is a body the product of all the finalities in dominant positions meeting themselves in four subordinated ones?

A substantial grounding seems to be prior to all others, so far as the understanding of a world of bodies is concerned. If so, the question of bodies comes down to understanding the meeting of a dominating grounding, with Substance as subordinated to the other finalities. The simplest way to begin, it would seem, is to start with a dominating substantial grounding, meeting Substance in four subordinated roles, leaving the other possibilities to ground the way in which the result exhibits Being, etc. That means, for the time being, accepting a priority for Substance, though perhaps only with respect to the problem of the origin of a plurality of bodies.

*   *   *

I have just returned from a department meeting where my colleagues tried to determine what status they had, and how much freedom they had over against the university and particularly over against the Vatican. They are trying to maintain a distance, but it is not clear to what degree the distance can be maintained while still remaining a department and a university under pontifical jurisdiction. On and off, and later, I continued to think about today's reflections. For the moment, I think I will conclude with saying that each finality in a dominant position meets itself as subordinated by others. To make a match between itself as dominant and itself as dominated, on meeting, the two break up into a plurality of entities. There are five of these matches, ending in five kinds of entities—substantial, self-maintained, intelligible, self-bounding, and assessive. All occur at the same time. It is not therefore correct to suppose that there are just bodies, or that these underly the self-maintained, etc. pluralities.

A plurality of entities is the outcome of a five-fold fractionization, initially of a dominated component, and secondarily of the dominating as that which is to express itself through the dominated. The units, with this five-fold status, have their own integrity, and as such are in a position to interplay with the dominating conditions, both as having a universal application and as specialized. The units all have a limited reality because they are prevented from being further fractionated by the exercise of the power of a dominating finality on itself as dominated.

We could conceivably begin with a plurality of self-maintained beings, intelligible natures, limited existences, or particular values, and take the others (as well as substantial beings) to qualify them, to be alongside them or, as I think is correct, to be moments within substantial units. An interest in bodies leads to an emphasis on substantial units and to a limited use for other kinds of unit. But if we start with say, intelligible natures, we will be able to view substantial bodies as special cases of such intelligible natures, just as we can view these as special cases of substantial actualities. Only because we are interested in understanding how ultimate particles could provide the initial material for all there is, do substantial actualities, and thus the interplay of a dominant and dominating Substance, come to the fore.

January 25

In the manuscript I mentioned the other day, I treated dominated finalities as though they were in an hierarchy. That is part of the reason why the whole became mechanical—I tried to go through all the variations. But there is no need to suppose that they do form an hierarchy; conceivably, they could all be dominated together. Or one can imagine the differences in the items in an hierarchy being so small as not to make it worthwhile to attend to them.

If there are five groups of finalities, with one dominant and the others dominated, we start at a position Hegel thinks he must arrive at. He supposed that the dominant finality not only was singular, but that it divided itself against itself; just why or how, it is not easy to see. It had, he thought, to make itself be for itself. Let this be granted. Why does it not do the job at once? The answer I suppose is that to be for itself it must be spelled out in detail. But once again, why doesn't this spelling out occur all at once? Isn't Hegel's just a system of categories? Could he possibly tell us why there are many unit entities, and particularly bodies? I don't see how he could.

If there are five finalities, each dominating over the other four, each will be divided from itself, not because it did something to itself but because it is inevitably caught in a subordinated position in four groups. The effort to make itself one with all its subordinated forms requires it to struggle against the dominance of other finalities over its dominated forms. The meeting of a dominating and dominated finality is never entirely successful, for the dominated never can be made to measure up to the dominating. The remedy is to have the two together avoid the other dominating finalities by so joining that they constitute a plurality of unit actualities.

Each actuality is the product of a union of a dominating finality with itself as dominated. As dominating it has the status of an active privacy; as dominated it has the status of a body. Bodies are loci of the dominated forms of a finality made one with a dominating form. The match is not perfect, for the dominating finality, even when it is specialized in the form of a common potentiality, needs its dominated forms to be on a footing with it. But bodies, though continuous with privacies, lack the power to act on a dominant finality with the same force and intensity that it acts on all of them. Still, something is achieved. A plurality of bodily actualities, each with its own privacy, is produced, all under the possessive control of the dominating finality in the form of a privacy in each.

If this is right, a body is a finite four-fold dominated finality continuous with a dominant finality. Is this not close to Hegel and his all-encompassing categories? Must bodies be analyzed as consisting of nothing but dominated finalities? How would it be possible for the five groups of finalities to be together? How could there even be five to come together were there not a One apart from them all? And if the One for them is, as I have held in *First Considerations,* an actualtiy, how could the actuality be the outcome of the meeting of the finalities?

We must say both that the explanation of the presence of bodies does not make a reference to what comes later in time; and that once finite entities are in existence, they have their own integrities and therefore can act on one another and function as a One for all the finalities.

There never are just finalities or groups of them; there also are actualities with privacies and bodies. But if we wish to explain the latter we must have recourse to the former in an analytic account. If that is so, must we not also say that we can start with actualities having privacies and bodies, and understand the finalities as generalized variants of these? Yes. But unlike those who suppose that philosophy is the discipline which makes such generalizations, it is here being maintained that the generalized variants are ontological, distinct, and functioning, just as surely as actualities are the finalities condensed and in a relation of dominating to dominated.

Must we not also go on to say that, though Substance, for example, can be understood to be an active potentiality in the guise of a private insistent power, and that the bodies of actualities are substantial dominated forms of this, each actuality is also subject to the dominating forms of all the other finalities? I think so. But it is not clear whether this adds anything to the claim that each of the finalities separately acts on each actuality.

Bodies are not categories and they cannot be produced by deduction; finalities are not categories either, and cannot be reached simply by generalization. But once they both are granted to be real, we can account for the one as the outcome of the activity of the other, and can account for that other as an intensive form of what is found in the one. If the first move is called a 'deduction' it is a deduction that is dialectical; if the second is called a 'generalization', it is one which moves by intensification.

January 26

I am not yet satisfied with the account of the origin of a plurality of bodies. Any finality is faced with itself as subordinated by four other finalities. There is then some kind of plurality to begin with, where a finality is somehow sundered from itself. Since its subordinated forms are subject to different dominant finalities, must it not, as dominant, act on the other groups of finalities in different ways? And must it not solidify all its subordinated versions to make them into a single matching counterpart? Can it do this in any other way than piecemeal, and thus by fractionating itself (into privacies) which forge single appropriate bodies out of the subordinated versions? If these questions are answered in the affirmative, it seems that we must then recognize that the epoch in which a finality finds one solution to the problem of joining itself to its own four subordinated versions, could give way to another where another effort was made, with another result. If this is possible, we would have the problem of knowing when and how such a new effort was made.

The idea of five groups is perhaps misleading. It is better, perhaps, to see a finality as being subjected to other finalities and, as a consequence, attempting to achieve an equilibrium by accepting itself as subordinated, but on its own terms. This will require it, as a distinct finality, to deal with itself as subject to the other finalities on its own terms. It must possess those subordinated versions. The acceptance of the subordinated versions as its own is one with the having of many passive versions of itself subject to many versions of itself as active. But it is not yet evident to me that there has to be a fractionization.

Suppose a finality could not get all the subordinated versions on a footing? There seem to be two alternatives: it could continue the effort again and again until they were on a footing, or it could accept the result, and match it with an appropriate subdivision of itself. The pluralization of the finalities and the contingency of the result could then be seen to be the outcome of the need to accept whatever subordinating there is, and to make the result somehow continuous with itself.

Perhaps the alternatives are: a finality, being faced with different ways in which it is being subordinated, possesses them in different ways to make itself one with all those subordinated forms; or it breaks up into a multiplicity of units, each of which is a unit possessing itself as a unit. Where a single finality might conceivably possess all its subordinated versions in different ways, a subdivision of that finality could itself unite with a fractionated form of all the subordinated versions together. The two are compatible. As a finality possesses in different ways all the other subordinated versions of itself, it breaks up into a plurality of units, each of which possesses in only one way one fraction of all the subordinated versions. The leaving over of the initial finality provides a reservoir for the latter. In the one way, a finality yields to the subordination of itself by others, and keeps itself one by matching the subordination with cor-responding acts of possession; in the other way, it breaks up into a plurality of distinct acts of possession of distinct parts of the solidified union of all the subordinated versions. When broken up into a multi-plicity of distinct acts of possession, the possessive act can be more insistent and be in more effective control than is the case when the finality merely matches subordinations of itself with appropriate balancing acts.

This is not yet right. A finality, as a unit, can do no more than adjust itself to the limitations it suffers due to other finalities. If it could do more, it would somehow be stronger than they are, and the finalities would not be on a footing. The only way it can insist on itself despite what the other finalities do to it, is to defeat them by not dealing with the result of their subordinating. To do this it must act, not only by subordinating the other finalities as they subordinate it—something that occurs regardless of what they are doing to it and therefore when the finality is being subordinated by them—but by possessing what has been subordinated. But it cannot possess this except as something less than itself. Instead, as single it can do no more than adjust itself to the result. But to adjust itself to itself as a subordinated finality is to adjust itself to what is itself in a lesser mode. Consequently, it must supplement the adjustment with acts of possession. These cannot be directed at the subordinated versions of itself; it is to these it adjusts itself unsatisfactorily and beyond which it cannot go in view of the insistence of the other finalities. As insistent, it multiplies itself to make corresponding parts of the subordinated versions into multiple continuations and possessions. To be insistent, and therefore not to be just submissive to the outcome of the subordination of itself to other finalities, it divides into multiple insistent privacies, each possessing itself in the form of a subdivision of the finality as subordinated, limited, not sufficiently insistent. The result is single entities in which the privacy and body are on a footing, the one insistent, the other marked by qualifications of other finalities, and the two made one by an act of possession by the insistent privacy. If there were no finality left over, able to function as a unit, each would be self-destructive. Not only would there be no finalities any more, but the finite entities would have no reserve, no common reservoir of power of which use could be made. Each ultimate particle would not only have made itself into a single unity of an insistent privacy and a body, which is qualified by the other finalities, but would have no capacity to change, to interact, or to make possible wholes and complex individuals.

An outline of these ideas would look something like this:

1. Each finality dominates over all the others.

2. The result is that each finality has an insistent undivided form, and four distinct qualified forms.

3. To be a single finality it must not be divided against itself.

4. No finality can free itself from the domination of the others.

5. If there were nothing else it could do, it would have to adjust itself to the situation, without losing its claim to be insistent. But such an adjustment makes it give up something of itself for the sake of being harmonized with versions produced by others.

6. To remain insistent, not divided against itself, it can have no other recourse but to possess what the others produced through the subordinating of it.

7. It must insist on itself, make that which it reaches to be continuous with itself, consistently with its continuing to be subordinated to the other finalities.

8. It succeeds by dividing itself into a multiplicity of insistences, each effectively possessing a portion of itself as subordinated.

9. Each unit of the multiplicity has its own integrity; each can therefore be under the control of the finality, and offer it and others a One for their Many.

10. As not used, an undivided, insistent finality is a common potentiality in the form of a reservoir, which the finite entities could use in helping to constitute wholes, and which may itself become insistent in a limited form as the privacy of individuals.

11. The body of a substantial actuality is a possession of a division of an insistent finality.

12. Four other kinds of finite entities are also produced.

January 27

Yesterday's suggestion allows one to say that created works are the individual caught in an alien context. In order to recover the individual's full creative meaning, he will have to free the work from the alien influence, and make it his own in acts of appreciation. Conversely, from the side of the world, an individual artist's intention is a physiological occurrence subordinated to personal considerations. Its status as such an occurrence is to be recovered in the history of art.

A state's laws are met by the people as subject to a society. The state must therefore act in individualized ways in order to make the people be the public side of itself. Conversely, a society takes the people to be subject to the alien control of the state, and must try to recover the people as the purely subjective side of itself.

The recognition of the reciprocals in both cases points up the fact that we cannot take an actual entity to be just a substantial privacy with a possessed body. That overemphasizes Substance, and ignores the equal standing of the other finalities. Where then is the unity of an actual entity? It cannot lie in some alien power, without denying the entity its integrity. It cannot be provided by the several finalities without denying the actualities a power to act on those finalities. It cannot be the outcome of a constant shifting of power amongst the insistencies, for not only are they all present at the same time and with the same force, but the result would make the actuality a mere arena and not a unit reality. Instead, we must, I think, say that there is a midpoint where the substantial privacy ends and the body begins. It is at that point that the other finalities also are as active as they are passive. An actuality is a one, at the point of intersection of all the finalities as active with themselves as passive, and thus as subject to the others. At that common point, each actuality continues into what others had subjugated, at the same time that it moves to subjugate these others. As a consequence, we have four insistencies meeting at a single point where each makes the others passive, at the same time that each lays hold of its own converted states.

January 31

The attempt to speak of all things in cosmological terms, whether these be framed by philosophers or scientists, tacitly makes the supposition that what occurs in local situations is not real, is a complication of what happens cosmologically, is just an arbitrarily demarcated place, or has only a derivative status. But if, instead, aware that individual entities have an integrity even in those cosmologies, we affirm that as in limited regions, items are distinctively constituted, and that the conditions with their boundaries help constitute what is occurring in those regions, we can recognize islands of activity having their own laws. We can still allow that when we abstract from those regions, the items can be in the cosmos on the same terms as others, and therefore as denuded of the distinctive natures they have in those regions. A man is distinctive in his milieu but is a congeries of units in a cosmological frame. Substituting the latter for the former would be like substituting a collection of books for a library, two people together for a brother and sister, husband and wife, or child and parent.

If, with the Wittgensteineans, anthropologists, sociologists and those who take some one discipline alone to yield truth, we take one bounded area and its contents to be primary, all others will have to be viewed as complications or abstractions of this. But the others, with equal warrant, can take themselves to be basic. If we allow that all contexts have legitimacy, and that the scientific universe is the largest of all, whether or not we take it to provide defining characteristics for what is within its confines, we are faced with the question of how to deal with them all. What I have been doing these last years could be seen as providing those universal principles which apply to any situation, and taking the principles to be specialized in distinctive ways, to interact with a limited number of items, and to produce a complex 'we' in the different cases. The items, as apart from all the conditions, are the actualities in themselves; the conditions, as apart from the actualities, are intensive, unitary, and final. Dealing with the two as joined in a metaphysical scheme yields, not what is real, but a schema of the real, that which is made concrete by being contracted within the limits of special domains.

February 2

Often explicitly, but sometimes implicitly, I have been following the lead of a number of principles. The following come to mind immediately:

1. Unities are intensified versions of a multiplicity of expressions.

2. Entities are translators of different expressions into one another.

3. Wherever we stop we also engage in a premonitional thrust beyond, toward an object or conditions, i.e., toward what is alongside, or toward what is at the other side of the boundary at which we end.

4. Every entity and every group of entities forms an enclave or domain with its own distinctive laws and activities. To deal with those entities within a larger set requires one to ignore the distinctive unities, tensions, qualities, and behaviors that occur within the enclaves.

5. The contents we deal with are two-sided, each side offering the beginning of an evidential move to its source.

6. All movement is directed and supported by that at which one is to arrive, if what is sought is real.

7. There are universal conditions determining the ways in which beings can be together with one another.

8. Universal conditions are specified in limited cases.

9. Universal conditions are grounded in final realities.

10. The final realities have one another in subordinated forms.

11. A specialization of the subordinated forms as together with and met by the dominant is the body of an actuality possessed by a privacy.

12. A plurality of beings can concurrently mediate a common potentiality to yield a single whole.

13. The effects of the conditioning finalities are internalized by actualities.

14. Any common condition functions as a simple 'we'. This interplays with a plurality of entities (already governed by a condition making it possible for them to be together) to constitute a complex 'we', able to interact with others.

15. No words in language refer: 'designating' terms are coordinate with 'predicates'. Together, they articulate what is adumbratively reached in a thrust, so that what refers is the whole articulated expression inseparable from a continuation into the object.

16. A proper name, of which the best example is 'me', adheres to its object.

17. The absolutely perfect needs the entities which seek to realize it, and is therefore less than perfect.

18. Ontology presupposes epistemology, and conversely.

19. Actualities provide One's for all the finalities; each finality provides a One for all the actualities.

20. The identity of a being lies in an indefinite privacy, specialized over the course of its career in the form of specific epitomizations.

21. An epitomization of a privacy clings to it and thereby gives it the form of a promise for the next stage of determination.

22. Limited domains are constituted by mathematics, art, culture, history, and indeed every enterprise other than metaphysics. In those domains entities are constructed by joining conditions and conditioned, and thrusting backwards and forwards to constitute the area where other constructions have occurred or are to occur.

23. Each actuality in itself has a power appropriate to the matching of what is externally imposed: the distension of an actuality matches the undivided extension that Existence provides.

24. Knowledge never stops at the surface; it always penetrates toward the unitary intensive, possessing, expressive reality.

25. All beings seek to be complete by making their own thrust and what this terminates in, into part of themselves.

26. Nothing can be all-conquering; there comes a point where what has been dominated begins to dominate.

Is there an underlying common theme here? Is there an *ur*-principle? If there is, how are the various items related to it? What kind of warrant could be provided for the principle and its dependents?

February 7

Apart from teaching and some occasional reading, I have done hardly anything these last days but to try to see if I could get into focus the basic method behind my recent views. I have now come to what seems to me a reasonable answer, particularly so far as the consideration of the various depths of human privacy is concerned. Each stage of human privacy has behind it a promise. The realization of that promise, in the form of another determinate stage, is one with the conversion of the earlier stage into a representative of the later. As such a representative it anticipates, prepares, signals, reports what the higher stage needs for guidance and success. This activity in an actual man has something like a reciprocal in the finalities. Each of these engages in acts of subordination of the other finalities and, in order to be consistent with itself, makes what is subordinated be continuous with itself, and thus so far not under the control of other finalities. While still bearing the marks of their presence, it divides into a plurality of actualities. Since this is what each finality does, an actuality turns out to be the totality of dynamic forms continuous with the finalities in their subordinated forms, but divided against other similar totalities.

I am not as clear about the finalities as I think I am about the actualities' progressive stages of intensification, perhaps in good part because I do not see that I am providing anything like a correlative to the idea of representativeness. This can be done by taking each of the divisions to be an agency for the finalities, enabling these to become reconciled with their subordinated forms. There is a progress in the achievement of reconciliation so far as there is a progress in excellence in actualities. The ultimate particles at one extreme, and matured men at the other, express different ways at which the objective of the finalities, to recover their subordinated forms through divided modes of acting, is attained to a higher and higher degree. Only when we come to the highest degree, the living, do we have the achievement of representativeness. Man differs from other living beings in carrying out the activity of representativeness from sensitivity to the I.

We have then a production of a mere agent in the form of particles, and anything to which these might give rise. But since it is a contingent matter that there be living beings, we must also say that there is no further activity required by the finalities. But they are better served when the agents are able to make subordinated parts of themselves have the status of representatives, for then the stage of an agent is carried out most completely. Until there are living beings, the finalities yield a world of particles and of wholes which have no internal subtlety, and therefore no capacity to be agents in a superior way.

If this is right, the stages of representativeness are contingently produced, and yet answer to a primary need. There will be a promise for the higher stages but it will await contingent occurrences before those higher stages can be attained. But the finalities do not depend on contingencies in order for them to divide and produce unities of themselves in agents, at once active and passive.

February 8

The problem of relating mind and body is part of a larger, unless 'mind' be understood to include every private activity from thinking to feeling, creative activity to perception. If we distinguish what is scientifically known from what is perceived, we must not only find a way of relating them in something objective but also in individuals, unless we are to suppose that only one of them tells us something about what is real apart from us, and what is true about ourselves. The achievement of an answer to that duality is faced with the fact that values and events do not fit in with these, and that if scientific claims are set alongside perceptual ones, values and events, too, must be set alongside. But this is still not enough. There are also the worlds of art, religion, social living, and politics.

I think we must recognize that there are many different domains, each of which continues beyond itself into a base that it shares with others. When we deal with a few of those domains and neglect the others, we begin to think of men as primarily moral, creative, reflective, active, and the like. Each of these is to be envisaged as underlying more than one distinguishable domain having its own rhythms, laws, relationships, and objects. But then we must go further and find what is at the root of these various bases. We must not rest with the idea of man as a creative being who is at the base of all art and perhaps also of such inquiries as science, but see him as having the creative activity itself grounded in something even more basic. We come to the end of such groundings in deeper and deeper bases, underlying a number of diverse modes of activity, themselves at the base of a multiplicity of disciplines or topics, when we arrive at man, as a radically private being. He is directed at an objective, the realization of which may take the form of a life involved with some more limited objective, such as the making of a work of art, or having a knowledge of nature, or being successful in practice. Each of these limited enterprises has its own boundary, within the limits of which there is a multiplicity of occurrences bunched together, and functioning in ways that cannot be understood, except so far as account is taken of the fact that they are subject to the boundary. The converse is also true; the activity of a unitary bounded whole is limited by the ways in which the parts within it function. The basic fact is unity with distinct parts all confined and bunched in a distinctive way, at the same time that they are related to other similar entities outside the confines of that unity. What is true of the unity and parts from the side of the individual is matched by what is true of a unity and parts on the side of what is produced, or is objectively real. These considerations seem to have been included in the account I have given in *You, I, and the Others* of the nature of the complex we.

The primary private unity of man—indeed any objectively real actuality—is to be understood as a source directed at an indeterminate prospect. The realization of the prospect, through an expression of the source, yields some such basic ground as morality, faith, thought, creativity, all limited forms of the initial unity. Specializations of the morality, etc., yield domains which require for their explanation and presence a joining by the limited forms of what is actual and what is final. A work of art is a domain produced by a creative being who joins together what he discerns of what is actual and what is eternal, the joining being guided by a pertinent objective, that of making something excellent.

February 10

If the fundamental principle is that all realities, whether actual or final, seek to become self-complete, the effort will have two forms, because of the different ways in which the actualities and finalities are constituted. A finality has determinate bases and expresses a determinate control, the two being mediated by an indeterminate condition. An actuality, in contrast, has an indeterminate promise and an indeterminate thrust, the two being mediated by a determinate body. The progressive development of finalities involves the making of the conditions determinate, with preceding stages serving as relatively less effective mediators. The progressive development of actualities, instead, involves the making the promise and the thrust more determinate with the preceding stages serving as representatives.

All determinations involve boundaries effectively binding what is within their confines. We can account for the presence of actualities as being the result of the need for finalities to be in possession of their subordinated forms, since this can be achieved only if they divide into effective private beings in possession of their bodies. Conversely, we can account for the presence of finalities as being the result of the need of actualities to function in harmony, since this requires their solidification, with the promise becoming a determinate base, the determinate bodies becoming indeterminate conditions, and the indeterminate thrusts becoming determinate powers. But the two are in fact always present and always interactive, with the determinate bodies meeting the determinate conditions and thereby producing determinate appearances.

February 11

Men are both responsible and accountable from the position of a common social good. Whatever they decide and whatever they do is measured by their measuring up to the requirements of that good. A man, consequently, must be said to have a responsibility to realize the absolute good, an accountability to do what his society requires, and a union of these two directed toward a social good.

A man is directed at what has a private determination and a public role. His identity as a being in society is one with his continuing to have a role there. If he changes over the course of his life, in mind, body, intent, or act, he still remains self-same, one who fits in society as defined by its good. That good has a collective and a distributive role. Those of his decisions and acts which preclude the realization of that good in all, continue to measure him, since he is a man in that society only so far as the good is definitory of what he is to aim at.

The higher good of sheer responsibility and the lower good of acknowledged accountability are united and measured as more or less idle and more or less narrow, at the same time that they measure the degree to which a society is at once ethical and moral. There are many societies, each with its own good. Subtending them all is the good of a society of civilized men. It is that good which makes it possible to say that Eichmann was doing what was evil, even though it was approved by his Nazi society, and even though it did not hold him accountable.

February 13

All realities can be viewed as stretching from a private center to a limit where they are most attenuated. Actualities have the stretch in the form of an indeterminate, and finalities have it in the form of a determinate. Both have their stretches broken by an intermediary. For the actualities the intermediary is a determinate body; for a finality it is an indeterminate form of itself resulting from its subordination to other finalities.

All realities seek to be more unified. The finalities consequently seek to be in possession of themselves as subordinated by the others. But to do this they must divide into a multiplicity of actualities. The actualities, themselves, seek to be harmonized with one another. To do this they solidify in the form of finalities. Neither the actualities nor the finalities produce the other; the account of each as yielding the other is the result of an analysis made from its position. Each type is real apart from the other; it is not derived from it, though it can be understood in terms of it.

Taken in their severalty, the two types of reality seek to express what they are at their most intensive and thereupon produce more specialized forms of themselves. The actualities mature so far as they are able to make their indeterminate privacies be specialized in specialized powers. The achievement of those powers is one with the conversion of what is not specialized as a promise for a higher stage and the conversion of the specialization into an agent when the promise becomes a higher specialization. A finality, in contrast, makes its indeterminate intermediary more and more determinate, and thereby makes its subordinated form more and more effective. The subordinated form then has the role of a structure for a domain. Different grades of structure are related to one another as promises to agents. All intermediaries are bounded; the boundaries are effective, binding what they contain; the intermediaries, whether determinate or indeterminate, are relatively passive.

It is the being which feels that desires; what has satisfied desire also needs; what has satisfied need has an environment—and so on until we come to responsibility. We then have a promise that there will be a use of the finalities. One then is unified by virtue of the addition of new kinds of unities.

None of this is very clear to me. But I discern a need to change the view that all beings attempt to become self-complete, to the view that they all attempt to become more unified by making what is now indeterminate determinate—the actualities by specializing their privacies, the finalities by insisting on themselves as subordinated by others. The failure of each to attain its goal, requires it to take account of the other. Actualities reach their limit in a man who is able to make private use of the finalities; the finalities reach their limit in creases within themselves which answer to the existence of actualities. Alternatively: beings seek to become self-complete, and they succeed best when they become more unified by making provision for the use of the other type of reality.

An Hegelian would like to take the finalities and actualities to be correlatives. My account of them does allow for the view that they are correlatives, but it denies that they could ever be actually united, made into a single One. The One for them both, I have held and think it necessary still to hold, is an ideal perfection in which they could be fully together only at the price of losing their independence and distinctness. Might one not maintain that this is exactly Hegel's view? A sheer absolute without distinctions is for him only an abstraction. It is concrete only so far as it is articulate, and the articulation continues as we progress closer and closer to the position where there is only the absolute. To arrive at that absolute is to arrive at a pivotal position, forcing us to leave it behind. All the absolute, as undifferentiated, would then be a lure and a beginning of a pluralization. But Hegel does want the absolute itself to generate a pluralization, and does not allow that what is less than the absolute could have an integrity of its own, maintained against the absolute and never caused or produced by it. Nor is it entirely evident that for him there is a steady progression of more and more unified forms with the absolute as the limit. Most important: the power exhibited by actualities and finalities is their own, and not a limited form of an absolute power. Hegel does not take the actualities seriously. His different limited forms of the absolute, though something like the finalities, are really only categories.

February 15

Every view sooner or later comes to acknowledge something just simply 'brute', 'had', 'sheer data', 'what is undergone', 'lived through', 'the immediate', 'the irrational', 'the inexpressible', 'the occasion', 'the manifold', all referring to what Wittgenstein at one place says is not something but also not nothing. One way of dealing with the matter is to suppose that what has such a status from a particular point of view is nevertheless quite intelligible and of a different order when dealt with from an opposite position. What is taken to be an undergone pain by linguistic philosophers is, from the standpoint of classical thought and introspection, something known. One here accepts the position of those who treat the 'brute' as a limit, while claiming to have a special access to it, thereby enabling one to deal with it in a distinctive way. It accepts the position of the other without examination, to end with a radical dualism.

The problem I think can be solved by being made more complex. Instead of acknowledging only one limit, we should acknowledge two. What is intelligible is midway between two extremes, the position from which we begin and that at which the object does. If we start with an expression of pain, we have this between the extreme of a living of the pain and a terminal listener. If, instead, we were to start with the experiencing of the pain, we would have this between the extreme of an act of consciousness, a kind of private 'intentionality' and the body or the mind that is sustaining the pain. If we take all knowledge to have a ground in an I or in a Lockean substance, these will have the roles of limits for one another, with assertions, claims and the like serving as intermediaries. If we turn to the I and takes this to be what is known, intelligible, communicable, and explicable, we will start with an unexamined me on the one side and the self, which the I epitomizes, on the other.

The last illustration prompts the suggestion that what is intermediary might have as its limits the same item approached from different sides. 'Me' is approached from the outside by the very I which also sustains it from within. Might it not always be the case that an intelligible item is pivotal, coming to a limit in two directions? This need not preclude its also having two limits beyond itself in opposite directions. As having limits beyond itself in opposite directions, it can be seen as a precipitate of what is at the extremes, the way appearances are in between the actualities and finalities which help constitute them. As pivots, the appearances measure the truth of judgments.

If all judgments involve an adumbrative component leading into the object beyond, what is the status of the adumbration? Is it something immediate? The acknowledgment of a limit requires that use be made of a connection between it and what is intermediary, representative, or intelligible. It seems reasonable to begin by saying that adumbration can be credited to the judgment or to the object, and thus to either limit. It can also be distinguished from these, with judgment having the judger as its other limit, and with the object having itself as in itself as the other limit. Can it be taken to be something like an I, sustaining that at which it itself arrives?

The foregoing was written this morning before I went off to class. I have been thinking about the questions raised while going to and from class, and for some time after it, so that what follows is in part an entirely new effort.

We can view anything as a kind of limit that is sustained by another kind of entity coming to that item from another side. The result is a single item with a thickness. To know that something is just 'had' or undergone is to face it as a limit of our knowing, a limit that is part of a thick content filled out by an alien insistence. If we start from that alien insistence, we arrive at the 'had' from the opposite side, and there find that it has a thickness due to the presence of what before was our own insistence. What is immediately undergone, then, is something known to be there only because we approach it as a limit. But if we arrive at as such a limit, we find that it is only the surface of a content that is filled out by an alien insistence. If we are concerned with language or knowledge, what is public and the like, we arrive at the 'had', a pain e.g., as undergone, as that which is the unity for the articulations of the language or knowledge. If, instead, we are concerned with our own private life we arrive at the 'had' as the unity for that private life at that moment.

The 'had' is also a ground for itself in the form of a surface that it reaches and sustains. It is therefore like the I when it moves toward itself via the me—or better, it is an instrument for such an I. We come to that 'had' from a thicker version of itself, at the same time that we sustain it by that thicker version.

Combining these two approaches, it can be said that any supposed limit, faced as an immediate, beyond what we are ourselves having as knowledge or in some other articulate or usable, dissectable form, is actually spread out both horizontally and vertically. Contextualists approach pain as a limit of an alien insistence; it is the unity of their expressions, but of which they can say nothing as apart from the expressions. Those who take themselves to be primarily minds or privacies take the pain to be the content of, and thus to be the limit of their private insistence. The very same pain can also be viewed as having a depth from which we begin in order to have that pain as something attended to, and as being sustained from that depth, thereby enabling us to know what we are as pained. In the first way, we treat the immediate as something like an appearance (but not constituted by the finalities and actualities); in the second way we deal with it as something like a me, but not itself able to act or to sustain, but to be instead used by something which can act and sustain.

Adumbration, reachings, sustainings, etc., can be credited to the insistencies or the limit, or dealt with by themselves. When dealt with by themselves they have to be understood as thick contents resulting from the meeting of one kind of thrust from an adumbrating, etc., and being with another thrust from the object. If the previous discussion can serve as a model, we will have to recognize that adumbration and the others cannot be dealt with from only two points of view. Instead of saying, for example, that adumbration takes us only from judgment or assertion to the unitary being which these articulate, we will have to say as well that it is the surface of a more basic relation between the knower and known, a relation which we use to allow us both to attend to that adumbration and to sustain it. We will have isolated the adumbrative factor because we had begun below it to have it as a datum, and as that which is sustained. This will occur when and as we have that very surface in the role of a spread between the articulation and what it articulates. If this is correct, we must recognize that the dimensions of what were recognized to be distinctive of the me—its being arrived at from the outside and sustained from the inside by the same I—are only two of four. The me, too, would have to be said to be a limit for the external world, the point where it stops, and a limit for subjectivity, that which is more subjective than the me itself.

Most compendiously: Any item can be isolated and then dealt with as a unity at the limit of a subjectivity and objectivity, at the same time that it is the surface of itself as able to both sustain and approach it, either unaided or backed by some such power as the I.

*　*　*

Over the years I have remarked on the state of my health. I think I am now going through a significant change. I find I must rest many times during the day, even after I have had a long night's sleep. I find, too, that there are some days when I feel too weak to walk or do any exercise at all. There have been a few days when I found myself suddenly falling, or so weak and tired that I just wrapped myself up in blankets and stayed in bed, sleeping most of the day without affecting my ability to sleep at night. I seem to teach as well as before; whether I am thinking as well, the present work and my current writing reveals. I am about the same weight as always, perhaps a pound or two lighter; I do not drink except occasionally, at dinner with company. Many days, though, when the weather is inclement, I ride from 6 to 8 miles on my stationary bicycle. Often enough I find that I have a dull ache in my legs the next day, and sometimes I feel I cannot do any exercises then. At those times, I usually do manage to engage in my setting up exercises. I think I look much older than I did a year or so ago. I also have almost daily pains in my chest, which I assume are gas pains, do not have the appetite I had a year or so ago, and do not seem to have the energy to paint. Yet all the while I am as cheerful as before, do not worry, and continue to struggle with philosophic questions.

February 16

Every finite entity has a brutality to it; it is just that and nothing else. We reach it as brute in the guise of a limit. What is at that limit can be explicated. It is midway between two different kinds of insistencies. One of these is subjective and the other objective. The finite entity is a brute ultimate when approached as a limit from one or the other but is explicable as the product of the two together. If we attend to these factors, we find that each itself is a brute immediate, and is to be explicated in a somewhat similar way as the initial item. But an absolute subjectivity, unlike the initial item, is at a position between the finalities and objectivity, while an absolute objectivity is between the finalities and subjectivity.

Every finite occurrence is also explicable as an immediate surface externally entered into and inwardly sustained from a greater depth. When the deepest level is an I, the surface is a me. But well before and apart from the I, there is a reaching and accommodating. Each actuality, by accommodating the final conditions, makes the terminal surface, that these condition, into its own surface. Appearances are not to be understood as simply credited to actualities; they are possessed by them via the conditions. At its deepest level, an actuality is a limiting surface for finalities. Those finalities reach it via the expressions of that actuality.

A me exists because other beings are used by the I as surrogates for the finalities. When other actualities are used by subjectivity as surrogates for the finalities, we have a me which differs from other limits because it is reached by an I making use of other epitomizations of the privacy. Denied these other epitomizations, the I would be just the deepest level of an individual, arriving at its sustained limit via the finalities.

This account can be applied to insistence, adumbration, and expressions. Though they are all continuations of subjectivity and objectivity, and have surface and depth, each can be dealt with as a brute immediate. But, because they are parts of larger realities, they are to be viewed primarily as different positions where subjectivity and objectivity meet, but not as reached and sustained limits. They are derivative items, dependent on others, without independent standing or reality.

Does this kind of approach to actualities have a duplicate or counterpart in relation to the finalities? If it had a duplicate, those finalities would be just grandiose actualities. One can view them in this light from the position of actualities, just as surely as one can see the actualities as so many distinguished fragments of the finalities. But viewed objectively, from the position of an absolute ideality or perfection, the finalities and actualities are inverses of one another. I do not now see this as clearly as I think I see how finite entities are to be dealt with. Is it satisfactory to say that a finality is a ground for a plurality of actualities, each otherwise just a brute immediate? Does each finality give itself a brute surface and base? Are these relative to actualities?

Just as an actuality uses the finalities in order to have a surface for itself, so the finalities use actualities to maintain themselves apart from all else. And just as 'brute' actualities are in between their own subjectivity and an objectivity provided by others, so a 'brute' finality has each of the other finalities as dominated and dominating. And just as absolute subjectivity and objectivity of actualities require a reference to each of the finalities, so the understanding of a finality as in between dominating and dominated requires a reference to a plurality of actualities. This is not yet entirely in focus, perhaps because I am trying at one and the same time to deal with the finalities as having something analogous to subjectivity and objectivity, base, and surface, and yet need to refer to something quite different in order to express the fact that the finalities are not entirely understood in terms that are pertinent to actualities. Finalities are oppositional to actualities both in nature and role.

One way of speaking of the finalities with terms used in connection with the actualities is to give them a different placement and use: the finalities, by virtue of their relation to the actualities, give themselves a depth, something like an I, and by virtue of their presenting themselves between other finalities in the role of dominating and dominated, make themselves into brute realities.

February 17

Every unit has the status of an ultimate in four ways: It is a limit for an external approach to it, that where another's action stops—the content, the immediate, the experienced. It is also that which is present, given, data, where the unit is presented, making something available to others. The unit is also that which is being sustained, presented, something at its most attenuated. And it is a sheer 'essence', that which is detached, held on to by being approached as the beginning of a move to what is sustaining it. It is dealt with in these various ways from special positions, with its unitary status ignored, as though it were just itself, just present, just presented, or just detached.

When philosophers try to solve the problem of the relation of mind and body by reducing the former to pains and the latter to brains or brain waves, they suppose that only the pains are ultimates, and are either to be understood to be the objects of a special experience, an intentionality, or private knowledge, or to just provide an occasion for an expression or knowledge. But the intentionality, occasion, and expression all have their own unit status and thus yield to the same analysis.

Were there initially only one reality, God, he would have to withdraw himself into himself in order to be able to have something which is himself as related to the world. The withdrawal could itself be understood to be a way of enabling the supposed created world to be apart from him; he would then have an I because he allowed for an area beyond himself where he could be a me. One could hold that this area was in fact a nothing; that God had first to hold himself away from the nothing in order to be able to be a God who could distinguish himself from that nothing, by sustaining himself at the limit of that nothing and approaching himself via it. He would have the status of a creator only so far as he was at a limit between himself in himself and what he was from the position of the creation. He could, contrary to what I maintained in *You, I, and the Others* properly say to Moses, "I am that [or what] I am," meaning by that, "I am an I because and so far as I adopt what I am for you as (the limit of) myself." This says in another way that a finality makes itself have an internal density by concentrating itself in itself and thereby becoming able to accept actualities via the limit of that finality. This from which it is withdrawn is also inwardly and outwardly constituted.

Everything, it is here being maintained, is where the objective and the subjective meet, and where something sustained is approached from without by and thereby made to adhere to the entity which provides the sustaining. What is difficult to see is just how the inward constituting differs from the sustaining. Is it that the inward constituting has the item as something thrust toward, where the sustaining is passive, merely allowing the limit to be? The outward thrust would then match the thrust from what was beyond the entity, to make the meeting point a constituted unit item. The sustaining, instead, would have the unit holding on to itself as it spread, expressed itself, diversified itself, and would be countered by an externally expressed insistence that the diversified be made the beginning of a convergence toward the original source.

Every unit, instead of being an irreducible immediacy, is analyzable into a component coming from the inside, another from the outside, a third from a sustainer, and a fourth from an act in which the item is brought toward the source of the sustainer. Also, every unit, no matter how complex or basic, is capable of being faced as a limit in a four-fold way. A pain, a sense datum, an aesthetic content, what is undergone, is no less analyzable than an actual man. An actuality, human or subhuman, though functioning on its own, and serving as a base in terms of which other entities are to be understood, is also approachable as a limit from four directions. There is, of course, a difference between a dependent, derivative item, an outcome of the interplay of realities, or some distinguished factor, and actualities. This difference seems to be primarily in the capacity of actualities to provide sustainers and ways of arriving at their own limits so as to begin an approach to themselves—in short, in the ability of actualities to detach themselves from one another.

If a sharp distinction is to be made between what is brute, immediately, and the like, and what is not, it should be between what is not an actuality and therefore cannot, and what is an actuality and can therefore provide a sustainer, as well as approach itself from the outside. The brute, if not a reality, must have its sustaining and the approach to it, produced by others. To know whether or not a pain is a reality, we must determine whether or not it has a deeper side that sustains what is evident, and whether it can come to itself from its depths to have itself as its own surface. One can readily conceive of it to be but the most evident, forward aspect of what has a greater depth, but it does not seem to be a medium by which what is at a greater depth is able to approach itself. It is not detachable, an item all by itself. Constituted from within and from without, by the experiencer and the bodily occasion or the experience of this, it lacks the status of something which can be distinct from all else.

Those who speak of a private access to 'mental' occurrences, such as pains, rightly argue for the constitution of these from within. Those of their opponents who speak of public criteria and direct public manifestations of the pains rightly claim that the pains are constituted from without. They need one another. And they should be supplemented by those who speak of pains being experienced and thereby being constituted by a sensitive being. Pains are also part of the content of a me which an I both sustains and arrives at from the outside on the way toward itself as more than a mere sustainer.

Every actuality, apart all knowing, is present for others because it is presented from within and conditioned from without, and keeps itself detached from others by both sustaining what is at its limit and by passing through that limit from the outside on the way to a recovery of the limit as its own surface. Each could be said to have a private access to every other, since each faces all else as its limit. That at which it stops, is constituted from within by the others from their side. If an entity is an actuality, it will have both to sustain and to arrive at what is itself, as present for others.

February 18

I confront items at a limit. It makes no difference whether they occur in my privacy or in the external world. But when I confront items in my privacy I usually do not supplement them with a judgment whose adumbrative component overlays a directly confronted factor. When I dream, have a mere aesthetic experience, live through a tonality of my body, the judgment is minimal and perhaps absent. It is also minimal and perhaps absent when I suddenly confront an obstacle or am attentive to some particular item in the world. The limit, whether in my privacy or in an external world, is one to which I have a 'private access', for though the object is available to others, and though they and I can both make the same statements about it, we come to it from our own positions and have it as a limit to our own perceiving. That limit is maintained apart from all of us, by virtue of the fact that the object sustains it from its own side.

If we stress the fact that an encountered entity sustains the limit at which we arrive directly, whatever is encountered is 'objective'; if instead we stress our own direct coming to a limit, whatever is encountered is 'subjective'. Some items may be available only to one individual; there is a 'private access' to pains, thoughts, dreams, willings, assumption of accountability, and the like, in the sense that, though these have an objectivity by virtue of being sustained from the opposite side, others do not have the opportunity to be blocked by them.

I have 'private access' to everything, but what I arrive at may be sustained by what in fact sustains that at which others also directly arrive at. We call that 'external' which has such a backing. It is then not the fact that I experience a pain that distinguishes the pain from an experienced color or an apple but the fact that it is sustained by what does not sustain the content directly had by others.

It is possible, of course, for others to arrive at what is sustaining my pain, say certain physiological occurrences, by taking another route. They will then arrive at a different counterpart of this from what I do when I have a pain. If they confront my body directly, they will come to a sustainer of a limit—on the hypothesis, the same sustainer that I come to—but as the other side of a limit different from that at which I arrive. I come to a pain backed, let us say by the physical occurrence, which sustains that pain and allows me to face it as that at which I arrive as an intensified limit. He will come to that very occurrence sustaining his experience of the physical occurrence. Were he and I to attend to the same physical occurrence in my body, he and I would both have this as the direct object of an experience. I, in addition, can have another experience of the physiological occurrence, the experience of a pain which, on the hypothesis, is being sustained by that occurrence. The experiences of the physiological occurrence will be different for both of us, but will be sustained by the same item; I, in addition, will have another experience of that item. He might also be pained, but we would then look for the base of this, not in that initial physiological occurrence, but in one that it might cause in his body. But even if the very physiological occurrence which I experienced directly via my pain was experienced by him via his own, that occurrence would have to be distinguished from the experience each of us has of that occurrence as something observed. He would be pained at or by it. I would have it painfully.

I can be said to have a direct encounter with a physiological occurrence in two ways. It is what I arrive at via a pain, and that which I arrive at via attention. (I can, of course, attend to the pain, but then it will be directly confronted as that which could be reached via another pain or some other 'psychical' occurrence.) Both can be said to be 'subjective', possible only to me, though if another is pained at the sight of the physical occurrence and also attends to it, he too will have 'subjective' experiences which terminate at the same place mine do.

My pain does not allow for a full overlay of the experience of it by the adumbration of an assertion; it accompanies any experience I might have of the physiological occurrence that another might also terminate at. One can, though, conceive of a pain so slight that the experience of it is hidden by or is merged with the adumbration, and of the experience of the occurrence in me by another as being so vivid that it can be distinguished despite his judgment or assertion. Since he can be pained at what he notes is occurring in my body, he too can have a pain while he attends to that occurrence. But where my pain is my termination at the occurrence, his is only occasioned by the occurrence; otherwise it would make sense to say that there could be pains which were not grounded in one's own physiology.

The pain I undergo stretches from my having it to it as a terminus; the pain as at the terminus is the pain experience continued. Another, who is pained by what he observes in me, while he too has a pain experience of his own continued into his own actual terminating pain, does not painfully reach me. I am connected with the pain at which I terminate; he is connected with that terminated pain by shock, irritation, and the like, while being connected with the pain he feels in the same way that I am connected with the pain I feel.

A pain, then, is an experience terminating in a more concentrated form, sustained beyond itself by what comes from the other side. The painful experience can be accompanied by a judgment or assertion, whose adumbration will ride on the back of the painful experience. The pain, of course, is but a special case of a private occurrence. Its constitution is mine alone; that at which it terminates, though continuous with the entire experiencing as a more concentrated and limiting form of this, can also be terminated at in an adumbration, continuing an assertion which can be accepted by others. It isn't then an intention, a private access, or a supposed purely phenomenological character exhausted in the experiencing that characterizes pain and other so-called private or mental occurrences, but the fact that they terminate intensive versions of themselves. These cannot be entirely obscured or merged with the adumbration which is inseparable from a communicable articulation of that terminus.

I have a private and even a secret access to my pain in the sense that I constitute it, but when I try to know it, I approach it from the outside. Beginning with myself, I then have a private access to it, but not one that is secret, since I can begin with what others can note, my bodily activities. Theories of intentionality seem to confound the constituting of what is directly and individually confronted with what is known. But any terminus, even the constituting stretch to it, can be known, just as anything else can; we can formulate propositions having any terminus as the limit of an adumbration.

Though everything is constituted from a subjective as well as from an objective side, and though both of these could be said to continue to the point where they join, the result is not a concentrated form of one of them, with the other in a subordinated role, as is the case with a pain or other so-called private experience. A pain is a product, with a subjective and objective factor meeting to constitute it, but the role of the objective here is mainly that of a carrier. The opposite emphasis is found when we take a physiological occurrence to provide the measure of the appropriateness of our approaches to it. Is there any situation where the two are in balance, where the subjective and objective constitutions are equal? I have maintained there is—in *Beyond All Appearances.* I called them 'phenomena'.

February 19

Any object of experience, whether this be encountered in privacy, in the body, or outside it, can be viewed in a number of ways. A pain, for example, is:

1. Constituted from within and from without, the one by the experiencer, the other by the body.

2. The inward constituting is, for the experience, overwhelmingly dominant.

3. As that which is being experienced, it is an intensified and unified form of the experiencing itself.

4. It can be referred to through the agency of an assertion by means of an adumbrative component that converges the components of the articulated assertion at it.

5. It is passively sustained from a deeper level by the being.

6. It is approached by going to it from the outside and thereby made into a surface.

7. As at once sustained and approached it is detached.

8. It can be penetrated toward from the outside both by oneself and by others.

9. It cannot be entirely obscured by the adumbrative factor in an articulative affirmation of it.

10. It is different in mature men from what it is in those not mature, for it is then related to an actual and not merely a potential realization of other aspects of the privacy.

11. It is different in humans from what it is in subhumans, for only the humans have it related, at the very least, to a potentiality of having a psyche and a self.

12. When another is sympathized with, the inward constituting by him takes over; to sympathize is to touch on the inward constituting of the pain, but not to mesh with it.

13. It has some bodily act or part function as its representative, warning, directing, anticipating its occurrence.

14. It acts as the representative of desire, warning, directing, and anticipating what might ensue on the expression of the desire.

15. It is evidenced by what is publicly discernible. Moaning and similar occurrences are not criteria; they are it in a public guise.

These are not all equally evident; no.6 for example seems far less obvious than no.2.

The above characterizations are made from the position where something is accepted as a unit and its constituents distinguished. Should there not also be other ways of dealing with the experienced, or any entity whatsoever? Instead of accepting it as a unit can one begin by treating it as an irreducible ground, something distinct, intelligible, and an existent? An irreducible ground will allow one to distinguish aspects of it—a boundary cutting it off from all else, a nature, an activity, and a status. As distinct, it can be analyzed into a privacy, an intelligibility, a presence, and a state of priority over others. As intelligible, it provides an explanation, acts as a representative, is predictable, and encompasses what it explains. As existent, it is a source, that which is self-maintained, a specialized nature, and related to an objective. This is a list of headings and nothing more. Do they answer to what is the case?

What is treated as a unit, could be part of a continuum. This does not change the fact that when it is focused on, we face it as a unit, a ground, a separated item, an intelligible, or an existent. The very fact that it is a terminus of the experience means that it has all these positions. If it is the base in terms of which everything else about it is to be understood, it will have a dimension where it is distinct: be one of a kind; make its presence felt; be insisted on over against others; and offer a measure for the assessment of others. It will also be a distinct entity with its own privacy and nature, which presents itself, and is the orientation point for an ordering of others. As that which is considered, something made into an object for ourselves, it provides an explanation for others, represents some other occurrence, has predictable outcomes, and is at the beginning of an hierarchy of values. As having its own insistence, it is a point of origin, maintains its separateness, specializes something more general, and is inseparable from some objective. Once more, I am just listing, and not, as I did when I took pain to be a unit, really focusing on it and therefore giving genuine experiential content to what theory makes it desirable to distinguish. A proper procedure will require me to take up each of these four sets of characterizations in turn, in the light of what the facts require or justify.

An obvious difficulty: there are derivative occurrences, adjectival to others. They cannot have the status of substantial entities, or dynamic existents. At the very least, one would have to deal with them as part of what is substantial or existent.

February 21

Both an experiencer and an organic body are conditions for content, the one terminating in it, the other encompassing it. The experiencer is insistent while the body is limitative; content for the one plays a minor role, for the other a major. If we try to make the condition and content equal, we must bring the experienced up to the level of the conditioning experiencer and strengthen the bodily encompassment so that it governs the content. We will then have two specialized cases of conditions with content, each restricted in range, the one because of the specialization of the condition to be an experiencer, the other because the units are only part of a larger set. To reconcile the two, we will have to make both the condition and the content cosmic, the one as a universal, the other as an all-inclusive set.

The union of mind and body becomes intelligible only if it serves to unite a universal condition with all the actualities, thereby escaping from the individual's limitation of both the condition and content. If this is correct we should be able to arrive from the world of appearances at the mind by specializing finalities and minimizing the actualities, to make them just terminal points, and arrive at the organic body by isolating a limited number of actualities while making the body be an encompassment of them. The one would be like a 'qualia', the other like a space, with the 'qualia' still subject to a brute obstinacy and the 'space' having a power to encompass.

Since a privacy reaches to and controls a body, it is also possible to take the organic body to be enriched by the privacy and, as so enriched, to be more in consonance with the parts within it, both controlling and encompassing them. On the other side, the physical units can enrich the terminal experienced content by providing them with a singular obstinacy and independence of movement. As a consequence, we can view the result indifferently as an experiencing which faces enriched obstinate entities, or as an enriched body facing real physical units. The two at their limits should be identical, differing only in the way they are reached.

The final fact will be a condition which, like the 'mind', is controlling and, like an organic body, is encompassing; and a content which, like the experienced, is terminal and, like actual entities, is pluralized, each item having its own irreducible integrity.

*   *   *

No one knows how successful he will be in a life devoted to art or any other enterprise. But if he is really devoted, he will be involved in a process of purging himself so that what he does will be maximized. It is true, of course, that there have been great creative men who were petty, mean, unstable. But so far as they were involved in the making of their works, they were free of these, perhaps because they freed themselves from their daily lives by drugs and similar agencies. One cannot be sure that the pettiness will not carry over. The best policy is to try to be as honest with oneself as one can, while engaged in the activity, to give oneself to it in such a way that one's emphases on oneself are bypassed. If this is done, even if it turns out that one is only second-rate, one will have succeeded in becoming a more complete human being. There is, therefore, a fail-safe position for every practitioner who gives himself, while risking failure in the pursuit of some good outside himself: he will succeed in becoming more of a man, and in that sense will have succeeded in becoming what he otherwise would not have become had he not devoted himself to producing a great work. It was in the attempt to do this that he succeeded in achieving a stage where he was free of the petty vices that might otherwise characterize him.

It is conceivable that, in the case of the mean or petty great creators, they had to sacrifice the achievement of a higher moral state. But no one can take as his goal the sacrifice of such a possible state in order to achieve something first rate; there is no warrant for supposing that the pettiness etc., is a precondition for great achievement. At most, we can say that a great creator is able to immerse himself so deeply in a making that there is no opportunity to do more than force any pettiness he has into the background. While one is engaged in anything like a conscious occupation with the making of something excellent, one is involved in a self-purging, so that even if the result is second-rate one incidentally achieves the status of becoming a better, more complete, a fuller human being.

Both the first rate person, who is not a decent human being in relation to others or in other situations, and the mediocrity, who gives himself fully to his task, become improved by their occupation in bringing about what is excellent. As long as they remain so occupied, they are good. If the goodness does not carry over, at least it is the case that during the period of their devotional activity, they are as good as men can be, to the extent that they give themselves unstintingly to producing what is as excellent as it can be. The failure to produce it and the incapacity to carry the achievement of excellence into other fields do not detract from the fact that, while engaged in the activity, they have achieved an honesty and a selflessness worthy of a man.

* * *

Returning to the discussion of this morning, one can say that a private insistence misses the obstinacy of ultimates and gets only to the terminus of an experiencing. Ultimates, in contrast, as within the body, miss the governance of the privacy. The getting to the obstinacy and the governance are one with attaining a universal situation where the privacy and the ultimates are properly matched. And this is the 'phenomena', appearances which are due equally to conditions and actualities.

If, instead of dealing with insistence, one were to attend to experiencing, one would lose the encompassment of the body and the obstinacy of the irreducibles. If, instead of dealing with ultimates, one were to deal with the body, one would lose the governance that an insistence provides, as well as the terminal nature of the experienced. Once again, the reconciliation involves a universalization of the conditions and an inclusion of all ultimates. The resultant phenomena have conditions which are governing and encompassing, and units which are terminal and obstinate. Phenomena are not then just neutral, as was suggested in *Beyond All Appearances*; they have obstinate terminal content and governing encompassing conditions and make a single set.

If we start with phenomena, whether they be viewed as in fact occurring or as representing an ideal stage of equilibrium, and we pass toward a compound actuality, such as a man, we begin to lose the obstinacy, the brute physical presence of something; narrow the number of irreducibles; contract and specialize a condition; and lose its encompassing power. The limit is a qualia which seems almost completely terminal, but governed by a condition. If we move, instead, in the opposite direction, toward a finality, we begin to lose the terminal nature of items and their being part of an experience. And we increase the scope of units to be dealt with, to make the conditions more and more encompassing, thereby losing their governing function. The final fact is a single totality of phenomena in which conditions are universal, governing and encompassing, and irreducibles are all dealt with, as at once brute and terminal.

'Mind' is a concentrated form of a mere governance; "body" is the concentrated form of a mere irreducible. They are reconciled by adding encompassing to governance, and termination to irreducibles, and placing no limitations on either. The additions are produced either by dealing with 'mind' and 'body' separately, and then seeing how they could have both condition and content and be in equipoise; or by dealing with a possessive privacy terminating in physical units, and with physical units which give the privacy the status of a mere encompassment. We must then go on to see these two emphases balanced through a universalization of the conditions and an inclusion of all irreducibles.

There is no antecedent neutral stuff. If we suppose that from the very beginning there are phenomena, though, we will begin at a neutral position. This is derivative from the interplay of actualities and finalities, and will be utilized, not by being organized in different ways, but by losing aspects while it is being specialized and limited in range.

Does encompassing always require distinct units? Does experiencing always involve a stretching from experiencer to experienced? Does governance always require a lack of fixed borders? Does irreducibility always require a place in a cosmic totality? Does my appearance of myself express both 'mind' and body? Is the merely bodily appearance an organized set of actual units in a limited context? Can I appear as just a privacy or 'mind'? It seems as if the answers to all but the last must be in the affirmative. But there cannot be an appearance of anything like a finality or a condition, except so far as it is countered by irreducibles. To appear as a privacy and thus as insistent on the unitary body and, through this, on the parts of that body, or as a mind and thus as an experiencing which terminates in itself as concentrated and unified, one needs the mediation of the unitary body for the one, and brute distinct resistances by physical entities for the other. The phenomena seem quite close to what Kant calls by that name, except that he did not take the conditions governing them to be encompassing, i.e., bunching them within boundaries, making them all one set, and did not take them to be distinct by virtue of a brute non-experienced component, enabling them to resist the conditions.

Any conditioning which is less than cosmic in its reach is biased. Both experiencing and private intrusion on the body are biased; so are an organic body and the parts within it. Each type of bias involves a loss of a factor present in the other. Bodies are not wholly passive; they always have a resistant component expressing a brute presence. Nor are conditions wholly active; they always have an encompassing role, and therefore have their activities determined by bodies.

The meeting of insistent, private conditioning and the body as having its own integrity, yields a kind of internal phenomenon, the emotions. The appearance of an individual, if it results from the meeting of his privacy (mediated through his body) with conditions, will give way to a phenomenon when external conditions are united with the expression of the privacy. The one will be at once governing and bounding, the other at once terminal and obdurate. The latter involves a contribution by the body and another by the privacy; the contribution made by the individual always involves both. The man who appears is a man whose body is manifested no less than his privacy, though the latter will be in ascendancy. His emotion is a limited humanized compressed and privately undergone counterpart of the world of phenomena.

I have maintained elsewhere that the emotions, particularly such primary emotions as awe and reverence, take us to the conditioning finalities. Why? How? Do they not answer to the phenomena? And when they reach these, do they tend in the direction of the final conditions or of what is irreducible, thereby compensating for their initial joining of the individual privacy with his oppositional body?

At the objective pole one rarely gets to the irreducibles, stopping instead with complex individuals, particularly men, but sometimes also with groups of individuals, such as a forest or a herd, and with the final conditions only so far as they are pertinent to man's welfare. Does this not answer to an inadequate joining on the subjective side? Apparently. The privacy and the body continue to function apart from the emotion that is joining them, and that fact is caught in the passage beyond the phenomena toward actual individuals and the finalities. A man's emotions are incomplete in the double sense of not fully joining the privacy and the body, and of not being able to remain within the individual but having to be projected outward toward its counterpart in the guise of the phenomena. On reaching the phenomena, the emotions are directed toward the components of these, though we concentrate on one side or the other, getting to the neglected side only afterwards.

We begin our movement toward actualities or finalities by beginning with appearances, which are biased more toward one or the other. If we start, instead, with phenomena we attend to the factors of governance and encompassment on the one side, and terminations and obduracy on the other, and seek to understand how there can be insistent privacies and complex bodies without appealing to the emotions which blur the two, rather than respecting the factors they should embody.

The distinguishing of a 'mind' and a body is in effect the analyzing away of the emotions. Not to consider the emotions or the recovery of the different factors in a world of phenomena is like trying to get a royal flush in a card game where there are no aces—an essential part of the solution is antecedently precluded. 'Mind' and body are united in the individual emotionally, while leaving each with some integrity and separate functioning. But the understanding of them as distinct, with their several powers and limitations, requires an intellectual solution that takes us to the phenomena as together in a single setting where each is terminal and obdurate, and the setting is encompassing and governing.

A similar elimination of phenomena will leave one with laws integrated with the data—the cosmos in fact. We can now envisage various combinations—emotions facing the variegated cosmos, distinct minds and bodies facing phenomena, and emotions facing phenomena.

February 23

Both phenomena and emotions are to be analyzed in two ways. They are to be dealt with as a. as joining units with final conditions, and thereby acquiring the status of units in a context, and thus as having the status of termini, and as giving the conditions the status of bounding conditions encompassing just those termini. b. They are also to be analyzed as expressing an equilibrium in the domination of one of their factors over the other, and thus to be a kind of neutral appearance, an appearance not biased toward one or the other.

a. If we dissolve phenomena to attend to the metaphysical ultimates of actual units and finalities, and thus to the constituents of the phenomena freed from one another, we also lose the fact that the phenomena make up a particular set of items, and that these items have a terminal or immediate nature to them. Similarly, if we dissolve the emotions to attend to just a privacy and a mere body, we lose the fact that the privacy was limited to a particular body with its distinctive active parts, and that parts of the body were actually reached as termini by the privacy as it governs the body.

b. If we analyze the phenomena as points of equilibrium between opposing forces, we can see them as at the midpoint between differently constituted appearances, with those at one extreme being preponderantly expressive of actualities and those at the other being preponderantly expressive of finalities. A similar analysis of emotions is possible, with one extreme expressing the body maximally, and the other extreme expressing an experiencer. In both cases, we always have two opposing factors, but with one more or less dominating the other. There will then never be a mere body or experiencer, or a mere set of biological occurrences and a mere mind. All together produce emotions which make the body provide termini for the experiencer and keep the experiencing 'mind' limited to what can be bodily provided.

In order to make advances into privacy on the basis of available evidence, we begin with the recognition that the body encompasses with different strengths, and thus behaves in different ways. We move to deeper and deeper grounds to attend to objectives which enable one to ignore the body's use of items. Similarly, in order to make advances into the finalities, we recognize that the actualities are bunched in various ways, and that we need consider deeper and deeper levels of finalities if all the actualities are to be dealt with as together.

A possible method: Start with appearances biased toward actualities or finalities, or emotions biased toward the experiencer or bodily conditions, move to phenomena by balancing the contributions of actualities and finalities, or to a tonality by balancing the biases characteristic of the emotions. (If we move to the factors of either, we lose the limited range of one factor and the terminal role of the other. The attainment of an equilibrium is thus one with the recognition that phenomena and tonality add a limitation in range to the governing component and the role of terminus to the governed component. These additions are relative to one another.) We move toward the stage of having mere finalities or mere privacies by freeing the finalities from being limited to just those particular phenomena bunched in such and such ways, and by freeing the privacy from being limited by the body to just such and such units. We move to the stage of having mere actualities or mere bodies, by freeing them from being governed to having them just confined, and from being termini to being just brute. The stages in this move require a freeing of them from controls, and making them have the status of termini. The one is achieved by moving through grades of self-containedness, the other by moving into the cosmos of bodies.

A rational understanding of mind and body requires the translation of emotion into a world of phenomena, with a concurrent translation of the mind and body into final conditions and a totality of joined actualities. The emphasis on one rather than the other of these yields the confrontable appearances of actualities or the contextualizing appearances of the finalities. The arrival at a particular privacy and its particular body is one with a specialization of the conditions and a restriction in the number of items. The privacy and the bodies retain the additions by the way in which they affect one another, the one passing beyond mere private termini, the other beyond mere bodily encompassment.

* * *

I followed the above with a four-mile walk (I will do another four miles or so on my stationary bicycle) and lunch. The fact that I seem to be in as good a shape as ever makes me think that my troubles of the other day were due to a touch of the flu, and that I had milder cases the other days. There is a flu epidemic and people report symptoms similar to mine, though they usually are not back to normal the next day, perhaps because they do not just wrap themselves up and stay in bed for a day as I did.

* * *

The exhibitions of an actuality should be treated as the product of a privacy and a body; the exhibitions of a finality, similarly, should be treated as the product of a dominant finality involved with itself as dominated. To get to the privacy or the finalities one must abstract from the tone or phenomena and thus lose the encompassment and terminal character, to leave one with just a governing power and irreducibles.

Are these limiting ideas, answering to nothing in fact? Is the root fact the intrusive presence of each side in the other, more or less, with the phenomena and the emotions expressing midpoints? No. The power and reality of actualities and finalities, in comparison with the phenomena and appearances, show that they are realities, with the encompassment and terminal features being produced when the opposing realities meet.

Phenomena, and therefore appearances, have an underside, an ontological dimension, where realities effectively join. Phenomena and their biased forms—the appearances—are products able to encompass and to be termini. They have no independent status as units. The fringes of the appearances, where I first detected the two powers as not yet intermixed, are aura produced at the appearances by the underlying juncture of the finalities and actualities, each complex in the sense that it is not entirely alone, the one being connected with itself in a subordinated role, the other joining privacy and body. We move to realities from the fringes, but once we get to the realities we must move toward the position where the finalities are without a subordinated component, privacy is not involved with body, actualities are in themselves, and bodies have no efficacy. These moves require a series of steps freeing the finalities and the privacies from that with which they are involved. So far as one succeeds in freeing them, one has the finalities as terminating in themselves as subordinated, without the subordinated status having any efficacy, and the privacy as terminating in intensive versions of its terminating acts, without these being able to offer any resistance. We then have something close to what are taken to be the factors in the so-called mind-body problem. The problem cannot be solved without recovering the tonality of the product of the two. This is the result of their direct interplay, having its outcome in phenomena or emotions.

The mind-body problem, as it has been accepted from Descartes, starts with a detached experiencer and his experienced content on one side, and a governing body with its parts on the other. This is a special case of what we have in art and other fields. A work of art is produced by using muscles and tools; it can be understood to be a whole of parts. But there is also another kind of unity, that of the maker or appreciator, terminating in the work as that which is experienced and made. Their separation is artificial. The unfied work is just one component; the encountering and experience are other components. Each produces a single result, which more or less dominates the other, to yield a series of appearances. If we are to get to a mere artistic creator and mere material on which he works, we will have to ignore the limits of the work and the fact that the muscles and tools have the role of terminal points (the limits and the termini together helping constitute the work as it appears).

I had supposed, as late as *First Considerations,* that actualities and finalities had simple expressions, and that all one had to do was to free the expressions from one another's influence in order to get back to their sources. It is now becoming evident that a separation out of the factors in an appearance yields only exhibitions of what is itself complex, and that if we want to get into the actualities and finalities as they are apart from one another, we must sacrifice tonality or emotion in the course of an act of freeing each side from the factor with which it is involved. We must distinguish between the move toward *components,* which never allow us to escape from appearances and therefore from finalities involved with their own subordinated forms, from a move toward emotions, and therefore from privacies involved with their bodies. These are to be distinguished from a move toward *constituents.* Such a move involves a separation of a primary element out of each component—a dominating finality or an insistent privacy, each with its own internal termini. These are the analogues of a traditional cosmic or individual mind respectively, leaving behind a dominated finality or a mere body, the first an analogue of the traditional world of bodies, and the second of irreducible bodies.

We should separate out dominant-dominated finalities on the one side, and privacies and possessed bodies on the other, and then get to the dominant finalities and the privacies as they are apart. That requires us to go through a process of freeing the dominant finalities from their restriction to a particular set of occurrences (to which the dominated finalities contribute a factor of encompassment) and of freeing privacies from a restriction to their appropriate bodies (to which the bodies contribute a factor of brute irreducibility). The one move passes from smaller groupings to wider groupings, to end finally with what is restricted to none, while the other passes from one degree of encompassment by the body to lesser and lesser degrees, until we get a privacy which is directed only to what is itself in a terminal concentrated form.

Is the evidenced a finality in a subordinated form? If so, must the progress to the finality not consist in a separation from that subordinated form by a retreat within the finality, so that it is less and less restricted, not made to have an encompassing form, pertinent to the world of evidences? Will we then not have degrees of inwardness attained in the finality matching the extent to which its activities are restricted by its subordinated form?

We must distinguish the components of the appearances. This is best done by first moving to the phenomena where their biases are mutually counteracted, and then moving from there to the constituents by gradually freeing dominant from subordinated forms of finalities, or by gradually freeing the privacy from the restrictions imposed by the body. Only the attempt to reach the limits of reality in the universe or in the individual requires the second. The first keeps us with both constituents either in the phenomena and appearances, or the tonality and emotions.

February 24

There are a number of neutral positions that deserve distinguishing, each with its own distinctive biased forms:

1. Phenomena, where actualities and finalities meet, with appearances as biased forms.

2. Self-possession, where dominating and dominated forms of a finality are balanced, with limitation as a biased form.

3. Equilibrium where a finality is midway between its depth and surface, with biased forms in density and attenuation.

4. Integrity, where privacy and body of an actuality are balanced, with the biased forms of potentiality and passivity.

5. In itself, where an actuality is between a maximum and a minimum density, with different densities as biased forms.

6. Tonality where the privacy and body are in equilibrium, with emotions as biased forms.

7. Private health where a privacy is balanced between the extremes of a mere experiencing and a mere aesthetic content.

8. Whole, where a body is balanced between a governing unity and a control by the parts.

We start with appearances, and move to a midpoint, the phenomena (1), or to a finality (2), or actuality (4), and then to the neutral forms (3, 5). If we attend to the actualities in the guise of humans, we pass from (4) to (6), and from there either to (7) or (8).

The move to private health is a move into the depths of a privacy, as the outcome of a series of dislodgements from tonality, and the arrival at a position where one is able to keep all epitomizations in balance. It is now possible to distinguish five different procedures:

a. We attend to the biased forms at their minimum in order to see the various distinctions that have to be made in the least effective factor, so that it is seen to be at its most effective. This is what is done when we try to understand the different divisions in the privacy of men or in the finalities at different depths.

6. We attend to the midpoints when we are interested in distinguishing the different contributors as apart from one another, and thereby having the limits of an enterprise—finalities and actualities, privacy and irreducibles, active potentiality and passive bodies.

c. We credit the distinguished items with the characters found in the midpoint—governance and terminal roles—in order to be able to use them as explanatory bases.

d. We start with biased cases where one contributor is most influential, and thus where the bias is maximally in its favor, in order to be able to penetrate most readily into it.

e. When we want to account for the existence of a bias in one direction-or-another, we emphasize the unity of the source of that bias.

These five procedures reveal the use of categories reflective of Substance, Being, Possibility, Existence, and Unity. They focus on distinct interior regions, ultimate realities, explanations, direct penetrative encounters, and origins of biases. I concerned myself with part of the first in *Beyond All Appearances* and *You, I, and the Others,* but neglected examining the finalities in depth. I emphasized the ultimate realities in *First Considerations* where the explanatory task was taken up primarily in accounting for the togetherness of actualities, beginning with *Modes of Being*. In *First Considerations,* there are scattered efforts made to use the two types of reality as explanations, but rarely using actualities, though the view of actualities as providing unities for all the finalities is one such attempt. In *You, I, and the Others,* I carry on the effort to penetrate into realities. An initial effort was made in *Beyond All Appearances,* particularly with reference to actualities. Finally, the way in which each of the oppositional realities imposes itself as a condition on the others lies behind the explanation of the occurrence of appearances, initially presented in *Beyond All Appearances.* I did not, of course, have these distinctions and procedures in mind when I was working on those books.

Alternatively: We begin with an appearance in which we are most insistent on ourselves (d) with a corresponding lesser emphasis on finalities (a). This makes it possible to penetrate into the finalities, but sets a problem for a more complete separation of ourselves, since that requires a number of steps where the hold by the body is overcome. The double activity yields two realities (b), one articulated, the other penetrated. Each of these can provide explanations (c), or unitary insistent expressions (e).

When dealing with actualities other than men, we would be inclined to begin at the phenomena, or to move to the position where we impose a lesser emphasis, and then to where there is a lesser emphasis on finalities, thereby enabling us to penetrate each as a reality. The explanatory and unitary states pertain to both the dominated-dominant finalities and to the private-bodily actualities, or to the dominant finalities and the privacy, depending on whether we want to deal with the finalities as at once dominant and dominated or as just dominant, and with ourselves as units in a world or as just human individuals.

If we move, in accordance with (b), to a privacy and body together, the starting point must be with the individual as involved in a larger world. This would require a distinguishing of grades in the privacy-body of an actuality. And there would have to be a penetration begun, not at the finalities, but at what is beyond them—with the evidence—if we are to attend to the finalities as at once dominant over and dominated by one another.

An account of the individual should, strictly speaking, begin with him as minimally affecting the world about and being maximally affected by it. One will then be able to move to the individual as a detached unit of privacy and body, and will then once again be able to take account of a minimal efficacy by the privacy, thereby leading to an understanding of it as having different grades of independence from the body. At both times we would free it from what was alien and brute. Similarly, if we start with the world as maximally affected by the finalities, but these in the state of being dominant and dominated, we will have to penetrate to them in this guise, and then find where the dominated aspect is maximally dominant in order to have a set of steps leading to the grasp of them as more and more in themselves. When we get to equal complex realities (privacies-bodies or dominant-dominated finalities) or portions of these (privacies or dominant finalities), we will be in a position to see how they can provide explanations or be unitary sources.

One could also begin with the individual as private and bodily, and only minimally involved with the finalities. This will allow for a penetration to him as apart, and will allow one to begin with an examination of the way to free the privacy from an initial maximum subordination to the body. Conversely, one could begin with dominant-dominated finalities as being maximally involved with the individual as both private and bodily, and gradually arrive at the stage where they are fully articulated.

There are the following to consider: starting with maximally involved privacies and bodies and going on to maximally or minimally penetrated privacies; starting with minimally involved privacies and bodies and going on to minimally or maximally involved privacies; and to another set of four for the finalities. The independents are privacies-bodies, privacies, dominating-dominated finalities, and dominating finalities. Each of these can be used to provide explanations, or to act as a source.

More consideration should have been given by me to bodies and dominated finalities as apart from the privacies and the dominating finalities. These, too, have grades, to be understood by starting with the bodies and the dominated as maximally involved with privacies and dominants, respectively. Though relatively passive, they have a status of their own and are able to be in ascendancy with respect to the privacies and dominant finalities. If so, they require these to engage in a series of acts of dislodgement involving recourse to deeper and deeper levels.

February 25

The Empedoclean principle maintains that there are two basic opposing forces which encroach on one another, with one now dominant and later the other. When one of them reaches maximum dominance, that other begins to take other; when this becomes maximally dominant, the initial power takes over, and so on without end. The force which is overwhelmed could not possibly begin the reverse move, of course, unless it had power in reserve. The awareness of that reserve makes possible the understanding of the different degrees of a self-maintained epitomization characteristic of a human privacy; it should also make possible the understanding of the different degrees of density characteristic of a finality.

We detach ourselves from our governing sensitized bodies so as to act more effectively on larger areas. The beginning is with the aesthetic sensitivity; the end is with a submission to a final governance of all bodies. Responsibility is connected with a finality which controls it. Finalities (as we ourselves) are least in control of our sensitized bodies, we failing to control them as brute, and the finalities failing to control each of them as just one among the many over which they exercise a common rule. Since, when we retreat from the body, the finalities are in control of us, on recovering ourselves from dominance by the body we become dominated by the finalities as ideal ends. A state is at the midpoint between men's increased separateness from their bodies while extending the range of men's governance through a greater and greater identification of finalities as their counterparts, and the finalities' narrowing of their range so as to be pertinent to this or that body.

Men escape the control or limitation by their bodies, species, environment, milieu, society, and state, by retreating to a higher ground in themselves where they face the finalities as privately experienced objectives. If this is correct, one should apeak of an experienced pain as a kind of congealed finality brought under private control. Something similar would have to be said about the object of desire as not yet reached, the efficacy of the species, and even of obligation. The references here, of course, are to the termini of experiences, and not to what is occasioned by a body or is a condition apart from it.

How does one know that another who does not conform to conditions set by his body, society, state, etc. does not understand the conditions, incorrectly responds to them, or just fails to have something pertinent to do with them? How do we know when he is denying them for the sake of recovering himself and engaging in other, presumably more appropriate tasks? Must one not assess the conditions as those to which one would conform?

A protestor of a state's assignment of duties or guilt provides a condition to which the state should conform—or if it cannot, a condition requiring the state's modification or abolition. One who paid no attention, or who incorrectly understood, would offer no such condition.

When a chimpanzee gives the wrong answer to a question, one could warrantedly say it was playing, deceiving, etc., only if it could be shown that it was engaged in playing, trying to deceive, etc., and thus that a number of its activities were joined together under the conditions of playing or deceiving, etc. To this, it might be objected that one might make a single playful gesture, offer just one isolated protest against the state, and so on. But then the issue is ambiguous, or the individual is already known to be one who freely conforms and therefore can freely not conform. If a chimpanzee does not really understand what it is signalling, then its failure to do what is expected does not show that it is playful. But to know that it is freely conforming is already to know that it is able to be playful, etc. If we know that a man conforms to the demands of a state from a position which the state does not control, we know that when he does not conform he can be making use of the same freedom that he used to conform, or that he is employing it to carry out a series of activities, all of which fit inside a new pattern.

The Empedoclean principle seems to operate with respect to the dominating-dominated finalities as they meet the privacy-bodies to produce appearances oriented toward the one or the other, with the midpoint at phenomena. It seems to work, too, with reference to the relation of the dominating to the dominated finalities, and with respect to the privacies and their bodies. We escape it only when we take the phenomena, not as midpoints between the appearances, but as the produced juncture of the finalities and actualities, and when we take the privacies and bodies not to make a continuous being, but to be productive of and joined by the emotions.

February 26

'From subjugation to sources' could well be the motto for the procedure I have been following, for I begin with an appearance, biased toward actualities or finalities, or with a human being, biased toward the body, and by a series of steps showing stages of freedom from the subjugating power, I move into the realities and privacy by stages, supplementing the penetration in which I can engage when the subjugated is in fact dominant. (More should have been done by me to deal with the stages to be distinguished in the actualities and finalities. A beginning, though, was made in the distinguishing of the in-itself, etc., and of the transcendentals from qualifiers, etc. in *First Considerations*.)

If a state be viewed as a neutral place where individual assumption of accountability is countered by the finalities' restriction to men, we could begin an account of the state by attending to the way in which individuals in their interplay dominate over a common 'we', or to the way in which their grouping dominates over them individually, and then move to the position where the we is more extensive and has its own power, or to the position where the individuals present themselves as grounding rights.

If one were to follow this procedure, he would begin a study of man's privacy at the end of *You, I, and the Others,* where one is overwhelmed by the others, and proceed by steps to get to the individual as a body, a living body, and a lived body, and move on to the privacy with its various epitomizations, ending finally with an account of the *idios,* man at his most inward and effective. *You, I, and the Others,* from this perspective, penetrates to the individual as a you and proceeds inward to an I, without making many intermediate stops or justifying the view that there is an I, except as that which is in fact being employed in all claims, knowing, possessings, and the like. It then moves outward, to end with the individual as overwhelmed by all the others.

April 3

Since the last entry I have been rewriting 'Private Powers' from the beginning. During that time I have also been thinking on and off about what I called the problem of 'domains'. It now seems to be desirable to distinguish three distinct types, which I will tentatively call 'achievements', 'concentrations', and 'disciplines'. *Achievements* are the outcome of unions of final conditions with the daily world produced by men. *Concentrations* are unions of finalities and men produced by the daily world. *Disciplines* are unions of men and the daily world produced by the finalities. Because there are no less than five finalities, we will have a number of cases under each. And because the unions can be produced with a bias toward one or the other of the united items there will be two basic types under each head. A summary:

Achievements which unite Substance with the daily world will join together various items so as to subject them to an affiliating condition. If the emphasis is on Substance, and therefore on affiliation, we will have the technology forming various subgroups; if the emphasis is on the daily world, the primary consideration will be on equipment. Replacing Substance by Being yields coordinate items, pertinent to a *morality,* if we emphasize the finality; if the emphasis is on the daily world, we have *customary justice*. If we replace Being with Possibility and emphasize this, we get *pure mathematics;* if the emphasis is on the daily world, an *applied mathematics*. If we replace Possibility by Existence, and emphasize this we get *art;* if we emphasize the daily world, *craftsmanship*. If, finally, we replace Existence by Unity, we get *religion*, if we emphasize it, and *ritual* if we emphasize the daily world. In these different cases, one might begin with one emphasis and end with another. In art, for example, we engage in work or craftsmanship, initially, and then move over to art where the primary fact is the embedding of the work in a field provided by Existence. As this illustration shows, the use of one finality does not preclude the presence of the others in subordinated roles.

In all these cases, the outcome involves the union of distinct factors. That outcome, instead of being just some particular item, focuses on this at the same time that it projects backward and forward to provide a setting in which other similar products will be set. A work of art, a mathematical formula, a prayer, e.g., are the outcomes of the union of the daily world with a finality, due to the action of a man. All end with items in an appropriate area. Were there no men occupied with the outcome, it would still have some kind of reality, since the projection backwards and forwards will remain, and therefore will continue to allow for what the men produced. Art continues to be even when no one is attending to it, because it is in a distinctive area. Similar observations apply to the others. Achievements occupy a midpoint between factors used to constitute it. Though dependent on man to produce them, they continue to be apart from men.

Concentrations are unions of men with the daily world, produced by the action of the finalities. If the finality is Substance, we get *classification* if the emphasis is on men, *groupings* if it is on the daily world. If the finality is Being, we get *economics* if the emphasis is on man, *analysis* if on the daily world. If the finality is Possibility, we have *natural language* if the emphasis is on the daily world, linguistics or speech and communication if on man. If the finality is Existence, an emphasis on the daily world will yield a *milieu;* if on man what is *available*. If the finality is Unity, an emphasis on man yields *evaluations;* an emphasis on the daily world yields the *desirable* and undesirable.

Disciplines result from the union of finalities with men, produced by the daily world. An emphasis on Substance yields *society;* on men, *accountability*. An emphasis on Being yields *law;* on man, *duty*. An emphasis on Possibility yields *logic*; on man *epistemology*. An emphasis on

Existence yields *history;* on man, *anthropology.* An emphasis on Unity yields *axiology;* on men, *tradition.*

These various names are just headings; many undoubtedly will have to be changed. What they make evident is that, as is true in the daily world, men and finalities are determinate, and have relations to one another. Although the daily world is the outcome of the interplay of actualities (i.e., of men and other unit real, finite entities) these yield new items which are determinate in another sense. An emphasis on man, e.g., in a concentration, will yield classifications when, under the influence of Substance, he is joined with the daily world. The classification is something new, but it uses material obtained from men. As just a classification, it occupies its own area, but this is not entirely separable from the kind of bunchings the men already produced.

I am here evidently on the edge of something new—and not altogether in focus.

If we concentrate on a few cases, and deal particularly with emphases on one factor or the other, we can come a little closer to clarity: In mathematics we emphasize Possibility, making some use of the daily world to obtain units, even where we have mathematical results having no direct bearing on what is familiar. A non-Euclidean geometry goes back, as does the Euclidean, to original configurations and numbers taken as limits, generalizations, or boundaries of ordinary objects, though it then subjects them to final conditionings to bring them into new relationships not exemplified in the daily world. In art, we begin, instead, by working over things in the daily world; emphasizing the demands of a final Existence we are able to bring the work inside a domain where it consorts with others of the same kind. When, instead, we emphasize Existence, making some use of what we know of man, the daily world allows us to have a governing language. In linguistics, the emphasis is on Possibility, though with this as not unaffected by the way men in fact have used language. Law makes use of Possibility, emphasizing man but with some use of the daily world, thereby making the law pertinent to what in fact is occurring in the world with which man is involved. History, instead, makes use of Existence, emphasizing man, and making use of the daily world in order to operate with what is plausible, not too alien to what we now know.

The crucial cases, perhaps, are mathematics and art. Mathematicians are inclined to be Platonists because they seek a pristine purity and necessity. The attempt by linguistic philosophers and Hegelians to try to bring mathematics down into the dross of language or the world should not be construed to deny the fact of a pure mathematics, but to point up the truth that a mathematics can also be applied. The application preserves some of mathematics' integrity. It does not make mathematics a function of language or practice. Pure mathematics, and applied mathematics as well, are domains in which one constructs limited expressions, having a necessary relation to one another.

In art, instead of beginning, as one does in mathematics, with what is formal, one begins with what is available, and tries to make this be self-sufficient, to incorporate within itself a final excellence. This is done by working on the material that is available, and finally turning this into a unit in a domain. As something made, a work of art is subject to conditions through the agency of man, but as in the work, making determinate what occurs there, and doing so in a new way by relating it to finalities. The acknowledgment of the result of his working, as a work of art, involves a shift, so that the made item is seen to be not simply affected by a finality but to be pulled away from the world to become part of a domain. Where mathematical items are forged in domains and subsequently made to apply, art works are made in the world and subsequently brought into a domain apart from this.

June 12

The more appearances are freed from the contributions of actualities, the purer are the conditions which the final realities had expressed. If men fixate those conditions, and then fill them out with distinctive activities, they are able to produce a domain in which the distinctive features of the finalities are allowed to characterize a plurality of particulars. Mathematics, particularly when understood constructively as involving the production of diagrams, formulae, and the like, and embodying a rational necessity, is one such domain. The world of sport, with its multiple games, all governed by the objective of having a game well contested, with men at their bodily best, is another. So is the world of art with its works, each of which accumulates the union of an aim at beauty with the creative activities of men.

In every domain complexes are produced, each of which thrusts beyond itself to provide an area where other complexes can be. Each play in a game has this role; so do the games themselves. Each formula has this role in mathematics; so does a particular branch. Each work of art has this role; so do all the works of a particular kind, and so do all the kinds.

Outside the domains are men with different aptitudes toward an occupation with one or a few domains. The totality of men with these aptitudes constitutes the spirit of the time. The history of each domain records the ways in which the different particulars there are produced and related. When the result is read back into the men, as the realization of their aptitudes, we have a culture, whose course is the topic of a general history.

* * *

This entry comes over two months after the last. In part, this is due to the fact that I have been reluctant to write any more entries, since there seems little likelihood that this set of them will be published; in part because I have been involved in writing and rewriting 'An Exploration of Human Privacy'; and in part because I did not find myself thinking what was an advance on anything I had done, or was sufficiently different to merit recording. But I have just finished a paper on the nature of a game, to be read in Karlsruhe next month, and find myself maintaining that the plays of a game join together the rules, the energies provided by the men, and the objective of producing a game well played. It then became evident that the games themselves are related to one another in somewhat the ways in which the plays were, and that each offered a solution to the problem of the One and the Many, *ambulando*. The present entry results from my asking myself how the different domains are related to one another. Though the domains do not thrust toward one another, the men who occupy themselves with one of them can have aptitudes toward others. At a given time, men have aptitudes which some of them realize in the production of different domains. We never know just what the spirit of a people is except by coming back from the totality of domains they have sustained, and seeing what potentialities must have been there, to make possible the particularized domains that were in fact produced.

* * *

I had a birthday almost a month ago, rather quiet. I had a check-up a week ago; I am somewhat of the same health, with blood pressure of 110-70, and no symptoms of anything untoward. I have begun to paint again after an interval of about a year, perhaps somewhat more boldly and non-representationally than I had before.

Recently I have been employing a device of surprising simplicity and effectiveness, at least for myself. I say to myself, "I love everybody". I do not in fact; if I tried, I would be frustrated within hours. But when I say this I find that I break into smiles, and that I begin to look at various odd characters, who might otherwise have annoyed me or displeased me or, at the very least, made me try to avoid them, as interesting human oddities. I know that this is not the kindest of attitudes, and that it is far from showing any love. But I am not contending that I do love everybody or even many, but only that, when I say to myself that I do, it has a beneficial effect on me. The day becomes brighter, I feel gayer, and others seem more interesting. I do not aim at these results, nor do I in fact try to love everybody. All I do is say to myself "I love everybody", and these desirable results follow. I wonder whether this would work for every one, or most.

July 13

Dan Dahlstrom has remarked that *You, I, and the Others* fails to "give an account of the human experience of a non-erotic form of love". Jonathan's objection to 3.9 apparently has the same thrust. I think they are right. As a consequence, I have looked into some of my previous writings to see what I have had to say about love, and have now begun to think of it afresh. I think the results are compatible with what is said in *You, I, and the Others* and, contrary to what I first supposed, are not alien to my earlier view that an individual seeks to be self-complete.

When a man loves, he continues the process begun in expressing himself in and through his body. He makes himself continuous with the body and what lies beyond it. The outcome would be identical with the result of an Eastern identification of the self with (or even a loss of it in) an all-encompassing, undifferentiated absolute, were one not able to love, since the individual would then just spread endlessly outward. I think he could never lose all hold of himself. If so, 'enlightenment' in its complete form is never possible. At most, one ends with oneself as a mere point inseparably melting into an all-comprehensive undifferentiated totality.

One must love in order to remain oneself, for in the loving, one is directed at this or that individual, and so far, remains distinct from an undifferentiated totality. Could one love every item in the universe, one would engage in differentiated activities, with lines directing one to a plurality of distinct actualities. We perfect ourselves by loving, because we then, while allowing ourselves to merge into the totality, remain distinct and directed toward distinctive termini.

One who is loved is loved as an individual; So far he is completed, since he remains himself and yet receives the other without reserve. Where the lover becomes more himself, since he does not stand opposed to his body or to what is beyond it, but continues into these as integral to himself, the beloved becomes more complete, obtaining, through the gift of the lover, the lover himself, and thus what the beloved lacks as one who is just alongside other beings.

If this is correct, lover and beloved gain different things. The lover becomes more himself, no longer distinguished from some others, but melting into them, while the beloved becomes more complete, possessing in a new way and with more intimacy and directness the lover who is outside, and who defines him to be less than all there is. Only if the beloved loves as well, and only if the lover is himself beloved, do they gain in self-completeness. In no instance, of course, is any real being in fact made part of another. The acts always leave the real world as rich as before. But where, in knowing, we complete ourselves by adopting the articulated known content provided by what is present, in being loved we complete ourselves by adopting what is in fact a real other, in the form of an attentuated continuation of itself.

* * *

The entry before this, I notice, was also about love. That does not mean that I was thinking about the subject in the interval.

I have spent the month and much of the time before in going over the revised text of 'Explorations of Human Privacy', interspersing it with a trip to Karlsruhe to attend the first international meeting of the Philosophical Society for the Study of Sport—a most pleasant occasion, where I read a paper, and heard a number of others, most of which were not memorable. Hans Lenk was a splendid host and the German government and the university were generous in their support. There were no more than a few dozen members present at any session, from about a dozen countries.

I will try to refrain from writing in this work until I hear from the new director of the So. Ill. Univ. Press. If he agrees to having it published, and perhaps even to my planning volume 9, I will begin to think in terms of it. In the meantime, I will spend my extra energies, apart from revising the book in progress, in painting.

July 16

I have changed my mind. I will continue to write in this journal, even if the publisher decides that he will not print it. Firstly, it will eventually be seen by somebody, and what is worthwhile in it will surely be picked out and saved. Apart from that, I gain from writing down my vagrant thoughts, since I then get them into better focus. There is also some value in having them set down, and thus seen in some relation to what I am systematically writing.

*   *   *

Kant, it could be said with justice, tried to relate the One (of conditions) with the Many (of an extensionalized manifold). His metaphysical deduction of the categories tries to unite them from the side of the One, while his transcendental deduction tries to unite them from the side of the Many. His schematism tries to have them meet in a common time, with judgment bringing them together as controlling and controlled.

Kant supposed that the conditions were formal and the content spatio-temporal. But as the discussion of the We in *You, I, and the Others* makes evident, there are other than formal conditions, and other than existential content to which the conditions can apply. Kant's account falls within the discussion of 4.6, d,· e, and f, pages 302-6 of *You, I, and the Others.* I there take the conditions to operate in something like the way conditions function in a Kantian judgment, but not, as he held, to be due to the exercise of a mysterious power of the imagination. Real conditions have a power of their own; a genuine 'metaphysical deduction' does not stop at categories but at content that would otherwise be set in contrast with the Kantian 'logical categories'.

By applying the different cases distinguished in the discussion of the We, it is possible to produce a large number of variants on the Kantian position. We could, for example, take a 'judicious mind' to begin with an equitable simple we and bring this to bear on content that was purely formal. We would then have something like the outcome of mathematical thinking in topology, where different formal properties are equated. Or we could take an 'evaluative mind' to bear on content which was affiliated. (I pick these illustrations arbitrarily.) The outcome would be different kinds of aesthetic unities of different grades. Artists engage in such activity when deciding if one aesthetic whole of related items is better than another.

If there are five primary conditions which characterize distinctive uses of the mind, we should have minds that are affiliative (the minds of the associationalistic psychologists?), judicious, formalistic, spatial, temporal, causal, and assessive. Each should be seen to be able to be brought to bear on any one of seven different kinds of content, through distinctive acts of subordinative judgment.

Is there any point in going through a 'metaphysical' or a 'transcendental' deduction if in fact one is able to bring the formal at once to bear on content in a judgmental act? It does not seem so. But if there is some value in trying to see how far one can go by starting with one of the factors and subjecting it to various other factors short of the judgment, we can multiply the cases already indicated by giving each of them a 'metaphysical' and a 'transcendental' deduction, and supplementing the results with distinctive schematisms.

If it be recognized that a 'metaphysical' deduction cannot occur without a continued grasp of content which will direct and guide the deduction, and that a 'transcendental' deduction cannot occur without a 'transcendental unity of apperception', which is a condition guiding and controlling it, we can add to the above possibilities. We can then have deductions which begin with a condition or content, and proceed toward the other, while being guided and controlled by it. We could, for example (to take another case arbitrarily), start with a causal condition and objects of different values, and try to get more and more concrete forms of the first by specifying them through the agency of the second. Or we could try to get more and more comprehensive forms of the second by making them more and more subject to the first. Neither of these efforts will end with their union; all that one would succeed in doing would be to see how close one could get to the other while never escaping the confines of that with which one began. We would always remain either with the causal condition or with the valuable objects, but would understand each as at the limit of an approach to the other.

*   *   *

I have now seen the ascendancy and decline of a number of philosophical movements. First there was idealism, then pragmatism, then positivism, and just now analysis. I am speaking primarily of course, about the United States, and am referring to dominant views. Analysis has been defeated politically for the moment at the last meeting of the Eastern division of the American Philosophic Association, where the members rejected the official slate—a slate produced, as such slates had been for over a decade, by analysts. And now Rorty's book appears exposing bankruptcy of the entire movement by pursuing the implications of the views of its leaders to the bitter end. Rorty thinks that he has also shown that speculative thought is bankrupt and willful, but this he merely assumes, taking no account of the views of the speculative thinkers of his time. Another movement will surely soon come to the fore, also somewhat simplistic, for this is the way in which academics find it easiest to engage in what they call 'philosophy'. I have no idea just what this new view will be like.

July 21

A domain is a humanly produced set of items. There are at least fourteen domains, each with many subdomains dealing with specialized objects and relations. In each something essential to final realities—their ability to provide prescriptive relations among actualities—is joined by men to something essential to actualities—their unduplicable singularity. There are seven cases where the contribution of the finalities is dominant, and seven where the contribution of the actualities is. There can of course be many grades between, with a limiting one where the two are equally effective. And we can have cases where the contribution of the finalities or of the actualities has its own insistency. But these various grades and cases I will now ignore, to concentrate solely on those where one or the other is dominant and the two are joined through the efforts of men.

1. A *society* is a domain in which the primary condition is affiliative, and the individuals assume roles. The primary emphasis here is on the affiliative condition, the designated roles enabling the condition to have application to actual men. (This seems to make unnecessary the 'harmonics' spoken of in *First Considerations*.) Society, in this guise, is what interests sociologists and anthropologists.

2. A *class*, (in somewhat of a Marxian sense) is a domain in which individuals, through their work, sustain a distinctive type of interrelationship. Here the stress is on the individuals, with the relationship enabling them to make contact with an affiliative condition of wider scope and greater insistence, and allowing one to relate the class to other classes. Where a society is primarily structural, a class is primarily dependent on the actions of its individual members.

3. *Economics* is a domain where the primary condition is coordinative and equalizing, and the individuals present different goods which are there connected. Economics in this sense is also a system of (civil) justice. The application of it takes us to living individuals who are considered only as the producers and consumers of goods.

4. *Convention* is a domain in which the emphasis is not on a coordinative condition but on individuals facing one another, thereby giving a function to a coordinative relation. Convention allows one to attend to justice as that which is to provide convention with lodgement, generalization, and correction.

5. *Mathematics* is a domain where necessity is combined with variables and their values, to constitute a system that can be empirically used by taking individuals to be the loci for the values. As is true of the other domains, the domain of mathematics is constituted by the actions of men. Men, primarily by working on diagrams, in Peirce's sense, produce abstract units related to one another by thrusts beyond themselves to others which, with them, are terms in the necessitating relation.

6. *Theory,* as constitutive of formal science, is a domain where the emphasis is on what is occurring. Theory makes possible the envisagement of mathematical necessity as that in which the theory will eventually be imbedded. But as just a theory, it remains attached to individuals, insisting on their unduplicability as it connects them formally.

7. *Spatial arts* put primary emphasis on space in its purity, filled out with colors and figures that are less concrete than any actuality. They can be brought to bear on actualities when used representatively, or when they allow one to grasp what it is to occupy space by laying hold of it from within an unduplicable privacy.

8. *Geography* reverses the emphasis of the spatial arts to emphasize actual, occupied, related spatial regions and, incidentally, to make possible a better grasp of sheer spatiality.

9. *Temporal arts,* and most evidently story and poetry, emphasize the sheer passage from past to present to future, filling them out with counters which could be embodied in actual men and other finite entities.

10. *Sport* places emphasis on particular games with an incidental incorporation of the rules. The games make it possible to articulate the nature of a pure time.

11. *Causal arts,* most clearly musical performances and the dance, emphasize the productiveness, the dynamism which is punctuated by symbols of particulars.

12. *History* reverses the stress of the causal arts, to emphasize particular kinds of occurrences related by causation. To know history is to know a domain which can illuminate the nature of a primary dynamic condition.

13. *Theology* is a domain where emphasis is placed on final values organized in dogma so as to be able to apply to individuals.

14. *Religion* is a domain where emphasis is placed on individuals and their needs, joined together in rituals, thereby becoming pertinent to a final value.

Not all of the above designations or even their descriptions will, I fear, withstand detailed examination. There is, particularly with reference to the arts, a singular neglect here of the ideal of excellence that guides the making of works. Indeed, in all the cases, something of the factors pertinent to other domains must be given a role. There is also something too formal about the presentation, obscuring the fact that every one of these domains is the product of vital activity on the part of men.

All the domains have their own boundaries. To move from one to another, the items in that one must be transformed. We cannot, e.g., get an art work into history without setting it in within a causal whole where the primary determination is the way in which the work enables a dynamism to be illustrated, and this regardless of the merits of the work.

There is an all-encompassing domain of human culture or civilization. Because of the distinctive boundaries of specialized domains, the domain of human culture cannot be a sum of these. Culture is presupposed by them all, but is filled out by them separately, without regard for the culture which they together articulate.

If I understand Nelson Goodman correctly, he would hold that there is nothing more or less than a plurality of domains, but this he cannot say unless he can occupy a position outside all of them—and that must be the as yet unarticulated position of a single culture. But even this is not enough. There is more to the 'mixed' than domains. Not only are there situations where there are no men and which men never did help bring about, but there are actualities and finalities out of which the domains must be produced, and objective appearances which the actualities and finalities together constitute even when there are no men.

Only an identification of scientific objects with the variables or values of scientific theories will allow one to suppose that the world of science is nothing but a domain. Just as mathematics incorporates a necessity that is part of a final rationale, and in such a way as to make it applicable to actualities, so scientific theories incorporate the singularities of actualities in such a way as to make a combination of them illuminate the nature of a final necessity. In mathematics the necessity connecting the terms is laid bare; in theory that necessity is specialized, limited, bounded within laws which are oriented toward what is actual.

In all domains, the primary fact is the activity of producing units within larger fields which, when filled out, allow either for the presence of an essential dimension of a finality or some specialized bounded version of this, and therefore for the presence of some abstraction from actualities or of an essential dimension of actualities.

We avoid entrance into domains by avoiding an emphasis on human constructions and attending, instead, to what is before one. The claim

of Wittgensteineans, in effect, is that this is not possible. They seem to
hold that there is in fact only one domain, the domain of language in
which one participates, apparently more or less passively, and that there
is no going outside it and therefore no understanding of how it is constituted. One simply is in the domain and carries out its requirements.
But you can't play a 'language game' (or any other kind of game) without
entering into it from somewhere, respecting its rules, and making use
of material (speech, writing) outside it.

The outline of the fourteen domains suffers, too, I think from the
too ready assumption that in each case there is a possible application to
singular actualities, or an approach to final conditions. But music and
other arts need make no reference to any actuality. And there may be
no occasion for a history to illuminate or to take us to some final state.
Mathematics can be applied, but not every part of it; much of it just
remains biased toward a formal necessity, leaving governing variables
and their values without any necessary bearing on any matter of fact.

July 22

Yesterday's listing of domains requires considerable refinement.
It mixes references to actual states of affairs with references to disciplines.
It should refer to sociology rather than to society if there is to be a
matching with mathematics; and to classification rather than class if there
is to be a matching with theory. There should also have been consideration given to those cases where the contribution of the relational component is about equal to that of the units. And once it is seen that art
cannot be understood without taking account of an excellence to be
achieved, a matter repeated on connection with sport, and undoubtedly
present in mathematical constructions in the form of importance, the
presence or absence of such a factor in other domains should be examined, and not put aside with the comment that all factors undoubtedly
have some role.

A mathematical domain involves deliberate acts of men in the creation of a new self-enclosed field in which units are subject to a necessity
in relation to one another. Were one to look for a match with society,
one would have to find a domain where necessity related men. Conversely, if we take mathematics to be our model for a domain, we must
replace society by sociology, since sociology is a product resulting from
a combining of factors (that had been abstracted from actualities) with
an affiliative power obtained from a finality.

July 23

Kant's transcendental deduction of the categories—more correctly, of 'categoreality'—depth grammar, structuralism, Schenker and Zuckerkandl's dissection of what is at the 'forefront' in music, and my own probing of the emotions in *Cinematics* seem all to be occupied with the same task. The original of all these is obviously Plato's ascent to the good in the *Republic*. It is what occupies me in my attempt to move (in the book I am now writing) from what is publicly manifested to private sources, ending finally with the self, I, and the *idios*, that which governs all expressions of a common privacy. In all the cases, the move seems to be toward what provides a unity for what otherwise would be an inexplicable assemblage. The problem in each is to discover more and more basic unities or 'synthetizing powers'.

Kant differs from the others in starting with what is supposedly more or less unorganized and trying to find out what would be required to organize it so that one finally comes to have genuine categoreal knowledge of the kind needed in science in its classical guise. The others start with the fully complete but not intelligibly organized content found in direct experience, and try to understand it as involving the imposition or expression of more and more basic unities in alien situations which introduce dispersions.

If one were to bring Kant's approach in accord with the others, one would start, not with the 'manifold', but with common experience, and try to show that it is the product of layers upon layers of unities which the 'manifold' filled out. If the 'manifold' and the 'transcendental unity of apperception' are taken to be his ultimates, Kant could be said to be trying to account for the existence of a domain of scientific knowledge. Where the others, so as to understand what is initially confronted, suppose that what they are using is more real, more basic—Zuckerkandl is an exception—than the product, Kant apparently wants to hold that it is the product alone that is real, and that the 'manifold' and the 'transcendental unity of apperception' are 'givens', presuppositions, or something of that order. One could reasonably also hold that Kant accepted the fact that there was objective scientific knowledge, and looked for the layers of unity which made it possible, by seeing what was lacking to sheer content spread out in space and time. If we followed something like this line, we could start with just a body and ask ourselves what makes it be a human body. If we followed the other method, we would start with the human body and try to isolate factors, powers, etc., which must originate elsewhere, because they control or unify the body. We find evidence in what we confront of what is determinative of and has been imposed on it, so as to turn, what would otherwise not be anything more than an inexplicable plurality, into what is unified. If Kant followed that method, he would start with scientific objective knowledge and show that the content of it was unified in a series of more and more basic forms of knowledge.

Is there one set of unities that must be exhibited no matter whether we are dealing with music, knowledge, social practices? Is there some principle which tells us just what steps to take in a move from initial data to the conditions which make it possible? I have not found one.

The deeper the source of principles, the broader their range. If one begins with a man making his body living and sensitive, and moves on to him using his body to become social, or to enable him to fulfill his obligations, one moves in somewhat of a Kantian way, looking for what makes richer and richer outcomes. One, though, should avoid the Kantian attempt to begin with what is not organized at all, or is merely spatio-temporal, and begin instead with what, from the first, is subject to some kind of controlling condition. But then the subsequent moves can be rather Kantian. My own approach can be said to be non-Kantian in that I start with what is already organized, but to be Kantian in making a progressive acknowledgment of conditions having possibly richer or wider reaching results. A non-Kantian approach takes man in state and society as initial data; a Kantian takes him to be a body. I take him to be an expressive sensitive being, and look with Kant for principles warranting the acknowledgment of, and explaining what it is like for him to be more, and finally to be in a state or a society. In the different ways, one looks for the same set of unities. The problem then is: is there a necessary set of more and more basic unifying conditions which we can use to explain everything we already have—music, man in state and society, language, emotional organizations, private dimension? I don't know.

It is better to take a step by step approach than to begin with the richest possible content and try to discover its conditions. The richest possible content so incorporates the other stages that it does not let us see them working on their own. It also tends to make us overlook the fact that those other stages are exercised at times as the limit of what can be done, either by some kind of living being, or by man in some activity or in some not fully matured stage.

Though, in the various ways in which the move to what is explanatory and basic, there are cases where attention is paid only to man in his depths, and other cases where attention is paid to what is final, no one seems to have tried to engage in both movements. I, who have tried, never did spend much time trying to see what the layers in the finalities have to be in order to account for the ways in which those finalities in fact function in the world—though there is some suggestion of this in *Beyond All Appearances,* when I try to show how to move toward pure space.

In order to constitute a domain, a man must act from his depths. The discovery of levels in his privacy is one with the discovery of powers in him. These, among other things, can unite derivatives from actualities with essential features of finalities. If there are levels in a man, they will apparently differ in their effectiveness in uniting what is obtained from the actualities and finalities. But there need not be any consideration of the levels in these, since domains are constituted, not by them in their concreteness, but by facets derived from each.

Perhaps there is no need to consider different levels in men, for what is required of them in connection with domains is only creativity? What is less than this, the mechanical, habitual, conventional, derivative, or inadvertent, can be understood to be the outcome of a hardening of the creativity. Our interest in different levels in man is then evidently not due to an interest in domains, but to an attempt to understand what man himself is, beginning with what is constituted by some level in him in interplay with resistant material provided by his body and what is beyond this.

A man's fundamental power will be expressed in one way when it is occupied with producing units in domains; in another way when he is speculative (to follow the suggestion in *Cinematics*); in a third way when he is self-controlling and active at the same time; in still another way, when he acts representatively for others in a state; and in a fifth way when he insistently imposes himself as a possessor and measure of all else. These five ways match distinctions based on Existence, Possibility, Substance, Being, and Unity, respectively. This observation suggests that we move to man at his most inward from content that exhibits him as involved with what is affected primarily by one finality or another. But if all domains are the outcome of the action of men who, as creative, are primarily existentialized, the difference between one type of domain and another will not only depend either on what is derived from actualities or what factor one is able to obtain from a finality, but will deny to creativity a role in the other types of activity—and that seems not to be correct.

A man is creative when making domains. He is also creative when he speculates, is self-governing, functions as a representative, and measures all else. We must, at the very least, evidently distinguish between the acts of men involved in uniting various factors to produce a domain, and their equally creative acts directly imposed on content in order to make this serve their purposes. Suppose then that a man has as his purpose the making of a domain? Must we not say that he then faces an ideal of excellence whose creative realization is achieved in the course of a creative production of units in a domain?

July 24

One ought to use the richest possible result as a guide. At the same time, one should start with the thinnest result in order to isolate the lowest form of a contribution. This is to be used to constitute the first step on the way to reaching the richest possible result in fact. Hegel engaged in something like that procedure in the *Phenomenology of Mind*. But he took the beginning of the move which was to reach the richest possible result to be itself due to the action of the richest reality. Yet both the richest possible and the richest actual result are products of two distinct powers, the results differing form one another in that the first has one of the factors in a radically indeterminate, while the second has it in a maximally determinate form. The goals sought by men are prospects; the actions of men, in accord with what they had introduced into those prospects, add determinations to those prospects to turn them into actual outcomes.

Hegel also held that earlier stages were transcended and yet preserved in what came after. It is hard to see in what way they could be preserved. So far as he held a doctrine of internal relations, what was achieved lost its boundaries to become merged with all else. (If what is achieved continued to hold on to its boundaries, it becomes less clear just what his dialectic accomplishes.) I think we must say that what is achieved never loses its boundaries, and that when we advance beyond one stage to a 'higher' more determinate, richer one, we provide another context in which that determinate result can be.

There seem to be a number of 'richest possible outcomes'. There is the perfection of a man; the Confucian community of civilized men or the Epicurean society of friends; a religious community; a social group; a state; culture; civilization; the cosmos where all realities preserve their boundaries at the same time that they encompass units related to one another by cosmic laws; (despite the negativity of the expressions) Tao, Nirvana; the Day of Last Judgment; the Absolute; the world of commonsense or experience; the world open to scientific knowledge. How are we to choose amongst these? Can they be comprehended within one account?

Is not the richest, the whole of civilization, viewed as within the cosmos and as having a history, and within which men, their societies, states, domains, culture all have their bounded realities? To say this is, of course, to go beyond the position which I have for the most part assumed in the past, that the beginning of philosophy (and therefore, on the present account of a proper beginning, the richest) is in common sense. As I have previously remarked, common sense is somewhat chaotic and indeterminate, and contains the various disciplines only in incipient forms. Common sense is only part of the richest content, and then only so far as it is one with what a reasonable man knows or takes for granted. At best, it is only one among the 'richest possible outcomes' and then only if viewed as the product of men in interplay with one another in a milieu.

If the proper start is at an historically grounded civilization, set in the cosmos, we must look to limited areas within it to provide beginnings for limited inquiries. In these, individuals will be privately matured; be in control of themselves; be self-contained while together with their fellows; and be representative of the rest. There will be a cosmos; actualities; a set of the most comprehensive domains; separated domains in which men can be creative to a degree they otherwise could not; and a set of all the finalities, each conditioning and encompassing the others. Can the number be reduced? Can the various cases be interrelated?

We could start with men by themselves as most mature inwardly, and therefore able to be most completely involved with other men and finalities. Or we could start with men as subject to the cosmos or to their bodies and other actualities, and thus most subject to these in situations at their richest. Similarly, we could start with finalities at their inward richest, enabling us to get to what other finalities, all actualities, men, and the cosmos are—or conversely, with the finalities as involved with all else, thereby leading us to a knowledge of what they are at their richest by themselves. We could take our start with a cosmos of men, finalities, actualities, and ultimate units. And finally, we could start with actualities as involved with men, finalities, other actualities, and men. Domains would be found only where men at their richest dealt with finalities and actualities, and were sustained by a cosmos and other men.

These various suggestions are now being only vaguely apprehended; they are really just blind stabs in the dark. One problem is that the richest possible situation for one type of being will involve its dominance over other types. We will either have to allow for a plurality of situations where different realities are dominant, or start with one in which all are in equilibrium, neither dominant nor dominating. We must apparently either start with the prospect of men, matured, healthy, self-controlled, dominating over all else, or with such men so far as they can be members of a single civilized world. The latter allows for the maximum rights of all other beings to be maximally satisfied, with universal conditions operating on all levels of relationship and in individuals, and being subject to one another. A move deep into actualities and finalities is a third alternative, where, in each member of a disjunctive set of situations, one contributor is dominant. We will then have: a mature, healthy self-controlled individual; a civilized world; the maximum rights of all other beings maximally satisfied; universal conditions operating on all levels in the form of relations and in the form of individualized determinants; and finally, each finality dominant over the others. In this way we can envisage the richest possible results which will lead to the understanding of fundamental realities at their most powerful.

Since the actual beginning will be with the least rich manifestation of an entity, and therefore with one where others are maximally manifest, we should be able to find all the other realities at their maximum there, and together; if they could not be maximal and together there, the entity would be minimal in a number of disjunctive ways. Though there is no one conjunctive set of all the realities at their maximum, are there no sets in which one is minimum and all the rest are maximum? Is it possible for a human to just live his body sensitively, as an embryo might, and his body there exhibit in maximum form the other actualities, the finalities, and other men? Might a domain be one of the ways in which men deal with a number of dominant powers together, becoming dominant over them by starting within himself at a deep level and isolating dimensions of them which it will unite?

July 25

If we begin with man as primarily bodily, and therefore as exhibiting only a private sensitivity, we should find his body to be a place where his sensitivity is dominated by other actualities, the various finalities, and other men. As dominated by the other actualities, his body will be in a world with others; as dominated by the finalities, it will be subject to a plurality of universal conditions, which both qualify and relate it to all others; as dominated by other men, it will be a body that could be held accountable by them and therefore be subject to rewards and punishments for occurrences which need not in fact originate with that body. The privacy of a man will be able to overcome that dominance and, in turn, dominate over what was dominating its body, by making use of powers more basic than that of the sensitivity—desire, mind, will, etc. The more an individual achieves such domination, the more will he be involved with what has reality apart from his body.

A body has different dominant forces together impinging on and affecting it on one side, and a sensitivity affecting it on the other. As the privacy achieves more and more control, it will not only use the body on behalf of various private deeper and deeper powers, but will be involved in a number of distinct areas. As dominated, the body is one. As expressing itself in and by means of the body, the privacy is one. But as imposed on different items—other actualities, the various finalities, or other men—privacy is involved in a number of distinct situations. The commonsense world is to be found somewhere along the route.

The commonsense world is one where men and other realities effect one another in various degrees, all hovering around the position where they are equally influential. One could make an 'unofficial' beginning there, remaining alert to those cases where some one type of item was subject to all the others, and then tracing this back to the point where the dominance was at its maximum. This would be the place to make an 'official' beginning of an investigation into the nature of an individual man, the nature of final realities, the nature of other actualities, or the ways in which men or other actualities are together. This 'official' beginning would be directed at the opposite state of affairs, where the dominated item would be dominant. But where the 'official' beginning is dominated by all the other types of being, an end which is to guide the move to have the dominated become dominant, has just one of those types operating. Were the body dominated by other actualities and men, for example, a man's privacy would be directed either toward the other actualities or toward the other men.

In *Beyond All Appearances* I offered a gradation of eight steps showing how actualities and space affected one another in different degrees. But the move there was too swift. If the foregoing discussion has merit, I should have begun with an occupied space in which space itself was dominant, and moved from this to the position of a private occupant that expressed itself by making the whole of space be that for which it provides an orientation point. To get to pure space we must move from such an oriented space to the position where the occupant of space is subject to a condition over which it has no control.

Both the 'official' and the 'unofficial' beginnings would be 'mixed', in Plato's sense. At both times there would be distinct powers in various positions of dominance. Plato held, and I have as well, that one can get to the pure cases, where other factors were not present. But each should also be seen to reach toward the other factors, and to dominate them. If we start with any item in its purity, we will end with it being expressed in a dominant way over the largest possible region. But we should begin, with the mixed where some one type of item is dominated by others. We will then be able to start with that dominated item and, guided by the prospect of its being fully dominant over one of the items which dominated it, move into the item so as to identify powers which allow it to become dominant progressively, over a number of stages. To know what a man is in his privacy we begin with his sensitized body and move gradually deeper and deeper into that privacy to find those powers which enable one to become more and more dominant over what had dominated that body. If, instead, we sought to know some finality, we would have to begin where it was dominated. We would then move into the finality in order to identify a power in it that would enable the finality to be less dominated, and would progress along those lines until we came to where the finality was able to dominate over every type of being.

If it be true that domains are the result of individuals trying to master both actualities and finalities at the same time, should we not also have other products of efforts to master other pairs of entities? Should there not be representative individuals who join mankind with basic types of relations; standard individuals who envisage mankind in an alien world; purposive individuals who relate mankind and finalities; observing individuals who connect actualities and relations; and specializing individuals who join relations and finalities and thus deal with conditions? I don't know. What is evident is that, if men do nothing more with respect to what is other than themselves than pair dimensions of actualities and finalities, other alternatives are not dealt with. To be sure, it is only domains which need individual men in order to be at all. Actualities and finalities, as together making a world of appearances, parallel these other products. Why then are there domains, resulting from men's use of factors of what would otherwise function to produce appearances? If men produce domains, ought they not produce, by similar uses of abstracted dimensions, something from mankind and relations; mankind and actualities; mankind and finalities; actualities and relations; and finalities and relations?

More directly pertinent to the previous discussions of domains is the question whether or not different distinguishable private powers—sensitivity, sensibility, need, desire, understanding, resolution, autonomy, responsibility, and the I—to list some of those that I have distinguished in the current 'Explorations of Human Privacy'—do not answer to different levels of a union of actualities and finalities, and thus provide different domains in which the united factors have different roles. We seem, for example, to have an hierarchy of mathematics, theoretical science, language, conversation, all involving the creative acts of men. These make use of different private powers and, therefore, make the necessity derived from Possibility and the singularity derived from actualities become modified by virtue of the different ways and different degrees to which they interplay with one another. But now it seems we must consider, not only various essentialities, each to be derived from a different finality, but the different degrees in which each is exhibited. The different degrees enable them to constitute domains having different units and connections produced by men making use of different powers of unification in themselves, and imposed on the derived factors. The same factors would be derived from actualities and a particular finality, but the two would be joined together in different ways, depending on what private dimension of the individual was being used to unite them.

Faced with a domain that made use of powers not at the deepest level in a man, we could engage in a 'depth analysis' so as to arrive at what were purer forms of the dimensions derived from the actualities and a finality. We would move from language, let us say, to theoretical grounds and then to a mathematical base. But such analysis is not exactly what 'depth' studies seek; they want to remain with a language, music, science, or experience while dissecting and analyzing it into more basic elements. It is one thing to pass from language to mathematics, and another to pass from language to depth grammar. What is that difference?

If the world of art depends on the creative exercise of sensibility, the depth analysis of the product will continue to involve sensibility, but instead of giving the factors an equal role, depth analysis will emphasize one of them to the disadvantage of the other. The 'mathematics' found at the root of an art is one in which necessity is related by sensitivity to the singularity of actualities. The patterning and the relations of the patterns to one another, that are expressible mathematically, are related to one another by a creative thrust. This bunches and separates the necessities of the mathematical in accord with the demands of sensibility.

July 26

I am near the very end of my current revision of 'An Exploration of Human Privacy'. At present it is a very uneven book, with long sections that need to be rewritten. I will put it aside for a while, particularly since I want to develop the ideas which I have been struggling with these last days. I found that, as I progressed in the revising of the manuscript of AEHP, I also became somewhat bored and was not engaged in any vital thinking. But now I have begun, not only to think, but to find life more exciting just because I am struggling. I do not want to paint, visit anyone, go to any shows, do anything but think and write. I find that I am happiest then, more so than I am at any other stage in writing, and surely in any other kind of activity.

* * *

Granted that there are five finalities, that a domain is produced by men joining an essential feature of one of the finalities with the singularity of actualities, that the joining has various degrees (formal, theoretical, structural, and segregational) and that it makes use of a man's creative powers as initiated by some limited private power in him, making use of his body and material, we have the following schema to consider:

A man unites an affiliativeness with singularity to produce items joined to one another segregationally. If sensitive, he groups items which are congenial and makes other groups of those which are not. He engages in a depth analysis when he moves from that segregational result to structural, theoretical, and finally to formally controlled domains. Another segregational result is produced when an equilibriating factor is joined to a singularity, yielding units of stimulation, all on a footing. Emphasizing the need to analyze, we move to a purely formal structure, creatively united by sensibility with singularity. A segregational result is also obtained by sensitivity when it is used to join a purely prescriptive condition with singularity, to yield groups of approved or disapproved items. Here, too, we can move through analysis to the stage where the initial condition plays a dominant role. The prescription then has the guise of a formal rule pertinent to the singularity. It is reached by going through the stages where it is first seen to be structural, and then to have a theoretical role.

A segregational result is obtained by sensitivity when it is used to join some form of extension with singularity to produce a field. The result is a domain of the usable or available, which can be analyzed in depth. A segregational result, finally, is obtained by sensitivity when it joins a determination of value, in the form of a grading, with singularity. Once again a depth analysis will lead to a formal principle, but now one pertinent to singular values.

Sensitivity is here being understood to join affiliative, coordinative, prescriptive, extensionalizing, and grading agencies with singularity, so as to constitute limited groups of entities. Analysis is then employed to get to the agencies in their most formal guise, by going through the stages where they function as structures and theories. The sensitivity is used in the different cases to yield domains of the congenial/uncongenial; units of stimulation; the approved/disapproved; the available or useful; and the better and worse.

We have here an outline which can be used with appropriate alterations in connection with a creative use of sensibility in the arts, by the understanding in abstract disciplines, and by resolution in the playing of games. In AEHP I have also found warrant for distinguishing need, desire, positioning, sociality, sagacity, accountability, responsibility, and the I. If what is said there is sound, there ought to be cases where these are also used creatively to constitute domains, each characterized by an essential feature of some finality, and able to be subject to a depth analysis. But there is no point in going through a purely abstract set of possibilities, except to make one alert to possibilities. What is most desirable is a careful examination of the different types of created domain, each making use of a distinctive power in man. If this cannot be done, at least such well-known domains as art, mathematics, sport, economics, history, must be dealt with. To see whether or not it can be done, an effort to carry out the schema in all cases must be made.

It is best to put aside the question of depth analysis. So far as I have gone, it seems to have the same stages in all cases. The created domain has the factors most effectively together and of rather equal strength in segregated situations, and to take us toward the contribution of a finality when we pass through the stages where that contribution serves to provide first a structure and then a theory. It will suffice then for the time being to concentrate on domains of segregated items (each the product of a distinctive creative power making use of an essential feature of one finality at a time) and joining each to singular entities. If now we return to the initial case of a creative sensitivity, we will acknowledge the same five cases listed, but will ignore the fact that they can be subject to a depth analysis. Most important, an effort must be made to see the creative power at work. How does a man, using his sensitivity, act in and through his body, so as to produce a distinctive domain?

*   *   *

I have now returned from a seven-plus mile walk, have had my lunch, and read a few pages in a book on structuralism to see if my view of it was on the right track. I am now ready, I think, to make a fresh start, emphasizing the actual creation and nature of domains, and remembering (as I did not in the schema with which I started today) that what one does is guided by an ideal having an initial subjugated item in a position where it is no longer hemmed in by other factors but, instead, has them as possible subordinates.

1. A man's sensitivity has a private origin and some controlling effect on his body. But that body dictates how it will be expressed. It is a body, too, which should not be viewed in isolation, but as under the dominance of other actualities, other men, and whatever final conditions control and relate whatever there be. It is a body, too, which functions as an agent for the sensitivity, enabling this to take account of the presence of the concrete singularity of other individuals, human and non-human, and of the demands of ultimate conditions. Sensitivity is creative when it joins the two. If we ignore the different degrees to which conditions are dominant, we can say of the result that it is a domain of what is acceptable or not acceptable to all men as exercising their sensitivities with reference to the two factors.

A domain is a produced field in which created items thrust forward and backward to provide possible places where other items can be. Produced by men, the domains exist apart from them, just so far as the items do. The items project beyond themselves. and when any part of the projection is filled by other items, there is an objectivity to them all. The domain continues to exist, but it is not identifiable with anything basically real. It is a product having its own integrity, within which one can distinguish variants or subdomains by changing the emphasis on one or the other constitutive factor. Men work within the frame of a domain just so far as they focus on the end to be attained while starting with the nature of that end as subordinated to other powers.

The world of utilitarians is a domain produced by sensitive men. The ethicists amongst those utilitarians emphasize the prescriptive character of formal principles. But ordinary men attend to that variant where the prescriptive rules are weak, and there is a merging of rules with content. A utilitarianism is the product of a depth analysis or, alternatively, a transcendental deduction, as is sometimes tacitly recognized when a reference is made to the ordinary man's occupation with what brings pleasure or pain. The ordinary man faces a segregated situation, occupied by a limited number of objects in which the presence of the prescriptive principles is hardly discernible. But it is with this that one must begin if utilitarianism is to have an empirical gounding.

The productive creative work of sensitivity, with respect to the factors obtained from actualities and finalities, is not usually recognized to yield a domain, because the relationship of one item to another is not often noted. But what is acceptable helps define the suitability of other items, particularly since the items accepted make room for the others, directed toward an ideal of what is finally acceptable. The result is sources of the pleasurable and painful, within which one can distinguish relations connecting items by affiliation, coordination, prescription, availability, and value.

2. Sensibility is the creative power utilized by artists. Musicians, painters, sculptors, and so on, differ from one another, not in their sensibility, but in the bodily organs and the material they use to produce what is in consonance with an ideal of the superlatively agreeable. Works of different arts are all members of distinctive domains, themselves together within the single domain of *works of art*. Each work is produced through the exercise of creative powers. Each is set in a field provided for by other works. Each makes possible positions where other works can be placed. Here, perhaps more conspicuously than in other domains, the initial situation in which we find ourselves is one where principles and rules are inextricably involved with the content.

Art works are extensional. In *Nine Basic Arts* I divided them into the spatial, temporal, and dynamic arts. But if this is so, there would seem to be no use for the other final conditions. There is such use, yielding, not works of art, but ways of dealing with them. An affiliative condition allows us to bring works of art together in schools, influences, cultures, and the like. A coordinative condition allows us to present them as on a footing, in a museum perhaps, as equally open for appreciation and enjoyment. A prescriptive condition allows us to see them as conforming to various canons. And an evaluative condition allows us to grade them. If these are to be considered to be equally basic with a domain which embraces works of art—products of a sensibility working on material so as to bring about a sensuous excellence—we will have to treat them as alternative to a world of art. But they are parasitical on such a world. Does this mean that the five types of domain, produced through the exercise of some one private power, are not alternatives? Do different types of creative power favor the use of some one kind of condition, and allow for the use of the others only in parasitical guises? Looking back at the first case, dealing with the action of sensitivity, is this not concerned primarily with what is evaluated? If we could answer these questions in the affirmative, we would simplify the examination of cases considerably, but would have to make good decisions as to just which condition is in fact basic.

The problem arose because I supposed that affiliations and the like had to do with art objects. But suppose, instead, one were to view the affiliations, which sensibility was joining to singularity, as having to do, not with works of art primarily, but with objects of design, appreciation, prescription, and approval? We would then have alternatives to a world of art, but apparently of an inferior nature. Should we say, then, that though there are five genuine alternatives for each mode of creation, they may be of unequal interest and that one of them might, as seems true of art, have the others as specialized cases—for a work of art takes account of designs, appreciation, prescriptions and approvals? Or should we say that a work of art stands out because of the fact that it radically transforms recalcitrant material? Might there not be works which sensibility creatively produces as loci of singularity, affiliation, etc.; and conversely, might there not be sensibly created products of extension and singularity which do not require an extensive working over of material? If we can make sense of these, we can go on to hold that a work of art combines all the final conditions, not only extensions. This seems plausible. What kind of union is produced by minimal work done in order to join extension and singularity? And if a work of art can combine all the conditions, should there not be something similar found when we use other creative powers?

One can unite extension and singularity without producing a *work of art*, and yet do this by making creative use of the sensibility, by conceiving attractive distributions of items in space, time, and becoming. And one can envisage sensitivity to be involved in a genuine making involving all conditions by taking it to be occupied with producing what will enhance pleasures to a degree not possible naturally. Is this not what we attempt to do when we provide means for producing?

If these ruminations can withstand criticism, we must, in addition to considering the five conditions severally, also take account of them as functioning together in an object requiring difficult creative work.

3. Need is a privately grounded power occupied with making good some lack of the body. Functioning creatively, it aims at bringing about satisfaction, contentment, the overcoming of tension. Used creatively, it unites singularity with an affiliative condition to produce a domain where items supplement or cancel one another; with a coordinative condition to provide a domain of substitutable items; with a prescriptive condition to provide a domain of permissible or tabooed items; with an extensional condition to provide occasions in which the need can be satisfied; and with an evaluative condition to grade satisfactions of need as better and worse. If a work is to combine all the conditions, and if this is where the need is at its most creative, reference perhaps has to be made to technology, inventions, and the like. The industrial world, it could then be said, is a domain in which individual men creatively join need to final conditions. If this is correct, we have sources of amusement, works of art, and technology on a par, all involving the creative use of private powers. But need seems to be a power more basic than sensibility, and yet a technological product is not a greater achievement than a great work of art. Must we not go on to say that a work of art not only has all conditions creatively used by sensibility, but that sensibility must be enhanced by a multitude of deeper powers? If so, what does mere sensibility produce when it creatively combines all final conditions with the demand that they be exhibited in particular cases? Will this not be just pleasant, folk art, the readily appreciated? If so, must we not also consider cases where sensitivity and need are also enriched by deeper powers? A world where *reasonable men* are produced who are occupied with what pleases and pains is perhaps what is achieved by the first; a need enriched by deeper powers, in somewhat the way in which sensibility is, will yield a technology or *industrial society* 'with a human face', in accord with what man himself is—the kind of technology or society that the Marxists envisage as coming about eventually.

I have now progressed to the point where, instead of concentrating on how distinct conditions are joined with a need for punctuation and concreteness (what I have termed 'singularity'), it seems desirable to concentrate on those cases where real work is required in order a. to have all five conditions operative, and b. to see creative power sustained and quickened by other powers. So far as I have now gone, this results in viewing sensitivity as a creative power ending with *reasonable men* occupied with *sources of pleasure and pain, works of art,* and *technological works* 'with a human face'. All require a beginning with a creative power, constrained by the body as conditioned with others and affected by what

is alongside. That power operates with the guidance of an ideal, in which
it is dominant over what now constrains it.

4. Desire is a private power serving the species primarily. That species, too, was operative in previous stages, serving to constrain the body,
and requiring sensitivity, sensibility, and need to free themselves from
it in order to become dominant in fact, and to act as ideals guiding its
activities in and through the body. What is the work that the species
requires so that desire, backed by other powers, is able to join all five
conditions with singularity? Biologists answer that it is the work of selecting, mating, and surviving. But this occurs without creative effort,
and does not seem to be directed at the realization of an ideal. The
biological answer, no matter how satisfactory for various purposes, is
therefore not altogether pertinent to the present issue. What is now
being sought is the work that a creative desire can bring about, so utilizing
the human species that it limits its range and power of that species.

Is the domain a story? Myth? But if story, how distinguish it from a
work of art? If myth, how take care of the creative acts of individual
men? Must we not, as was the case with technology, think of individuals
making their contribution to a common, larger work? Alternatively, must
we not think of technology as the domain in which men's creative works
fit? If so, the works pertinent to a creative desire will be individual
contributions to such common activities as ritual, dance, hunting, family-
making, and the like. These give desire an embodiment.

Freud seemed to suppose that desire was captured in sexuality and
that even works of art expressed this in some way or form. One need
not deny such a view, and still hold that works of art are the outcome
of a creative use of sensibility, with sexuality providing only a motivation,
a stimulus, or an occasion. In any case, we are still faced with the question
as to just what kind of creative work is produced through the use of
human desire, backed by other more recessive powers, and not directed
at the preservation of the species. Would it perhaps be religious objects
and a vital participation in religious rituals, without any necessary reference to some transcendent being?

5. For want of a better term I have spoken of 'positioning' in AEHP
to refer to a man's involvement in his environment and milieu. A creative
use of that positioning would, if it is to join all five conditions to singularity, have to involve some work on recalcitrant material. The needed
work here seems to be the *habitat* of men. The making of such a habitat
could of course be subsumed under architecture, but only if it was the
outcome of a creative use of sensibility rather than, as is now the case,

the creative use of that power which enables a man to find a satisfactory place in an environment. Freed from its involvement with the environment, positioning is able to join conditions with singularity in a distinctive way. What is the work that results when the positioning is used to change recalcitrant material so as to realize the ideal end of being a mere positioning, no longer limited to an environment or milieu, if it is not the habitat treated, not as something worked over with sensibility but solely to secure the position, make a man be within his own self-enclosed whole? I can think of no alternative for the moment.

6. Sociality, I have come to suppose, is a power behind the others in the person, and gives man a role in a society. Freed from its confinement to society, and given a creative role with respect to all the conditions and singularity, it too should be expressed in some created work. What can this be? Does it lie in the carrying out of a role in a fresh way? Would this be enough to constitute an item in a domain? Or does it require a man to carry out the role on behalf of others?

July 27

I spent last evening with Dr. Harvey and Candace Sherber. I am the godfather of their child, Nöelle. Harvey was a student at Yale toward the end of my stay there, and was a phtographer for the college newspaper. He took some pictures of one of my paintings and plans to take a good number more next Saturday morning, when the light may be better. I saw their new house, which is in the process of being completed; it looks as if it will be outstanding. Then they took me to dinner. It was a great evening, but I got to bed at 11:30. Not I feel a little more muddled than usual. I have decided not to walk today—I skip my daily walk about a half dozen times a year, when I don't feel up to scratch. If the weather is bad, I use my stationary bicycle. But today I will not, and hope that I will be able to continue from where I left off yesterday afternoon.

Two problems must be faced: why are the stages of analysis the three I have fastened on, (the structural, theoretical, and formal) once we start from a confrontation of limited data in which principles are merged? Why are there just these stages of effective creative powers, beginning with sensitivity, and going through sensibility, need, desire, and so on? The first of these questions is to be answered, I think, in some consonance with Kant's transcendental deduction. We must retain the dispersed content that we confront; structure it so that it has a stable nature; subject it to conceptualizations which give it a theoretical role; and end with what will enable us to see it as objective. Unlike Kant, the content is not to be thought of as something itself 'subjective', and the analysis should answer to what is already present. The analysis does not move us to what in fact is constitutive of an objective situation. Instead, it allows us to acknowledge something present, and tries to see what in fact would be the case if submerged conditions were in fact dominant.

The second problem is also to be answered by attending to what is objectively the case. The various stages of private creative powers answer to distinct external controls—the body, undifferentiated content, need of the individual, desire pertinent to the species, and so on, until we come to the I. This reaches toward whatever there be. Its expression is initially subject to the dominating presence of the entire cosmos. But this is to anticipate, and perhaps misstate, what I was in the process of finding out yesterday. The right answer to the second question is to be provided only after one has in fact gone through the various stages already isolated, by considering the different ways in which men express themselves. The creativity of men makes use of these different stages, not to overcome what was dominant, but to enable the individual to deal with two types of ultimates by uniting them in items within domains.

I ended yesterday with the creative power of sociality, the most deeply grounded power of the person. The next set of creative powers are in the psyche, which I have distinguished as sagacity, understanding, and resolution.

7. Sagacity is close to what Aristotle dealt with as practical wisdom. It is occupied with bringing about a harmony of body and privacy by becoming involved with what has the two together under a single control. That control is provided by a society in which men are full participants. When we free sagacity from an involvement with what is socially present and with which men are to adjust themselves, and deal with it as a creative power, the best work that is produced is perhaps the transformation of conventionally set rules into expressions reflecting individual emphases in games within the domain of sport. It is not to be supposed that athletes are models of sagacity; all that is being maintained is that sagacity is exhibited as a creative power by them when they act so as to incorporate the rules of a sport. Freeing the rules from an involvement in particulars under the creative control of sagacity allows for pure expressions of rules of greater generality. I am not sure whether or not one escapes in this way from the limits of sport proper, and moves into the world of convention with its various languages.

July 28

8. One comes to the idea of a domain perhaps most readily when one begins to deal with mathematics as at once having its own integrity, is able to be applied (at least in various of its parts), and involves creativity expressed in the manipulation of symbols, and the making of diagrams. This does not mean that one need maintain that the initial situation with which one begins is where the mathematical is hardly discernible. But that situation could be taken, with historic justification, to be where men are involved in mensuration and thus, in a pre-Euclidean period, where they were concerned with the properties of figures, and by extension, with the interplay of various numbers or numbered objects. It would be better perhaps to hold that the initial situation is the living use of language, *parole,* where excellence takes the form of expressions which convey what one means. One can then view the Egyptian geometers as dealing with a living language restricted to figures to which their language could be seen to be precisely appropriate. If we take this tack, semiotics, *langue,* will be obtained by allowing the grammar and syntax of a language to be laid bare. Beyond this, there is theoretical science and therefore an ideal mathematical physics in which any mathematics used will have an application and, indeed, will be confined to what is actual. If one takes this line, one can, in accord with modern linguistic, analytic philosophers, see both science and mathematics as having their roots in language. But, in opposition to them, one will also see that physics, etc., are distinct domains and, in any case, even if they were derived from a living language in actual use, existed as domains where distinctive items were related to others. The interrelations of mathematical units are not reducible to the relations of language units to one another.

The analysis of domains, produced through the creative use of private powers other than the understanding, ends with something formal. This could have a mathematical form. Such a form, though, unlike the structures used in a pure mathematics, is tied to the singularities of the world by creative powers, such as sensitivity. The creative powers do not provide a mathematics to be carried out for its own sake. Instead, they give a mathematical articulation to what was initially encountered as having an almost indiscernible constant structure, theoretical underpinning, or formal dimension. The situation produces a difficulty for depth grammarians. If they start with an actual language and seek its ultimate components, they must deal with language, not as a product of a creative use of the understanding, but of sociality. But then, in some accord with

Wittgenstein, they will have to use living discourse and communication as a kind of game in which each interchange is like a plan in it, and the game itself is part of the ongoing history of a sport, with its established rules. But if what is sought is language, as the creative product of an understanding, they will have to move to a semiotics. This provides a structural or grammatical formulation of the rules that are initially imbedded in the living language.

The creative work of the understanding, at its most concrete, is involved in the production of a used language, through the understanding's combining of singularity with a grammar; a semiotics, in which the rules that were submerged in the used language are seen to structure what is being said; a theoretical science, in which the rules attain the status of distinctive theoretical principles inseparable from the actual world; and manipulated units interrelated by mathematical necessity.

9. Resolution is a power expressed in the form of preference, choice, or will. Each of these has its own distinctive creative use, with its own domain and objects. Preference involves the election of means to an appealing goal. A creative use of the preferential power requires techniques, instruments, tools, machinery. These are to be distinguished from technology, which is frozen in the instruments. Techniques allow for the use of instruments in creative ways.

10. In choice, one elects actions which are in accord with an obligated set of values. To choose properly, one must persistently live a type of life where the values one is obligated to promote are in fact produced. We must look therefore to the acts of a man of character to find a domain of created work which choice produces out of the various final conditions and singularity. The totality of value governing the proper choice is the ideal counterpart of the character of a man.

11. By will, a man attaches himself to an end governing what he does with both his privacy and body. He thereby becomes dedicated. The work carrying that dedication incorporates the meaning of the dedicated end. That is usually an object vested with the powers of the divine or, in the absence of a religion, with the power to enable a man to live a full life. A Confucian group and an Epicurean society of friends are illustrations of the ways in which men can express their wills creatively and thereby produce outcomes where a primal obligation is joined to a world encompassing distinct individuals. In different ways, the objects exhibit human dignity, man at his willed best.

12. With autonomy, one enters the area of the self, the most recessive of the major divisions of a man's privacy. An autonomous man assumes

accountability for what he publicly does. To use his autonomy creatively, he joins the conditions with singularity to produce works in a domain, all of which exemplify his moral character, the degree to which he lives up to doing what he ought to do to fellowman in the present world.

13. Responsibility, unlike autonomy, does not attend to that for which one might be held to be publicly accountable. It is occupied solely with what ought to be, defined in terms of what is absolutely good. The work that is created responsibly is produced by an ethical man, one who privately initiates what ought to be done, no matter what the judgment of others. The state of affairs in which men for the moment find themselves plays a role in their judgments, decisions, and acts. There men find values which must be taken into account. Where a moral man has a status in a world of actualities, an ethical man stands apart from all, making himself be in the light of what all men should be, regardless of what they hold him accountable for.

14. Finally, the I, the representative of the self, can be used creatively, uniting all conditions together with singularity to constitute a humanized world, where whatever is confronted is subject to the single unifying possessiveness of an I. The value that items have in that world serve as units in a single domain, encompassing all there is, but as oriented toward the private I.

We have, then, the sources of pleasure and pain; art; technology; religious objects and activity; habitats; roles; games; language-semiotic; theoretical science; mathematics; instruments; men of character; human dignity; moral character; ethical men; and a humanized world, all as objects in domains, or domains themselves. Some of these terms need to be changed so that there is more of a parity among them; and there should be a set of terms clearly referring to the items in domains and another set to the domains themselves.

Each domain is bounded off from the others. Together, they constitute a single civilized world. They do not merge into that world. That world extends beyond all of them, and they exist within it as limited areas. Civilization in one sense is an aggregate. But it is an aggregate which has a temporal stretch to it, sometimes reaching far beyond the limits of a particular domain in it.

Outside civilization is the cosmos, to be dealt with as the locus of ultimate units governed and interrelated by the action of finalities in the role of cosmic conditions. That cosmos is no domain. The theoretical science that deals with it, though, constitutes a domain. The one is objective, the other purports to understand it within the limits of scientific articulations.

In the cosmos, there are only ultimate units, and these may not be known to science. A cosmology, such as Whitehead's, tries to tell what the functioning of the units is like. But he fails to make adequate provision for the civilization, with which he was equally concerned. It is not enough to so understand the ultimate units that civilization could be treated as the outcome of complicated unifications of these. The units themselves, as in the cosmos, apart from men and their science, are bunched and separated. So far as one remains only with the cosmos one cannot account for the bunching and separation. (The recognition that the bunching and separation are inexplicable for a 'deterministic science' is prompted by Peirce.)

There are two kinds of bunchings and separations. One is due to the existence of complex unitary beings, within whose confines ultimate parts are compelled to be together and to act in ways not cosmically determined; the other is the bunching and separation that is due to civilization and therefore to all the domains this encompasses.

The cosmos is the totality of all ultimate units under universal conditions. Nature is the totality of those units as ordered, and thus as bunched and separated by the beings within which they are encompassed. The natural cosmos is the two together. When the civilized world of domains is added to the natural cosmos, we have the humanized cosmos in which one can at last account, not simply for the way ultimate items are bunched and separated, but for the ways in which those bunches and separations are themselves bunched and separated, with indirect effects on the ways in which ultimate particles will act and where they will be, without affecting their functioning as so many units in the cosmos.

INDEX OF NAMES

Acher, J., 4
Aebischer, S., 149
Anderson, W., 295
Aristotle, 8, 9, 41, 44, 45, 59, 62, 83, 97, 106, 119, 153, 191, 238, 239, 285, 327, 329, 330, 357, 370, 454
Aquinas, T., 75, 97, 105, 115, 285, 331
Augustine, 285

Berkeley, G., 285
Bernstein, R., 4
Bergson, H., 241, 307, 330
Bradley, F. H., 307
Brentano, F., 27
Brumbaugh, R., 184

Cavett, D., 7
Christ, 84
Christian, W., 150
Clarke, N., 35
Compton, J., 329
Confucius, 330, 357, 440, 456
Cua, A., 10, 11, 315

Dahlstrom, D., 429
Darwin, C., 209
de Chardin, T., 369
Descartes, R., 109, 348, 417
Dewey, J., 343
Dougherty, J., 131
Dozoretz, J., 295

Empedocles, 421, 423
Epicurus, 440, 456

Fermat, P. de, 300
Ford, L., 35
Foucalt, M., 186

Francis, St., 97
Freud, S., 97, 113, 114, 115, 283, 452

Galileo, G., 75, 145, 189
Goodman, N., 435

Haberman, J. O., 84
Hartshorne, C., 83
Hegel, G. W. F., 8, 31, 34, 35, 36, 37, 42, 53, 60, 61, 83, 97, 113, 114, 115, 116, 117, 142, 155, 280, 285, 286, 330, 351, 357, 369, 383, 384, 396, 426, 440
Heidegger, M., 115, 142, 155
Heisenberg, W., 124
Hendel, C., 184
Hill, R., 295
Hitler, A., 99, 375
Hobbes, T., 148
Hume, D., 103, 141, 281, 306
Husserl, E., 27, 142, 155, 280, 329

Joyal, P., 4, 7
Jesus, 84

Kant, I., 5, 8, 103, 122, 142, 157, 158, 160, 195, 285, 301, 306, 307, 344, 412, 431, 437, 438, 454
Kierkegaard, S., 36, 58, 141

Leibniz, G. W., 285, 306, 369
Lenk, H., 430
Lessing, G. E., 1
Lewis, C. I., 295, 301, 307
Locke, J., 148, 285, 397
Lowell, R., 98

Marx, K., 97, 337
Matisse, H., 43

Merleau-Ponty, M., 329
Michelangelo, 97
Mill, J. S., 8
McMullin, E., 329

Occam, Wm., 283, 317

Peirce, C. S., 45, 117, 325, 434, 458
Piaget, J., 107
Plato, 5, 7, 153, 218, 224, 285, 426, 437, 444
Plotinus, 369
Poe, E. A., 85
Prall, D. W., 340

Quine, W. V., O. 8

Riley, F., 4, 7
Rorty, R., 432
Russell, B., 8

Sartre, J.-P., 58, 142, 186
Schilpp, P. A., 5, 6
Schopenhauer, A., 64, 202, 330

Schulz, R., 295
Scotus, D., 74, 75
Shakespeare, W., 96, 97
Sherber, H. C. and N., 453
Smith, E., 295
Sontag, S., 186
Spinoza, B., 109, 112, 281, 369
Sternberg, V., 183 ff.
Stevens, W., 86, ff, 98, 101, 102
Surber, J., 149, 295

Theresa, Sr., 97

Van Gogh, V., 88, 98

Weiss, J. A., 4, 36, 316, 427
Weiss, T., 86
Whitehead, A. N., 35, 41, 59, 60, 217, 220, 369, 370, 457
Wittgenstein, L., 155, 233, 338, 387, 396, 436, 456, 458

Zuckerkandl, V., 437

INDEX OF SUBJECTS

Abduction, 45
Aberrations, 167, 213, 243
Abilities, 90
Abortion, 162
Absenting, self- 229, 311
Absolute, the 34, 35, 37, 55, 60, 61, 113, 115, 304, 354, 367, 396, 429, 441; see also, *Tao*
Absorptions, 83
Abstractions, 292
Abyss, 339
Acceptable, 126, 261
Acceptance, self- 108, 220, 447
Access, 406; private, 403, 404; secret, 406
'Accidents', 37, 38, 45, 79, 83, 153, 160, 269, 270, 272, 321, 331
Accommodation, 138, 400
Accountability, 14, 113, 126, 129, 140, 159, 187, 194, 202, 203, 204, 230, 231, 266, ff., 279, 392, 404, 425, 443, 447; and responsibility, 211; assumed, 210, 232, 241, 242, 245, 254, 257, 260, 296, 340, 343, 346, 365, 370, 371, 373, 424, 456; evidence for, 253, 257; private, 124, 128, 129, 188, 225; responsible, 164
Achievement, 112, 410, 424, 425
Acknowledgment, 135
Acquaintance, 28
Actors, 99
Action, 13, 15, 17, 21, 100, 143, 220, 234, 337, 348, 355, 398, 440; aberrational, 213; and thought, 349; creative, 50, 52, 392; ethical, 14, 17, 73; free, 159; individual, 179; levels of, 204; political, 181; practical, 43; public, 234, 242; religious, 3; responsible, 349
Actualities, 42, 118, 170, 229, 271, 311, 328, 390, 391, 393, 403, 404, 417, 420, 426, 439; and finalities, 28, 37, 38, 48, 66, 74, 172, 173, 227, 230, 236, 271, 272, 288, 290, 294, 384, 388, 391, 395, 396, 400, 401; attenuation of, 29; bodily, 240, 385; by themselves, 172, 173; complex, 73, 74; compound, 410; creased, 394; depth of, 403; determi-

nate, 50; development of, 394; distended, 173; evidenced, 165, 318; exhibitions of, 416; expressions of, 173; grades of, 236, 237, 239; harmonized, 395; hierarchy of, 237; incomparable, 229; indeterminate, 192; in themselves, 8, 172, 173, 389; inwardness of, 142; knowledge of, 28; limit of, 396; mediated, 393; move into, 442; mediated, 393; origin of, 383, 384; promise of, 393; self-bounded, 173; singularity of, 433, 435; solidification of, 395; specializing, 396; stretch of, 395; subordinated, 66; thrust of, 393; understanding of, 354; unified, 396
Address, terms of, 151, 225
Adjudication, 268, 269, 273
Adjustment, 92, 197, 266, 273, 339, 386, 387
Adoption, 158, 159, 255, 256, 311
Adults, 81
Adumbration, 26, 38, 76, 116, 156, 308, 310, 312, 397, 399, 400, 405, 406, 407
Aesthetic, the, 255, 334, 337, 338, 340, 403
Affiliation, 12, 145, 313, 357, 358, 424, 433, 446, 447, 449, 450
Agents, 170, 353, 391, 395
Aggregates, 39, 61, 64, 112, 323, 388, 457
Aggression, 93, 94, 107, 108
Aid, mutual, 357
Alienation, 46, 102, 103, 179, 203, 350, 421
Amendment, First, 147
American Philosophic Association, 134, 432
Analysis, 19, 20, 21, 118, 169, 188, 306, 403, 432, 446, 453; depth, 445, 446, 447; Freudian, 19; linguistic, 30; stages of, 453
'An Exploration of Human Privacy', 315, 316, 447, 452
Animals, 126, 128, 152, 157, 196, 197, 209, 214, 236, 319, 371; and things, 358; conscious, 240; domestic, 163; freedom of, 157; groups of, 209; humanized, 376;

knowledge by, 209; lives of, 209; lower, 239, 240; pain of, 345; playful, 423; privacy of, 239, 240, 371, 379; reasoning of, 351; rights of, 162, 252; sensitivity of, 367, 373, 378; trained, 158; world of, 371

Anomalies, 165, 166, 171, 172

Anthropology, 18, 308, 389

Anthropocentrism, 282, 366

Anxiety, 243

Appearances, 8, 27, 28, 30, 37, 50, 76, 77, 80, 81, 83, 120, 122, 127, 142, 144, 156, 157, 160, 167, 168, 172, 173, 218, 235, 269, 276, 288, 290, 313, 316, 320, 329, 352, 398, 400, 412, 413, 414, 415, 416, 417, 420, 423, 427, 444; adventitious, 178; components of, 418; constituents of, 112; context for, 313; determinations of, 156; domain of, 120, 172; objective, 38, 170, 270, 276, 302, 303, 306, 435; ordered, 277; subjective, 171, 270, 304, 305, 307; you as, 243

Apperception, 122

Approval, 450

A priori, 366

Appreciation, 51, 52, 99, 117, 135, 164, 283, 331, 333, 334, 335, 336, 340, 346, 366, 387, 417, 449, 450

Architecture, 450

Art, 2, 5, 25, 26, 39, 49, 50, 53, 107, 117, 164, 203, 204, 219, 222, 224, 261, 271 ff., 334, 426, 427, 431, 435, 445, 451; and existence, 32; and nature, 48, 49, 52, 53, 283; and science, 57; beautiful, 54, 269 f., 275, 288; domain of, 271, 291, 388; ethical, 39; folk, 451; great, 52; history of, 270, 273; making of, 56; material of, 272; object of, 38; power of, 271; realm of, 57; right to, 161; types of, 434, 449; works of, 48, 49, 52, 58, 61, 104, 220, 271, 288, 269, 276, 283, 284, 298, 332, 334, 335, 391, 417, 425, 449, 450, 451; unity of, 269; world of, 51, 57, 58, 277, 331, 392, 445

Articulation, 29, 139, 305, 398, 399, 421

Artifacts, 104

Artists, 65, 97, 272, 332, 387

Assemblage, 437

Assertiveness, 100, 128

Assertion, 395, 397, 406, 407; self-, 108, 260

Assessments, 176, 240, 244, 254, 267, 309, 312, 349, 350, 351, 357

Assimilation, 43

Association, 11, 145

Atheism, 171

Athletes, 111, 452

Atomism, 69, 270, 306, 320

Attention, 235, 339, 402, 418

Attitudes, 18, 102, 108, 235, 428

Attribution, 126

Autobiographical, 4 ff., 12, 29, 33, 35, 37, 43, 44, 57, 112, 131, 148 ff., 158, 160, 165, 171, 183 ff., 187, 189, 202, 211, 220, 221, 229, 237, 254, 273, 274, 279, 284, 295, 296, 297, 316, 333, 336, 337, 377, 399, 425, 427, 430 f., 446, 448, 449, 453

Authenticity, 168

Autonomy, 457

Awe, 18, 20, 413

Axiology, 293, 426

Background, 116

Backing, 32

Balances, 419

Ballet, 316

Bases, 323, 408; explanatory, 419; mathematical, 445

Baseball, 316, 317

Basketball, 317

Beauty, 51, 54, 92, 275, 286, 288, 289, 291, 427; created, 269; knowledge of, 297; natural, 53; production of, 234

Behavior, 12, 101, 154, 164

Behaviorism, 8, 103, 118, 154, 155, 233, 234, 282

Being, 11, 18, 19, 43, 76, 78, 108, 123, 173, 214, 228, 229, 237, 288, 296, 297, 308, 354, 382, 424, 425; and actualities, 228; creative, 391; evidencing, 154; humanized, 151; individual, 13; living, 53, 238, 293, 325, 357, 391, 392; mature, 375; organic, 112, 130, 318, 319; origin of, 112; private, 223; political, 290; power of, 229; private, 154, 222, 231; public, 214; realization of, 75; social, 53, 54; unity of, 231

Belief, religious, 217

Benefits, 13, 15

Beyond All Appearances, 4, 18, 21, 38, 79, 104, 124, 187, 195, 224, 237, 238, 311, 407, 411, 419, 420, 439, 443

Bias, 191, 412, 415, 418, 419, 423, 424

Binders, 118 ff., 334

Biology, 239, 359

Bodies, 209, 322, 376, 382, 387, 388, 390, 416; and conditions, 81; and desire, 248; and emotions, 109; and Existence, 296; and mind, 252; and person, 148; and privacy, 64, 69, 77, 79, 83, 323, 383; animal, 215, 234; as instrument, 216; capacity of, 251; complex, 67, 318, 320, 321, 326, 339; confronted, 246; constancy of, 83; control by, 454; dominated, 443; enlivened, 328; expressions of, 80, governed, 197, 214, 422; governing, 417; human, 61, 79, 191, 208, 210, 347; in world, 112; irreducible, 418; kinds of, 424; limitating, 409; lived, 108, 109, 112, 213, 214, 292, 320, 442; living, 21, 61, 69, 187, 196, 213, 214, 243,

329, 438; opacity of, 327; organic, 39, 40, 65, 80, 81, 292, 409, 411; origin of, 377; pained, 249, see also, sensitive; parts of, 414, 417; potentialities of, 233, 321, 322, 325, 326, 328, 345; power of, 76; public, 122, 123, 233, 246, 318; responsive, 247; resurrected, 105; right of, 208, 262; satisfaction of, 249; sensitive, 249, 422, 438, 442; social, 436; types of, 320; unity of, 73, 74, 81, 328; used, 109, 214, 235, 248, 261 f., 263, 290, 320, 347; you-ified, 235, 236; wisdom of, 196, 258

Bondage, humanized, 127, 357, 359, 362
Borders, 130
Boundaries, 63, 66, 68, 69, 74, 105, 140, 145, 195, 278, 306, 309 ff., 388, 394, 395, 408, 412
Bounding, 69, 395; self-, 69, 121, 122, 123, 125, 128, 129, 173, 243, 320, 359
Brain, 234, 402
Brute, the, 396, 397, 400, 403, 418, 421
Bunchings, 51, 285, 287, 393, 412, 415, 446, 458

Canons, 449
Caprice, 111
Categories, 285, 301, 337, 353, 384, 419, 437; five, 311; Kantian, 122; series of, 34
Causality, 40, 48, 123, 281, 450; and freedom, 158, 160; kinds of, 48
Celebrations, 22, 222
Cells, 64, 66 ff., 320; origin of, 71
Centering, 204, 241
Centers, 28, 201, 227, 395
Change, 32, 325
Character, 100, 261, 457; class-, 133; moral, 456
Characterizations, 169
Children, 81, 128, 367; autistic, 150, 151; growth of, 107; insight of, 144; knowledge by, 158; language of, 139, 140, 141; sensitivity of, 377
Choice, 254, 256, 257, 265, 266, 269, 373, 374; and body, 251; creative, 456; knowledge of, 251
Christianity, 1 ff., 84, 85, 317
Cinematics, 204, 437
Citizens, 133
Civilization, 164, 289, 369, 370, 374, 375, 435, 440, 441, 442, 458
Claimant, 122
Claims, 100, 109, 121, 193, 230, 231, 234, 237, 241, 253, 343, 353, 371, 397, 424; essential, 163; just, 260; private, 177
Class, Marxian, 132, 433
Classifications, 425, 426, 436
Closure, 87
Clusters, 42, 108, 291, 292
Collections, 61

Collectivity, sense of, 317
Color, 60, 61, 83, 84
Comedy, 26
Commitment, 257, 347
Commonsense, 312, 441; world of, 288, 410, 441, 443
Communication, 106, 161, 455
Community, 2, 47, 107, 129, 132, 135, 140, 163, 456; civilized, 330; Confucian, 440; human, 356; language, 161; moralistic, 330; of appreciators, 340; religious, 440; scientific, 334
Completion, 225, 354; need for, 218, 223, 224; self-, 108, 111, 114, 215, 216, 231, 241, 243, 258, 261, 263, 390, 393, 395, 396, 429, 430
Complexes, 67, 68, 73, 74, 110, 119, 124, 130, 272, 325, 326, 335, 427, 458; artificial, 320; interaction of, 335; kinds of, 319; origin of, 58; potentiality of, 326; privacy of, 68; relational, 154; types of, 322
Components, 415
Composites, 327, 329
Computers, 252, 291, 355, 460
Conatus, 112
Concentrations, 424, 426
Concepts, 294 ff., 355, 356
Conceptualization, 83, 350, 351, 453
Concern, 241, 351, 365
Conclusions, acceptance of, 38; backed, 24; use of, 340, 342
Condensations, 190
Conditions, 312, 334, 388, 389, 427; adoption of, 80; and art, 53; basic, 144; bodily, 415; and body, 81; common, 10, 11, 14, 83, 103, 125, 130, 134, 144, 146, 174, 314, 318; controlling, 133; cosmic, 412, 457; dominant, 448; ethical, 12, 13; final, 12, 28, 80, 124, 323, 377, 400, 413, 414, 450, 451; five, 112, 113, 125, 145; functioning, 429; general, 319; governing, 11, 53, 60, 125, 129, 133, 145, 146, 197; human, 137, 139; indeterminate, 393, 394; individual, 83; insistent, 322; intelligible, 11; internalization of, 11, 13, 15, 82; knowledge of, 14; primary, 112, 431, 434; realization of, 80, 125; shared, 99; social, 53, 127, 146; specialized, 125, 409, 415; transcendent, 328; types of, 435; union with individuals, 13; universal, 7, 108, 304, 368, 389, 411, 412, 443, 458; utilization of, 17
Conditioning, 268
Conformity, 421
Confrontation, 8, 102, 107, 307, 308, 334, 335, 404, 405, 453
Confusion, 348, 350
Consciousness, 83, 127, 128, 129, 138, 139, 161, 164, 187, 189, 192, 193, 196, 199, 204, 206, 209, 223, 225, 231, 241, 245,

252, 255, 260, 266, 280, 296, 397; ac-
knowledgment of, 249; evidence of, 250;
origin of, 205; responsible, 250; self-,
106, 127
Consortia, 337
Constituents, 302, 417
Constituting s, 402, 406, 407
Constructions, 44, 272, 435; mathematical,
27, 436
Contained, self-, 225, 240, 359, 415
Contemporaneity, 34
Content, aesthetic, 417; bounded, 308 ff.;
kinds of, 430; objectified, 314; won-
drous, 28
Contentment, 448
Contexts, 54, 89, 91, 92, 142, 172, 180,
314, 316, 372, 389, 414, 415; five-fold,
313; social, 173, 319
Contextualism, 346
Contingencies, 35ff., 44, 117, 307, 391,
392
Continuum, 408; of outcomes, 49
Control, 10, 13, 100, 234, 241, 261, 320,
336, 349, 357, 415; self-, 108, 111, 439,
441, 442
Convention, 164, 433
Convergence, 403
Conversation, 445
Coordination, 145, 228, 357, 424, 433, 447,
449, 451
Copula, 9
Copyist, 292
Corpse, privacy of, 324
Correctness, 212
Correlation, 40
Cosmology, 2, 5, 20, 21, 186, 458; phil-
osophical, 18, 19, 21, 22
Cosmos, 168, 170, 227, 271, 276, 283,
319, 324, 325, 335, 409, 411, 413, 440,
454, 458; man in, 320; organic view of,
71, 72; units in, 70, 173, 291, 458
Craftsmanship, 425
Creationism, 119
Creativity, 34, 41, 49, 50, 59, 88, 89, 162,
176, 203, 205, 212, 218, 265, 283, 284,
331, 334, 362, 392, 398, 440, 445, 446,
447, 449 ff., 454, 455, 457; right to, 161
Creators, 402, 403, 417
Creatures, 80
Creed, 3
Criminals, 103, 367
Criteria, 403, 408
Culture, 161, 272, 289, 390, 428, 435, 439,
440
Cures, 32, 43, 284
Custom, 138, 140

Dance, 432, 450
Datum, sense, 312
Death, 69, 71, 76, 78, 79, 104, 105, 106,
163, 321
Decision, 187, 188, 196, 199, 210, 223,

225, 227, 241, 244, 245, 246, 253, 264,
281, 296, 351, 365; and sensitivity, 247;
evidence for, 255, 256; free, 254, 255
Decisiveness, 198, 231
Dedication, 88, 337, 338, 456
Deduction, dialectical, 382; Kantian, 431,
432, 437, 449, 453; types of, 432
Definiteness, 219
Delimitation, 309
Demands, 12, 194, 195, 204, 260, 363
Demiurgos, 286
Demythologizing, 279
Denotation, 8, 155
Density, 308, 309, 418, 419, 422
Denver, Colorado, 131, 221
Denver, University of, 274, 294, 295
Depth, movement in, 116
Descriptions, theory of, 9
Designation, 338
Desirable, the, 247, 255, 260, 265, 425
Desire, 109, 178, 187ff., 194, 196, 198,
204 ff., 208, 223, 225, 230 ff., 237, 241,
247, 255, 260, 266, 337, 340, 346, 351,
357, 365, 371, 377, 395, 408, 422, 443,
447, 452 ff.; and body, 248, 249; and
preference, 249; and rights, 200; and self,
200; and sensitivity, 247; control by, 454;
control of, 248; creative, 452; expression
of, 26, 338; free, 249
Destruction, self-, 384
Desubjectification, 309
Detachment, 312, 403, 404, 407, 422
Determinateness, 47, 48, 57, 90, 91, 123,
173, 174, 192, 248, 426, 458
Determination, 10, 87, 172, 192, 194, 247,
257, 393, 395, 396, 440; limiting, 169;
private, 245, 246, 394; production of,
221; self-, 260
Determinism, geographic, 84
Deterrents, 182, 183
Devil, the, 171
Diagrams, 17, 293, 384, 427, 434, 455
Dialectic, 115, 117, 132, 355, 360; and
time, 36, 38; Hegelian, 37, 42, 60
Difference, 41; all-pervasive, 63; identity
in, 35; symmetry of, 63
Dignity, 107, 108, 109, 225, 241, 258, 261,
357, 359, 371
Diligence, 90
Disciplines, 17, 18, 101, 104, 110, 286,
424, 425, 436; basic, 19; pure, 19, 20,
22, 30
Disconnection, 27
Discourse, 234, 315, 456
Disjunctions, 442
Display, animal, 39
Dispositions, 91, 96, 97 ff., 106, 109, 110,
113, 345; bodily, 105; common, 103,
108; knowledge of, 101 ff.; private, 105;
set of, 104
Disruptions, 166
Distances, 11, 335

Distancing, 145; self-, 353
Distension, 76, 78, 121 ff., 173, 213, 214, 238, 241, 244, 328, 329; self-, 41
Distinctions, 144; basic, 145, 146; private and public, 143
Distinctness, 308, 309, 408, 412
Distributions, 450
Disturbances, 167
Diversification, 159, 160, 169, 170, 403
Dogma, 432
Domains, 8, 13, 17, 37, 150, 152, 165, 175, 177, 271f, 277 f, 283 ff, 314, 316, 317, 337, 389, 390, 392, 393, 424, 441f, 444, 445, 447, 448, 449, 451, 452, 453 ff.; all-encompassing, 435, 457; bounded, 455; kinds of, 17, 27, 42, 54, 164, 169, 279, 289f., 292f., 299, 300, 433, 435, 439; of appearances, 120, 172; production of, 435, 439, 444; units in, 427
Dominance, 108, 145, 172, 240, 377 ff., 387, 390, 416, 421f., 424 ff., 433
Dreams, 297, 304, 404; access to, 300
Drives, 91, 92, 109, 111, 112, 114, 115, 202; basic, 107, 110, 113
Dualism, 101, 286
Duration, 44
Duties, 203, 422, 425
Dynamism, 54, 213, 434

Economics, 55, 219, 425, 433, 447; and politics, 59
Education, 5, 161, 181
Egg, privacy of, 67, 69, 71
Ego, 202
Élan Vital, 330
Election, 257
Elements, ultimate, 120
Embryo, 78, 81, 104, 137, 139, 145, 367, 376, 440
Emotions, 18, 20, 83, 94, 100, 103, 116, 203, 204, 208, 275, 286, 332, 333, 413 ff., 419, 423, 437; levels of, 204, 205; lists of, 109, 110; mediative, 108; of artist, 334; origin of, 205
Empiricism, 8, 142, 278, 312
Enactments, 175
Encompassment, 412, 413, 415, 416, 418
Encounters, 352, 402, 419; direct, 405; penetrative, 241
Encyclopedia of Philosophy, 71
Endorsement, 353
Ends, 454; accepted, 45; kingdom of, 14; governing, 269; ideal, 422, 453; realization of, 107, 108; subordinated, 448; willed, 258 f.
Energy, 72, 319; and mass, 120
Enjoyment, 337, 341
Enlightenment, 429
Entelechy, 239
Entities, distended, 121, 123, 124; ex-
tended, 121; indeterminate, 123; internalization by, 238; kinds of, 380; physical, 73, 233, 238; see also particles; private, 121; public, 121, 123
Enumerations, 145
Environment, 167, 308, 319, 395, 422, 453
Episodes, historic, 277
Epistemology, 5, 286, 390, 425
Epitomizations, 76, 77, 83, 108, 109, 112, 113, 193, 316; degrees of, 422; knowledge of, 353
Equalization, 228, 229
Equilibrium, 206, 228, 258, 385, 411, 412, 414, 415, 418, 419, 442, 446
Equipment, 336, 424
Error, 31, 75, 182, 206, 288, 304
Essay, French, 186, 187
Essence, 62, 286, 326, 327, 402
Ethics, 10 ff., 39, 202 ff., 212, 448, 457; origin of, 205
Evaluation, 145, 193, 234, 235, 306, 425
Events, 390; crucial, 343
Evidence, 22, 28, 29, 30, 37, 40, 46, 56, 100, 154, 164, 169, 170, 171, 174, 234 ff., 242, 244, 250, 251, 253, 260, 296, 317, 318, 339, 344, 354, 355, 360, 366 ff., 374, 389, 408, 415, 418; of animal sensitivity, 365; of actualities, 315, 316; of finalities, 172, 173; theory of, 165; types of, 359; use of, 219
Evidenced, the, 21, 22, 25, 159, 173, 174, 219, 221, 294, 315, 316
Evidencing, 169, 353
Excellence, 15, 107, 241, 243, 258, 366, 411, 436, 440; achievement of, 111, 231, 263; ethical, 38, 39; final, 425; progress toward, 389; sensuous, 58, 269, 449; striving for, 107, 108, 216, 223
Existence, 26, 37, 43, 51, 54, 57, 58, 76, 107, 108, 206, 224, 229, 230, 277, 286, 288, 312, 333, 335, 380, 390, 425, 426; and art, 32, 218; dimensions of, 238; modalities of, 123; power of, 173; social, 101
Existentialism, 18, 118, 141, 286, 301, 408, 409
Experience, 141, 142, 143, 298 ff., 332, 340, 342, 345, 403, 405, 406, 407, 417; aesthetic, 301, 304, 404; common, 437; crucial, 342; dream, 301; object of, 407; private, 3 ff.; religious, 300 f.
Experienced, the, 399, 408
Experiencing, 141 ff., 304, 307, 309 ff., 339, 409, 411, 413, 415; reach of, 314; termini of, 422
Experiment, 332
Explanation, 45, 188, 192, 239, 290, 308, 348, 351, 408, 420, 438
'Exploration of Human Privacy', 279, 291, 296, 297, 298, 377, 428, 430, 445, 446
Expressions, 98, 359, 361, 363, 389, 400,

402, 403, 420; asserted, 273; bodily, 79; confronted, 273; emotional, 18; free, 160; of animals, 157; public, 255; self-, 108, 156, 338; sources of, 108

Extensions, 119, 173, 246, 308, 328, 333, 378, 390, 446, 447, 450, 451; occupied, 76, 78

External, the, 404

Externalization, 115, 169

Failure, 89, 90

Faith, 154, 203, 217, 347, 393

Fall, free, 292, 318, 345

Fallacy, intentional, 102

Family, 130, 133, 135, 271

Fanaticism, 282

Fantasy, 347

Fear, 243

Features, 271; adventitious, 191; global, 172

Feelings, 192, 205, 206, 281, 392

Feminists, 155

Festivals, 174

Fetus, 138, 162, 367, 372, 376; privacy of, 162; rights of, 78, 162; social status of, 163; viable, 370

Fictions, 55, 97

Fields, 118 ff., 122, 124, 229, 314, 323, 447; action of, 123; five-fold, 123; nuances in, 119, 120

Fillings, 29, 30, 31, 32, 33

Film, 82

Finalities, 2, 8, 11, 21, 22, 25, 29, 40, 46, 64, 71, 79, 86, 100, 103, 108, 115, 124, 141, 142, 168, 172, 173, 191, 213, 218, 219, 221, ff., 226, 227, 235, 258, 265, 286, 287, 303, 304, 308, 311, 316, 337, 352, 379, 387, 392, 402, 411, 412, 415, 419, 422, 439, 441, 445, 446, 447, 457; acceptance of, 220; action of, 64, 386, 391; adoption of, 80, 83; adjustment to, 28, 383; and actualities, 28, 37, 38, 48, 66, 159, 172, 218, 227, 229, 230, 236, 271, 288, 290, 294, 297, 383, 384, 391, 393, 394, 395, 396, 400, 401, 444, 445; see also: Appearances, Domains, Phenomena, Mixed, the; and bodies, 81, 386; and conditions, 53, 390; and domains, 433 f.; and privacies, 65, 68, 70, 74, 75, 105, 106, 225; and men, 46, 231, 434; and time, 105; and wholes, 70; articulating, 293; as guides, 42; as measures, 350; as qualifiers, 173; division of, 345, 383, 384, 386, 387; dominant, 383, 384, 385, 386, 392, 416, 417, 418, 420, 421, 423; evidences of, 165, 172, 173, 205, 225, 315, 394, 418; insistence of, 386, 387; instantiated, 72, 73 ff., 76, 77, 78, 220; internalized, 65, 74, 80, 225, 236, 237, 263, 340; intrusion of, 39, 77, 217; knowledge of, 28, 74, 442; levels of, 415, 438; moves into, 442; nuanced, 68, 105;

objective of, 391; power of, 229, 337; presence of, 73 ff.; receptivity of and to, 207, 218, 222, 223, 231, 236; self-possession of, 395; specialization of, 73, 78; stretch of, 395; subordinated, 173, 289, 379 ff., 391, 395, 396; surrogates for, 400; use of, 242, 396

Finitude, 400

First Considerations, 21, 37, 38, 66, 74, 80, 124, 141, 142, 159, 172, 173, 187, 189, 218, 220, 230, 235, 294, 295, 297, 315, 341, 353, 384, 417, 420, 423, 433

Foci, 231

Football, 317

Force, 180, 421

Form, 75, 119, 329; and matter, 59; Aristotelian, 8; indeterminate, 305; mathematical, 455

Formualae, 427

Fractionization, 380

Freedom, 127, 129, 202, 212, 252, 254, 257, 350, 353; and causality, 156, 160; and necessity, 344; animal, 157, 158; evidence for, 255; expression of, 156; human, 128; private, 244; stages of, 423

Freudians, 202

Friends, 456; society of, 440

Fringes, 30, 38, 156, 270, 339

Frustration, 348, 349, 350, 352, 355, 364

Fulgurations, 120

Full and Empty, 278

Future, the, 46, 118, 315

Games, 108, 164, 272, 316, 331, 427, 428, 434, 454, 456

Gender, 62, 84, 153

Generalization, 382

Genes, 71, 83, 84

Genius, 88

Geography, 293, 434

Geometry, 314, 426, 455

Given, the, 399

Goals, 42, 43, 249, 255, 256, 260, 440, 452

God, 2, 12, 16, 19, 31, 55, 84, 103, 106, 113, 155, 159, 171, 219, 282, 296, 297, 304, 306, 315, 347, 369, 402; acts of, 267; and man, 113; as finality, 220; control by, 315; cosmological, 35; idea of, 280; love by, 106, 107, 171; names for, 26; omnipresent, 41; ontological, 35; process view of, 220

Good, the, 218, 219, 304, 437; absolute, 394, 457; apparent, 265; common, 179; doing, 13; evidence for, 174; Platonic, 8, 11; roles of, 394

Goodness, 92, 288, 289, 411

Governance, 72, 134, 192, 211, 261, 337, 412, 413, 415, 422; self-, 439

Grace, 31, 203

Grades, 145, 420, 421, 447, 449

Grammar, 455, 456; depth, 8, 139, 445, 455
Groundings, 189, 191, 379
Grounds, 190, 207, 408
Groups, 293, 315, 370, 418, 423, 425, 440, 447, 456, see also Wholes
Growth, 107, 238, 240, 345
Guidance, 234, 315, 339
Guides, 38, 339, 341, 440, 443, 448, 451, 452
Guilt, 203, 251, 422; and innocence, 337, 351, 373

Habit, 45, 133
Habitat, 452, 453
Habituation, 81, 84
Had, the, 397, 398
Happiness, 376
Harmonics, 218, 219
Harmony, 59, 78, 394, 433
Health, 188, 261, 281, 336, 337, 338, 347, 354, 365; private, 264, 419
Hegelianism, 29, 30
Hermeneutics, 144
Hierarchies, 78, 123, 238, 361f., 366, 374, 383, 408, 445
History, 36, 37, 47, 54, 132, 280, 286, 288, 289, 293, 426, 428, 434 ff., 441, 447; Christian view of, 315; domain of, 42, 388; sedimented, 334; stages of, 42; world of, 329; written, 293
Honesty, 212, 409
Hope, 213, 224, 225, 231, 243
Horizons, 151, 169
Humanism, 144, 302
Humankind, 127, 356, 362, 364
Humans, 128, 131, 132, 133, 201, 407; knowledge of, 215, 356; identity of, 129; immature, 157, 362, 366, 371
Humility, 18, 20
Hypotheses, 287

I, 15, 63, 77, 96, 104, 106 ff., 110, 112, 114, 127, 128, 138, 139, 158, 164, 187, 188, 189, 191, 193, 195 ff., 201, 204, 206, 210, 221, 223, 227, 228, 230, 231, 232, 237, 241, 254, 260, 261, 266, 281, 283, 323, 337, 340, 350, 351, 360, 363, 365, 366, 370, 371, 373, 374, 381, 391, 397 ff., 404, 424, 437, 447, 454; actions of, 199, 200, 284; and desire, 283, 284; and domain, 283, 284; and identity, 197, 199, 200; and interest, 200; and others, 102; and you, 202; creative, 457; divisions of, 207; dominant, 195; evidence of, 362; expressions of, 199, 200; functions of, 228; insistent, 225; possessive, 124, 200, 205, 296; power of, 199
Idealism, 5, 72, 190, 280, 306, 307, 432
Ideals, 38, 39, 44, 179, 180, 181, 217 ff., 231, 347, 440, 448; and finalities, 221,

222; control by, 216; guiding, 451, 452; identification with, 220; realization of, 44, 221; sanctioning, 178; specification of, 220; sustained, 219, 220, 222
Ideas, 202, 296; and concepts, 294; and finalities, 80; Cartesian, 143; correction of, 342; exhibited, 76; formation of, 344; guiding, 342, 343, 344; inadequate, 294; use of, 343
Ideality, absolute, 401
Identity, 74, 77, 96, 104, 105, 127, 128, 130, 138, 154, 164, 187 ff., 193 ff., 197, 198, 201, 202, 205, 206, 210, 225, 227, 231, 236, 241, 245, 255, 258, 260, 261, 390, 394; and I, 195, 199, 200; and responsibility, 200, 224; and rights, 195, 198; empty, 195; in difference, 94; kinds of, 207; self-, 83, 223
Ideology, 182
Idio, the, 351, 353, 354, 357, 365, 366, 371, 374
Idios, the, 424, 437
Ignorance, knowledge of, 174
Imagination, 107, 203, 431
Imitation, 17
Immaturity, 369, 370
Immediacy, 394, 398, 400, 401, 403
Immortaloit, 79, 104, 105
Importance, 349, 436
Imprisonment, 181, 182
Inadvertent, the, 439
Incarnation, 84
Indeterminacy, 122, 123, 124, 245, 357, 440
Individual, 10, 15, 63, 74, 99, 108, 130, 132, 133, 138, 139, 148, 150, 157, 168, 174, 177, 180, 190, 200, 202 ff., 212, 221, 227, 237, 240, 254, 282, 317, 330, 334, 360, 375, 387, 393, 420, 421, 424, 444; being of, 108; center of, 231; claims of, 164; completion of, 201; complex, 413; depth of, 182; divisions of, 192, 210, 211, 243; existent, 108; identity of, 77; intelligible, 108; in itself, 196; origin of, 39; paradigmatic, 11, 14; public, 164; rectifying, 261; , 179; standard, 192; substantial, 107
Individuality, 65, 68, 69, 77, 190, 191, 214, 241
Individuation, 62, 72, 73 ff., 78, 112, 196, 238, 329
Infants, 81, 147, 148, 353, 367, 370, 371, 372; sensitivity of, 363
Inference, 25, 26, 38, 142, 252, 253, 342; and time, 44; creative, 263; intensive, 203
In-itself, the, 196, 421
Injustice, 177
Innocence, 22, 25
Inquiry, 22, 26, 203, 293; philosophical, 232

Insanity, criminal, 267 f.
Insight, 102, 203
Insistence, 77, 157, 164, 172, 173, 245, 309, 310, 322, 337, 388, 395, 396, 399, 400, 403, 408, 409, 411 ff.; alien, 172, 398
Inspiration, 16, 17, 88
Instantiation, 72, 73, 76, 77, 79
Instrumentalism, 344, 348
Instruments, 456
Integrity, 417, 214, 261
Intelligibility, 12, 204, 217, 285, 325, 408
Intelligible, the, 12, 325, 396, 397
Intensification, 62, 65, 83, 163, 164, 384, 404, 417
Intension, 9
Intensive, the, 390
Intention, 14, 76, 81, 102, 178, 187, 188, 199, 223, 336, 406, 407
Intentionality, 27, 142, 397, 402, 406
Interaction, 335, 337
Interest, 18, 20, 181, 188, 195, 196, 198, 199, 204, 210, 223, 225, 227, 230, 237, 241, 255, 260, 340, 365, 371, 377; expression of, 338; harmony of, 351; responsible, 250
Interinvolvement, 330 ff., 334, 335, 339
Interiority, 287
Intermediaries, 395, 397
Intermingling, 287
Internalization, 13, 14, 16, 65, 66, 80, 147, 160, 220, 223, 230, 236, 237, 240, 241
Interplay, 443
Interpretation, 301
Introspection, 397
Intrusions, 77, 83, 106, 166, 172, 192, 338, 412, 416
Involvement, 164, 190, 332
Irreducibles, 403, 411, 412, 413
'is', 157
'It', 9

Japanese, 82
Judaism, 1ff., 84, 85, 315
Judgment, 9, 26, 30, 76, 203, 305, 312, 337, 357, 399, 404, 406, 440; aesthetic, 298, 300; final, 171; Kantian, 431; last, 315, 441; origin of, 205; perceptual, 337; social, 337
Justice, 2, 116, 181, 222, 288, 289, 425, 433

Kenosis, 117
Kinds, 357, 408
Knots, 36, 38, 42
Knowledge, 14, 29, 30, 116, 117, 118, 253, 302 ff., 306 f., 349, 390, 424, 430; limit for, 398; origin of, 205; scientific, 335, 392, 437, 438; self-, 97, 98, 203, 204, 210; transcendental, 47
Knower and known, 122, 305, 399

Language, 26, 104, 125, 137, 138, 139, 143, 145, 148, 150, 151, 153, 161, 164, 182, 209, 233, 234, 272, 338, 425, 426, 454, 456; common, 339; dimensions of, 146, 147; domain of, 315, 436; foreign, 279; formal, 145; function of, 145; of animals, 150, 151; rules of, 454; structure of, 133; used, 456
langue, la, 453
Laws, 2, 151, 175, 286, 354, 414, 425, 426; biological, 137; chemical, 137; conformity to, 107; context of, 359; enacted, 147; evaluation of, 325; international, 375; living, 164; of cosmos, 291; of nature, 137, 145, 230; positive, 164; power of, 145; social, 82; state's, 385
Legalism, 279
Lemmings, 357
Liberty, 202
Liberty, creative, 164
Libido, 110, 113, 283
Life, civilized, 330, 333; commonsense, 302; daily, 88, 202; good, 15, 34; private, 398; right to, 148, 162; social, 203, 279; successful, 89; world, 329
Limit, 43, 170, 397 ff., 418; adopted, 333
Limiting, self-, 121
Linkages, 321
Linguistics, 8, 425, 426
Listening, 155
Literature, 280
Living, 69; civilized, 331, 337; social, 390
Location, 127, 308
Logic, 17, 19, 22, 25, 65, 145, 203, 204, 252, 425; and metaphysics, 24; intensional, 295; modal, 307
Love, 106, 107, 155, 219, 428 ff.
Lucidation, 38

Machines, 252, 253
Macrocosm, 293, 297
Madness, 262 ff.
Magic, 282
Maintenance, 83, 121, 205, 206, 261, 313, 357
Making, 417, 490
Malefactors, 356
Man, see Men
'Man', 145
'Man: Private and Public', 33, 38, 43, 57, 113, 164, 173, 273
Manifestations, 403
Manifold, 121, 122, 437
Mankind, 133, 135, 168, 170, 179, 356, 374, 444
Man's Freedom, 185, 256
Many, the, 30, 120; and One, 19, 72, 118, 224, 225; and privacy, 225
Market, 175, 176, 178
Marxism, 42, 449
Mass-objects, 73, 75

Mastery, self-, 111, 223 ff.
Materialism, 116, 285
Mathematics, 2, 27, 100, 203 ff., 224, 258, 277, 288 ff., 293, 304, 340, 425, 433 ff., 445, 447, 455; and nature, 145; applied, 425; constructionistic, 37; domain of, 336, 390; relevance of, 289; reports of, 298 ff.
Matter, 74, 325; prime, 329, 330
Maturation, 62, 96, 129, 138, 148, 197, 441; right to, 162
Maturity, 367
Maximization, 107
Me, 27, 28, 32, 33, 77, 106, 124, 129, 158, 159, 187, 188, 201, 204, 210, 212, 216, 225, 232, 323, 337, 379, 390, 397 ff.
Meaning, 4, 9, 28, 29, 53, 75, 116, 142, 155, 234
Means, 45, 247, 250, 251, 256, 454
Measures, 102, 103, 145, 192, 348, 359, 367, 368, 394, 408, 439, 455
Mechanical, the, 439
Mediators, 83, 102 ff., 108, 153, 412
Medicine, 284
Medium, 106
Memory, 51
Men, 53, 59, 121, 129, 134, 137, 139, 144, 147, 151, 188, 189, 230, 290, 336, 359 ff., 391 ff., 411, 434, 439; active, 437; and animals, 126, 163, 214; and finalities, 46; and nature, 57, 190, 332; and others, 112, 237; anomalous, 167; bodies of, 76, 79, 190, 320, 413; civilized, 331, 333; claims of, 161; commonsensical, 86; complex, 339; creative, 88, 89, 99, 359; dignity of, 152, 359; dimensions of, 84, 97, 99, 225, 392; dispositions of, 96, 97; distinctness of, 350; dominating, 442; essence of, 59, 61; ethical, 12, 89, 457; evaluation of, 124; evidences for, 365; free, 359; good, 45, 105; governance of, 130; great, 88; history of, 209; identity of, 105, 290; incompetent, 89; independence of, 78, 100; individuality of, 100; in society, 209; inspired, 15, 16; instantiation of, 139, 140; intelligibility of, 78; interiority of, 187; in world, 57, 114; irreducibility of, 359; judicious, 168; knowledge of, 91, 125; levels of, 443; manifested, 96; mature, 45, 104, 128, 391, 407; model, 14 ff.; moral, 89, 457; nature of, 59, 112, 327, 438; origin of, 367; perceptive, 167; perfection of, 440; power of, 439; practical, 287; privacies of, 76, 112; produced, 58; properties of, 61; public, 112, 178; reasonable, 167, 451; reflective, 168; self-control of, 439; sensitive, 365, 446; similarity of, 101; species, members of, 98, 150, 162, 163, 173; task of, 58; together, 57, 114, 138, 146, 167, 175; totality of,

428; types of, 218; understanding, 34, 91; uniqueness, 97; unity of, 86, 96, 107; value of, 78; whole, 95
Messiah, the, 171, 315
Metaphysics, 2, 19 ff., 30, 65, 298, 301, 303, 304, 330 ff., 335, 382; aim of, 25; and logic, 24; beginning of, 155; domain of, 27; forms of, 19; method of, 21; system of, 341
Method, 5, 26, 116, 127, 158, 165, 188, 204, 208, 210, 237, 239, 244, 246, 286, 297, 310, 329, 330, 338, 341, 342, 355, 357, 358, 360, 364 ff., 372, 374, 376, 389, 391, 397, 408, 409, 415, 416, 419, 420, 421, 423, 432, 437, 438, 440, 441, 442, 444; genetic, 128; Hegel's, 35
Microcosm, 230, 293
Midpoints, 19, 21, 35, 414, 422, 423, 425
Milieu, 127, 151, 209, 388, 422, 425, 441, 452
Mind, 8, 56, 77, 78, 80, 81, 106, 113, 129, 138, 140, 147, 162, 164, 187, 188, 196, 198, 199, 206, 210, 223, 225, 227, 230 ff., 241, 243, 260, 276, 277, 281, 285, 286, 296, 398, 443; animal, 253; /body, 99, 100, 104, 108, 118, 226, 252, 275, 286, 287, 392, 402, 409, 412, 414, 415, 417; cosmic, 415; domain of, 276, 277, 280; evaluation of, 431; evidence for, 252, 253, 256 f., 281; individual, 415; intermediating, 223; judicious, 431; personalized, 106; structure of, 305; types of, 431; use of, 257
Mixed, the, 7 ff., 287, 297, 336, 342, 343, 435, 444
Models, 15 ff.,
Modes of Being, 173, 184, 229, 420
Molecules, 40, 121, 320
Monism, 280
Morality, 10, 175, 181, 203, 280, 293, 395, 424, 457; origin of, 205
Movement, 44, 156, 169, 243, 389; intensive, 167, 192, 233, 312, 348, 353
Music, 276, 436, 445
Musicry, 47, 49
'My', 283
Mysticism, 1, 3, 18, 20 ff., 55, 144, 204, 282, 298
Myth, 2, 18, 104, 175, 176, 452
Names, 76; arresting, 231; honorific, 230; proper, 8, 9, 26, 83, 126, 132, 163, 353, 390
Naming, 76
Narcissism, 99, 107
Nature, 47, 48, 54, 131, 145, 156, 167, 332, 334, 368, 382, 458; and art, 48, 49, 52; and men, 48, 57, 190; grounding of, 190; human, 16, 61, 130, 132 ff., 148; individual, 10; knowledge of, 335, 393; laws of, 145, 174, 293, 325; philosophy of, 60; sustained, 191

'Nature', 54
Natures, 319, 408; sharable, 214
Nation, 280
Nazis, 96, 97, 102, 103, 133, 375, 394
Necessity, 260, 426, 433, 435, 445; rational, 427, 434, 436, 456
Needs, 178, 202, 351, 394, 451, 497; bodily, 347; control by, 454; creative, 450, 451
Negation, 10
Neglect, 34
Neoplatonism, 8, 22
Neuroses, 196
Nine Basic Arts, 47, 449
Nirvana, 441
Nominalism, 282, 319
Nothing, the, 41, 354, 402
Novels, 97
Novelty, 46
Now, 25; the eternal, 41
Nuances, 226, 227
Obduracy, 411
Obedience, 15
Objectification, 312, 314
Objectives, 222, 225, 250 ff., 258, 259, 265, 266, 320, 393, 402, 406; 427, 453; final, 217, 223, 234, 241, 264; non-bodily, 246
Objectivity, 25, 399, 400, 401, 404, 448
Objects, 17; art, 53, 335;artificial, 320; daily, 21; familiar, 166, 167, 170; intentional, 27; known, 305; mass, 73, 75; natural, 52, 53; obligating, 265; religious, 452; scientific, 435; terminal, 166; willed, 265
Obligations, 202, 203, 211, 251, 258, 265, 266, 269, 337, 365, 373, 375, 422, 456
Observers, 166
Obstacles, 404
Obstinacy, 409, 411
Occupancy, 213, 234, 238, 240, 328, 443
Occurrences, crucial, 340, 344
Omnipresence, 41
One/Many, 19, 61, 72, 224, 226, 227, 286, 287, 344, 387, 428, 431
One, the, 29, 56, 226, 227, 369, 384, 390; and privacy, 225
Ontology, 2, 5, 18, 19, 20, 22, 288, 290, 416
Openness, 18, 20, 339
Opinion, public 174, 175
Opposition, 352, 413
Order, social, 163
Organisms, 40, 61, 63, 70, 72, 73, 118, 119, 121, 283
Organization, 204, 287, 288, 323, 437, 438
Orientation, 31, 32, 74
Overinsistence, 110, 111, 113
Others, 107, 117, 125, 135, 159, 160, 161, 224, 351
Ought, the, 217, 344, 351, 363, 457

Our Public Life, 147, 148, 161
Outcome, the best, 115, 440, 441
Pain, 3 ff., 43, 109, 164, 209, 315, 337, 339, 345, 357, 372, 396, 397, 398, 402 ff., 422; and pleasure, 249, 338, 348, 351, 448, 449, 451, 457; animal, 240, 345; expression of, 359; privacy of, 315
Painting, 49, 84
Panpsychism, 72
Pantheism, 281, 282
Paradigms, 11, 12
Parole, la, 455
Particles, ultimate, 40, 65, ff., 70, 71, 73 ff., 118, 124, 306, 318, 320, 321, 323, 324, 368, 380 ff., 386, 391, 458; and finalities, 72; privacy of, 67, 68, 238
Particulars, 38, 41, 42, 56, 434
Particularization, 220
Parts, 137, 318, 321, 322, 323, 326, 419
Passivity, 419
Past, the, 59, 315
Pattern, cosmic, 172
Peace, 223 ff., 231
Pelagianism, 282
Penetrations, 26, 32, 33, 35, 116, 126, 142, 157, 192, 293, 307, 331, 349 ff., 353, 356, 357, 390, 407, 419, 420, 423, 424
People, 385, 428
Perception, 203, 204, 206, 337, 347, 392; extrasensory, 40
Perfection, 13, 109, 124, 369f., 390, 396, 401; self-, 16, 429
Performance, 316, 434
Persistence, 109, 112, 126, 318
Person, 67, 76, 77, 78, 83, 108, 113, 114, 128, 129, 132, 138, 140, 147, 148, 161, 165, 167 ff., 188 ff., 193, 195, 196, 197, 201, 205, 206, 209, 214, 221, 227, 232, 236, 237, 241, 243, 281, 282, 284, 296, 316, 351, 353, 370 ff., 454; and body, 78, 148; and fetus, 162; center of, 231; claims of, 162, 164; controlling, 148; distinctions in, 164; divisions of, 148; epitomizations of, 108, 109; evidences of, 170, 174; intensifications of, 164; knowledge of, 163; rights of, 162, 163, 199, 256; public, 148; rectifying, 261; stages in, 374
Personalism, 281
Personality, 290
Phenomena, 407, 411, 413, ff., 418, 420, 422
Phenomenology, 118, 141, 142, 302
Philosophical Society for the Study of Sport, 430
Philosophies, classification of, 8
Philosophy, 115 ff., 141, 144, 202, 290, 382; analytic, 453; and science, 287; history of, 117, 432; linguistic, 26, 118, 396, 397, 455; process, 35, 220, 245, 281; science of, 116, 117; systematic, 5, 286

Philosophy in Process, 37, 38, 158, 430
Photography, 82, 83
Physicalism, 163, 285
Physics, 118, 455
Physiology, 4, 62, 405, 407
Piety, 289
Pivots, 27, 28, 31, 33, 283, 342, 397
Plans, 120
Plants, 237 ff.
Platonism, 424
Play, 164
Pleasure, 339, 340, 450, see also Pain
Plurality, 224, 381f, 384f., 396, 437
Poetry, 5, 86 ff., 101, 102, 434
Points, focal, 237
Politics, 55, 202, 203, 283, 288, 289, 337, 392; and economics, 59; domain of, 280; origin of, 205
Positioning, 447, 452, 453; self-, 357
Positions, 167, 299, 418
Positivism, 8, 278, 432; legal, 267 f.
Possession, 29, 76, 215, 349, 365, 367, 387, 424; self-, 225, 418
Possibility, 18, 27, 43, 46, 51, 54, 59, 75, 78, 108, 173, 229, 230, 275, 288, 305, 379, 425, 426, 445; articulation of, 305; internalization of, 237, 239; realized, 90
Potentialities, 66, 320, 322, 323, 368, 380 ff., 419; active, 384; common, 323, 370, 377, 383, 387; dormant, 376; grades of, 375; kinds of, 326; realization of, 326, 370; substantial, 381
Power, 73, 119, 130, 278, 281, 282, 283, 390; common, 177; creative, 447, 449, 451, 453, 454; final, 173, 280; grades of, 374; individual, 63; of species, 133; political, 133; private, 113, 144, 171, 246, 445; reserve, 422; social, 175; stages of, 451; unifying, 70, 437
Practice, 290
Pragmatism, 117, 337, 343, 432
Praise and blame, 125, 128, 129
Prayer, 155
Predicaments, 152, 153, 156
Predicates, 388
Predication, 305
Prediction, 257, 337, 408
Predisposition, 9
Preference, 255, 265, 266, 269, 373; and desire, 249; creative, 248, 456; kinds of, 250; knowledge of, 251
Prehistory, 230
Premiss, truth of, 24
Preparations, 234, 240, 357
Prescriptions, 234, 239, 241, 242, 246, 251, 252, 356, 357, 371, 373, 378, 446 ff.; common, 362, moral, 374, final, 363
Presence, 129, 309, 408, 411
Present, the, 46, 47, 334, 401
Presentation, 241; self-, 234, 247, 408
Preservation, 53; self-, 114, 215

Presupposition, 203
Principles, 15, 451, 456; basic, 389, Empedoclean, 423, ethical, 10, 11, 12, 16, formal, 447 source of, 438, universal, 15, 389
Privacies, 16, 56, 63, 66, 67, 108, 111, 112, 120, 122 ff., 127, 130, 138, 139, 140, 147, 151, 157, 164, 165, 179, 187, 190, 195, 196, 202, 206, 221, 228, 230, 234, 238, 260, 266, 276, 278, 309, 315, 317, 318, 321, 331, 340, 345, 357, 383, 388, 391, 393, 398, 404, 408, 411 ff., 416, 417, 418, 419, 437; action of, 258, anatomy of, 232, and art, 32, and bodies, 39, 68, 69, 75, 76 ff., 83, 121, 226, 323, 343, 409, 413, 421, 443, 454, 456, and nature, 190, and finalities, 64, 65, 68, 106, 225, 293, and privacies, 74, ff., 105, 106, and Unity, 296; animal, 69, 77, 374; being of, 241; centering, 241, 243, 258, 261; common, 319, 324, 325, 368; communication of, 106; complete, 227; concern of, 81; constancy of, 80, 83, 290; dimensions of, 178, 358 ff.; divisions of, 351; dominance of, 337, 377, 441; eptomizations of, 139, 353, 354, 358, 424; evidence of, 239, 337, 343, 347; existence of, 67, 68; governing, 270; hierarchical, 246; human, 63, 77, 80, 239, 240, 249, 250; identity of, 106; indeterminate, 368, 373, 374, 390; individual, 78, 80, 368; intensifications of, 62, 79, 80, 190; internalization by, 236, 237; irreducible, 69; knowledge of, 444; levels in, 439; matured, 243, 263; mediated, 79, 80, 322, 413; nuanced, 106, 225; of particles, 238; of sperm and egg, 67, 69, 71; orientation of, 68; origin of, 40, 63 ff., 71; ought of, 212; penetration of, 355; possessive, 412; potentiality of, 329; power of, 68, 254, 263, 267; primordial, 368; reception by, 83; rectifying, 258, 259, 261, 263, 266, 269, 298; representative, 152; resistance of, 77; rights of, 161; roles of, 265; self-bounding, 66; self-divisive, 76; self-maintaining, 77; shared, 368; specialized, 83, 395; stages in, 353; subdivisions of, 235; subhuman, 63, 64, 69, 240, 376; subordinated, 64; surplus, 162, 319, 368, 369, 371; traits of, 329; thrust of, 223; triangle of, 188, 198; types of, 320; unitary, 80, 236
'Private Powers', 422
Probability, 40, 41
Procedure, see Method
Procreation, 359
Projection, 13 ff., 17, 27, 288, 333, 334, 336, 413, 425, 448
Promise, 45, 296, 390 ff., 395
Proof, 17, 100, 301, 314
Property, 176, 265; right to, 148, 174, 175

Prophets, 14
Prospects, 122, 219, 248, 251, 440; inviting, 154; realization of, 393
Provincialsim, 282
Prudence, 241
Psyche, 296, 316, 340, 351, 371 ff., 375, 407, 454; animal, 196, 197
Psychiatry, 203, 204
Psychic, 196, 403
Psychology, 55, 203, 204, 277
Public and private, 234
Punishment, 180, 181 ff., 374
Purpose, 439, 440, 444
Qualia, 314, 407, 409, 415, see also Limits
Qualifiers, 172, 413
Qualities, 274 ff., 285
Quantity, 275;
'Quantity', 286
Ranges, 314, 415, see also Limit
Rational, the, 117
Rationale, 41, 42, 214, 326, 435
Realism, 31, 133, 134, 317
Realities, 24, 117, 142, 185, 340 f., 418, 425, 448; absolute, 369; depth of, 116; irreducible, 270; knowledge, 116; primary, 325; reference to, 341; recess of, 32; sets of, 442; stretch of, 395; transcendent, 190; types of, 8, 270, 420; ultimate, 16, 57, 166, 167, 294, 343; undifferentiated, 332
Reality, 99, 107, 118, 121, 216
Realm, 57, 58; basic, 55; human, 55, 56, 58, 363
Reason, 107, 167, 188, 203, 204, 223, 230, 241, 242; and intention, 199
Reasonableness, 241, 351
Reasoning, see Inference
Rebellion, 181
Receptivity, 99 ff., 206, 217, 218, 222, 223, 232, 236, 237, 241
Rectifications, 204 ff., 208, 228, 241, 243, 254, 258, 259, 261, 263, 264, 266, 269, 273, 296
Reductionism, 55, 118, 292, 322, 323, 330, 364
Reference, 9, 155, 353
Rehabilitation, 181
Relations, 83, 125, 129, 130, 131, 169, 191, 227, 231, 278, 313, 326, 399, 436, 449; aberrational, 243; epitomizing, 131; internal, 440
Relativism, 301
Relevance, 84
Religion, 1ff., 5, 12, 17 ff., 80, 114, 117, 153, 171, 175, 203, 204, 212, 217, 219, 222, 225, 261, 282, 286, 291, 304, 392, 425, 434, 456, 457; report of, 298, 299; state, 147; world of, 329
Remedies, 25, 349
Repercussions, 397
Reports, 300, 301

Representatives, 132, 134, 135, 151 ff., 335, 339, 391, 392, 394, 408, 440, 444
Repression, 196, 213
Resistance, 77, 412
Resolution, 44, 76, 337, 340, 371, 373, 454, 456
Responsibility, 14, 77, 108, 113, 125, 126, 127 ff., 132, 138, 140, 154, 162, 167, 188, 196, 197, 200, 202 ff., 210, 211, 213, ff., 220, 221, 223, 225, 226, 227, 231, 241, 247, 251 ff., 255, 258 ff., 279, 281, 337, 340, 346, 359, 366, 370, 371, 373, 374, 394, 422, 447, 457; and action, 266; and body, 262, 346; and I, 200; and identity, 224; and punishment, 442; and rights, 242; and you, 212; evidence of, 247, 264 f., 260, 268, 361; governing, 217, 242; knowledge of, 244 f.; legal, 266 ff.; objective, 217; operative, 268; primordial, 347; prominence of, 243; scope, 216, 217
Responsiveness, 234, 244
Restraints, 213, 228
Reverence, 18, 20, 21, 22, 116, 413
Review of Metaphysics, 7
Revolution, 181
Rewards and punishments, 121, 254, 337, 351, 443
Right and wrong, 266, 267, 288
Rights, 19, 77, 78, 82, 109, 124, 127, 128, 138, 148, 152, 188, 193 ff., 198, 200, 202, 204 ff., 225, 230 ff., 237, 241, 243, 260, 261, 289, 350, 351, 371, 442; acquiring, 175; and choice, 256; and duties, 176, 177; and I, 199; and identity, 198; and person, 199; and preference, 256; animal, 162, 197, 252; evidence for, 174, 256,; expression of, 189, 245; fetal, 162; ground of, 188; human, 116, 162, 245; inalienable, 148, 152, 169, 251; individual, 177, 179; insistence on, 108; kinds of, 207, 208;knowledge of, 126; location of, 162; native, 147, 148, 203, 209; personal, 163, 296; private, 177, 178; property, 176; system of, 176, 177, 179 ff.; viability of, 161; violation of, 182
Rites, 163
Ritual, 2, 82, 217, 315, 425, 452
Roles, 140, 156, 157, 159, 160, 163, 167, 170, 175, 176, 180, 203, 219, 360, 371, 417, 433, 453; and evidence, 165; dominant, 178; human, 363, 364; internal, 14; public, 153, 154, 192, 394; sex, 153
Romanticism, 118
Rules, 11, 334, 428, 449, 454 ff.; and values, 12; conformity to, 107; ethical, 10 ff.; formal, 446; inferential, 38; social, 175, 178
Sacraments, 203
Sacrifice, 216, 357
Sagacity, 447, 454

Saints, 96
Satisfactions, 180, 337, 450
Schematism, 431
Schizophrenics, 99
Science, 5, 164, 203, 286, 304, 323, 332 ff.; domain of, 55, 57, 280; formal, 432; knowledge by, 144; mathematical, 144; occult, 101; philosphic, 287; reports of, 298, 299; right to, 161; soft, 203; theoretical, 290, 445, 455 ff.
Sedimentation, 315
Segregations, 446 ff.
Selections, 343
Self, the, 63, 73, 76, 78, 81, 83, 103, 108, 113, 114, 124, 132, 138, 147, 148, 160, 165, 187, 190, 195 ff., 202, 206, 210, 214, 221, 227, 237, 241, 243, 254, 281, 282, 289, 296, 316, 351, 354, 371 ff., 397, 407, 437, 456, 457; -absenting, 229; acceptance of, 108, 220, 261; -articulation, 205; assertive, 108; -bounding, 120, 123, 128, 129, 212, 246, 320, 357; center of, 201, 231; -completion, 107, 108, 216, 218, 231, 241, 243, 258, 261, 263, 390, 393, 395, 396, 429, 430; -consciousness, 127; -contained, 122, 152, 225, 240, 359, 415, 441; -control, 108, 442; -determination, 260; -destruction, 386; -distancing, 353; divisions of, 164; epitomizations of, 96, 108, 196, 296, 374; evidence of, 258; -expression, 308, 340; -governance, 439; grounding, 214; -identity, 77, 83, 96, 223, 258; -indulgence, 107; -knowledge, 204, 210; -legislation, 203; -limiting, 121; -maintenance, 78, 83, 115, 120, 205, 206, 213, 261, 315; -mastery, 223 ff.; -perfection, 429; -positioning, 357; -possessed, 201, 225, 418; -presentation, 215, 234, 408; promise for, 375; rectifying, 243, 261, 264; resistant, 32; -respect, 212; rights of, 162; sufficient, 261, 427
Selfishness, 179
Semantics, 155
Semiotics, 456, 457
Sensibility, 340, 348, 445, 449 ff.; creative, 451
Sensitivity, 72, 77, 109, 128, 148, 161, 187 ff., 193, 194, 196, 204, 206, 209, 223, 225, 231, 237, 240, 241, 244, 245, 266, 273, 283, 296, 315, 339, 340, 348, 357, 377, 391, 443, 447, 449 ff., aesthetic, 345, 346, 360, 365, 371, 422, see also Sensibility; and consciousness, 199; and responsibility, 211, 258, 260; bodily, 346, 371, 374; creative, 447, ff., 455; evidence of, 338, 360 ff.; expression of, 164, 247, 338, 339; objects of, 347; primordial, 347; protective, 107, subhuman, 247
Sensuality, 111
Sentences, 146

Separations, 359, 407, 409, 414, 420, 425; humanistic, 53; types of, 362
Shape, 328
Signs, use of, 150
Sincerity, 212
Singularity, 445 ff., 450 ff., 457
Slavery, 3, 36
Social, the, 132, 289, 340, 447, 451, ff
Society, 10, 49, 58, 62, 104, 125, 130, 131, 143, 154, 175 ff., 182, 284, 320, 323, 337, 338, 370, 371, 375, 387, 394, 422, 425, 433, 436, 441, 453; and men, 176, 178; and state, 180, 182; and structure, 369, 433; civilized, 357, 369, 394; controlling, 133, 454; good of, 394; governance by, 127; human, 370, 371; of friends, 440; organic, 72; power of, 175; strands of, 178, 179
Sociobiology, 132, 283, 287, 293, 377, 389
Sociology, 2, 18 ff., 436, 457
Solidification, 334 ff., 394; of privacies, 66
Soul, 75, 105, 153, 327, 329
Sound, 275, 276
Sources, 169, 421
Southern Illinois University Press, 184 f., 430
Space, 118, 121, 122, 213, 281, 409, 434, 439, 444, 450; cosmic, 325; kinds of, 48, 444; whole of, 54
Species, 319, 321, 338, 340, 351, 357, 370, 374, 422, 452, 454,; articulated, 150; biological, 152; fixed, 239; human, 125, 132 ff. 138, 161, 164; intensified, 150; interests of, 249; privacy of, 368; promotion of, 337
Speculation, 25, 142, 219, 240, 242, 270, 346, 347, 439
Speech, 139, 140, 234; right to, 148, 161
Sperm and egg, 39, 137, 145; privacy of, 39, 67, 68, 69, 71
Spirit, absolute, 41, 115, 117; common, 315, 334, 337
Sport, 5, 107, 108, 111, 272, 280, 324, 336, 427, 434, 447, 454, 456
Sport: A Philosophical Inquiry, 107, 111, 216
Standards, 234, 337
State, the, 58, 61, 92, 125, 130, 175, 209, 256, 272, 284, 318, 320, 323, 347, 371, 375, 422, 424, 440, 441; action of, 385; and conditions, 53; and rights, 161, 180, 181; and society, 180; controlling, 133; corrupt, 181; Hegelian, 369; organic view of, 71, 72; power of, 133; privacy of, 369; task of, 125, 181, 182
Statistics, 293
Status, 357
Stimulation, 446, 447
Stoics, 43
Story, 434, 452
Strands, 175, 178, 179
Striving, 213

Structuralism, 8, 446
Structure, 41, 151, 287, 315, 320, 321, 322, 324, 326, 327, 334, 433, 447, 453, 455; common, 326; five-fold, 146, 147; formal, 333; grades of, 395; linguistic, 133; political, 318; public, 144; social, 145, 148, 153, 157, 164, 209, 315, 369
Subhumans, 247, 448
Subjective, the, 402, 406
Subjectivism, 281
Subjectivity, 77, 397 ff., 404, 405
Subjects, 117; and objects, 29
Subjugation, 423
Sublimation, 92,
Sublime, the, 52
Submission, 203, 220, 337
Subordination, 169, 334
Subrealms, 55, 59
Substance, 11, 18, 38, 43, 51, 63, 64, 76, 117, 173, 214, 229, 237, 268, 286, 358, 372 ff., 381, 384, 388, 408, 424, 425, 426; internalization of, 237, 240, 241; possessive, 296; unification by, 78
Substantializing, self-, 261
Substitution, 152, 451
Suffering, 338
Sufficiency, self-, 261
Suitability, 125
Suppression, 91, 113
Surfaces, 398, 407
Surplus, 191, 368, 369, 374
Sustainers, 164, 403, 405 f.
Sustainings, 27, 216, 389, 404, 405; evidence of, 165
Symbols, 76, 353
Sympathy, 116, 135, 160, 407
Synthesis, 53, 122
Systems, 178; philosophical, 330, 340
Tao, 19, 64, 116, 441
Tasks, 58, 377
Tautology, 295
Taxation, 148
Taxonomy, 219
Teams, 317, 320, 321, 323, 324, 331, 334
Technology, 424, 451, 452, 456, 457
Teleology of behaviorism, 154, 155
Tendency, 91 ff., 197
Terminations, 349, 350, 413
Termini, 192, 193, 352, 361, 406, 409, 411, 414 ff.
Terms, 9
Texts, 279
'The Days of Heaven', 82
The Making of Men, 376
Theology, 2, 17, 18, 20, 21, 22, 31, 202, 332, 434
Theories, 334, 434, 435, 447
The World of Art, 38, 57, 212, 218, 333, 335
'They', 174
Thing-in-itself, 121, 122

Things, 126, 127, 236; action of, 318; privacy of, 69, 318; relation to, 126, 127; world of, 367
Thomism, 35
Thought, 24, 143, 231, 253, 307, 339, 340, 366, 392, 393, 404; and action, 351; private, 297; responsible, 262 f., speculative, 430; systematic, 203
Thrust, 25, 26, 29, 31, 32, 46, 116, 141, 188, 194, 223, 288, 292, 293, 294, 308, 331 ff., 336, 348 ff., 352, 389, 393, 394, 399, 400, 402, 427, 434, 446, 448; kinds of, 349
Time, 44, 51, 57, 115, 120 ff., 213, 277, 281, 434, 450; and dialectic, 38; and finalities, 105; common, 431; continuum of, 50, 51, 54; kinds of, 47 ff., 54; undifferentiated, 277; whole of, 50, 54
Togetherness, 56, 118, 173, 320, 396
Tonality, 113, 128, 339, 404, 415, 417, 419
Tools, 417
Topology, 431
Totality, undifferentiated, 429
Tradition, 104, 203, 209, 272, 315, 426
Tragedy, 26, 116
Training, 82, 83, 111
Transcendentals, 8, 37, 170, 199, 218, 274, 286, 302 f., 421,
Transcendents, 55, 56, 58, 77, 133, 134, 172, 173, 195, 198, 203, 275; receptivity to, 200, 201, 204, 205, 210, 212, 217, 218
Triangle, analytic, 194, 198
Truth, 5, 92, 127, 233, 288, 289, 304, 340 ff., 389; aesthetic, 300; and error, 203; established, 289; evidence for, 174; in inference, 296; locus of, 74; mathematical, 298, 300; of premiss, 22, 24; scientific, 300; universal, 4
Ugliness, 288, 340
Ultimates, 168, 400, 401, 411, 454
Unconscious, the, 196, 202, 203
Understanding, 127, 142, 191, 203, 454 ff.
Unifications, 11, 228, 294, 321, 337, 395, 407, 445
Unions, 11, 58, 424, 450
Uniqueness, 97
United States Constitution, 147
Units, 284, 287, 308, 330, 387, 401, 402, 408, 409, 411; contextual, 414; cosmic, 458; detached, 291, 292; in domains, 272; kinds of, 382; origin of, 283; physical, 409, 412; pure, 278; reality of, 38; social, 271, ultimate, 283, 291, 292, 458
Unity, 11, 12, 18 ff., 51, 54, 64, 76, 78, 80, 173, 188, 220, 226, 229, 230, 237, 241, 288, 289, 308, 310, 312, 322, 358, 372, 382, 386, 388, 389, 393, 398, 417, 425, 426, 437, 438; aesthetic, 431; bodily, 73, 74, 81; controlling, 59; divisible,

321; encompassing, 118, 192; governing, 121, 137, 419; human, 59; intensive, 80; internalization of, 240; inwardness of, 296; layers of, 437; multi-dimensional, 76; organic, 81; social, 318
Universals, 8, 62, 63, 155, 317, 409
Universe, 24, 389
Urge, primary, 100
Utilitarinism, 14, 374, 449
Utopia, 259
Value, 11, 12, 84, 120, 176, 204, 214, 225, 229, 246, 256, 307, 310 f., 350, 351, 392, 408, 447, 449, 456, 457; aesthetic, 255, 260; final, 434; hierarchy, 193; loss in, 251; public, 359; totality of, 257
Variables, 334, 433, 435
Variants, 102
Verification, 343
Victims, 182
Virtue, 4, 112, 113, 202, 203
Want, 249, 260
War, 25, 178, 375
Warnings, 339
We, 202, 269 ff., 272, 277, 319, 323, 324, 330, 334, 335, 381, 431; common, 424; complex, 129, 389, 390, 393; power of, 130, 424; simple, 390, 431
Weltanschauung, 332
Wholes, 75, 130, 131, 133, 134, 135, 317 f., 322, 417, 419; bounded, 393; encompassing, 70; humanized, 131; interacting, 337; overlapping, 333, 334; political, 204; social, 133, 204, 316
Will, the, 14, 81, 108, 127, 138, 162, 164, 171, 258 ., 264, 346, 375 ff., 404, 443, 456; and responsibility, 258, 259, 260; and self, 258; creative, 454; evidence of, 258, 259, 264; exercise of, 266;

free, 113, 259; practical, 454; Schopenhauerian, 330; weak, 258
Withdrawals, 107, 309, 336, 348 ff., 402
Wonder, 18, 21, 22, 24, 25, 28, 109, 203, 204, 207;
Words, 146
Work, 44, 145, 146, 153, 337; creative, 88, 385, 427; public, 14; right to, 161
World, 168, 332, 430; alien, 444; awareness of, 339; civilized, 335, 457, 458; common, 176, 330, 331commonsense, 165, 334, 443; confronted, 334, 336; daily, 45, 343, 424, 425, 426; external, 27, 190, 191, 399, 404; human, 196, 364, 457; industrial, 451; intrusion of, 338; limit of, 153; objective, 174, 332; physical, 144, 282, 364, 367; public, 00, 107, 192, 233, 243, 331, 339; scientific, 410; social, 254, 374
Worship, 22;
Yale University Press, 184
You, 31, 128, 187 ff., 192 ff., 198, 200, 204, 205, 206, 209, 210, 213 ff., 223, 224, 225, 232 ff., 235 ff., 247, 253, 256, 381, 424; acting, 216; and me, 32, 33, 201, 232; and responsibility, 212; controlled, 232; depth of, 243, 244; embodied, 208, 213, 216, 232; evidenced, 235, 236; grounded, 205; inwardness of, 28; knowledge of, 28, 31, 32, 226, 231, 356; levels of, 241; presentation of, 192, 205, 233; privacy of, 227; public, 214; responsibility of, 222; roles of, 241; sustained, 232
You, I, and the Others, 12, 33, 35, 37, 43, 57, 58, 187, 202, 269, 287, 315, 319, 381, 393, 402, 419, 420, 424, 429, 431